DSM-5™ in Action

DSM-5™ in Action

SOPHIA F. DZIEGIELEWSKI

WILEY

Cover design: Wiley

Cover photograph: Chad Baker/Getty

This book is printed on acid-free paper. ♾

Published by John Wiley & Sons, Inc., Hoboken, New Jersey.

Published simultaneously in Canada.

For general information on our other products and services please contact our Customer Care Department within the U.S. at (800) 762-2974, outside the United States at (317) 572-3993 or fax (317) 572-4002.

Wiley also publishes its books in a variety of electronic formats. Some content that appears in print may not be available in electronic books. For more information about Wiley products, visit our website at www.wiley.com.

Library of Congress Cataloging-in-Publication Data:
Dziegielewski, Sophia F., author,
DSM-5 in action/Sophia F. Dziegielewski.
1 online resource.
Includes bibliographical references and indexes.
Description based on print version record and CIP data provided by publisher; resource not viewed.
ISBN 978-1-118-13673-7 (pbk.: alk. paper)
ISBN 978-1-118-76074-1 (pdf)
ISBN 978-1-118-76066-6 (epub)
I. Title.
[DNLM: 1. Diagnostic and statistical manual of mental disorders. 5th ed. 2. Mental Disorders—diagnosis. 3. Mental Disorders—classification. 4. Patient Care Planning. WM 141]
RC469
616.89'075—dc23 2014015479

Printed in Singapore

10 9 8 7 6 5 4 3 2 1

A Tribute to Dr. Cheryl Green

I have come to believe that intelligence consists of the knowledge that one acquires over a lifetime. Wisdom, however, is far greater. Wisdom requires having intelligence, but realizing it means nothing if it is not shared. In wisdom, there is a natural sense of giving where there is no fear of loss. It means realizing that the knowledge is measured purely by what we can teach and share with others.

For Dr. Cheryl Green, her intelligence made her a social work scholar. It was her wisdom, however, that touched my soul and made her one of my colleagues and dearest friends. Her sense of humor and "Cherylisms" made the time fly by. Cheryl passed on before the formulation of this book. Through her teaching and writing, the hearts of so many social workers like me will never be the same. Although not a day goes by that I do not miss my dearest friend, I remain comforted by the time we shared together.

Contents

Preface

The pages that follow will introduce the reader to the diagnostic assessment, with its obvious strengths as well as its limitations. Although the concept of diagnosis and assessment is rich in tradition, the connection between diagnostic procedures and behavioral-based outcomes calls for a practice strategy that recognizes the importance of the relationship between the problems and concerns of the person and his or her environment. Continually assessing and reassessing how to best address context changes related to emotional, physical, and situational factors regarding client well-being is paramount.

This book stresses a multidisciplinary and interdisciplinary focus that invites all medically and nonmedically trained professionals, social workers, and other mental health practitioners to join in a collaborative team-based approach. By working together, teams best serve clients' needs by providing a comprehensive diagnostic assessment that ensures high-quality care.

This book utilizes the diagnostic nomenclature outlined in the *Diagnostic and Statistical Manual of Mental Disorders* (*DSM*) and goes beyond the *DSM* to clearly suggest treatment planning and application. The diagnostic assessment is embedded in the use of supporting texts, also referred to as the bibles of mental health, such as the *Diagnostic and Statistical Manual of Mental Disorders*, 5th ed. (*DSM-5*; American Psychiatric Association, 2013) and the *International Classification of Diseases,* ninth and 10th editions (*ICD-9-CM* and *ICD-10-CM*; World Health Organization, 1993, 2008). These books have been the standards for mental health practice for decades. Therefore, it should come as no surprise to mental health professionals that the new edition, the *DSM-5,* which crosswalks insurance billing with the *ICD-10,* with its latest mandatory requirement for usage in October 2015, will bring what some consider earth-shaking changes.

Familiarity with these books is important for completing the diagnostic assessment, and all mental health professionals need to understand this information and how to incorporate it to provide a competent, efficient, and effective practice strategy. To assist in this process, this book outlines the basic diagnostic information related to the *DSM-5* and suggests treatment strategy.

Similar to previous editions, this edition of this text continues to serve as a handbook that extends beyond just learning the criteria for a diagnosis. After providing an overview of the basics, the text extends to treatment strategy with the creation of treatment plans, including suggestions for individualizing the best therapeutic services available. In using the *DSM,* concerns remain about misdiagnosis, overdiagnosis, and labeling clients—all practices that can have severe repercussions personally, medically, socially, and occupationally—and the need for informed, ethical practice has never been more important. The early stages of transition to the *DSM-5* will require balancing the knowledge of both books, the *DSM-IV-TR* and *DSM-5.* Mental health practitioners believe strongly in allowing ethical principles, environmental factors, and a respect for cultural diversity to guide all practice decisions. From this perspective, the diagnostic assessment described in this book embodies concepts such as individual dignity, worth, respect, and nonjudgmental attitudes.

For social workers and other mental health counselors (often referred to as practitioners), recognizing these values is the cornerstone from which all treatment planning and intervention is built. Many times these concepts remain subjective and require professional acknowledgment, interpretation, and application extending beyond the formal diagnostic criteria and requiring interpretation and application strategies that lead to efficient and effective practice strategy. What is most important to remember is that the *DSM,* regardless of the version, does not suggest treatment. My hope is that this book will help to further the crosswalk as the *DSM* works with the *ICD* in terms of billing and that this book will outline a comprehensive diagnostic assessment leading directly to the treatment and treatment planning essential for the implementation of practice strategy.

OVERVIEW

To start this endeavor, the four chapters of Section I introduce the reader to the major diagnostic assessment schemes utilized in the profession and through this diagnostic lens outline both support and resistance issues. In these introductory chapters, the basics of diagnosis and assessment are exemplified in relation to how these terms are applied in current health and mental health practice. The learning process begins with an understanding of how terms such as *diagnosis* and *assessment* are combined in relation to current health and mental health practice. A historical perspective provides the background of the *DSM,* comparing the similarities and differences from previous editions and the rationale for the latest version, the *DSM-5.* Further, this section summarizes the current expectations and controversies surrounding the *DSM-5.* Taken into account in *DSM-5* is the importance of including supporting information, such as use of the dimensional assessment, crosscutting of symptoms, and use of the Cultural Formulation Interview (CFI). It ends with an overview of how the "In Action" connection is made, linking the diagnostic impression to treatment planning and practice strategy. Case examples show the application of the theoretical concepts and demonstrate how these principles relate to practice strategy.

Section II provides comprehensive diagnostic information for each selected category of disorder, identifying commonly seen psychiatric mental health conditions. Each chapter contains *Quick References* designed to highlight the most important diagnostic criteria clearly and concisely. The case examples show how the criteria can manifest. For each category of disorders outlined in the application chapters, at least one disorder highlights the "In Action" focus of the book. The case example provides a comprehensive diagnostic assessment and treatment plan that reflects the related practice strategy.

Additional treatment plans were one of the most popular features of previous editions of this book, and they have been expanded. Treatment planning is essential to practice strategy, and regardless of whether the *DSM* or the *ICD* is used for diagnostic purposes, the treatment plans and intervention strategy will remain similar. Therefore, the appendix covers selected disorders not addressed in the individual chapters, and also added are selected quick references that clearly outline the criteria. Each treatment plan explains the signs and symptoms that should be recorded, what the short- and long-range goals for the client are, and what needs to be done by the client, the practitioner, and the family.

Uniqueness of This Book

What remains unique about this book is that it challenges the practitioner to synthesize information into a complete diagnostic assessment that bridges the diagnostic assessment to current treatment planning and practice strategy. Each chapter, along with the quick references, is designed to give health and mental health practitioners a sense of hands-on learning and participation. This book is not meant to include all aspects of a mental disorder and its subsequent treatment. Rather, it provides a framework for approaching the disorder, with suggestions for the treatment that will follow.

Therefore, this book provides a reader-friendly comprehensive reference to the most commonly diagnosed mental disorders, as well as specific applications designed to show how to apply the diagnostic framework toward current practice strategy. Each disorder was carefully selected, based on what is most often seen in the field and taught in the graduate-level classroom. In addition, based on the prevalence of these diagnoses, the disorders covered in this book are often included on social work and other mental health–related licensing exams.

On a personal note, I believe creating a reader-friendly, practice-based handbook of this nature is never easy—nor should it be. Creating the best diagnostic assessment takes a lot of hard work, and all practice wisdom must be grounded in individualized, evidence-based practice strategy. Therefore, the actual drafting of chapters of this edition from the first proposal to the end product covered a span of well over 4 years, with numerous rewrites and edits. This book represents more than 25 years of my professional practice and teaching experience. In addition, I have worked with all the contributing authors of the application chapters, all are fellow practitioners in the area, and together we have spent countless hours deciding on how best to transcribe practice experience into the written word. All the contributors to this text are passionate about our profession and agree that much needs to be learned from the clients served. We all believe strongly that diagnostic skill will always fall short if it is not linked to practice strategy.

Case examples are used throughout this book to help the reader see the interface between what is written in the text and how it applies to practice. Many of the struggles that other professionals have noted are highlighted, and the case examples present information in a practical and informative way that is sensitive to the client's best interests while taking into account the reality of the practice environment. Thus, the contributors invite the reader to begin this adventure in learning and to realize that diagnostic assessment needs to be more than "the Blind Man and the Elephant."

There will always be a subjective nature to diagnosis and assessment, just as there is a subjective nature to individuals and the best-employed intervention strategy. The person-in-situation stance provides the strongest link to the successful diagnostic assessment, which can often be overlooked. This edition, like the ones before it, is intended to take the practitioner beyond the traditional diagnostic assessment and ignite a creative fire for practice strategy and implementation, similar to what it has done for those in our profession. The importance of the person-in-environment and of including supportive characteristics related to individuals, families, and the related support system will always stand in the forefront of the successful application of treatment strategy. Welcome to this latest edition, and with each client served, I hope you never forget the importance of the three Rs: Recognition, Respect, and Responsibility.

REFERENCES

American Psychiatric Association. (2013). *Diagnostic and statistical manual of mental disorders* (5th ed.). Arlington, VA: American Psychiatric Publishing.

World Health Organization. (1993). *International classification of diseases: Mental disorders* (10th ed.). Geneva, Switzerland: Author.

World Health Organization. (2008). *ICD-10: International statistical classification of diseases: Clinical modification* (10th rev. ed.). New York: NY: Author.

Acknowledgments

I am very grateful for all the help I have received from the coauthors on the applications chapters included in this text. The sharing of such experienced practitioners' firsthand experiences has been invaluable. I would also like to thank the 18,000 social workers and counselors that I have trained for professional practice in supervision and for taking the social work licensure exams. Their wonderful feedback in terms of what they are seeing in the field and the problems they have encountered has helped me to become a stronger teacher and practitioner. For this input, I will always be thankful and intend to continue to give back as much as possible to help others along their professional journey. As mental health practitioners, regardless of discipline, not only do we have a clear path set before us to deal with the challenges of this changing environment but also we bear the burden of exploring and subsequently influencing how these changes will affect our professional practice and the clients we serve.

I would like to thank my clients for teaching me the importance of going beyond what is expected and recognizing the uniqueness of each individual I have had the privilege of serving. Seeing firsthand the stigma and subsequent danger of placing a label on a client has left me sensitive to ensuring that the diagnostic assessment is not done haphazardly and always takes into account the person-in-situation or person-in-environment perspective. This means that each encounter must first recognize the uniqueness of the individual, show respect for the client and his or her situation, and take responsibility for providing the most comprehensive diagnostic assessment and subsequent treatment available.

Furthermore, the final product is only as good as those who work diligently behind the scenes on the editing and production of this book. First, I would like to thank Barbara Maisevich, MSW, for her second set of eyes and technical support in completing this manuscript. I would also like to thank Rachel Livsey, Senior Editor, Social Work and Counseling, and Kim Nir, editor "extraordinaire" at John Wiley & Sons. I would like to thank both of these individuals for their openness to new ideas, high energy level, drive, ambition, and perseverance making them both wise teachers, mentors, colleagues, and now my friends.

Last, I want to thank my family members, friends, and colleagues who understood and supported me when I said I could not participate because I had to work on this book. Special thanks to my husband who for 35 years always listens and understands the stress another deadline places on our time together. I am a firm believer that the more we share with others, the greater the gifts we receive in return. Therefore, it comes as no surprise that I am blessed with knowing and working with so many caring and supportive family members, friends, and colleagues. With that level of encouragement and support, all things really are possible.

Sophia F. Dziegielewski

Quick Reference List

SECTION I

UTILIZING THE *DSM-5*: ASSESSMENT, PLANNING, AND PRACTICE STRATEGY

CHAPTER 1

Getting Started

INTRODUCTION

This chapter introduces the concepts and current application principles relating psychopathology to clinical mental health practice. This application is supported through the use and explication of diagnosis-assessment skills found in today's behavioral-based biopsychosocial field of practice. The major diagnostic assessment schemes utilized in the profession, along with support and resistance issues, are introduced. Diagnosis and assessment are applied to current mental health practice. A historical perspective is explored, and the type of diagnostic assessment most utilized today is outlined. Practice strategy is highlighted, and considerations for future exploration and refinement are noted.

BEGINNING THE PROCESS

The concept of formulating and completing a diagnostic assessment is embedded in the history and practice of the clinical mental health counseling strategy. Sadler (2002) defined the traditional purpose of the psychiatric diagnosis as providing efficient and effective communication among professionals, facilitating empirical research in psychopathology, and assisting in the formulation of the appropriate treatment strategy for the client to be served. The importance of the diagnostic assessment is supported by estimates related to the prevalence of mental disorders in our population and the effects it can have on human function and productivity. It is estimated that each year, a quarter of Americans are suffering from a clinical mental disorder. Of this group, nearly half are diagnosed with two or more disorders (Kessler, Chiu, Demler, & Walters, 2005). Paula Caplan (2012), a clinical and research psychologist, wrote in the *Washington Post* that about half of all Americans can expect to get a psychiatric diagnosis in their lifetime. Although on the surface these numbers may seem alarming, some researchers question whether these incidences of mental disorders are simply a product of our times and related primarily to the taxonomy used to define a mental disorder (Ahn & Kim, 2008). In practice, this rich tradition related to making the diagnostic impression has been clearly emphasized by compelling demands to address practice reimbursement (Braun & Cox, 2005; Davis & Meier, 2001; Kielbasa, Pomerantz, Krohn, & Sullivan, 2004; Sadler, 2002). For example, whether a client has health insurance can be a factor in whether he or she gets a mental health diagnosis and the supporting treatment received (Pomerantz & Segrist, 2006). Also, use of the *DSM* and creating a psychiatric diagnosis continue to go basically unregulated and open to professional interpretation (Caplan, 2012).

To facilitate making the diagnostic impression, numerous types of diagnosis and assessment measurements are currently available—many of which are structured into unique categories and classification schemes. All mental health professionals need to be familiar with the texts often referred to by those in the field as the bibles of mental health treatment. These resources, representing the most prominent methods of diagnosis and assessment, are the ones that are most commonly used and accepted in health service delivery. Although it is beyond our scope to describe the details and applications of all of these different tools and the criteria for each of the mental disorders described, familiarity with those most commonly utilized is essential. Furthermore, this book takes the practicing professional beyond assessment by presenting the most current methods used to support the diagnostic assessment and introducing interventions based on current practice wisdom, focusing on the latest evidence-based interventions utilized in the field.

MAKING THE DIAGNOSTIC ASSESSMENT: TOOLS THAT FACILITATE THE ASSESSMENT PROCESS

Few professionals would debate that the most commonly used and accepted sources of diagnostic criteria are the *Diagnostic and Statistical Manual of Mental Disorders, Fifth Edition* (*DSM-5*) and the *International Classification of Diseases, Tenth Edition* (*ICD-10*) or the *International Classification of Diseases* (*ICD-11*). Across the continents, especially in the United States, these books are considered reflective of the official nomenclature designed to better understand mental health phenomena and are used in most health-related facilities. The *DSM-5* (American Psychiatric Association [APA], 2013) is the most current version of the *Diagnostic and Statistical Manual of the American Psychiatric Association* (APA), which replaced the *DSM-IV-TR* (APA, 2000).

Today, the *DSM* has similarities to the criteria listed in the *ICD* in terms of diagnostic codes and the billing categories; however, this was not always the case. In the late 1980s, it was not unusual to hear complaints from other clinicians related to having to use the *ICD* for clarity in billing while referring to the *DSM* for clarity of the diagnostic criteria. Psychiatrists, psychologists, social workers, and mental health technicians often complained about the lack of clarity and uniformity of criteria in both of these texts. Therefore, it comes as no surprise that later versions of these texts responded to the professional dissatisfaction over the disparity between the two texts, as well as the clarity of the diagnostic criteria. To facilitate practice utility, the *DSM-5,* like its previous versions, serves as a crosswalk between the two books, utilizing the criteria from the *DSM* to facilitate forming the diagnostic impression and utilizing the *ICD* for billing. Balancing the use of these two books is essential in formulating a comprehensive diagnostic assessment. Use of these two books, clearly relating them to each other with their closely related criteria and descriptive classification systems, crosses all theoretical orientations.

Historically, most practitioners are knowledgeable about both books, but the *DSM* is often the focus and has gained the greatest popularity in the United States, making it the resource tool most often used by psychiatrists, psychologists, psychiatric nurses, social workers, and other mental health professionals.

ROLE OF SOCIAL WORKERS AND OTHER MENTAL HEALTH PROFESSIONALS

The publisher of the *DSM* is the American Psychiatric Association, a professional organization in the field of psychiatry. Nevertheless, individuals who are not psychiatrists buy and use the majority of copies. Early in the introductory pages of the book, the authors remind the reader that the book is designed to be utilized by professionals in all areas of mental health, including psychiatrists, physicians, psychiatric nurses, psychologists, social workers, and other mental health professionals (APA, 2013). Since there is a need for a system that accurately identifies and classifies biopsychosocial symptoms and for using this classification scheme as a basis for assessing mental health problems, it is no surprise that this book continues to maintain its popularity.

Of the documented 650,500 jobs held by social workers in the United States, more than 57% are in the area of health, mental health, substance abuse, medical social work, and public health, where many are directly involved in the diagnostic process (Bureau of Labor Statistics, U.S. Department of Labor, 2012). When compared with psychiatrists, psychologists, and psychiatric nurses, social workers are the largest group of mental health providers with a significant effect on diagnostic impressions related to the current and continued mental health of all clients served.

Mental health practitioners (also referred to as clinicians), such as social workers, are active in clinical assessment and intervention planning. Back as far as 1988, Kutchins and Kirk reported that when they surveyed clinical social workers in the area of mental health, the *DSM* was the publication used most often. Furthermore, since all states in the United States and the District of Columbia require some form of licensing, certification, or registration to engage in professional practice as a social worker (Bureau of Labor Statistics, U.S. Department of Labor, 2012), a thorough knowledge of the *DSM* is considered essential for competent clinical practice.

Because all professionals working in the area of mental health need to be capable of service reimbursement and to be proficient in diagnostic assessment and treatment planning, it is not surprising that the majority of mental health professionals support the use of this manual (Dziegielewski, 2013; Dziegielewski, Johnson, & Webb, 2002). Nevertheless, historically some professionals such as Carlton (1989), a social worker, questioned this choice. Carlton believed that all health and mental health intervention needed to go beyond the traditional bounds of simply diagnosing a client's mental health condition. From this perspective, social, situational, and environmental factors were considered key ingredients for addressing client problems. To remain consistent with the person-in-situation stance, utilizing the *DSM* as the path of least resistance might lead to a largely successful fight—yet would it win the war? Carlton, along with other professionals of his time, feared that the battle was being fought on the wrong battlefield and advocated a more comprehensive system of reimbursement that took into account environmental aspects. Questions raised include: How is the *DSM* used? Is it actually used to direct clinical interventions in clinical practice? Or is the focus and use of the manual primarily limited to ensuring third-party reimbursements, qualifying for agency service, or avoiding a diagnostic label? Psychiatrists and psychologists also questioned how the *DSM* serves clients in terms of clinical utility (First & Westen, 2007; Hoffer, 2008). Concerns evolved that clients were not always given diagnoses based on diagnostic criteria and that the diagnostic labels assigned were connected to unrelated factors, such as individual clinical judgment or simply to secure reimbursement. These concerns related directly to professional misconduct caused ethical and legal dilemmas that affected billable and nonbillable conditions that had intended and unintended consequences for clients. To complicate the situation further, to provide the most relevant and affordable services, many health care insurers require a diagnostic code. This can be problematic, from a social work perspective, when the assistance needed to improve mental health functioning may rest primarily in providing family support or working to increase support systems within the environment. The *DSM* is primarily descriptive, with little if any attempt to look at underlying causes (Sommers-Flanagan & Sommers-Flanagan, 2007).

Therefore, some mental health professionals are pressured to pick the most severe diagnosis so their clients could qualify for agency services or insurance reimbursement. This is further complicated by just the opposite trend, assigning the least severe diagnosis to avoid stigmatizing and labeling (Feisthamel & Schwartz, 2009). According to Braun and Cox (2005), serious ethical violations can be included, such as asking a client to collude with the assigning of mental disorders diagnosis for services. A client agreeing to this type of practice may be completely unaware of the long-term consequences this misdiagnosis can have regarding present, continued, and future employment, as well as health, mental health, life, and other insurance services or premiums.

Regardless of the reasoning or intent, erroneous diagnoses can harm the clients we serve as well as the professionals who serve them (Feisthamel & Schwartz, 2009). How can professionals be trusted, if this type of behavior is engaged in? It is easy to see how such practices can raise issues related to the ethical and legal aspects that come with intentional misdiagnosing. These practices violate various aspects of the principles of ethical practice in the mental health profession.

Although use of the *DSM* is clearly evident in mental health practice, some professionals continue to question whether it is being utilized properly. For some, such as social workers, the controversy over using this system for diagnostic assessments remains. Regardless of the controversy in mental health practice and application, the continued popularity of the *DSM* makes it the most frequently used publication in the field of mental health. One consistent theme in using this manual with which most professionals agree is that no single diagnostic system is completely acceptable to all. Some skepticism and questioning of the appropriateness of the function of the *DSM* is useful. This, along with recognizing and questioning the changes and the updates needed, makes the *DSM* a vibrant and emerging document reflective of the times. One point most professionals can agree on is that an accurate, well-defined, and relevant diagnostic label needs to reach beyond ensuring service reimbursement. Knowledge of how to properly use the manual is needed. In addition, to discourage abuse, there must also be knowledge, concern, and continued professional debate about the appropriateness and the utility of certain diagnostic categories.

DEVELOPMENT OF THE *DSM* CLASSIFICATION SYSTEM: HISTORY AND RESERVATIONS

The *DSM* was originally published in 1952, with the most recent version, the *DSM-5,* published in 2013. The publications of the *DSM* correspond to the publications of the *ICD,* with an uncertain time frame for the next version of the *DSM,* which will accompany the adopting of the *ICD-11* published by the World Health Organization.

DSM-I *and* DSM-II

The *ICD* is credited as the first official international classification system for mental disorders, with its first edition published in 1948. The APA published the first edition of the *DSM* in 1952. This edition was an attempt to blend the psychological with the biological and provide the practitioner with a unified approach known as the psychobiological point of view. This first version of the *DSM* outlined 60 mental disorders (APA, 1952). In its spiral-bound format, it captured the attention of the mental health community. After the popularity of this first edition, the second edition of the book was published in 1968. Unlike its predecessor, the *DSM-II* did not reflect a particular point of view; it attempted to frame the diagnostic categories in a more scientific way. Both *DSM-I* and *DSM-II,* however, were criticized by many for being unscientific and for increasing the potential for negative labeling of the clients being served (Eysenck, Wakefield, & Friedman, 1983). The mind-set at the time centered on understanding the mental health of individuals based on clinical interpretation and judgment. From this perspective, symbolic and professional meaningful interpretations of symptoms were highlighted. This perspective relied heavily on clinical interpretation while taking into account the client's personal history, total personality, and life experiences (Mayes & Horwitz, 2005). With their focus on the etiological causations for identified mental disorders, these earliest editions were often criticized for the variance in the clinical and diagnostic interpretation within the categories. The fear of individual interpretation leading to a biased psychiatric label that could potentially harm clients made many professionals cautious. The situation was further complicated by the different mental health professionals who were using this book as a diagnostic tool. Originally designed by psychiatrists, for psychiatrists, the related disciplines in mental health soon also began using the book to assist in the diagnostic process. These other disciplines, as well as some psychiatrists, warned of the dangers of using guides such as the *DSM,* arguing that the differences inherent in the basic philosophies of mental health practitioners could lead to interpretation problems. For example, Carlton (1984) and Dziegielewski (2013) felt that social workers, major providers of mental health services, differed in purpose and philosophical orientation from psychiatrists. Since psychiatry is a medical specialty, the focus of its work would be pathology-based linking with the traditional medical model, a perspective very different from social work, a field whose strengths-based perspective historically has focused on how to help clients manage their lives effectively under conditions of physical or mental illness and disability. (See Quick Reference 1.1 for a brief history of the *DSM.*)

DSM-III *and* DSM-III-R

According to Carlton (1984):

> Any diagnostic scheme must be relevant to the practice of the professionals who develop and use it. That is, the diagnosis must direct practitioners' interventions. If it does not do so, the diagnosis is irrelevant. *DSM-III*, despite the contributions of one of its editors, who is a social worker, remains essentially a psychiatric manual. How then can it direct social work interventions? (p. 85)

These professional disagreements in professional orientation continued, with further divisions developing between psychiatrists and psychoanalysts on how to best categorize the symptoms of a mental disorder while taking into account the professional's theoretical orientations. Some professionals, particularly psychiatrists, argued that there was insufficient evidence that major mental disorders were caused by primarily psychological forces; other psychiatrists, especially those skilled in psychotherapy, and other mental health professionals refused to exclude experience and other etiological concepts rooted in psychoanalytic theory (Mayes & Horwitz, 2005).

Other professionals argued that the criteria for normalcy and pathology were biased and that sex-role stereotypes were embedded in the classification and categories of the mental disorders. They believed that women were being victimized by the alleged masculine bias of the system (Boggs et al., 2005; Braun & Cox, 2005; Kaplan, 1983a, 1983b; Kass, Spitzer, & Williams, 1983;

QUICK REFERENCE 1.1

BRIEF HISTORY OF THE *DSM*

- *DSM-I* was first published by the American Psychiatric Association (APA) in 1952 and reflected a psychobiological point of view.
- *DSM-II* (1968) did not reflect a particular point of view. Many professionals criticized both *DSM-I* and *DSM-II* for being unscientific and for encouraging negative labeling.
- *DSM-III* (1980) claimed to be unbiased and more scientific. Many of the earlier problems still persisted, but they were overshadowed by an increasing demand for use of *DSM-III* diagnoses to to qualify for reimbursement from private insurance companies or from government programs. *DSM-III* is often referred to as the first edition that utilized a categorical approach and in previous research studies was often considered the model for comparison.
- *DSM-III-R* (1987) utilized data from field trials that the developers claimed validated the system on scientific grounds. Nevertheless, serious questions were raised about its diagnostic reliability, possible misuse, potential for misdiagnosis, and ethical considerations.
- *DSM-IV* (1994) sought to dispel earlier criticisms of the *DSM*. It included additional cultural information, diagnostic tests, and lab findings and was based on 500 clinical field trials.
- *DSM-IV-TR* (2000) did not change the diagnostic codes or criteria from the *DSM-IV*; however, it supplemented the diagnostic categories with additional information based on research studies and field trials completed in each area.
- *DSM-5* (2013) presented major changes in diagnostic criteria and highlighted a shift toward a dimensional approach over the previous categorical one.

Williams & Spitzer, 1983). The biggest argument in this area came from the contention that research conducted on the *DSM-III* (1980) was less biased and more scientific.

To address these growing concerns, the *DSM-III* (APA, 1980) was noted as being highly innovative. In this edition, a multiaxial system of diagnosis was introduced, specific and explicit criteria sets were included for almost all of the diagnoses, and a substantially expanded text discussion was included to assist with formalizing the diagnostic impression (Spitzer, Williams, & Skodol, 1980). This edition clearly emphasized the importance of using criteria sets based in observational and empirically based research, disregarding underlying psychic mechanisms and causes (Helzer et al., 2008). This edition was considered an improvement over the earlier versions (Bernstein, 2011); however, even this shift from a psychodynamic perspective to the medical model failed to differentiate between classification of healthy and sick individuals (Mayes & Horwitz, 2005). Therefore, many professionals believed that the earlier problems persisted and that observation data and precise definitions were not really possible, as these criteria generally were not grounded in evidence-based practice principles. However, these concerns about application were overshadowed by an increasing demand for use of the *DSM-III* for clients to qualify for participation and reimbursement from insurance companies and governmental programs and for the treatment requirements for managed care delivery systems and pharmaceutical companies.

The APA was challenged to address this issue by an immediate call for independent researchers to critically evaluate the diagnostic categories and test their reliability. The developers initiated a call of their own, seeking research that would support a new and improved revision of this edition of the manual, the *DSM-III-R* (APA, 1987). Some professionals who had originally challenged the foundations of this edition felt that this immediate designation for a revised manual circumvented attempts for independent research by aborting the process and making the proposed revision attempt obsolete. Therefore, all the complaints about the lack of reliability concerning the *DSM-III* became moot because all attention shifted to the revision.

The resulting revision, the *DSM-III-R* (1987), did not end the controversy. This edition did, however, start the emphasis on reporting the results of field trials sponsored by the National Institute of Mental Health (NIMH). According to Mayes and Horwitz (2005), these field trials included information from more than 12,000 patients and more than 500 psychiatrists from across the country. These researchers were familiar with the *DSM-II* and had actually participated in its preliminary drafts. Pleased to see the focus on research-based criteria, critics were still concerned that those who did the criteria verification were the same individuals who supported the narrowly defined set of criteria originally identified as the disorder symptoms (Mayes & Horwitz, 2005). Others felt strongly this was a positive step toward using field trials and evidence-based research, which would allow better statistical assessment of incidence and prevalence rates of mental disorders in the general population (Kraemer, Shrout, & Rubio-Stipec, 2007).

Despite these criticisms, *DSM-III* started the trend that was followed in later versions. It outlined a common language for all mental health providers to use and to define mental disorders for professionals using the book, as well as for the systems in which it was to be utilized in the delivery of mental health services for all parties (Mayes & Horwitz, 2005).

The data gathered from these field trials helped to validate the system on scientific grounds while also raising serious questions about its diagnostic reliability, clinical misuse, potential for misdiagnosis, and ethics of its use (Dumont, 1987; Kutchins & Kirk, 1986; Mayes & Horwitz, 2005). Researchers, such as Kutchins and Kirk (1993), also noted that the new edition (*DSM-III-R*) preserved the same structure and all of the innovations of the *DSM-III,* yet there were many changes in specific diagnoses, resulting in more than 100 categories altered, dropped, or added. The complaint noted that no one would ever know whether the changes improved or detracted from diagnostic reliability when comparing the new manual with the old. Attempts to follow up on the original complaints and concerns about the actual testing of overall reliability of the *DSM-III* were not addressed, even after it was published. Specifically, Kutchins and Kirk (1997) continued to question whether these new revised versions still created an environment where diagnosis might be unnecessary or overapplied. Some researchers believe that these complaints may have evolved from a misunderstanding or misapplication of the statistical component of the *DSM* and how it related to the clinical decision making that was to result (Kraemer, Shrout, & Rubio-Stipec, 2007).

DSM-IV

Less than 1 year after the publication of the *DSM-III-R,* the APA initiated the next revision. The *DSM-IV* was originally scheduled for publication in 1990, and the expectation was that it would carry a strong emphasis on the changes that occurred, grounded by empirical evidence. In addition to the *DSM-IV* itself, a four-volume *DSM-IV* sourcebook provided a comprehensive reference work that supported the research and clinical decisions made by the work groups and the task force responsible for updating the *DSM.* This publication included the results of more than 150 literature reviews, as well as reports outlining the data analysis and reanalysis and reports from the field trials. The four volumes of the sourcebook were the culmination of final decisions made by the task and work groups, presenting the rationale in an executive summary (APA, 1995). Because of this emphasis on evidence-based diagnostic categories and the resulting criteria, publication of *DSM-IV* was delayed until May 1994. The time period waiting its publication (1990–1994) caused some professionals to question whether this publication delay would detract attention and efforts toward substantiating earlier versions of the manual. They felt that more was needed than simply waiting for this newer version of the *DSM,* and this lack of attention could have the same disruptive impact in regard to the manual's overall reliability (Zimmerman, 1988). Most professionals agreed that the *DSM-IV* (1994) did indeed place greater emphasis on empirical evidence as a basis to amend diagnostic rules. The short time period between *DSM-III* and *DSM-III-R* and the subsequent revisions, the paucity of relevant studies, and the lack of a coherent plan to involve statistical consultation in the process limited the feasibility and impact of statistical input (Kraemer, Shrout, & Rubio-Stipec, 2007, p. 259). The *DSM-IV* was hailed for its great improvements, but whether the research-based changes were really enough to address the shortfalls identified was questioned.

DSM-IV-TR: *Another Text Revision*

The *DSM-IV-TR* (the *Diagnostic and Statistical Manual of Mental Disorders, Fourth Edition,* text revision) was published by the American Psychiatric Association in 2000. The *DSM-IV* was published before it had more than 400 mental diagnoses, and the actual number of diagnoses did not change with the revision to *DSM-IV-TR.* The *DSM-IV* and *DSM-IV-TR* clearly had come a long way from the original volume (*DSM-I*) with its 60 diagnostic categories. To prepare for the publication of the *DSM-IV-TR,* with the work starting in 1997, the work and assignments for the task groups for this version, referred to as a text revision, were assigned. Since the *DSM* has historically been used as an educational tool, it was felt that updating this version with the most recent research was essential. The APA originally expected *DSM-5* to be published in 2005, and, with delay after delay, the eventual publication in 2013 left a big gap needing updated information. Surprisingly, even though during this period there was much new research and information, the *DSM-IV* was still considered to be relatively up-to-date, and the text revision did little to update the actual diagnostic criteria. (See Quick Reference 1.2, Reasons for the Publication of the *DSM-IV* and the *DSM-IV-TR,* and Quick Reference 1.3, Intent of the *DSM-IV-TR.*)

There were five primary reasons for releasing the *DSM-IV-TR.*

1. The authors corrected factual errors that cropped up in the *DSM-IV.* For example, there was a diagnosis termed Pervasive Developmental Disorder Not Otherwise Specified, and under this category an error was corrected that had allowed the diagnosis to be given in cases in which there was a pervasive impairment in only one developmental area rather than multiple related areas (APA, 2000). Other areas in which factual inconsistencies were corrected

QUICK REFERENCE 1.2

Reasons for the Publication of the *DSM-IV* and the *DSM-IV-TR*

1. Corrected factual errors.
2. Allowed the work study groups to review each diagnostic category to ensure that information was timely and updated.
3. Incorporated new information from literature reviews and research studies.
4. Enhanced the educational value of the book.
5. Incorporated the updated coding changes from *ICD-10 (ICD-10-CM)*, which at the time was believed to be implemented in 2004.

included Personality Change Due to a General Medical Condition and Bipolar Disorders with Melancholic Features. Comorbidity information related to a disorder was also an important addition in the *DSM-IV-TR* that clearly provided the basis for the more comprehensive diagnostic supporting information provided in *DSM-5*.

2. The authors updated the information in the *DSM-IV* with the latest supporting documentation. Better examples of the different types of behavior were added under a category outlined in this version called Autistic Disorder. Similar data were added to many of the diagnostic categories in an attempt to assist practitioners in forming a more accurate diagnostic impression.
3. At the time the *DSM-IV* was published in 1994, some of the field trials and literature reviews were still under way. The *DSM-IV-TR* included the latest research results from the period between 1994 and 2000 and integrated how this information related to the clinical diagnostic category. The majority of the categories and information from the *DSM-IV*, however, remained up-to-date without modification.
4. Since the *DSM* is often used in educational settings to teach professionals about diagnostic categories, more information was added to support this use.

QUICK REFERENCE 1.3

Intent of the *DSM-IV-TR*

According to the American Psychiatric Association, the intent of this revision was:

- To review existing information posted in the *DSM-IV* and ensure that information was up-to-date for the period and included the latest research and supporting information available.
- To make educational improvements that enhanced the value of the *DSM* as a teaching tool and included in the text the new *ICD-9-CM* codes (as many of these codes did not become available until 1996—the year after the publication of the *DSM-IV*).

5. Not all the *ICD* codes were available until 1996. Thus, those who bought early copies of the *DSM-IV* did not receive the complete *ICD* coding. Later printings included the *ICD* update. It is easy to check whether the *ICD* codes are included in the *DSM-IV* of the book by simply looking at the front cover. If the coding update is included, the cover should have a round orange stamp stating "Updated with *ICD-9-CM* Codes." The *DSM-IV-TR* incorporated the *ICD-9-CM* codes into the text.

In summary, in formulating the text revisions, none of the categories, diagnostic codes, or criteria from the *DSM-IV* changed. What was updated, however, was the supplemental information for many of the categories listed. In addition, more information was provided on many of the field trials introduced in the *DSM-IV* that were not yet completed by the original 1995 publication date. Publishing the *DSM-IV-TR* allowed the inclusion of updated research findings. Furthermore, special attention was paid to updating the sections in terms of diagnostic findings, cultural information, and other information to clarify the diagnostic categories (APA, 2000). Yet with all these changes, Muller (2008) still warned that special caution was needed, regardless of the pronounced efforts to make the *DSM* more research based. Muller clearly outlined the dangers of taking the reports of patients with abnormal thoughts, feelings, and behaviors and stretching them to fit the symptoms related to one or more checklists.

DSM-5—*Long Awaited: Change and Controversy*

Although Chapter 2 discusses the application of the latest version of the *DSM-5* in greater detail, a brief summary of the controversy and changes related to the *DSM-5* is provided here. Similar to previous versions, the American Psychiatric Association continues to develop the *DSM* to reflect clinical approaches to diagnosis and training. Furthermore, similar to its history, the *DSM* continues to strive to be compatible with (but not identical to) the issues presented in the International Classification of Diseases (*ICD-10*) and, to be preemptive, also includes the codes for the *ICD-11* scheduled to be published in 2017.

Prior to the publication of this latest version, *DSM-5,* criticism remained strong. Debates were extensive about what changes needed to occur. Hoffer (2008) encouraged inclusion of additional supportive information, such as medical and diagnostic tests, that could better clarify the diagnoses identified. Sadler, Fulford, and Phil (2004) requested a more comprehensive approach that would take into account the perspective of patients and their families to support both sound policy and public concerns. Shannon and Heckman (2007) warned about the continued danger of being too quick to "pathologize" behaviors and label them. In the midst of this discussion related to the expected changes, Zachar and Kendler (2007) stated it was probably best to just accept that mental disorders are highly complicated concepts that need to be determined. From this perspective, it becomes possible to accept that some aspects of this mental disorder taxonomy will need to be determined (as opposed to discovered) with practical goals and concerns at the forefront of the diagnostic assessment (Ahn & Kim, 2008). Last were the concerns written in open letters to the APA discussing the long-term hazards that can occur when highlighting neurobiology as the standard basis for treatment, while de-emphasizing sociocultural variations and how they can affect the completion of a comprehensive diagnostic impression.

To support this controversy, Caplan (2012) warned that just having the word *statistical* in the title could give professionals and the lay public alike a false sense of hope that the professionals who used the book could do so with scientific precision. Because making a mental health diagnosis remains an unregulated diagnostic category, significant differences in professional acumen and judgment would continue. These differences could easily result in differential diagnostic criteria in research and clinical practice and, similar to previous versions of the *DSM,* could affect problem awareness, knowledge, reporting, and subsequent generalizability of the clinical diagnostic assessments made. Bernstein (2011) questioned how the *DSM-5* work groups would recognize the importance of facilitating communication across what could be considered "restrictive diagnostic silos" (p. 29). Yet she remained optimistic that this could be addressed at least to some degree by recognizing the clusters of symptoms that might best characterize what a client is feeling.

Listening carefully to these concerns, the American Psychiatric Association made some significant changes in the *DSM-5* to both form and content. Consistent with the professional call for modification, to start this process, major changes were made to the structure and the format of the book, resulting in all chapters being organized in the life span order. For example, within this new organizational structure, the mental disorders that can occur in infants, children and adolescents are now listed first in each chapter. This led to the elimination of the Child Disorders section outlined in *DSM-IV* and *DSM-IV-TR.*

Also, relative to Bernstein's (2011) request for clustering of symptoms, crosscutting was introduced, where symptoms relative to a closely related disorder could be taken into account without formulating a new diagnostic condition. In addition, the introduction of the dimensional approach may also help with firming up the diagnosis. This change was one of the revision's most active debates, as it directly surrounded extending the categorical approach to a more dimensional approach (Helzer et al., 2008). The work groups for *DSM-5* hope that the dimensional approach will allow greater flexibility and recognition that mental disorders cannot be easily described by a single diagnostic category (Helzer et al., 2008). Dimensional assessments also appear to permit the practitioner to assess the severity of the symptoms in a particular client while crosscutting or taking into account symptoms relative to a number of different diagnoses that can influence current presentation and behavior. The following chapters of this book will explain many of these pronounced changes in greater detail.

Despite much controversy, the newest edition of the *DSM* was unveiled at the APA conference at the end of May 2013 and has been restructured and divided into three sections (see Quick Reference 1.4). These proposed revisions within the *DSM-5* were supported by a task force of more than 160 world-renowned

QUICK REFERENCE 1.4

DSM-5 THREE SECTIONS

- Section I: Introduction and Directions on How to Use the Updated Manual
- Section II: Outline of the Categorical Diagnoses That Eliminate the Multi-Axial System (20 Disorder Chapters and Two Additional Supporting Information Categories)
- Section III: Conditions That Require Future Research, Cultural Formulations, and Other Information

QUICK REFERENCE 1.5

CATEGORICAL SECTIONS: 20 DISORDERS AND TWO ADDITIONAL CATEGORIES

***DSM-5* Chapters**	
Neurodevelopmental Disorders	Gender Dysphoria
Schizophrenia Spectrum and the Other Psychotic Disorders	Disruptive, Impulse Control, and Conduct Disorders
Bipolar and the Related Disorders	Substance-Related and Addictive Disorders
Depressive Disorders	Neurocognitive Disorders
Anxiety Disorders	Personality Disorders
Obsessive-Compulsive and the Related Disorders	Paraphilic Disorders
Trauma and Stressor-Related Disorders	Other Mental Disorders
Dissociative Disorders	*Medication-Induced Movement Disorders and Other Adverse Effects of Medication
Somatic Symptom Disorders	*Other Conditions That May Be a Focus of Clinical Attention
Feeding and Eating Disorders	*Includes other conditions and problems that require clinical attention but are not considered mental disorders.
Elimination Disorders	*Not considered mental disorders.
Sleep-Wake Disorders	
Sexual Dysfunctions	

practitioners and researchers who were selected members of 13 work groups. These work groups reviewed the research literature, consulted with a number of experts, and for the first time sought public comment. Section One provides an introduction to the manual, some rationale for the changes, and instructions on how to use the updated manual. It is followed by 21 chapters that outline the documented mental disorders found in Section Two (see Quick Reference 1.5). The last section of the manual, Section Three, outlines the conditions that require future research, cultural formulations, and other information.

DIAGNOSTIC LABELS

Regardless of the controversy surrounding the use of the earlier, current, or future versions of the *DSM* as a diagnostic assessment tool, such tools continue to be used. One of the biggest concerns remains: Categorizing an individual with a mental health diagnosis can result in a psychiatric label that is difficult to remove. Many practitioners believe that they must always consider the implications of making the diagnosis. When used properly, the identification of disorders and the acquisition and reimbursement of delivered services results. Consequences that are not intended can lead to social stigma and loss of other opportunities (Caplan, 2012; Moses, 2009). There is no question that labeling an individual with a mental health diagnosis can result in personal and public stigma (Hinshaw & Stier, 2008). In fact, some mental health professionals feel so strongly about labeling clients that they continue to resist using this assessment scheme in their practices. For example (as is discussed later in this text), if a child is given the diagnosis of conduct disorder in youth, many professionals believe that this condition will continue into adulthood, resulting in the classification of a lifelong mental health condition known as antisocial personality disorder. What complicates this diagnosing pattern further is that clients who receive such a diagnosis may start acting that way, creating a negative feedback loop that leads the individual to act in accordance with the condition given (Tsou, 2007).

Such a label, whether accurate or inaccurate, can be very damaging to the client because of the negative connotations that characterize it and because of what then becomes expected of the client for himself or herself and others. The negative connotations that sometimes accompany the diagnostic label of conduct disorder (e.g., generally unresponsive to intervention, lack of moral standards, and lack of guilt) may result in conduct-disordered behaviors that may not have been present to begin with (e.g., severe aggression toward people or animals). These types of behaviors are unacceptable by all societal standards, yet if legitimized as part of a diagnosis, the effect can be twofold: If in conduct disorder it is expected that the client has no control over the behaviors exhibited, these overt actions may be viewed as acceptable or unchangeable. When unacceptable behaviors are considered an inevitable part of the diagnosis, there may be less hope for the individual's capacity for growth and change. Also, if the condition is not present but the individual was incorrectly classified with the diagnosis of conduct disorder, the client may begin to develop behaviors viewed as unacceptable and unchangeable, thus acting in accordance with the diagnosis. Regardless, these behaviors are accepted or tolerated because they are related to a mental disorder. (See Quick Reference 1.6 for a list of some Positive Aspects (pros) and Negative Aspects (cons) of the *DSM*-5.)

One common misconception that remains true about each edition of the *DSM* diagnostic scheme is that "the classification of mental disorders classifies people, when actually what are being classified are the disorders that people have" (APA, 2000, p. xxxi). Professionals must be sensitive to the labels placed and utilized when referring to people who have a mental health disorder. For example, never refer to an individual as "a schizophrenic" but rather as "an individual with schizophrenia" or "an individual who suffers from schizophrenia." Consideration should always be used to ensure that terms are not used incorrectly and that individuals who have a mental disorder are not referred to or

QUICK REFERENCE 1.6

DSM-5: Positive Aspects (PRO) and Negative Aspects (CON)

PRO: Leads to uniform and improved diagnosis.

CON: Leads to diagnostic labels.

PRO: Improves informed professional communication through uniformity.

CON: Can provide limited information on the relationship between environmental considerations and aspects of the mental health condition.

PRO: Provides the basis for a comprehensive diagnostic and educational tool.

CON: Does not describe intervention strategy.

treated in a careless or derogatory manner. It is important to guard against this type of labeling and to remind others to do so as well.

When mental health assessment schemes are utilized, a diagnostic label is placed on the client. In the ideal situation, labels would not exist, nor would treatment for certain mental health conditions be more likely than others to be reimbursed. Often in health and mental health practice, much of the assessment and diagnosis process is completed based on service reimbursement needs. Many health care professionals feel the pressure and focus on more reimbursable diagnostic categories, although there can be serious consequences for these pressures. For mental health practitioners, careful evaluation of what is actually happening with the client is essential. The diagnostic assessment starts with providing an accurate diagnosis (despite reimbursements as a criterion and incentive to diagnose). In this process, care is taken to prepare the client for the stigma that can occur with trying to overcome a diagnostic label with negative connotations or a label for which reimbursement is typically not allowed.

ANOTHER MENTAL HEALTH ASSESSMENT MEASURE

Social workers believe strongly in design and base all practice strategy on the recognition of the person in the environment or person in the situation (Colby & Dziegielewski, 2010; Dziegielewski, 2013). From this perspective, the individual is believed to be part of the social environment, and his or her actions cannot be separated from this system. The individual is influenced by environmental factors in a reciprocal manner.

Impetus toward the development of this perspective may be partially related to dissatisfaction with the reliance on psychiatric-based typologies, which failed to account for environmental influences. The categorical approaches within the *DSM* did not appear to give such influences proper attention. Because these existing categories did not involve psychosocial situations or units larger than the individual within a system, problems were not viewed from an environmental context, thereby increasing the probability of such problems being classified as a mental illness (Braun & Cox, 2005). In such a system, mental health practitioners could diagnose an individual with a mental health condition due to some general medical or symptom-based concern but were given no leeway to address a mental health condition based on life events and/or situational factors.

What transpired with the dynamic changes starting in the *DSM-III* encouraged social workers and other mental health professionals to provide aggregate parts to a diagnostic classification system. This focus on the individual tended to minimize the psychological and social causation, focusing more strongly on the reductive and biological causations of the disorders, hence its specific focus on symptom-based typologies (Brendel, 2001). Clear demarcation of symptom-based criteria for diagnosing and classification encouraged by insurance companies became an efficient and cost-effective measure for the treatment of mental disorders. Because insurance companies required a medical diagnosis before service reimbursement, social workers, psychologists, and other mental health professionals waged a long and difficult fight to use *DSM* independently for third-party payment purposes and their distinct services.

Originally developed through an award given to the California chapter of the National Association of Social Workers (NASW) from the NASW Program Advancement Fund (Whiting, 1996), a system was designed to focus on psychosocial aspects, situations, and units larger than the individual. It was called the Person-in-Environment Classification System, or PIE (Karls &

Wandrei, 1996a, 1996b). It is built around two major premises: recognition of social considerations and the person-in-environment stance—the cornerstone on which all social work practice rests. Knowledge of the PIE is relevant for all mental health social workers regardless of educational level because of its emphasis on situational factors (Karls & O'Keefe, 2008, 2009).

The PIE system calls first for a social work assessment that is translated into a description of coding of the client's problems in social functioning. Social functioning is the client's ability to accomplish the activities necessary for daily living (e.g., obtaining food, shelter, and transportation) and fulfill major social roles as required by the client's subculture or community (Karls & Wandrei, 1996a, p. vi).

Originally designed to support the use of the *DSM-IV* rather than as a substitute for it, the PIE's purpose was to evaluate the social environment and to influence the revisions of the *DSM*. Essentially, the PIE provided social workers and social work educators with a tool that allowed environmental factors to be considered of primary importance. The PIE, an environmentally sensitive tool, supplemented the descriptive system of the *DSM* that related the mental illness to the human condition, utilizing a holistic, ecological, and pluralistic approach rather than just the diagnosis-focused (medical) foundational basis of the *DSM* (Satterly, 2007).

Social workers proposed an ecosystems perspective incorporating the assumption that clinical practice needs to include the individual within his or her social environment and that his or her actions cannot be separated from his or her support system. Therefore, the PIE adopted features of the *DSM-IV* and *DSM-IV-TR* multiaxial diagnostic system in its assessment typology and had a notable influence on *DSM* revisions, particularly in the area of recognizing environmental problems. One concrete example of the PIE's influence on the *DSM-IV* is the change of Axis IV of the diagnostic system to reflect "psychosocial and environmental problems" where the problem is clearly listed; in the past the *DSM-III-R* Axis IV merely listed the "severity of psychosocial stressors" and ranked the problem on a scale. Although the multiaxial system has been deleted in *DSM-5*, Chapter 22 lists "Other Conditions That May Be a Focus of Clinical Attention," which continue to be used.

The PIE was formulated in response to the need to identify client problems in a way that health professionals could easily understand (Karls & Wandrei, 1996a, 1996b). As a form of classification system for adults, the PIE provides:

- A common language with which social workers in all settings can describe their clients' problems in social functioning.
- A common capsule description of social phenomena that can facilitate treatment or ameliorate problems presented by clients.
- A basis for gathering data to be used to measure the need for services and to design human service programs to evaluate effectiveness.
- A mechanism for clearer communication among social work practitioners and between practitioners, administrators, and researchers.
- A basis for clarifying the domain of social work in human service fields (Karls & Wandrei, 1996a).

In professional practice, tools such as the PIE can facilitate the identification and assessment of clients from a person-in-environment perspective that is easy for social workers to accept as comprehensive. When compared with the *DSM-IV-TR* and *DSM-5,* the PIE provides mental health professionals with a classification system that enables them to codify the numerous environmental factors considered when they look at an individual's situation. Classification systems like the PIE allow mental health professionals to first recognize and later systematically address social factors in the context of the client's environment. The PIE can help professionals to obtain a clearer sense of the relationship the problem has to the environment in a friendly and adaptable way.

PROFESSIONAL TRAINING IN THE PROFESSIONAL COUNSELING FIELDS

This book is written as a guide for several different disciplines of health and mental health professionals. Similar to the *DSM,* this book is designed to support use in medicine and psychiatry, psychology, social work, nursing, and counseling. This type of integration, with so many diverse yet similar fields, is no easy task because different professions follow different practice models and methods. Yet regardless of which discipline a professional is trained in, there is often great overlap of therapeutic knowledge and skill. In the next chapter, special attention is given to how to apply the diagnostic framework outlined in *DSM-5.*

If practitioners are going to continue to utilize diagnostic assessment systems in the future, there are major implications for professional training and education. MacCluskie and Ingersoll (2001) are quick to remind us that, if professionals of different disciplines are going to use the *DSM,* training and adequate preparation in its use in classroom instruction and as part of a practicum or internship is required. This requires adopting a more homogeneous approach to education and application among all helping disciplines. Other professionals, such as Horn (2008), remind us that all current interpretations must remain flexible and that, as we adopt the new version, *DSM-5,* we must remain vigilant of the ethical concerns that can result from misuse of this important diagnostic tool.

In today's practice environment, most would argue that the interdisciplinary approach of professionals working together to help the client is here to stay. To provide this homogeneity from a practice perspective, almost all professional helpers share one goal: to "help clients manage their problems in living more effectively and develop unused or underused opportunities more fully" (Egan, 1998, p. 7). Now, to extend unification while ensuring competent, ethical, and homogeneous practice, these helping disciplines will also need to unite in terms of professional education, mission, and goals. The first principle for the unification of professional education across disciplines is that (regardless of whether it is for social work, psychology, or other fields of professional counseling) training programs need to be more uniform and specific about what professional training entails and the effect it has on those who participate. When training can be defined in a reasonably specific manner and measured empirically, these professions will better assess its effects on client behavior. With the contemporary emphasis on professional accountability, the effort to predict and document specific outcomes of professional training is timely as well as warranted. The data also suggest that one way professional training can be further enhanced is through differential selection of specified treatment methods. Training in these different treatment methods allows different causative variables (i.e., feelings and actions) to be identified in the course of assessing the client's behavior. Some researchers believe that sticking primarily to traditional methods, which are still a great part of professional training that emphasizes dispositional diagnoses (i.e., the direct relationship of the diagnosis and how it will relate to discharge), may result in diminishing accuracy of behavior assessment (Dziegielewski, 2013).

Educators can improve the accuracy of client behavioral evaluations through the introduction of specific training in behavioral assessment. This may be the primary reason that in health care, the behaviorally based biopsychosocial approach has gained popularity. Clinical assessment, particularly when it emphasizes client behaviors, is a skill that can easily be taught, transmitted, and measured. Therefore, professional training that includes behavioral observation on how to construct observable and reliable categories of behavior and various systems of observation is recommended.

SUMMARY

As emphasized in this chapter, the *International Classification of Diseases* and the *Diagnostic and Statistical Manual of Mental Disorders* reflect the official nomenclature used in mental health and other health-related facilities in the United States. Diagnostic assessment systems such as the *DSM,* the *ICD,* and the PIE are three descriptive (categorical) classification schemes that cross all theoretical orientations.

The concept of understanding mental disorders; their taxonomical categorization; the formulation and completion of a diagnosis, assessment, or the diagnostic assessment; and their definitions and meanings are embedded in the history of the *DSM.* Exactly what constitutes *diagnosis* and what constitutes *assessment* remains blurred and overlapping, with the words used interchangeably yet remaining distinct and interrelated. For all professional practitioners, compelling demands and pressures related to practice reimbursement clearly emphasize the need for coordination in providing mental health care and subsequent intervention. Despite the differences among the disciplines, all mental health professionals need to be familiar with and able to apply the criteria used in the *DSM* diagnosis.

Because of the increasing demands related to evidence-based practice to achieve outcomes to assess quality, the effectiveness of service delivery, and the collection of data, numerous diagnosis and assessment measurements are currently available. Many are structured in unique categories and classification schemes. Whether this categorical approach used in the *DSM* is replaced by a dimensional one in the *DSM-5* still remains to be seen (Helzer et al., 2008). Utilizing the current system, this text demonstrates the application of these classification schemes and describes how assessment, treatment planning, and intervention become intertwined (Dziegielewski, 2008). Because assessment and treatment are based primarily on the practitioner's clinical judgment and interpretation, a thorough grounding in these classification systems will help the practitioner make relevant, useful, and ethically sound evaluations of clients.

Practitioners need to remain familiar and update their knowledge with some of the major formal methods of diagnosis and assessment, especially the ones most commonly used for billing of mental health services. The changes made over time and efforts toward betterment within the criteria outlined in the *DSM* have moved it toward becoming the best diagnostic tool possible. All mental health practitioners, regardless of discipline, can benefit by utilizing this information to systematically interpret and assist clients in understanding what the results of the diagnostic assessment mean and how best to select empirically sound and ethically wise modes of practice intervention.

No matter whether we call what professional practitioners do assessment, diagnosis, or a combination resulting in the diagnostic assessment, the function remains a critical part of the helping process. Diagnosis and assessment is the critical first step to formulating the plan for intervention (Dziegielewski et al., 2002; Dziegielewski & Leon, 2001). The plan for intervention sets the entire tone and circumstances of the professional helping process. As Dziegielewski (2013) has stated, based on the general context of reimbursement or fee for service, is it wise for all professionals to continue to struggle to differentiate diagnosis and assessment? Unfortunately, with the shift in mental health care to market-based services, practice and methods have evolved to reflect specialization, integration, and cost-effectiveness as part and parcel of service delivery. Now the question that arises is: Who is eligible to make a diagnosis or an assessment? Professionals are lobbying, and professional licensures reflect this transition and can help to provide public accountability.

Today, the role of the practitioner is twofold: (1) ensure that high-quality service is provided to the client and (2) provide the client access and opportunity to see that his or her health and mental health needs are addressed. Neither of these tasks is easy or popular. Amid this turbulence, the role and necessity of the services that the practitioner provides in assessment and intervention remain clear. All helping professionals must know and utilize the tools of diagnostic assessment and demonstrate competence in properly completing diagnostic assessment—the first step in the treatment hierarchy. To achieve this, it is crucial that health and mental health professionals have comprehensive training in this area to meet current requirements and service needs in an environment filled with limitations and shortages. The question remains: How can we best help the clients we serve?

QUESTIONS FOR FURTHER THOUGHT

1. Is there a difference between the terms *diagnosis* and *assessment?* How would you define the diagnostic assessment, and what client-relevant factors are the most important to identify?
2. Are these terms treated differently and assumed to have different meanings if the practitioner is in a particular health or mental health setting?
3. What do you believe is the most helpful aspect of using manuals such as the *DSM-5* in the diagnostic process?
4. What do you feel are the least helpful aspects of using manuals such as the *DSM-5* in professional practice?
5. Do you believe that use of the *DSM* as a diagnostic/assessment tool will facilitate your practice experience? Why or why not?

REFERENCES

Ahn, W., & Kim, N. S. (2008). Causal theories of mental disorder concepts. *Psychological Science Agenda, 22*(6), 3–8.

American Psychiatric Association. (1952). *Diagnostic and statistical manual of mental disorders*. Washington, DC: Author.

American Psychiatric Association. (1980). *Diagnostic and statistical manual of mental disorders* (3rd ed.). Washington, DC: Author.

American Psychiatric Association. (1987). *Diagnostic and statistical manual of mental disorders* (3rd ed., rev.). Washington, DC: Author.

American Psychiatric Association. (1995). *Diagnostic and statistical manual of mental disorders* (4th ed., rev). Washington, DC: Author.

American Psychiatric Association. (2000). *Diagnostic and statistical manual of mental disorders* (4th ed., text rev.). Washington, DC: Author.

American Psychiatric Association. (2013). *Diagnostic and Statistical Manual of Mental Disorders* (5th ed.). Arlington, VA: American Psychiatric Publishing.

Bernstein, C. A. (2011). Meta-structure in the *DSM-5* process. *Psychiatric News, 46*(5), 7–29.

Boggs, C. D., Morey, L. C., Skodol, A. E., Shea, M. T., Sanislow, C. A., Grilo, C. M., . . . Gunderson, J. G. (2005). Differential impairment as an indicator of sex bias in *DSM-IV* criteria for four personality disorders. *Psychological Assessment, 17*, 492–496.

Braun, S. A., & Cox, J. A. (2005). Managed mental health care: Intentional misdiagnosis of mental disorders. *Journal of Counseling and Development, 83*, 425–433.

Brendel, D. H. (2001). Multifactorial causation of mental disorders: A proposal to improve the *DSM. Harvard Review of Psychiatry, 9*(1), 42–45.

Bureau of Labor Statistics, U.S. Department of Labor. (2012). *Occupational outlook handbook, social workers, 2012–2013 ed.* Retrieved from: http://www.bls.gov/ooh/community-and-social-service/social-workers.htm#tab-3

Caplan, P. J. (2012, April 27). Psychiatry's bible, the *DSM*, is doing more harm than good. *The Washington Post.* Retrieved from http://www.washingtonpost.com

Carlton, T. O. (1984). *Clinical social work in health care settings: A guide to professional practice with exemplars.* New York, NY: Springer.

Carlton, T. O. (1989). Classification and diagnosis in social work in health care. *Health and Social Work, 14*(2), 83–85.

Colby, I., & Dziegielewski, S. F. (2010). *Introduction to social work: The people's profession* (3rd ed.). Chicago, IL: Lyceum Books.

Davis, S. R., & Meier, S. T. (2001). *The elements of managed care: A guide for helping professionals.* Belmont, CA: Brooks/Cole.

Dumont, M. P. (1987). A diagnostic parable: First edition, unrevised. *Journal of Reviews and Commentary in Mental Health, 2,* 9–12.

Dziegielewski, S. F. (2008). Brief and intermittent approaches to practice: The state of practice. *Journal of Brief Treatment and Crisis Intervention, 8*(2), 147–163.

Dziegielewski, S. F. (2013). *The changing face of health care social work: Opportunities and challenges for professional practice* (3rd ed.). New York, NY: Springer.

Dziegielewski, S. F., Johnson, A., & Webb, E. (2002). *DSM-IV* and social work professionals: A continuing education evaluation. *Social Work in Mental Health, 1*(1), 27–41.

Dziegielewski, S. F., & Leon, A. M. (2001). Time-limited case recording: Effective documentation in a changing environment. *Journal of Brief Therapy, 1*(1).

Egan, G. (1998). *The skilled helper: A problem management approach to helping* (6th ed.). Pacific Grove, CA: Brooks/Cole.

Eysenck, H. J., Wakefield, J. A. Jr., & Friedman, A. F. (1983). Diagnosis and clinical assessment: The *DSM-III. Annual Review of Psychology, 34,* 167–193.

Feisthamel, K. P., & Schwartz, R. C. (2009). Differences in mental health counselors' diagnoses based on client race: An investigation of adjustment, childhood, and substance-related disorders. *Journal of Mental Health Counseling.* Retrieved from http://www.thefreelibrary.com/Differences+in+mental+health+counselors%27+diagnoses+based+on+client . . . -a0193182088

First, M. B., & Westen, D. (2007). Classification for clinical practice: How to make *ICD* and *DSM* better able to serve clinicians. *International Review of Psychiatry, 19*(5), 473–481.

Helzer, J. E., Kraemer, H. C., Krueger, R. F., Wittchen, H. U., Sirovatka, P. J., & Regier, D. A. (Eds.). (2008). *Dimensional approaches in diagnostic classification: Refining the research agenda for* DSM-V. Washington, DC: American Psychiatric Association.

Hinshaw, S. P., & Stier, A. (2008). Stigma in relation to mental disorders. *Annual Review of Clinical Psychology, 4,* 269–293.

Hoffer, A. (2008). Child psychiatry: Does modern psychiatry treat or abuse? *Journal of Orthomolecular Medicine, 23*(3), 139–152.

Horn, P. (2008). Psychiatric ethics consultation in light of the *DSM-V. HEC Forum, 20*(4), 315–324.

Kaplan, M. (1983a). A woman's view of *DSM-III. American Psychologist, 38,* 786–792.

Kaplan, M. (1983b). The issue of sex bias in *DSM-III*: Comments on articles by Spitzer, Williams, and Kass. *American Psychologist, 38,* 802–803.

Karls, J. M., & O'Keefe, M. E. (2008). *The PIE Manual.* Washington, DC: NASW Press.

Karls, J. M., & O'Keefe, M. E. (2009). Person in environment system. In A. R. Roberts (Ed.), *Social workers' desk reference* (2nd ed., pp. 371–376). New York, NY: Oxford University Press.

Karls, J. M., & Wandrei, K. M. (Eds.). (1996a). *Person-in-environment system: The PIE classification system for social functioning problems.* Washington, DC: NASW Press.

Karls, J. M., & Wandrei, K. M. (1996b). *PIE manual: Person-in-environment system: The PIE classification system for social functioning problems.* Washington, DC: NASW Press.

Kass, F., Spitzer, R. L., & Williams, J. B. W. (1983). An empirical study of the issue of sex bias in the diagnostic criteria of *DSM-III* Axis II personality disorders. *American Psychologist, 38,* 799–801.

Kessler, R. C., Chiu, W. T., Demler, O., & Walters, E. E. (2005). Prevalence, severity, and comorbidity of twelve-month *DSM-IV* disorders in the national comorbidity survey replication (NCS-R). *Archives of General Psychiatry, 62,* 617–627.

Kielbasa, A. M., Pomerantz, A. M., Krohn, E. J., & Sullivan, B. F. (2004). How does clients' method of payment influence psychologists' diagnostic decisions? *Ethics and Behavior, 14,* 187–195.

Kraemer, H. C., Shrout, P. E., & Rubio-Stipec, M. (2007). Developing the diagnostic and statistical manual V: What will "statistical" mean in the *DSMV*? *Social Psychiatry and Psychiatric Epidemiology, 42,* 259–267.

Kutchins, H., & Kirk, S. A. (1986). The reliability of *DSM-III*: A critical review. *Social Work Research and Abstracts, 22*, 3–12.

Kutchins, H., & Kirk, S. A. (1988). The business of diagnosis. *Social Work, 33*, 215–220.

Kutchins, H., & Kirk, S. A. (1993). DSM-IV and the hunt for gold: A review of the treasure map. *Research on Social Work Practice, 3*(2), 219–235.

Kutchins, H., & Kirk, S. A. (1997). *Making us crazy. DSM: The psychiatric bible and the creation of mental disorders.* New York, NY: Free Press.

MacCluskie, K. C., & Ingersoll, R. E. (2001). *Becoming a 21st century agency counselor.* Belmont, CA: Brooks/Cole, Thompson Learning.

Mayes, R., & Horwitz, A. V. (2005). *DSM III* and the revolution in the classification of mental illness. *Journal of the History of the Behavioral Sciences, 41*(3), 249–267.

Moses, T. (2009). Stigma and self-concept among adolescents receiving mental health treatment. *American Journal of Orthopsychiatry, 79*(2), 264–274.

Muller, R. J. (2008). *Doing psychiatry wrong: A critical and prescriptive look at a faltering profession.* New York, NY: Analytic Press.

Pomerantz, A. D., & Segrist, D. J. (2006). The influence of payment method on psychologists' diagnostic decisions regarding minimally impaired clients. *Ethics and Behavior, 16*(3), 253–263.

Sadler, J. Z. (Ed.). (2002). *Descriptions & prescriptions: Values, mental disorders and the DSMs.* Baltimore, MD: Johns Hopkins University Press.

Sadler, J. Z., Fulford, B., & Phil, M. B. (2004). Should patients and their families contribute to the *DSM-V* process. *Psychiatric Services, 55*, 133–138.

Satterly, B. A. (2007). The alternative lenses of assessment: Educating social workers about psychopathology. *Teaching in Social Work, 27*(3/4), 241–257.

Shannon, S., & Heckman, E. (2007). *Please don't label my child: Break the doctor–diagnosis–drug cycle and discover safe, effective choices for your child's emotional health.* New York, NY: Rodale.

Sommers-Flanagan, R. S., & Sommers-Flanagan, J. (2007). *Philosophical foundations.* Hoboken, NJ: Wiley.

Spitzer, R. L., Williams, J. B. W., & Skodol, A. E. (1980). *DSM-III*: The major achievements and an overview. *American Journal of Psychiatry, 137*, 151–164.

Tsou, J. Y. (2007). Hacking on the looping effects of psychiatric classifications: What is an interactive and indifferent kind? *International Studies in the Philosophy of Science, 21*(3), 329–344.

Whiting, L. (1996). Foreword. In J. M. Karls & K. M. Wandrei (Eds.), *Person-in-environment system: The PIE classification system for social functioning problems* (pp. xiii–xv). Washington, DC: NASW Press.

Williams, J. B. W., & Spitzer, R. L. (1983). The issue of sex bias in *DSM-III*: A critique of "A woman's view of *DSM-III*" by Marcie Kaplan. *American Psychologist, 38*, 793–798.

Zachar, P., & Kendler, K. S. (2007). Psychiatric disorders: A conceptual taxonomy. *American Journal of Psychiatry, 164*, 557–565.

Zimmerman, M. (1988). Why are we rushing to publish *DSM-IV? Archives of General Psychiatry, 45*, 1135–1138.

CHAPTER 2

Basics and Application

The concept of formulating and completing a diagnostic assessment is richly embedded in the history of mental health practice (Ahn & Kim, 2008; Dziegielewski, 2010). The desire to master this process has been strengthened by its necessity for practice reimbursement (Dziegielewski, 2013). Therefore, all mental health practitioners need to become familiar with the major formal methods of diagnostic assessment, especially the ones used and accepted in health and mental health service delivery. This chapter outlines the issues that contribute to the hesitancy and reluctance to determine what constitutes a mental disorder and how the terms *diagnosis* and *assessment* relate. If these two terms are seen as a dichotomy, obvious difficulty in practice focus and strategy may result. The purpose of this chapter is to explore the relationship between diagnosis and assessment and to introduce a more comprehensive term, the diagnostic assessment. The diagnostic assessment describes a combination approach that utilizes the meaning inherent in each term.

Once the terms are clearly defined, the information gathered during the diagnostic assessment becomes central for identifying and classifying mental health disorders, as well as reporting this information systematically to insurance companies for reimbursement. In completing the diagnostic assessment, factors such as race, ethnicity, culture, and gender can affect the diagnostic impression derived. With the rapid changes related to globalization, culture has become so embedded in the human experience that separating it out is almost impossible (Pare, 2013). Recognition of this supporting information is essential to ensure the comprehensive diagnostic assessment that is vital for high-quality care. The information gathered through a comprehensive diagnostic assessment can also be utilized to understand the client and, in turn, better help the client understand himself or herself. Once completed, the diagnostic assessment becomes the foundation for identifying problem behaviors that will be utilized in establishing treatment plan considerations, as well as the best course of intervention for a particular client. Because most fields of practice utilize the *DSM* as the basis of the formal diagnostic assessment system, this text focuses on this classification scheme.

UTILIZING THE *DSM-5* IN THE PRACTICE SETTING

In the United States, most health and mental health practitioners use the *DSM* to classify mental health problems. However, as described in Chapter 1, the *DSM*, which was originally designed for statistical and assessment purposes, does not suggest treatment approaches. This makes the *DSM* essential as a starting point for determining the nature of a client's problem, as well as providing supportive information on prevalence rates within the larger population to inform policy decisions. Thus, the book is valuable for clinicians, practitioners, and researchers. For researchers, the interest lies in understanding the etiology and pathophysiology of the disorders; for clinicians, the focus remains on the immediate and pragmatic, such as identifying clinically significant symptoms that affect human behavior and functioning (Nunes & Rounsaville, 2006). The *DSM* does, however, fall short on treatment strategy and options. Therefore, supportive books are required to address this important aspect of comprehensive, efficient, and effective care. In addition to the information provided in the *DSM-5*, practitioners need to be familiar with the latest and most effective forms of treatment and practice strategy based on relevant diagnostic criteria.

Professional Use: Who Can Use the DSM-5?

The *DSM-5* states clearly that it was designed to be used in a wide variety of settings, including inpatient and outpatient settings and consultation and liaison work. Furthermore, the *DSM-5* was designed for use by professionals, not as a self-help book for the lay public. The *DSM* is very complex and could overwhelm a client unfamiliar with the technical jargon. Therefore, use by the lay public is discouraged. Historically, the role of the professional is to interpret the diagnostic criteria, inform the client, and work with the client on what the best course of action would be.

The *DSM-IV-TR* and *DSM-5* both clearly state this philosophy, although Paris (2013) questions it. He believes that clients have a right to know their own diagnoses and that the more they know, the more they are empowered to participate in self-help strategies. Also, with the Internet and other forms of information so readily accessible, clients often actively gather information related to their own mental health. This supports the notion that clients should not be kept unaware of their diagnoses and the contributing criteria. To do this creates a disservice that forces them to be passive consumers of their own health and mental health care. Most practitioners would agree wholeheartedly that client participation in their own health care is essential, so why not their own mental health care? Arguments that the *DSM* is very complex and could overwhelm a client unfamiliar with the technical jargon have been questioned, and active client participation has become expected (Paris, 2013).

This active involvement is confirmed by the use of technology. Many clients are savvy in using the Internet to look up information, and it makes sense that they would not hesitate to look up information related to their own health and mental health needs, as well as those of family members. Unfortunately, this opens up the client to information that may or may not be accurate, adequate, or entirely relevant to his or her situation. Or clients may be in a compromised cognitive position that does not allow them to fully integrate this information. To further complicate this picture, the Internet is such an open venue that the information gained may not be reputable and may be misleading or confusing to the client or his or her family. Although *DSM* information is designed for the professional, when questioned about a diagnostic assessment and information is shared with the client, professional awareness and support are essential for the best treatment outcomes.

In certain types of therapy, it is not uncommon to share diagnostic information with the client. For example, in some cognitive behavioral approaches, a client may be presented with a list of criteria reflecting the symptoms of a diagnosis and asked which ones he or she has. Once self-identified, how to behaviorally address the symptoms may be the next step. From this, a treatment plan with a clear practice strategy related to how to either control the symptoms or avoid them may be implemented. Therefore, regardless of whether the *DSM* is designed for professionals, client-initiated interactions related to this information may occur. Knowing how to best handle this situation for the client and his or her family members is an important part of the therapeutic process.

This book is designed for professional practitioners who use the *DSM-5,* including psychiatrists and other physicians, psychologists, social workers, occupational and rehabilitation therapists, and other health and mental health professionals. Although they may all have different training and expertise, they still are expected to use this categorical and dimensional approach by applying clinical skill and judgment to achieve similar determinations. These professionals need to be trained in how to use this categorical and dimensional approach and be aware of its potential for misuse before putting it into practice. Special care and consideration are necessary to protect the rights of clients while identifying issues to be addressed to ensure client benefit and progress.

WORKING AS PART OF A TEAM: CONNECTIONS AND COLLABORATIONS

Serving as part of a team, social workers and other mental health professionals have a unique role in the assessment and diagnostic process. Most professionals agree that a comprehensive diagnostic assessment starts with taking into account the complexity of the human condition and situational factors that affect behavioral health (Pearson, 2008). As part of a collaborative team, the mental health professional gathers a wealth of information regarding the client's environment and family considerations. The practitioner also needs to remain aware that whether taking a leadership or supportive role, all efforts must resonate with the culture of the team (Conyne, 2014). Therefore, the practitioner can serve as the professional bridge that links the client to the multidisciplinary, interdisciplinary, and transdisciplinary teams and the environment (Dziegielewski, 2013).

The term *multidisciplinary* can best be explained by dividing it into its two roots, *multi* and *discipline. Multi* means "many" or "multiple"; *discipline* means "the field of study a professional engages in." When combined, professionals from multiple disciplines work together to address a common problem. In health care settings, multidisciplinary teams were part of a cost-effective practice response to the shifts from institutional care to community and home care through the delivery of specialized services (Rosen & Callaly, 2005). This type of team collaboration may also improve patient care outcomes (Burns & Lloyd, 2004). The multidisciplinary team is often recognized as a preferred form of service delivery, especially in complex health and mental health service delivery systems (Orovwuje, 2008). Multidisciplinary teams include health and social welfare professionals from various disciplines: psychiatrists, physicians, nurses, social workers, physical therapists, occupational therapists, and so on.

When serving on a multidisciplinary team, each member has a distinct professional role and refers to other professionals in the same or other agencies in a loose yet semistructured manner. Each professional generally works independently, sometimes in isolation, to solve the problems and related needs of the individual. At the same time, the professionals share what is learned about the client to improve treatment progress and overall team concerns. A key feature of multidisciplinary teams is participants' network-style group interaction (Rosen & Callaly, 2005), in which the boundaries within professional disciplines are maintained, with each providing a perspective of the client's problem to address key features in the delivery of care. This process of patient care planning provides a comprehensive method of service delivery for the client. In multidisciplinary teamwork, "a team manages its resources collectively according to

QUICK REFERENCE 2.1

Multidisciplinary Teams	A group of professionals working together for a common purpose, working independently while sharing information through formal lines of communication to better assist the patient/client/consumer.

Definition from *The Changing Face of Health Care Social Work: Opportunities and Challenges for Professional Practice (3rd edition)*, by S. F. Dziegielewski, 2013, New York, NY: Springer (p. 35).

client needs or along professional discipline boundaries" (Whyte & Brooker, 2001, p. 27). Communication and goals are consistent across disciplines, with each contributing to the overall welfare of the client. (See Quick Reference 2.1.)

In the current mental health care system, which stresses evidence-based practices and outcomes to measure quality, multidisciplinary approaches are limited in meeting the current standards of care secondary to their structural makeup and style of approach to service delivery. Measurement is difficult when the interpretation of the stated goals and how to best achieve them differs among varied professionals. These professionals are all committed to working together to help the client, but in this type of teamwork, there may be different approaches and expectations for what is considered high-quality care and how to best achieve it. And while communication is evident, cohesion in multidisciplinary teams is not always feasible in service delivery, especially with normal differences in worldviews, professional identities, salaries, status, attitudes, and educational backgrounds (Carpenter, Schneider, Brandon, & Wooff, 2003; Lankshear, 2003). The multidisciplinary team is still often used to provide services from a team perspective in mental health care, yet a more collaborative and integrative approach, known as the interdisciplinary team approach, is gaining in popularity (Dziegielewski, 2013; Molodynski & Burns, 2008; Rosen & Callaly, 2005).

Similar to the multidisciplinary team, the interdisciplinary team includes a variety of health care professionals. An interdisciplinary approach takes a much more holistic approach to health care practice. "An interdisciplinary team in a modern mental health service brings specialist assessments and individualized care together in an integrated manner and is the underlying mechanism for case allocation, clinical decision-making, teaching, training and supervision and the application of the necessary skills mix for the best outcomes for service users" (Rosen & Callaly, 2005, p. 235). Interdisciplinary professionals work together throughout the process of service provision. Generally, the entire team develops a plan of action. This type of teamwork involves a collaborative coordination of care; team-related activities, such as treatment planning; and shared leadership and power (Zeiss & Gallagher-Thompson, 2003).

In service provision, the skills and techniques that each professional provides often overlap. Interdependence is stressed throughout the referral, assessment, treatment, and planning process rather than through networking. This is different from the multidisciplinary team, where assessments and evaluations are often completed in isolation and later shared with the team. Boundaries in the formation of interdisciplinary teams are often blurred. In the interdisciplinary team process, each professional team member is encouraged to contribute, design, and implement the group goals for the health care service

QUICK REFERENCE 2.2

Interdisciplinary Teams	A group of health care professionals who work together for a common purpose, working interdependently where some degree of sharing roles, tasks, and duties can overlap with both formal and informal lines of communication to better assist the patient/client/consumer.

Definition from *The Changing Face of Health Care Social Work: Opportunities and Challenges for Professional Practice (3rd edition)*, by S. F. Dziegielewski, 2013, New York, NY: Springer (p. 35).

to be provided (Dziegielewski, 2013; Mezzich & Salloum, 2007).

Within the interdisciplinary team, each member may also supervise each other's work—a key difference from multidisciplinary teams, in which each member is measured and supervised independent of each discipline and agency (Rosen & Callaly, 2005). Interdisciplinary teams can facilitate high-quality care by gathering participatory information related to the analysis of the client's problem. A variety of multidisciplinary skills are available that work in a mutual and reciprocal educational fashion and produce viable and demonstrable results. This allows implementation and problem-solving capabilities that encourage collaboration among providers to decrease and avoid isolation and to generate new ideas. (See Quick Reference 2.2.)

The transdisciplinary team is similar to the interdisciplinary team in that it also has a variety of health care professionals. The primary difference is the degree of openness between the team members, with all openly sharing information and participating in the client-helping strategy. With this holistic approach to practice, all of a client's health and mental health needs are treated together, and case allocation and clinical decision making, teaching, training, and supervision are done collaboratively as a team. This is more common in health care but may continue to gain in importance as the need for more collaborative teamwork grows. (See Quick Reference 2.3.)

Regardless of the type of team utilized, multidisciplinary, interdisciplinary, or transdisciplinary mental health professionals should

QUICK REFERENCE 2.3

Transdisciplinary Teams	A group of health care professionals and the patient/client/consumer and identified members of his/her support system freely share ideas and work together as a synergistic whole where ideas and sharing of responsibilities are commonplace in routine care.

Definition from *The Changing Face of Health Care Social Work: Opportunities and Challenges for Professional Practice (3rd edition)*, by S. F. Dziegielewski, 2013, New York, NY: Springer (p. 35).

always emphasize client skill building and strength enhancement. A team approach helps to build satisfaction among members and provides leadership enhancing satisfaction among all team members (Baran, Shanock, Rogelberg, & Scott, 2012). If client needs are addressed from this perspective, each team member will be well equipped to contribute accordingly to the diagnostic assessment, supporting the development of the treatment plan, which will guide and determine future service delivery. Attending to the dynamics of the team collaboration as well as the contributions each team member makes can only lead to enhanced service delivery (Packard, Jones, & Nahrstedt, 2006). These types of collaborative teams can be utilized in service delivery and provide fertile ground for understanding how service delivery can be unsuccessful when fragmentation occurs (Bunger, 2010).

DIAGNOSIS AND ASSESSMENT: IS THERE A DIFFERENCE?

Identifying a Mental Disorder

Diagnostic assessment starts with defining what constitutes a mental disorder. The terms consistent with problematic behaviors within a mental disorder include distress and disability leading to a harmful dysfunction, abnormality, or aberration (Cooper, 2004; Kraemer, Shrout, & Rubic-Stipec, 2007). From a biological perspective, a medical disorder is generally defined as a biological or evolutionary disadvantage to an organism that interferes or reduces the quality of the life span or fitness (Lilienfeld & Landfield, 2008). Few would disagree that a clear definition can help to guide decisions that determine the boundary between normality and pathology (American Psychiatric Association [APA], 2013). Clearly defining the criteria for a mental disorder is no simple task while taking a strengths perspective that respects the worth and dignity of each client (Corcoran & Walsh, 2010). Similar to the problems that occur in trying to identify a medical disorder, the actual criteria can be subject to individual interpretation by the client as well as by the provider. For the client, self-reporting of symptoms can be confused by what the client thinks he or she is experiencing and what is actually happening. From the perspective of the practitioner, using a categorical approach to defining symptoms indicative of a mental disorder can also lead to differences. Experienced practitioners can have very different interpretations on how symptoms are identified and what they believe meets the criteria for the diagnosis (Rashidian, Eccles, & Russell, 2008).

When starting with the definition of what constitutes a mental disorder, it is important to note the distinction between disorder and disease (Kraemer, Shrout, & Rubio-Stipec, 2007). Making this distinction plays a fundamental part in determining whether a disease or a disorder is present in the individual. According to Cooper (2004), making a distinction between these two terms is not easy because related disciplines continue to challenge what constitutes a mental disorder. Furthermore, there is disagreement about how using the taxonomy of categorizations within the *DSM* influences the subsequent diagnostic process. As early as the *DSM-II*, a condition was considered a disorder when the condition influenced role formulation and application of the diagnostic impression. Factors identified focused on distress or disability. Starting with the publication of the *DSM-III*, the term *disorder* was used interchangeably with the term *disease*. Regardless of the term used, disease or disorder, it relates directly to harmful, dysfunctional behavior from an evolutionary psychology perspective (Cooper, 2004). To simplify the definition most often used today, it appears that disease indicates a known pathological process; a disorder may be two or more separate diseases, but generally there is a pathological process that is either known or unknown.

For medical professionals, especially those working in primary care, the difficulty in identifying a mental disorder rests within the diagnostic impression and the variability among professionals in identifying characteristics, traits, and behaviors relative to the disorder (Mitchell, Vaze, & Rao, 2009). Because identification and recognition rates can vary, the actual presence of a mental disorder can be difficult to ascertain, leading to incidents where professionals either over-report or under-report these symptoms. In addition, the flexibility within formulating the diagnostic impression leads to the question of what exactly is the diagnostic impression? And is the formulation of the evaluation completed by the mental health professional more accurately termed *diagnosis* or *assessment?*

When we look specifically at terms like *disease* and *disorder* in mental health practice, confusion results when the two terms are not considered distinct. In such cases, the concepts inherent in each tend to blur and overlap in application. This is complicated further by the multiplicity of meanings of the terms used to describe each aspect of what a client is experiencing and whether it is related to a disease or a disorder. The imprecision of definitions can result in applied social, personal, and professional interpretations in health and mental health practice that are varied rather than uniform. Like problems with defining disease and disorder, the debate on what to call the outlining of a client's mental health problems, such as diagnosis or assessment, continues. In today's practice environment, it is not uncommon to use these words interchangeably (Dziegielewski, 2013; Dziegielewski & Holliman, 2001).

Concrete definitions for all these terms and for their relationship to each other facilitate the diagnostic process. Practitioners must be careful not to be too quick in categorizing an individual's problems, which may result in diagnostic bias and an inaccurate diagnostic label. The symptoms with which an individual may present for treatment may differ, based on numerous variables, including psychological, social, cultural, and environmental circumstances.

Diagnosis and the Diagnostic Process It is easy to see how the actual definition, criteria, and subsequent tasks of assessment and diagnosis are viewed as similar and overlapping, thereby creating a shared definition. Rankin (1996) believed that in most cases, if viewed separately, the assessment has been considered to come before the diagnosis. Most would agree that completing a psychological assessment provides a process by which the client's functioning is catalogued. From this perspective, the practitioner examines important aspects of individual functioning, such as cognitive, emotional, and psychological strengths and weaknesses (Wright, 2011). The psychological assessment is then the initial building block on which the diagnosis is established. In other cases, the diagnosis is historically thought to include both an assessment and a diagnosis. Regardless of whether health or mental health practitioners truly subscribe to or support the distinction between the terms *assessment* and *diagnosis,* awareness of the difficulty in trying to separate these two terms and define their uniqueness continues. One commonly accepted definition of *diagnosis* in the field of social work is in *The Social Work Dictionary* (Barker, 2003):

> Diagnosis: The process of identifying a problem (social and mental, as well as medical) and its underlying causes and formulating a solution. In early social work delineation, it is one of the three processes, along with social study and treatment. Currently, many social workers prefer to call this process

> assessment because of the medical connotations that often accompany the term diagnosis. Other social workers think of diagnosis as the process of seeking underlying causes and assessment as having more to do with the analysis of relevant information. (Barker, 2003, p. 118)

The most widely accepted definition of *diagnosis* is in the medical model because it is based on the representation of a presenting medical concern. This is changing, however, and is more likely to be viewed as a collaborative process when working together both the client and the therapist can change (Corey, 2012). Yet Perlman's (1957) warnings about bridging the gap between viewing diagnoses in isolation remain salient. Her reminder still rings true, and caution should always be exercised not to perceive that determining and formulating a diagnosis "would magically yield a cure to any conclusion beyond an impression . . . grasping at ready-made labels" (p. 165). Perlman defined *diagnosis* as the identification of both process and product. According to Perlman, the diagnostic process is defined as "examining the parts of a problem for the import of their particular nature and organization, for the interrelationship among them, for the relationships between them and the means to their solution" (p. 164).

In mental health assessment, historically the emphasis has been placed on measuring the diagnostic product. Falk (1981, as cited in Carlton, 1984) suggested 14 areas to address in providing diagnostic impressions: life stage, health condition, family and other memberships, racial and ethnic memberships, social class, occupation, financial situation, entitlements, transportation, housing, mental functioning, cognition (personal), cognition (capability), and psychosocial elements. Utilizing a biopsychosocial spiritual perspective, the areas are organized into three primary categories: biomedical, psychological, and social factors (Dziegielewski, 2013). Because all mental health professionals are responsible for assisting in providing concrete services, recognizing these factors is often considered part of the practitioner's role in assessment with the addition of a fourth area that addresses the functional/situational factors affecting the diagnostic process.

Historically, relating the diagnosis to the client's needs has always been essential. A diagnosis is established to better understand and prepare to address the probable symptoms of the mental disorder. Factors resulting from the diagnostic procedure are shared with the client to assist with goals related to self-help or continued skill building. From a medical perspective, the diagnostic process examines symptoms and the situation and provides the basis to initiate the helping process. The formal diagnostic process yields and contributes to formal diagnostic and functional assessment based on the information learned. The diagnostic information gathered facilitates establishing the intervention plan.

Carlton (1984) further exemplified the issue of process in the diagnostic procedure:

> To be effective and responsive, any clinical social work diagnosis must be a diagnosis "for now"—a tentative diagnosis. It is the basis of joint problem solving work for the practitioner and client. To serve this purpose, the diagnosis must be shared with the client(s) and, as their work gets under way and proceeds through the various time phases of clinical social work process, the diagnosis must change as the configuration of the elements of the problem change. Thus clinical social work diagnosis is evolutionary in character and responsive to the changing nature of the condition or problem in which it relates. (p. 77)

In addressing the diagnostic process, clear results that lead to a *diagnostic product* must be obtained. The diagnostic product is the obtained information gained through the diagnostic assessment. It includes drawing logically derived inferences and conclusions based on scientific principles from the information obtained. Corey (2012) reminds practitioners that psychotherapy and any assessments that are derived need to remain part of a collaborative process. Specific questions to start the process include asking:

- What is the most important problem the client wants to address?
- What does the client hope to gain from solving this problem?

Corey (2012) believed that any interview process needs to remain collaborative between the client and the practitioner. This interchange allows the diagnosis and assessment to be joined in a tentative hypothesis; these educated hunches can be formed and shared with the client throughout the treatment process. To establish a firm foundation for the diagnostic process, the professional therapist must be skilled in obtaining and interpreting the information acquired, identifying the client's concerns while ruling out differential diagnoses (Owen, 2008). Dziegielewski (2013) stressed the importance of recognizing four factors: biomedical, psychological, social, and spiritual. To understand the health and mental health of all we serve, professionals need to understand the biopsychosocial spiritual approach to health care practice and obtain balance between these factors. This balance does not have to be equal, and the area of emphasis can change. Working with the whole person in his or her environment requires flexibility. As the environment changes, so can the person's needs and impressions. Understanding the situation experienced by the client is always the most important area to address first.

For example, a client diagnosed with HIV can have many concerns that need prioritization. First, practitioners must clarify what is related solely to the medical aspects of the condition and what is related to the mental health aspects. The biomedical information will stress the need to get the client information and the implications of the positive findings of the medical test used. Medical tests will determine the T-cell count (a type of body protection factor) and establish a baseline for current and future levels of self-protection from the illness and opportunistic infectious diseases and treatment. Once the biomedical condition is clarified, emphasis will shift to education, providing information on the effects of the disease, what the illness means, and what to expect if the illness progresses. Here treatment adherence strategy becomes essential to making sure that the client gets and continues to utilize needed services. Adherence issues such as disease management, provider–client relationships, and other individual factors become essential to treatment success (Gilbert, Abel, Stewart, & Zilberman, 2007). In many cases, only after the immediate medical needs have been addressed can mental health needs be assessed and later addressed.

As the total needs of the client are considered, the diagnostic focus will shift to address the social aspects of the client's condition. The practitioner has to decide which is the most effective approach to assessment—whether categorizing strengths and weaknesses or describing a person's personality forms a more comprehensive approach (Corcoran & Walsh, 2010). For this client, components of transmission will be addressed, including sexual contacts and practices, and addressing these with the partners who are or have been sexually active with the client. Doing this requires educating the client on disclosure of the illness and exploring the implications that having a contagious disease presents to him or her and to all parties involved. The focus is how to explain to loved ones what has happened and address what this illness means for present and future social relationships. This focus involves a complex process of interpersonal and intrapersonal and emotional issues with the client that will occur in response to the illness and which must be resolved. Regardless of what area is emphasized and with what intensity, understanding and integration of the biopsychosocial approach is essential in the diagnostic assessment.

Overall, mental health professions have embraced the necessity for diagnosis in practice—although this need is often recognized with caution. While accepting the requirement for completion of a diagnosis, much discontent and dissatisfaction among professionals continues. Some mental health professionals fear that when the diagnosis is referred to in the most traditional sense, reflective of the medical or illness perspective, it will be inconsistent with professional values and ethics. For these professionals, an illness-focused perspective detracts from an individual's capacity for initiative based on self-will or rational choice. Today, however, this view is changing. Many mental health professionals struggling for practice survival in a competitive, cost-driven health care system disagree. They feel that practice reality requires that a traditional method of diagnosis be completed to receive reimbursement. In a fee-for-service environment, the capacity for reimbursement determines and therefore influences what professionals will be compensated for providing the service. The climate within a pressured service environment can make determining the right choices difficult and ethical dilemmas more prevalent, making professional decision making an important skill (Strom-Gottfried, 2014).

In documenting treatment for reimbursement, however, it is probably better to use the term *assessment* or *diagnostic assessment* in place of *diagnosis* (Dziegielewski & Leon, 2001). *Assessment* is often not directly related to the medical model, whereas the term *diagnosis* often is (Barker, 2003). Assessments are usually related to practice models, based on clinical expertise and training designed to recognize the patient's holistic situation and taking into account individual strengths and family support (Corcoran & Walsh, 2010; Siebert, 2006).

Assessment Most mental health practitioners obtain and complete assessment within the general context of diagnostic considerations (Corey, 2012). According to Barker (2003), *assessment* involves "determining the nature, cause, progression, and prognosis of a problem and the personalities and situations involved," as well as understanding and making changes to minimize or resolve it (p. 30). Assessment requires thinking and formulating from the facts within a client's situation to reach tentative hypotheses and a logical conclusion (Owen, 2008; Sheafor & Horejsi, 2012). Therefore, assessment is an essential ingredient in the therapeutic process and the hallmark of all mental health professional activity. An assessment is a collaborative process as it becomes part of the integrated interactions among client, therapist, multidisciplinary and interdisciplinary teams, and support systems (Corey, 2012). It controls and directs all aspects of practice, including the nature, direction, and scope; however, the assessment and diagnosis cannot be separated and must be continually updated as part of the intervention process (Corey, 2012).

For practitioners who often fill many different roles as part of a collaborative team, the process of assessment must reflect diversity and flexibility. Environmental pressures and changes in client problem situations require examining and reexamining the client's situation for accuracy. If the process of assessment is rushed, superficial factors may be highlighted while significant ones are de-emphasized or overlooked.

Professionals bear administrative and economic pressures to make recommendations for consumer protection while balancing fiscal and reimbursement concerns. Consumer protection is paramount and should never take second place to cutting costs—health care quality should always be preserved.

The problem of differentiating between diagnosis and assessment is not unique to any one of the counseling disciplines. Because none of the helping professions developed in isolation, the individual assessment process has been influenced by many disciplines, including medicine, psychiatry, nursing, psychology, and social work. Historically, assessment has been referred to as *diagnosis* or the *psychosocial diagnosis* (Rauch, 1993). Although further similarities seem to exist, professional helpers should not accept the terms as interchangeable. Diagnosis focuses on symptoms and assigns categories that best fit the symptoms the client is experiencing. Assessment is broader and focuses on the functional ability of person-in-situation or person-in-environment to achieve activities of daily living.

This blurring of terminology is becoming customary, and even the previous version, *DSM-IV-TR* (APA, 2000), used both words. At times, these words appear interchangeable throughout the books when used to describe the diagnostic impression. It seems that terminology as well as the resulting helping activities and subsequent practice strategies have been forced to adapt to the dominant culture (Dziegielewski, 2013) and the models for service delivery, which guide their structure and implementation. Because these expectations deal with the pressures of reimbursement for service, they influence and guide practice intervention and strategy. Therefore, the role of assessment and diagnosis, regardless of what we call it, is a critical one because it can determine what, when, and how services will be provided.

A COMBINATION APPROACH: THE DIAGNOSTIC ASSESSMENT

The features inherent in a diagnostic assessment can overlap with the subsequent practice strategy. The distinction, which is present, is that the term *diagnosis* is utilized to describe a presenting condition, and an *assessment* is utilized to acquire information to describe and/or verify the presence of a condition. Furthermore, *assessment* can be used more broadly to include taking into account a larger context at each step of the process, including understanding a client's personality, problems, strengths, and related information about relevant social and interpersonal considerations that influence his or her mental health (Corcoran & Walsh, 2010; Dziegielewski, 2013). These terms are often used interchangeably, but the primary difference lies in the fact that the focus of the assessment is applied to practice strategy. In this text, the term *diagnostic assessment* is used simply as a combination of both terms.

In diagnostic assessments, the foundation and goals for therapy are established, and confirmatory and disconfirmatory strategies are utilized to elicit information to confirm diagnosis and/or test the viability of an alternative diagnosis (Owen, 2011). Much of the client–provider interaction is asking questions, establishing mutual goals for therapy and alliance, and acquiring information to formulate a diagnostic impression. In addition to the diagnostic criteria, a comprehensive assessment goes further by seeking information on a wide variety of personal and environmental factors. Gathering this additional information contributes to increased understanding of the mental health disorder and supplements the treatment context by taking into account the influence of the individual's relational systems.

Five factors guide the initiation of accurate diagnostic assessment that will ultimately relate to the implementation of practice strategy.

When working with individuals and preparing to complete the diagnostic assessment, professional practitioners should:

1. Examine carefully how much information the client is willing to share and the accuracy of that information. This ensures the depth and application of what is presented, as well as the subsequent motivation and behavioral changes that will be needed in the intervention process. Gathering information from the *DSM* and evaluating whether it matches what the client is reporting requires an awareness of this phenomenon as it relates to how the symptoms are reported. Focusing on information that is readily available and forming quick impressions and conclusions can lead to incomplete or inaccurate information (Owen, 2008). Pay special attention not only to what the client is saying but also to the context in which this information is revealed. What is going on in the client's life at this time? What systemic factors could be influencing certain behaviors? What will revealing the information mean to family and friends, and how will it affect the client's support system? Gathering this information is important because a client may fear that stating accurate information could have negative consequences. For example, clients may withhold information if they feel revealing it may have legal ramifications (imprisonment), social consequences (rejection from family or friends), or medical implications (rehospitalization).
2. Gather as accurate a definition of the problem as possible. It will guide not only the diagnostic assessment but also the approach or method of intervention that will be used. Furthermore, the temptation to let the diagnostic impression or intervention approach guide the problem rather than allowing the problem to guide the approach should always be resisted (Sheafor & Horejsi, 2012). So much of the problem identification process in assessment is an intellectual activity. The practitioner must never lose sight of the ultimate purpose of the assessment process, which is to complete an assessment that will help to establish a concrete service plan to address the client's needs.
3. Be aware of how a client's beliefs can influence or affect the interpretation of the problem. An individual's worldview or paradigm shapes the way the events that surround the situation are viewed. Most professionals agree that what an individual believes creates the foundation for who he or she is and influences how he or she learns. In ethical and moral professional practice, these individual influences must not directly affect the assessment process. Therefore, the practitioner's values, beliefs, and practices influencing treatment outcomes need to be clearly identified at the onset of treatment. Practitioners need to ask themselves, "What is my immediate reaction to the client and the problem expressed?" Clients have a right to make their own decisions, and the helping professional must do everything possible to ensure this right and not allow personal opinion to impair the completion of a proper assessment. Because counseling professionals are often part of an interdisciplinary team, the beliefs and values of the team members must also be considered. Awareness of value conflicts that might arise among team members is critical to prepare for how

personal feelings and resultant opinions might inhibit them from accurately perceiving and assessing the situation. As part of a team, each member holds the additional responsibility of helping others on the team be as objective as possible in the assessment process. Values and beliefs can be influential in identifying factors within individual decision-making strategies; they remain an important factor to consider and identify in the assessment process (Sue & Sue, 2013).

4. Openly address issues surrounding culture and race in the assessment phase to ensure that the most open and receptive environment is created. Simply stated, the professional practitioner needs to be aware of his or her own cultural limitations, open to cultural differences, and able to recognize the integrity and uniqueness of the client while utilizing the client's own learning style, including his or her own resources and supports (Dziegielewski, 2013; Sue & Sue, 2013). Ethnic identity and cultural mores can influence behaviors and should never be overlooked or ignored. For example, in utilizing the *DSM-5*, cultural factors are stressed prior to establishing a diagnosis. The *DSM-5* emphasizes that delusions and hallucinations may be difficult to separate from the general beliefs or practices related to a client's specific cultural custom or lifestyle. For this reason, the *DSM-5*, like the *DSM-IV-TR*, includes an appendix that describes and defines culture-bound syndromes affecting the diagnosis and assessment process (APA, 1995, 2000, 2013).
5. The assessment process must focus on client strengths and highlight the client's own resources for addressing problems that affect his or her activities of daily living and for providing continued support (Lum, 2011). Identifying strengths and resources and linking them to problem behaviors with individual, family, and social functioning may not be as easy as it sounds. There is a tendency to focus on the individual's negatives rather than praising the positives, which is further complicated by time-limited intervention settings in which mental health professionals must quickly identify individual and collectively based strengths (Dziegielewski, 2008). Accurately identifying client strengths and support networks in the diagnostic assessment is critical, as they will be incorporated into the suggested intervention plan to provide a means for continued growth and wellness beyond the formal treatment period.

In the diagnostic assessment, three aspects must always be considered:

1. Determine the existence of a disorder, disease, or illness supported by somatic, behavioral, or concrete features.
2. Ascertain the cause or etiology of the disorder, illness, or disease based on features in the client that are severe enough to influence occupational and social functioning.
3. Base any diagnostic impression on a systematic, scientific examination of the client's reported symptoms, always taking into account the client's situation (Kraemer, Shrout, & Rubio-Stipec, 2007).

DSM-5 UPDATES AND STRUCTURAL CHANGES

To complete a diagnostic assessment, the actual information presented in each criteria set must be utilized. When the *DSM-5* task force began to set the stage in 2006 by appointing chairs for the 13 diagnostic work groups, the work of the committee began. At this time, an emphasis was placed on creating a more multidisciplinary task force where any conflicts of interest were disclosed. In 2010, the work of the task groups was opened to the public for professional viewing and opportunities for public comment of the review. In 2010, for the first time in the history of the *DSM,* the professional community, through postings on the APA website (http://www.dsm5.org), allowed other professionals to comment. More than 8,000 submissions were received, and each was systematically reviewed by the work groups. Among other supportive efforts, each work group had the opportunity to view the original classifications and correct factual errors. In the organizational structure outlined in the *DSM-5* introductory pages, it is clear that the APA took extensive painstaking steps to ensure that the professionals engaging in this process had the latest in terms of information based on research and evidence-based practice.

This allowed work teams to complete (a) comprehensive and systemic reviews of the published literature, (b) reanalysis of the already collected data sets, (c) public professional and expert review with feedback from community professionals, and (d) extensive issue-focused academic and public field trials (APA, 2013). As stated clearly in *DSM-IV-TR,* projective testing alone was insufficient as supporting evidence for placement in a diagnostic category. In forensic settings and regardless of the supporting criteria, a diagnostic label should be used with caution, because of the symptom variation among those suffering from a mental disorder. Therefore, in forensic settings, the risks and limitations of doing so should be clear, and other supportive measures such as adaptive functioning should be utilized. In forensic settings, caution should be at the forefront when criteria are being applied as a legal definition of a mental disorder or mental disability. Therefore, a mental disorder alone should never be used to determine competence, criminal responsibility, or disability. Information needs to describe a person's behavioral problems and other functional impairments.

DSM-5: *Based in Research Evidence*

As explained in Chapter 1, one of the major weaknesses in earlier editions of the *DSM* is that they generally focused on descriptive rather than etiological factors. This was somewhat addressed in *DSM-IV*, and to further this progress, *DSM-IV-TR* addressed this shortfall by updating the supportive information using (a) literature reviews, (b) data analysis and reanalysis, and (c) field trials. Like *DSM-5,* in the *DSM-IV* and the *DSM-IV-TR,* literature reviews were conducted to elicit clinical utility, reliability (did the same criteria continue to present from case to case?), descriptive validity (did it actually describe what it was meant to describe?), and psychometric performance criteria (were common characteristics of performance on psychometric tests listed in the criterion?). Similar to *DSM-IV* and *DSM-IV-TR,* a number of validating variables were identified and studied. This research, including systematic and computerized reviews, ensured that evidence-based information was utilized to support the suggestions made by the individual work groups.

Thus, the two most recent editions of the *DSM,* unlike their predecessors, include efforts to incorporate the best mix of practice wisdom and research for determining the criteria and characteristics of the categories presented. This trend was exemplified in *DSM-5,* including not only clinical field trials but also large academic field trials. In addition, special attention was given to establishing reliability information related to the criteria included and the modifications made. Similar to *DSM-IV*, the literature

QUICK REFERENCE 2.4

BASIS FOR CHANGES IN THE *DSM-5*

The* DSM-5 *changes are based on:

Clinical field trials

Large academic field trials

Professional, public, and expert feedback

Improved reliability of the assessments

reviews were conducted to elicit clinical utility and reliability (did the same criteria continue to present from case to case?), as well as testing new measurement instruments and criteria related to psychometric performance. What *DSM-5* added in this area was the benefit of almost two decades of new research that culminated in an intensive 6-year process of additional literature reviews, data analysis, and periodic public professional comment. All information from these sources was treated with importance, especially when evidence was either lacking or inconclusive in supporting work group recommendations (see Quick Reference 2.4).

Changes to Organizational Structure

The structure and presentation of the *DSM-5* may appear significant to those skilled in using the previous version of the *DSM*. One of the biggest structural changes rests in the assumption that diagnoses need to flow in a developmental order, taking into account development and life span considerations. From this perspective, disorders that can generally manifest in infancy or childhood come before those most likely to occur in adolescence, young adulthood, and so on. Within this organizational structure, the mental disorders that can occur in infants, children, and adolescent disorders are listed first in each respective chapter. This lead to the elimination of the Child Disorders section outlined in *DSM-IV* and *DSM-IV-TR*. Terminology that may be helpful to note in *DSM-5* is *neurodevelopmental* and *neurocognitive* (see Quick Reference 2.5).

Presenting diagnoses across the life span is intended to help practitioners take into account the natural order of occurrence and assist with the clinical assessment. Using a developmental life span approach has required many of the chapters in *DSM-IV-TR* to be collapsed, separated, or moved. One major reason for this organizational restructuring is the task force's desire to improve clinical utility. For example, a new disorder was added to the *DSM-5* termed disruptive mood dysregulation disorder (DMDD),

QUICK REFERENCE 2.5

BASIC DEFINITIONS

Neurodevelopmental: Examines diagnoses across the life span.
Disorders most frequently diagnosed in childhood.

Neurocognitive: Disorders most frequently diagnosed in adulthood.

which is a type of persistent depressive irritability that is generally diagnosed in children and adolescents between the ages of 7 and 18 years. With the young age of onset and the pediatric course, it is listed first in the chapter on the depressive disorders and followed by other depressive disorders that are not only found in childhood and adolescence.

Another major change in *DSM-5* that resulted in organizational changes was the attempt to clarify the boundaries between what constitutes normal human functioning and what constitutes a mental disorder. This is an important distinction, especially for working with children and adolescents. For example, when does the agitated teenager represent what could be considered a typical impulsive act in response to a problem, and when is it assessed to be something more? Depressive symptoms in the adult simply may not present the same as in adolescents. In the 30-year-old male, for example, the mood may be depressed and the congruent affect is sad or blunted, whereas in the adolescent the mood may still be depressed but may present as angry and agitated. This angry and impulsive behavior could in turn result in one or more repeated acts that are interpreted as mood swings similar to bipolar disorder. Fine distinctions to clarify criteria as relevant were included in each section, and criteria were reformulated, moved, or deleted to facilitate diagnostic decision making.

In summary, four major premises guided all revisions in this edition of the *DSM*. The first involved clinical utility. Since the book was designed to be used by practitioners, all revisions had to be applicable and feasible for use in the clinical practice setting. This premise was central to getting professional feedback in the open windows of opportunity provided. Second, multiple clinical and academic field trials were conducted to test current and past diagnostic criteria. This information was to be added to a rich database of existing studies, and analysis and reanalysis were conducted. Therefore, all recommendations were to be guided by research evidence. The third premise was the simple contention that the *DSM-IV* and *DSM-IV-TR* had been deeply embedded in current diagnostic procedures, and when possible, continuity between the two volumes should be maintained. Fourth, the need for openness and functional changes rested in the expectation that no prior constraints should be placed on the degree of change between the *DSM-5* and its predecessors *DSM-IV* and *DSM-IV-TR* (see Quick Reference 2.6). Thus, this latest version of the *DSM* has continued the effort to incorporate the best mix of clinical practice wisdom and research for determining the criteria and characteristics of categories presented.

The Dimensional Assessment

A purely categorical approach is limited to individual interpretation on the part of the client as well as the practitioner. Reporting symptoms

QUICK REFERENCE 2.6

***Supporting the Changes and Use of* DSM-5**

- Highest priority is clinical utility—useful to clinicians
- All changes based in research evidence
- Keep continuity with *DSM-IV* and *DSM-IV-TR* as much as possible
- No predetermined constraints on changing structure or format if problematic
- Adopt a development life span approach
- Help to differentiate what constitutes normal human functioning

can be confusing for clients and make it difficult to quantify experiences and what is actually happening. Many times clients are not thinking clearly, and the influence of physical or mental pain or discomfort can affect all subsequent interpretations of what they believe is happening to them. Subsequently, this confusion and ambiguity can also affect the decisions clients make and how they are viewed. Picking from a list of symptoms at one point in time can easily fall short of understanding the context of what is happening, thereby limiting treatment application. A categorical approach can also fall short when it comes to the practitioner's interpretation. If a diagnostic assessment is limited to the information the client presents, it can fall short in terms of treatment. When information is limited, from the perspective of the practitioner, no matter how experienced he or she is, the diagnostic assessment can target different symptoms that result in different interpretations (Rashidian et al., 2008). Regardless, the diagnostic assessment must take into account information from the client, the family system, and other confirmatory methods, and it is here that some feel the categorical approach may come up short.

Therefore, the emphasis of the *DSM-5* and inclusion of the dimensional assessment would allow the patient's full range of symptoms to be reported, and these symptoms can be noted in terms of severity with specific criteria to establish what constitutes mild, moderate, severe, and very severe. This also allows noting important factors that can affect the diagnostic assessment as well as the individual's behavior, such as depressed mood, anxiety, sleep level disturbances, and other factors that could easily be overlooked in a strictly categorical assessment. Noting these factors allows the full range of symptoms to be evaluated and documented. Examining this full spectrum of pathology enables inclusion of dimensionalization, a concept that explains the importance of recognizing comorbidity (Paris, 2013).

DSM-5: SECTIONS AND APPENDICES

Section I

In its latest version, the *DSM* is broken down into three sections and ends with seven appendices (see Quick Reference 2.7). Section I provides an introduction to the manual, some rationale for the changes, and instructions on how to use the updated manual. It provides an overview of the structure, content, and applications of the manual that are at the core of understanding each chapter

QUICK REFERENCE 2.7

DSM-5: *Three Sections*

Section I: Introduction and directions on how to use the updated manual

Section II: Outline of the categorical diagnoses that eliminated the multiaxial system (20 disorder chapters plus 2 supporting chapters)

Section III: Subsections covering assessment measures, cultural formulation, an alternative *DSM-5* model for personality disorders, highlights of the changes from *DSM-IV* to *DSM-5*, a glossary of terms, and an alphabetical listing of *DSM-5* diagnoses and codes (*ICD-9-CM and ICD-10-CM*).

Appendices: Seven appendices providing supporting information.

and properly supporting the mental health diagnosis. A review of the research and attempts at harmonization, as previously explained in this chapter, are presented. This new edition takes some of the aspects of the older edition and expands them to provide a more comprehensive view of making the diagnostic impression, while deleting the formulation of the multiaxial diagnosis that many practitioners had come to depend upon. Section I also adds information related to the dimensional assessment that was introduced previously in this chapter.

Section II

Section II has 20 chapters that outline the documented mental disorders with 2 other related chapters, for a total of 22 chapters (see Quick Reference 2.8). For chapters 1 to 20, all disorders listed must match the definition of a mental disorder. The *DSM* warns that deciding on a diagnosis can be multifaceted and requires the skills of a trained practitioner. In *DSM-5,* a mental disorder is defined as "a syndrome characterized by clinically significant disturbance in an individual's cognition, emotional regulation, or behavior that reflects a dysfunction in the psychological, biological or developmental processes underlying mental functioning" (APA, 2013, p. 20). In addition, it must be accompanied by clinically significant impairment in social, occupational, and other daily activities. Therefore, each of the first 20 chapters provides an overview of the types or spectrum of disorders that can be classified in the chapter. Because each mental disorder in the chapter was placed there on account of its similarities, the specific criteria for the individual diagnoses follow, where differences are highlighted. Each

QUICK REFERENCE 2.8

DSM-5, SECTION II

- Neurodevelopmental Disorders
- Schizophrenia Spectrum and the Other Psychotic Disorders
- Bipolar and the Related Disorders
- Depressive Disorders
- Anxiety Disorders
- Obsessive-Compulsive and the Related Disorders
- Trauma and Stressor-Related Disorders
- Dissociative Disorders
- Somatic Symptom Disorders
- Feeding and Eating Disorders
- Elimination Disorders
- Sleep-Wake Disorders
- Sexual Dysfunctions
- Gender Dysphoria
- Disruptive, Impulse Control, and Conduct Disorders
- Substance-Related and Addictive Disorders
- Neurocognitive Disorders
- Personality Disorders
- Paraphilic Disorders
- Other Mental Disorders
- Medication-Induced Movement Disorders and Other Adverse Effects of Medication*
- Other Conditions That May Be a Focus of Clinical Attention**

*Not considered mental disorders.
**Includes other conditions and problems that require clinical attention but not a mental disorder.

disorder within the chapter is listed separately, and the criteria for the diagnostic assessment are outlined to show how it relates, identifying clearly the criteria that must be present for it to cause significant distress or disability. It also takes into account specific supporting information such as diagnostic features that are described later in this chapter.

The only chapter with a slightly different format is Chapter 20, "Other Mental Disorders." This chapter has been included to address the broad range of mental disorders that are directly or indirectly linked to a medical cause and the degree to which this medical cause affects the mental health symptoms displayed. In these conditions, there is a clear (other specified mental disorder due to a medical condition) documented medical condition. It can also be used when the practitioner is not comfortable diagnosing a mental disorder because of the medical symptoms that may complicate its presentation (unspecified mental disorder due to another medical condition) or there is not enough information at the time to clearly say what the mental disorder is. This chapter also identifies the term "Other Specified Mental Disorder" as a provisional category where the practitioner decides to not list the mental disorder for a variety of reasons or the individual does not fully meet the criteria for a disorder. When this diagnosis is used, documenting the reason for selecting it is required. This differs from "Unspecified Mental Disorder," which would be used in situations where not enough information exists or there is an emergency situation that will not allow a full comprehensive assessment.

The last two chapters are not considered mental disorders but rather provide supportive information for completing a comprehensive diagnostic assessment. The first of the two chapters is related to medication usage and the adverse effects that can complicate mental health conditions. Because it is often difficult to determine whether the medication used to treat a mental health condition actually caused the resulting medical condition, a causal relationship is difficult to ascertain. What is most important, however, is recognizing how these medication-related conditions can influence the mental health condition the client is experiencing. These medications important to treatment can also complicate and create other medical conditions.

Conditions related to medication that are listed in this chapter are not mental disorders, and this information is provided for supportive reasons only. Disorders listed in this chapter include neuroleptic-induced Parkinsonism and other medication-induced Parkinsonism, which involves a characteristic set of side effects such as tremors and muscle rigidity that generally occur within a few weeks of either starting or reducing the dosage of a neuroleptic medication. Other medication-related conditions in this chapter include neuroleptic malignant syndrome, medication-induced disorders, medication-induced acute dystonia, and medication-induced acute akathisia, which are often related directly to the dosage of the medication received. Tardive dyskinesia, tardive dystonia, tardive akathisia, and other medication-induced movement disorders are generally related to characteristic movement-related symptoms. Medication-induced postural tremor is often seen with anxiety symptoms related to excessive caffeine and other stimulants. Also highlighted in this chapter is antidepressant discontinuation syndrome, symptoms seen after the abrupt discontinuation of antidepressant medications after taking them for at least a month. This chapter concludes with other adverse effect of medication; this category is reserved for side effects that are not movement related but can have other effects on the body, such as severe hypotension, cardiac arrhythmias (heart rate and rhythm concerns), and priapism (a prolonged and painful penile erection that can last from a few hours to days).

The last chapter in this section is "Other Conditions That May Be a Focus of Clinical

Attention." This chapter in *DSM-5* has been rearranged and takes on increased importance in highlighting the circumstances that may relate directly to the occurrence of a mental disorder and subsequently affect its care and treatment. Areas presented include relational problems; abuse and neglect; educational and occupational problems; housing and economic problems; problems related to crime or interaction with the legal system; other health service encounters for counseling and medical advice; problems related to other psychosocial, personal, and environmental circumstances; and other circumstances of personal history. This chapter and the circumstances presented are further highlighted in the next chapter; when present, these factors could affect the diagnostic assessment.

For those familiar with *DSM-IV* and *DSM-IV-TR*, the new structure and division of the chapters in Section II may at first seem confusing. For example, in *DSM-IV*, there was one chapter for the Mood Disorders that included both the bipolar disorders and the depressive disorders. This is not the case now, as in *DSM-5* they have been separated into individual chapters. The same is true for the anxiety disorders. This restructuring is accompanied by numerous reclassifications and the addition of several new disorders. It appears that careful thought went into not only separating the disorders into individual chapters but also rearranging selected disorders to match the new focus on the life span approach, along with research evidence. Each individual chapter has a short description of what was in *DSM-IV-TR* just to help bridge the changes in structure and format for those familiar with the older version.

Section III

The last section of the manual, Section III, provides supportive information to enhance the clinical decision-making process. Subsections covered in Section III include assessment measures, cultural formulation, an alternative *DSM-5* model for personality disorders, and conditions for further study.

In Section III, the first subsection begins by outlining the importance of assessment measures and explains the purpose and basics of using a dimensional assessment. This is coupled with the crosscutting of symptoms. The supporting information provided in this subsection is designed to bridge the primarily categorical assessment system of its predecessor to a more dimensional one. From this perspective, the practitioner is encouraged to acknowledge the diagnostic criteria while documenting the crosscutting or overlapping of symptoms. This emphasis allows for explication of the relationship between symptom characteristics of more than one disorder without the creation or addition of a second disorder. For example, how many times have you worked with a depressed client who was also anxious? Documenting with the dimensional assessment and taking into account the crosscutting of symptoms enable noting all evident symptoms, even those that might be more consistent with a different diagnosis. Therefore, a primary diagnosis of major depressive disorder could be cross-tabulated with symptoms of anxiety without requiring a second diagnosis. Being able to document all symptoms related to a primary diagnosis and any secondary symptoms allows the practitioner to make a stronger diagnostic assessment while avoiding an unnecessary label indicative of a second diagnosis.

In taking into account the crosscutting of symptoms, *DSM-5* gives practitioners the possibility of two levels of symptom assessment and rating. The first level involves a brief survey of 13 domains for measuring symptomology in adult patients and 12 domains for child and adolescent patients. Level two provides a more in-depth level of assessment of certain domains. To supplement the written text, *DSM-5* also offers some aspects of this second level of assessment for crosscutting online (http://www.psychiatry.org/dsm5).

Because the *DSM* does not suggest treatment, for practitioners it becomes essential to realize that, for the most part, many treatments just treat the symptoms, not the underlying mental disorder. Similar to treating most medical conditions by addressing the symptoms, mental disorders can follow a similar path. For example, whether we use antidepressants for the treatment of a diagnosed anxiety disorder or a depressive disorder, the benefits for the patient may be similar, regardless of the diagnosis assigned. If we used cognitive behavioral therapy to treat either of these diagnosed mental disorders, the outcome could also be the same, regardless of the specific diagnosis. A dimensional assessment with the use of crosscutting of symptoms provides a more complete diagnostic assessment that will more easily relate to a symptom-focused treatment regime, regardless of the specific diagnosis.

The second measurement option provided is the "Clinician-Rated Dimensions of Psychosis Symptom Severity." This dimensional measurement may be particularly helpful in supporting diagnoses related to Schizophrenia spectrum and other psychotic disorders because it measures the degree of cognitive or neurobiological factors related to an illness. This particular assessment can help in completing a more comprehensive assessment by identifying multiple dimensions of psychosis, including positive symptoms (hallucinations, delusions, and disorganized speech), abnormal psychomotor behavior (such as catatonia), and negative symptoms (restricted emotional expression or activity). The scale measures eight specific domains and measures information over a 7-day period. Each domain including hallucinations, delusions, disorganized speech, abnormal psychomotor behavior, negative symptoms such as avolition and restricted emotional affect, and impaired cognition, depression, and mania are recorded on a scale from 0 (not present) to 4 (present and severe). It is expected that this scale will be completed upon initial assessment and as needed each 7-day period afterwards. Consistent high scores in a particular area can help the practitioner to target interventions.

The third assessment measure presented in Section III is a scale designed to measure individual disability for adults age 18 and older. This scale, referred to as the WHODAS 2.0, is published by the World Health Organization. More information related to this scale and how it applies to the diagnostic assessment is presented in the next chapter. The fourth assessment measure in Section III is related to culture. "Cultural Formulation" presents a measurement instrument termed the Cultural Formulation Interview (CFI) and goes into depth on how to best identify and measure cultural information. An outline for how to gather cultural information is presented, and for the first time in the *DSM,* a scale is included to help measure it. This CFI and how to best utilize it for taking into account the cultural aspects of a problem are outlined further in the next section of this chapter.

Next in Section III is an "Alternate *DSM-5* Model for Personality Disorders." This subsection addresses the problem of how some personality disorders may have overlapping traits with others. Although the *DSM-5* did not change the chapter describing the personality disorders significantly from what was in *DSM-IV* and *DSM-IV-TR*, this additional subsection provides the potential for an expanded approach. It focuses on personality functioning and personality traits and identifies specific criteria. An alternative model takes the 10 primary personality disorders and reduces them to 6 primary disorders (antisocial, avoidant, borderline, narcissistic, obsessive-compulsive, and schizotypal personality disorder). Specific criteria are outlined, and if the criteria for the diagnosis are met and other traits exist that do not meet full criteria, they can be noted as specifiers. This option is not present in the current classification but included in this section as an alternate approach that provides further modification and re-classification of the personality disorders currently listed in Section II.

To help classify these trait disorders, the Level of Personality Functioning Scale is presented. This scale looks at 4 elements (identity, self-direction, empathy, and intimacy) and rates them on a scale from 0 (little or no impairment) to 4 (extreme impairment). Examples related to each area are outlined. In addition, there is a listing of personality trait domains and facets with definitions for each. More regarding this typology and its potential application is presented in Chapter 13 of this text.

Section III ends with a list followed by detailed explanations of Conditions for Further Study. The diagnoses in this section, although not present in the disorder chapters of the text, are to make the practitioner aware of these potential disorders and to provide common grounding for further development as research continues to emerge.

Appendices

The *DSM-5* ends with seven appendices used to support the information in the text. This differs from the 11 appendices in *DSM-IV* and *DSM-IV-TR*. In this latest version, the appendices have been deleted or changed and do not match the previous version. For example, one major change is the deletion of the previous Appendix G, which contained the *ICD-9-CM* codes for selected general medical conditions and medication-induced disorders. It listed the general medical conditions and matched these conditions with the *ICD-10-DRC* codes. This section also allowed for coding concerning certain medications (prescribed at therapeutic doses) that can cause substance-induced disorders. The effects of these medications are coded (E-codes) as optional and, when used, would have been listed on Axis I. This appendix has been completely deleted, and no medical codes from the *DSM* are listed in the new version of the appendix section. To document these accompanying medical conditions, the practitioner is advised to go directly to the relevant edition of the *ICD*. Also deleted was the appendix about decision trees that could be used to assist with differential diagnosis. With the inclusion of the dimensional assessment criteria and crosscutting of symptoms, it is hoped that decision trees will not be needed to supplement the existing criteria and, if needed, can be ascertained from other supportive sources.

Of the seven appendices that are included, the first highlights the changes from *DSM-IV* to *DSM-5*; to help the reader compare the two versions, all changes and the descriptions are listed in the same order as presented in *DSM-5*. This appendix is followed by a "Glossary of Technical Terms" that defines words used throughout the book to ensure that a clear and concise definition is outlined, especially when actual text definitions may be limited. The third appendix is a "Glossary of Cultural Concepts of Distress" that have been adapted and updated from *DSM-IV*, where they were termed cultural-bound syndromes. Because these cultural concepts of distress, if unrecognized, can complicate the diagnostic assessment, they are discussed further in the next section of this chapter. The next three appendices are related to numerical listings and comparison to the *ICD*. The first is an alphabetical listing of the *DSM-5* diagnoses and codes (*ICD-9-CM* and *ICD-10-CM*); the second and third are numerical listings of the *ICD-9-CM* and the *ICD-10-CM*, respectively. The last appendix is an extensive list of the *DSM-5* advisers and others who contributed to the updates in this latest edition.

IMPORTANT SECTIONS IN THE *DSM-5*

The *DSM-5* has 20 chapters that are dedicated to each category of disorders listed. At the beginning of each chapter is an overview of the disorders outlined in that particular chapter, listing what they are and what they have in common. For example, in the chapter on schizophrenia spectrum and other psychotic disorders, key features that define all of the psychotic disorders in the chapter are outlined, highlighting what they share, with each listed and organized along a gradient of psychopathology. For those familiar with *DSM-IV* and *DSM-IV-TR*, this presents, in some cases, a very different order for listing. One reason for this change is the commitment that the *DSM-5* task force made to base placement of the diagnoses on two primary factors: developmental life span and the gradient of psychopathology. For each disorder in the *DSM-5*, the authors describe the primary characteristics of the disorder and provide additional available diagnostic information (see Quick Reference 2.9). Depending on the information available and the importance to the diagnosis, some of the sections for each of the disorders may vary.

When available, the diagnostic criteria are divided under separate headings with categories such as diagnostic features, which is always listed for each individual diagnosis. The information under the diagnostic features helps to clarify the specific criteria of a disorder with examples of relevant behaviors that further explicate the criteria.

Another important section with supporting information is termed "Associated Features Supporting the Diagnosis." In this section, characteristics that support the diagnosis are informally divided into three sections: descriptive features, laboratory findings, and information associated with features related to the physical examination or other medical conditions. The section on lab findings is further broken down into three areas: diagnostic (tests available to determine etiology), confirmatory of the diagnosis (tests supporting the diagnosis but not providing etiological basis), and complication(s) of the disorder (conditions often found in conjunction with or as a result of

QUICK REFERENCE 2.9

Presentation of the Disorders

- Diagnostic Features (outlines specific criteria)
- Associated Features Supporting the Diagnosis (characteristics)
- Prevalence (adults, males, females, etc.)
- Development and Course (signs and how long it lasts)
- Risk and Prognostic Factors (temperamental, environmental, genetic, and physiological)
- Course Modifiers
- Culture-Related Diagnostic Issues
- Gender-Related Diagnostic Issues
- Diagnostic Markers (sleep history and a sleep diary)
- Suicide Risk
- Functional Consequences
- Differential Diagnosis
- Comorbidity

it, such as electrolyte imbalance and anorexia). This section, along with the diagnostic features, is a must read for all clinicians because it presents the descriptive features of the mental disorder, as well as predisposing factors and complications. Awareness of the associated laboratory findings can help to ensure that, as part of collaborative team, aspects important to the diagnosis have been addressed and the most common medical conditions that can accompany the condition are noted.

For example, under the disorder schizophrenia (listed in Schizophrenia Spectrum and the Psychotic Disorders), "Associated Features Supporting the Diagnosis" note symptoms that may accompany this disorder, such as inappropriate affect, mood, and other types of symptoms that can impair perceptions of reality, judgment, and insight. Also in this section, the text highlights that there are no radiological, laboratory, or psychometric tests for the disorder. This is an important section to read. There are no tests for this particular disorder, but for other disorders, this may not be the case, and recognition of them may be central to a complete diagnostic assessment. In the diagnostic assessment, the practitioner should be alert to these factors and how they affect the diagnostic criteria being exhibited (see 2.10).

In addition to "Diagnostic Features" and "Associated Features Supporting the Diagnosis," other categories of supportive information relative to the diagnosis presented might be helpful. These sections may vary somewhat on the information available. Of particular importance is "Prevalence." For the practitioner, this section is rich with information. It can help to define how often the diagnosis occurs and with whom, whether it is more common in certain groups based on age and gender, and the types of symptoms that could accompany this categorization. In the section on "Development and Course," signs of the disorder related to age of

QUICK REFERENCE 2.10

Associated Features Supporting Diagnosis

Associated descriptive features and mental disorders: This category can include features associated with the disorder but not critical to making the diagnosis.

Associated laboratory findings: This section can also provide information on three different types of laboratory findings. First, when diagnostic tests are presented in a section, they explain the cause of the etiology of the disorder. Second, the diagnostic tests presented may not clearly be related to the disorder but seem to appear in other groups of individuals who suffer from this disorder. Third, when relevant this section can present the laboratory findings that are associated with complications resulting directly from the disorder. These tests are presented because they help the practitioner make a more comprehensive diagnostic determination. But when all three areas are addressed, these findings are not generally required for formulating the diagnosis. For the most part, tests provided in this category are associated with the diagnosis but do not necessarily reveal the cause of etiology (e.g., computerized tomography [CT] scans to assist in classification of types of neurocognitive disorders).

Associated physical exam findings and medical conditions: Awareness of these findings related to the disorder can have significance in treatment.

onset, how long it lasts, and the essential features as the disorder progresses are outlined. When available, "Risk and Prognostic Factors" are described. Depending on the particular diagnosis, this section can describe temperamental, environmental, genetic, and physiological factors and other risk factors related to the diagnosis. Other sections are "Culture-Related Diagnostic Issues," "Gender-Related Diagnostic Issues," "Suicide Risk," "Functional Consequences," "Differential Diagnosis," and "Comorbidity." Other optional sections, depending on the diagnosis, include diagnostic markers, sleep disturbance, and other conditions. For example, in comorbidity an individual can suffer from two or more diagnoses that may or may not be related but can complicate the assessment as well as treatment. If the potential for comorbidity is not taken into account, the practitioner may have difficulty determining the symptoms that are central to the presenting diagnosis and those that may be situation-dependent. Because the definition of dimensional is symptom-specific and rooted in data-based observation rather than biological markers, the clinician needs to be careful not to allow overquantification of the behavior to push it to the higher level of severity. For example, with Cannabis Use Disorder, under comorbidity, *DSM-5* warns the practitioner that cannabis is often referred to as a gateway drug because an individual who uses this drug is more likely to use drugs such as opioids and cocaine. Equipped with this knowledge, the practitioner knows to assess for the potential of other drug usage and, when it exists, how it can affect treatment outcomes. The section on differential diagnosis clearly points to the problem of identifying whether it is nonproblematic use, especially when it is linked to problems with school, employers, or the legal system. Information provided can be helpful in improving the diagnostic assessment as well as the treatment plans and strategy to follow.

Meaning of Clinically Significant

The practitioner needs to be well versed in the use of the *DSM* and situational factors that need to be part of the diagnostic assessment process. Knowing how to address these factors in clinical practice is critical. Knowledge of the potential damage that can occur from placing a diagnostic label inappropriately is essential. The term *clinically significant* indicates that a practitioner has clearly linked the symptoms present in the mental disorder with how they stop or impair a client's current level of functioning. An individual who exhibits the symptoms matching the criteria of a mental disorder yet his or her individual, social, or occupational functioning is not impaired should not be given a diagnosis. A diagnosis should be given only when the symptoms are severe enough to interfere with or disturb functioning. This makes the incorporation of environmental circumstances essential to support or negate the use of a diagnostic category. Next, important sections and diagnostic features associated with the *DSM-5* are introduced. Remember, however, that regardless of the diagnostic symptoms a client is experiencing and whether these symptoms are related to factors such as culture, age, and gender, if the behavior is not considered clinically significant, no diagnosis should be given.

CULTURE, AGE, AND GENDER-RELATED INFORMATION

Culture has been defined as the "sum total of life patterns passed from generation to generation within a group of people and includes institutions, language, religious ideals, artistic expressions, and patterns of thinking, social and interpersonal relationships. Aspects of culture are often related to people's ethnic, racial and spiritual heritage" (Kirst-Ashman, 2008, p. 36). Many individuals are confused regarding the differences among culture, ethnicity, race, and the development of an ethnic identity.

Ethnicity generally refers to one's roots, ancestry, and heritage. *Culture* generally relates to values, understandings, behaviors, and practices (Ton & Lim, 2006). Although race and culture are related, they are not the same. In ethnicity, the groups have generally accepted similar beliefs (Yeager, Cutler, Svendsen, & Sills, 2013). To provide a comprehensive diagnostic assessment, all social workers need to take into account clients' personal beliefs about the etiology and prognosis of their symptoms (Chang-Muy & Congress, 2009).

Race is defined as a "consciousness of status and identity based on ancestry and color," and ethnicity is all of that (e.g., religion, customs, geography, and historical events) minus color (Lee & Bean, 2004). Racial identity is not static and can be fluid, depending on specific contexts. These certainly are influenced by location of residence, developmental stage, context of being asked, and the perceived benefit or loss (Mays, Ponce, Washington, & Cochran, 2003).

The development of *ethnic identity* stems from the continuum of acceptance of a person's ethnicity. *Ethnic identity* is generally defined as a common thread of heritage, customs, and values unique to a group of people (Queralt, 1996). These commonalties define and bond members, producing an ethnic backdrop to everyday life. Ethnicity can influence thinking and feeling and pattern behaviors in both obvious and subtle ways (Canino & Alegria, 2008). Culture, on the other hand, is an umbrella term that can include racial and ethnic identity (Congress & Gonzalez, 2013).

Many individuals either embrace or reject their ethnicity, relating it to personal and ascribed identity or a particular reference group, which dictates the primary support group to which they turn for clarity of decisions (Helms, 1990). No two people seem to experience their culture in the same way. And as race and ethnicity are more fluid than otherwise posited, *situational ethnicity* addresses changing race or ethnic identity within specific contexts (Mays et al., 2003). Counselors must be careful not to approach the client with any preconceived bias or textbook definition of exactly what to expect (Swartz-Kulstad & Martin, 1999).

The classifications of race and ethnicity change dramatically with the new fluctuations of immigration in the United States and the frequency of intermarriage. A new cultural paradigm related to a blended society and multiracial considerations seems to be emerging. Every culture has processes, healers, medications, and prescribed medical practices that enter into the shared view of what constitutes daily living. These shared lifestyle patterns are reflected in daily behaviors. Patterns of response can easily be misinterpreted for something they are not, such as reflective of pathology.

Taking into account the possibility of this multifaceted presentation, practitioners continue to encounter a wide range of ethnic minority clients who present varied mental health problems and concerns. Although this book cannot do justice to the unique characteristics, issues, and challenges that each of these groups presents, practitioners must be aware of the major considerations for mental health practice with these populations. This section of the chapter will sensitize the reader to some of these considerations and how they can affect the course of mental health treatment.

Addressing Cultural Aspects in the DSM-5

In the *DSM-5,* each diagnostic category seeks to be sensitive to issues related to culture, age, and gender and the effects these variables can have on the client's symptoms. This is particularly important in terms of cultural diversity. Knowledge of

QUICK REFERENCE 2.11

Identifying Cultural Aspects

Practitioners Need to Help the Client:

Identify and discuss the impact of current life circumstances that can affect daily functioning.

Self-report race and ethnicity, respecting the self-identification of multiracial individuals, in a manner consistent with how the client thinks of himself or herself (Mays et al., 2003).

Identify and acknowledge any psychological problems stemming from adaptation to a new environment.

Identify and explore the degree to which the client has positive and supportive peer relationships contributing to or reducing feelings of isolation and facilitating transition.

Identify social variables for which race or ethnicity serves as a proxy (e.g., social status, neighborhood context, perceived discrimination, social cohesion, social capital, social support, types of occupation, employment, emotional well-being, and perceived life opportunities) (Mays et al., 2003).

Identify willingness to explore new coping skills to help negotiate his or her environment.

and sensitivity to cultural aspects that can contribute to a client's overall diagnostic picture are critical in completing an accurate diagnostic assessment. (See Quick Reference 2.11 on how to identify cultural aspects.) Each diagnostic category briefly addresses cultural variables. For additional information, practitioners are referred to Section III of the manual and the Cultural Formulation and the Cultural Formulation Interview (CFI) and to the glossary of Cultural Aspects of Distress in Appendix 3 in *DSM-5*.

Being culturally sensitive in completing the diagnostic assessment requires clearly outlining the client's culture-based behaviors that correspond to diagnostic criteria for a mental disorder. Then the practitioner can rule out disorders for which the client might otherwise qualify. It becomes more and more difficult as cultural practices and mores of different races and ethnic groups overlap.

The practitioner needs to work with the client to help him or her examine issues related to *personal identity,* where the individual sees himself or herself in a certain way(s), and *ascribed identity,* where the individual indicates how the society values or perceives behaviors and actions. In current society, ethnic identity is not easily determined, and the degree to which it can influence life factors and behavior changes can remain elusive. It can be further complicated by acculturation, which is often described as an adjustment process that involves adopting customs of an alternate culture (Locke & Bailey, 2014). Disadvantaged populations can be affected by poverty, lack of access, and limited health care. Adopting a culturally sensitive approach can help reduce misperceptions.

Remember that both the client and the practitioner are products of the society in which they live. Societal influences can directly affect individual cultural mores and beliefs. Culture and its mechanisms of integration influence not only a client's behaviors but also the practitioner's. Most of the beliefs and values that helping professionals hold closely resemble those beliefs and values espoused by the greater society. Based on this assumption, practitioners from other ethnic groups, as well as those with a heritage in a similar cultural group, may look at the client's behaviors through a culturally limited lens. This perspective may prevent the professional from gaining a clear picture of the importance of helping the client to differentiate that which is cultural and that which is a disorder. Professional helpers must be aware of a tendency to assess the client based on the professional's own values, beliefs, societal biases, and stereotypes (Mays et al., 2003). If practitioners do not take care to avoid this bias, the lack of awareness of client ethnicity and culture may lead to distorted perceptions, misdiagnosing, and labeling these clients and their family dynamics (Canino & Alegria, 2008; Sue & Sue, 2013).

The key to completing the best diagnostic assessment is addressing how to work best with the client in his or her cultural context (Congress, 2008). Some considerations for completing the diagnostic assessment and integrating helping activities with clients from different cultural backgrounds are (a) becoming familiar with the client's cultural values and points of reference, (b) being aware of and sensitive to the traditional role of the client when in the client's environment, (c) identifying areas of conflict that can result from changes in environmental considerations, and (d) gaining familiarity with how the client is encouraged to express feelings of grief, stress, or unhappiness. To accomplish this, the mental health practitioner must first recognize aspects of the client's culture and incorporate this meaning into the diagnostic assessment and any change efforts to follow.

According to the APA (2013), one major change in *DSM-5* was clarifying and updating the cultural information needed to assess the client and adding a measure to Section III to help measure culture and the influences it can have on an individual's mental health. To update the information needed to accomplish a comprehensive cultural formulation, five areas were identified. The first requires the practitioner to take into account the *cultural identity of the individual*: the clinically relevant aspects of a client's identity and the unique challenges, conflicts, or predicaments it may present. Aspects of identity include religious affiliation, sexual orientation, socioeconomic family background, and other aspects of a client's circumstances that could affect behavior. The second area to be considered was *cultural conceptualizations of distress,* where the client's perceptions are treated as essential toward understanding the problem. For example, how do clients interpret their symptoms and communicate them to others? What are their current help-seeking behaviors, and how comfortable are they with discussing what they are feeling? The third area is recognizing *psychosocial stressors* and *cultural factors of vulnerability and resilience.* From this perspective, attention is given to exploring a client's cultural environment and the role recognized support systems play in all aspects of a person's life, including vulnerabilities and strengths leading to resilience. The fourth area is sometimes referred to as cross-racial awareness and considers the *cultural features of the relationship between the individual and the clinician.* Taking into account differences is central to this area of assessment, as is being careful to remember that as products of a system, fears of racism, unequal treatment, or misinterpretations of what is culturally relevant can occur. Accounting for all of these factors can help to establish the rapport needed to complete the most accurate and comprehensive diagnostic assessment possible. The fifth area summarizes the information gathered from the first four and brings them together into a synergistic whole that provides the *overall cultural assessment.* Whether a formal diagnostic tool is used or not, *DSM-5,* like previous versions, recognizes the importance of cultural mores and expectations in the diagnostic assessment process. These five areas can help a practitioner look specifically at how these factors can influence the behaviors exhibited and the treatment that results. They can also avoid misplacing a diagnostic label of a mental disorder on behaviors and expectations that may be directly related to a client's cultural values and beliefs.

After field testing for diagnostic usefulness and patient acceptability, *DSM-5* went beyond the descriptions in *DSM-IV* and introduced a systematic assessment called the Cultural Formation Interview (CFI). The CFI is followed by the Cultural Formulation Interview (CFI)–Informant Version, which gathers collateral information from someone familiar with the client who is capable of providing information the client is unable to share. Both measures take into account the client and the influences his or her culture can have on behavior, as well as the influences of members of his or her support system. The CFI–Informant Version may be particularly helpful when the client cannot give the information because of age, mental status, or cognitive impairment. This assessment system recognizes the influence significant others, family, friends, and other members of the client's support system can have. Furthermore, this clinical measure is a semistructured interview with no right or wrong answer. All questions are designed purely to better understand the client. There is also no hard-and-fast format that must be followed, and flexibility in both asking the questions and probing the responses is allowable.

Prior to starting the CFI, background demographic information such as age, gender, racial/ethnic background, marital status, and education should be gathered. Having this information from the start allows the interviewer the flexibility to tailor the questions to what is most relevant for the client. Both instruments can be used in their entirety, or aspects can be used to facilitate the diagnostic process. For the CFI, supplementary modules can be accessed online with formats designed for children and adolescents, elderly individuals, immigrants, and refugees. The informant version asks questions designed for family members, friends, and others familiar with the client's situation, whereas the CFI asks questions directly to the client. There are 16 questions in the CFI and 17 questions in the CFI–Informant Version (see Quick Reference 2.12).

After a brief introduction, the instrument is presented to the informant. Both versions of the CFI examine four domains of a problem (see Quick Reference 2.13). For the CFI, the first three questions seek to elicit the cultural

QUICK REFERENCE 2.12

CULTURAL FORMULATION INTERVIEW

Cultural Formulation Interview (CFI) (16 questions)/Cultural Formulation Interview (CFI)–Informant Version (17 questions)

- Semistructured interviews
- No right or wrong answers
- Gather demographic information first as it can help to select questions
- Can use entire instrument or just what is needed to supplement the interview
- Supplementary modules are available online for children and adolescents, elderly individuals, immigrants, and refugees

QUICK REFERENCE 2.13

TAKING INTO ACCOUNT CULTURE AND CULTURAL FORMULATION INTERVIEW (CFI) [LOCATED IN SECTION 3, PP. 749–759 OF *DSM-5*]

Examines four domains:

1. Cultural definition of the problem.
2. Cultural perceptions of the cause, context, and support (circumstances and background).
3. Cultural factors affecting self-coping and past help seeking.
4. Current help seeking.

definition of the problem, helping the client to feel at ease while asking what troubles the person most. The second domain, questions 4 to 10, ask cultural perceptions of the cause, context, and support (circumstances and background) questions. Here the questions focus on perceptions of significant others and what causes the problem to become more significant. The third area, questions 11 to 13, addresses the cultural factors affecting self-coping and past help seeking and whom the individual is most likely to look to for help. The last area, questions 14 to 16, examines current help-seeking behaviors, identifying client preferences as well as the clinician–patient relationship.

In addition to identifying the factors related to completing a comprehensive diagnostic assessment, attention should always be given to the practitioner's cultural sensitivity. *Countertransference* problems may present challenges for both the client and the practitioner, especially when the practitioner is not familiar with the norms and mores of the client's culture. The best-meaning practitioner may assess and treat the client using his or her own cultural lens. *Countertransference* related to over-identification with the client's culture and values may cause the practitioner to lose objectivity and not encourage the client to examine and make changes to improve his or her psychological well-being. It is important not to accept a dysfunctional pattern as a cultural one; with this acceptance, the practitioner may not help to identify alternative coping strategies. This concept is discussed further in the next section; however, the danger rests in the potential violation of the client's right to self-determination (Hepworth, Rooney, Rooney, Gottfried, & Larsen, 2010). Completing an ethnic-sensitive diagnostic assessment requires the practitioner to very clearly assess the client, his or her family, the role of culture and environment, and how each affects the client's behaviors and responses.

In terms of training professionals, graduate education and preparation to deal with multicultural issues is central to competent practice. Regardless of the helping discipline, cultural competence training focusing on cultural awareness and the various ways professionals can respond, as well as taking into account their preconceived notions, can lead to improvement in the diagnostic process and subsequent treatment (Qureshi, Collazos, Ramos, & Casas, 2008).

If mental health practitioners are truly committed to enhancing the lives of people—as individuals, groups, families, and communities—they must also be committed to enabling clients to maximize their capabilities as full and effective participants in society. If there is a spiritual aspect of human life, and it is interrelated with other aspects of life, practitioners need to be trained to take this into account to help clients reach their

QUICK REFERENCE 2.14

CREATING CULTURAL COMPETENCE IN PRACTITIONERS

Value diversity in all individuals and the strengths that can be found in differences.

Seek out experiences and training that will facilitate understanding the needs of diverse populations.

Conduct a cultural self-assessment, identifying one's own values, beliefs, and views.

Be sure to include aspects of cultural identity, as self-reported and self-identified by the client, and the influences it can or does not have on the diagnostic assessment.

Become aware of the limits of one's areas of competence and expertise. If the problem behavior(s) the client is experiencing is beyond the understanding of the practitioner, it is up to the practitioner to seek ethnic group consultation or to make referrals to more appropriate services or helping professionals.

goals and potential. Although many practitioners may accurately assess relevant cultural, religious, or spiritual issues, they may not understand the relevance of a client's spiritual beliefs, values, and perceptions. What a client believes can influence the way he or she responds, and these behaviors may be inseparable from the environmental system. Without specific education, professional training, and preparation in this area, mental health practitioners are just as ill equipped to practice as they are to deal with policy issues or other types of psychological or culturally related problems. Mental health practitioners need to be aware of their own strengths and limitations and remain active in seeking education to prepare themselves to deal effectively with cultural, spiritual, and/or religious issues in the lives of their clients. (See Quick Reference 2.14.)

CONCEPTS OF DISTRESS

Practitioners have to be aware that viewing a client through a narrow cultural lens can lead to misinterpreting a client's cultural traditions and problem-solving processes as abnormal or dysfunctional. The revisions and changes in the *DSM-III-R* (1987), *DSM-IV* (1994), and *DSM-IV-TR* (2000) show that experts clearly acknowledged that powerful cultural influences could negate a mental health diagnosis. The term *culture-bound syndrome* was introduced in *DSM-IV* to represent recurrent, locality-specific patterns of behavior that can result in troubling experience(s) potentially linked to a particular *DSM-IV* diagnostic category (APA, 2000). Culture-bound syndromes were examples of extreme forms of cultural expression that could be seen as dysfunctional in mainstream society. Yet when these forms of cultural expression were compared among various cultures, culture-bound syndromes shared more similarities and commonalities than differences in physiological manifestations. In *DSM-5*, the term *cultural-bound syndromes* has been dropped. This term has been replaced, however, with a glossary of Cultural Concepts of Distress. This section lists nine cultural concepts of distress that could clearly influence the perception of or mimic a mental disorder (see Quick Reference 2.15).

Two common concepts of distress are *ataque de nervios* and *nervios*. *Ataque de nervios* is a

QUICK REFERENCE 2.15

Selected Cultural Concepts of Distress

- ***Ataque de nervios*** (anxiety often related to a trauma [Latino])
- ***Nervios*** (similar to *ataque de nervios* but chronic in nature [Latino])
- ***Dhat syndrome*** (discharge and impotence [Southeast Asia])
- ***Khyai cap*** (windlike attacks [Cambodian])
- ***Kufungisisa*** (similar to *brain fag* [Nigeria] anxiety attacks, brain-tiredness [Zimbabwean])
- ***Maladi moun*** (humanly caused illness, sent sickness, jealous [Haitian])
- ***Shenjing shuairuo*** (stress related, imbalances [Chinese])
- ***Susto*** (stress-related frightening traumatic event [Latino, Mexico, Central or South America)
- ***Taijin kyofusho*** (unrealistic fears, body odor [Japan])

Source: Abbreviated definitions summarized from the *Diagnostic and Statistical Manual of Mental Disorders, Fifth Edition.* Copyright 2013 by the American Psychiatric Association.

syndrome principally reported among individuals of Latino descent. Often referred to as an "attack of the nerves," it generally occurs after a very stressful event, such as news of the death of a close relative, divorce, conflicts with family members, or witnessing an accident involving a family member. The individual often expresses the concern that he or she has lost control. Symptoms are usually similar to a panic attack, where he or she may experience uncontrollable shouting, attacks of crying or laughing, trembling, heat in the chest rising into the head, and verbal or physical aggression. Individuals may also have a type of dissociative experience, with seizure-like episodes or fainting. It is not uncommon for some individuals to express suicidal gestures. People may experience amnesia during the *ataque de nervios* but return rapidly to their usual level of functioning, or they may report out-of-body dissociative experiences where the conscious mind appears to separate from the event and it does not feel like things are really happening to them. In *DSM-5,* conditions this most likely might be confused with are disorders that involve panic attacks related to the symptoms of anxiety and panic (specified or unspecified anxiety disorder), stress-related disorders due to the response accompanying a traumatic event (e.g., specified or unspecified trauma disorder and stressor-related disorder), and disorders with dissociative symptoms (e.g., specified or unspecified dissociative disorder or conversion disorder); due to the unpredictable possibility of uncontrollable outbursts, it may have similarities to intermittent explosive disorder.

Sometimes confused with *ataque de nervios* is *nervios. Nervios* is a cultural concept of distress found among Latinos in the United States and Latin America. In these cases, people report feeling vulnerable and unable to handle stressful life events, saying that events in their lives seem out of their control. The symptoms reported can vary, and some may mimic a depressive or anxiety disorder, such as emotional distress, irritability, stomach disturbances, problems either falling or staying asleep, easy tearfulness, inability to concentrate, trembling, and tingling sensations.

Somatic (bodily) disturbances may include headache sometimes reported as "brain aches." The term *mareos* is used to explain bouts of dizziness with occasional vertigo-like exacerbations. One distinction between *ataque de nervios* and *nervios* is that in *nervios* the problem tends to be chronic and ongoing, whereas in *ataque de nervios* it is generally abrupt and related directly to a stressful event. In *DSM-5,* conditions it is most likely to be confused with include major depressive disorder and persistent depressive disorder (dysthymia) related to the long-term chronic nature of the depressive symptoms, the anxiety disorders and social anxiety disorder related to the anxiety and inability to target one particular stressor related to the onset, and other disorders such as specified or unspecified dissociative disorder, somatic symptom disorder, and schizophrenia.

Dhat syndrome, an idiom of distress coined in Southeast Asia, occurs typically in young males who may exhibit a multitude of symptoms of anxiety and distress, resulting in weight loss and other somatic complaints. These symptoms are generally related to *Dhat*, a white discharge noted on defecation or urination that is believed to be connected to semen loss in these young males and resultant impotence.

Khyal cap, often referred to as *Khyal attacks*, are often described as windlike attacks that go through the body quickly and leave the individual with a series of serious effects. If the windlike attacks go through the lungs, the individual may report feelings of lung compression that leave the individual with shortness of breath and asphyxia. If it enters the brain, it could cause tinnitus (a ringing in the ears), dizziness, blurred vision, and fear of a fatal syncope (fainting). When presenting, the individual is most likely of Cambodian decent, and the practitioner should be aware that the perceived attacks can mimic severe mental and physical reactions that result in considerable disability.

Kufungisisa is a term that originated with the Shona of Zimbabwe that can explain feelings of anxiety, depression, and body-related concerns. Similar to what was originally listed in *DSM-IV* and *DSM-IV-TR* and not listed officially in *DSM-5* is a condition called *brain fag*. Both syndromes share the identifier of "thinking too much"; worries overwhelm the individual, resulting in symptoms such as anxiety, panic, and irritability. There are many similarities between these two syndromes in that both cultural concepts describe an anxious distress. What is different between *kufungisisa* and *brain fag* (most common to Nigeria as opposed to Zimbabwe) is that the latter is most directly related to excessive study habits and behaviors. *Kufungisisa*, on the other hand, could have more global worries, such as trying to take care of the family or other interpersonal and social problems. There may also be some differences in presentation: With *brain fag*, complaints may extend beyond simple "brain tiredness" and include heat or crawling sensations in the head.

Maladi moun can be defined as "humanly caused illness," where in Haitian communities the individual believes the symptoms he or she is experiencing have been sent by someone who is jealous or envious. The belief rests in the idea that another individual has sent symptoms such as psychosis or depression, and these symptoms will cause the person to lose the recent success they have just had. The symptoms experienced can vary depending on the reason they were sent and are often related to someone's social status, good fortune, attractive appearance, or other enviable assets.

Shenjing shuairuo, defined in its most traditional sense, has its origins in Mandarin Chinese and results when the body channels (*jing*) that hold the essential vital forces (*shen*) becoming dysregulated. Simply stated, the stressors an individual is experiencing become more than the individual can handle, and his or her internal balance cannot adjust. There can be multiple reasons, including social or occupational stressors, family stressors, or simply losing the ability to save face when the individual or his or her family feels public embarrassment, as others may know what should be kept private or as a family secret. The anxiety and stress-related reactions can be similar to *brain fag*. Unlike *brain fag*, however, *shenjing shuairuo* may not be solely related to academic performance and can have other causes. Depression and symptoms of anxiety, as well as stress-related disorders, may be confused with this cultural syndrome. Also, the private nature of the culture may not allow the individual to discuss important issues related to the stressors with the practitioner; the client may present with a strong desire for saving face and protecting his or her family or anyone within the family system who may be contributing to or directly causing the reactions.

Susto in its simplest definition is generally related to a traumatic, frightening event so severe that the soul or "life-blood" leaves the individual's body. In this culturally related condition, there can be numerous psychological and medical symptoms, although the symptoms reported can vary. At times, a preoccupation with a physical condition that does not appear to be medically consistent causes the individual great distress. Often this cultural condition can be easily confused with a somatic disorder or the trauma-related disorders. *Susto* was originally linked to Latinos, although Latinos from the Caribbean in particular do not see it as an illness. It may be seen among people in Mexico and Central and South America. In extreme cases, the incident is so frightening it can result in death. It requires clear identification of the cultural implications of this idiom of distress that avoids the potential for misdiagnosis.

Taijin kyofusho is a cultural idiom that may have originated in Japan that focuses on an unrealistic fear that is so severe it stops the person from interacting with others, while avoiding interpersonal situations. There are two primary types. The sensitive type leads people to avoid social situations because of extreme sensitivity. In the offensive type, people are extremely concerned about offending others with their own body odor (olfactory reference syndrome). The concerns are so pronounced that they can appear delusional and, according to the APA (2013), can easily be misdiagnosed as a delusional disorder, obsessive-compulsive disorder, or disorders related to social anxiety.

Regardless of the exact definitions, if practitioners are not sensitive to these syndromes and their limitations, they may inaccurately assess such symptoms as a *DSM-5* diagnostic category. In these syndromes, cultural beliefs and mores influence the symptoms, course, and social response to the behaviors. Each family system seeks to maintain a homeostatic balance that is functional and adaptive for that system. The practitioner, therefore, must guard against impulses to reorganize a client's family system based on his or her expectations or on standards set by the larger society. Awareness of cultural differences and acceptance of diversity are essential in establishing a culturally sensitive practice (Congress, 2008; Sue & Sue, 2013). This awareness can prevent giving a client an inappropriate diagnostic label. In addition, practitioners can increase their understanding of cultural expectations by examining culturally related behaviors and breaking them down into subgroupings, since differences among groups that appear similar may also exist (Alegria et al., 2007). Appendix 3 of the *DSM-5* lists some of the best-studied culturally related syndromes and idioms of distress that may be encountered in clinical practice.

In summary, a comprehensive diagnostic assessment needs to take into account the client's cultural identity. This is particularly important for immigrants and ethnic minorities who exhibit communication problems in terms of foreign language acquisition, understanding, content, and stress due to the loss of social networks in new settings (Breslau et al., 2007). Also, adjusting to a new culture can cause acculturation adjustment problems serious enough to end in suicide attempts (Leach, 2006). The practitioner must also be sensitive to the predominant idioms of distress through which problematic behaviors are identified or communicated in what is called cultural concepts of distress, especially when clients report problems with nerves, being possessed by spirits, multiple somatic complaints, and a sense of inexplicable misfortune. The meaning these symptoms have to the client need to be explored in relation to norms of his or her cultural reference group.

When addressing any symptoms that may be culturally related, the practitioner should exercise care to interpret the symptoms displayed and not use a biased cultural perspective that rests on stereotypes and pathologies rather than responding to the actual situational factor. For example, in *ataque de nervios* found among people of Latin American and Caribbean descent, what appears to be an extreme response to the situation of distress may occur. This extreme response can include dissociative symptoms, suicidal gestures, seizures, or fainting spells related to a distressing event such as interpersonal conflict or the death of a loved one (Keough, Timpano, & Schmidt, 2009).

To take into account the cultural context of the client's response, the practitioner should question: How is this extreme response influenced by the client's cultural surroundings and ethnic identity, and how do these factors lead to the exhibited response of grief and loss? What makes this response a different cultural representation and/or syndrome? How does it differ from pathology? When examining these factors, connecting how these factors can be related to psychosocial and environmental stressors and the client's level of individual, social, or occupational functioning is important. The *DSM-5* outline of cultural concepts and the CFI may be of assistance in forming the most comprehensive history. Always be sure to note differences in culture and social status between the client and the practitioner and problems these differences may cause in the diagnostic assessment. The diagnostic assessment should always conclude with an overall cultural assessment, using the CFI to quantify the responses and thereby acknowledging how these factors directly or indirectly influence behavior and further comprehensive diagnosis and care.

CULTURE AND OTHER DIAGNOSTIC ASSESSMENT FACTORS RELATED TO AGE

Regardless of their cultural or racial background, individuals both young and old use their cultural experiences to interpret their immediate surroundings, their interaction with others, and the interpersonal patterns of society (Holt & Green, 2013). Culture and family are the first two powerful influences that determine how all individuals understand, internalize, and act on what is expected of them by their family, community, and the larger society (Sue & Sue, 2013). Discriminatory experiences may provide additional information and feelings to decipher and understand in individuals who are considered minorities. During times of emotional or psychological turmoil, human nature is such that all individuals, regardless of age, strive for meaning in their lives using their cultural lens: their values, beliefs, and experiences. In assessing both the elderly and children in therapeutic situations, the practitioner must first accept that these individuals present a rich and complex picture that requires examination of the biological, psychological, and social factors within a historical and cultural framework. During the diagnostic assessment, helping professionals must ensure that lack of historical and cultural sensitivity does not hinder the good intentions of the intervention or the research process.

Age and culture in the diagnostic assessment are similar and need to be assessed and treated

QUICK REFERENCE 2.16

Diagnostic Assessment With Children

Carefully assess changes in self-esteem or confidence levels.

Assess dysfunctional behavioral patterns, taking into account the family system and other support system influences (including peer pressure).

Be aware that the child is not solely responsible for many of the difficulties he or she encounters.

Understand the role that cultural differences and expectations can play in each family system.

effectively and rapidly. Personal stereotypes about age and aging and discriminatory practices can affect the welfare and progress of the individual for whom assessment or treatment is provided (Sue & Sue, 2013).

Cultural and Other Diagnostic Assessment Factors Related to Children

Recognizing, understanding, and appreciating the effects that geographic and regional differences can have on children help to develop age-sensitive practices and provide effective services. When assessing children, the family's place of origin should not be minimized. Family values may reflect differences in urban versus rural expectations and traditions. Congress and Gonzalez (2013) recommend that practitioners identify appropriate tools to conduct culturally sensitive assessments. Children's actions are guided by the values and norms established within the family system. For example, if a child's family of origin is not supportive of mental health treatment and holds negative beliefs surrounding professional assistance, a child may not independently ask for help. If a parent or the extended family does not support the provider's assessment or treatment for the child, gaining family support may be more complicated than simply having an uninvolved parent (Locke & Bailey, 2014). A more accurate assessment may be possible in the family home and/or through collaboration with other significant people in the community (e.g., clergy). Taking into account religious and cultural worldviews can help a practitioner access the family's extended helping network and use this information to benefit the family (Suarez & Lewis, 2013). See Quick Reference 2.16.

Culture and Other Diagnostic Assessment Factors with Older Adults

Growing old is often viewed negatively in our society, including some health and mental health care professionals. Victimized by societal attitudes that devalue old age, many individuals (young and old) will do almost anything to avoid or deny old age. Such prejudices are the result of both rational and irrational fears. Rational fears about declining health and loss of income, loved ones, and social status can be exaggerated by negative stereotypes, as are irrational fears such as changes in physical appearance, loss of mobility, loss of masculinity or femininity, and perceived mental incompetence. Older adults continue to be oppressed by myths and misinformation and by real obstacles imposed by various biological, psychological, social, and economic factors.

Practitioners need to examine their own attitudes toward aging. They need to recognize older adults as valuable resources in our society and provide services and advocacy to assist them in maximizing their degree of life satisfaction and well-being. Many older adults fear loss of activity and may deny the actual loss. Older adults may suffer from chronic conditions where improvement is unlikely. They may also suffer from continuous life stresses, such as widowhood, social and occupational losses, and progressive and declining physical health problems. Lack of access and transportation creates barriers for older adults with psychiatric problems who attend community mental health centers for checkups and medication.

Knowledge of the problems that elderly individuals face is critical. Practitioners need to know what is normal and what is not as far as changes in sexuality (Clay, 2012). Education can help to address problems that can occur, as well as the perceptions and attitudes of ascribed asexuality in older adults by family, friends, peers, and caregivers. Patronizing attitudes about elderly individuals increase the tendency to deny terminal problems rather than help them develop ways to cope. A diagnostic assessment should take into account the individual's health conditions and environmental factors, among other aspects of his or her life.

Assessing lethality with a suicidal older client is essential. Older adults may not openly discuss feelings of hopelessness and helplessness, and these must be screened. If suicidal ideation and a concrete plan (the way to carry out the suicidal act) are expressed, steps to ensure hospitalization must be taken immediately, as for any client at serious risk for suicide. Many older adults may not be forthcoming with situational criteria, and the practitioner may remain uncertain of the seriousness of the client's thoughts with respect to his or her actions. Regardless of whether the client's behavior is action focused, some type of immediate protective measure needs to be employed. This topic is discussed in detail in the chapters on intervention strategy. (See Quick Reference 2.17.)

CULTURE AND OTHER DIAGNOSTIC ASSESSMENT FACTORS RELATED TO GENDER

Most professionals would agree that girls and boys are often subjected to early differential treatment and identification. Parents and the larger societal network deal differently with girls and boys, and children often are expected to model themselves according to accepted gender lines. Most inquiry into gender has focused on the importance of outlining the actual differences between male and female characteristics and whether there are true physical, cognitive, and personality differences between the sexes. From a medical-biological perspective, most professionals would say that such differences do exist. Although the physical differences (e.g., physical structure and anatomy) between males and females are obvious, other differences are not. In medication use, although factors such as size and dose are controlled for, therapeutic response to certain drugs can differ between males and females (*Physicians' Desk Reference*, 2009). Furthermore, from a social-psychological perspective, stereotyping can lead to unfair practices of sexism.

During the diagnostic assessment, it is difficult to avoid gender bias because of sex role representations. Even though gender-neutral influences may be considered products of the society at large, individuals continue to have definite ideas about sex role deviance. It is critical to acknowledge the influences that gender may have on the diagnostic assessment process. Practitioners must be careful to rule out bias, such as viewing the male as the doer who is always rational, logical, and in control and the female as the nurturer who is often emotional, illogical, and dependent.

A gender-sensitive diagnostic assessment includes behaviors as naturally occurring phenomena. From a feminist perspective, gender and power relations are paramount to effective assessment and intervention. To summarize

QUICK REFERENCE 2.17

Diagnostic Assessment With Older Adults

Identify life circumstances that can complicate the diagnostic assessment process.

Retirement issues: Identify problems with work role transition and retirement status.

Chronic conditions: Identify an individual's chronic medical conditions and how these conditions can affect his or her level of daily functioning.

Physical health conditions: Identify physical health conditions, especially vision and hearing problems that can complicate or magnify current problems.

Mental health complaints: Identify mental health problems, looking for signs such as feelings of sadness, loneliness, guilt, boredom, marked decrease or increase in appetite, change in sleep behavior, and a sense of worthlessness. Be aware that signs of depression in elderly persons can be situational (the etiology of the depression is related to life circumstances), and screen for problems related to tragic life experiences, including the loss of loved ones, job, status, and independence, as well as other personal disappointments. Screen for confusion that may be a sign of dementia.

Medication use and misuse: Identify the use and misuse of prescription medication because commonly prescribed medications can present such side effects as irritability, sexual dysfunction, memory lapses, a general feeling of tiredness, or a combination of these.

Sexual problems: Be open to the identification of sexual problems.

Suicide: Identify the probability of accumulated life losses and be cognizant of a client's abilities and/or problems in coping with grief.

feminist theory in our society, four elements are generally considered:

1. Gender inequality is highlighted, and women are oppressed by a patriarchal society.
2. The individual experiences of men and women are considered the cornerstone of all social science understanding.
3. The primary emphasis is to improve the conditions women experience.
4. Feminism acknowledges that gender bias exists and that, as products of the society, practitioners cannot be objective observers (McCann & Kim, 2013).

Feminist contributions have been a major force in rethinking gender and power relations and the importance of recognizing the influences of politics, as well as how feminist theory can be used to inform effective politics (McCann & Kim, 2013). With perceived power imbalances so ingrained in a culture, every effort should be made to ensure they do not influence traditional methods of assessment and intervention.

To be gender sensitive in the diagnostic assessment process, the practitioner must first identify power differentials contributing to the source of the problem area. According to feminist theory and thought, power differentials create and/or are the source of distress that the person experiences within the system. They may

QUICK REFERENCE 2.18

Gender and the Diagnostic Assessment I

Practitioners Need to:

Identify the individual's perception of gender and how this belief affects values, beliefs, and behaviors.

Identify an individual's traditional roots and acknowledge how that can influence the way issues are addressed and discussed.

Identify adaptive and maladaptive behaviors.

Identify the environmental or interpersonal circumstances supporting the behavior.

Help the individual to acknowledge family or societal perceptions of his or her behavior and how it may detract from or contribute to current problem behaviors.

be found in relationships, roles, the cultural hegemony, and what are generally referred to as discourses. The primary focus is placed on power differentials and how they influence the individual as a source of distress and disorder. The practitioner would encourage the client to address how these power differentials affect and play a role in relation to self and others. The practitioner is responsible for interpreting and finding meaning in what is said and must listen and respond by helping the client to problem-solve what is determined to be the real situation.

When practitioners complete the diagnostic assessment, they must consider gender as a basic building block, along with such concepts as generation (age) and ethnic and cultural implications. Operating with this foundation or mind-set, practitioners can assess the behavior patterns that are reinforced in this contingency pattern. (See Quick References 2.18 and 2.19.)

QUICK REFERENCE 2.19

Gender and the Diagnostic Assessment II

Practitioners Need to:

Realize that individuals are products of their family and societal context.

Make a conscious attempt to recognize their own behavior paradigms and their conscious or unconscious sexual stereotypes.

Strive to be as objective and tolerant as possible regarding the uniqueness of clients and their rights, acknowledging that the behavioral paradigm of the practitioner is not necessarily the correct or ideal one.

Be aware of how gender (the practitioner's or the client's) can affect the diagnostic assessment process and the information shared.

Be aware of the personalities of those in the family and their effect, significant or otherwise, on the client and how these personalities can influence the client's views, actions, and performance of the activities of daily living.

In the diagnostic assessment process, the practitioner is responsible for interpreting and finding meaning in what the client says, and this interpretation is not based solely on what the client has stated. The practitioner must listen and respond by helping the client to problem-solve what is determined to be the real situation. Developing rapport during the diagnostic assessment is critical because it makes clients feel more comfortable and gives them permission to state how they feel and how those feelings are affecting their behaviors. Wright (2011) warns, however, that building rapport, while important in all settings, may not be quite the same in the assessment phase as in the therapeutic phase. Building rapport in the assessment phase can be more limited than in the therapeutic setting because the role of an assessor is focused on completing the diagnostic process.

Although differences between men and women do exist, many differences can be traced to situations in which men and women find themselves; in these situations, even if they behave identically, they are perceived and judged by different standards (Aronson, 2008). The practitioner is also a product of the social environment and influenced by the culture natural to him or her. It is important not to impose double standards of interpretation or, worse yet, interpretation without realizing the influence of gender at all. The inclusion of gender is imperative within the mind-set incorporated in diagnostic assessment.

Use of Other Specified and Unspecified Disorders

Sometimes the practitioner completing a diagnostic assessment cannot neatly categorize all the symptoms into a particular diagnosis, and for such cases, the option for selecting other specified or unspecified disorders has been added. However, when the specified category is used, the specific reason the client does not meet the criteria must be reported. If the practitioner is not comfortable with or unable to state the exact reason, the unspecified disorder may be selected. These diagnostic options have replaced the previous term *not otherwise specified* (NOS) that was introduced in *DSM-IV-TR*. Similar to the previous NOS category, these new disorders have been added as an option at the end of the diagnostic categories listed in the *DSM-5*. Even though the criteria for its use rest in sound clinical judgment, coding these disorders can remain subjective and variable, as they may change with time and circumstances. This makes continued assessment with the application of skilled clinical judgment a key factor in the determination to use or maintain it. This is particularly relevant to the unspecified disorders, where the actual reason that the individual does not meet the diagnosis is not required. In both cases, constant monitoring is necessary to see if changes have occurred that now allow a more specified diagnosis.

Helpful hints for using this category include the following: For specified disorder, the client will meet the general guidelines for the disorder, yet all of the criteria may not be met. In this case, the ones not present, which the clinician suspects exist but are not fully displayed, need to be documented. In the unspecified type, the practitioner may use his or her clinical judgment to not place a more diagnostic label. This decision may be based on the situation and any mitigating circumstances that may be present. Once given, and later more information is gathered, the practitioner may decide to change the diagnosis from the unspecified category to the specified one or change it to the specific one it most fits. Regardless, to place a specified or unspecified diagnosis similar to any mental disorder, the behaviors exhibited must be significant enough to affect social and occupational functioning. Generally, using either category involves the practitioner making a decision regarding the information presented, and although there may be insufficient information to fully support assigning behaviors to a particular mental disorder in the category, the general criteria for the category of disorders are evident. For example, it is clear that an individual suffers from a type of bipolar disorder, but the specific criteria for a particular type cannot be clearly identified.

Similar to use of the NOS category introduced in *DSM-IV*, there may be many reasons this new category is utilized. For example, in a crisis situation or in an emergency room, the practitioner may feel he or she has inaccurate information with no time to verify or confirm it. Also, in a crisis situation, the individual may be too upset to report symptoms accurately. There may not be a family or support system available to help complete or verify the accuracy of the information needed for the diagnostic assessment.

Although using the specified or unspecified category in *DSM-5* is not discouraged, a caution based on experienced practice reality must be noted. Like the discontinued NOS category outlined in *DSM-IV*, it appears this new category will also be scrutinized in billing and reimbursement practices. With the advent of coordinated care, service providers well aware of the criteria required for a diagnosis may shy away from reimbursement. This means that medical reviewers will be looking closely to see why the client is given this category. Monitoring such diagnoses in terms of the time frame, current and past criteria, and the duration of symptoms should be ongoing and updated regularly. Reimbursement patterns will most likely show that these diagnoses are given the greatest scrutiny, and reviewers may expect this diagnostic category to be updated with justification as to why it remains more appropriate than the others in the same classification. Practice reality will probably dictate very cautious use of this diagnostic category.

Updating and Consistency with ICD-11

The *DSM-IV-TR* (2000) was the standard for assessment until the latest revision (*DSM-5*) was released in May 2013. Historically across the United States, the *DSM* has been used to classify mental health disorders. True to its historical roots, the most current version of the *DSM* supports this premise with the stated purpose being for statistical and assessment purposes, as well as educational support. It also provides supportive information on prevalence rates within the larger population that has been gathered to inform policy decisions. This makes the *DSM* an important reference for students, researchers, clinicians, and practitioners.

The International Classification of Diseases (*ICD*) is credited as the first official international classification system for mental disorders and remains the global standard for diagnostic classification and is recognized for service reimbursement. The *ICD-10* was originally released in 1990 and received full endorsement by the World Health Organization (WHO) in 1994 (WHO, 1993). In 2002, it was published in 42 languages, and in 1999 the United States implemented it for mortality (death certificates). Currently, it has three volumes. Volume 1 has tabular lists of cause-of-death titles and the codes that accompany the cause-of death-titles. Volume 2 has description guidelines and coding resources. Volume 3 provides an alphabetical index to diseases and the nature of injury, external causes of injury, and a table of drugs and chemicals. The *ICD-10* hosts more than 141,000 codes, with many different diagnostic categories, compared with the 17,000 codes in the *ICD-9-CM* (CMS, 2013).

The *ICD* is a classification system that creates a global linkage and enables disorders across the world to be viewed at one point in time. Scientific progress ultimately requires revision and updates (Sartorius et al., 1992). Similar to the *DSM*, the *ICD* has also gone through many changes and updates. The latest version of the *ICD* is ICD-10, which replaced *ICD-9-CM* (WHO, 1979). The *ICD-11* is expected to be released in 2017. During the work on the revisions to the *DSM*, interest was focused on creating a crosswalk to the book that would serve as the greatest link to the future. Because the *ICD-9-CM* and the *ICD-10-CM* would be replaced shortly and the *ICD-11* is scheduled to be implemented in 2017, this version became the focus.

In the past, the *DSM-IV-TR* was similar to the *ICD* in terms of diagnostic codes and the billing categories. Concerns have been voiced that although the codes are listed for both the *ICD-9-CM* followed by the codes for *ICD-10-CM,* the criteria needed for the diagnosis may not match what has been updated in *DSM-5*. The concentration on *DSM-5* is to be in harmonization with *ICD-11* with its expected release in 2017. Because these two books need to go hand in hand, categories with criteria listed in one book that are not listed in the other can be extremely problematic for proper coding and reimbursement. These two books have to work together, and when practitioners use the *ICD* for billing while referring to the *DSM* for clarity of the diagnostic criteria, both books need to have matching criteria. This cross-referencing is where the term *crosswalk* between the two books was derived. Although the APA states clearly that the categories are general enough to match the categories in the *ICD*, ensuring clarity and uniformity between the two texts may once again become a concern. This will be most evident to those trained on *DSM-IV* and *DSM-IV-TR*, as these texts closely match the *ICD-9-CM*. For billing purposes, there were few discrepancies between the categories listed, and the books could be used interchangeably. Working with *ICD-11* will bring major changes, and initially when it is adopted, care will be needed to ensure the categories match. They need to match based on the simple fact that the billing codes used for reimbursement are based on the *ICD*, not the *DSM*.

So What About Billing?

For diagnostic classification and billing, *ICD* is considered the global standard. It is expected that in October 2015, the *ICD-10* codes for service will replace the *ICD-9-CM* codes used previously across the United States. This date has changed several times as originally it was expected to begin in October of 2014 (CMS, 2013). The reason for adopting the newer version is threefold: (1) It is expected to provide improved data for measuring health care and service quality, (2) it will help information technology (IT) systems to record more specific and comprehensive diagnostic information, and (3) it can improve documentation and billing information by helping to better identify specific health conditions (United Health Care, 2013). The *ICD* conforms to the Health Insurance Portability and Accountability Act (HIPAA) of 1996 that seeks to protect consumers by, among other things, creating standardized mechanisms for electronic data exchanges involving the transfer and subsequent use of data related to consumer private health care. In 2000, *ICD-9-CM*, inclusive of its three volumes, was adopted for reporting diagnoses, other health problems, causes of injury, diseases, and impairments in all standard billing transactions. Furthermore, according to the secretary of the Department of Health and Human Services, a ruling was released and published in the *Federal Register* on January 16, 2009, to adopt the *ICD-10-CM* standards and the Procedural Coding System (PCS). The final rule is posted on http://www.gpo.gov/fdsys/pkg/FR-2009-01-16/pdf/E9-743.pdf. This means that everyone covered by HIPAA must be *ICD-10* compliant.

Some professionals may question why it took so long to adopt the *ICD-10,* but there is no simple answer. For the most part, the original push to make *ICD-10* the standard was in 2003. The pushback was great, however, with concerns that having to work with HIPAA as well as changes in the *ICD,* all at the same time, was too big a change. The implementation date has been pushed back several times, and when sponsors tried to make it happen in 2013, the inpatient version of the *ICD-10-PCS* was so complicated to incorporate into the Content Management Systems (CMS), it was agreed to wait till October 2014. To date, for the conversions that were already made, billing systems were told they could use either the *ICD-9-CM* or *ICD-10* codes but will need to complete the transition by the due date scheduled currently for 2014.

In summary, for the most part *DSM-IV* and *DSM-IV-TR* parallel the *ICD-9-CM; DSM-5* does not clearly parallel *ICD-9-CM* or *ICD-10* but is geared to more closely relate to *ICD-11.* The *ICD-11* will be released in 2017, and the hope is that it will be adopted shortly after its release. Training for billing staff is highly recommended and clearly beyond the scope of this chapter. For clinicians without billing staff, training on *ICD-10-CM* and familiarity with both books, the *ICD* and the *DSM,* are highly recommended.

Coding the Diagnosis in the DSM-5

All mental health practitioners must be familiar with the numeric coding utilized in the *DSM*-5. This coding provides quick and consistent recording, leading to service recognition and reimbursement. Coding can also assist with describing the client's injury or illness. It can be helpful in gathering prevalence and research information and can assist other health care professionals in providing continuity of care (Rudman, 2000). When a mental health practitioner completes or assists in completing a claim form, the proper diagnostic and procedural claim codes must be utilized. There are two primary types of coding: diagnostic (what a client suffers from) and procedural (what will be done to treat it). The *DSM-5* and the *ICD-10-CM* are most concerned with the diagnostic codes. *Current procedural terminology* (CPT) codes are related to the services that mental health practitioners often use for assessing clients. Although closely linked to the *ICD-9-CM* and *ICD-10-CM* codes, these codes correspond to procedures rather than to diagnostic categories.

The CPT codes are divided into four procedural categories: (1) evaluation and management services, (2) surgical care, (3) diagnostic services, and (4) therapeutic services (Rudman, 2000). For example, in billing for Medicare reimbursement, the CPT codes are primarily responsible for documenting practice strategy. The *DSM-5* has been updated with the latest diagnostic codes. Updated CPT codes assist with procedural recording in inpatient and outpatient settings, denoting the setting where the service is provided (APA Online, 2001). One myth in the practice setting is that since the CPT codes represent procedure, use of certain CPT codes can restrict reimbursement. Although there is some truth to this statement, the code itself does not restrict reimbursement—it is the reimbursement provider. Therefore, each insurance company or service reimbursement system determines what service is covered and what is not. This makes it critical for the mental health practitioner who practices or facilitates billing to be aware of not only what the major service reimbursement systems utilized will cover but also which providers are authorized to dispense these services.

With the expected release of the *ICD-11* in 2015, the decision was made to list the codes from the *ICD-9-CM* and *ICD-10-CM* in the latest revision of the *DSM.* With the release and subsequent application of *ICD-11,* the codes will also be updated in the *DSM-5* and then appropriately applied to each category. During the transition, both the *ICD-9-CM* and the *ICD-10-CM* codes are important. Since *ICD* conforms to HIPAA,

QUICK REFERENCE 2.20

EXAMPLE OF CODING IN *DSM-5*

Diagnosis or Related Condition	*ICD-9-CM* Code	*ICD-10-CM* Code
Schizotypal Personality Disorder	301.22	(F21)
Medication-Induced Acute Akathisia	333.9	(G25.71)
Homelessness	V60.0	(Z59.0)

this is the coding that will be needed, based on electronic data exchanges, when the billing diagnoses involve the use and transfer of data related to consumer private health care. For billing, this is very important for practitioners to know and understand, as *DSM-5* utilizes the current version of the *ICD* needed for mental health billing.

To facilitate billing for the mental disorders in *DSM-5,* both codes are listed with the *ICD-9-CM* codes first, followed in parentheses by *ICD-10-CM* codes. The 20 chapters that list the mental disorders provide a brief overview of the chapter, followed by specific information related to the individual diagnoses that can help determine what criteria flow best with either the *ICD-9-CM* or the *ICD-10* billing codes. There are 22 chapters in the *DSM,* and the last two chapters—the medication-induced movement disorders and other adverse effects of medication (Chapter 21) and the other conditions that may be the focus of individual attention (Chapter 22)—are not mental disorders. These two chapters are included to help the practitioner provide the supportive information considered essential for a complete diagnostic assessment. These two chapters list the codes as relevant, and the chapter on other conditions that may be the focus of clinical intervention lists both the V codes outlined in *ICD-9-CM* and the Z codes relevant to the *ICD-10-CM.* These last two chapters are not comprehensive and do not constitute mental disorders. The information in these chapters is provided purely to support a more comprehensive diagnostic assessment and the treatment planning and practice strategy to follow. (See Quick Reference 2.20.)

SUMMARY

This chapter gives the mental health practitioner the background information needed to complete the most accurate diagnostic assessment possible by using the *DSM-5.* An accurate diagnostic assessment is the critical first step to identifying behaviors that disturb individual, occupational, and social functioning and to formulating the plan for intervention. Thus, the diagnostic assessment sets the tone for treatment planning and therapy. To compete in today's current mental health care service environment, the role of the practitioner is twofold: (1) ensure that high-quality service is provided to the client and (2) ensure the client's access and opportunity to address his or her health needs. Neither of these tasks is easy or popular in today's environment. The push for mental health practice to be conducted with limited resources and services, along with the resultant competition among providers, has stressed the role of the mental health service practitioner (Dziegielewski, 2013). Amid this turbulence, the importance of a comprehensive assessment that takes environmental circumstances into account remains clear. Chapter 3 discusses in detail the application of the diagnostic system utilized in *DSM-5* in terms of documentation and the development of treatment plans that can assist with and guide the intervention process.

QUESTIONS FOR FURTHER THOUGHT

1. Is it important for mental health practitioners to be aware of the *DSM* and the *ICD*, and if so, why?
2. What are the differences among diagnosis, assessment, and using a diagnostic assessment?
3. Why is it critical to realize and incorporate the mind-body connection when completing the diagnostic assessment?
4. Explain the differences among race, racial identity, and culture and how it could affect the diagnostic assessment.
5. List two reasons that culture is so important to consider in the diagnostic assessment.
6. Can you list at least two substantial changes between the *DSM-IV* and the *DSM-IV-TR* and *DSM-5*?

REFERENCES

Ahn, W., & Kim, N. S. (2008). Causal theories of mental disorder concepts. *Psychological Science Agenda, 22*(6), 3–8.

Alegria, M., Shrout, P. E., Woo, M., Guarnaccia, P., Sribney, W., Vila, D., . . . Canino, G. (2007). Understanding differences in past year psychiatric disorders for Latinos living in the US. *Social Science and Medicine, 65*, 214–230.

American Psychiatric Association. (1995). *Diagnostic and statistical manual of mental disorders* (4th ed., rev). Washington, DC: Author.

American Psychiatric Association. (2000). *Diagnostic and statistical manual of mental disorders* (4th ed., text rev.). Washington, DC: Author.

American Psychiatric Association. (2013). *Diagnostic and statistical manual of mental disorders* (5th ed.). Washington, DC: Author.

APA Online. (2001). *Practice coding*. Retrieved from Practice central: http://www.apapracticecentral.org/reimbursement/billing/index.aspx?__utma=12968039.270164585.1399907347.1399907347.1400002716.2&__utmb=12968039.4.10.1400002716&__utmc=12968039&__utmx=-&__utmz=12968039.1399907347.1.1.utmcsr=google|utmccn=(organic)|utmcmd=organic|utmctr=suicide risk and clients&__utmv=-&__utmk=136117041

Aronson, E. (2008). *The social animal* (10th ed.). New York, NY: Worth.

Baran, B. E., Shanock, L. R., Rogelberg, S. G., & Scott, C. W. (2012). Leading group meetings: Supervisors' actions, employee behaviors, and upward perceptions. *Small Group Research, 43*(3), 330–335.

Barker, R. L. (2003). *The social work dictionary* (5th ed.). Washington, DC: NASW Press.

Breslau, J., Aguilar-Gaxiola, S., Borges, G., Castilla-Puentes, R. C., Kendler, K. S., Medina-Mora, M., . . . Kessler, R. C. (2007). Mental disorders among English-speaking Mexican immigrants to the US compared to a national sample of Mexicans. *Psychiatry Research, 151*(1–2), 115–122.

Bunger, A. C. (2010). Defining service coordination: A social work perspective. *Journal of Social Service Research, 36*(5), 485–401.

Burns, T., & Lloyd, H. (2004). Is a team approach based on staff meetings cost-effective in the delivery of mental health care? *Current Opinion in Psychiatry, 17*(4), 311–314.

Canino, G., & Alegria, M. (2008). Psychiatric diagnosis—Is it universal or relative to culture? *Journal of Child Psychology and Psychiatry, 49*(3), 237–250.

Carlton, T. O. (1984). *Clinical social work in health care settings: A guide to professional practice with exemplars.* New York, NY: Springer.

Carpenter, J., Schneider, J., Brandon, T., & Wooff, D. (2003). Working in multidisciplinary community mental health teams: The impact on social workers and health professionals of integrated mental health care. *British Journal of Social Work, 33*(8), 1081–1193.

Chang-Muy, F., & Congress, E. P. (Eds.). (2009). *Social work with immigrants and refugees: Legal issues, clinical skills, and advocacy*. New York, NY: Springer.

Clay, R. A. (2012). Later-life sex. *APA: Monitor on Psychology, 43*(11), 42. Retrieved from http://www.apa.org/monitor/2012/12/later-life-sex.aspx

CMS: Centers for Medicare & Medicaid Services. (2013). *FAQs: ICD-10 Transition Basics*. Retrieved from http://www.cms.gov/Medicare/Coding/ICD10/Downloads/ICD10FAQs2013.pdf

Congress, E. (2008). Assessment of adults. In K. M. Sowers & C. N. Dulmus (Series Eds.) & W. Rowe & L. A.

Rapp-Paglicci (Vol. Eds.), *Comprehensive handbook of social work and social welfare: Vol. 3. Social work practice* (pp. 310–325). Hoboken, NJ: Wiley.

Congress, E., & Gonzalez, M. (Eds.). (2013). *Multicultural perspectives in social work practice with families* (3rd ed.). New York, NY: Springer.

Conyne, R. K. (2014). *Group work leadership: An introduction for helpers*. Thousand Oaks, CA: Sage.

Cooper, R. (2004). What is wrong with the *DSM*? *History of Psychiatry, 15*(1), 5–25.

Corcoran, J., & Walsh, J. (2010). *Clinical assessment and diagnosis in social work practice*. New York, NY: Oxford University Press.

Corey, G. (2012). *Theory and practice of counseling and psychotherapy* (9th ed.). Belmont, CA: Brooks/Cole.

Dziegielewski, S. F. (2008). Brief and intermittent approaches to practice: The state of practice. *Journal of Brief Treatment and Crisis Intervention, 8*(2), 147–163.

Dziegielewski, S. F. (2010). *Psychopharmacology and social work practice: A person-in-environment approach* (2nd ed.). New York, NY: Springer.

Dziegielewski, S. F. (2013). *The changing face of health care social work: Opportunities and challenges for professional practice* (3rd ed.). New York, NY: Springer.

Dziegielewski, S. F., & Holliman, D. (2001). Managed care and social work: Practice implications in an era of change. *Journal of Sociology and Social Welfare, 28*(2), 125–138.

Dziegielewski, S. F., & Leon, A. M. (2001). *Psychopharmacology and social work practice*. New York, NY: Springer.

Gilbert, D. J., Abel, E., Stewart, N. F., & Zilberman, M. (2007). More than drugs: Voices of HIV-seropositive individuals with a history of substance use reveal a range of adherence factors. In L. S. Ka'opua, & N. L. Linsk (Eds.), *HIV treatment adherence: Challenges for social services* (pp. 161–179). Binghamton, NY: Haworth.

Helms, J. E. (Ed.). (1990). *Black and White racial identity: Theory, research, and practice*. Westport, CT: Praeger.

Hepworth, D. H., Rooney, R. H., Rooney, G., Gottfried, K., & Larsen, J. A. (2010). *Direct social work practice: Theory and skills* (8th ed.). Belmont, CA: Brooks/Cole.

Holt, T. C., & Green, L. B. (Eds.) (2013). *The new encyclopedia of Southern culture: Vol. 24. Race*. Chapel Hill: University of North Carolina Press.

Keough, M. E., Timpano, K. R., & Schmidt, N. B. (2009). Ataques de nervios: Culturally bound and distinct from panic attacks? *Depression and Anxiety, 26*(1), 16–21.

Kirst-Ashman, K. K. (2008). *Human behavior, communities, organizations, and groups in the macro social environment: An empowerment approach* (2nd ed.). Belmont, CA: Wadsworth/Brooks Cole.

Kraemer, H. C., Shrout, P. E., & Rubio-Stipec, M. (2007). Developing the *Diagnostic and Statistical Manual V*: What will "statistical" mean in the *DSM V*? *Social Psychiatry and Psychiatric Epidemiology, 42*, 259–267.

Lankshear, A. J. (2003). Coping with conflict and confusing agendas in multidisciplinary community mental health teams. *Journal of Psychiatric and Mental Health Nursing, 10*(4), 457–464.

Leach, M. M. (2006). *Cultural diversity and suicide: Ethnic, religious, gender, and sexual orientation perspectives*. Binghamton, NY: Haworth.

Lee, J., & Bean, F. D. (2004). America's changing color lines: Race/ethnicity, immigration, and multiracial identification. *Annual Review of Sociology, 30*, 221–242.

Lilienfeld, S. O., & Landfield, K. (2008). Issues in diagnosis: Categorical vs. dimensional. In W. E. Craighead, D. J. Miklowitz, & L. W. Craighead (Eds.), *Psychopathology: History, diagnosis, and empirical foundations* (pp. 1–33). Hoboken, NJ: Wiley.

Locke, D. C., & Bailey, D. F. (2014). *Increasing multicultural understanding* (3rd ed.). Thousand Oaks, CA: Sage.

Lum, D. (Ed.). (2011). *Culturally competent practice: A framework for understanding diverse groups and justice issues* (4th ed.). Pacific Grove, CA: Brooks/Cole, Thomson Learning.

Mays, V. M., Ponce, N. A., Washington, D. L., & Cochran, S. D. (2003). Classifications of race and ethnicity: Implications for public health. *Annual Review of Public Health, 24*, 83–110.

McCann, C. R., & Kim, S. (Eds.). (2013). *Feminist theory reader: Local and global perspectives* (3rd ed.). New York, NY: Routledge.

Mezzich, J. E., & Salloum, I. M. (2007). Towards innovative international classification and diagnostic systems: *ICD-11* and person-centered integrative diagnosis [Editorial]. *Acta Psychiatrica Scandinavica, 116*(1), 1–5.

Mitchell, A. J., Vaze, A., & Rao, S. (2009). Clinical diagnosis of depression in primary care: A meta-analysis. *Lancet, 374*, 609–619.

Molodynski, A., & Burns, T. (2008). The organization of psychiatric services. *Medicine, 36*(8), 388–390.

Nunes, E. V., & Rounsaville, B. J. (2006). Comorbidity of substance use with depression and other mental disorders: From *Diagnostic and Statistical Manual of Mental Disorders*, fourth edition (*DSM-IV*) to *DSM-V*. *Addiction, 101*(Suppl. 1), 89–96.

Orovwuje, P. R. (2008). Contemporary challenges in forensic mental health: The ingenuity of the multidisciplinary team. *Mental Health Review Journal, 13*(2), 24–34.

Owen, D. W. (2011). The role of assessment in mental health counseling. In A. J. Palamo, W. J. Weikel, & D. P. Borsos, *Foundations of mental health counseling* (4th ed., pp. 333–353). Springfield, IL: Charles C. Thomas.

Owen, J. (2008). The nature of confirmatory strategies in the initial assessment process. *Journal of Mental Health Counseling, 30*(4), 362–374.

Packard, T., Jones, L., & Nahrstedt, K. (2006). Using the image exchange to enhance interdisciplinary team building in child care. *Child and Adolescent Social Work Journal, 23*(1), 86–106.

Pare, D. A. (2013). *The practice of collaborative counseling & psychotherapy: Developing skills in mindful helping*. Thousand Oaks, CA: Sage.

Paris, J. (2013). *The intelligent clinician's guide to the* DSM-5™. New York, NY: Oxford University Press.

Pearson, G. S. (2008). Advocating for the full-frame approach [Editorial]. *Perspectives in Psychiatric Care, 44*(1), 1–2.

Perlman, H. H. (1957). *Social casework: A problem solving process*. Chicago, IL: University of Chicago Press.

Physicians' Desk Reference [PDR]. (2009). *Physicians' desk reference* (63rd ed.). Montvale, NJ: Medical Economics.

Queralt, M. (1996). *The social environment and human behavior: A diversity perspective*. Boston, MA: Allyn & Bacon.

Qureshi, A., Collazos, F., Ramos, M., & Casas, M. (2008). Cultural competency training in psychiatry. *European Psychiatry, 23*(Suppl. 1), 49–58.

Rankin, E. A. (1996). Patient and family education. In V. B. Carson & E. N. Arnold (Eds.), *Mental health nursing: The nurse patient journey* (pp. 503–516). Philadelphia, PA: Saunders.

Rashidian, A., Eccles, M. P., & Russell, I. (2008). Falling on stony ground? A qualitative study of implementation of clinical guidelines' prescribing recommendations in primary care. *Health Policy, 85*, 148–161.

Rauch, J. (1993). Introduction. In J. Rauch (Ed.), *Assessment: A sourcebook for social work practice*. Milwaukee, WI: Families International.

Rosen, A., & Callaly, T. (2005). Interdisciplinary teamwork and leadership: Issues for psychiatrists. *Australasian Psychiatry, 13*(3), 234–240.

Rudman, W. J. (2000). *Coding and documentation of domestic violence*. Retrieved from http://www.endabuse.org/userfiles/file/HealthCare/codingpaper.pdf

Sartorius, N., Kaelber, C. T., Cooper, J. E., Roper, M. T., Rae, D. S., Gulbinat, W. M., & Regier, D. A. (1993). Progress toward achieving a common language in psychiatry: Results from the field trial of the clinical guidelines accompanying the WHO classification of mental and behavioral disorders in ICD-10. *Archives of General Psychiatry, 50*, 115–224.

Sheafor, B. W., & Horejsi, C. J. (2012). *Techniques and guidelines for social work practice* (9th ed.). New York, NY: Allyn & Bacon.

Siebert, C. (2006). Functional assessment: Process and product. *Home Health Care Management and Practice, 19*(1), 51–57.

Strom-Gottfried, K. (2014). *Straight talk about professional ethics*. Chicago, IL: Lyceum.

Suarez, Z. E., & Lewis, E. A. (2013). Spirituality and culturally diverse families: The intersection of culture, religion, and spirituality. In E. Congress & M. Gonzalez (Eds.), *Multicultural perspectives in social work practice with families* (pp. 231–244). New York, NY: Springer.

Sue, D. W., & Sue, D. (2013). *Counseling the culturally diverse: Theory and practice* (6th ed.). Hoboken, NJ: Wiley.

Swartz-Kulstad, J. L., & Martin, W. E. (1999). Impact of culture and context on psychosocial adaption: The cultural and contextual guide process. *Journal of Counseling and Development, 77*, 281–293.

Ton, H., & Lim, R. F. (2006). The assessment of culturally diverse individuals. In R. F. Lim (Ed.), *Clinical manual of cultural psychiatry* (pp. 3–31). Arlington, VA: American Psychiatric Press.

United Health Care Online. (2013). ICD-10. Retrieved from https://www.unitedhealthcareonline.com/b2c/CmaAction.do?channelId=6fa2600ae29fb210VgnVCM1000002f10b10a

Whyte, L., & Brooker, C. (2001). Working with a multidisciplinary team: In secure psychiatric environments. *Journal of Psychosocial Nursing and Mental Health Services, 39*(9), 26–34.

World Health Organization. (1979). *International classification of diseases, 9th revision, (ICD-9-CM): Clinical modification. Mental Disorders*. Geneva, Switzerland: Author.

World Health Organization. (1993). *International classification of diseases, 10th edition: Mental disorders*. Geneva, Switzerland: Author.

Wright, J. A. (2011). *Conducting psychological assessment: A guide for practitioners*. Hoboken, NJ: Wiley.

Yeager, K. R., Cutler, D. I., Svendsen, D., & Sills, G. M. (2013). *Modern community mental health: An interdisciplinary approach*. New York, NY: Oxford University Press.

Zeiss, A. M., & Gallagher-Thompson, D. (2003). Providing interdisciplinary geriatric team care: What does it really take? *Clinical Psychology: Science and Practice, 10*(1), 115–119.

CHAPTER 3 Completing the Diagnostic Assessment

The purpose of this chapter is to apply the diagnostic criteria from *DSM-5* utilizing the principal and the provisional diagnosis, along with other supporting information, to start the process toward a comprehensive diagnostic assessment within the parameters of current mental health practice. Professional record keeping by all mental health practitioners in the 21st century is characterized by time-limited services, coordinated care requirements, cost containment practices, and quality assurance and improvement procedures (Dziegielewski, 2008, 2013; Shlonsky, 2009). To complete comprehensive diagnostic assessments, learning how best to document mental disorders and supporting information makes practitioner training mandatory in how to best utilize this system. Skill in professional documentation becomes essential for social workers, psychologists, mental health therapists, professional counselors, and other clinicians and practitioners. Training in this area is a functional building block for effective, efficient, and cost-controlled service provision, as well as representing the legal, ethical, and fiscal concerns inherent in all service provision (Braun & Cox, 2005; Dziegielewski, 2010; Sheafor & Horejsi, 2012).

In addition to presenting information on how to best complete the diagnostic assessment, this chapter outlines the changes from *DSM-IV* (APA, 1994) and *DSM-IV-TR* (APA, 2000) to *DSM-5* (APA, 2013); awareness of these changes enables a smoother transition in maintaining the proper application of the diagnostic assessment. Similar to previous editions of the *DSM,* many of the changes are shrouded in controversy (Mallett, 2014). This chapter at times outlines this controversy but focuses primarily on how these changes relate to completion of the diagnostic assessment. Therefore, completion of the assessment is presented with the changes between the earlier and later versions of the *DSM* described. The application of this information is highlighted, allowing practitioners to clearly identify and apply each step of the diagnostic system.

BASICS FOR COMPLETING A COMPREHENSIVE DIAGNOSTIC ASSESSMENT

This book assumes that the diagnostic assessment begins with the first client–practitioner interaction. The information gathered provides the data-based observations and reporting to be used to determine the requirements and direction of the helping process, as well as the data collection. The professional is expected to gather information about the current situation, take a history of past issues, and anticipate service expectations for the future. This diagnostic assessment should be multidimensional, include creative interpretation, and provide the groundwork for the possible strategy for service delivery. The information gathered follows a behavioral biopsychosocial approach to practice (Pearson, 2008). Utilizing the *DSM-5* can provide the starting point for accurately creating the diagnostic impression that will later provide the basis of the treatment planning and practice strategy to follow.

Starting the Process: Gathering Information

Biomedical Information In a comprehensive diagnostic assessment, the biomedical factors highlighted often start with a client's general physical health or medical condition. (See Quick Reference 3.1.) Such information should be considered from both the practitioner's and the client's perspective. All initial information needs to show the relationship between the biological or medical factors and the functioning level attainable that will allow the completion of certain behaviors that will maximize independence. Assessing the biomedical problems allows the practitioner to become aware of how medical conditions can either influence or complicate mental health conditions. Although most counseling professionals are not qualified to examine or diagnose biomedical information, they are expected to document and note it and provide referrals as needed to ensure comprehensive care. All practitioners are expected to know how some medical symptoms present and what needs to be done in the referral process. Whether the practitioner is working collaboratively in a team or independently, the first referral for a physical exam is given the highest priority. For example, when an older adult client very quickly shows behaviors that are delusional and disorganized, before the practitioner diagnoses a serious mental disorder, a good physical exam may reveal that the individual has a urinary tract infection (UTI). This medical condition that may mimic a mental health one would certainly be treated differently than a neurocognitive or a type of delusional disorder.

Taking the medical condition into account is essential, and often a comprehensive physical exam, if it is not completed at the initial assessment, should be done soon afterwards. Also, how does the client view his or her own biomedical health? What is the client's self-reported health status, and is there any interest in preventive medical care and intervention? Practice wisdom dictates that the professionals who are trained in the medical area spend the most attention on the medical aspects of a client's health, whereas those trained in mental health also stick with what they know best, the mental health aspects. Special attention should always be given to recognizing these roles. In addition, what otherwise might be considered normal

QUICK REFERENCE 3.1

Biomedical Factors in Assessment

Medical conditions	The physical disability or illness the client reports and what specific ways it affects the client's social and occupational functioning and activities of daily living
Perceived overall health status	Encourage the client to assess his or her own health status and what he or she is able to do to facilitate the change effort
Maintenance and continued health and wellness	Measurement of functional ability and interest in preventive health

QUICK REFERENCE 3.2

Psychological Factors in Assessment

Mental functioning	Describe the client's mental functioning. Complete a mental status assessment. Learn and identify key cultural factors related to the client.
Cognitive functioning	Does the client have the ability to think and reason about what is happening to him or her? Is the client able to participate and make decisions in regard to his or her own best interest?
Assessment of lethality	Would the client harm himself or herself or anyone else because of the perception of the problem he or she is experiencing?

human responses should not be medicalized (Horowitz & Wakefield, 2012).

Taking the whole person into account is well complemented by a collaborative team. To facilitate the process for nonmedically trained professionals, be sure to ascertain whether the client has had a recent physical exam. If so, does the client have a copy of it, or is there a way to get the record so it can be reviewed? Were there any laboratory findings, x-rays, or other tests completed related to the symptoms experienced? If the client has not had a recent physical exam, suggest or take steps to make sure that one is ordered. Once the information is obtained, it needs to be shared with the collaborative team to ensure that it is discussed in terms of how this biomedical information may influence the mental health condition presented. In addition, assess for medication side effects, substance use, or medical conditions that contribute or in some cases cause the mental health problems evident (Frances, 2013). To provide a comprehensive biomedical assessment and take into account the mind–body connection, all aspects of the person must be considered, including social and environmental factors. To start the process and address the biomedical aspects, a thorough medical checkup or workup is always recommended as close to the initial assessment as possible.

Psychosocial Information The second area of a comprehensive diagnostic assessment relates directly to the psychological factors a client is exhibiting. To start the diagnostic assessment in this area, psychological functioning is noted. Cognitive health functioning is recorded, along with its effects on occupational and social functioning. Although we attempt to do so in an assessment, separating the psychological and the social-spiritual factors can be difficult. To facilitate the diagnostic impression, the psychological is related to the resulting mental functioning, cognitive functioning, and the assessment of lethality. To start the mental health process, a mental health status exam needs to be completed. Specific information related to lethality for a client who may be at risk for suicide or harming others must be gathered and processed. If these behaviors exist, immediate action is needed. (See Quick Reference 3.2.)

Social, Cultural, and Spiritual Information Behavioral-based biopsychosocial and spiritual approaches to assessment emphasize aspects highly influenced by a client's environment, such as social, cultural, and spiritual factors. Most professionals would agree that environmental considerations are very important in measuring and assessing all other aspects of a

QUICK REFERENCE 3.3

Social and Environmental Factors in Assessment

Social/societal help seeking	Is the client open to outside help? What support system or helping networks are available to the client from those outside the immediate family or the community?
Occupational participation	How does a client's illness or disability impair or prohibit functioning in the work environment? Is the client in a supportive work environment?
Social support	Does the client have support from neighbors, friends, or community organizations (e.g., church membership, membership in professional clubs)?
Family support	What support or help is expected from relatives of the client?
Ethnic or religious affiliation	If the client is a member of a cultural or religious group, will this affiliation affect medical intervention and compliance issues?

client's needs. Identifying family, social supports, and cultural expectations are important in helping the client ascertain the best course of action (Colby & Dziegielewski, 2010). (See Quick Reference 3.3.) A comprehensive assessment in this area starts with the basic assumption that people are social creatures. Therefore, how the individual responds in the social environment and within his or her support system provides important information for problem identification. In defining diversity, the possibilities for defining people and how they will behave are unlimited (Dudley, 2014). As discussed in Chapter 2, *DSM-5* offers several ways to not only recognize culture but also measure it by using focused culturally based questions, the Cultural Formulation Interview (CFI), and definitions in the appendix Glossary of Cultural Concepts of Distress. Therefore, *DSM-5* can be helpful in assessing the situation, which is especially important for working with certain cultures. For example, Alegria et al. (2007) warn that living in what the client perceives as an unsafe area can clearly influence the behaviors the client exhibits. The social situation is discussed in more detail later in this chapter in reference to the chapter in the *DSM-5* about the other disorders that may be the focus of clinical attention.

Gathering the Data Because the client is the primary source of data, be sure to take the time to assess the accuracy of the information and determine whether the client may either willingly or inadvertently withhold or exaggerate the information presented. Assessment information is usually collected through verbal and written reports (Owen, 2011). Verbal reports may be gathered from the client, significant others, family, friends, or other helping professionals. Critical information can also be derived from written reports, such as medical documents, previous clinical assessments, lab tests, and other clinical and diagnostic methods. Furthermore, information about the client can be derived through direct observation of the client's verbal or physical behaviors or interaction patterns with other interdisciplinary team members, family, significant others, or friends. When a practitioner is seeking evidence-based practice, recognizing directly what a client is doing can be a critical factor in the diagnostic assessment process. Viewing and recording these patterns of communication can be extremely helpful in later establishing and developing strengths and resources, as well as in linking problem behaviors to concrete indicators reflecting a client's performance (Corcoran & Walsh, 2010). Remember that in addition to verbal reports, written reports reflective of practice effectiveness often are expected. Background sheets, psychological tests, or tests to measure health status or level of daily function may be used to more concretely measure client problem behaviors.

Although the client is the first and primary source of data, the current emphasis on evidence-based practice necessitates gathering information from other sources. Taking a team approach involves examining previously written information and records, as well as sharing the responsibility for talking with the family, significant others, and other health providers to estimate planning support and assistance. From this perspective, task effectiveness is measured in how successful the team is in achieving its outcomes (Whyte & Brooker, 2001). As part of a team, collecting information from other secondary sources, such as the client's medical record, is important. To facilitate assessment, the nonmedically trained practitioner must work with those who are medically trained to make sure he or she understands the client's medical situation (Dziegielewski, 2005, 2006). Knowledge of certain medical conditions and when to refer to other health professionals for continued care is an essential part of the assessment process.

DSM-5 AND COMPLETING THE DIAGNOSTIC ASSESSMENT

The information presented in this chapter is not meant to include all the possibilities for use of the *DSM-5*. It is, however, designed to give practitioners a practical introduction to facilitating and identifying how to best complete the diagnosis assessment, taking into account all aspects of the client. Proper use of the *DSM-5* requires diagnostic classification of both the principal diagnosis and the reason for visit, as well as other supporting information as needed. This chapter describes and compares and contrasts what is required today within the assessment process to past requirements. The intent is to use this information to support the completion of the comprehensive diagnostic assessment that leads to the treatment plan and practice strategy.

Elimination of the Multiaxial System

One of the most significant changes in *DSM-5* is the elimination of the multiaxial assessment system. This assessment system and the five axes required for use have a long history, starting with *DSM-III* and *DSM-III-R*. Practitioners familiar with the *DSM* have used this system for more than 25 years. To review, the multiaxial assessment system identified five separate axes. Axes I and II had the primary mental health diagnoses, Axis III was the medical information, and Axes IV and V documented the information that supported the diagnosis. (See Quick Reference 3.4.)

In many practice settings in the 1980s and 1990s, the first three axes were considered sufficient as the formal diagnostic process. The practitioner completed a diagnostic impression of the client that involved Axes I, II, and III, leaving the use of Axes IV and V as optional. With the later editions of the *DSM* (*DSM-III* and *DSM-III-R*), it was recommended that all five axes be addressed

QUICK REFERENCE 3.4

***DSM-IV-TR:* Multiaxial Assessment**

Axis I:	Clinical disorders, pervasive developmental disorders, learning, motor skills, and communication disorders
	Other conditions that may be the focus of clinical attention
Axis II:	Personality disorders; Mental retardation
Axis III:	General medical conditions
Axis IV:	Psychosocial and environmental problems
Axis V:	Global assessment of functioning (GAF)

as part of the diagnostic assessment. In the multiaxial system in *DSM-IV* and *DSM-IV-TR,* the first three axes alone were not considered acceptable as a practice standard, and working with that multiaxial framework required using all five axes. The APA (2000) has always clearly said that the first three axes, although separate in documentation, were unrelated, and diagnoses were placed on either Axis I or II just to facilitate coding. The multiaxial system was simply a system of convenient systematic documentation, yet many professionals did not feel that way.

For example, the diagnosis of a personality disorder, coded on Axis II, was avoided, as its lifelong behaviors were often avoided for diagnostic coding because it could hamper reimbursement. There were also times when using the multiaxial diagnostic assessment was not appropriate. For example, with special population groups (e.g., troubled youth) or in specialized settings (e. g., assisted residential care with elderly persons), having such a formal diagnostic assessment did not seem appropriate and was considered unnecessary. It could also be problematic in other settings, such as some counseling agencies that focused directly on problem solving, which entails helping individuals gain the resources needed to improve functioning. In this type of setting, use of the multiaxial system was considered disadvantageous and optional. In updating the manual, despite widespread use of the multiaxial system, the work groups decided to eliminate it in favor of a format more relevant to simply writing the diagnosis and the supporting information. In *DSM-5,* coding diagnostic impressions on a multiaxial system has been eliminated and is no longer an option. It now emphasizes only the free listing of the mental health diagnosis without the restrictions of utilizing the multiaxial system.

DSM-5: *The Diagnostic Impression*

With the elimination of Axes I, II, and III that were used in earlier versions of the *DSM,* the replacement requires all three of these axes to be combined by simply listing the relevant diagnosis as either the *principal diagnosis* or in some cases adding a *provisional diagnosis* (see Quick Reference 3.5). Listing the principal diagnosis eliminates the need for Axes I and II. Also, combining any medical conditions and listing them with the principal diagnosis eliminates the need for Axis III, which included any related medical conditions. Eliminating Axes I, II, and III helped to clarify that Axis II specifically was never meant to be a separate set of diagnoses, nor was it the intent of the multiaxial system to separate medical and mental health conditions in assessment or

QUICK REFERENCE 3.5

PRINCIPAL AND PROVISIONAL DIAGNOSIS

The Practitioner can Use Either of These Terms When the Diagnostic Criteria are Met:

Principal diagnosis: Symptoms related to the disorder are the primary reason for the diagnostic assessment and often denotes the request for treatment/intervention.

Provisional diagnosis: Diagnosis is determined on the criteria used to verify the duration of the illness or when there is not enough information to substantiate a principal diagnosis.

treatment. What many professionals do not realize is that this new coding system presented in *DSM-5* is not completely new. Both *DSM-IV* and *DSM-IV-TR* offered two ways of coding: the multiaxial system and simply listing the diagnosis, similar to what is now required in *DSM-5*. In *DSM-5,* listing the mental disorders and the relevant medical conditions are combined, thereby avoiding the artificial distinction suggested by listing them on separate axes. The diagnostic assessment starts with identifying either the principal or the provisional diagnosis.

THE PRINCIPAL DIAGNOSIS

The reason an individual is seen by a mental health professional or admitted to an inpatient facility is in *DSM-5* termed the *principal diagnosis*. Listing the principal diagnosis and just listing any subsequent diagnoses eliminates the need for Axes I and II, which were part of the multiaxial diagnosis in *DSM-IV* and *DSM-IV-TR*. This change helps to clarify that in *DSM-IV,* Axis II was never intended to separate medical and mental health conditions in assessment or treatment. When the principal diagnosis is listed according to *DSM-5,* it is listed first, but there can be more than one diagnosis as long as each meets the criteria. If there is more than one diagnosis, they should be listed in terms of attention. At times, determining which diagnosis is the principal one may be difficult. There may also be some confusion related to which mental health diagnosis is the reason for the visit. In *DSM-5,* always remember to list the principal diagnosis first. It is generally the "reason for the visit" that is most often linked within the inpatient situation to admission status; in the outpatient setting, it is also the reason the medical services are provided.

The principal diagnosis should always be qualified with "(principal diagnosis)" added after it; if it is the reason for the visit, it should be qualified by "(reason for visit)" given after it. There may also be more than one diagnosis, and taking into account comorbidity (when two mental disorders are related and often occur together) is essential. When there is comorbidity (or co-occurrence) and the two diagnoses both present prominent symptoms that need to be addressed, determining which is the primary or principal diagnosis may be even more difficult (Cipani, 2014). Noting all relevant mental and medical conditions present is essential for the treatment planning to follow. When there is more than one mental disorder, be sure to always list the primary (principal) diagnosis first. (See Quick Reference 3.6.) If both diagnoses seem equally relevant, use clinical judgment to decide which one is more important to the course and treatment, and list that one first.

QUICK REFERENCE 3.6

Helpful Tips for Documenting the Principal Diagnosis

- Principal diagnosis is most ofen the reason for the visit and is generally listed first.
- If there are multiple diagnoses, the reason for the visit should always be listed first.
- For the principal diagnosis, use the phrase (principal diagnosis) or (reason for visit).
- If there are multiple diagnoses, list them after the principal diagnosis in terms of focus and attention.
- If there is a medical condition or disorder that appears to be the cause of the mental health disorder, according to the ICD, the medical disorder should be listed before the mental disorder.
- List the mental disorders that interfere with functioning first, and then list other medical condition(s) that are complicating or are directly or indirectly related to the mental health condition but not the direct cause.

In *DSM-5,* Axis III—where the medical disorder was listed on a separate axis—was eliminated. Therefore, if the principal diagnosis is a mental disorder that is directly attributed to a medical disorder, the medical disorder (according to the *ICD*) is listed first. From this perspective, the medical disorder is given the appropriate focus, as the mental disorder is considered to be secondary and may or may not resolve once the medical disorder is addressed. Previously, in *DSM-III* such a disorder was referred to as *physical disorders and related conditions.* In *DSM-IV* and *DSM-IV-TR,* they were referred to as *general medical conditions.* In *DSM-5,* these medical or physical conditions are now referred to as *another medical condition.*

Because the term *mental disorder* means a condition that is not directly due to a medical condition, all nonmedically trained practitioners need some knowledge of the most common medical conditions that can complicate the diagnosis of mental health conditions. Furthermore, the practitioner needs to be acquainted with the relationship these conditions can have to a mental disorder. Pollak, Levy, and Breitholz (1999) were quick to warn that in the diagnostic assessment, alterations in behavior and mood that mimic a mental disorder may be directly related to a medical illness. This difference is particularly important to distinguish in that many times clients suffering from a mental disorder may be confused about the symptoms they feel and may not report them clearly. Because most mental health practitioners do not have extensive training in medical disorders and what to expect from one, the misdiagnosis of a medical disorder as a mental health disorder can be fairly common.

Clients at the greatest risk for misdiagnosis in this area include women who are pregnant or after pregnancy (prenatal, perinatal, or neonatal), indigent individuals because of limited resources and access to continued health care, individuals who engage in high-risk behaviors, individuals with a medical illness who exhibit symptoms that might be confused for mental illness, and individuals with chronic conditions, such as those who suffer from major mental disorders and older adults (Pollak et al., 1999). For example, clients who have been diagnosed with mental disorders such as schizophrenia or bipolar disorder may be unable to perceive, may misperceive, or may simply ignore warning signs of a medical problem (Dziegielewski, 2010). Many of the chronic conditions older adults exhibit may be de-emphasized or ignored as a normal part of aging or as chronic disease progression.

For example, I will never forget a client who presented in a severe acute phase. He had been seen numerous times at the clinic, and his diagnosis was Schizophrenia. He constantly complained of demons invading his brain and voices that would not allow him to think independently. He was convinced that placing a piece of tinfoil under his baseball hat could help to deter the demons' rays that penetrated his brain with disparaging thoughts. One night while I was working in the crisis unit, he came in for assistance and was extremely delusional, begging for help. He was experiencing auditory hallucinations that were so pronounced he felt his brain would explode. He tried to help himself by wrapping an entire roll of tinfoil on his head with the hope it would turn aside the rays from the demons that were causing him so much discomfort. Upon assessment, he was so agitated and difficult to assess that I immediately suspected he had stopped taking his medications, but he swore he had not. An immediate referral for a physical exam determined he had a sinus infection that was causing the signs prevalent of his mental disorder to worsen. Once the sinus infection was treated with an antibiotic, his perceptions of demon rays and voices in his head subsided greatly. This client needed an antibiotic, and receiving an antipsychotic medication would have been secondary to his mental health presentation. Because of his previous mental health disorder, he believed that all his pain was demonic and did not understand that there could be other reasons for it. In presentation, it would have been a true disservice if the medical condition had not been addressed first. Within 3 days of the antibiotic, his previous symptoms almost disappeared. For cases such as this, whether trained in medical areas or not, practitioners must rule out the signs and symptoms most relevant to a medical condition before the mental health condition can be treated. Therefore, when listing the principal diagnosis as the reason for the visit, practitioners should always list the medical disorder first when a medical disorder is coded "due to another medical condition."

In summary, according to the *ICD,* if there is a medical condition that causes the mental health disorder, it has to be listed first. If there are other medical conditions important to the diagnosis, they can be listed as well after the principal diagnosis. As previously stated, in *DSM-5* these conditions are referred to as "another medical condition," replacing the previous listing in *DSM-IV* as a "general medical condition."

The Provisional Diagnosis

Many times when a client is interviewed and the initial diagnostic assessment is completed, a principal diagnosis cannot be determined. In these cases, a provisional diagnosis can be assigned. A *provisional diagnosis* (often referred to in the field as the best-educated clinical guess) is based on clinical judgment and reflects a strong suspicion that an individual suffers from a type of disorder that, for some reason or another, either the actual criteria are not met or the practitioner does not have information available to make a more informed diagnostic assessment. In practice, a provisional diagnosis can be particularly helpful when information from family or the support system is not available to confirm the diagnosis. There are also disorders for which specific time periods must be met to assign a diagnosis. For example, the criteria for schizophrenia outline that the duration of the illness must be at least 6 months or more. With the first episode or the onset of the disorder, all criteria may be met except for the time frame. Therefore, the provisional diagnosis allows the practitioner to use the term *schizophreniform disorder,* which meets the same criteria as schizophrenia but has a shorter time frame (less than 6 months and remission does not occur).

The most important thing for the practitioner to remember, however, is that a provisional diagnosis is *temporary*. Once a provisional diagnosis is given, every attempt must be made to monitor its course and remove it if symptoms are no longer present. When the needed information is gathered or the suggested time frame has been met, the provisional diagnosis should be changed to the primary diagnosis most relevant to current problem behaviors and future treatment.

Information Supportive of the Diagnosis

In *DSM-III, DSM-IV,* and *DSM-IV-TR,* supportive information about the diagnosis was listed on Axis IV and Axis V. In *DSM-5,* by contrast, the nonaxial system of diagnosing a mental disorder simply requires adding this supportive information related to the diagnostic assessment. Separating the stressors experienced and the level of disability on a separate axis is no longer required. The APA (2013), however, states quite clearly that just listing the diagnosis is not enough, and supportive information, although not formalized on a multiaxial system, is still expected. To assist with providing supporting information, Chapter 21, "Medication-Induced Movement Disorders and Other Adverse Effects of Medication," and Chapter 22, "Other Conditions That May Be a Focus of Clinical Attention," may be of help. The criteria outlined in these two chapters may help to document the medication-related influences, stressors, and other circumstances that can influence the mental health condition and the diagnostic assessment. In addition to the conditions listed in these two chapters, a new measurement instrument has been introduced to address the level of disability that was previously outlined with the Global Assessment of Functioning (GAF) in *DSM-IV* and *DSM-IV-TR*. This measure of disability, which is more quantifiable than the GAF, is published by the World Health Organization and called the World Health Organization Disability Assessment Schedule (WHODAS).

Medication-Induced Movement Disorders and Other Adverse Effects of Medication

Chapter 21 and the medication-related conditions listed in *DSM-5* are not considered mental disorders. The information presented, however, is important, as it may support the diagnostic assessment. Lacasse (2014) warns that placing a diagnosis of a mental disorder can create a pathway to treatment with psychiatric drugs. Two important diagnostic areas most often associated with these medications are in schizophrenia spectrum disorders and use of neuroleptics and in the depressive disorders and discontinuance syndromes related to stopping antidepressant medications. The conditions listed in this new chapter were previously covered in *DSM-IV* and *DSM-IV-TR* in a combined section, Other Disorders That May Be a Focus of Clinical Attention. In addition, when used with the previous multiaxial system, they were coded on Axis I. These conditions were reorganized and placed in their own chapter to emphasize the conditions' prominence, and designating a separate chapter for them clearly highlights the importance of recognizing medication effects and how the resulting presentation can affect and confuse the mental health diagnosis. The medication-related conditions listed in this chapter can lead to a temporary or permanent movement-based disorder or influence behavior because of the adverse effects being experienced.

The APA (2013) gives two primary reasons for including these in a separate chapter. The first is the helpful information these categories can provide in management and subsequent treatment of client problems. In these conditions, the medications are either the primary or secondary effect and clearly influence any subsequent

QUICK REFERENCE 3.7

Typical Antipsychotic Medications*

Chlorpromazine (Thorazine)

Thioridazine (Mellaril)

Trifluoperazine (Stelazine)

Fluphenazine (Prolixin)

Haloperidol (Haldol)

Loxapine (Loxitane)

Thiothixene (Navane)

Side Effect Profiles and Parkinsonian Symptoms Include:

Dystonia—Acute contractions of the tongue (stiff or thick tongue)

Akathisia—Most common form of extrapyramidal symptoms (e.g., inner restlessness)

*Generic medications listed first.

diagnosis. The second reason is how helpful acknowledgment of these medication-related conditions can be for making the diagnostic impression. Recognizing these conditions can assist with the differential diagnosis and completing a more comprehensive and accurate diagnostic impression. For example, a client suffering from an anxiety disorder may report feeling restless and fidgety. These types of symptoms may be consistent with extreme anxiety. If the symptoms alone are assessed without a good supporting history, the abnormal fidgety and rocking movements' relationship to medication may be missed. The medication-related condition most representative of these symptoms is neuroleptic-induced akathisia. Therefore, recognizing the etiology of symptoms can clarify what is medication related and what may be symptoms consistent with a mental disorder.

In Chapter 21, several different categories are all termed *neuroleptic-induced;* the conditions in this area are medication related, and the types of medications are the neuroleptics. Because the term *neuroleptic* may be considered outdated in some of the literature, the reader is cautioned that often this term is used interchangeably with the term *antipsychotics* (APA, 2013). Although explaining all the differences between the types of antipsychotic medication is beyond the scope of this chapter, it is important to distinguish between typical and atypical types. The newer medications in this category, referred to as atypical medications, may also have some serious side effects but fewer neuroleptic or movement-related symptoms, which are the focus of this chapter. (See Quick References 3.7 and 3.8).

Medications often referred to as traditional or neuroleptic antipsychotic medications are *dopamine inhibitors* that block other neurotransmitters, including acetylcholine, histamine, and norepinephrine. For example, this chapter describes medication-induced acute dystonia and medication-induced acute akathisia; both conditions are related to medications used to treat extrapyramidal symptoms. These problematic symptoms may develop a few days after starting a medication or increasing or decreasing the dosage of a medication.

QUICK REFERENCE 3.8

Selected Atypical Medications*

Clozapine (Clozaril)

Risperidone (Risperdal)

Olanzapine (Zyprexa)

Quetiapine (Seroquel)

Ziprasidone (Geodon)

Aripiprazole (Abilify)

Pimozide (Orap)

Selected Side Effects Include:

Weight gain

Diabetes

*Generic medications listed first.

The term *extrapyramidal symptoms* (EPS) describes a side effect profile that affects a client's motor movements and can accompany use of the neuroleptic medications. *Dystonia,* which is characterized by sudden and painful muscle stiffness, may present in clients as grimacing, difficulty with speech or swallowing, *oculogyric crisis* (upward rotation of the eyeballs), muscle spasms of the neck and throat, and extensor rigidity of the back muscles (Carpenter, Conley, & Buchanan, 1998). Clients may also complain of a thick or stiff tongue that impairs their ability to speak. These reactions often occur within the first few days of treatment.

Another symptom is *akathisia,* which is often considered less obvious than dystonia, although it is the most common form of EPS. Akathisia is an extreme form of motor restlessness that may be mistaken for agitation (National Alliance on Mental Illness [NAMI], 2003). The individual feels compelled to constantly move, and many times clients report an inner restlessness evidenced by a shaking leg or constant pacing. During assessment, these clients cannot sit still, and the restlessness in their legs can result in uncontrollable foot tapping. Although akathisia generally appears early in the course of treatment and can be related to other EPS, it can also occur independently (Carpenter et al., 1998).

Another form of EPS listed in Chapter 21, which results from long-term treatment with older antipsychotic medications, is *tardive dyskinesia* (TD). This condition involves pronounced involuntary movements of any group of muscles, most commonly the mouth and tongue (NIMH, 2009).This syndrome generally occurs with elderly individuals, especially women. Prolonged use of these medications can also result from movement-related symptoms characteristic of dystonia and akathisia referred to as tardive dystonia and tardive akathisia.

A less frequent side effect associated with the older or traditional antipsychotic medications is *neuroleptic malignant syndrome* (NMS). Recognizing this syndrome can be difficult. It often includes serious medical complications and illness (pneumonia, etc.) and untreated or unrecognized symptoms related to the EPS mentioned earlier

QUICK REFERENCE 3.9

Medication-Induced Movement Disorders

Neuroleptic-Induced Parkinsonism	Coded 332.1 (G21-11)
Other Medication-Induced Parkinsonism	Coded 332.1 (G21.19)
Neuroleptic Malignant Syndrome	Coded 333.92 (G21.0)
Medication-Induced Acute Dystonia	Coded 333.72 (G24.02)
Medication-Induced Acute Akathisia	Coded 333.99 (G25.71)
Tardive Dyskinesia	Coded 333.85 (G24.01)
Tardive Dystonia	Coded 333.72 (G24.09)
Tardive Akathisia	Coded 333.99 (G25.71)
Medication-Induced Postural Tremor	Coded 333.1 (G25.1)
Other Medication-Induced Movement Disorder	Coded 333.99 (G25.79)
Antidepressant Discontinuance Syndrome	Coded 995.29 (T43.205A)
Initial encounter	Coded 995.29 (T43.205D)
Subsequent encounter	Coded 995.29 (T43.205S)
Sequelae	

(PDR, 2013). Benzer (2007) reported that although NMS occurs in only 0.1% to 0.04% of cases, one of four cases of NMS can end in death. This condition is typically more common in males. Symptoms of NMS include severe rigidity of the muscles, high fever, confusion, pallor, sweating, and rapid heart rate. One early sign of the condition is high blood pressure. Once a client has been assessed with NMS, any further drug treatment must always be monitored closely by a medically trained professional.

The last conditions to be coded in Chapter 21 are the other medication-induced movement disorders. In this classification, like the other groups in this chapter, the movement disorders are related to medications. These problematic medication-influenced movements, however, are caused by medications other than the neuroleptics. Another category in this section is antidepressant discontinuation syndrome, the set of symptoms that occur after an antidepressant medication has been taken for at least a month and then reduced or discontinued. In this condition, the discontinuation of these medications can result in a multitude of symptoms that were not present before the medication was taken initially, including a variety of somatic symptoms such as nausea and hypersensitivity to noise and light. (See Quick Reference 3.9.)

Other Conditions That May Be a Focus of Clinical Attention

The last chapter in this section is a brief compilation of the disorders that may be the focus of clinical attention. This group of conditions (Chapter 22), similar to the Chapter 21, are not mental disorders. Probst (2013) highlights the importance of this chapter in that there may be a fine line between a life problem and a mental disorder. Life transitions are rich with behavioral transitions, material deprivations, and

QUICK REFERENCE 3.10

General Categories

Other Conditions That May Be a Focus of Clinical Attention

Relational Problems
- Problems Related to Family Upbringing
- Other Problems Related to Primary Support Group

Abuse and Neglect
- Child Maltreatment and Neglect Problems
- Adult Maltreatment and Neglect Problems

Educational and Occupational Problems
- Educational Problems
- Occupational Problems

Housing and Economic Problems
- Housing Problems
- Economic Problems

Other Problems Related to the Social Environment

Problems Related to Crime or Interaction With the Legal System

Other Health Service Encounters for Counseling and Medical Advice

Problems Related to Other Psychosocial, Personal, and Environmental Circumstances

Other Circumstances of Personal History
- Problems Related to Access to Medical and Other Health Care
- Nonadherence to Medical Treatment

Source: Summarized from the *Diagnostic and Statistical Manual of Mental Disorders, Fifth Edition.* Copyright 2013 by the American Psychiatric Association.

abandonments that could easily be documented as a mental disorder to facilitate service reimbursement (Probst, 2014). This incentive provides fertile ground for documenting the effects ethical dilemmas and abuse can have on the diagnostic assessment.

To facilitate use of these codes, the list has nine main subject areas: relational problems; abuse and neglect; housing and economic problems; educational and occupational problems; other problems related to the social environment; problems related to crime or interaction with the legal system; other health service encounters for counseling and medical advice; problems related to other psychosocial, personal, and environmental circumstances; and other circumstances of personal history. For a comprehensive list of the main categories that outline the other disorders that may be a focus of clinical attention, see Quick Reference 3.10. For a complete list of all the codes and subcategories possible in each area, see the *DSM-5.*

With the elimination of the multiaxial diagnostic system used in *DSM-IV* and *DSM-IV-TR,* this newly revised chapter (Chapter 22) of other conditions can be helpful. Conditions that document stressors and contributing factors that would have been previously placed on Axis IV allow for some aspect of recognition. In *DSM-5,* the V codes remain reflective of the *ICD-(CM),* and the Z codes are related to *ICD-10.* See the *DSM-5*'s Other Conditions That May Be a Focus of Clinical Attention (pp. 715–727) for a full listing of these disorders. When coding for billing or simply documenting these conditions in the record, the practitioner needs to be sure that the criteria to justify this support diagnostic category are met. Often to support this effort, as discussed later in this chapter, further information may be needed, including psychometric testing such as rapid and self-administered assessment instruments.

Listing other conditions that may be a focus of clinical attention pertinent to the diagnosis can assist in documenting the supportive information that needs to be in the record. Although these conditions are not mental disorders, the symptoms the client is experiencing may initially present in a severe enough form to make the professional consider assigning a diagnosis. The circumstances listed in this section are broken into categories. For example, when information is listed under the relational disorders, these supporting circumstances can influence the presentation of the disorder. Once a practitioner is aware of these circumstances, they can influence and in some cases change the disorder identified, as well as the course of treatment. For example, an older client's reaction to the death of a loved one may be significant enough to meet the criteria for bereavement or major depressive disorder (MDD).

In uncomplicated bereavement, however, the individual often recognizes what is happening and contributing to the symptoms reported. Although the symptoms may clearly match what might be present in a major depressive disorder, such as trouble sleeping, lack of appetite, and weight loss, these symptoms could be considered a normal reaction to the death of a loved one. In uncomplicated bereavement, the symptoms experienced become the focus of clinical attention, and all supportive treatment is related directly to the recent death (APA, 2013). Yet, the individual may ask for treatment and management of these symptoms as a way to speed the grief process and regain his or her prior level of functioning. The symptoms combined with the grief reaction make it difficult to determine whether it is uncomplicated bereavement or indicative of something greater (Wakefield & Schmitz, 2014).

As Frances (2013) summarized so succinctly, when there is clinical doubt, underdiagnosing is always better than overdiagnosing. The label given to a client could last a lifetime. In the case of the grief reaction, this mistake could be costly. As part of normal life transitions as people age, the likelihood of experiencing repeated losses of partners, family, and friends increases. Repeated losses and the constant adjustment process can easily lead to feelings of sadness, disturbed sleep, and loss of appetite—all symptoms that can resemble depression. Although the individual eventually learns to cope with these changes and losses, the responses that occur in the adjustment process vary considerably. One major change in *DSM-5* was the change of name for this category from bereavement to uncomplicated bereavement. This change in title was made to highlight that the symptoms experienced are not beyond a normal reaction to the death of the loved one.

Furthermore, taking research evidence into account, the task group also agreed to delete the 2-month bereavement exclusion from major depressive disorder (MDD). The time frame in the previous edition of the *DSM* was questioned because research evidence was lacking to support what constitutes normal bereavement, especially in terms of the time frame (2 months versus 6 months versus 1 year) (Wakefield & Schmitz, 2014). Whether clearly supported in the literature or not, taking this information into account and utilizing it provided one important reason for eliminating the bereavement exclusion. Elimination of the 2-month waiting period was formalized in *DSM-5* when grief-related systems could be better explained by normal reactions to the death of the loved one. See Chapter 7 on depressive disorders and MDD criteria for a more comprehensive explanation of this change and how it relates to the manifestation of depression and suicidal ideation and intent.

The revised categories such as uncomplicated bereavement are intended to help the client and family and friends within his or her support system, as well as other professional and nonprofessional helpers, to better understand and explain the individual's behaviors. This diagnostic category can also avoid giving the client a label that might not be appropriate.

Another example of this category under other circumstances of personal history, further subdivided into nonadherence to medical treatment, is malingering (coded as V65.2 or Z76.5). Although a client may present with multiple severe individual, occupational, and social problems, if the client meets the criteria for the condition of malingering, careful evaluation and documentation are required. Malingering is not a mental disorder. It involves "the intentional production of false or grossly exaggerated physical or psychological symptoms, motivated by external incentives such as avoiding" (APA, 2013, p. 726). Acknowledging and clearly documenting these intentionally created symptoms is essential for the practitioner. Examining these symptoms and contrasting them with any external incentives is important for a comprehensive diagnostic assessment.

This category also outlines several situational and environmental conditions where avoidance is most likely to occur, such as military duty, employment, seeking financial compensation, or trying to avoid criminal prosecution. To apply this further, consider a client who wants to qualify for a documented disability in order to receive a disability check. In desperation, the client may feign or grossly exaggerate what he or she is feeling to obtain thc disability status. In actuality, with this type of planned, deliberate behavior, the client would not qualify as having a mental disorder related to the reason for visit. In such cases, the client's behaviors are viewed as primarily manipulative. Therefore, a diagnosis of a mental disorder would be inappropriate.

When the chapter is utilized properly, it is easy to see that the conditions that may be the focus of clinical attention can support completion of a thorough comprehensive diagnostic assessment. Although important for use, these conditions should not be applied haphazardly. For example, to better define malingering, *DSM-5* goes beyond what was described in the previous version. The current version defines four circumstances that can help to identify malingering. The first is identifying the reason for the referral. Referrals that come from an attorney with litigation pending or self-referrals in similar circumstances are suspect. The second area is the actual assessment, especially when discrepancies do not match the overall presentation and the practitioner questions if the client is accurately presenting information. The third area relates directly to the client's attitude and whether he or she is cooperative and interested in the assessment process. Does the client either avoid pertinent questions or providing information that could facilitate the diagnostic assessment? Fourth, the client who qualifies for antisocial personality disorder would not meet the criteria supportive of malingering. Using a combination approach and taking into account all four of these items could make a difference in whether this term is applied.

In summary, conditions that may be the focus of clinical intervention can be used to support the diagnosis. This chapter discusses only some of the supportive conditions. In this chapter and throughout the rest of the book, documenting these conditions is considered essential for completing a comprehensive diagnostic assessment. Although they are not mandatory for inclusion, I believe they should be. Use of this supplemental supporting information is highly encouraged, as life circumstances can often impede any clinical presentation. When they are present, be sure to note them. All practitioners should be familiar with them and able to utilize them in the supportive and supplemental way intended.

SUBTYPES AND COURSE SPECIFIERS

Developing a diagnostic impression involves assessing whether there is a mental disorder, supported by gathering information from collateral sources such as family and friends. When this is coupled with a strong and dynamic relationship between the practitioner and the patient, the best therapeutic assessments result (Frances, 2013). Because the *DSM* continues to utilize distinct diagnostic categories, mental disorders may not precisely fit into a particular area (Garland & Howard, 2014). Or there may be times when the presentation tends to follow a similar or recognized pattern. In such cases, a *subtype* or *course specifier* may be warranted.

Use of subtypes and course specifiers is encouraged in utilizing the *DSM-5*. A subtype clarifies a diagnosis when the phenomenological criteria are mutually exclusive and exhaustive (APA, 2013). Using the subtype qualifiers allows homogeneous groupings of disorders. Therefore, a subtype can be considered a subgroup within a diagnostic category. Subtypes are easy to recognize in documenting, as the coding starts with "*specify* whether."

One consideration to note in documenting is that subtypes are often linked to specifiers. Specifiers, however, are not mutually exclusive and exhaustive, and they differ from the subtype in that there is often more than one. For example, in the diagnosis of schizophrenia, the *DSM-IV* and *DSM-IV-TR* established five identified subtypes (paranoid type, disorganized type, catatonic type, undifferentiated type, residual type). The subtypes were defined by the prominent symptomatology at the time of evaluation. In *DSM-IV-TR,* discussion of eliminating these subtypes began, and in *DSM-5,* these subtypes were eliminated. This is one of the major changes in regard to updating research information that supports a diagnosis. In this case, the subtypes were deleted, although the categories were not changed. For example, the subtype of schizophrenia, paranoid type, was deleted because research did not support it; the symptoms of paranoia were so extensive in all subtypes that it could not meet the criteria for mutually exclusive and exhaustive. In *DSM-IV-TR,* the actual subtyping found in *DSM-IV* did not change; however, to support the diagnosis, the latest information not previously available in the earlier version was added. The reader was made aware that in *DSM-5* these subtypes would most likely be eliminated. Because the previous subtypes of schizophrenia appeared to be limited in terms of stability and prognostic value, in *DSM-5,* they were eliminated to more accurately reflect the research field trial results.

Although the subtypes were deleted for schizophrenia, in *DSM-5* the value of using a subtype, when relevant, remains. Therefore, in *DSM-5* several subtypes are used in schizophrenia spectrum and the other psychotic disorders. For example, although the diagnostic criteria relevant to schizophrenia do not have any subtypes, delusional disorder does. In delusional disorder, the expectation is to specify whether the mental disorder is best classified as erotomanic type, grandiose type, jealous type, persecutory type, somatic type, mixed type, or unspecified type. In addition to the subtypes noted, these categories can be further broken down and the condition linked to a specifier such as bizarre content.

The second grouping for diagnostic categories is the course specifier. Unlike the diagnostic subtype, the course specifier is not considered mutually exclusive and exhaustive. It is provided to show how criteria that are similar within a diagnostic category can be grouped. These homogeneous (or similar) subgroupings can highlight certain shared features. There are many examples of specifiers added in *DSM-5,* but not all diagnoses have them. Also, the specifier coded "specify if" should not be confused with "specify current severity," which is designated by the criteria that result in categorizing some diagnoses as mild, moderate, or severe. An example of a specifier in *DSM-5* is the mental disorder persistent depressive disorder (previously termed dysthymia in *DSM-IV* and *DSM-IV-TR*) that has several possible specifiers to assist with clarification of the disorder. The coding allows specifying if there is partial remission, early onset or late onset, or pure dysthymic syndrome with further clarifying of the type of episode. This also provides a good example of the use of *specify current symptoms,* as it can also be further quantified and listed after the diagnosis with severity such as mild, moderate, and severe.

Other terms may also be used to quantify a particular diagnosis, such as labeling the type of presentation "with psychotic features" or noting whether the condition is in partial or full remission. These additional terms can help the practitioner point out important features that may require attention. The term *remission* is particularly useful when the criteria for a past disorder are not currently met, yet the practitioner's clinical judgment is that the criteria will shortly be met, the condition is dormant but still there, and it could soon match what has occurred before.

When applying any of the additional qualifiers or specifiers, the practitioner needs to make sure the application is related to the current level of problem behavior and must clearly document the frequency, intensity, and duration of the reason the specifier was noted. Diagnostic codes, usually three to five digits, are often used to report statistical information and facilitate retrieval of information. The fourth and fifth digits of the code can be assigned to the subtype. (See Quick Reference 3.11.)

QUICK REFERENCE 3.11

Subtypes and Specifiers

- Subtypes ***"Specify whether"***
    - Mutually exclusive and exhaustive
    - Homogeneous subgroupings within a diagnosis
- Specifiers ***"Specify if"***
    - Not mutually exclusive and exhaustive
    - Can have more than one and better explains the particular diagnosis
- ***Specify current severity:*** mild, moderate, and severe

Examples of subtypes and specifiers

- **Subtypes "specify whether"**

    DSM-5: Schizoaffective Disorder

    Specify whether: Bipolar Type or Depressive Type

    Specifiers "specify if"

    DSM-5: With good prognostic features, without good prognostic features

    Specify current severity: mild, moderate, severe

Because many of the subtypes and specifiers listed in the *DSM* are not listed in the *ICD* system, there may not be corresponding codes for these subtypes and specifiers. The practitioner who wants to specify a client problem by utilizing the subtype or specifier should simply write it out (e.g., in the posttraumatic stress disorder, the subtype possible is with dissociative symptoms, and the specifier is with delayed expression).

Application of Crosscutting of Symptoms and the Dimensional Assessment

As outlined in the third section of the *DSM-5,* when the dimensional assessment is coupled with crosscutting of symptoms, the change from primarily a categorical assessment system to a dimensional one is made even stronger. Acknowledging the diagnostic criteria, while documenting the crosscutting or overlapping symptoms, allows explication of the relationship between symptoms characteristic of more than one disorder to be documented without the creation or addition of a second disorder. For example, how many times have you worked with a depressed client who did not have sleep difficulties that could be confused with the diagnosis of insomnia? Documenting with the dimensional assessment and taking into account the crosscutting of symptoms, while clearly noting those related to depression and disturbed sleep, can make a stronger diagnostic assessment while avoiding an unnecessary label indicative of a second diagnosis.

In taking into account the crosscutting of symptoms, *DSM-5* pushes use of the dimensional assessment further by utilizing different measures designed to quantify a client's behaviors. To help with this task, some of the measures are self-completed while others are completed by the practitioner. To improve the comprehensive nature of what is available for a dimensional assessment, a specific way to measure crosscutting of symptoms has been introduced. This measure of symptom assessment allows acknowledging and recording symptoms that do not neatly fit into one category while also assessing severity. The severity measure, often depicted as mild, moderate, or severe, can help to determine how often a behavior occurs and what it involves. Three important measurement instruments can be used to support the dimensional assessment and crosscutting of symptoms: the crosscutting measures, the Clinician-Dimensions of Psychosis Symptom Severity, and the World Health Organization Disability Assessment Schedule 2.0 (WHODAS 2.0).

Cross-Cutting of Symptoms Measures

The first measurement instrument in this area provides two levels of symptom assessment and rating. In the academic field trials conducted for *DSM-5,* this measurement instrument demonstrated good reliability across the United States and Canada. The first level, termed *Level 1 Cross-Cutting Symptom Measure,* has an adult self-report version, a brief survey with 23 questions assessing 13 common symptom domains, which often have overlapping symptoms. It includes having the client record during the last 2 weeks feelings of depression, anger, mania, anxiety, somatic symptoms, suicidal ideations, psychosis, sleep problems, memory, repetitive thoughts and behaviors, dissociation, personality functioning, and substance use. Each domain is further divided into subquestions that further clarify the 13 psychiatric domains identified above and how often these symptoms occur over a 2-week period. Once symptoms are identified using the sub-questions, they are then rated on a scale from 0 to 4, with 0 being no symptoms or not at all, up to 4 for very severe and occurring nearly every day. Of the 13 symptom domains, there are three (substance use, suicidal ideation, and psychosis) that when assessed as problematic at the slight level (as

QUICK REFERENCE 3.12

CROSS-CUTTING OF SYMPTOMS: LEVELS I AND II

Adult version and child and adolescent version (self-completed and/or parent or guardian can complete).

Two Levels:

Level 1: A brief survey of 13 symptom domains for adult patients and 12 domains for child and adolescent patients.

Level 2: More in-depth level of assessment of certain domains. This is available online: http://www.psychiatry.org/dsm5

opposed to the assessment of mild or greater for the others) might require further assessment. If the severity of the symptoms warrants a more extensive assessment, the Level II measure is utilized. Level II provides a more in-depth level of assessment of certain domains. To supplement the book and Level II symptoms, *DSM-5* also offers some aspects online (http://www.psychiatry.org/dsm5). It is beyond the scope of this chapter to explain exactly how to use this scale. The reader is urged to use the copy provided in *DSM-5* in Section III (pp. 733–744) and apply it to assist with completing of a comprehensive mental status exam, which is part of the comprehensive diagnostic assessment.

In addition to the adult version of the cross-cutting measurement, there is a parent-guardian version for children and adolescents age 6 to 17 designed to measure behaviors similar to those of adults. In this version, there are 25 questions, and the number of domains is decreased by one. The same types of domains are measured, but this version adds irritability and inattention, which are more commonly exhibited in this age group, and personality functioning was removed. Added to suicidal ideation is the potential for an actual suicidal attempt. In this version, the parent or guardian is asked to rate how much the child or adolescent experiences these symptoms over the same 2-week period. Also, there is a related measure that the child can complete. To access this measure, the practitioner has to go to the APA website (http://www.psychiatry.org/dsm5) and locate it online. (See Quick Reference 3.12.)

In summary, regardless of which measurement instrument is used to assist with the cross-cutting of symptoms, always keep in mind that the *DSM* does not suggest practice strategy. For the most part, practitioners focus on treating the symptoms and not the underlying mental disorder. Like treating most medical conditions by addressing the symptoms, mental disorders can follow a similar path. The measures for cross-cutting of symptoms can help to identify symptom domains and provide a comprehensive assessment that can assist in completing the mental status exam. These measures are not included as part of diagnostic billing but remain central for providing supporting information in completing the comprehensive and inclusive diagnostic assessment, In treating the symptoms, whether we use antidepressants for the treatment of a diagnosed anxiety disorder or a depressive disorder, the benefits for the client may be similar, regardless of the diagnosis assigned. Or if we use cognitive behavioral therapy to treat either of these diagnosed mental disorders, the outcome could also be the same, regardless of the specific diagnosis. Although not critical to the diagnostic label utilized, assessing the symptom domains and monitoring changes in clinical severity provide a more comprehensive mental status assessment that can facilitate the assessment application and guide the treatment strategy to follow.

Clinician-Rated Dimensions of Psychosis Symptom Severity

A second scale that may be used to assess symptom domains is designed for the clinician or practitioner to complete. The symptoms often seen in the disorders in schizophrenia spectrum may cross into other disorders, and the scale titled "Clinician-Rated Dimensions of Psychosis Severity" may help. This scale has eight domains (utilizing Roman numerals I–VIII) that help to identify important aspects for confirming a diagnosis. The instrument measures symptoms reported as experienced during the previous week. Like the other measurement instruments in Section III of *DSM-5,* this scale follows a similar pattern and ranking system by identifying the symptom domain and rating it from 0 (not present) to 4 (present and severe). On the instrument, the eight domains include positive symptoms (hallucinations, delusions, disorganized speech), abnormal psychomotor behavior, negative symptoms, impaired cognition, depression, and mania. All of these symptoms can overlap into other diagnoses, and this measure can assist in securing the frequency and intensity duration data needed in completing a comprehensive cross-cutting of symptoms as part of the dimensional assessment.

To measure the positive symptoms, the practitioner is expected to identify the presence, as well as the frequency and intensity, of symptoms such as hallucinations, delusions, disorganized speech, and abnormal psychomotor behavior. For example, the most common form of hallucination in the schizophrenia spectrum disorders is auditory. When auditory hallucinations are present, clients often express concern that the voices they hear in their heads are persecutory and commanding. Clients can be tortured by uncontrollable voices that tell them they are stupid, ugly, and no one cares. When hallucinations are of a command nature, the voices can cause clients to act out against themselves or others, and the control they feel is limited. Using a rating scale from 0 (not present) to 4 (present with severe pressure to respond to the voices that cannot be avoided), the practitioner can outline the frequency and intensity of these symptoms in a critical 7-day window.

Identifying this window of symptom presence and intensity can be essential to identifying the active phase of a disorder. The scale can also be given every 7 days retrospectively until the amount of time needed to secure the criteria for an active phase is met. Time frames, part of the criteria in many of these disorders, can be difficult to quantify. This scale can assist by identifying the time frames that are an important distinction between the basic criteria for distinguishing one disorder from another. To explicate the importance of the time frame in making the distinction between schizophreniform and schizophrenia is not always easy. The time frame in this example becomes essential because in the criteria needed for a diagnosis of schizophrenia, the individual would need to display clear active symptoms for a period of 6 months. Yet, what if this is the individual's first psychotic break, and the symptoms have been active for a month but not 6 months? In these cases, the diagnosis schizophreniform, often referred to as provisional, would be used, as opposed to schizophrenia. This scale can assist in differentiating the symptom severity as well as the time frame, providing a richer, more evidence-based diagnostic assessment.

Within the eight (I–VIII) identified domains of symptomatology, V addresses the importance of identifying the negative symptoms that are essential to differentiating this spectrum of diagnoses. The two negative symptoms selected for identification in the scale are restricted emotional expression and avolition. Since these two symptoms often occur together, they are measured with the same scale and allow for examining concerns related to facial expressivity, prosody, and gestures or self-initiated behaviors. Restricted emotional expression is often evidenced in decreased facial expression or in prosody, where the individual has difficulty with phonetics and other aspects of speech such as pitch, loudness, and tempo; listeners have difficulty interpreting what is being said. Gestures that facilitate communication may also be problematic, and avolition, a clear lack of goal-directed behavior, can occur. With avolition, the ability to start and complete tasks is always problematic. As volition is essential in daily functioning, it is often a part of any mental status exam.

The scale also measures impaired cognition (VI), depression (VII), and mania (VIII). In impaired cognition, the clinician is expected to rate an individual's ability to engage and respond in regard to cognitive functioning. In assessing this measure, two factors should always be taken into account: age and socioeconomic status (SES). Functioning is compared with what would be considered average for the client's age and SES and the degree to which it goes outside the normal range of variation and deviates from the average (mean) level of functioning. If the presentation is not clearly outside the clinical judgment of the rater (using an estimate of standard deviation of 0.5), a rating of 1 is assigned. If extensive and severe reduction (using an estimate of standard deviation greater than 2) in cognitive functioning is present, a score of 4 is utilized. The simplest way to think of the severe range is that 95% to 97% of people with a similar age and SES would do better than an individual given a rating of 4.

In depression, an individual's feelings of sadness and hopelessness can impair his or her functioning. When severe, these feelings can result in delusional thought patterns that are grossly out of proportion to the events at hand. The depression rating scale (VII) allows assessment of these types of circumstances and how often the individual engages in self-blame and self-reproach.

The last domain (VIII) assesses mania. Particularly in schizoaffective disorder, there is a clear link between bipolar-related symptoms, especially depression and mania. In schizoaffective disorder, this distinction is further highlighted by the subtypes (specify whether bipolar type or depressive type). Therefore, this scale, similar to the one that measures depression, highlights the importance of noting the presence, degree, and severity of manic-like symptoms. The clinician is expected to rate over a 7-day period the symptom severity for elevated, expansive mood and how irritable or restless the client appears.

This Clinician-Rated Dimensions of Psychosis Symptom Severity is new to the *DSM* and provides another option for clinicians to measure problematic and overlapping symptomatology and the intensity and duration with which it occurs. Directions on how to use this scale are limited in the *DSM,* but its intent is clear in providing another step toward quantifying symptoms. In the mental status assessment, measuring these symptoms is primary, and having a standardized way to do this is a welcome addition to all practitioners. Although limited in scope because it gives minimal guidance in how to assess the symptoms being recorded in the identified domain, it can still be very helpful in highlighting the symptoms often seen across mental disorders and facilitating the use of the crosscutting of symptom scales, as previously discussed.

WHODAS: Assessing Disability

In *DSM-5,* the multiaxial diagnostic system was eliminated as an option for diagnostic coding, and with this deletion was the expected recording of the individual level of functioning. The purpose of Axis V in the previous version of the *DSM* was to measure the behavioral functioning of an individual over the previous year. To complete this task, the Generalized Assessment of Functioning (GAF) scale was designed to enable the practitioner to differentially rank identified behaviors from 1 to 100, with higher ratings indicating higher overall functioning and coping levels. By rating the highest level of functioning a client had attained over the past year and then comparing it to his or her current level of functioning, this measure provided helpful, repeated comparisons of changes in functioning. The GAF was first introduced in *DSM-IV*. One major change between *DSM-IV* and *DSM-IV-TR* related to the supplemental use of this scale, providing more detailed instructions on how to apply the GAF.

According to the *DSM-5* task force, the major problem with the GAF that resulted in its being dropped was the lack of clarity in the numbered divisions and what each 10-digit interval actually stood for, leading to questionable psychometric properties (APA, 2013). To replace the GAF, a global measure of disability, the WHO Disability Assessment Schedule (WHODAS, version 2.0), was adopted and included in Section III. The WHODAS is based on the International Classification of Functioning, Disability and Cognitive Health (ICF) and can be used with adults and, in a separate version, with caregivers. The adult version is a 36-item self-administered measure for those age 18 and older that assesses disability across six domains. The first domain involves understanding and communicating and utilizes six questions designed to measure the results of an individual's cognitive domain. Answers to these six questions can be rated from no disability to so extreme that at its most severe point cognitive functioning can prohibit performance.

The second area involves five questions related to how well the client can get around. This subsection follows a similar scoring format, and questions assess for problems with standing, moving, and walking inside and outside the home. The third area is performance of self-care and how capable the client is with basic skills required for grooming, such as bathing and dressing, and the degree to which self-feeding is possible. The fourth area involves getting along with people and how the person interacts with people in his or her support system, as well as how he or she makes new friends and interacts with people he or she does not know. There is also one question related to sexual activities. The fifth area relates to basic life activities, including household tasks, school, and work, and gathers information related to the appropriate life situation. The sixth area has eight questions on how the individual sees his or her role in society, along with any concerns or preoccupations with health. What all six sections of the adult version of the WHODAS share is that they assess behaviors over the past 30 days and can be given as often as needed to examine changes in individual perceptions and functioning.

The hope is that the WHODAS will assist with measuring individual functioning and replace the need for the GAF. Measuring the term *clinically significant* and how it relates to impairment in social and occupational functioning has always been difficult. The use of this measure is recommended, along with other possible assessment measures listed online (http://www.psychiatry.org/dsm5). When these measures are combined with getting information from third parties such as family members and others in the client's support system, the most comprehensive diagnostic assessment will be obtained.

Documentation of Information

In documenting the mental health disorder, the reason for the visit, generally referred to as the principal diagnosis, is listed first. Other existing mental disorders can be coded by simply listing them based on relevance to treatment. In addition, any supportive information and circumstances affecting the diagnosis can be documented. In practice, most clients usually present with a principal diagnosis, and it is often labeled the reason for visit. Regardless of whether the practitioner is working with adults or children, acceptable proficient documentation when there is more than one diagnosis requires that the principal diagnosis, which is also considered the reason for visit, should always be listed first.

When documenting the diagnostic assessment, three situations need to be examined.

1. For each primary diagnosis given, the practitioner should note the major psychiatric symptoms the client is displaying that support its use. In the *DSM-5,* each of the 20 chapters that outline the mental disorders have specific criteria associated with it that need to be reviewed, applied, and assessed for symptom occurrence.
2. These presenting symptoms should be clearly noted and documented concerning frequency, intensity, and duration. The measurement scales described in this chapter can assist with this.
   - **a.** When looking at issues of frequency, it is critical to document how often the problem behaviors occur during a specific time period. Are the behaviors happening, for example, once a week or once a day? How does the frequency of occurrence of these problem behaviors directly affect individual, occupational, or social functioning? Many of the diagnostic categories say that the behaviors must occur once or more; others say they must be frequent occurrences. To be safe, always document the frequency of the behavior and how it is documented to have occurred and relate it directly to level of functioning.
   - **b.** Intensity is another critical aspect to be clearly identified in assessing diagnostic criteria. To address intensity, the practitioner must gather information about the magnitude of the strength, power, or force with which a problem behavior is occurring and relate this directly to the way it affects daily functioning. Is the behavior affecting the client's abilities to form and maintain relationships, or is it more severe, thereby affecting the client's ability to perform routine daily activities such as self-hygiene?
   - **c.** For duration, the practitioner should document the time between the onset and stopping of the behavior (Wright, 2011). Specifically, addressing duration requires that the period of time that something lasts or exists be measured. This period is very important in terms of identifying the criteria for a disorder because often specific time frames must be met (e.g., for schizophrenia, the symptoms must last approximately 6 months; if less than 6 months, the diagnosis of schizophreniform is utilized). Suggested measures and standardized tools can assist with this. One particularly helpful tool outlined in the *DSM* is the Clinician-Rated Dimensions of Psychosis Symptom Severity scale discussed earlier. Such measures can help the practitioner measure incidence and problem behaviors (in terms of frequency, intensity, and duration). Other rapid assessment instruments are presented in Chapter 4, as well as in each subsequent chapter as relevant.
3. When substantiating the categorization of diagnostic criteria supportive of the

mental health diagnosis, environmental, cultural, and social factors must always be assessed. As discussed in Chapter 2, it can be difficult to separate behaviors that are culturally based from those that are not. In the diagnostic assessment, the expectation is not to diagnose disorder(s) when an individual's behaviors are related to a cultural situation or syndrome. In the diagnostic assessment process, if the practitioner believes the behavior is culture related, no clinical syndrome or formal diagnosis constituting a mental disorder based on those symptoms alone is given. Use of the CFI is highly recommended, and based on the results, caution should be used in terms of diagnosing someone with a mental disorder, even if the symptoms displayed seem to suggest it. (See Quick Reference 3.13.)

For all clients, misdiagnosis or absence of the proper diagnosis can have devastating effects. When a client is extremely agitated and uncooperative, the practitioner should assess to see if this type of behavior is characteristic of any other time in the client's life. If it is not, the behaviors could be related to an unknown trauma such as a closed head injury. Nonrecognition of the medical aspects of a mental disorder could also result in severe legal, ethical, and malpractice considerations. It is essential for nonmedically trained mental health practitioners to have some background in medical conditions, particularly the influence these conditions have on mental health symptoms.

To guide the diagnostic assessment and screening inquiries that help to identify the relationship between medical factors and mental health–related behaviors, Pollak et al. (1999) suggested three guidelines that remain relevant.

1. The practitioner should look for risk factors and whether the client falls into a high-risk group as identified earlier.
2. The practitioner should consider whether the presentation is suspicious or inconsistent and therefore suggestive of a neurodevelopmental or medical condition.
3. After gathering initial screening information, the practitioner should decide whether further testing is warranted to

QUICK REFERENCE 3.13

Questions to Guide the Process

- What are the major psychiatric symptoms a client is displaying?
- What are the frequency, intensity, and duration of the symptoms or problem behavior?
- Do the symptoms identified fit the dimensional criteria outlined for the disorder in the *DSM-5*?
- Has a complete diagnostic assessment been conducted that utilizes assessment measures such as Cross-Cutting of Symptoms, the WHODAS, and the Symptom Severity Scale?
- Has supportive information been evaluated such as environmental factors, cultural and social factors, and have these apects been considered as a possible explanation?

QUICK REFERENCE 3.14

Helpful Hints: Clinical Presentations Suggestive of a Mental Disorder

- Previous psychosocial difficulties not related to a medical or other type of developmental disorder.
- Chronic unrelated complaints that cannot be linked to a satisfactory medical explanation.
- A history of object relations problems, such as help-rejecting behavior, codependency, and other interrelationship problems that significantly impair social functioning.
- A puzzling lack of concern on the part of the client as to the behaviors he or she is engaging in with the tendency to minimize or deny the circumstances.
- Evidence of secondary gain where the client is reinforced by such behaviors by significant others, family, or members of the support system.
- A history of substance abuse problems (legal or illegal substances such as alcohol or prescription medication abuse).
- A family history of similar symptoms and/or another mental disorder.
- Cognitive or physical complaints that are more severe than what would be expected for someone in a similar situation.

address the physical or medical basis of the symptoms a client is experiencing. In this case, a physical exam should always be considered.

Once the practitioner makes a referral, the client will need to sign a release for the physician to share this information with the mental health practitioner. The practitioner is also advised to use client information from previous history and physical exams, medical history summaries, radiological reports, and lab findings. The most valuable advice for the practitioner is to first establish when the client last had a physical exam. When this information cannot be verified and the practitioner is not sure whether the condition is medically based, referral for a physical exam should be made.

Although the mental health practitioner can assist in identifying and documenting medical conditions, remember that the original diagnosis of any such medical condition always rests with the physician or the medical provider (see Quick Reference 3.14). Also, please keep in mind that *DSM-5* no longer gives the "*ICD-9* Codes for the Selected Medical Conditions and Medication-Induced Disorders" that were in Appendix G of the *DSM-IV-TR*. Therefore, where using the *ICD-10* medical condition codes is essential for diagnostic and billing purposes, obtaining the codes from *ICD* would be expected.

Pollak et al. (1999) suggested several factors to help a practitioner separate mental health clinical presentations that may have a medical contribution. Eight points should always be considered in completing the diagnostic assessment:

1. Give special attention to clients who present with the first episode of a major disorder. In these clients, particularly when symptoms are severe (e.g., psychotic, catatonic, and nonresponsive), close monitoring of the original presentation, when compared with previous behavior, is essential. Note if the client's

symptoms are acute (just started or relative to a certain situation) or abrupt with rapid changes in mood or behavior. Examples of symptoms that fall in this area include both cognitive and behavioral symptoms, such as marked apathy, decreased drive and initiative, paranoia, labile mood or mood swings, and poorly controlled impulses.

2. Pay particular attention when the initial onset of a disorder or serious symptoms occurs after the age of 40. Although this is not an ironclad rule, most mental disorders become evident before the age of 40; thus a later onset of symptoms should be carefully examined to rule out social or situational stressors, cultural implications, organic concerns, or other environmental or medical causes.
3. Note symptoms of a mental disorder that occur immediately before, during, or after the onset of a major medical illness. The symptoms may be related to the progression of the medical condition. It is also possible that symptoms could be medication- or substance-related (Dziegielewski, 2010). Polypharmacy can be a problem for individuals who are unaware of the dangers of mixing medications and substances that they do not consider medications (e.g., herbal preparations) (Dziegielewski, 2010).
4. In gathering information for the diagnostic assessment, note whether there is an immediate psychosocial stressor or life circumstance that may contribute to the symptoms the client is experiencing. This is especially relevant when the stressors present are so minimal that a clear connection between the stressor and the reaction cannot be made. One very good general rule is to remember that anytime a client presents with extreme symptomology of any kind, with no previous history of such behaviors, assessment and possible attention and monitoring for medical causes is essential.
5. Pay particular attention in the screening process when a client suffers from different types of hallucinations. Basically, a hallucination is the misperception of a stimulus. In psychotic conditions, auditory hallucinations are most common. When a client presents with multiple types of hallucinations—such as visual (seeing things that are not there), tactile (referring to the sense of touch, e.g., bugs crawling on them), gustatory (pertaining to the sense of taste), or olfactory (relative to the sense of smell)—this is generally too extreme to be purely a mental health condition. It could be substance related or medically based; therefore, a referral of collaborative teamwork with a medically trained professional is expected. Be sure a medically trained practitioner is aware of these symptoms and how they can relate to the mental health diagnosis.
6. Note any simple repetitive and purposeless movements of speech (e.g., stuttering or indistinct or unintelligible speech), the face (e.g., motor tightness or tremors), and hands and extremities (e.g., tremor, shaking, unsteady gait). Also note any experiential phenomena such as derealization, depersonalization, or unexplained gastric or medical complaints and symptoms, such as new onset of headache accompanied by nausea and vomiting.
7. Note signs of cortical brain dysfunction, such as aphasia (language disturbance), apraxia (movement disturbance), agnosia (failure to recognize familiar objects despite intact sensory functioning), and

visuoconstructional deficits (problems drawing or reproducing objects and patterns).

8. Note any signs associated with organ failure, such as jaundice related to hepatic disease or dyspnea (difficulty breathing) associated with cardiac or pulmonary disease. For example, a client who is not getting proper oxygen may present as very confused and disoriented; when oxygen is regulated, the signs and symptoms begin to decrease and quickly subside.

Although mental health practitioners are not expected to be experts in diagnosing medical disorders, being aware of the medical complications that influence mental health presentations is necessary to facilitate the most accurate and complete diagnostic assessment possible.

Coding Medical Conditions: Making the Mind–Body Connection

In using the *DSM-5,* several issues need to be explored. Perhaps most important is remembering the importance of *linking the mind and the body.* People are complex beings. When a categorical approach to identifying and classifying disorders is utilized, the temptation is great to apply concrete and discrete criteria that do not include the full range of an individual's existence or situation. Adding the concepts of the dimensional assessment and crosscutting of symptoms enables considering a greater range of symptomology without a formal diagnosis. It also allows factors related to another medical condition to be considered.

Making the connection between mind and body and studying the resulting relationship is crucial to a comprehensive diagnostic assessment. A medical disorder can clearly affect individual functioning, and vice versa. The medical disorder and its subsequent symptoms as reported by the client can easily become confused. Just having a medical disorder can affect the mental disorder, which in turn can influence the course of many diseases leading to short-term or long-term disability. In addition, mental health conditions can influence other medical conditions, such as cardiovascular disease, diabetes, HIV/AIDS, tuberculosis, and malaria. According to Prince et al. (2007), mental health conditions and the behaviors that are characteristic can influence reproductive and sexual health with the development of conditions such as dysmenorrhea (disturbed menstrual cycles) and dyspareunia (genital pain during intercourse and other sexual activities).

In professional practice, it is easy to see how the line between what constitutes good *physical health* and what constitutes good *mental health* might be blurred (Dziegielewski, 2010). Separating the mind from the body is impossible, and the concept of wholeness must be considered. Achieving healthy outcomes requires positive and healthy mental health, and vice versa. Integrating these medical components into diagnostic assessment can increase the application of this connection. For example, for a client who has all the symptoms of depression but was recently diagnosed with cancer, a mental health diagnosis of this nature could be premature if not simply inaccurate. A diagnosis alone is never enough, and each practitioner must also assess a situation completely, taking into account system variables that include a person's physical health.

The *DSM-5* no longer uses the multiaxial diagnostic system that was previously clearly delineated and coded on Axis III; however, listing a medical condition still remains relevant when it affects or compounds the mental health diagnosis. Listing a medical condition remains relevant when the mental disorder appears to have a physiological relationship or bearing on the mental health diagnosis listed. It is also important to note when the medical condition actually causes, facilitates, or is part of the reason for the development and continuation of the

QUICK REFERENCE 3.15

General Categories for Medical Diseases and Conditions

Diseases of the nervous system

Diseases of the circulatory system

Diseases of the respiratory system

Neoplasms

Endocrine diseases

Nutritional diseases

Metabolic diseases

Diseases of the digestive system

Genitourinary system diseases

Hematological diseases

Diseases of the eye

Diseases of the ear, nose, and throat

Musculoskeletal system and connective tissue diseases

Diseases of the skin

Congenital malformations, deformations, and chromosomal abnormalities

Diseases of pregnancy, childbirth, and the puerperium

Infectious diseases

Overdose

Additional codes for the medication-induced disorders

**ICD* medical codes are no longer listed in *DSM-5*.

Source: List of topics reprinted with permission from the *Diagnostic and Statistical Manual of Mental Disorders, Fourth Edition, Text Revision*, Copyright 2000 by the American Psychiatric Association.

mental health condition. In this situation, according to the *ICD*, the medical condition that causes the mental health condition would be listed first as the reason for visit. One sure way to establish whether the medical condition is the reason for visit is when the relationship between the medical and mental disorder is such that when the medical condition is resolved, the mental health condition is resolved as well. This premise sounds easy to the beginning professional, but for those more experienced, it is clear this simple distinction is not always so simple. Although conclusive, this relationship can be complicated, and there is often no simple pathway, especially when the damage from the general medical condition may not be curable. Regardless, it is important to document all related medical conditions that are important or can influence forming the mental diagnosis (APA, 2013). (See Quick Reference 3.15.) For

QUICK REFERENCE 3.16

Important Questions in Assessing Medical Symptoms

Has the client had a recent physical exam? If not, suggest that one be ordered.

Does the client have a summary of a recent history and physical exam that can be reviewed? If not medically trained, does the practitioner have someone to consult and review these with? Be sure to examine whether the etiology could be medically related.

Are there any laboratory findings, tests, or diagnostic reports that can assist in establishing a relationship between the mental and physiological consequences that result? If not medically trained in this area, does the practitioner have someone medically trained to consult or refer?

the coding and specific categories of such disorders, see the *ICD-10* and most probably after 2015 the *ICD-11*.

When assessing medical conditions, nonmedically trained mental health practitioners may find it helpful to receive support from an interdisciplinary or multidisciplinary team that includes medically trained professionals (Dziegielewski, 2013). Individuals who have training in the medical aspects of disease and illness can be valuable resources in understanding this mind–body connection. (See Quick Reference 3.16 and Case Example 3.1.)

When medical conditions are listed and recorded as part of the diagnostic assessment, there should always be hard evidence to support

CASE EXAMPLE 3.1 - IMPORTANCE OF ASSESSING FOR MEDICAL FACTORS

In a comprehensive diagnostic assessment, the importance of examining complicating or interacting medical conditions cannot be underestimated. Consider this example. Late one night, a client who was extremely unkempt, delusional, and paranoid was brought to the emergency room. He reported bizarre delusions: Demons had invaded his teeth and were trying to capture his mind. The client had a past history of schizophrenia and often reported persecutory auditory hallucinations. This time, however, the delusions he was reporting were extreme compared with previous presentations. He was so convinced that demons were inside his mouth that he had started to tear at his gums with his fingers in an attempt to get at the demons inside. In his state of poor hygiene and malnourishment, it was not hard to see how he had managed to remove most of his teeth from his mouth, ripping them out with his fingers. Immediately on admission, a physical exam was ordered, along with an X-ray of his teeth to see the extent of the damage he had created by ripping the teeth from his mouth. The X-ray revealed that the client had an extensive sinus infection and made it obvious how much pain the untreated infection was causing. The pressure the sinus discharge placed on the roots of his teeth was causing him extensive pain and heightening the paranoid delusion of demons occupying his teeth. Once the sinus infection was treated, the severity of the paranoid delusions subsided.

As can be seen in this example, it is critical that medical issues, especially when clients present with extreme signs and symptoms, be clearly assessed and documented as part of the comprehensive diagnostic assessment process.

its inclusion. The practitioner should query whether a recent history and physical exam has been conducted and, when one is available, review the written summary, which can be helpful in identifying medical conditions that may be related to the symptoms and behaviors a client is exhibiting. As stated earlier, if a physical exam has not been conducted prior to the assessment, it is always a good idea to refer the client for a physical or suggest that the client see a physician for a routine examination. A review of the medical information available, such as lab reports and other findings, as well as consulting with a medical professional, may be helpful in identifying disorders that could complicate or prevent the client from achieving improved mental health. When looking specifically at the relationship between the mental and the medical disorder, mental health practitioners should be prepared to inquire into the signs and symptoms of these conditions and to assist in understanding the relationship of this medical condition to the diagnostic assessment and the planning processes that evolve.

Special Considerations

Two areas of the diagnostic assessment are often overlooked and neglected, yet they are critical to a well-rounded comprehensive diagnostic assessment. In *ICD-9,* the first of these medical conditions fell under diseases of the eye and had to do with *visual loss* (coded 369.9) or *cataracts* (coded 366.9). Visual loss is related to a decrease in vision (sight), yet the apparent loss of visual acuity or visual field is not related directly to substantiating physical signs. This problem may be best addressed with client reassurance (WebMD, 2008). Cataracts relate to the loss of transparency in the lens of the eye. Both conditions result in vision impairment. Keep in mind that decreased or impaired vision may lead individuals to interpret daily events incorrectly. For example, have you ever sat near a window only to look up and be startled by your reflection? For a moment, you are shocked and frightened that someone is watching you. As you look closer, however, you realize that it is only your reflection. Now imagine that you are vision impaired and cannot see well. Or imagine that you are not wearing your glasses because you cannot remember where you put them. Or that you have developed a cataract that has grown so dense your vision is obstructed, and what you can see is clouded or shadowed. Is it possible that no matter how hard you try, you are still unable to see that the reflection in the window is really you? Since you are unable to distinguish the shape in the window as your own, imagine how frightened you might become as you now convince yourself that a stranger is watching your every move. Would you not be suspicious of why you were being watched, and what this person or people might be after? Now imagine how someone who is vision impaired might feel if he or she is troubled by symptoms that cannot be easily explained. The frustration with the present situation can lead to symptoms being misperceived or misinterpreted. For mental health practitioners, the most salient issue to identify once the vision difficulty is recognized or corrected is whether the problem resolves itself. As part of the diagnostic assessment, special attention should always be given to screening for vision problems that may cause distress to the client in terms of individual and social functioning.

The second medical area that is often overlooked in the diagnostic assessment is related to hearing loss (coded 389.9 in *ICD-9*). A client with hearing impairment or hearing loss experiences a reduction in the ability to perceive sound that can range from slight impairment to complete deafness (WebMD, 2008). Many times a client who is having hearing difficulty may not want to admit it. Many individuals may rely on hearing enhancement devices such as hearing aids, which amplify sound more

QUICK REFERENCE 3.17

Assessing Hearing and Vision Problems

In the Diagnostic Assessment Process for Hearing and Vision, Practitioners Need to Ask the Client:

Do you have any problems with your hearing or vision?

How would you rate your current hearing and your vision?

Can you give examples of specific problems you are having?

When did you have your last vision or hearing checkup?

Have you noticed a difference between what you used to be able to hear or see in the past and what you can process now?

Risk Factors in Children and Hearing Loss

Has the child had repeated ear infections that could have resulted in hearing loss?

Has the child had repeated operations and tubes placed in their ears?

Has the child ever had an eardrum burst?

Risk Factors with Adults and Potential Hearing Loss:

Has the adult been exposed to loud noises and the ears were unprotected (e.g., military/ combat soldiers, machinists)?

Could these exposures have resulted in mild hearing loss that may not be obvious to others?

effectively into the ear. Such hearing aids may not be able to differentiate among selected pieces of information as well as the human ear. Furthermore, as a normal part of aging, high-frequency hearing loss can occur. Most noises in a person's environment, such as background noise, are low frequency. Therefore, an individual with high-frequency loss may not be able to tune out background noise, such as television sets or side conversations. He or she may get very angry over distractions that other people who do not have a similar hearing loss do not perceive. (See Quick Reference 3.17.)

During the diagnostic assessment process, the practitioner should ask very specific questions about hearing and vision problems, as these medical problems can be misinterpreted as signs of a mental health problem.

ETHICAL AND LEGAL CONSIDERATIONS

Professional efforts require that all activities performed and judgments made are within an ethical and legal framework. Practitioners must avoid any hint of malpractice. *Malpractice* is negligence in the exercise of one's profession. All the legal requirements and the problems that can occur is beyond the scope of this book. However, professionals should (a) be aware of the rules and requirements that govern professional practice activity in their state and (b) be well versed in the code of ethics that represents their profession's moral consensus (Reamer, 2001, 2009). It is not enough for helping professionals to assume that their ethical practice will be apparent on the basis of their adherence to their professional code of ethics.

Two common sayings about documentation are:

1. If you documented it, it happened.
2. If you did not document it, it did not happen.

When documenting client information, be sure it is accurate and reflects the nature of the ethical services provided, as this can be the best way for mental health practitioners to protect against malpractice. Practitioner documents must ensure that client confidentiality and privacy are protected (Dziegielewski, 2013). One helpful rule is to remember that at any time, all records may be subpoenaed in a court of law, where private client information may be divulged. Regardless of the employment setting, all helping professionals should consider maintaining personal malpractice insurance in addition to what may be provided through agency auspices. Even with the best of intentions, mental health practitioners may find themselves in legal proceedings defending the content of notes, subjective assessments, or terminology used in the diagnostic assessment. It is always best to record objective data and refrain from using subjective terminology (i.e., what you think is happening). When documenting, always use direct client statements; do not document hearsay or make interpretations based on subjective data (Dziegielewski, 2008). Practitioners need to be familiar with specific state statutes that do not allow professionals to elicit or document specific client information. For example, mental health professionals are prohibited from documenting the medical condition of AIDS patients without client consent. In record keeping, the ultimate legal and ethical responsibility of all written diagnostic and assessment-based notes always starts and stops with the mental health practitioner.

PULLING IT ALL TOGETHER

For a comprehensive diagnostic assessment, it is assumed that the screening begins with the first client–mental health practitioner interaction. The information the mental health practitioner gathers is assembled into a database that facilitates the diagnostic assessment and determines the requirements and direction of future treatment planning and intervention efforts. The diagnostic assessment assists in ordering information on the client's present situation and history in regard to how past behaviors can relate to present concerns. This comprehensive assessment is inclusive, supporting both clinically based judgments and interpretation of perspectives and alternatives for service delivery.

To start this process, the problem must be recognized as interfering with daily functioning. Here the practitioner must be active in uncovering problems affecting daily living and engaging the client in self-help or skill building, changing behaviors, or both. The client has to acknowledge that the problem exists. Once this is done, the definition of the problem becomes clear, allowing for exploration (Hepworth, Rooney, Rooney, Gottfried, & Larsen, 2010).

In addition, the problem must be clearly identified. The problem of concern is what the client sees as important; he or she is the one who is expected to create the behavior change. It is common to receive referrals from other health care professionals, and special attention should always be paid to referrals that clearly recommend a course of treatment or intervention. This type of focused referral may limit the scope and intervention possibilities available. Often such focused referrals that limit intervention scope can provide the basis for reimbursement as well. Although referral information and suggestions should always be considered in your discussion with the client in identifying the problem, in terms of assessment and the resulting plan, the client's best interest is paramount, and he or she should participate to identify the end result.

Generally, the client is the primary source of data. This information can be supplemented through direct observation of verbal and physical behaviors and through interaction patterns with other interdisciplinary team members, family, significant others, or friends. Viewing and recording these patterns of communication can be extremely helpful in later establishing and developing strengths and resource considerations. In addition to verbal reports, written reports such as background sheets, psychological tests, and tests of health status or level of daily functioning can be used. Although the client is perceived as the first and primary source of data, the need for information from others cannot be underestimated. This means talking with the family and significant others to estimate planning support and assistance. Gathering information from other secondary sources, such as the client's medical record, is also important. To facilitate the diagnostic assessment, the practitioner must be able to understand the client's medical situation and the relationship that medical symptoms can have with mental health symptoms. Knowledge of certain medical conditions and when to refer to other health professionals for continued care is an essential part of the diagnostic assessment process.

Completing a comprehensive assessment has three primary steps:

1. Problem or behavior recognition. Here the practitioner must explore and be active in uncovering problems that affect daily living and will later be targeted in engaging the client in self-help or skill-changing behaviors. The client has to acknowledge that the problem exists. Once the problem is acknowledged, the boundaries related to the problem become clear (Hepworth et al., 2010).
2. Problem or behavior identification. In the diagnostic assessment, problems that affect daily functioning are identified. What the client sees as the problem of concern is important for helping the client to develop change behavior. In the mental health field, referrals that often provide the basis for reimbursement are common, and sometimes the referral source establishes how the problem is viewed and what should be the basis of intervention. Sound, efficient, cost-effective clinical practice takes referral information into account because it can lead to better problem identification.
3. Treatment plan. Once the diagnostic assessment is complete, how will the information be related to the intervention plan and strategy to follow? According to Sheafor and Horejsi (2012), the plan of action is central to bridging the diagnostic assessment with the resultant practice strategy. Here the practitioner focuses on the goals and objectives to be attained in the intervention process. In the initial planning stage, emphasis on the outcome is essential.

The outcome of the diagnostic assessment process is a plan to guide, enhance, and in many cases determine the course of intervention to be implemented. Given the complexity of human beings and the problems they encounter, a properly prepared multidimensional assessment is the essential first step to high-quality service delivery. The diagnostic assessment should never be considered a static entity, or else it may become too narrow in focus, thereby decreasing its utility, relevance, and salience. The process of diagnostic assessment must continually be examined and reexamined to ensure its quality. This process should not be rushed because when it is, superficial factors may be highlighted and significant ones de-emphasized or overlooked. Mental health practitioners owe it to their clients that diagnostic efforts and the helping strategy that develops are quality driven, no matter what the administrative and economic pressures may be. This support is just one of the ways practitioners are working not only to assist in developing a comprehensive strategy to help clients but also to ensure that high-quality service is available and obtained.

SUMMARY

Mental health practitioners must know how best to proceed with completing a comprehensive diagnostic assessment and evaluation. In mental health, all practitioners are expected to do so for all their clients. For many professionals, the role of assessment leading to diagnosis in mental health counseling can be a complicated one; it can be particularly problematic for practitioners in solo practice who do not have access to collaborative teams or referral sources (Dziegielewski, 2013). Regardless of the practice setting, all mental health practitioners are being called on to be more knowledgeable and interactive and to utilize evidence-based diagnostic tests to support practice strategy (Dudley, 2014). The role of the practitioner in linking the client to environmental considerations is an essential one. As well, all mental health practitioners need to be keenly aware of updates in diagnostic criteria and act as advocates for the client throughout the diagnostic assessment and intervention process.

Equipped with a basic knowledge of the use and misuse of the *DSM-5* in the creation of a diagnostic impression, the mental health practitioner can more constructively participate in the consultation process. Knowledge of diagnostic impressions and criteria can assist the practitioner in enhancing the client's overall functioning level. Because mental health practitioners often have regular and subsequent contacts with their clients, they can be essential in helping the interdisciplinary team to reexamine or reformulate previous diagnostic impressions and the relationship these original impressions can have on the client's future treatment potential. As a team member, the mental health practitioner is aware of the environment and the importance of building and maintaining therapeutic rapport with the client. This makes the practitioner's input in understanding the mental disorder an essential contribution to intervention effectiveness. The mental health practitioner remains in a key position to allay the client's and his or her family's fears and to elicit their help and support (Dziegielewski, 2013).

Moreover, coordinated care continues to increase the emphasis on behavior-based care with limited time frames for treatment (Dziegielewski, 2008, 2013). Use of the two supplemental chapters (21 and 22) is essential for documenting supportive information and conditions not attributable to a mental disorder. These circumstances and conditions are not attributable to a mental disorder yet remain the focus of clinical treatment. Because they historically have not been considered reimbursable, some practitioners have avoided their use. Nevertheless, the current practice emphasis on brief time-limited treatment (Dziegielewski, 2008) makes understanding these conditions essential.

Information gathered must always extend beyond the client. Special consideration should be given to the needs of family, significant others, and the client's identified support system. Family members not uncommonly have limited information about mental health diagnosis and treatment. Information gathered from outside sources such as the Internet can be misleading and biased, and family members may feel uncomfortable telling health care professionals that they believe another mode of treatment might be better. The well-informed practitioner can correct distortions and foster cooperation in the treatment plan (Dziegielewski, 2013). When practitioners are knowledgeable about different mental health conditions, they can better serve their clients and make the most appropriate treatment decisions and system linkages. With an updated knowledge of mental health diagnosis and subsequent intervention, they can help prepare, as well as educate, clients and family members about the responsible use and expectations for psychiatric care. Professional schools that train mental health practitioners need to include course work on how to complete a comprehensive diagnostic assessment that focuses on identifying the principal diagnosis and any supportive information that can affect the diagnosis. Because practitioners are held accountable for their own practice actions, they must strive to achieve the highest standards of their profession (Reamer, 2009).

QUESTIONS FOR FURTHER THOUGHT

1. What is your opinion of the deletion of the multiaxial system as part of the diagnostic assessment? What strengths and weaknesses do you see related to simply listing a diagnosis?
2. What two medical conditions that are often overlooked could have significant implications for the diagnostic assessment? Give an example related to adults and one related to children.
3. Does the *DSM-5* suggest treatment?
4. In completing the diagnostic assessment, how important is listing the supportive factors relative to a client's situation? Why and how would this be done?

REFERENCES

Alegria, M., Shrout, P. E., Woo, M., Guarnaccia, P., Sribney, W., Vila, D., . . . Canino, G. (2007). Understanding differences in past year psychiatric disorders for Latinos living in the US. *Social Science and Medicine, 65*, 214–230.

American Psychiatric Association. (1994). *Diagnostic and statistical manual of mental disorders* (4th ed.). Washington, DC: Author.

American Psychiatric Association. (2000). *Diagnostic and statistical manual of mental disorders* (4th ed., text rev.). Washington, DC: Author.

American Psychiatric Association. (2013). *Diagnostic and statistical manual of mental disorders* (5th ed.). Arlington, VA: American Psychiatric Publishing.

Benzer, T. (2007). *Neuroleptic malignant syndrome*. Retrieved from http://emedicine.medscape.com/article/816018-overview

Braun, S. A., & Cox, J. A. (2005). Managed mental health care: Intentional misdiagnosis of mental disorders. *Journal of Counseling and Development, 83*, 425–433.

Carpenter, W. T., Conley, R. R., & Buchanan, R. W. (1998). Schizophrenia. In S. J. Enna & J. T. Coyle (Eds.), *Pharmacological management of neurological and psychiatric disorders*. New York, NY: McGraw-Hill.

Cipani, E. (2014). Comorbidity in *DSM* childhood mental disorders: A functional perspective. *Research on Social Work Practice, 24*(1), 78–85.

Colby, I., & Dziegielewski, S. F. (2010). *Introduction to social work: The people's profession* (3rd ed.). Chicago, IL: Lyceum.

Corcoran, J., & Walsh, J. (2010). *Clinical assessment and diagnosis in social work practice*. New York, NY: Oxford University Press.

Dudley, J. R. (2014). *Social work evaluation: Enhancing what we do*. Chicago, IL: Lyceum.

Dziegielewski, S. F. (2005). *Understanding substance addictions: Assessment and intervention*. Chicago, IL: Lyceum.

Dziegielewski, S. F. (2006). *Psychopharmacology for the non-medically trained*. New York, NY: Norton.

Dziegielewski, S. F. (2008). Brief and intermittent approaches to practice: The state of practice. *Journal of Brief Treatment and Crisis Intervention, 8*(2), 147–163.

Dziegielewski, S. F. (2010). *Psychopharmacology and social work practice: A person-in-environment approach* (2nd ed.). New York, NY: Springer.

Dziegielewski, S. F. (2013). *The changing face of health care social work: Opportunities and challenges for professional practice* (3rd ed.). New York, NY: Springer.

Frances, A. (2013). *Essentials of psychiatric diagnosis: Responding to the challenge of DSM-5.* New York, NY: Guilford Press.

Garland, E. L., & Howard, M. O. (2014). A transdiagnostic perspective on cognitive, affective, neurobiological processes underlying human suffering. *Research on Social Work Practice, 24*(1), 142–151.

Hepworth, D. H., Rooney, R. H., Rooney, G., Gottfried, K., & Larsen, J. A. (2010). *Direct social work practice: Theory and skills* (8th ed.). Belmont, CA: Brooks/Cole.

Horowitz, A. V., & Wakefield, J. C. (2012). *All we have to dear: Psychiatry's transformation of natural anxieties into mental disorders.* New York, NY: Oxford University Press.

Lacasse, J. R. (2014). After *DSM-5:* A critical mental health research agenda for the 21st century. *Research on Social Work Practice, 24*(1), 5–110.

Mallett, C. A. (2014). Child and adolescent behaviorally based disorders: A critical review of reliability and validity. *Research on Social Work Practice, 24*(1), 96–113.

National Alliance on Mental Illness. (2003). *Tardive dyskinesia.* Retrieved from http://www.nami.org/Content/ContentGroups/Helpline1/Tardive_Dyskinesia.htm

National Institute of Mental Health. (2009). *How is bipolar treated?* Retrieved from http://www.nimh.nih.gov/health/publications/bipolar-disorder/how-is-bipolar-disorder-treated.shtml

Owen, D. W. (2011). The role of assessment in mental health counseling. In A. J. Palamo, W. J. Weikel, & D. P. Borsos (Eds.), *Foundations of mental health counseling* (4th ed., pp. 333–353). Springfield, IL: Charles C. Thomas.

Pearson, G. S. (2008). Advocating for the full-frame approach [Editorial]. *Perspectives in Psychiatric Care, 44*(1), 1–2.

Physicians' Desk Reference. (2013). *Physicians' desk reference* (67th ed.). Montvale, NJ: Medical Economics.

Pollak, J., Levy, S., & Breitholtz, T. (1999). Screening for medical and neurodevelopmental disorders for the professional counselor. *Journal of Counseling Development, 77,* 350–357.

Prince, M., Patel, V., Saxena, S., Maj, J., Phillips, M. R., & Rahman, A. (2007). No health without mental health [Global Mental Health Series Article 1]. *Lancet, 370,* 859–877.

Probst, B. (2013). Walking the tightrope: Clinical social workers use of the diagnostic and environmental perspectives. *Clinical Social Work Journal, 41*(2), 184–191.

Probst, B. (2014). The life and death of Axis IV: Caught in the quest for a theory of mental disorder. *Research on Social Work Practice, 24*(1), 123–131.

Reamer, F. G. (2001). Ethics and values in clinical and community social work practice. In H. Briggs & K. Corcoran (Eds.), *Social work practice: Treating common client problems* (pp. 85–106). Chicago, IL: Lyceum.

Reamer, F. G. (2009). Ethical issues in social work. In A. Roberts (Ed.), *Social workers desk reference* (2nd ed., pp. 115–120). New York, NY: Oxford University Press.

Sheafor, B. W., & Horejsi, C. J. (2012). *Techniques and guidelines for social work practice* (9th ed.). New York, NY: Allyn & Bacon.

Shlonsky, A. (2009). Evidence-based practice in social work education. In A. Roberts (Ed.), *Social workers desk reference* (2nd ed., pp. 1169–1176). New York, NY: Oxford University Press.

Wakefield, J. C., & Schmitz, M. F. (2014). Uncomplicated depression, suicide attempt, and the *DSM-5* bereavement exclusion debate: An empirical evaluation. *Research on Social Work Practice, 24*(1), 37–49.

WebMD. (2008). *Webster's new world medical dictionary* (3rd ed.). Hoboken, NJ: Wiley.

Whyte, L., & Brooker, C. (2001). Working with a multidisciplinary team: In secure psychiatric environments. *Journal of Psychosocial Nursing and Mental Health Services, 39*(9), 26–34.

Wright, J. A. (2011). *Conducting psychological assessment: A guide for practitioners.* Hoboken, NJ: Wiley.

CHAPTER 4

Applications

Beyond the Diagnostic Assessment

Completing the initial diagnostic assessment is paramount, as it is the foundation for the treatment planning and practice strategy that will follow. Accurate and successful documentation shows what progress is being made in therapy and provides the groundwork for establishing efficiency and effectiveness of treatment. Many professionals falsely assume that the *DSM-5* suggests treatment strategy, but similar to previous versions of the text, this assumption is not correct for *DSM-5*. Neither the *DSM-5* nor any of the previous versions of the *DSM* suggests treatment strategies or courses of action regarding the intervention or treatment phases of the helping process. Because the mental health practitioner is expected to assist in the diagnostic assessment, treatment planning, and selection of the intervention and practice strategy, some background knowledge in this area is essential.

This chapter provides an overview of the importance of documentation in terms of treatment planning and practice strategy. In Section II of this book, direct application is made to many of the specific diagnostic conditions that integrate many of the principles and practice techniques described in this chapter. Once the mental health practitioner has completed the diagnostic assessment, this information must be recorded and applied accordingly.

DOCUMENTATION, TREATMENT PLANNING, AND PRACTICE STRATEGY

Throughout the history of mental health practice, practitioners have relied on some form of record keeping to document information on client situations and problems. Although the formats professionals use have changed, the value of documentation in maintaining case continuity has remained a priority (Dziegielewski, 2010, 2013). In its most basic form, thorough documentation provides a map indicating where the client and practitioner have traveled in their treatment journey. Treatment is not just breaking things down into small parts; it is also putting them back together in a holistic way that benefits the client served (Magnavita & Anchin, 2014). Clearly documenting what is done is the first step in this process. Collaborative therapeutic assessments help to link the client's concerns and history to the documented data (Martin & Jacklin, 2012). Because a client's experiences are never static, written words need to allow flexibility and change when possible. Understanding and recording the client's problems, the counseling interventions used, and the client's progress enables the practitioner to assess the interventions and make necessary changes in counseling strategies. It is also crucial in terms of client safety, especially when clients are depressed and might attempt to hurt themselves or someone else. As part of the assessment process, developing a safety plan that takes into account the client's short- and long-term situation is emphasized (Yeager, Roberts, & Saveanu, 2009). Creating a comprehensive assessment involves a delicate balance of clinical judgment and the latest research into practice (Schore, 2014).

In addition, in the courts, the medical record may be central to portraying and defending what was done or not done with a client in the treatment setting. The old saying "If you did not document it, it did not happen" remains an important reminder of the power of the written word. It is often followed with the reminder, "if you did document it, it did indeed happen." Therefore, the exact words used must be chosen carefully, making the primary goal of case documentation an evolving process. Reamer (2005) suggested thinking about the various audiences for the case record and then striking a balance between too little information, which might compromise the work of a team member or other professional who reviews the record, and too much information, which might prove detrimental to a client if the record is used for other purposes, such as a custody hearing.

Wiger (2005) outlined four functions of case documentation: (1) to monitor treatment, (2) to assist in determining treatment outcomes, (3) to aid in communicating with other professionals, and (4) to help with regulatory compliance. Additionally, case records serve as the basis for determining eligibility for services by coordinated care companies and provide evidence of the practitioner's accountability (Dziegielewski, 2008). Sheafor and Horejsi (2008) state that good record keeping must give an accurate and standardized account of the information gathered and support this information with prospective and retrospective data collection.

In the diagnostic assessment and throughout the intervention, practitioners must be aware that without accurate case documentation, most third-party payers will not reimburse for the start or continuation of services. Therefore, all documentation within the diagnostic assessment and subsequent practice strategy must clearly identify specific information related to problem severity that will lead and guide continued intervention efforts. This emphasis on accountability is mandated by health care organizations and other external reviewing bodies that monitor client services (Sommers-Flanagan & Sommers-Flanagan, 2009). All mental health practitioners are expected to justify and document client eligibility for service, including diagnosis, symptoms, and functional impairment; appropriateness for specific services and their continuation based on client progress; the intensity of services, including length of treatment and level of care; interventions provided; and specific, objective, behavioral outcome criteria that serve as goals for discharge (Wiger, 2005).

Increasingly, coordinated care organizations expect mental health providers to justify treatment decisions in terms of medical or therapeutic necessity, which means that services are needed because of the severity of impairment or dysfunction, rather than simply the diagnosis (Wiger, 2005). The case record is critical in demonstrating therapeutic necessity. Records that specifically document impairment and symptoms and their persistence over time can demonstrate the need for continuation of services. If a record lacks this level of specificity, a reviewer may conclude that the impairment no longer exists, and payment for services may be denied or discontinued (Wiger, 2005).

Utilizing a holistic framework that stresses the client's behavioral and biopsychosocial spiritual factors allows mental health practitioners to play an important role in the efficient delivery of interdisciplinary psychological and social services

(Straub, 2012). Mental health practitioners can also assist other team members in documenting effectively while collaborating with them on client progress and problems (Dziegielewski, 2013). Accurate, up-to-date, and informative records are vital to the coordinated planning efforts of the entire team. Comprehensive care that incorporates measurement instruments and other types of outcome verification has transformed mental health care and the services provided (Davidson, Tondora, Lawless, O'Connell, & Rowe, 2009).

As expected in behavior-based systems of coordinated care, high caseloads and shorter lengths of stay continue to cause mental health practitioners to adopt a style of documentation that is brief yet informative (Dziegielewski, 2013). The challenge is to summarize important client information in meaningful yet concise notes and treatment plans. Given our litigious society, informative records that demonstrate treatment interventions and reflect legal and ethical values and concerns can become important documents in legal proceedings long after the therapeutic intervention has ended (Bernstein & Hartsell, 2013). The pressure for accurate documentation comes from the growing emphasis and pressure to use evidence-based professional practice and justification for the course of intervention that will follow. In evidence-based practice, clear documentation as reflected in the case record can be used for numerous purposes. Regardless of the helping discipline or practice setting, five generic rules for efficient and effective documentation must always be employed (Dziegielewski, 2008).

1. Clear and concise record keeping is essential to distinctly document problem behaviors and coping styles.
2. The behavioral symptoms and impairments in functioning identified within the diagnostic assessment set the tone and give concrete justification for the goals and objectives in the treatment plan. Recording supporting information in the case file is essential for supplementation of the treatment plan. The relationship between case notes and the treatment plan is critical to the justification for service delivery.
3. The treatment plan shows progress indicators and time frames, which once again must be supported in the written case record. In this section, the review of current goals and objectives, as well as whether the therapeutic tasks assigned can be completed, is discussed.
4. The case notes and the treatment plan must clearly document and show response to interventions and whether changes are needed to continue to help the client to progress.
5. Case notes are used to assess goal accomplishment and to evaluate the efficiency, treatment, and cost-effectiveness of the service delivered.

(See Quick Reference 4.1.)

Problem-Oriented Recording

Among the various types of record-keeping formats, many mental health facilities still commonly use problem-oriented recording (POR) (Dziegielewski, 2008, 2010, 2013). Developed first in health care and medical settings, this type of recording was used to encourage multidisciplinary and interdisciplinary collaboration and to train medical professionals. As members of either multidisciplinary or interdisciplinary teams, helping professionals find that problem-oriented case documentation enables them to maintain documentation uniformity within a team approach to care. Problem-oriented documentation also satisfies health care organizations' demands for accountability (Kane, Houston-Vega, & Nuehring, 2002).

QUICK REFERENCE 4.1

OVERVIEW OF GUIDING PRINCIPLES FOR EFFICIENT DOCUMENTATION

Use the information gathered in the diagnostic assessment as the foundation for treatment planning and practice strategy. Be sure to use concrete behaviors and impact on functioning as indicators of client progress when designing treatment or intervention plans.

Complete periodic updates; report and change those interventions and treatment strategies that do not appear to be working for the client.

Be sure that the goals the client is to accomplish are stated in concrete, measurable terms and that the client can complete the therapeutic tasks assigned.

Monitor problem behaviors and behavior changes to continually review and update the intervention process.

Be sure to always assess goal accomplishment and evaluate the efficiency, treatment, and cost-effectiveness of the service delivered.

Problem-oriented recording emphasizes practitioner accountability through brief and concise documentation of client problems, services, and interventions, as well as client responses. In any of the numerous formats for POR, always keep comments brief, concrete, measurable, and concise. Many professionals feel strongly that POR is compatible with the increase in client caseloads, rapid assessments, and time-limited treatment. By maintaining brief but informative notes, practitioners are able to provide significant summaries of intervention progress. The mental health practitioner does not select the type of POR to be utilized. The choice of a specific problem-oriented format for case recording is based on the agency, clinic, or practice's function, need, and accountability. In today's practice environment, clear and concise documentation reflects the pressure of evidence-based practice. This makes it critical that mental health practitioners be familiar with the basic types of POR and how to utilize this format within the case record.

All POR formats start with a problem list that is linked to the behavioral-based biopsychosocial intervention. Whether completed electronically or in writing, this problem-oriented documentation helps the practitioner to focus directly on the presenting problems and coping styles the client is exhibiting, thereby limiting the recording of abstractions and vague clinical judgments. (See Quick Reference 4.2.) This type of documentation should include an inventory reflective of current active problems that are periodically updated. Although many client problems overlap and are interrelated, listing each problem separately allows more focused treatment planning and intervention (Sheafor & Horejsi, 2008). When a problem is resolved, it is crossed off the list with the date of resolution clearly designated. Noting the active problems a client is experiencing and maintaining self-contained files are considered the basic building blocks for case recording within the problem-oriented record. (See Quick Reference 4.3).

QUICK REFERENCE 4.2

INFORMATION TO BE INCLUDED IN THE POR

In a Complete Problem-Oriented Mental Health and Medical Record, Regardless of the Recording Format Used, the Following Should Always be Included:

Client identifying information and initial assessment information.

A complete behavioral-based biopsychosocial diagnostic assessment.

A psychosocial history recording important past and present information.

A list of client problems with suggestions for problem resolution.

Progress notes that encapsulate intervention strategy and progress.

A termination summary.

Copies of supporting data and information (e.g., consent forms, releases, summaries of recent medical or physical exams, and laboratory results).

Supervision and consultation reports (if applicable).

Although numerous formats for the actual progress note documentation can be selected, the subjective, objective assessment plan (SOAP) remains the most commonly used. (See Quick Reference 4.3.)

QUICK REFERENCE 4.3

SOAP, SOAPIE, AND SOAPIER RECORDING FORMATS

Subjective, Objective, Assessment, Plan (SOAP) or Subjective, Objective, Assessment, Plan, Implementation, Evaluation (SOAPIE) or Subjective, Objective, Assessment, Plan, Implementation, Evaluation, Review (SOAPIER)

S = Subjective data relevant to the client's request for service; client and practitioner impressions of the problem.

O = Objective data such as observable and measurable criteria related to the problem. If client statements are used, put the statement in quotes.

A = Assessment information of the underlying problems; diagnostic impression.

P = Plan outlines current intervention strategy, and specific referrals for other needed services.

I = Implementation considerations of the service to be provided.

E = Evaluation of service provision.

R = Client's response to the diagnostic process, treatment planning, and intervention efforts.

The Subjective Objective Assessment Plan (SOAP) first became popular in the 1970s. In this format, the practitioner utilizes the S (subjective) to record the data relevant to the client's request for service and the things the client says and feels about the problem. The mental health professional can use his or her clinical judgment in terms of what appears to be happening with the client. Some professionals prefer to document this information in terms of major themes or general topics addressed rather than making specific statements about what they think is happening. Generally, intimate personal content or details of fantasies and process interactions should not be included here. When charting in this section of the SOAP, mental health practitioners should always ask themselves, "Could this statement that I record be open to misinterpretation?" If it is vulnerable to misinterpretation or it resembles a personal rather than professional reaction to what is said, it should not be included.

The O (objective) includes observable and measurable criteria related to the problem. These are symptoms, behaviors, and client-focused problems observed directly by the practitioner during the assessment and intervention process. In addition, some agencies, clinics, and practices have started to include client statements in this section. If a client statement is to be utilized as objective data, however, exact quotes must be used. For example, if in the session the client states that he will not harm himself, the practitioner must document exactly what the client has said. What is said must be placed within quotation marks. Under the objective section of the summary note, it is also possible to include the results of standardized assessment instruments designed to measure psychological or social functioning. These instruments can support the process of gathering objective data.

The A (assessment) includes the therapist's assessment of the underlying problems, which often involves developing a *DSM*-5–based diagnostic impression. As described in Chapter 3, clearly identifying the principal diagnosis and the reason for visit assists in identifying the mental disorder, and the information from "Other disorders that may be the focus of clinical intervention" should always be reviewed and considered for inclusion.

In P (plan), the practitioner records how treatment objectives will be carried out, areas for future interventions, and specific referrals to other services needed by the client. Time frames or deadlines for interventions are often included (Shaefor & Horejsi, 2008).

For today's increased emphasis on time-limited intervention efforts and accountability, two new areas have been added to the original SOAP format (Dziegielewski, 2013). This extension, referred to as SOAPIE, identifies the first additional term as I (implementation considerations of the service to be provided). Here the mental health practitioner explains exactly how, when, and who will implement the service. In the last section, an E represents service provision evaluation. Here all health care professionals are expected to identify specific actions related to direct evaluation of progress achieved after any interventions are provided. When treatment is considered successful, specific outcomes-based objectives established early in the treatment process are documented as progressing or checked off as attained. In some agencies, a modified version of the SOAPIE has been introduced, SOAPIER. In this version, the R outlines the client's response to the intervention provided.

Another popular problem-oriented recording format used in some health care facilities today is the data, assessment, and plan (DAP) format. The DAP encourages the mental health practitioner to identify only the most salient elements of a practitioner's client contact. Using the D (data), the practitioner is expected to

QUICK REFERENCE 4.4

DAPE Recording Format

Data, Assessment, and Plan (DAP) or Data, Assessment, Plan, and Education (DAPE)

D = Data gathered to provide information about the identified problem.

A = Assessment of the client in regard to his or her current problem or situation.

P = Plan for intervention and what will be completed to assist the client to achieve increased health status or functioning.

E = Professional education that is provided by the mental health practitioner to ensure that problem mediation has taken place or evaluation information to ensure practice accountability.

record objective client data and statements related to the presenting problem and the focus of the therapeutic contact. Information related to the A (assessment) is used to record the diagnostic assessment information, the client's reactions to the service and intervention, and the practitioner's assessment of the client's overall progress toward the treatment goals and objectives. Specific information on all tasks, actions, or plans related to the presenting problem and to be carried out by either the client or the helping professional is recorded under P (plan). Also recorded under P is information on future issues related to the presenting problem to be explored at the next session and the specific date and time of the next appointment (Dziegielewski, 2013). Similar to the SOAP, the DAP format has undergone some changes. For example, some counseling professionals who apply the DAP are now being asked to add an additional section. This changes the DAP into the DAPE, where E reflects what type of educational and evaluative services have been conducted. (See Quick Reference 4.4.)

Two other forms of problem-based case recording formats are the problem, intervention, response, and plan (PIRP) and the assessed information, problems addressed, interventions provided, and evaluation (APIE). Both formats (see Quick Reference 4.5) can also be used to standardize case notes. Their structure is similar to the SOAP and the DAP. All four of these popular formats of problem-oriented case recording support increased problem identification and standardizing what and how client behaviors and coping styles are reported. Thus they provide a greater understanding of mental health problems and methods of managing them. This type of problem-oriented record brings the focus of clinical attention to an often-neglected aspect of recording, allowing all helping professionals to quickly familiarize themselves with a client's situation (Dziegielewski, 2008).

For mental health practitioners, utilizing a problem-focused perspective must go beyond merely recording information that is limited to the client's problems. When the focus is limited to gathering only this information, important strengths and resources that clients bring to the therapeutic interview may not be validated (Dziegielewski, 2013). In providing effective mental health treatment, identifying and utilizing a client's strengths stands at the forefront of every intervention (Jones-Smith, 2014). Furthermore, looking at a problem and ignoring the situation that surrounds the problem,

QUICK REFERENCE 4.5

PIRP AND APIE RECORDING FORMAT

Problem, Intervention, Response, and Plan (PIRP)

P = Presenting problem(s) or the problem(s) to be addressed.
I = Intervention to be conducted by the mental health practitioner.
R = Response to the intervention by the client.
P = Plan to address the problems experienced by the client.

Assessed Information, Problems Addressed, Interventions Provided, and Evaluation (APIE)

A = Documentation of assessed information in regard to the client problem.
P = Explanation of the problem that is being addressed.
I = Intervention description and plan.
E = Evaluation of the problem once the intervention is completed.

sometimes referred to as *partialization* of the problem, presents the risk that other significant aspects of a client's functioning will be overlooked in treatment planning and subsequent practice strategy. To understand the entire client situation and presenting problem, as mentioned in Chapter 3, all practitioners need to take into account a client's personal beliefs about the etiology and prognosis of symptoms (Chang-Muy & Congress, 2009). These beliefs can influence a client's interpretation of information about health and mental health (Chang et al., 2012). Therefore, problem-oriented forms of case recording need to extend beyond the immediate problem, regardless of whether agencies require it (Dziegielewski, 2008; Rudolph, 2000).

In recent years, a number of sourcebooks for documentation of mental health services have been published (see, e.g., Jongsma, Peterson, & Bruce, 2006; Wiger, 2005). These sourcebooks provide templates for treatment plans and progress notes and can assist in meeting the requirements of third-party payers and regulatory agencies (Berghuis & Jongsma, 2008a, 2008b). In general, the templates provided fit within a problem-oriented recording framework.

Maintaining Clinical Records

Because records can be maintained in more than one medium, such as written case files, audiotaped or videotaped material, and computer-generated notes, special attention needs to be given to ensuring confidentiality and maintaining ethical release of client information. Probably the greatest protection a mental health practitioner has in terms of risk management for all types of records is maintaining accurate, clear, and concise clinical records. This means that an unbroken chain of custody between the practitioner and the file must always be maintained. The mental health practitioner will ultimately be held responsible for producing a clinical record in case of litigation, and this policy cannot be overemphasized.

Documentation in the record should always be clearly sequenced and easy to follow. If a mistake occurs, never change a case note or treatment plan without acknowledging it. When changes need to be made to the diagnostic assessment, the treatment plan, or any other type of written case recording, clearly indicate that a change is being made by drawing a thin line

QUICK REFERENCE 4.6

Helpful Hints: Documentation

Accurate and ethical documentation ensures continuity of care and ethical and legal aspects of practice and provides direction for the focus of intervention. Here are some pointers on how to best write the information to be recorded in the client's file:

Date and time of entry.

Interview notes that clearly describe the client's problem(s).

A complete diagnostic assessment that is evidence-based.

A treatment plan with clearly established overall goals, objectives, and intervention tasks.

Print and sign your name (if electronic, use approved electronic signature), title, and credentials with each entry that is made.

Document all information in the case record as if you might someday have to defend it in a court of law.

Making changes or corrections in a record for paper records:

Always use ink that does not run (ballpoint pens are best), and never erase or use Wite-Out to cover up mistakes.

Draw a line through an error, mark it "error," and initial.

through the mistake and dating and initialing it. When correcting computer-generated records, do not delete the mistake; instead, insert the correct information, and include the date and your initials in parentheses (Bernstein & Hartsell, 2013). Records that are legible and cogent limit open interpretation of the services provided. (See Quick Reference 4.6.) In addition, the mental health practitioner is always required to keep clinical case records (including written records and computerized backup files) safeguarded in locked and fireproof cabinets. The mental health practitioner might consider archiving types of storage systems, such as encrypted data or secure remote (cloud) storage to preserve records and maximize space. States have varying legal requirements regarding the length of time records must be maintained. Many authorities, however, suggest that records be maintained indefinitely as a protection in the event of a lawsuit (Bernstein & Hartsell, 2013).

Computer-Generated Notes As computer-generated notes are considered commonplace, varying forms of problem-oriented case recording are linked directly into computerized databases (Gingerich, 2002). In terms of convenience, this can mean easy and immediate access to the client's treatment record, as well as fiscal and billing information. For working with computerized records, Hartsell and Bernstein (2008) suggest six pointers:

1. When recording client information on a hard drive or disk, be sure to store it in a safe and secure place.
2. Be sure to secure any passwords from detection.

3. If you are treating a celebrity or a famous individual, use a fictitious name and be sure to keep the key to the actual name in a protected place.
4. Always maintain a backup system and keep it secure.
5. Be sure that everyone who will have access to the client's case file reads and signs an established protocol concerning sanctity, privacy, and confidentiality of the records.
6. Take the potential of computer theft or crash seriously, and establish a policy that safeguards the information being stored and notes what will need to happen if a breach of confidentiality should occur.

The convenience of electronic records produces another major concern. Because clinical case records are portable and so easy to access, unauthorized access to recorded information presents a genuine problem. Every precaution should be taken to safeguard any information that is shared and stored electronically. In terms of convenience, this can mean immediate access to fiscal and billing information, as well as client intervention strategy, documentation, and treatment planning. Caution is always needed. Despite such easy access, one simple rule should always be applied: Never access anything unless there is a clearly identified clinical need to know that is directly related to patient care. Also, be sure the basic concepts related to electronic records—creation and maintenance—are clearly outlined. To be sure all aspects of privacy are met and the client's information is protected, working closely with the professionals responsible for protecting such information is highly recommended.

Protected Health Information

This easy accessibility, however, has fueled concerns about confidentiality and privacy. To address these concerns, Congress enacted the Health Insurance Portability and Accountability Act (HIPAA) in 1996, which established new rules for the privacy and security of electronic medical records. Under HIPAA, the Privacy Rule requires mental health practitioners to develop procedures for controlling the disclosure and use of client information, and the Security Rule requires the implementation of administrative, technical, and physical safeguards to protect client information (Bernstein & Hartsell, 2013). The term *protected health information* (PHI) relates to how private individual health information is recorded and processed.

The Privacy Rule requires that practitioners and agencies provide clients with a written notice of the providers' privacy policy about the disclosure of private health information. In general, providers can disclose this information without obtaining a specific consent for the purposes of treatment, payment, and health care operations, such as quality review. However, psychotherapy notes require a specific written authorization for disclosure or use (Bernstein & Hartsell, 2013; Yang & Kombarakaran, 2006). As medical records are kept for the benefit of the client, access to the record by the client is generally allowed without consent under HIPAA (Wiger, 2005). Some authorities, however, suggest that obtaining written consent from clients before allowing access to their records is always the most prudent policy. Practitioners should be familiar with HIPAA and state regulations that allow withholding information from clients when it is deemed harmful (Bernstein & Hartsell, 2013).

TREATMENT AND INTERVENTION PLANNING

Once the diagnostic assessment information has been gathered, it is used to start a treatment or intervention plan. Each treatment plan must be individualized. It must also reflect the general as well as the unique symptoms and needs the client is experiencing. A formal treatment plan helps to determine the structure and provide focus for the mental health intervention. Furthermore, a clearly established treatment plan can deter any litigation by either the client or a concerned family member (Bernstein & Hartsell, 2013; Reamer, 2005). When the treatment plan is clearly delineated, the client's family and friends may feel more at ease and agree to participate and assist in behavioral interventions.

Experts urge practitioners to adopt a risk-management approach to documentation (Reamer, 2005). Of particular importance is developing the skills to assess and document threats of suicide or homicide. Any statements suggesting a client's threat of violence to self or others should be documented in the case record without delay, preferably in the client's own words. Additionally, the record should reflect the practitioner's inquiry into the statement. Documentation of intent and any potential plans are essential and should lead to action almost immediately if a specific plan is outlined. The practitioner's plan of action should also be documented. It may include consultation with supervisors or others, compliance with agency protocols for these situations, referrals for further evaluation, and compliance with state statutes regarding duty to warn potential victims and notify police or other authorities (Bernstein & Hartsell, 2013). The client's reaction to any subsequent discussion should also be noted. Despite a practitioner's best efforts, a client may act violently. Documentation that reflects compliance with current standards of care and legal obligations can minimize the practitioner's risk. Also, when there is a potential for violence, keep in mind that practitioner safety should always be given priority over any other types of intervention or immediate documentation.

Assessing for Suicide and Creating a Safety Plan

Regardless of the reason for completing the diagnostic assessment, assessing for the possibility of danger to self or others is essential. When danger to self is suspected, the first step is to screen for suicidal thoughts or plans. If the individual makes reference to suicide, appears seriously depressed, reports starting to feel better after experiencing a more pronounced depression, or has a history of suicide attempts, the practitioner needs to be sure to assess for the possibility of danger to self or others. For the most part, regardless of whether the client is a child, adolescent, or adult, assessment for suicidal thoughts requires asking direct questions.

When you ask direct questions, it is most important to clients not just that they are listened to but that they are heard (Papadatou, 2009). Speaking clearly and slowly and paraphrasing what is said in response will help the client to connect with the practitioner (Dziegielewski, 2010).

Critical questions to ask are:

- Have you considered killing yourself or someone else?
- If so, what would you do?
- How would you do it?
- Have you ever tried to do this before? What did you do that time?
- What would stop you from trying to kill yourself?
- Have you ever considered killing anyone else? If so, what would you do, and why? (It is important to determine if clients have access to the means for action or self-harm and whether a concrete plan exists.)

If the potential for suicide is suspected, regardless of whether the client has a formal plan, a safety plan is required. It may include elements of a no-harm, no-risk agreement;

QUICK REFERENCE 4.7

No-Harm, No-Risk Behaviors: Discussion Points

- Discuss with the client what he or she is feeling.
- Determine a clear safety plan of what to do if he or she starts to think about harming self or others.
- Is the client aware of the circumstances that could trigger a dangerous reaction and, if so, what can be done to avoid this situation?
- Does the client know who to call for help, such as the police or a mental health treatment facility? Does the client have a name and number to call?
- Do you have the client's permission to let a family member know of the potential situation and the plan?

however, this should not constitute a separate record and always be documented as part of the file. All documentation should always involve controlling unpredictable behavior and creating a clear safety plan. (See Quick Reference 4.7.)

The effectiveness of talk related to a no-harm, no-risk script is only as strong as the safety plan that supports it (Dziegielewski, 2010). If this type of formalized behavioral rehearsal helps to clearly outline the safety plan, then use it. Be sure to use referrals as needed and seek inpatient treatment when there is a clear plan. To have a comprehensive safety plan, be sure that all questions related to safety have been asked, the responses addressed, and all information obtained is documented.

Always make sure family and others in the support system are aware of the safety concerns and the efforts in place to address them. Generally, the practitioner needs to get a client's permission to notify the family, but this is an important step to ensure that the support system is available to the client. On the surface, the client may not show visible depressive symptoms, which may give family members a false sense of security that the family member is okay and any difficulties can be addressed. When family and other members of the support system are not aware of the difficulties the client is having, they may expect him or her to resume normal family and occupational activities, resulting in emotional overload for the client. Many times clients do not respond as actively to these expectations as they did in the past, which may result in frustration for the client and other members of the environmental support system (Dziegielewski, 2010).

Furthermore, there are inherent risks in working with depressed clients that become particularly problematic when energy starts to return. When the client is taking medications to treat depression, for example, the symptoms being experienced may start to lift within the first few weeks of treatment. Then the client may want to discontinue the medication. Although all clients have the right to self-determination in medication and other aspects of their treatment, practitioners can educate them about the triggers and risk of relapse (Dziegielewski, 2010). Medication alone may not be enough to address some of the factors that caused the depression. It can help the client feel better with a resultant energy increase, but if only medication is used and the underlying problem is not addressed, the renewed energy could result in danger to self or others (Dziegielewski, 2010). Medication interventions should always be considered as part of the intervention and not all of it.

The danger inherent when the client's mood lifts too quickly without adequate support is further complicated when depression is grief-related. Grieving in general does not follow a particular pattern, and stages and responses can vary. What is considered normal grieving and its interpretation of life circumstances can change across the life span. For more in-depth reading in this area, see the work of Walter and McCoyd (2009). In addition, certain cultural groups grieve very differently from other cultural groups, and some awareness of what is considered normal for a culture versus what is considered pathological is required. The reactions a client experiences can easily become confused with what is considered a culturally acceptable response (Vazquez & Rosa, 2011). Application of the CFI, introduced in *DSM-5*, may be helpful in measuring cultural responses.

Honoring Self-Determination and Confidentiality: Danger to Self and Others

Many practitioners struggle with what can be revealed and what should not be revealed when they work with a suicidal client. Whether to involve family members and other members of the client's support system is always a difficult call to make, especially when the client does not want them notified. Questions of what can and cannot be shared can be difficult to answer. In terms of confidentiality, although statutory laws can differ across the states, Gamino and Ritter (2009) describe eight exceptions that allow the release of confidential information:

1. Client-authorized release of information
2. Imminent danger to self
3. Imminent danger to others
4. Neglect or abuse of children and vulnerable adults
5. Complaints or litigation against the counselor
6. Litigation concerning emotional pain and suffering
7. Court-ordered or statutory requirements to disclose
8. Requirements of third-party payers

For a complete discussion of these exceptions, see the work of Gamino and Ritter (2009).

Always try to get a client-authorized release of information. For any safety plan, it is important to get client permission to contact the family and make sure they are aware of the situation, any intervention efforts, and the safety plan itself. In addition, when establishing a safety plan assessing for danger to self or others, it is crucial to ensure that not only does the assessment involve information about what a client might do to himself or herself but also whether others are at risk.

Practitioners struggle with vague threats and whether the person would actually act on what he or she says would happen. Gamino and Ritter (2009) identify several factors that are particularly relevant to the seriousness of the threat. A combination of factors may complicate or worsen the potential for problems. For example, is the client male; recently divorced or separated, single, or widowed; over the age of 60; and lacking social support (especially no young children in the home)? Does the individual or another family member have a history of attempted suicide, unemployment, or financial difficulties? Is there a history of depression, a recent admission and discharge from a hospital, and/or alcohol use and abuse? Are firearms present?

When a practitioner is dealing with danger to self and others, issues surrounding the *Tarasoff v. The Regents of the University of California* (1976) are often cited. In this landmark case, an individual and the family were not warned by a therapist of a potential threat a client made against another individual that resulted in death.

To avoid the potential for harm, gathering a comprehensive summary of the situation while getting up-to-date information is essential. Expectations for protecting clients and duty to warn can differ among the states, and researching this topic and relating this information directly back to professional conduct is paramount. Also, on legal issues, always consult with an attorney. On professional or ethical issues, consult with a colleague or supervisor before you act in good faith to protect another from harm. Addressing the practitioner's professional code of ethics is mandatory. As a general rule, when debating whether to take action on duty to warn and when ethics are involved, before taking a specific action, always ask this question:

If I were held to a jury of my peers, would they do the same thing I am doing?

If so, be sure to outline the rationale for your decision.

Once professional ethical and legal implications have been addressed, and danger to self or others is suspected and ascertained, the individual(s) at risk, the police, and those involved may need to be notified. Gamino and Ritter (2009) remind the counselor to ask two critical questions before taking any action to protect others: (1) Is there a previous history of violent behavior toward people or animals? (2) Does the individual have possession of a firearm? If a client threatens to harm a member of a vulnerable population, such as children, an elderly individual, or a mentally impaired adult, mandatory reporting requires immediately addressing the situation and calling the local protective agency.

DEVELOPING THE TREATMENT PLAN

In developing the treatment plan for clients who suffer from mental health problems, several critical steps need to be identified (Jongsma et al., 2006).

1. Problem behaviors that are interfering with functioning must be identified. The ones that should receive the most attention are those that impair independent living skills or cause difficulties in completing tasks of daily living.
2. Once problem behaviors are identified, these behaviors need to be linked to the intervention process.
3. Involving the family and support system in treatment plan formulation and application can be especially helpful.

First, problem behaviors that are interfering with functioning must be identified. In practice, the client and his or her family must participate and assist in identifying the issues, problem behaviors, and coping styles that are either causing or contributing to the client's discomfort. Of all of the problem behaviors a client may be experiencing, the ones that should receive the most attention are those that impair independent living skills or cause difficulties in completing tasks of daily living. Once identified, these behaviors need to be linked to the intervention process. The identification of specific problem behaviors or coping styles can provide an opportunity to facilitate educational and communicative interventions that can further enhance communication between the client and family members. Involving the family and support system in treatment plan formulation and application can be especially helpful and productive because at times individuals experiencing mental confusion and distortions of reality may exhibit bizarre and unpredictable symptoms. If support systems are not included in the intervention planning process and the client's symptoms worsen, increased tension, frustration, fear, blame, and helplessness may develop in the connections between the client and the family system. To avoid the client withdrawing from his or her support systems, all components of the

QUICK REFERENCE 4.8

Sample of Identified Problem Behaviors

Identified problem behaviors often include:

Ambivalent feelings that impair general task completion related to independent living skills.

Affect disturbances, such as feelings of depression or a difficulty in controlling anger.

Problems with coping related to poor concentration and limited insight.

Associative disturbances, particularly in terms of inability to respond to being touched or approached by others.

family system of support need to be made aware of the treatment plan goals and objectives that will be used with the client. Also, the client must agree to share this information with the family system and allow current and continued involvement in each step of the intervention plan.

Second, not only do family and friends need to be aware of the treatment plan initiatives but also they need to be encouraged to share input and support to ensure intervention progress and success. Family education and supportive interventions for family and significant others can be listed as part of the treatment plan for an individual client. The multiple interventions available to the family members of the individual with mental illness are beyond the scope of this chapter; however, interested readers are encouraged to refer to Dziegielewski (2010), which provides strategies for working with individuals and families who have a relative suffering from mental illness that is also under medication management.

Third, to assist in treatment plan development, state the identified problem behaviors in terms of behavior-based outcomes (Dziegielewski, 2008). In completing this process, the assessment data that led to the diagnostic impression, as well as the specific problems the client often experiences, have to be outlined. Once identified, the client's problems are prioritized so that goals, objectives, and action tasks can be developed. Fourth, the goals of intervention, which are the basis for the plan of intervention, must be clearly outlined and applied. These goals must be broken down into specific objective statements that reflect target behaviors to be changed and ways to measure the client's progress on each objective. As subcomponents of the objectives, action tasks must clearly delineate the steps to be taken by the client and the helping professional to ensure successful completion of each objective.

Once the problem behaviors have been identified, the mental health practitioner must identify the goals and the behavior-based objectives that can be used to measure whether the identified problems have been addressed and resolved (see Quick Reference 4.8). If the problem behavior is ambivalent feelings that impair general task completion, for example, the main goal may be to help the client decrease feelings of ambivalence. A behavioral objective that clearly articulates a behavioral definition of ambivalence, ways that the ambivalence will be decreased, and the mechanisms used to determine if the behavior has changed must be documented. The therapeutic intervention is assisting the client in developing specific and concrete tasks geared toward decreasing this behavior and consequently meeting the objective. The outcome measure simply becomes establishing whether the task was completed. Each of the chapters in the applications section of this text and the appendix include hints on creating sample intervention plans for clients who suffer from different types of mental disorders. The treatment plan is not designed to be all-inclusive; rather, it provides guidelines for effective documentation of the assessment and intervention process. Treatment plans are to be viewed as starting points. Each diagnostic assessment and the treatment plan that results must be individualized for the client, outlining the specific problem behaviors and how each of these behaviors can be addressed.

In summary, the key to documenting the diagnostic assessment, treatment plan, and practice strategy is brevity while providing informative data. Documentation should record only the most salient issues relevant to client care and progress. Information should focus directly on content covered in the therapeutic sessions, as well as the interplay of the client's progress with the counseling interventions. The practitioner has to include the intervention strategies in the primary treatment plan. Always link the therapeutic interventions to the original problems, goals, and objectives identified. Today, approval of services is often related directly to documented treatment progress, goals, and objectives, and the need for clear documentation of these steps cannot be overemphasized (Russell-Chapin & Ivey, 2004).

Brief, accurate, and informative documentation that includes the diagnostic assessment, the treatment plan, and the practice strategy requires skill and training. Mental health practitioners must learn to document important information that will assist other professionals and oversight processes in providing the most effective interventions for clients. Doing this requires that vital client information gathered during the diagnostic assessment and intervention recommendations be combined in documentation that clearly identifies the client's problems, signs and symptoms, and past and current mental health history. Although the specific documentation format used by mental health practitioners often is determined by their practice setting, they should closely examine the format of choice and learn to integrate biopsychosocial and spiritual information that will be helpful in understanding the client and assist in formulating an effective intervention strategy. Van Dijk-deVries et al. (2012) note the importance of including this approach and getting the client's participation, especially with conditions that require chronic and continued care.

Outcome Measures

With the emphasis on treatment efficacy and accountability in today's practice environment, mental health practitioners must learn to include objective measures that help to evaluate the effects of counseling therapies on the client's functioning. Included in these measures are standardized scales, surveys, and rapid assessment instruments (RAIs). These tools provide evidence-based data that identify the changes over the course of the intervention. Mental health practitioners have to become familiar with and integrate measurement instruments in their practice and in their documentation to determine if treatment interventions have impacted baseline behaviors and problems (Dziegielewski, 2008). Furthermore, for specific populations, such as children, all measurement instruments are not created equal. Make sure that the measurement tool selected is appropriate for the population being examined as well as for the problem being elucidated. For more information on this topic, LeCroy and Okamoto (2009) outline specific considerations and measurement tools that are most sensitive to children.

Gathering pretreatment and posttreatment data on a client's course of treatment enables both the practitioner and the client to examine whether progress has occurred and provides regulatory agencies with tangible, objective evidence of client progress or decompensation. This single-system methodology, or the intensive or practice-oriented design, is used to draw conclusions about effectiveness in individual cases over time (Fischer, 2009). Designs such as this, along with standardized instruments, help satisfy the requirements of managed care organizations (Kane et al., 2002). By using a holistic framework that stresses the client's biopsychosocial factors, mental health practitioners play an important role in the efficient delivery of interdisciplinary health and mental health services.

Accurate record keeping increases effective communication and collaboration with other interdisciplinary health care team members on client progress and problems. Accurate, up-to-date, informative records are vital to the coordinated health care planning efforts of the entire team and most important to the client's health. (Sample Treatment Plan 4.1 provides an example of how to define the condition and break down problem behaviors into goals, objectives, and interventions for the client.)

SELECTING AN INTERVENTION FRAMEWORK

Most counseling professionals, regardless of discipline, agree that all practitioners should be familiar with multiple practice modalities and frameworks for utilization in therapy. Sommers-Flanagan and Sommers-Flanagan (2009) state that a broad range of training experience in a variety of settings allows utilization of multiple methods. The mission of all helping professionals is to engage in activity that enhances opportunities for all people in an increasingly complex environment. Because mental health practitioners can work with a variety of human systems, including individuals, families, groups, organizations, and communities, some type of orientation that guides practice structure is needed. Fischer (2009) suggests using a framework that can compare and analyze theories to determine which can best serve a client's needs. Regardless of which overarching framework is eventually used, it needs to be consistent with the professional values and ethics of the practitioner's discipline and respect the cultural differences of all involved. Defined simply, a *theoretical practice framework* is the structured ideas or beliefs that provide

SAMPLE TREATMENT PLAN 4.1

Uncomplicated Bereavement (V62.82 [*ICD-9-CM*] and Z63.4 [*ICD-10-CM*])

Definition: Clinical attention focusing on an individual's reaction, emotionally, behaviorally, and cognitively, to the death of a loved one. This is considered a normal reaction to the bereaving process.

Signs and Symptoms to Note in the Record:

Characteristics of a major depressive episode, including problems sleeping (insomnia), lack of appetite, and weight changes (particularly weight loss).

Guilt surrounding the death of the loved one.

Conversational superficiality with respect to the loved one's death.

Excessive emoting when the loved one's death is discussed.

(*continued*)

SAMPLE TREATMENT PLAN 4.1 (*Continued*)

Difficulty concentrating due to domination of thoughts surrounding loved one's death.

May seek professional when experiencing functional impairment(s).

Goals:

Acknowledge and accept the death of loved one.

Begin the grieving process and start to adjust to the death.

Resolve feelings over the death of loved one.

Reconnect with previous relationships and activities.

Objectives:

Identify and state individual steps to take in the grieving process.

Apply current feelings and actions that are related to the steps in the grieving process.

Express at least two emotions and feelings associated with this loss.

Problem-solve feelings of anger and guilt associated with the loss of loved one.

Interact and discuss the death of loved one with at least two significant others or family system members.

Interventions (Practitioner Initiated):

Practitioner will work with the client on gaining increased knowledge of the grieving process, specifically reviewing the stages of grief and how it relates to the client's thoughts and behaviors.

Practitioner will work with the client and ask the client to participate in "empty chair" exercise, where he or she verbally expresses feelings not verbalized to the deceased loved one in life.

Practitioner will recommend and assist the client in getting started with tasks to be completed and discussed in therapy (e.g., writing a letter to the loved one, selecting a family member or friend to discuss the grieving process).

Interventions (Client Initiated):

Client will seek out at least one other person who has experienced the loss of a loved one to discuss what she or he is feeling and how that individual has tried to cope.

Client will create a journal of emotions related to this loss to be discussed in individual therapy.

Client will write a letter to the lost loved one, expressing feelings and emotions, memories, and regrets associated with loss to be discussed in individual therapy.

Client will attend a bereavement support group.

Client will interact with one mutual friend of the client and the deceased and share feelings about this loss, discussing the impact it has had on the living.

the foundation for the helping activity that is to be performed. Clients need assistance in functional recovery. With whichever method is used, an emphasis on self-motivation and empowerment, especially for those who suffer from a mental disorder, should be at the heart of the strategy (Kern, Glynn, Horan, & Marder, 2009).

In mental health practice, many people use the words *theory* and *practice methods* or *strategy* interchangeably. Because they coexist (and in practice, one without the other cannot exist for long), this linking is understandable. However, theory and methods of practice strategy are not the same thing. A theoretical foundation provides the practitioner with the basics or the concepts of what can be done and why it is essential. The method or practice strategy is the doing part of the helping relationship. It is the outline or the plan for the helping activity that is generally guided by theoretical principles and concepts.

In mental health practice, attention needs to be given to selecting the best treatment approaches that form the basis for practice (Mandell & Schram, 2006). The diversity of clients and the uniqueness of each helping relationship require the practitioner to be well versed in theory and practice and resilient in his or her ability to adapt this foundation to the needs of the client and the situation. Mental health practitioners have a delicate balancing act in blending theoretical concepts and frameworks that direct practice strategy. Doing this requires practitioners to be flexible in their approach as they deal with a multitude of different clients and different problems (Sommers-Flanagan & Sommers-Flanagan, 2009). To design and initiate professional practice strategy, practitioners must often go beyond the traditional bounds of their practice wisdom.

Utilizing DSM-5 *When Selecting a Practice Framework*

The *DSM-5* is a diagnostic tool that can help practitioners develop a comprehensive diagnostic assessment. Once established, the diagnostic assessment can be used to develop an appropriate intervention plan. Developing an intervention plan and selecting appropriate practice strategies require using the information gathered from the diagnostic assessment to decide how to formulate the intervention plan and identify the best ways to engage the client. To begin this process, helping professionals must first be aware of the theoretical principles that underlie certain types of helping activity. Practitioners need to be prepared to pick and choose which theoretical concepts and practice strategies will offer the greatest assistance in formulating the helping process. Thus, practitioners should review theoretical principles in terms of their application to the problem behaviors noted. They cannot marry a particular theoretical model or its subsequent treatment—"one size fits all" is not suitable here.

First and foremost, the helping strategy must be firmly based within the reality of the client's cultural expectations and his or her environment (Vazquez & Rosa, 2011). At times, however, making this link may seem difficult or time consuming. Regardless, considering the impact of the client's environment on the practice method selected remains essential. For example, if a client is diagnosed with substance abuse and, after receiving treatment, is discharged back into an environment that is conducive to their once again beginning to abuse a substance, much of the influence of the intervention is negated. In one case, a client diagnosed with problematic substance use was admitted repeatedly to alcohol rehabilitation and treatment centers. The client always responded well to treatment while in the program but upon discharge quickly relapsed. After numerous intervention failures with this client, the mental health practitioner thoroughly assessed his situation and home environment. The practitioner quickly learned that the client was unable to maintain a bank account as a result of his instability and troubles with alcohol. He used the street address of a local bar to have his

QUICK REFERENCE 4.9

DEFINITIONS OF THEORETICAL CONCEPTS

Cognitive-behavioral therapy: A method of practice that uses the combination of selected techniques incorporating the theories of behaviorism, social learning theory, and cognition theories to understand and address a client's behavior.

Crisis intervention: A practice strategy used to help clients in crisis regain a sense of healthy equilibrium.

Educative counseling: A loosely defined approach to practice that focuses on helping the client become an educated consumer and through this information be better able to address his or her own needs.

Interpersonal therapy: A form of time-limited treatment often used in the medical setting. Generally, this method involves an assessment that includes a diagnostic evaluation and psychiatric history. In this type of therapy, the focus of treatment is interpersonal problem areas, such as grief, role disputes, role transitions, or deficits.

Psychotherapy: A form of therapy that involves understanding the individual in regard to his or her personal situation.

Social Security check sent. When his check arrived each month, he went to pick it up and cash it. To complicate matters further, the bar had a policy that it would cash checks only if a purchase was made, which contributed to the client's relapse. Awareness of the client's environment was a critical component in applying an appropriate helping strategy. Thus, anticipating the effect that a client's environment can have on intervention outcome is essential (Colby & Dziegielewski, 2010; Dziegielewski, 2013). In addition, trying to reconnect with friends and family has traditionally involved alcohol at the dinner table or present at other gatherings. When environmental factors were not previously addressed and behaviors on how to handle them were not rehearsed, avoiding alcohol on these occasions became a difficult task, leading to relapse. Without addressing the cultural and family system dynamics, he could easily fall back into patterns that seemed to work for other family members but were not possible for him.

In selecting a framework for the practice strategy, a second ingredient that is essential for formulating constructive helping activity is that all efforts are guided by theoretical concepts that are consistent with the needs and desires of the individual, group, family, or community being served (see Quick Reference 4.9). Furthermore, the theoretical framework must be consistent and reflect the values and ethics of the practitioner's profession. Selection of a theoretical framework to guide the interaction may not be as simple as knowing what models and methods are available and selecting one. When choosing a method of practice, feeling influenced and subsequently trapped within a system that is driven by social, political, cultural, and economic factors is not uncommon. With the numerous demands of today's practice environment, it is difficult not to be influenced by these factors, and often they can dictate the practice basis that is employed.

Mental health providers are often presented with problems as diverse as the individuals they treat. We live in a world filled with diversity, and treatment needs to include how diversity can affect both the client and the practitioner (Locke & Bailey, 2014). Once identified, these problems must be addressed within the framework of a client's unique circumstances (e.g., indigent or disadvantaged clients or clients who are culturally different from the majority culture in terms of ethnicity, race, or sexual orientation). How might all or any of these factors affect the helping relationship and practice strategy? How do mental health practitioners maintain the dignity and worth of each client and balance their own feelings and possible prejudices so that those feelings and prejudices do not compromise the helping relationship? To address these questions thoroughly would fill several books. In short, each situation must be dealt with individually, and mental health practitioners should take care to identify potential problems and seek supervisory help when needed.

PRACTICE STRATEGY AND APPLICATION

Selecting the most appropriate practice method requires helping professionals to consider a multitude of factors related to the individual and his or her family and support system. The treatment plan is the first step in this process, and the practice strategy accomplishes the services outlined. Important in every step of the assessment process and treatment strategy is recognition of the support system. Taking it into account as part of the assessment and helping activity maximizes overall client well-being. In some cases, families may be resistant to counseling and remain unconvinced that this type of intervention is necessary. For example, in the case of parents working with the problematic behaviors of their child, keeping the family as a nurturing unit as well as a rule-setting unit can be a difficult balance that can lead to frustration on many levels (Landy & Bradley, 2014).

In addition, other helping professionals may not recognize the importance of mental health professionals in improving clients' functioning (Lambert, Bergin, & Garfield, 2004). As mental health services are demystified and affirmed by the media, public policy makers, and the general public, access to these types of services will continue to improve. Most clients and their families, as well as other helping professionals, now recognize the importance of counseling (Dziegielewski, 2013; Lambert et al., 2004).

A basic assessment, intervention plan, and referral process initiated by the mental health professional can help clients promote and protect their physical as well as mental health. No matter how seasoned a practitioner may become, determining how to best handle a client's situation in the helping relationship will never be an easy task. It requires a constant process of assessing, reassessing, and collaborating with other professionals. Furthermore, in a professional team, professional opinions vary on how to interpret, best select, and apply these strategies for helping. Working together as a team and incorporating the helping ideas and strategies of each of the members improve the care available to vulnerable populations (Malone, Marriott, Newton-Howes, Simmonds, & Tyrer, 2009).

Although explaining how to select from among the many theoretical and practice frameworks available to mental health practitioners is beyond the scope of this chapter, a brief presentation of several of the most common methods of practice and how they can be related to client intervention follows. Practice principles are presented to stress the importance of inclusion when selecting a practice method prior to embarking on the direct application of process to outcome.

Mixing Art and Science: Utilizing an Empowering Approach

In most schools that train mental health practitioners, students have traditionally been taught that the practice application can be defined in phases (even when they are not clearly established), with each application having a beginning, middle, and end. This format is often presented in time-limited practice models. One of the greatest lessons professionals learn is that many times when applying the *science* of practice (i.e., identifying clear goals, objectives, and indicators for practice strategy), the intervention process has a predictable beginning, middle, and end. However, the *art* of practice acknowledges that at times nothing is predictable and even the best-made intervention plans need constant modification and renegotiating. Balancing art and science requires understanding that addressing and subsequently assisting in solving clients' problems is never as easy as it might seem to the untrained observer.

In mental health practice today, *client empowerment* is very important. The uniqueness of the individual must always be accentuated and highlighted in each step of the helping process, regardless of the method of practice that is selected. Almost all clients respond favorably to being acknowledged for their strengths and challenged to maximize their own potential (Jones-Smith, 2014).

Utilizing Time-Limited Practice in Behavioral Health Care

Mental health practitioners must recognize that current practice will be brief and all intervention strategies must be linked to behavior-based outcomes (Dziegielewski, 2008). There are many reasons for this trend. Probably the most significant reason is trying to control today's health care expenses, which continue to rise. In 2012, health care spending rose 50% faster than the gross national product and is already close to 20% of the economy (Hixon, 2012). Critics are quick to point out that the United States continues to spend far more per person on health care than any other country in the world (Hofschire, 2012). As the reality of our current situation sinks in and the budget implications grow, managed care philosophies appear to once again be gaining popularity (Dziegielewski, 2013). Insurers are responding to pressures from the public and employee organizations, and costs for health care are shifting more to the employee, with the promise that this shift will result in lower premiums (Mathews, 2012).

Regardless of the type of treatment provided, to receive reimbursement, practitioners must follow the expectations and subsequent limitations to service imposed by insurance reimbursement patterns (Sommers-Flanagan & Sommers-Flanagan, 2009). Insurance companies usually will not pay for long-term treatment. To ensure that practitioners are reimbursed for their services, very specific time-limited approaches are essential. Following this trend, behavioral contracts have gained popularity because they clearly allow outlining of costs for all, including the insurance provider, the program, and the client (Houmanfar, Maglieri, Roman, & Ward, 2008). In defense of this trend, many clients (especially the poor) do not have the time, desire, or money for long-term treatment. Many individuals are not willing to commit the extra time or energy to go beyond addressing what is causing the problem. For mental health practitioners who believe in long-term, comprehensive clinical helping relationships, this trend is very frustrating. Today, there is little emphasis on amorphous clinical judgments and vague attempts at making clients feel better, as these efforts are no longer supported. In most areas of mental health practice, the days of insurance-covered long-term therapy have ended.

For all professionals, starting the helping activity can be complicated by the fact that in today's turbulent and changing practice environment, selecting a practice framework depends on more than just what is best for the client. With the advent of coordinated care plans, practice strategy will need to balance the quality and effectiveness of the care provided with the cost-effectiveness of the service being delivered. A further complication is the advent of coordinated care, where insurance purchase has become mandatory. Because it is hard at times to quantify the helping benefits that clients receive, many professionals believe that even with coordinated care policies, in the battle between quality and cost-effectiveness, generally the latter wins. Therefore, even the most seasoned practitioners have to battle the expectation of providing what they believe is the most beneficial and ethical practice possible, while being pressured to complete it as quickly and efficiently as reasonable.

A further complication to selecting a method of practice in mental health is that defending a type of treatment viewed as in the best interest of the client may not truly reflect the client's wishes. Promises of lower premiums and health care expenditures have changed clients' perspectives and expectations for treatment. This pressure makes it crucial for practitioners to work quickly in setting up and outlining a course of treatment (Sommers-Flanagan & Sommers-Flanagan, 2009). Clients now may request a specific type of intervention or therapy that addresses only certain problems because they are concerned about whether their insurance plan covers the service. It is not uncommon for clients to be more interested in receiving a service that is time-limited or reimbursable, regardless of the expected benefit that may be gained from an alternate, possibly longer-term, intervention strategy.

Practice reality dictates that the duration of most practice sessions, regardless of the methodology used or the orientation of the mental health practitioner, remains relatively brief. Research on treatment duration and effectiveness suggests that 13 to 18 sessions are needed for client change to occur, but in a large multisite study, the average number of sessions clients attended was less than five and a third attended only one (Hansen, Lambert, & Forman, 2002). For many practitioners, seeing a client only once is becoming commonplace. Furthermore, so much of what practitioners do can no longer fall under the heading of brief therapy because much intervention no longer has clear beginnings and endings. Formal types of brief therapy have been replaced by intermittent types of therapy, where intervention is provided when a client comes in, and each session is considered to stand alone. Regardless of exactly what type of theoretical framework is utilized, a realization that most practice encounters are going to be brief and self-contained is essential (Sommers-Flanagan & Sommers-Flanagan, 2009). Planning for this short-term or single-session duration in implementing the helping strategy is critical (Dziegielewski, 2013). Without it, lack of planning can result in numerous unexpected and unplanned endings for the client (Wells, 2010). It can also contribute to feelings of failure and decreased job satisfaction for mental health professionals.

Time-Limited Brief Therapies

Many mental health practitioners who practice traditional forms of psychotherapy, particularly those who support psychoanalytic therapy, believe that time-limited expectations and subsequent counseling practice remain biased against them. Many practitioners trained in traditional forms of therapy and counseling believe that making changes in a person takes time and that rushing into changes could lead to complications in a client's future health and wellness. Yet given the practice reality of time-limited expectations, some practitioners continue their search for the Holy Grail, highlighting the one theory that does the most to help the client (Magnavita & Anchin, 2014). Yet all practitioners, regardless of their approach, realize that practice delivery in today's big business practice environment must be comprehensive and reflect best practices, regardless of the approach.

At times, traditional forms of psychotherapy such as long-term therapy can present a particular problem for poor and disadvantaged clients. They generally do not have the time or finances to afford long-term therapy, referred to in some circles as a long-term luxury. Today, the majority of practitioners have for years shunned the traditional approaches in favor of the applicability and effectiveness of time-limited practice methods (Dziegielewski, 2013; Wells, 2010). Studies suggest that practitioners who are successful in the managed care environment use problem-solving, short-term treatment models (Chambliss, 2000).

Time-limited therapies have the overall objective of bringing about positive changes in a client's current lifestyle with as little face-to-face contact as possible. This emphasis on effectiveness and evidence-based treatments with applicability leading to increased positive change has helped to make briefer treatments popular (Sommers-Flanagan & Sommers-Flanagan, 2009). In general, time-limited approaches are the most often requested forms of practice in use today.

The foundations for traditional psychotherapy and time-limited or intermittent approaches are quite different. This difference requires practitioners to reexamine some basic premises about long-term therapeutic models in a more traditional format. According to Dziegielewski (2013), seven factors highlight the differences between these two methods.

1. A primary difference is the way the client is viewed. Traditional psychotherapeutic approaches often link individual problems to personal pathology. In a time-limited perspective, the client is seen as a basically healthy individual with an interest in increasing personal or social changes or both (Budman & Gurman, 2002; Roberts & Dziegielewski, 1995). In current mental health practice, the focus on empowerment extends the belief that clients are not only capable of change but also aware and active participants in this process. Traditional psychoanalytic approaches emphasize that the client is often unaware and unable to access this information because it lies beneath the surface of the client's awareness at a preconscious or unconscious level. These approaches make empowerment difficult to foster and do not highlight the client's strengths in becoming an active participant in the practice strategy employed.
2. Time-limited approaches are most helpful during critical periods in a person's life (Roberts & Dziegielewski, 1995). A time-limited framework provides a basic difference from traditional psychotherapies, which are seen as necessary and continuing over a much longer period.
3. In time-limited brief treatment, the goals and objectives of therapy are always mutually defined by both the client and the therapist (Wells, 2010). In traditional psychotherapeutic approaches, goals are often first recognized and defined by the therapist and later shared with the client (Budman & Gurman, 2002).
4. In time-limited therapy, goals are concretely defined and often addressed outside the actual therapy session in the

form of homework or other activities (Jacobs, 2008; Tompkins, 2004). One example is bibliotherapy (the use of outside reading materials as an adjunct to office sessions). In traditional psychotherapeutic approaches, issues are generally addressed during the sessions only, not outside them (Budman & Gurman, 2002). The presence of the therapist is seen as the catalyst for change. When bibliotherapy is used as part of the treatment, particularly in cognitive-behavioral approaches (CBT), treatment manuals that outline what is to be done are often used (Papworth, 2006).

5. Time-limited intervention, regardless of the model, places little emphasis on insight. This difference between brief approaches and traditional psychotherapy is one of the hardest to accept for mental health practitioners who were educated with a traditional psychotherapeutic methodology. In traditional psychotherapy, problem-oriented insight is considered necessary before any type of meaningful change can take place.
6. Time-limited approaches to practice are seen as active and directive. Here the mental health practitioner often goes beyond active listening and assumes a consultative role with the client (Wells, 2010). This approach results in the development of concrete goals and problem-solving techniques and is very different from traditional psychotherapeutic approaches that emphasize a more nebulous inner representation of satisfaction.
7. In time-limited settings, termination is discussed early in the therapeutic process (Wells, 2010). Often the practitioner begins to plan for termination in the first session, and termination issues are discussed continually throughout the intervention process. By contrast, traditional psychotherapy may never address termination issues in advance. Preparation for termination is not typically considered an essential part of the therapy process.

TYPES OF TIME-LIMITED THERAPY IN MENTAL HEALTH PRACTICE

Here several models usually linked to the provision of time-limited counseling services are reviewed. However, these models do not represent all of the major models of practice for mental health counseling. This review briefly describes the types of models and methods available, as well as the tradition from which they were developed. Regardless of the method used, all practice approaches share the desire for change that will reduce pain or suffering for the client (Herbert, Forman, & England, 2008). In Section II of this book, each of the mental health disorders and conditions presented describes a currently accepted treatment or intervention strategy. To provide an overview of several current therapeutic approaches, these models for practice will be briefly summarized: interpersonal psychotherapeutic or psychodynamic approaches; strategic or solution-oriented therapies; cognitive-behavioral approaches; crisis intervention; and health, education, and wellness counseling. Cases highlight each of these approaches. In the psychodynamic aspects of therapeutic practice, emphasis is placed on understanding the internal workings of the individual. In the solution-focused therapies, the solution (or course of action) is identified, and specific attempts are made to attain it. In the cognitive-behavioral approaches, the focus is on understanding the complex relationship between socialization and reinforcement as it affects thoughts and behaviors in the current environment. In crisis intervention the focus is on helping to establish an improved way of coping when the usual practices for doing so do not work. The final application is a form of time-limited therapy in which practitioners focus on providing health counseling and education based on the principle of creating and maintaining wellness.

No method of practice can call itself a clean mental health practice theory. In mental health practice, ideas and theoretical concepts have been blended and altered to best serve the client. For example, Brandell (2004) warns that even psychodynamic approaches are compilations of multiple theories, models, and schemata. Thus, there is substantial overlap in the information presented for each approach. We are still in the process of developing and redefining standardized treatment guidelines based on empirical evidence, and just as professionals may be conflicted, imagine the concerns a client must feel in trying to select a therapist and follow an approach (Magnavita & Anchin, 2014).

When selecting an approach, the practitioner may first start using one mode of practice and then incorporate pieces of other methods of intervention to assist the client in the most efficient and effective way possible. Very often the mental health practitioner is expected to mix and match practice strategies, using what works to help the client. This can create a type of alphabet soup, where pieces or techniques become the focus (Magnavita & Anchin, 2014). There must be some theoretical understanding of why certain techniques are being used and how selecting these methods must be consistent with the practitioner's professional ethics and standards. When a type of therapy is used, the basic premises of the method should reflect not only the title but also what is actually being done (Simon, 2010).

Psychodynamic Approaches

Psychodynamic approaches allow past experiences to be blended with present ones (Brandell, 2004). These approaches are often credited as the foundation of mental health casework, and their premise is that focusing on history and past issues can lend credence to current problem-solving efforts. For utilizing a biopsychosocial perspective, this form of psychodynamic intervention gained credibility and recognition among many health care professionals as an interdisciplinary approach. For example, historically this type of approach to practice was used in medical settings where interdisciplinary teams assisted clients in addressing their needs. In this practice framework, helping professionals are seen as active, supportive, and a contributing factor in therapeutic gain. In general, these models are often used to directly address symptom removal and prevention of relapse and to help clients having difficulty relating to significant others, careers, social roles, and/or life transitions (Goldstein & Noonan, 2001).

Psychodynamic approaches focus clinical attention on the conscious (individual awareness) and the unconscious (beyond individual awareness). Next, these factors are identified, outlined, reviewed, and addressed as part of the practice strategy. For the most part, as evidenced by Case Example 4.1, most of the psychodynamic approaches used in practice today portray the unconscious as immediately accessible and changeable (Goldstein & Noonan, 2001).

In the case of John (see Case Example 4.1), the intervention addressed the client's present situation and focused on the here and now (Weissman, Markowitz, & Klerman, 2007). Similar to what was done in this case, the focus of the intervention is on recent interpersonal events (the death of John's mother) with a clear effort to link the stressful event to John's current mood and actions (crying out for attention by making obscene phone calls).

Information is gathered in the diagnostic assessment, along with a psychiatric history. When completing the diagnostic assessment,

CASE EXAMPLE 4.1 - CASE OF JOHN

Mr. Jones brought his 12-year-old son, John, for assessment after he discovered that his son had been making obscene phone calls. John had never been in trouble before, and after being charged legally and sent to court, a judge decided that John could benefit from a mental health assessment rather than proceeding with further legal action. It was obvious during the interview that the father was extremely frustrated with the situation and could not understand why John had been engaging in this type of behavior. During his interview, John became very nervous. He seemed embarrassed to talk about what he had done and kept his head down, looking directly at the floor, as he spoke.

The mental health practitioner asked John what had happened. John described exactly what he had done, the phone calls he had made, and the obscene comments he had made to the women who answered the phone. John seemed embarrassed by his behavior but appeared honest in telling what he had done. When asked how he had gotten caught making the calls, John calmly stated that when asked, he gave his name. The practitioner was surprised and tried to clarify what he said. Again John stated that when the recipient of the obscene phone call asked who was calling, John told her his name. After hearing John tell of what he had done and how he had gotten caught, John's father voiced his frustration, anger, and shock with his son's behavior. He openly stated that he was alarmed by the behavior and could not understand it. The fact that John was leaving his name when asked caused the practitioner to feel that there was more here than simply acting out, as the father had stated.

In gathering information for the diagnostic assessment, the practitioner asked if John had ever been in trouble before. John and his father agreed that he had not. Since this appeared inconsistent with his behavior, the practitioner asked if anything out of the ordinary had happened to upset John or disturb him. John stated he was not aware of anything. When asked specifically if there had been any changes in the past few months, John's father responded. According to him, John's mother had died approximately 6 weeks before. Once the practitioner began to explore the mother's death and the child's feelings, it became clear that John was indeed having difficulty adjusting to his mother's death. It appeared as if John was making the phone calls and leaving his name as an attempt to cry out for attention or help. After beginning to discuss the death of his mother with the practitioner, John was also able to voice his fear that his father might die as well and leave him alone. The practitioner concluded that John did not suffer from a mental disorder at all but rather was suffering from bereavement (related to the death of his mother), and his reaction was an adolescent antisocial act (making the obscene phone calls).

The role of the mental health practitioner is to gather a comprehensive assessment exploring why things are happening as they are. In this case, many issues surrounding the mother's death remained unresolved. Furthermore, it appeared as if the child might in his own way be crying out for help and attention from the father. The approach the practitioner took was to explore the relationship between John and his father, as well as look at how their past relationship could balance and strengthen the present one. This approach utilized the concepts relevant in ego psychology, a form of psychodynamic therapy. In this approach, the practitioner helped to address the situation, plant a seed as to what was happening, create a release of tension and energy for John and his father, and later help them to reintegrate, address, and discontinue the problematic behaviors that had resulted.

Minimally trained professionals should not engage in these types of psychodynamic approaches as graduate-level training and expertise are usually required. Professionals without graduate-level training and experience should refer clients to a qualified practitioner if they believe this type of approach would best serve the client. Overall, however, as can be seen in this case, the more a mental health practitioner knows in terms of practice strategy and frameworks, the more he or she can

(*continued*)

CASE EXAMPLE 4.1 - CASE OF JOHN (CONTINUED)

pick and choose the best helping approach. For John, exploring the reasons for his making the phone calls and the relationship between the problem behavior and his mother's death was crucial. In making this connection, John was helped to address his feelings, and he was able to stop making the phone calls as a means of getting attention. Once his feelings were addressed, a behavioral plan to stop problematic behaviors from occurring again was implemented.

---

the mental health practitioner is expected to pay particular attention to the client's family and support system interactions, including changes in relationships proximal to the onset of symptoms. In general, the focus of treatment is interpersonal problem areas such as grief, role disputes, role transitions, and deficits (Weissman et al., 2007). Focusing on one of these interpersonal areas allows the practitioner to identify problems in the interpersonal and social context that need to be addressed (Weissman et al., 2007).

Utilizing a psychodynamic approach, the mental health practitioner and the client work together to identify issues for the treatment plan and establish the goals and objectives that will later be addressed in the practice strategy. Practice strategy must be directly related to the identified interpersonal problem. For example, if a role conflict exists between a client and his or her family member in regard to substance use and abuse, practice strategy would begin by clarifying the nature of the dispute. Discussion of the problem would result in an explanation of usual limitations that often are beyond the client's control. Limitations that are causing the greatest disagreements are identified, and options to resolve the disputes are considered. If resolution does not appear possible, strategies or alternatives to replace the problematic behaviors are contemplated. In some cases, application manuals can be acquired and followed that give specific practice steps for approaching certain interpersonal problem areas (Weissman et al., 2007).

When applying the psychodynamic method of practice, mental health practitioners are expected to help clients identify issues of concern and provide the groundwork for how they can be addressed. Many times this includes helping the client to learn how to recognize the need for continued help and assistance through counseling, especially when problems seem greater than the client is capable of handling at the time (Dziegielewski, 2013). Regardless of who is actually assisting the client, the role of the practitioner in this form of practice is an important one. Most important, the practitioner must always remain influential in helping the client feel comfortable about seeking additional help when needed. This help-seeking behavior is an important step in establishing and maintaining a basis for continued health and wellness.

Solution-Focused Approaches

Solution-focused brief therapy (SFBT) is a short-term treatment intervention that focuses on creating solutions to a client's problems (de Shazer, 1988). From this perspective, solution building rather than problem solving is the focus (Iveson, 2002; Simon, 2010). In practice, solution-focused models are different in focus from the more traditional problem-solving methods because they do not spend much time on problem identification as the key ingredient to the practice encounter. The focus is on client's strengths and using these strengths to build solutions to current problems (Greenberg, Ganshorn, & Danilkewich,

CASE EXAMPLE 4.2 - CASE OF JIM

Jim was referred for a mental health assessment requesting help because he was having difficulty interacting with his child. His wife constantly complained that he did not show enough attention and concern for their disabled child. Jim stated he loved his son very much but was not particularly comfortable showing it. He did not like the way his son, who suffered from a moderate intellectual disability, always demanded to be hugged after completing tasks. When asked whether he believed that it was important to show affection, Jim agreed but stated that he just was not sure how to go about it. Furthermore, he felt that his son was expecting too much love and attention and should be able to function without always requiring that it be given.

When Jim sought intervention assistance, he made it very clear that his insurance company would allow only three sessions and that was what he was going to stick with. After completing a diagnostic assessment, the social work practitioner felt that a solution-focused approach to intervention would be best for Jim. Although his symptoms were problematic, they did not seem severe enough to affect Jim's overall functioning. In helping Jim develop a change strategy, the practitioner (a) focused on what Jim saw as the problem, (b) let Jim establish what he perceived as the desired outcome, (c) helped Jim begin to analyze and develop solutions focusing on his own individual strengths, (d) helped Jim develop and implement a plan of action, and (e) assisted with termination and follow-up issues if needed (Dziegielewski, 2013).

In summary, in this case, the social worker was active in helping the client find and identify strengths in his current functional patterns of behavior. A dialogue of change talk was created rather than problem talk (Walter & Peller, 1992). In change talk, the problem is viewed positively, highlighting patterns of change that appear successful for the client. Positive aspects and exceptions to the problem are explored, allowing alternate views of the problem to develop. Once the small changes have been highlighted, the client becomes empowered to elicit larger ones (de Shazer & Dolan, 2007). Jim looked at what he was doing, and the practitioner helped him establish alternative ways of acting and behaving when his son approached him. They also developed ways for him to discuss with his wife his feelings and his strategy for building independence in his son.

2001; Jones-Smith, 2014). Smock et al. (2008), similar to Metcalf (1998), believe SFBT is particularly helpful for individuals struggling with out-of-control behaviors such as substance abuse. This model is also used in settings such as schools, where short-term interventions are expected (Brasher, 2009). Solution-focused models assume that clients are basically healthy individuals who possess the skills they need to address their problems and who remain capable of change. Thus, this method focuses on identifying solutions to resolving the client's stated concern. This popular treatment strategy does not require a causal link between the antecedent (what comes before the problem behavior) and the actual problem. Since this causal connection is not made, a direct link need not be established between the problem and the solution (De Shazer & Dolan, 2007). (See Case Example 4.2.)

Cognitive-Behavioral Approaches to Mental Health Practice

Cognitive-behavioral therapy often involves concrete and focused strategies to help clients change irrational thoughts or behaviors that can complicate the helping process. This type of practice approach gained popularity in the early 1970s, when the focus was originally on the applied behavior and the power of reinforcement on the influence of human behavior (Skinner, 1953). However, many theorists believed that behavior alone was not enough and that human beings acted or reacted based on an analysis of the situation and the thought patterns that motivated them. Here the thought process, and how cognitive processes and structures influence individual emotions, was highlighted (Roberts & Dziegielewski, 1995; MacLaren & Freeman, 2007). Over the past decade, a significant movement has emerged that focuses not only on changing cognitions but at times simply accepting them (Herbert et al., 2008). To understand the problem thoughts and related behaviors, a schema is developed. The schema is generally referred to as the cognitive structure that organizes experience and behavior (Beck, Freeman, & Associates, 1990). The treatment that follows is based on the way a client conceptualizes the problems and rests in the specific beliefs and patterns of behavior that result (Beck, 2011). When utilizing this perspective, the practitioner must be skilled and practice multiple approaches covering standard behavioral, cognitive, acceptance, and mindfulness strategies (O'Donohue & Fisher, 2008).

Overall, cognitive-behavioral approaches to practice focus on the present and seek to replace distorted thoughts and/or unwanted behaviors with clearly established goals (Beck, 2011). In the cognitive-behavioral approach, the goals and objectives set should always be based in evidence-based research that supports the practice (Magnavita & Anchin, 2014). In addition, these goals should always be stated positively and realistically to increase motivation for completion. To facilitate the measurement of

CASE EXAMPLE 4.3 - CASE OF JILL

Jill sought the assistance of a mental health practitioner after becoming extremely frustrated with her ability to take tests in college. She often became so anxious that she could not focus or concentrate, rendering her unable to put on paper what she really did know in her head. After interviewing Jill, the practitioner decided a type of cognitive-behavioral therapy would probably be best to address her test anxiety.

As the first step in this helping process, the practitioner asked Jill to keep a diary. In the diary, she was asked to record the specific thoughts, feelings, and emotions she experienced when she was put in stressful situations—particularly testing situations. Jill kept the diary for 7 days and brought it to her next session. At that session, the practitioner reviewed the comments Jill had written and realized much of what was noted was self-defeating phrases and thoughts. For example, Jill often reported feeling stupid and useless. She also stated that she could remember her older brothers telling her how stupid she was.

Jill's schema revolved around her feelings of inadequacy and her belief that she was not smart enough to succeed in college. Once it was triggered by the stress of a test, she could no longer function. It was her interpretation of these events that influenced her reaction, resulting in cognitive distortion when interpreting a current situation or event. Therefore, the role of the mental health practitioner in this framework was to help Jill identify her negative and self-defeating thoughts and to replace them with more productive and fruitful ones.

The mental health practitioner helped Jill look at each of the statements in her diary and analyze them. Many times they practiced rewriting the statements or inserting more positive self-statements. Basically, the practitioner helped Jill rethink the comments she was saying to herself and replace them with more positive and productive statements.

effectiveness of what is being done, objectives must be stated in concrete and functional terms. In setting appropriate objectives, the focus is not necessarily on process but rather on the outcome that is desired (Roberts & Dziegielewski, 1995). Often a behavioral contract, either oral or written, is developed to clearly outline the expectations, plans, and/or contingencies for the behaviors. These contracts help to ensure that goals are agreed on; can monitor progress; outline responsibilities such as time, effort, and money; and ensure all involved are committed to the plan that is to be completed (Houmanfar et al., 2008). Adapting cognitive and behavioral principles in the time-limited framework creates a viable climate for change (MacLaren & Freeman, 2007). (See Case Example 4.3.)

In working with client problems such as Jill's, a cognitive-behavioral approach can be very helpful, especially for professionals who must deal with clients who are suffering from a variety of personal and situational problems. Thoughts can be difficult to control, and often clients become extremely frustrated with their inability to control their own actions and behaviors and perform poorly in areas in which they previously were proficient. When faced with a medical situation, they may develop negative schemata or ways of dealing with the situation that cause conflicts in their physical, interpersonal, and social relationships. Specific techniques such as identification of irrational beliefs, cognitive restructuring, behavioral role rehearsal, skill training, activity scheduling, self-reinforcement, and systematic desensitization can help clients adjust and accommodate to the new life status that will result (MacLaren & Freeman, 2007). Cognitive and behavioral techniques can help clients recognize these needs for change as well as assist with a plan to provide the behavior change needed for continued health and functioning.

Crisis Intervention Approaches to Mental Health Practice

A *crisis* is defined as a period of psychological disequilibrium that results from a hazardous event or situation (Yeager, Roberts, & Grainger, 2008). Kanel (2012) takes this definition further and refers to it as a trilogy involving (1) the precipitating event, (2) the perception or interpretation of the event that causes the individual distress, and (3) a failure of previous coping methods that leaves the individual at a lower level of functioning than prior to the event. Often the person in crisis becomes frustrated as his or her usual ways of coping simply do not seem to work. The practitioner assists clients in crisis by focusing on the immediate or acute problem situations. From this perspective, clients are helped to discover an adaptive means of coping with a particular life stage, tragic occurrence, or other problem that generates a crisis situation. Crisis intervention techniques are employed in many settings: social and relief agencies, the military, private practice, shelters, hospitals (especially hospital emergency rooms), public health agencies, hospices, home health care agencies, and almost all other agencies and services that utilize mental health professionals. Professionals have used crisis intervention techniques with migrant workers; rape survivors; domestic violence victims; death and dying; mental illness; event trauma, such as plane crashes, floods, and tornadoes; and whenever immediate help and assistance is needed (Roberts, 2005).

By its very nature, crisis intervention is time limited. All efforts are directed at solving immediate problems, emotional conflicts, and distress (Green & Roberts, 2008). Therefore, the first criterion in this method is the realization that all practice approaches are often going to be intense over a time-limited duration (Roberts & Dziegielewski, 1995). In crisis intervention, practice strategy is dictated within a specific time frame for accomplishment. According to Parad and

Parad (1990), utilizing minimum therapeutic practice strategy during the brief crisis period can often produce the maximum therapeutic effect. When a client is suffering from a crisis, supportive social resources and focused intervention techniques to facilitate practice effectiveness are emphasized (Green & Roberts, 2008). (See Case Example 4.4.)

CASE EXAMPLE 4.4 - CASE OF JUAN

Juan was referred for a mental health assessment after a devastating tornado, when he was found wandering the neighborhood in a state of shock. For weeks, he would return and wander through the rubble of what was once his home, looking for belongings (now treasures of a previous time). Although it had been a month since the event, Juan reported that he could not put it behind him and move forward. Juan sought intervention because his wife was very concerned about his behavior. He often woke up in the middle of the night in a cold sweat and could not go back to sleep. Juan reported that since his home was destroyed by the tornado, he often felt like he was in a daze. He reported having recurrent flashback episodes day and night in which he would relive the night the tornado destroyed his home. He reported that he now avoided driving to the construction site where his home was being rebuilt. Whenever he tried to go there, he would feel overwhelmed with anxious feelings and had to stop his car.

After completing a diagnostic assessment, the mental health practitioner felt that Juan was experiencing a stress reaction, such as acute stress disorder (308.3 ICD-9-CM or F43.0 ICD-10-CM). Although Juan was able to go to work, it was apparent that his reaction was severe enough to impair his overall functioning.

As part of the helping strategy, crisis intervention requires a dynamic form of practice that focuses on a wide range of phenomena affecting individual, group, or family equilibrium. For Juan, the crisis was defined as a temporary state of upset and disequilibrium characterized chiefly by his inability to cope with a particular situation. During this crisis period, Juan's usual methods of coping and problem solving simply did not work. His perception was that the tornado was so devastating and intolerable that he could not cope with it. Juan viewed the tornado as a hazardous, threatening event that left him vulnerable. He stated that no matter how hard he tried, he could not seem to control his fears.

To help Juan, crisis intervention techniques were applied to enable him to reformulate the crisis situation within the context of growth. Ultimately, the mental health practitioner needed to help Juan reach a healthy resolution where he could emerge with greater strength, self-trust, and sense of freedom than before the crisis event (Gilliland & James, 1997).

When applied with clients such as Juan, crisis intervention techniques are centered on the assumption that acute crisis events can be concretely identified, controlled, and lessened. Successful resolution is therefore achieved when the practitioner helps the client reach a healthier resolution of the problem.

For Juan, learning to deal with the physical devastation that resulted from the recent tornado was an area that needed to be addressed. A crisis such as this one was so unexpected that many families like Juan's lost their homes and their personal possessions. In some cases, lives were lost. Juan worried repeatedly what he could have done differently and why this had to happen to him. With such an unanticipated catastrophe, Juan was concerned with understanding why this happened and how he could prevent it in the future. In such situations, the role of the helping professional is clear: to help the client once again return to that previous level of coping and adjustment.

For many clients, psychological suffering after a traumatic event can make them feel powerless and frustrated with their inability to restore their equilibrium to the previous balance. These are basically healthy people who are so disturbed by the event that functioning is impaired. If they are afraid of something, the threat to life and bodily integrity overwhelms normal adaptive capabilities, producing extensive symptomatology. For the mental health practitioner, an active problem-addressing and supportive role is essential. The practitioner helps the client become empowered, recognizing that the symptoms being experienced can be viewed as signs of strength and that symptoms can be both a danger and an opportunity (Kanel, 2012).

Educative Counseling

Mental health professionals are often called on to participate in a type of counseling that is not considered traditional. Health promotion educators, health promotion specialists, and other health-related professionals can be called on to educate clients and thereby increase their self-awareness in terms of promoting health and wellness (Simmons-Morton, McLeroy, & Wendel, 2012). This type of counseling can include many different theories and techniques, and the use of theory-based planning frameworks continues to show promise (DiClemente, Crosby, & Kegler, 2009).

According to Blonna and Loschiavo (2011), simply defined, health counseling serves two primary functions: (1) to help clients recognize, understand, and address their own health-related problems and (2) through increased understanding, help clients follow the health care regimens outlined for them. Simmons-Morton et al. (2012) advocate strongly that regardless of the professional's discipline, focus on practices grounded in theory needs to be at the heart of all health promotion activities and practices. Therefore, although varied in scope and content, all health counseling strategies at a minimum must be time-limited, goal-directed, and objective-focused. In this role, the practitioner is expected to assist clients in addressing present and future health and wellness issues. At times, this type of counseling can include influencing others to make the best choices for health and wellness (Blonna & Loschiavo, 2011). More mental health practitioners are being called on to provide educative counseling (Cowles, 2003). More attention to this method is needed, stressing its use in formal education through the curriculum in most schools. (See Case Example 4.5.)

CASE EXAMPLE 4.5 - CASE OF BILL

Mental health practitioners can assist in providing education to clients in many different areas. Consider the case of Bill, who would not follow his diabetic diet. The medical condition resulting from his noncompliance was so severe that he was hospitalized repeatedly. During each hospitalization, he met with a dietitian and was given a copy of his diet before discharge, but he was later readmitted for noncompliance. Upon referral to the mental health practitioner, a family assessment was completed. The practitioner discovered that the client's wife prepared the family's meals. His wife had been handed the diet but was not really sure of the relevance of strict adherence to Bill's continued health. After meeting with the family and helping to educate his wife about the need for assisting, Bill's diet compliance increased dramatically.

Bill's case is just one example of how practitioners can assist clients by educating not only clients and their families but also other members of a delivery team. Including a family member has been shown to increase patient adherence to treatment plans (Desmond & Copeland, 2000). Because promoting health behaviors needs to take into account the total picture related to a client, the focus on individual, interpersonal dynamics; family systems; and social, cultural, and community contents should come as no surprise (Simons-Morton & McLeroy, 2012). It is also important for practitioners to be willing to educate clients in areas such as child abuse, domestic violence, and incest dynamics. Practitioners need to go beyond the traditional bounds of counseling and assist in educating clients to be better prepared for maintaining safety, security, and health and wellness for not only themselves but also their entire family system.

Openly acknowledging the importance of client education can assist practitioners in identifying the need for this commonly provided service. Mental health practitioners are in a unique position to participate in education, particularly in the areas of prevention and continued health and wellness. The overall practice of education in mental health is oriented toward safety and health, both conceptually and philosophically. This makes the mental health practitioner an important link between the person and his or her attempts to achieve health and wellness.

SUMMARY

Case documentation and using the information gathered to provide the basis for intervention planning and the practice strategy to follow are never simple. Numerous cases and individual situations arise that professionals are not sure how to handle. It is never easy to decide where to begin, what to write and what not to write in the case record, and what goals and objectives to process and apply to practice strategy. The science of intervention is important in starting the process, but it is the art that will carry it to a successful end. A delicate balancing act is required between the needs of the client, the demands of the environment, and the skills and helping knowledge available to the mental health practitioner.

Furthermore, the art and science within practice strategy are more involved than being familiar with the practice frameworks and simply choosing what works. It takes knowing the client and the strategies and methods available, as well as how and when to best apply the theoretical foundations that underlie the practice techniques selected. In today's environment, many complicated problems need to be addressed, and there is a real urgency to address them as quickly and effectively as possible. All mental health professionals, regardless of their discipline, need to be trained in these methods of helping. This training cannot be viewed as static. All professional helpers must continue learning and growing to anticipate the needs of our clients.

Dziegielewski (2013) identified five factors that must guide the initiation of the diagnostic assessment, treatment planning, and the practice strategy:

1. **Clients need to be active and motivated in the diagnostic assessment, treatment plan formulation, and intervention strategy.** The client's support and participation will increase the likelihood of encouragement and completion of change efforts. Generally, the issues and behavioral problems a client is exhibiting may require him or her to exert serious energy in attempting to make behavioral change. This means that clients must not only agree to participate in the assessment process but also

be willing to embark on the intervention plan that will result in behavioral change.

2. **The information gathered in the diagnostic assessment will be used to guide the approach or method of intervention used.** Once symptoms are identified, different methods and approaches for clinical intervention can be selected. However, the approach should never guide the intervention chosen. Sheafor and Horejsi (2008) warn against practitioners becoming overinvolved and wasting valuable clinical time by trying to match a particular problem to a particular theoretical approach, especially since so much of the problem-identification process in assessment is an intellectual activity. The practitioner should never lose sight of the ultimate purpose of the assessment process. Simply stated, the purpose is to complete an assessment that will help to establish a concrete service plan to address a client's needs.
3. **The influence and effects of values and beliefs should be made apparent in the process.** Each individual, professional or not, is influenced by his or her own values and beliefs (Colby & Dziegielewski, 2010). These beliefs create the foundation for who we are and what we believe. In mental health practice, however, these individual influences must not directly affect the assessment process. Therefore, the individual values, beliefs, and practices that can influence intervention outcomes must be clearly identified from the onset of treatment. For example, consider an unmarried client at a public health clinic who finds out she is pregnant. The practitioner assigned to her case personally believes that abortion is murder and cannot in good conscience recommend it as an option to the client. The client, however, is unsure of what to do and wants to explore every possible alternative. The plan that evolves must be based on the client's needs and desires, not the mental health practitioner's. Therefore, the practitioner ethically should advise the client of her prejudice and refer her to someone who can be more objective in exploring abortion as a possible course of action.

Clients have a right to make their own decisions, and regardless of the specific discipline all mental health professionals must do everything possible to ensure this right and not allow personal opinion to impair the completion of a proper assessment. In addition to the beliefs held by the practitioner and the client, the beliefs and values of the members of the interdisciplinary team must also be considered. It is not uncommon for helping professionals to have value conflicts. These team members need to be aware of how their personal feelings and resultant opinions might inhibit them from addressing all of the possible options to a client. For example, in the case of the unmarried pregnant woman, a physician, nurse, or any other member of the health care delivery team who does not believe in abortion would also be obligated to refer the client. This is not to assume that mental health practitioners are more qualified to address this issue or that they always have an answer. The point is that mental health practitioners should always be available to assist other helping professionals and advocate for how to best serve the needs of the client. Values and beliefs can be influential in identifying factors within individual decision-making strategy and remain important factors to consider and identify in the assessment process.

4. **Issues surrounding culture and race should be addressed openly in the assessment phase.** The mental health practitioner needs to be aware of his or her own cultural heritage as well as the client's to ensure the most open and receptive environment is created (Paniaqua, 2014). Dziegielewski (2013) suggested that health and mental health professionals should consider the following points:
   - **a.** Be aware of one's own cultural limitations.
   - **b.** Be open to cultural differences.
   - **c.** Recognize the client's integrity and uniqueness.
   - **d.** Utilize the client's learning style, including his or her own resources and supports.
   - **e.** Implement the behaviorally based biopsychosocial approach to practice from an integrated and as nonjudgmental a format as possible.

   For example, with the *DSM-5,* cultural factors should be stressed prior to establishing a formal diagnostic condition. As stated earlier in this book qualitative assessment using measures such as the Cultural Formulation Interview (CFI) to better identify the problem and its cultural roots and subsequent effects upon treatment are always recommended. In addition, delusions and hallucinations may be difficult to separate from general beliefs or practices related to a client's specific cultural custom or lifestyle. For this reason, the mental health practitioner should not forget that an appendix is included in the *DSM-5* that describes and defines cultural concepts of distress that might affect the diagnosis and assessment process and subsequent intervention strategy (American Psychiatric Association, 2013).

5. **The assessment must focus on client strengths and highlight the client's own resources for providing continued support.** One of the most difficult things for most individuals to do is to find, identify, and plan to use their own strengths. People, in general, have a tendency to focus on the negatives and rarely praise themselves for the good they do. With the advent of behavior-focused care, health and mental health care workers must quickly identify the individual and collectively based strengths of clients. Once this has been achieved, these strengths should be highlighted and incorporated into the suggested treatment plan (Jones-Smith, 2014). The information gathered is utilized in the assessment and stressed in regard to the importance of individual support networks for the client. In this time-limited intervention environment, individual resources are essential for continued growth and maintenance of wellness after the formal intervention period has ended. In such settings, practitioners need to stay vigilant that quality of care is not compromised (Sommers-Flanagan & Sommers-Flanagan, 2009).

One such example in need of support and attention from practitioners is individuals suffering from AIDS. According to the Joint United Nations Programme on HIV/AIDS (UNAIDS, 2013), globally the number of new HIV cases is decreasing, although new HIV infections remain most pronounced among children. An estimated 35.3 million people around the globe are infected with HIV, the virus that causes AIDS, and there were more than 1.6 million deaths in 2012. Many individuals are forced either to confront this generally terminal illness themselves or see it progress in a loved one. Misconceptions and fear based on lack of education often stop family and friends from supporting individuals when they most need care and support. Practitioners must actively work to help these individuals and encourage support for them in their time of need. In this situation, practitioners need to be not only educated to varied theoretical approaches but also able to select which one to use and when.

Psychodynamic approaches can be used to help clients feel better and to assist in resolving previous relationship experiences that are affecting the development of new or current ones. Solution-focused methods can help individuals develop new ways of changing behavior, focusing positive energy and attention on how to make things better. Cognitive-behavioral approaches can help individuals and family members to look at dysfunctional thought patterns and how they complicate current interactions. The crisis intervention approach can assist the client and his or her family to return to a previous or healthier level of coping. Education can provide client empowerment while enhancing independence and control. To become better equipped in the helping activity, practitioners must be aware of the multiple frameworks and practice methods available.

QUESTIONS FOR FURTHER THOUGHT

1. In this chapter, gathering supporting information beyond that directly related to the diagnostic assessment is essential. List the types of supporting information that are most helpful for inclusion and explain why.
2. Apply the basics of the POR to a client you have seen or are seeing. Break down the factors in the case into either the SOAP or SOAPIE format. What are the major concerns with an electronic version of this type of record?
3. When working with a client and gathering information, what is PHI, and how should it be handled?
4. Take a problem that a client could face and describe how you would approach it utilizing:
   Solution-focused therapy
   Cognitive-behavioral therapy
   Crisis intervention
   Educative counseling
5. Compare and contrast the different types of therapy in handling clients.
6. Describe strategies you should use to protect client records and minimize your risk of legal action.

REFERENCES

American Psychiatric Association. (2013). *Diagnostic and statistical manual of mental disorders* (5th ed.). Arlington, VA: American Psychiatric Publishing.

Beck, A. T., Freeman, A., & Associates. (1990). *Cognitive therapy of personality disorders*. New York, NY: Guilford Press.

Beck, J. (2011). *Cognitive behavior therapy: Basics and beyond* (2nd ed.). New York, NY: Guilford Press.

Berghuis, D. J., & Jongsma, A. E. (2008a). *The severe and persistent mental illness: Treatment planner* (2nd ed.). Hoboken, NJ: Wiley.

Berghuis, D. J., & Jongsma, A. E. (2008b). *The severe and persistent mental illness: Progress notes planner* (2nd ed.). Hoboken, NJ: Wiley.

Bernstein, B. E., & Hartsell, T. L. (2013). *The portable lawyer for mental health professionals* (3rd ed.). Hoboken, NJ: Wiley.

Blonna, R., & Loschiavo, J. (2011). *Health counseling: A microskills approach for counselors, educators and school nurses*. Sudbury, MA: Jones & Bartlett Learning.

Brandell, J. R. (2004). *Psychodynamic social work*. New York, NY: Columbia University Press.

Brasher, K. L. (2009). Solution-focused brief therapy: Overview and implications for school counselors. *Alabama Counseling Association Journal, 34*(2), 20–30.

Budman, S., & Gurman, A. (2002). *Theory and practice of brief therapy* (2nd ed.). New York, NY: Guilford Press.

Chambliss, C. H. (2000). *Psychotherapy and managed care: Reconciling research and reality*. Boston, MA: Allyn & Bacon.

Chang, D., Kang, O., Kim, H., Kim, H., Lee, H., Park, H., . . . Younbyoung, C. (2012). Pre-existing beliefs and expectations influence judgments of novel health information. *Journal of Health Psychology, 17*(5), 753–763.

Chang-Muy, F., & Congress, E. P. (Eds.). (2009). *Social work with immigrants and refugees: Legal issues, clinical skills, and advocacy*. New York, NY: Springer.

Colby, I., & Dziegielewski, S. F. (2010). *Introduction to social work: The people's profession* (3rd ed.). Chicago, IL: Lyceum.

Cowles, L. A. F. (2003). *Social work in the health field: A care perspective* (2nd ed.). New York, NY: Haworth Press.

Davidson, L., Tondora, J., Lawless, M. S., O'Connell, M. J., & Rowe, M. (2009). *A practical guide to recovery-oriented practice: Tools for transforming mental health care*. New York, NY: Oxford University Press.

De Shazer, S., & Dolan, Y. (2007). *More than miracles: The state of the art of solution-focused brief therapy*. New York, NY: Haworth Press.

Desmond, J., & Copeland, L. R. (2000). *Communicating with today's patient*. San Francisco, CA: Jossey-Bass.

DiClemente, R. J., Crosby, R. A., & Kegler, M. C. (Eds.). (2009). *Emerging theories in health promotion practice and research* (2nd ed.). San Francisco, CA: Jossey-Bass.

Dziegielewski, S. F. (2008). Brief and intermittent approaches to practice: The state of practice. *Journal of Brief Treatment and Crisis Intervention, 8*(2), 147–163.

Dziegielewski, S. F. (2010). *Psychopharmacology and social work practice: A person-in-environment approach* (2nd ed.). New York, NY: Springer.

Dziegielewski, S. F. (2013). *The changing face of health care social work: Opportunities and challenges for professional practice* (3rd ed.). New York, NY: Springer.

Fischer, J. (2009). *Toward evidence-based practice: Variations on a theme*. Chicago, IL: Lyceum.

Gamino, L. A., & Ritter, R. H., Jr. (2009). *Ethical practice in grief counseling*. New York, NY: Springer.

Gilliland, B., & James, R. (1997). *Crisis intervention strategies*. Pacific Grove, CA: Brooks/Cole.

Gingerich, W. J. (2002). Computer applications for social work practice. In A. R. Roberts & G. J. Greene (Eds.), *Social workers desk reference* (pp. 23–28). New York, NY: Oxford University Press.

Goldstein, E. G., & Noonan, M. (2001). The framework: Theoretical underpinnings and characteristics. In B. Dane, C. Tosone, & A. Woolson (Eds.), *Doing more with less: Using long-term skills in short-term treatment* (pp. 2–55). Northvale, NJ: Jason Aronson.

Green, D. L., & Roberts, A. R. (2008). *Helping victims of violent crime: Assessment, treatment, and evidence-based practice*. New York, NY: Springer.

Greenberg, G., Ganshorn, K., & Danilkewich, A. (2001). Solution-focused therapy: Counseling model for busy family physicians. *Canadian Family Physician, 47*(11), 2289–2295.

Hansen, N. B., Lambert, M. J., & Forman, E. M. (2002). The psychotherapy dose–response effect and its implication for treatment delivery services. *Clinical Psychology: Science and Practice, 9*(3), 329–343.

Hartsell, T. L., & Bernstein, B. E. (2008). *The portable ethicist for mental health professionals: A complete guide to responsible practice*. Hoboken, NJ: Wiley.

Herbert, J. D., Forman, E. M., & England, E. L. (2008). Psychological acceptance. In W. T. O'Donohue & J. E. Fisher (Eds.), *Cognitive behavior therapy: Applying empirically supported techniques in your practice* (2nd ed., pp. 4–16). Hoboken, NJ: Wiley.

Hixon, T. (2012). The U.S. does not have a debt problem . . . It has a health care cost problem. *Forbes*. Retrieved from: http://www.forbes.com/sites/toddhixon/2012/02/09/the-u-s-does-not-have-a-debt-problem-it-has-a-health-care-cost-problem/

Hofschire, D. (2012). Why health care reform is critical for the U.S. economy. Retrieved from https://news.fidelity.com/news/article.jhtml?guid=/FidelityNewsPage/pages/viewpoints-healthcare-economy&topic=saving-for-retirement

Houmanfar, R., Maglieri, K. A., Roman, H. R., & Ward, T. A. (2008). Behavioral contracting. In W. T. O'Donohue & J. E. Fisher (Eds.), *Cognitive behavior therapy: Applying empirically supported techniques in your practice* (2nd ed., pp. 53–59). Hoboken, NJ: Wiley.

Iveson, C. (2002). Solution-focused brief therapy. *Advances in Psychiatric Treatment, 8*, 149–157.

Jacobs, N. N. (2008). Bibliotherapy utilizing cognitive behavior therapy. In W. T. O'Donohue & J. E. Fisher (Eds.), *Cognitive behavior therapy: Applying empirically supported techniques in your practice* (2nd ed., pp. 60–67). Hoboken, NJ: Wiley.

Jones-Smith, E. (2014). *Strengths-based therapy: Connecting theory, practice, and skills.* Thousand Oaks, CA: Sage.

Jongsma, A. E., Jr., Peterson, L. M., & Bruce, T. J. (2006). *The complete adult psychotherapy treatment planner* (4th ed.). Hoboken, NJ: Wiley.

Kane, M. N., Houston-Vega, M. K., & Nuehring, E. M. (2002). Documentation in managed care: Challenges for social work education. *Journal of Teaching in Social Work, 22*(1/2), 199–212.

Kanel, K. (2012). *A guide to crisis intervention.* Belmont, CA: Brooks/Cole.

Kern, R. S., Glynn, S. M., Horan, W. P., & Marder, S. R. (2009). Psychosocial treatments to promote functional recovery in schizophrenia. *Schizophrenia Bulletin, 35*(2), 347–361.

Lambert, M. J., Bergin, A. E., & Garfield, S. L. (2004). Introduction and historical overview. In M. J. Lambert (Ed.), *Bergin and Garfield's handbook of psychotherapy and behavior change* (5th ed., pp. 3–15). Hoboken, NJ: Wiley.

Landy, S., & Bradley, S. (2014). *Children with multiple mental health challenges: An integrated approach to intervention.* New York, NY: Springer.

LeCroy, C. W., & Okamoto, S. K. (2009). Guidelines for selecting and using assessment tools with children. In A. Roberts (Ed.), *Social workers desk reference* (2nd ed., pp. 381–389). New York, NY: Oxford University Press.

Locke, D. C., & Bailey, D. F. (2014). *Increasing cultural understanding* (3rd ed.). Los Angeles, CA: Sage.

MacLaren, C., & Freeman, A. (2007). Cognitive behavior therapy model and techniques. In T. Ronen & A. Freeman (Eds.), *Cognitive behavior therapy in clinical social work practice* (pp. 25–44). New York, NY: Springer.

Magnavita, J. J., & Anchin, J. C. (2014). *Unifying psychotherapy: Principles, methods, and evidence from clinical science.* New York, NY: Springer.

Malone, D., Marriott, S., Newton-Howes, G., Simmonds, S., & Tyrer, P. (2009). Community mental health teams for people with severe mental illnesses and disordered personality. *Schizophrenia Bulletin, 35*(1), 13–14.

Mandell, B. R., & Schram, B. (2006). *An introduction to human services: Policy and practice* (6th ed.). Boston, MA: Pearson.

Martin, H., & Jacklin, E. (2012). Therapeutic assessment involving multiple life issues: Coming to terms with problems of health, culture, and learning. In S. E. Finn, C. T. Constance, & L. Handler (Eds.) *Collaborative therapeutic assessment* (pp. 157–177). Hoboken, NJ: Wiley.

Mathews, A. W. (2012, August 2). Medical care time warp. Remember managed care? It's quietly coming back. *Wall Street Journal* (U.S. ed.), B1.

Metcalf, L. (1998). *Solution-focused group therapy.* New York, NY: Free Press.

O'Donohue, W., & Fisher, J. E. (2008). Introduction. In W. T. O'Donohue & J. E. Fisher (Eds.), *Cognitive behavior therapy: Applying empirically supported techniques in your practice* (2nd ed., pp. 1–3). Hoboken, NJ: Wiley.

Paniaqua, F. A. (2014). *Assessing and treating culturally diverse clients: A practical guide.* Los Angeles, CA: Sage.

Papadatou, D. (2009). *In the face of death: Professionals who care for the dying and the bereaved.* New York, NY: Springer.

Papworth, M. (2006). Issues and outcomes associated with adult mental health self-help materials: A "second order" review or "qualitative meta-review." *Journal of Mental Health, 15*(4), 387–409.

Parad, H. J., & Parad, L. G. (1990). *Crisis intervention: The practitioner's sourcebook for brief therapy.* Milwaukee, WI: Family Service America.

Reamer, F. G. (2005). Documentation in social work: Evolving ethical and risk-management standards. *Social Work, 50*(4), 325–334.

Roberts, A., & Dziegielewski, S. F. (1995). Foundation skills and applications of crisis intervention and cognitive therapy. In A. Roberts (Ed.), *Crisis intervention and time-limited cognitive treatment* (pp. 3–27). Thousand Oaks, CA: Sage.

Roberts, A. R. (2005). Bridging the past and present to the future of crisis intervention and crisis management. In A. R. Roberts (Ed.), *Crisis intervention handbook: Assessment, treatment, and research* (3rd ed., pp. 3–34). New York, NY: Oxford University Press.

Rudolph, C. S. (2000). Educational challenges facing health care social workers in the twenty-first century. *Professional Development, 3*(1), 31–41.

Russell-Chapin, L., & Ivey, A. (2004). *Your supervised practicum and internship: Field resources for turning theory into action.* Belmont, CA: Thomson Learning.

Schore, A. N. (2014). Introduction. In J. J. Magnavita & J. C. Anchin (Eds.), *Unifying psychotherapy: Principles, methods, evidence from clinical science* (pp. xxi–xliv). New York, NY: Springer.

Sheafor, B. W., & Horejsi, C. R. (2008). *Techniques and guidelines for social work practice* (8th ed.). Boston, MA: Allyn & Bacon.

Simmons-Morton, B., McLeroy, K. R., & Wendel, M. L. (2012). *Behavior theory in health promotion practice and research*. Burlington, MA: Jones & Bartlett Learning.

Simon, J. K. (2010). *Solution focused practice in end-of-life & grief counseling*. New York, NY: Springer.

Skinner, B. F. (1953). *Science and human behavior*. New York, NY: Macmillan.

Smock, S. A., Trepper, T. S., Wetchler, J. L., McCollum, E. E., Ray, R., & Pierce, K. (2008). Solution-focused group therapy for level 1 substance abusers. *Journal of Marital and Family Therapy*, *34*(1), 107–120.

Sommers-Flanagan, J., & Sommers-Flanagan, R. (2009). *Clinical interviewing* (4th ed.). Hoboken, NJ: Wiley.

Straub, R. O. (2012). *Health psychology: A biopsychosocial approach*. New York, NY: Worth.

Tarasoff v. The Regents of the University of California, 551 P.2d 334 (Calif. 1976).

Tompkins, M. A. (2004). *Using homework in psychotherapy: Strategies, guidelines, and forms*. New York, NY: Guilford Press.

UNAIDS. (2013). UNAIDS 2013: AIDS by the numbers. Geneva, Switzerland: UNAIDS. Retrieved from http://www.unaids.org/en/media/unaids/contentassets/documents/unaidspublication/2013/JC2571_AIDS_by_the_numbers_en.pdf

Van Dijk–de Vries, A., Moser, A., Mertens, V., van der Linden, J., van der Weijden, T., & van Eijk, J. (2012). The ideal of biopsychosocial chronic care: How to make it real? A qualitative study among Dutch stakeholders. *BMC Family Practice*, doi: 10.1186/1471-2296-13-14

Vazquez, C. I., & Rosa, D. (2011). *Grief therapy with Latinos: Integrating culture for clinicians*. New York, NY: Springer.

Walter, C. A., & McCoyd, J. L. M. (2009). *Grief and loss across the lifespan: A biopsychosocial perspective*. New York, NY: Springer.

Walter, J., & Peller, J. (1992). *Becoming solution focused in brief therapy*. New York: Brunner/Mazel.

Weissman, M. M., Markowitz, J. C., & Klerman, G. L. (2007). *Clinician's quick guide to interpersonal therapy*. New York, NY: Oxford University Press.

Wells, R. A. (2010). *Planned short-term treatment* (2nd ed.). New York, NY: Simon and Schuster.

Wiger, D. E. (2005). *The clinical documentation sourcebook* (3rd ed.). Hoboken, NJ: Wiley.

Yang, J. A., & Kombarakaran, F. A. (2006). A practitioner's response to the new health privacy regulations. *Health & Social Work*, *31*(2), 129–136.

Yeager, K. R., Roberts, A. R., & Grainger, W. (2008). Crisis intervention. In K. M. Sowers, & C. N. Dulmus (Series Eds.) & W. Rowe & L. A. Rapp-Paglicci (Vol. Eds.), *Comprehensive handbook of social work and social welfare: Vol. 3. Social work practice* (pp. 179–198). Hoboken, NJ: Wiley.

Yeager, K. R., Roberts, A. R., & Saveanu, R. (2009). Optimizing the use of patient safety standards, procedures, and measures. In A. Roberts (Ed.), *Social workers desk reference* (2nd ed., pp. 175–186). New York, NY: Oxford University Press.

SECTION II

DIAGNOSTIC AND TREATMENT APPLICATIONS

CHAPTER

5 Schizophrenia Spectrum and the Other Psychotic Disorders

SOPHIA F. DZIEGIELEWSKI

INTRODUCTION

This chapter provides information on children, adolescents, and adults suffering from the disorders that constitute schizophrenia spectrum and the other psychotic disorders. A brief overview of each disorder is provided, along with a case example that includes specific treatment planning and an intervention-related application. Although the definitions of what constitutes schizophrenia and the other spectrum related disorders continue to shift (Wong, 2013), these devastating illnesses can have far-reaching effects that go beyond the client. They can touch the very core of the individual, affecting the development of close relationships, talents, family relations, and economic independence. Further complicating the conditions, now referred to as the schizophrenia spectrum disorders, is that even with the best treatments known, repeated episodes of the illness will occur throughout a client's life (Menezes, Arenovich, & Zipursky, 2006). Also, the symptoms can vary so much among individuals that no single treatment can be considered the intervention of choice. This varied and unpredictable course of the illness and the label placed can affect those seeking and receiving treatment (Rusch et al., 2013).

Because the psychotic disorders involve some level of *psychosis* that results in distorted perceptions and affects the way an individual perceives reality (Walker, Mitial, Tessner, & Trotman, 2008), when experiencing these incorrect impressions, individuals often cannot function as others do. They can become lost in a world where they cannot communicate their basic needs. These types of communications are so basic to daily functioning and survival, and the variability of response and accomplishment has left many family members to question how this could happen. This lack of understanding of the symptoms related to the disease and the impaired communication further disturb family relationships and thereby alienate support systems critical to enhanced functioning (Dziegielewski, 2007).

This chapter highlights the guidelines for using the *Diagnostic and Statistical Manual of Mental Disorders, Fifth Edition* (*DSM-5*) (American Psychiatric Association [APA], 2013) to better understand and assess these conditions. It is beyond the purpose of this chapter to explore in depth all of the diagnoses that constitute schizophrenia spectrum and the other psychotic disorders and the treatment options specific to each. Rather, the purpose of this chapter is to introduce the primary disorders as listed in *DSM-5*: schizotypal personality disorder (listed in this chapter but described in the chapter on

Special thanks to Shirleyann Amos and George Jacinto for contributions to the previous version of this chapter.

personality disorders), delusional disorder, brief psychotic disorder, schizophreniform disorder, schizoaffective disorder, substance/medication-induced psychotic disorder, and psychotic disorder due to another medical condition. Of all the psychotic disorders, schizophrenia is the most common (Walker et al., 2008). Although this chapter presents a brief overview of this spectrum of disorders, the diagnosis and treatment of schizophrenia is the central focus.

The application section of this chapter provides a case example of an individual suffering from schizophrenia with specific recommendations for completing the diagnostic assessment and the subsequent treatment plan. The extent, importance, and the early predictors of problem behaviors and symptoms are explored. The various aspects of the disorder are presented with a case application that highlights the diagnostic assessment, treatment planning, and evidence-based treatment strategy. In addition, the latest practice methods and newest research and findings are highlighted to further the understanding of these often-devastating illnesses.

TOWARD A BASIC UNDERSTANDING OF THE CONDITIONS

Reading about diverse ancient cultures (e.g., Egypt, India, Greece, and China), makes it clear that strange and bizarre behavior, often referred to as madness or lunacy, has existed for thousands of years (Woo & Keatinge, 2008, p. 470). The term *demence precoce,* or early dementia (dementia praecox), was the general term for what we today call schizophrenia. Within the psychotic disorders, schizophrenia historically has always been the most clearly defined. Several subtypes that can occur within schizophrenia were identified and described by Kraepelin in 1899. Emil Kraepelin (1856–1926), using the earlier work of Morel, developed a formal diagnostic category in which he divided dementia praecox into different subtypes: disorganized type (previously known as hebephrenia), paranoid, and catatonic. This classification system lasted for many years. Not until a new generation of researchers voiced concerns with the consistency and uniformity of these earlier classification schemes was the *DSM* definition most similar to what we utilize today developed (Walker et al., 2008). In *DSM-5,* limited diagnostic stability and problems with reliability and validity were the primary reasons for dropping the five subtypes, resulting in the definition we use today (Tandon, 2012).

Over the years, many theories about the causes of these mental health conditions evolved (Lehmann & Ban, 1997). Some of the more current theories of causation are oxygen deficiency, biological causes related to its similarity to epilepsy, and an imbalance of natural neurochemicals within the brain, such as serotonin or dopamine disturbance or both (Hong, Lee, Sim, & Hwu, 1997; Lehmann & Ban, 1997). One reason defining the disorder may be so difficult is that when most researchers think of the psychotic disorders, they immediately think of schizophrenia; to complicate the matter further, many professionals agree that schizophrenia is an illness with a complex and heterogeneous nature (Glick, 2005; National Institute of Mental Health [NIMH], 2009c). Based on recent research, the conceptual definition of schizophrenia has broadened to include awareness that it is not one singular disease (Walker et al., 2008). Walker et al. (2008) acknowledge this research and agree that trying to make schizophrenia one disorder might confuse and complicate the diagnostic assessment process. Rather, it might be easier to classify the disorder as a group or cluster of disorders that lack a single cause. According to *DSM-5,* what this complex group of psychotic disorders share is at least some symptoms such as hallucinations, delusions, disorganized or abnormal motor behavior, and a cadre of negative symptoms.

UNDERSTANDING INDIVIDUALS WHO SUFFER FROM THE PSYCHOTIC DISORDERS

Receiving a diagnosis of schizophrenia or one of the psychotic disorders can be one of the most devastating experiences for an individual and his or her family. Unfortunately, no known prevention or cure exists for these disorders (Woo & Keatinge, 2008). The behaviors and coping styles characteristic of psychotic disorders such as schizophrenia, which include symptoms such as hallucinations, delusions, and disorganized or grossly disorganized, bizarre, or inappropriate behavior, can be problematic. The word *psychotic* can easily be misinterpreted. In the psychotic disorders, individual criteria must be met, and the definition and meaning of what constitutes a psychotic symptom can change, based on the diagnosis being considered. Further, the disorders in this category do not always stem from a common etiology. What diagnoses in this category share are problems with performing daily tasks, particularly those that involve interpersonal relationships. Symptoms related to the psychotic disorders often appear as a thought disorder, with poor reality testing, social isolation, poor self-image, problems in relating with family, and problems at work (Woo & Keatinge, 2008).

The individual who suffers from one of these disorders can experience states of terror that prevent daily interactions and create difficulty in distinguishing fantasy from reality. This resulting separation from reality makes the symptoms that an individual client suffers extend far beyond personal discomfort. These symptoms also affect the support system and all of the people who come into contact with him or her. This disorder has far-reaching effects; not only does it disrupt the life of the individual but also it can tear apart support systems and alienate the client from daily contacts with family and friends. These disorders are not static in symptomatology and presentation, and having a client misinterpret the signs and symptoms may frustrate family and friends (Wong, 2013). A further complication is not knowing the actual cause of psychotic disorders. This category of mental disorders, especially schizophrenia, has been documented as a leading worldwide public health problem.

The often-negative reaction by lay individuals, peers, family, and professionals toward individuals who suffer from schizophrenia and other psychotic disorders is extreme in comparison to what might be experienced by those who suffer from depression. Once diagnosed, clients with these disorders often need extensive monitoring and support that most primary care physicians and other practitioners are not able to provide or are not interested in providing (Dziegielewski, 2008). Furthermore, although they might not openly admit it, few professionals except in a mental health setting seek out this type of client to work with. Many professionals simply prefer not to work with clients suffering from a psychotic disorder because of the monitoring problems and the unpredictability of client responses, which makes it difficult to provide the support and supervision required in a nonspecialized treatment environment. On the more optimistic side, it appears that practitioner views toward this population are changing somewhat, although the process is slow. In psychopharmacology, however, new medications have brought relief for many clients who have this chronic and debilitating condition (Dziegielewski, 2010).

In summary, since first introduced in the earliest version of the *DSM* (APA, 1952), the diagnostic category of the psychotic disorders, especially schizophrenia, continues to raise many questions for practitioners. Concerns center on validity and application of criteria, as well as the detrimental and negative impact that this diagnosis or others in the schizophrenia spectrum can have on the future life of the individual. With all the information available to people on the Internet, self-labeling has become a practice reality; in schizophrenia and the bipolar disorders, however, it can have particularly problematic effects. Individuals may increase their use of mental health services because of their fear of psychosis or be stigmatized by an inaccurately placed label (Rusch et al., 2013). For many individuals who suffer from this disorder, complete or total remission is rare, and a chronic yet variable course of the illness is to be expected. Furthermore, schizophrenia spectrum and the other psychotic disorders appear to be an equal opportunity illness that affects rich and poor alike.

Biology and Etiology of Schizophrenia Spectrum and the Psychotic Disorders

Support for a biological component to schizophrenia spectrum disorders increased substantially when psychotropic medications showed a decrease in symptoms related to the disorder (Dziegielewski, 2010; Lehmann & Ban, 1997). Subsequently, the medications that had an effect on these symptoms also opened a window to further understanding the biological dynamics of disorders such as schizophrenia (Lehmann & Ban, 1997). Researchers took great interest in the role that neurotransmitters such as serotonin and dopamine, as well as noradrenaline, acetylcholine, and glutamate, had in establishing a biological basis for schizophrenia (Bishara & Taylor, 2009). For example, the autopsied brains of individuals who suffered from schizophrenia showed that the D-4 (dopamine) receptors (members of the G-protein family that bind with antipsychotic medications) were six times denser than in others' brains (Hong et al., 1997). In turn, this discovery led to the biological or dopamine D-4 hypothesis of schizophrenia (Lehmann & Ban, 1997).

Regardless of the exact relationship, a connection between schizophrenia and the neurochemical dopamine is clear. This connection remains ambiguous because many of the medications to treat the disorder can also increase dopamine receptor density. However, even never-medicated patients with schizophrenia, in particular, still show elevations in the dopamine receptors (Walker et al., 2008). Studies on the structure and function of the amygdala and anterior segment of the hippocampus, basal ganglia, and thalamus have noted differences in individuals with schizophrenia and their siblings versus the control group (Qiu et al., 2009). Qiu and colleagues concluded that there may be a schizophrenia-related endophenotype. Neuroendocrinology studies have offered another perspective on the etiology of schizophrenia. These studies focus on the workings of the pituitary gland as related to the hypothalamus and the central nervous system (CNS). These studies have looked at growth hormone (GH) and thyroid-releasing hormone (TRH), but results linked directly to a causal interpretation have been mixed (Keshavan, Marshall, Shazly, & Paki, 1988; Lieberman et al., 1992).

Neuroimaging studies, first introduced in the 1970s, have been helpful in identifying possible causative factors for schizophrenia (Raz & Raz, 1990). These studies are helpful in exploring both the functional and the structural changes in the brains of individuals who suffer from schizophrenia. Through these studies (e.g., magnetic resonance imaging [MRI] or cerebral blood flow [CBF]), specific areas of the brain can be identified and studied (Gur & Pearlson, 1993; Keshavan et al., 1997). For example, MRIs used to look specifically at individuals who suffer from schizophrenia revealed decreased frontal, temporal, and whole-brain volume (Lawrie & Abukmeil, 1998).

The hippocampus has consistently been identified as where people with schizophrenia can be differentiating from people without it (Crow, Chance, Priddle, Radua, & James, 2013). Some researchers believe that a genetic link contributes to the subsequent risk of developing schizophrenia (Brzustowicz, Hodgkinson, Chow, Honer, & Bassett, 2000; Kendler & Diehl, 1993; Nauert, 2007; Tsuang, 2004). Researchers conducting studies in the United States, Germany, Greece, and Ireland affirm findings that schizophrenia strongly runs in families (Baron et al., 1985; Kendler et al., 1993; Kendler, Gruenberg, & Tsuang, 1985; Maier, Hallmayer, Minges, & Lichtermann, 1990; Tsuang, 2004).

Twin studies also appear to support genetic transmission of schizophrenia; however, not all individuals with a genetic predisposition will experience symptoms of schizophrenia (Kendler & Diehl, 1993). Several accounts for this discrepancy have been posited, including the interplay of genetic and environmental considerations, where a biological child of an individual with schizophrenia has a similar risk for developing the disorder whether the child grows up in a home with that parent or not (Altschule et al., 1976; Gottesman, 1991). Brzustowicz et al. (2000) found a susceptibility point on a particular gene for schizophrenia, which lends support to the theory that schizophrenia is related to genetic as well as environmental factors.

Environmental issues are highlighted by family response to a person diagnosed with schizophrenia and how soon the person relapses following hospitalization. It appears that relapse occurs most quickly if there is a hostile family environment that is nonsupportive or overcontrolling (Weisman, 1997). Research on the brain supports neurodevelopmental damage during childhood as a possible antecedent to the diagnosis of schizophrenia in children, adolescents, and adults (Dutta et al., 2007; Hollis, 1995; Mental Health America, 2009). These environmental events associated with developmental delays or permanent neurological damage can increase the occurrence of schizophrenia, as well as the possibility of an individual being most susceptible to developing other mental illnesses.

Nonetheless, it is fairly well accepted that genetics may be a necessary, but not a sufficient, cause for schizophrenia (Kendler & Diehl, 1993). To acknowledge this link between the individual and the family, the term *schizophrenia spectrum* was added to the *DSM-IV-TR* (APA, 2000) under the familial pattern section. Schizophrenia spectrum represented the range of mental disorders that are more likely to occur in family members of individuals with schizophrenia, such as schizoaffective disorder and schizotypal personality disorder. In *DSM-5,* this term was expanded to include the types of disorders that fall into this category that often have a genetic component linking them.

IMPORTANT FEATURES RELATED TO THE PSYCHOTIC DISORDERS

When preparing for the diagnostic assessment and the appropriate diagnosis, the practitioner must first be aware of the key features prevalent in the psychotic disorders that are used to constitute the diagnosis. Creating any diagnostic impression and the treatment plan to follow always requires a delicate balance of groundbreaking research and the practitioner's judgment and experience (Schore, 2014). Starting this process requires familiarity with applying the five primary characteristics of each of the disorders listed in this chapter: delusions, hallucinations, disorganized thinking and speech, grossly disorganized or abnormal motor behavior (including catatonia), and negative symptoms.

Delusions

A primary feature of many of the diagnoses in this area is delusions. Simply stated, a *delusion* is a belief held with extreme conviction, although others do not believe it; when compared with evidence to the contrary, the belief is clearly incorrect or unfounded. The individual suffering from delusions often becomes anxious or angry when the delusion is challenged. The individual often holds on to the false belief with what is sometimes referred to as *delusional conviction.* Whether delusions can be addressed when challenged is debatable, and more research in this area is needed (Wong, 2013). What is most evident is the frustration and sense of hopelessness that many clients feel.

In the glossary section, *DSM-5* identifies several types of delusions (APA, 2013). (See Quick Reference 5.1.) This chapter further defines the most common types of delusions and gives examples of each. The most common fixed delusions are persecutory, referential, grandiose, erotomanic, nihilistic, and somatic. In completing the diagnostic assessment, establishing the difference between a delusion and strong culturally held belief can be difficult. The easiest way to differentiate between them is to break the thought patterns into two classes: fixed and bizarre. In fixed delusions, the person is convinced, no matter how contrary the evidence, that what he or she believes is accurate. In the bizarre type, even when compared with individuals of the same cultural group, their thoughts

QUICK REFERENCE 5.1

TYPES OF DELUSIONS

Fixed Belief Delusions

- **Persecutory delusions:** The self or someone close is being conspired against.
- **Referential delusions:** Related to an event or an object in the person's life situation that holds what others in a similar situation would term as having an incorrect or unusual meaning.
- **Grandiose delusions:** Places extreme self-importance on their own existence and what is forthcoming from their contributions.
- **Erotomanic delusions:** The individual believes falsely another person loves him or her.
- **Nihilistic delusions:** Belief a major catastrophe will occur.
- **Somatic delusions:** Related directly to bodily concerns or images.

Bizarre Thoughts

- **Thought withdrawal:** The individual becomes convinced that someone or something is removing ideas from their head that he or she cannot stop from happening.
- **Thought insertion:** The individual becomes convinced that someone or something is planting ideas in his or her head from which he or she cannot escape.
- **Thought broadcasting:** The individual feels his or her own thoughts are being revealed and others can hear their most personal and private thoughts.

Bizarre Thoughts That Lead to Dysfunctional Behaviors

- **Delusions of control:** The individual believes someone or something has mental control that is so strong it can affect the individual's daily functioning and the resulting social or occupational behaviors.

and behaviors still are reportedly outside the norm.

The most common of the fixed delusions is termed *persecutory*. In persecutory delusions, the individual or someone close to the individual is being conspired against. As in most delusional thinking, the frustration level increases, as the individual really believes this is happening. To avoid potential harm, the individual will try almost anything because he or she feels so powerless to do anything to prevent it. The thoughts are so overwhelming that the individual cannot escape from them; when the problem is discussed with others, the person is often not believed. Frustration builds; there appears to be no way to improve or stop the situation. The person is often desperate and overwhelmed with feelings of impending doom from which no escape seems possible.

In *referential* delusions, the false belief held with delusional conviction is related to an event or an object in the person's life situation that holds what others in a similar situation would term as having an incorrect or unusual meaning. In delusions of reference, an individual may fear that everyone is out to get him or her and so interpret normal everyday events as tied to his or her own life. These types of delusions are linked to important aspects or objects in a person's life, and it is difficult to escape from its influence. Referential delusions can become so severe that they stop an individual from performing daily activities and basic functioning; the individual applies special meaning to objects or events recurring in his or her life, thereby creating an inescapable cumulative effect directed personally.

Grandiose delusions are often related to inflated self-worth or self-esteem. The person may see himself or herself as a famous person or connected to a deity. In grandiose delusions, the individual places extreme self-importance on his or her own existence and contributions.

In *erotomanic* delusions, the individual is convinced that another person loves him or her. This belief is not reciprocated, and the individual with the delusional belief can become completely engrossed in a fantasy relationship. The belief is so strong that it becomes difficult for the person to see what is real and what is not.

In *nihilistic* delusions, there is a belief that a horrible catastrophe is about to come. The individual continually talks about it and prepares for the worst, and this preoccupation may prevent completing current requirements needed to maintain his or her current situation.

Somatic delusions relate directly to the body or concerns with bodily function. The individual may focus on an imagined body flaw and not be able to see himself or herself positively because of it.

The second classification of delusions is *bizarre*. Delusions that fall into this category and involve thought content seem strange to everyone, including those with similar beliefs in a similar cultural group. Delusions of this type include problems with basic cognitive processes: thought insertion, thought withdrawal, and thought broadcasting. In *thought insertion,* the individual becomes convinced that someone or something is planting ideas in his or her head from which he or she cannot escape. There is a constant nagging feeling that the thoughts are really not of the person's thinking them, but rather put there and influenced by somebody or something else. This thought is so powerful the individual cannot function without taking it into account. In *thought withdrawal,* the individual becomes convinced that someone or something is removing ideas from his or her head that the person cannot stop from happening. In *thought broadcasting,* the individual feels his or her own thoughts are being revealed, and others can hear the most personal and private thoughts. To the person experiencing thought broadcasting, his or her general and most intimate thoughts cannot be protected from others' knowledge. This causes the individual to withdraw from any social situations where this could occur.

The third classification is *delusions of control*. In this bizarre type of delusion, the individual believes he or she is mentally controlled by another, and this control is so strong it can affect the physical behaviors that result. The individual believes this outside force has tremendous control of him or her and escape from this mind-behavioral control is not possible.

Hallucinations

Hallucinations are sensory experiences that happen without the support of the appropriate stimuli (Woo & Keatinge, 2008). The majority (70–90%) of hallucinations exhibited are auditory. For the practitioner, measuring them can be difficult as people's self-report may be clouded cognitively by the mental disorder being experienced (Wong, 2013). The *DSM-5* limits discussion in the text to the auditory hallucinations simply because they are the most prevalent in the schizophrenia spectrum and other psychotic related disorders. Other types can also be noted. Rarer forms of hallucinations are visual, olfactory (related to smell), gustatory (related to taste), and tactile (related to touch). Visual hallucinations may exist in the schizophrenia spectrum and other psychotic disorders but are extremely rare. When a client is experiencing visual hallucinations, an assessment to rule out other potential causes should be conducted. For example, could the visual hallucinations be related to organic damage to the brain, substance use or abuse, or any other medical conditions? For hallucinations other than auditory, a drug test should be considered. After the drug test results are received, a complete assessment by a medically trained professional is always warranted.

The least common forms of hallucinations in schizophrenia, the psychotic disorders and in some cases of bipolar disorder are the tactile, gustatory and olfactory sensations (Lewandowski et al., 2009). Tactile hallucinations may also be indicative of an organic problem. In some cases, clients may report feeling tactile misperceptions, such as bugs crawling on them. In this case, a simple rule is that clients' reports of bugs on them may be related to "drugs" including substance use and abuse. Substance misuse can be a problem in schizophrenia, and when it co-occurs with the disorder, negative consequences can influence all aspects of the treatment process (Green, 2007). In these cases, a client should immediately be referred for a drug screen, physical examination, or both to determine if the resulting psychosis is related to the side effects of prescription medications, drug abuse, or a related type of delirium. Gustatory hallucinations result in the perception that something tastes a certain a way that others would not agree or recognize and is often perceived as unpleasant. For example, a client may report that the food he or she is eating is poisoned and therefore tastes rotten or bitter. Reasons for the development of these types of hallucinations can vary but generally an assessment to address possible medical causes such as seizures should always be explored.

Olfactory hallucinations sometimes referred to as phantosmia, occur when individuals perceive smells that do not actually exist in their environment. The smells can vary and there are multiple medical causes for this such as seizures, brain tumors, or migraines and these are seldom related to a mental disorder.

Disorganized Thinking and Speech

The disorganized dimension of a client's behavior can be seen in his or her disordered patterns of speech. Disordered speech can be expressed in a variety of ways. Clients may make loose associations and jump from one topic to another, or their speech may be tangential or even incoherent. The disorganized speech may be so pronounced that it is referred to as word salad: There is marked incoherence, and the practitioner is not sure what the client is trying to say or how to interpret it because it sounds like unconnected, irrelevant gibberish. The individual may also make up words and when added to other features of this grossly disorganized speech it may become almost impossible to understand what the client is trying to say. The disorganized dimension of a client's thought process relates to the primary symptoms most relevant with linking to speech to better understand the occurrence of problematic behaviors. For the mental health practitioner, these symptoms are often obvious and easy to detect in the diagnostic assessment process.

Negative Symptoms

In completing a general mental status exam, positive and negative symptoms are often at the forefront. In schizophrenia spectrum and the other psychotic disorders, negative symptoms can be not only difficult to assess but also difficult to treat with medications. The negative symptoms seen in these disorders are often more common than the positive symptoms, although they remain harder to detect. Negative symptoms involve behaviors that should be present but are absent. For example, one symptom is a flat or blunted affect characterized by *diminished emotional expression.* In diminished emotional expression, there can be restrictions in the range or intensity of facial expressions, initiation of speech, and other types of delayed movements. Additional negative symptoms include *anhedonia* (decreased ability to experience pleasure), *avolition* (lack of goal-directed behavior), and *asociality* (lack of interest in social interactions and emotional withdrawal), as well as poor rapport, passivity, apathy, social withdrawal, difficulty in abstract thinking, lack of spontaneity, and stereotyped thinking patterns. In addition, the *DSM-5* includes a negative symptom termed *alogia* (APA, 2000), which deals primarily with the fluency and productivity of speech.

Because the negative symptoms are typically more common but subtler than the positive symptoms, inability to control these symptoms often prevents clients from leading fruitful and productive lives (Malhotra, Pinsky, & Breier, 1996). Negative symptoms often overlap with symptoms of individuals who are depressed, such as reduced appetite, lack of energy, lack of pleasure, and inattention. Medications appear to be most helpful in controlling the positive symptoms and less effective in controlling the negative ones (Dziegielewski, 2010).

In summary, these disorders share symptoms such as delusions, hallucinations, and disorganized speech and behavior, as well as numerous negative symptoms. Differentiating overlapping of symptoms between mood and affect is critical. One simple way to think of this relationship is that mood can be considered the general feeling experienced (i.e., the climate) and affect is how it's shown (i.e., the weather). (See Quick Reference 5.2.)

DSM-5: ASSESSMENT OF SYMPTOMS MEASUREMENT

One particularly helpful addition to *DSM-5* that highlights both the dimensional approach and the crosscutting of symptoms is the newly introduced Clinician-Rated Dimensions of Psychosis Symptom Severity, a scale included in Section III (p. 743). This scale is a dimensional assessment measure that addresses the primary positive and negative symptoms of schizophrenia spectrum and the psychotic disorders. As first introduced in Chapter 2, this dimensional measurement may be particularly helpful in supporting the diagnoses related to schizophrenia spectrum and other psychotic disorders because it measures

QUICK REFERENCE 5.2

Psychotic Characteristics and Symptoms

Positive Symptoms

Delusions—strong beliefs held in spite of strong evidence to the contrary

Hallucinations—misperceptions

Disorganized speech—affecting thought content and delivery

Negative Symptoms

Diminished emotional expression

Asociality

Anhedonia

Avolition

Alogia

Other factors for assessment include:

Poor rapport

Apathy

Difficulty in abstract thinking

Stereotyped thinking patterns

Passivity

Lack of spontaneity

the degree of cognitive or neurobiological factors related to an illness. This particular assessment can help in completing a more comprehensive assessment by identifying the multiple dimensions of psychosis outlined in the preceding paragraphs, including positive symptoms (delusions, hallucinations, and disorganized speech), abnormal psychomotor behavior (such as catatonia), and negative symptoms (restricted emotional expression or activity). The scale measures eight specific domains, addresses symptom severity over the past 7 days, and is completed by the clinician. It uses a 5-point scale, rating symptoms from no symptoms = 0 to severe = 4. It can be used as a repeated measure to regularly measure progress.

In addition, it can clarify the presence of each domain, quantifying symptoms such as hallucinations, delusions, disorganized speech, abnormal psychomotor behavior, negative symptoms (avolition and restricted emotional affect), impaired cognition, depression, and mania. The scale is completed by the practitioner upon initial assessment and can be reassessed as needed in each following 7-day period. Scores consistently high in a particular area can help the practitioner to target interventions. For example, noting the initial score and any changes can quantify beginning levels of delusional thinking and whether subsequent treatment appears to be decreasing them. This standardized measure can be used to keep track of these thoughts and behaviors in a disorder that is prone to difference and fluctuates over time.

Catatonia

One of the most significant changes made to the diagnosis of schizophrenia was the elimination of the five subtypes of schizophrenia discussed further in this chapter. One of the subtypes, catatonic type, that was deleted provided symptomatology that helps to better explain behaviors. It also helped to outline psychomotor presentations that could be connected to several different disorders. Because these types of behaviors could be seen in conditions other than schizophrenia, it was decided in the *DSM-5* revision that a re-introduction with a clearer presentation was needed. In the revision, these symptoms were identified and related back directly to the parent diagnosis and the cause. Although catatonia is not recognized as a diagnosis by itself, it was included as related to the mental and medical disorder in which it manifests. Disorders that may either involve catatonia or result in it include several disorders in this chapter, as well as in several other chapters, such as the neurodevelopmental disorders, bipolar disorders, depressive disorders, and medical conditions (First, 2014; Tandon, 2012).

To address the importance of identifying catatonia and the symptoms it represents, 12 psychomotor symptoms were identified as characteristic of the condition: stupor, catalepsy, waxy flexibility, mutism, negativism, posturing, mannerism, stereotypy, agitation, grimacing, echolalia, and echopraxia (APA, 2013). Catatonia is then defined as the presence of three or more of the 12 identified psychomotor features. One prominent symptom of this disorder is *stupor,* in which the individual presents with limited psychomotor activity. When questioned, the client often does not respond, nor does the individual respond appropriately to other factors in his or her environment. Others may report that the person appears to be in a sleepy daze, making communication difficult.

Catalepsy and *waxy flexibility* are two symptoms of catatonia that are often confused because both refer to posture. In catalepsy, the individual assumes a posture that is difficult to hold and goes against gravity, whereas in waxy flexibility the individual assumes the position but with some resistance can be positioned by the examiner. For example, while working with the state hospital system, I was assigned a client who had catatonic features and often exhibited both catalepsy and waxy flexibility. Each morning I would visit my client, who was in the hospital unit. She had the diagnosis of schizophrenia. Rapport was developed with the client, and often she would assume odd positions, such as standing with her hands reaching upward (*catalepsy*) for long periods of time. When attempts were made to get her to sit down, she would not move. Since she was so resistant, we had several sessions with her in that position until she decided to change her posture and sit. At times, she would look at me and assume an odd-looking facial *grimace* while leaning over. She often assumed an unusual posture that looked uncomfortable, referred to as *posturing.* When she became restless in a session, she would walk around the room; her movements resembled a toy soldier and were *stereotypy* in nature, having no purpose for the repetitive movements that could be considered normal walking. If I tried to get her to sit down, she would stand firm in her position and resist being repositioned (*waxy flexibility*). Often, although capable of speech, she would not speak and exhibited *mutism.* At other times during the session, she would stare off into space in a *stupor* and not exhibit any movement or responses to my prompts.

One morning the client came to my office for an unscheduled visit as I was rushing off to a meeting. I explained that I had to leave and I would be back. She was standing there with both hands in the air and appeared quite *agitated* as she mumbled what sounded like someone had taken her blanket from her bed. I touched her hand as I went past, and she responded to my touch by barely shaking my hand. When I returned to my office about an hour later, the client was still standing in the same position as when I left, with her hand extended as if we had just finished shaking hands. When I later asked other staff members about the position of the client outside my door, they stated that when they questioned her as to why she was there, she would not move or respond. When I returned, however, she immediately walked into my office and again muttered what she wanted my help with. It became obvious to me that she was waiting for me to return, and the waxy flexibility was evident in her retention of the exact position for an extended period of time. Although this client did not display them, two other symptoms of catatonia are *echolalia* (parrotlike representation of someone else's speech) and *echopraxia* (parrotlike repetition of someone else's speech and movements).

In summary, catatonia by itself is not a mental disorder, nor is it any longer considered a subtype of schizophrenia. In assessment the initial task is to determine whether this syndrome is present (First, 2014). Catatonia has to be linked to the parent mental or medical disorder and coded appropriately. As described later in this chapter, the three diagnoses related to catatonia are catatonia associated with another mental disorder (catatonia specifier), catatonic disorder due to another medical condition, and unspecified catatonia.

OVERVIEW OF SCHIZOPHRENIA SPECTRUM AND OTHER PSYCHOTIC DISORDERS

The *DSM-5* provides the standardized classification system for psychiatric disorders across the United States. Using the criteria for the mental disorders as outlined in the *DSM-5* allows standardization across disorders and quick, standardized, effective determinations of individual psychopathology (Schmidt, Norr, & Korte, 2014). According to the *DSM-5,* the primary psychotic disorders are schizotypal personality disorder, delusional disorder, brief psychotic disorder, schizophreniform disorder, schizophrenia, schizoaffective disorder, substance/medication-induced psychotic disorder, psychotic disorder due to another medical condition, catatonia associated with another mental disorder, catatonia associated with another medical disorder, unspecified catatonia, other specified schizophrenia spectrum or other psychotic disorder, and unspecified schizophrenia spectrum or other psychotic disorder. The characteristic symptom of psychosis experienced by clients is being out of touch with reality, and it is characterized by behavioral problems and issues noted in one of the five following domains: "delusions, hallucinations, disorganized thinking (speech), grossly disorganized or abnormal motor behavior (including catatonia) and negative symptoms" (APA, 2013: p. 87). Although defining all psychotic disorders is beyond the scope of this chapter, a brief definition of criteria for each is in Quick Reference 5.3.

Those familiar with *DSM-IV* and *DSM-IV-TR* will note that this chapter has been reorganized to reflect the gradient of psychopathology of the disorders listed, ranking them from least to most severe. In addition, all of the severity dimensions have been updated. Also, although schizotypal personality disorder is explained in depth in the chapter on personality disorders, it is listed in this chapter because of its relationship to schizophrenia spectrum. A disorder termed *attenuated psychosis syndrome* was added to Section III as an area for further study. This potential disorder has the possibility of delusions, hallucinations, and disorganized

QUICK REFERENCE 5.3

TYPES OF SCHIZOPHRENIA SPECTRUM AND OTHER PSYCHOTIC DISORDERS

Schizotypal personality disorder: Individuals often exhibit odd and eccentric behavior. For a complete definition of this personality disorder, see the chapter on personality disorders in both this book and *DSM*-5.

Delusional disorder: An individual suffers from one or more delusions that last approximately 1 month or longer; however, the criteria for schizophrenia has never been met.

Brief psychotic disorder: A time-limited disorder in which the symptoms generally last at least 1 day (24 hours) but no longer than 1 month. Sudden onset may or may not be linked to a psychosocial stressor. Once the disorder ends, the client returns to a fully functioning state similar to what was present before the brief psychotic episode.

Schizophreniform disorder: Diagnosis is usually considered provisional because it generally refers to the first episode of psychosis that has lasted at least 1 month, and two or more symptoms must be present, with at least one of them being delusions, hallucinations, or disorganized speech. When the active phase of the episode extends beyond 6 months and the other criteria for schizophrenia are met, the diagnosis is changed accordingly.

Schizophrenia: Individuals suffer from characteristic psychotic symptoms and a noted deterioration in adaptive functioning. Two or more from a list of symptoms must be present, with at least one of them being delusions, hallucinations, or disorganized speech. The time frame is an active phase of the disorder lasting approximately 1 month and these symptoms, with possibly less intensity, continuing for a duration of at least 6 months.

Schizoaffective disorder: The individual suffers from the signs and symptoms prevalent in both schizophrenia and mood disturbance (major depressive episode or manic), with the symptoms of schizophrenia remaining prevalent.

Substance/medication-induced psychotic disorder: The psychotic symptoms an individual is experiencing are related directly to drug abuse, a medication, or toxin exposure.

Psychotic disorder due to another medical condition: The psychotic symptoms an individual is experiencing are related directly to a medical condition.

Catatonia associated with another mental disorder: This disorder and catatonia are not considered independent and should be documented with the mental disorder that accompanies it (neurodevelopmental, psychotic disorder, bipolar, depressive, or other mental disorder).

Catatonia associated with another medical disorder: Catatonia is not considered an independent diagnosis, and the medical disorder that accompanies it—cerebral folate deficiency, rare autoimmune (abnormal immune response against substances and

(continued)

QUICK REFERENCE 5.3 (*Continued*)

tissues in the body), or paraneoplastic disorders (related to consequence of cancer in the body)—has to be indicated.

Unspecified catatonia: Symptoms of catatonia cause significant distress, but the underlying mental or medical disorder is not clear.

Other specified schizophrenia spectrum or other psychotic disorder: The psychotic symptoms and client's presentation of them do not meet all the criteria for any of the specific psychotic disorders, or the information needed to confirm a clear diagnosis is either inadequate or contradictory. The specific reason is documented following the condition.

Unspecified schizophrenia spectrum or other psychotic disorder: The psychotic symptoms and the client's presentation of them do not meet all the criteria for any of the specific psychotic disorders, or information to confirm a clear diagnosis is either inadequate or contradictory. The specific reason is documented following the condition.

Source: Summarized criteria from the *Diagnostic and Statistical Manual of Mental Disorders*, 5th ed. Copyright 2013 by the American Psychiatric Association.

speech that can cause distress or disability, but the occurrences are not nearly as intense as in a psychotic episode (Woods & McGlashen, 2011).

Schizotypal Personality Disorder

In schizotypal personality disorder, individuals often exhibit odd and eccentric behavior. For a complete definition of this disorder, see the chapter on personality disorders. This diagnosis is dual listed in *DSM-5* because it is considered to be most like the diagnosis of schizophrenia, although the symptoms exhibited are significantly less severe. Also, this disorder is listed first in the schizophrenia-related disorders because developmentally it is most likely to have its onset in childhood. When the symptoms for schizotypal personality disorder first manifest in childhood or adolescence and continue into adulthood, remaining severe enough to disturb functioning, diagnosing this personality disorder may be considered.

Delusional Disorder

Delusional disorder is diagnosed when the client is experiencing one or more delusions with a duration of at least 1 month. This diagnosis is immediately differentiated from schizophrenia for two reasons. First, the time frame is 1 month but does not have to continue for 6 months as in schizophrenia. Second, the only symptom required is delusions, and none of the other characteristics consistent with schizophrenia is required. As the name indicates, delusional disorder is characterized by persistent delusions that may or may not seem believable or bizarre. The delusions generally take on a theme and can fall into seven delusion-based subtypes. Identifying a subtype in this disorder helps to clarify the diagnosis when the phenomenological criteria of the delusional thinking are mutually exclusive and exhaustive (APA, 2013). In addition, subtyping the kinds of delusions allows for homogeneous groupings of disorders. The subtypes are easy to recognize in documenting because the coding starts with *specify whether*. The subtypes for this disorder are erotomanic type, grandiose type, jealous type (belief that spouse or partner is unfaithful), persecutory type, somatic type, mixed type (multiple delusional themes present), and unspecified type (cannot determine specific type).

In delusional disorder, the subtypes are followed by specifiers. The specifiers are not mutually exclusive and exhaustive and can add information beyond the subtypes. This disorder has two types of specifiers possible, and when applicable, both are coded with *specify if*. The first is providing a specifier that the delusions are of a bizarre nature. When bizarre content is used as a specifier, the delusional beliefs are so implausible that no one would accept them to be real. For example, a woman who was pregnant stated that she was having another woman's baby. The woman wanted to have a child with her husband but believed that he did not want to have a child with her. This led to another woman taking her child and replacing it with the one she was now carrying. In describing this, she was adamant that no one else knew, but she did; she could feel the difference inside her and was convinced she knew exactly when it happened and who the other woman was who took and replaced her child. This is considered a bizarre delusion in that anyone hearing it would immediately see it as implausible. In situations such as this, it would be properly classified with bizarre content and written accordingly.

Specify if: With bizarre content

Utilizing this diagnosis in *DSM-5* also requires outlining a second specifier related to the episode being experienced. This specifier, however, can be used only if the individual has had the course of the illness for at least 1 year. When relevant for application, this specifier is divided into eight potential categories that relate directly to the onset of the episode exhibited when the diagnosis is first placed. The first three specifiers relate directly to the onset and course of the illness and can be labeled either acute, partial remission, or in full remission. These three specifiers relate to the occurrence of the first episode. An acute episode is defined as meeting the criteria of the disorder over a certain time frame. Partial remission means improvement is noted; in full remission requires that no previous symptoms be present.

Specify if: First episode, currently in acute phase
Specify if: First episode, currently in partial remission
Specify if: First episode, currently in full remission.

Other specifiers include more than one episode and do not focus on just the first episode's onset. When noting multiple episodes, link to the same pattern description of whether the course is acute, partial, or in full remission. The last two specifiers can be labeled continuous or unspecified. In the continuous specifier, the criteria thresholds can appear confusing, as they remain through the majority of the course of the illness. However, during certain periods the presentation may vary and may not meet the thresholds. In the unspecified category, the thresholds are not met, and the course of the illness, although present, remains difficult to quantify in terms of first episode or course. (For complete definitions of these specifiers, see *DSM-5,* page 91.)

Specify if: Multiple episodes, currently in acute phase
Specify if: Multiple episodes, currently in partial remission
Specify if: Multiple episodes, currently in full remission
Specify if: Continuous
Specify if: Unspecified

This diagnosis also requires specifying the current level of severity. The *DSM-5* suggests using the Clinician-Rated Dimensions of Psychosis Severity Scale mentioned earlier for symptom rating, but it is not required.

In terms of functioning, these individuals often perform well at work or in certain situations where the delusional beliefs can be controlled. However, when something happens to change this situation or disturb the individual's usual coping styles, problems with social or occupational functioning often result (Munro & Mok, 2006). For the most part, this disorder usually starts late in life. Although it does not generally cause problems with intellect or work-related deterioration, it does cause frequent domestic problems. Family members close to the client may constantly listen to the delusional train of thought and become frustrated because, although in the nonbizarre delusions it may sound believable to some, they know it is not true. Efforts to convince the client suffering from the disorder generally fall on deaf ears because the delusional thinking, although it is not bizarre, is a critical part of the client's belief system than cannot be shaken. Based on their strong beliefs, these clients are often involved in litigation within the legal system for what they believe are crimes committed against them. When the delusions are psychosomatic and they believe what has happened to them is medically related, they may have endless medical tests.

Chronic reduction of sensory input (e.g., blindness or deafness) may contribute to misinterpretations and the eventual development of what seem to be hallucinations and delusions. In addition, further misinterpretations may occur in conjunction with the client's experiences, especially when there is social isolation, as when an immigrant tries to adjust to a different culture. Be sure to consider a drug test to assess for substance use or misuse, as well as a consult with a medically trained professional to determine whether the symptoms are medically related.

Brief Psychotic Disorder

The key feature of a brief psychotic disorder is that the disturbance is the result of a sudden onset of at least one of the first three listed psychotic symptoms: delusions, hallucinations, markedly disorganized speech (e.g., frequent derailment or incoherence). Although not required to always be present to confirm the diagnosis, grossly disorganized or catatonic behavior is still part of Criterion A. An episode of the disturbance lasts at least 1 day but less than 1 month, and the individual eventually has a full return to the premorbid level of functioning (Criterion B). In addition, the signs and symptoms of the disorder are not better accounted for by another related mental disorder (e.g., major depressive or bipolar disorder with psychotic features or another psychotic disorder such as schizophrenia). Nor should the symptoms displayed be attributable to catatonia, the direct physiological effects of a substance (e.g., a hallucinogen), or another medical condition (Criterion C) (APA, 2013, p. 94).

The condition of brief psychotic disorder may at first be confused with the condition of schizophreniform or schizophrenia because of the overlap of criteria, but there is a difference in duration. For this disorder the duration must be at least one day but cannot extend beyond one month. Carefully assessing the symptoms for this disorder and differentiating it from other psychotic disorders, depression or mania is central as it can occur across the lifespan with the majority of the cases occurring at approximately age 35. Awareness of this diagnosis is significant because it can also develop further into another psychotic disorder, and since it has no prodromal period it may be immediately assessed as substance-related which results case closure neglecting the need to alert practitioners that an underlying cause of the psychosis is not clear. Also, when coding the diagnosis of brief psychotic disorder according to the *DSM-5* criteria, the practitioner should *specify* whether it is with or without marked stressors and whether it is occurring with postpartum onset. Individually documenting the stressor or whether there are multiple stressors is central to better understanding the diagnosis. It is also expected that onset during pregnancy or within 4 weeks postpartum should be documented.

Specify if: With marked stressor(s)
Specify if: Without marked stressors(s)
Specify if: With postpartum onset

A second specifier with this diagnosis is related to catatonia and whether 3 of the 12 characteristic symptoms of the condition exist. To apply catatonia as a specifier to this mental disorder, the 12 characteristic symptoms must be examined: stupor, catalepsy (rigid posture), waxy flexibility (resistance to positioning by the examiner), mutism, negativism, posturing, mannerism, stereotypy (repetitive non-goal-directed movements), agitation, grimacing, echolalia (mimicking the speech of another), and echopraxia (mimicking the movement of another). When three of these symptoms co-occur and the criteria for this disorder are met, the specifier can be used.

Specify if: with catatonia.

Once this is complete, the current severity level of the disorder is indicated. Similar to delusional disorder, the Clinician-Rated Dimensions of Psychosis Severity Scale mentioned earlier should be considered for assessing the severity of the symptoms. However, in *DSM-5,* a severity specifier is not required for this diagnosis.

Schizophreniform Disorder

The diagnosis of schizophreniform is used to describe clients who recover from the symptoms of psychosis completely within the 6-month period and have no residual effects. The criteria for schizophreniform disorder are the same as those for schizophrenia (Criterion A) except for two differences: the total duration of the illness (including prodromal, active, and residual phases) and impaired social or occupational functioning during some part of the illness, which is not required, although it may occur. In addition, in schizophreniform there is a specifier with good or without good prognostic features (good premorbid functioning and the absence of blunted or flat affect). Like brief reactive psychosis, it can also receive the specifier of with catatonia if 3 of the 12 criteria are met. Similar to brief psychotic disorder using the Clinician-Rated Dimensions of Psychosis Severity Scale for assessing the severity of the symptoms is recommended but not required, as the diagnosis can be made without using the severity specifier.

One major difference between this disorder, brief psychotic disorder, and schizophrenia is the time frame needed for meeting the diagnostic criteria. The duration requirement in schizophreniform disorder is considered intermediate; it bridges the time frame between the two other disorders. In brief psychotic disorder, the time frame for the active symptoms is less than 1 month; in schizophreniform, it is less than 6 months; and in schizophrenia, it is 6 months or more (APA, 2013). Because the time frame for the symptoms of brief reactive psychosis has been exceeded but not met for schizophrenia, this diagnosis is generally considered provisional. The expected course of symptoms should be monitored, and when and if the time frame is met and the symptoms persist, the diagnosis should be changed to schizophrenia. In these cases, schizophreniform characterizes the beginning phase of schizophrenia.

Because so many mental health practitioners confuse brief psychotic disorder, schizophreniform disorder, and schizophrenia, these disorders are differentiated with a brief case example. When approaching a client who may suffer from one of these disorders, look carefully at the time frame in which the client experienced the active problematic symptoms for each disorder:

- Brief psychotic disorder: less than 1 month.
- Schizophreniform disorder: less than 6 months
- Schizophrenia: more than 6 months

Wong (2013) reminds practitioners that this 6-month time frame is arbitrary and not based on research. Using the time frames may be helpful in separating these disorders, but the clinical relevance is questionable. In brief psychotic disorder, the symptoms are often severe but generally are brief, lasting at least 24 hours but less than 1 month. When the symptoms subside, the client generally returns to the premorbid level of functioning. In addition to the time frame criterion, in brief psychotic disorder there may or may not be a stressor, although if there is a precipitating stressor, it should be clearly identified. Onset of brief psychotic disorder is sudden and accompanied by positive symptoms such as hallucinations, delusions, or disorganized speech. In schizophreniform disorder, the symptoms are very similar to schizophrenia; however, this provisional diagnosis is usually applied to the first psychotic break. In a diagnosis of schizophreniform disorder, the criterion of 1 month has been met, but the 6-month period has not. There is no requirement in schizophreniform disorder, as in the criteria for schizophrenia, for a decline in either social or occupational functioning during some point in the illness. Schizophreniform disorder is considered primarily a provisional diagnosis because if the criteria and the time frame of 6 months are met, the diagnosis will be changed to schizophrenia.

To highlight the relationship of these three psychotic disorders, a brief clinical case example is provided of a military recruit. It is not uncommon for a recruit to experience his or her first psychotic breakdown during military basic training. In this 6-week intensive training experience, new recruits are placed under considerable stress, and extreme pressure is applied to change their usual style of coping and patterns of behavior. Recruits are forced to abruptly learn and adopt an entirely new lifestyle. Emphasis on the individual is negated in an effort to have recruits form a group identity. This pressure to conform is so intense that some new recruits experience what would appear to be a psychotic break. In this case, a female recruit became hysterical and actively delusional. When told that she would have to take a shower in a communal setting with other female recruits, she experienced auditory hallucinations that told her that others were plotting against her. She became so uncontrollable and volatile that after weeks of trying to calm her within the unit, she was referred for inpatient admission and evaluation. After the initial evaluation was completed, it was clear that she met the criteria for schizophreniform except that there was no documented history of this disorder. She had been experiencing the symptoms for over one month but the 6-month period had not been met. Thus, the diagnosis of schizophreniform seemed most appropriate.

There was clearly a severe stressor related to the incident; within several hours after she was placed in an inpatient setting and after problem-solving the situation, her delusional thinking (positive symptoms) subsided. In the in-patient setting she was allowed to shower alone in her own private facility and within 1 week, all previous discomfort was resolved. A diagnosis of schizophrenia or schizophreniform would be inappropriate because of the short time frame and the complete remission. The recruit's symptoms supported neither diagnosis. In addition to duration of symptoms, cultural factors should always be taken into account when making a diagnosis (Woo & Keatinge, 2008). This particular client, during an interview, stated that she was always taught that the naked body was sacred and should be viewed only by her mate. The recruit believed that by taking a communal shower, she would be violating this sacred trust and tainting her physical body, which she was saving for marriage. When she was permitted to take showers alone, the symptoms disappeared. Nevertheless, one additional condition that may be the focus of clinical attention in this case is acculturation difficulty (coded V62.4 or Z60.3). According to the *DSM-5* (APA, 2013), this category can be used when the focus of clinical attention is adjustment to a different culture. In the example, the recruit's difficulties occurred because of adjustment problems related to rapid integration into the military culture. Once the stressor was resolved, and the expectation which violated her own cultural norms was addressed, so were the symptoms.

If the client had been diagnosed with schizophrenia (at that time it was military policy to do so), she would have immediately been processed for discharge. However, by carefully looking at her symptoms and taking into account environmental and cultural factors, it was determined that a diagnosis of brief reactive psychosis, schizophreniform, and/or schizophrenia was inappropriate. This is an excellent example of how the mental health practitioner's clinical judgment always has to include examining the criteria for a diagnosis, along with a mixture of art and science.

SCHIZOPHRENIA

Since schizophrenia was first inltroduced in the *DSM,* many changes have occurred in practice related to this disorder, requiring revisions in the *DSM.* The *DSM-IV* (APA, 1994) and the *DSM-IV-TR* (APA, 2000) combined three sections (schizophrenia, delusional disorder, and psychotic disorder not elsewhere classified) that were listed separately in the *DSM-III-R* (APA, 1987). In the *DSM-IV* and the *DSM-IV-TR,* the essential features of schizophrenia were divided into five subtypes (paranoid type, disorganized type, catatonic type, undifferentiated type, and residual type), and, in *DSM-5,* based on research that did not support them, the previous five subtypes were eliminated. The *DSM-5* (2013) reports the typical age of onset is late teens to the mid-30s, with the first episode of schizophrenia in the early to mid-20s for men and the middle to late 20s for women. Children may be diagnosed with schizophrenia, but the condition is rare; they would be expected to meet the same criteria and time frames as an adult.

In *DSM-5,* the diagnosis is based on a mixture of five characteristic signs and symptoms (delusions, hallucinations, disorganized speech, grossly disorganized or catatonic behavior, and negative symptoms such as diminished emotional expression and avolition) (Criterion A). To meet the diagnostic criteria for schizophrenia, the individual must have at least two of the five symptoms, and at least one of those two must be delusions, hallucinations, or disorganized speech. The magnitude of the symptoms must be enough to impair occupational and social functioning, interfering with activities such as work or interpersonal and social relationships (Criterion B). Furthermore, the duration of the symptoms must be at least 6 months and include a period of 1 month with active-phase symptoms. This period can be less than 1 month if the client is successfully treated with medication and may include periods of prodromal or residual symptoms (Criterion C). Documenting this 1 month criterion is different from older versions of the *DSM,* which listed it as 1 week. Other conditions such as schizoaffective and bipolar with psychotic features must be ruled out (Criterion D), and what the client is experiencing cannot be related to a substance abuse problem or another medical condition (Criterion E). When there is a history of autism spectrum disorder (ASD) or a communication disorder, the relationship between these disorders and whether there are any overlapping symptoms must be clarified. For example, in schizophrenia, it must be determined that in addition to other related symptoms similar to ASD, the client must also be experiencing hallucinations and/or delusions (Criterion F).

Although in *DSM-5* there are no subtypes for the disorder, multiple specifiers can be utilized. Similar to the criteria for delusional disorder, the first group of specifiers is related to the course of the illness and cannot be used unless the illness has been present for at least 1 year. Because of the variability of this disorder, these specifiers are designed to better display the course of the illness and the symptoms. The first three specifiers discuss the first manifestation of the disorder and how it has progressed for at least 1 year. They are designed to help identify how the course of the illness is progressing and whether the client is actively in an acute phase (displaying active symptoms) of the disorder. For example, the first three specifiers relate to the occurrence of the first episode and require that the individual has had the illness for at least 1 year. An acute episode is defined as meeting the criteria for the disorder for the past year and now actively displaying the full symptoms of the disorder once again. This is referred to as the first episode, and the individual is currently in the episode. In the first episode, partial remission means improvement is noted, and in full remission the previous acute episode has resolved and no current disorder-specific symptoms are being displayed. Those familiar with *DSM-IV-TR* may be reminded of the term *in-remission.* In *DSM-5,* this is further clarified with the use of these specifiers. (For complete definitions of these specifiers, see *DSM-5,* page 99-100.)

Specify if: First episode, currently in acute phase

Specify if: First episode currently in partial remission

Specify if: First episode currently in full remission.

In schizophrenia, when the term *multiple episodes* is used, it means the client has had a series of acute episodes in which the criteria for the disorder have been met. In multiple episodes, the current status of the condition for the client can be rated.

Specify if: Multiple episodes, currently in acute phase

Specify if: Multiple episodes, currently in partial remission

Specify if: Multiple episodes, currently in full remission

Two additional specifiers can help explain the condition's course.

Specify if: Continuous (symptoms of the illness remain constant)

Specify if: Unspecified

A second option for using specifiers for the diagnosis of schizophrenia is to specify whether it is with catatonia. As described earlier, catatonia by itself is not a diagnosis, but the symptoms that occur when accompanying a mental or medical diagnosis could allow placement of a specifier related to it or a separate diagnosis relating it directly to the medical condition. Catatonia is described in more depth later in this chapter as it is related to the possible mental health and medical diagnoses that could accompany it. With the diagnosis of schizophrenia, making this distinction is important because many of the symptoms displayed in catatonia overlap the symptoms of schizophrenia. If the occurrence of catatonia is comorbid rather than complicated by it, a separate code for the catatonia can be used.

Specify if: With Catatonia

Like the other disorders in this section, rating the symptoms and the severity is essential to the proper diagnosis. In addition, given the variable course of this disorder, although not required, the Clinician-Rated Dimensions of Psychosis Severity Scale should be considered to assess the severity of the symptoms. In *DSM-5*, a severity specifier is not required for this diagnosis.

Regarding children, the prevalence of schizophrenia is rare prior to age 12, and the diagnosis increases 50-fold for those older than 15 (Clark, 2006). In adults, the prevalence of schizophrenia is reported to range from 0.3% to 0.7% of the population, with variations noted among certain population groups, geographic locations, and immigrant status (APA, 2013). Each of the age groups has different indicators associated with the onset of schizophrenia. The psychosis related to schizophrenia develops gradually in children, without the sudden psychotic break that may happen in adolescents and adults. The behavior of children with this illness may change over time and, in fact, often does.

Childhood-onset schizophrenia (COS) research has confirmed that those with early-onset schizophrenia experience a more complicated, clinically severe problem than those with the adult-onset disorder. The COS continues into adulthood yet manifests with special developmental and social challenges (APA, 2013). For this reason, COS is often chronic, persistently debilitating, and overwhelming to support systems. It affects the client's quality of life unless closely followed by combined medical, physical, social, and environmental treatments. Glick (2005) presented an etiologic pathway of targeted features of schizophrenia that discusses intervention at every level. He asserts that there is a hopeful picture for the natural course of the disease and that it tends to stabilize with age.

Although childhood schizophrenia is rarely diagnosed, several antecedent neurodevelopmental issues seem to be related to the condition (Mental Health America, 2009; Weiner, 1987). These neurodevelopmental antecedents include developmental delays in speech and motor development, problems with behavior and social development, emotional problems, and reports of psychotic-like experiences (Hollis, 1995; Laurens, Hodgins, Maughan, Rutter, & Taylor, 2009; Weiner, 1987).

In adolescents, schizophrenia may develop over time or have a rapid onset. Assessment of the adolescent for a diagnosis of schizophrenia must include a discussion of the adolescent's history and current functioning, such as disorganized thinking; poor interpersonal skills; inability to control ideas, behavior, and emotions; and impaired reality perception (Weiner, 1987). All adolescents have specific life circumstances and experiences that contribute to the symptoms they may experience in the development of schizophrenia.

Schizoaffective Disorder

The description of schizoaffective disorder clearly distinguishes it from the other psychotic disorders, and it is increasingly assigned to individuals in clinical settings. Schizoaffective disorder addresses individuals who have prominent features of both schizophrenia and either depressive or manic symptoms. Prior to *DSM-III*, this diagnostic category was often used to classify anyone who had symptoms of mood-incongruent psychotic features, together with signs of an affective disorder (Woo & Keatinge, 2008). Clients suffering from this disorder were considered to have a subtype of dementia praecox, yet they experienced good premorbid adjustment, rapid recovery, and subsequent achievement of good social and occupational function (APA, 2000). To clarify this disorder, the *DSM-III-R* identified it in relation to the timing and duration of the mood episodes that accompany the psychotic symptoms (APA, 1987).

In *DSM-IV* and *DSM-IV-TR,* the individual was expected to meet the criteria for the occurrence of both the psychotic and the affective symptoms. Symptomatology for both disorders (schizophrenia and the mood disorder) had to be clear, but schizophrenia was always prominent, while it met the criteria for a manic, mixed, or depressive episode (APA, 2000). In *DSM-5,* some of the diagnostic considerations have been met with one substantial change. In *DSM-5,* the symptoms related to the manic or depressive episodes must be evident through the entire course of the illness as opposed to just the assessment phase, as specified in *DSM-IV.* Also, attempts were made to clarify the longitudinal nature of the disorder (Tandon, 2012).

According to *DSM-5,* the symptoms required for the diagnosis of schizophrenia (listed in criterion A of that disorder) need to be met. Once this is established, a major depressive or manic episode must also be present and continuous throughout the period of the illness. In addition, the diagnosis of schizophrenia would remain prominent as specified in criterion B, and either delusions or hallucinations for 2 or more weeks without the symptoms of either the depressive or manic symptoms must be noted. This must occur throughout the duration of the illness (criterion C) and not just during the assessment phase, as was expected in *DSM-IV.* Similar to the other disorders in this category, criterion D requires that the effects of substances (medication or otherwise), along with potential medical conditions that could cause the situation, need to be assessed.

In diagnosing schizoaffective disorder, the importance of documenting the subtype is central to the diagnosis. Because the symptoms of schizophrenia are prominent in this diagnosis, the criteria for that diagnosis are evident. To facilitate this diagnosis, however, the subtypes may be of great assistance. The first subtype is related to whether the symptoms apply to the criteria for what would be considered a manic episode. In this subtype, the manic episode is predominant in the presentation, although there may be depressive symptoms that either meet or do not meet the criteria as outlined.

Specify whether: Bipolar type

A second subtype that is seen more commonly in women is the depressive type. In this subtype, the presence of major depressive episodes is part of the presentation. There should not be any symptoms related to a hypomanic or manic episode, and the presentation is depressive symptoms coexisting with schizophrenia.

Specify whether: Depressive type

The additional classifications for the specifiers are identical to those for schizophrenia, and the specifiers can relate to the first episode, multiple episodes, continuous, and unspecified. Symptom severity rating can be completed by using the same measurement instrument as the other diagnoses in this category. For this disorder, however, the diagnostic characteristics for schizophrenia must be met and the specifier applied before any further specifications can be made. Also, to complete a comprehensive diagnostic assessment, be sure to monitor the disorder for the required time periods and watch the display of symptoms accordingly. For the depressive subtype in particular, be sure the episode meets the full criteria for the depressive episode, as some of the negative symptoms are prominent in the diagnosis of schizophrenia as well. This fact makes it difficult to tell if the depressive symptoms actually coexist, as depression may be a co-occurring condition.

The *DSM-5* prevalence information states that schizoaffective disorder is about a third as common as the occurrence of schizophrenia (APA, 2013). A clear diagnostic history is needed, and careful attention should be given to the occurrences of the disorder and whether the individual actually meets the criteria of

1 year. For example, if the individual has a 4-year history of schizophrenia but does not meet the criteria for the affective/mood symptoms (manic or depressive), the diagnosis should not be given (APA, 2013, p. 107). Again, to place this diagnosis, monitoring the individual and the symptoms displayed over a course of time is required, and this may allow for the use of either a provisional diagnosis (see Chapter 3) or the specified or unspecified category to be discussed later in this chapter. One of the biggest concerns with this diagnosis is the overlap of symptoms and the confusion that can occur when putting these two major clinical syndromes into one (Woo & Keatinge, 2008). The practitioner is left to question whether the psychosis and affective components of these two conditions are really separate and how best to treat them to address all aspects of the condition and the symptoms being experienced. More research is needed in this area to attain a better focus on the treatment options for this group and how best to take into account the positive symptoms characteristic of this disorder, along with the affective component, which can clearly affect mood and presentation.

Substance/Medication-Induced Psychotic Disorder

In diagnosing substance/medication-induced disorder, the individual is expected to suffer from either hallucinations or delusions. In addition, an adequate history of what was taken is needed. In criterion B, the substance medication causing the condition must be confirmed by history, physical exam, or lab result. The individual also needs to experience the symptoms soon after ingestion or with resultant intoxication or withdrawal from the substance. Once the information is gathered, especially by history or physical exam, it needs to be confirmed that the substance taken is capable of displaying the side effects that resulted. Similar to other diagnoses in this area, it is central to determine that the substance is not related to another mental health condition such as delirium and that the symptoms are indicative of the substance ingested and not something else (criteria C and D). As with any diagnosis, the disturbance has to be severe enough to interfere with social, occupational, or other important areas of functioning, resulting in impairment or distress. The *DSM-5* outlines specific time frames that should be followed.

In addition, this disorder requires the specification of the onset and whether it is during intoxication or onset during withdrawal. The symptom severity rating scale is recommended for measurement of the severity of the symptoms. For this disorder, however, the hallucinations or delusions must be present, and attribution to the substance must be carefully supported and defined. Also, careful consideration and awareness of what constitutes a substance use disorder are important. If it is related to a substance use disorder and the hallucinations and delusions are not directly related to this disorder, the substance disorder should be utilized.

Psychotic Disorder Due to Another Medical Condition

Similar to the criteria for substance/medication-induced disorders, the individual is expected to suffer from either hallucinations or delusions (criterion A). In addition, there needs to be direct evidence from an adequate history, physical exam, or lab result that makes the connection to the medical condition causing it. For any medical condition, the nonmedically trained practitioner has to work collaboratively and consult with a medically trained practitioner skilled with identifying and addressing the medical condition that is causing the symptoms. Once the information is gathered, especially by history or physical exam, it must be confirmed that the medical condition is the cause, it is not based on a mental health disorder, and it is not occurring during the course of delirium (criteria C and D). As with any diagnosis, the disturbance has to be severe enough to interfere with social, occupational, or other important areas of functioning, resulting in impairment or distress. The *DSM-5* requires that the name of the medical disorder be documented before this particular mental health disorder or any other mental health disorders. This disorder does require determining subtypes and whether the hallucinations or the delusions are prominent. The symptom severity rating scale is recommended for measurement of the symptoms. A wide variety of central nervous system diseases, from both external poisons and internal physiologic illness, can produce symptoms of psychosis. The numbers of medical conditions that can cause or induce a psychotic disorder are many. To be classified as a psychotic disorder due to a another medical condition, however, the psychotic symptoms an individual is experiencing must be related directly to a medical condition.

Catatonia Associated With Another Mental Disorder (Catatonia Specifier)

When catatonia is related to a mental disorder, this is the diagnosis (referred to as catatonic specifier) that is to be used and recorded alongside the mental disorder. In listing the diagnoses, the mental disorder that is the principal diagnosis is listed first. To utilize this diagnosis, catatonia is listed first and then the mental health disorder following a pattern similar to the title. There is only one criterion (criterion A) needed to meet the criteria for the diagnosis. To correctly utilize this as a diagnosis, the 12 possible symptoms reflective of catatonia are reviewed, and when at least three are present, the diagnosis can be made (criterion A). Mental disorders that can be linked to catatonia include several schizophrenia spectrum disorders such as brief psychotic disorder, schizophreniform disorder, schizophrenia, and schizoaffective disorder. Other mental disorders that can be affiliated with catatonia include neurodevelopmental disorders, bipolar disorders, and major depressive disorder.

Catatonic Disorder Due to Another Medical Condition

Like catatonia associated with another mental disorder, this disorder utilizes the same criteria for criterion A. In criterion A, from the 12 possible symptoms of catatonia, only three or more need to be present for the diagnosis to be made. Since this condition involves a medical disorder, it also requires evidence of the medical disorder through history, physical exam, or laboratory findings that confirm the condition (criterion B). In addition, it is not better explained by a mental disorder (criterion C), nor can it occur exclusively during the course of delirium (criterion D). And, (criterion E) the symptoms of the catatonia must cause significant impairment in multiple areas of functioning. According to ICD, with this diagnosis and others of this type, the medical condition is always listed first.

Unspecified Catatonia

This category applies to both mental and medical disorders when there is insufficient information available to make a confirmatory diagnosis. In addition to not only being able to confirm the parent (medical or mental) diagnosis, the full criteria for catatonia are not met. This would often be used in an emergency room setting or where there is not a clear link to the actual cause.

Other Specified or Unspecified Schizophrenia Spectrum and Other Psychotic Disorder

The application of either of these diagnoses requires that the symptoms characteristic of the schizophrenia spectrum and the psychotic disorders be present. These two disorders both require persistent hallucinations in the absence of any other features. Delusions may also be present, and these severe thought patterns can be confusing to assess because they can overlap the symptoms of a manic or depressive episode. Also, it is important to distinguish the specified or unspecified schizophrenia spectrum from attenuated psychosis syndrome, which is a condition listed in *DSM-5* under areas for further study. Attenuated psychosis syndrome is suggested to require symptoms similar to brief reactive psychosis, although the duration is over a 1-week period, and the individual's reality testing remains intact. Distinguishing the delusional content from delusional disorder is valuable. Generally, in this disorder there may also be contradictory information or disorders with psychotic symptoms that do not meet the criteria for any specific psychotic disorder.

Professionals choose this category for symptoms or syndromes that do not meet the criteria for any of the disorders previously described in this chapter. It is generally used when there is inadequate information to assign a diagnosis, or the professional can assign it but simply chooses not to. The primary difference between the specified and the unspecified disorder is that in the specified disorder the practitioner documents the reason that it does not meet the criteria. The unspecified disorder is often used in a crisis situation or an emergency room setting or simply if the practitioner does not see the immediate benefit of listing the reason a formal diagnosis is not to be placed.

BEGINNING THE DIAGNOSTIC ASSESSMENT

Better understanding the schizophrenia spectrum and the other psychotic disorders requires examining the risk factors and symptoms, the diagnostic criteria, the problems identifying the disorder, and the different interventions that have been used to treat persons with this disorder. The case example and the rest of this section focus specifically on the condition of schizophrenia from a personal, community, and societal perspective. Based on this information, a treatment plan and practice strategy is developed that can efficiently embrace, identify, and effectively treat individuals who suffer from psychotic disorders such as schizophrenia.

A diagnosis of schizophrenia is commonly based on the presence of positive symptoms in juxtaposition with impaired social function and the absence of significant mood symptoms. To support a comprehensive diagnostic assessment, the practitioner should always make sure that a physical exam has been conducted to rule out any recognizable neurological illness or substance use that can account for the psychotic symptoms. Working collaboratively with a medically trained professional is always recommended.

Since the first onset of almost all the schizophrenia spectrum and the psychotic disorders occurs in the late teens, taking developmental responses into account is always critical. There may also be an overlap with other disorders, and diagnosing schizophrenia in particular may be complicated because of the overlapping symptoms mentioned earlier in this chapter. It can also be problematic that the time frames (active symptoms of 1 month for a continued period of 6 months) are arbitrary and not based in research (Wong, 2013). Recent research has begun to show connections between the etiology and the disease boundaries between schizophrenia and several other mental health disorders. For example, recent genetic research involving studies of the brain supports similar causes for schizophrenia, autism spectrum disorders, and mental retardation (currently renamed intellectual disability) (Guilmatre et al., 2009).

Continuous research and development of a database to keep up with the various studies and findings hold much promise for the care of these clients.

Characteristically, schizophrenia is a disturbance in perception, thought, emotion, affect, and social relatedness. The potential severity of schizophrenia spectrum disorders and its associated problems makes the information gathered in the diagnostic assessment and treatment plan crucial for an accurate diagnosis, especially identification of environmental factors that are important in the early assessment, prevention, and treatment of this disorder. Situation reporting and cognitive functioning in individuals with these disorders may be clouded; collateral information from others close to the individual is essential. Individuals who suffer from schizophrenia and members of their support system can all benefit from educational interventions and other intervention programs. The majority of individuals experience some type of prodromal phase, characterized by the slow and gradual development of several signs and symptoms. Most studies report that the course of schizophrenia may be inconsistent, with some experiencing exacerbation and remission of the disease and others remaining chronically ill (APA, 2013).

SCHIZOPHRENIA AND FACTORS FOR CONSIDERATION IN THE DIAGNOSTIC ASSESSMENT

In starting the diagnostic assessment for this disorder, two factors must be clearly understood:

1. Identification of a single disorder: Schizophrenia is probably not a single disorder (Woo and Keatinge, 2008). In professional practice, mental health practitioners quickly realize that the client with a single problem does not exist, nor does the client who clearly and concisely fits perfectly into an identified diagnostic category. Clients often have multiple problems that require a multifaceted approach to intervention. The same can be said for clients with schizophrenia who have multiple mental health problems and difficulties (Dziegielewski, 2010). Some of these problems can easily overlap other mental health conditions, such as the affective disorders (bipolar and depression) or the dementia- or delirium-based disorders. Because the etiology of schizophrenia is not yet fully understood, medications as a treatment modality should always focus on controlling the symptoms. As understanding of the causes and origins of schizophrenia and the psychotic disorders increases, so will the ability of mental health professionals to better treat this illness.
2. Cultural considerations: Because the diagnostic assessment will serve as the foundation for intervention with an individual who has schizophrenia, it is imperative to consider the cultural background and experiences of the client and how the client's culture may influence or affect subsequent behavior (Dutta et al., 2007; Locke & Bailey, 2014). Research suggests that there is a better prognosis for schizophrenia in developing societies than in more industrial societies (Cohen, Patel, Thara, & Gureje, 2008). Furthermore, some theorists have postulated that cultural factors can be directly involved in acculturation and adjusting to a new culture (Locke & Bailey, 2014). At times these cultural mores and cultural beliefs can be linked to misperception of either positive or negative symptoms (Dassori et al., 1998; Weisman, 1997).

Ethnic group identity, religion, and spirituality can help to establish culturally sanctioned behaviors that appear to be different from behaviors demonstrated in the dominant culture. For the practitioner, Lum (2011) notes that taking into account the cultural context or knowledge of the cultural environment is a critical factor in determining how one evolves as a cultural being. For example, there was an assumption that those who practice Catholicism in the Latino culture and suffer from mental health or medical concerns would first seek or confer with indigenous healers (*curanderos* or *espiritistas*). Organista (2007) questions this assumption, believing that they are often just as likely as others to seek medical care in a more traditional way. Furthermore, Locke and Bailey (2014), referring to African Americans but applying to all cultural groups, note that all individuals need to be taught that deviations from what is considered normal by the dominant culture does not indicate that what they believe is abnormal. The Cultural Formulation Interview (CFI), as described in Chapter 3, is very important. This interview format allows evaluation of the way the individual approaches and responds to the culture from a cultural perspective. In addition, the third appendix of the *DSM-5* contains some of the best-studied culturally related syndromes and idioms of distress that may be encountered in clinical practice. Being aware of these idioms of distress can help the practitioner be inclusive of the culture, as well as identify what could be considered problematic behaviors identified or communicated in more understandable cultural terms. In completing a comprehensive diagnostic assessment, the CFI and awareness of the cultural concepts of distress, especially when clients report problems with nerves, being possessed by spirits, multiple somatic complaints, and a sense of inexplicable misfortune, can be explored further. In these cases, unwarranted labeling of pathology can be avoided, and behaviors can be explored in relation to norms of the client's cultural reference group.

As times change and cultures become more blended, racial differences may blend, too. Standard definitions continue to be questioned, as evidenced by Paniagua (2014), who suggests eliminating the term *minority* altogether. Regardless of the current definition, cultural factors are central to both the diagnostic assessment and the intervention plan. Cultural factors always need to be identified and taken into account when working with individuals. The CFI may be particularly helpful in formulating a concrete measure to explore the definition of the problem, as well as past and current helping strategy. The ways cultural factors can affect or contribute to problematic behavior should not be underestimated. Grigorenko (2009) provides an excellent edited resource for assisting practitioners in making culturally sensitive assessments.

Special Concerns in Placing the Diagnosis for Schizophrenia

The diagnosis of schizophrenia is often complicated by the fact that symptoms remain susceptible to change during subsequent assessment. Depression and the symptoms relevant to it occur in 25% of the cases in which there is clear documentation of schizophrenia (Siris, 2000). To provide the best care, mental health practitioners need to realize that negative symptoms can overlap and be easily confused with other mental health conditions, such as depression (Woo & Keatinge, 2008).

Generally, most individuals who suffer from schizophrenia experience a characteristic deterioration in adaptive functioning that accompanies the psychotic symptoms. The first psychosis, or break with reality, usually occurs between ages 17 and 30 in men and 20 and 40 in women (Carpenter, Conley, & Buchanan, 1998). The course and variation of schizophrenia remain extremely variable. The first episode of this illness should always be assessed carefully because, after one episode, some individuals may not become psychotic again. The majority of individuals with schizophrenia improve after the first episode but continue to manifest symptoms and remain unpredictable with future occurrences.

Schizophrenia can have either a gradual and insidious onset or a rapid and sudden onset. As noted earlier, for a diagnosis of schizophrenia to be given, the active phase must last approximately 6 months and the person must present with psychotic symptoms for a significant portion of time during a 1-month period, or less if the client responds to treatment. If the time period is shorter, the individual should be diagnosed with schizophreniform disorder or brief psychotic disorder.

Mood disorders, substance abuse, and medical conditions can imitate schizophrenia and must be ruled out. Individuals who suffer from schizophrenia can also abuse alcohol and other drugs. Since substance abuse can reduce effectiveness of treatment, a clear and comprehensive assessment to rule out co-occurring conditions and complicating factors must be conducted.

Concerns Regarding Misdiagnosis and Treatment

Over the years, misunderstandings surrounding schizophrenia have resulted in individuals being treated primarily by trial and error with a variety of supposed remedies to alter body states. Some examples include substances such as cocaine, castor oil, turpentine oil, sulfur oil, and barbiturates; the injection of animal blood; carbon dioxide inhalation; and various methods designed to induce convulsions (Lehmann & Ban, 1997).

Schizophrenia has a lifelong chronic prevalence, with 20% to 30% showing continuing moderate-level symptoms for the rest of their lives (Walker et al., 2008). It is estimated that 50% of individuals with this diagnosis will suffer from relapse within the first year of their most recent episode, regardless of whether they are taking medication. In fact, relapse occurs so often that sufferers can expect to be in the hospital 15% to 20% of their lives. If a person with schizophrenia stops taking his or her medication, relapse tends to be longer, and most do not return to previous baseline functioning (Ayuso-Gutierrez & del Rio Vega, 1997). This finding is complicated further by what is often referred to as treatment-resistant schizophrenia. From 10% to 30% of patients prescribed antipsychotic medications have little if any response, and an additional 30% have only a partial response (APA, 2004). This makes using medication alone problematic and the use of supportive care essential. Many individuals with schizophrenia, especially those with treatment resistance, may have such poor responses to medications that they may be destined to suffer chronic yet variable courses of illness.

The chronic course of treatment and the high relapse rate make care for the individual who suffers from schizophrenia extremely costly within the health care system (Ayuso-Gutierrez & del Rio Vega, 1997). In the United States, it is estimated that mental health disorders are one of the costliest health care expenditures (Soni, 2009). According to the Medical Expenditure Panel Survey (MEPS), from 1996 to 2006, the expenses in this area rose from $19.3 million to $36.2 million (Soni, 2009). Mental disorders have been linked to the loss of $193 billion annually in terms of lost wages (Kessler et al., 2008).

In summary, clients who suffer from schizophrenia and other psychotic disorders are usually thought to be out of touch with reality and to have an impaired ability to evaluate the environment around them. Often these clients are not receptive to the intervention the mental health practitioner tries to provide, even though they require help. Schizophrenia remains a very complex disease that can manifest itself in numerous ways. Overall, the general understanding of schizophrenia and the related psychotic disorders has improved; however, schizophrenia and the psychotic disorders still remain a significant challenge to those who try to provide therapeutic treatment. To achieve a current, ethical, and efficacious practice, mental health practitioners must have a general understanding of the condition of schizophrenia and the resulting behaviors to accurately complete or facilitate the diagnostic assessment.

Use of the Dimensional Assessment

One essential part of the *DSM-5* is the switch from what would be considered a categorical diagnostic assessment to a dimensional one. In these disorders, the hope of introducing cross-cutting of symptoms and the dimensional assessment rests in the fact that schizophrenia spectrum disorders are complicated. They require careful assessment to identify the presenting symptoms an individual is experiencing. The dimensional assessment is intended to get a better understanding of the conditions across this spectrum and to better differentiate them. Given the specific criteria presented for each diagnosis, it is clear that the criteria to make the diagnosis have been tightened up. For example, two or more of the five symptoms identified in criterion A must be present, with at least one of them involving hallucinations, delusions, or disorganized speech. Firming up the criteria for each of the diagnoses, coupled with the specifiers, defines distinct stages and dimensions of the illnesses described (Tandon, 2012). This clarity that helps to formulate the diagnostic assessment assists in developing the symptom-specific treatment that will need to follow.

Completion of the Diagnostic Assessment

The diagnostic assessment starts with identifying a client's initial symptoms. To facilitate the

CASE EXAMPLE - CASE OF JACOB

Jacob is a 58-year-old divorced White man. He is of large build and tall, with brown hair and brown eyes. He is unshaven, with long, greasy hair, and appears to care little about his personal hygiene, as evidenced by his dirty and disheveled appearance and layers of sloppy clothing. Jacob was recently released from jail after being arrested for vagrancy and resisting arrest. Currently, Jacob states he was evicted from his apartment by his landlord several weeks ago and has been homeless and living on the streets.

Upon interviewing Jacob, he appeared guarded and suspicious of the police and his previous landlord. While in jail, Jacob had gotten into a fight with another inmate and suffered a black eye and two broken ribs. Officers in the jail referred him for an evaluation, as he appeared to have limited insight and judgment. He also stated that the prisoner who beat him up was taking orders from the devil. When they did a drug screen, Jacob did not show positive for any substances, including marijuana.

Upon arrival at the crisis stabilization unit, Jacob displayed suspiciousness and refused to answer any questions that could reveal any personal information about himself or his behaviors. He appeared agitated, showed bizarre posturing, and appeared unpredictable in terms of his reactions and movement. Upon admission, Jacob was given a drug screen, for which he again tested negative, and a basic physical did not reveal any pending medical concerns that needed to be addressed.

(*continued*)

CASE EXAMPLE - CASE OF JACOB (CONTINUED)

When left alone for a few moments, Jacob was observed talking to himself. When he was finally able to talk, Jacob told the practitioner that he played as backup musician for Bob Dylan in the 1960s. Jacob stated that his being locked up in jail was a plot to keep him away from his real brother in music, Elvis, who was really not dead, as everyone thought. He also stated that he wished he could turn off the voices in his head. Once he started to feel more comfortable with the interviewer, he stated that he could hear two voices during the interview in particular, a man and a woman both telling him he was never going to be successful.

After permission was obtained from Jacob to call his family, his father related that Jacob had a long history of mental illness since age 25 and had been previously diagnosed using in *DSM-IV* criteria with schizophrenia, paranoid type, and it was chronic. Jacob had reportedly been in and out of the state mental hospital, the Veterans Administration hospital, his parents' house, and various assisted living facilities for the past 15 years. Recently, Jacob had been doing so much better that he was discharged from an assisted living facility and moved into his own apartment. According to his father, around this time Jacob started hanging around with the wrong crowd and sharing his cigarettes. It was also reported he would drink wine and smoke marijuana. His new friends would help him cash his disability check; they would buy wine and then drink the wine and smoke the cigarettes Jacob had bought. According to his father, Jacob constantly reported that he could not sleep, as he often had nightmares of bombs exploding. Jacob's father suspected that Jacob had stopped taking his antipsychotic medication shortly after he got into his apartment, but he could not be sure of exactly when. After Jacob failed to pay his rent, his landlord threw him out. This led to Jacob being on the street and his subsequent arrest for vagrancy. According to his father, Jacob had become quite paranoid and frightened in jail. Jacob had never had any legal problems prior to being arrested for vagrancy.

Jacob is a veteran who did not have direct combat experience but spent a great deal of time on tactical training maneuvers. His father insists that Jacob was fine until he was discharged from the military at age 21. After leaving the military, Jacob had gradually increasing symptoms, particularly hearing voices. Jacob told family and friends that he was discharged from the military because he was caught trying to help prisoners of war being held in the United States. After the military discharge, he began to stay in his room all of the time, and his hygiene became very poor. Jacob began to express bizarre and paranoid thoughts. The family tried to ignore Jacob's behavior until one night when he had a psychotic episode and threatened to stab his mother with a kitchen knife, while alternating between cries for help and fiendish ranting. After this incident, Jacob was hospitalized numerous times with delusions and hallucinations.

Jacob was married for 6 months to another patient he met during one of his hospitalizations. Jacob said they divorced after her parents protested the marriage. Between his times in the hospital, Jacob has usually lived with his parents or alone. He has no children. Jacob's last hospitalization was 1 year ago. His father states that Jacob feels overwhelmed and does not know what to do. Jacob's father is elderly and legally blind, and he feels that he cannot handle Jacob anymore. He asked if permanent placement in the state hospital could be an option for Jacob because, if it was, then he would know that Jacob was safe. After a 3-day course of antipsychotic medication, Jacob presents as friendlier and more cooperative, although his affect is flat and he complains of being sleepy. Jacob says that he knows he is a worry to his father but begs not to be put back in the state hospital. He wants to get his own apartment back and asserts that he goes off his medication because it has such terrible side effects, and then he smokes and drinks in an attempt to self-medicate.

Table 5.1 Mental Status Description

Presentation	Mental Functioning	Higher-Order Abilities	Thought Form/Content
Appearance: Unkempt	Simple Calculations: Mostly accurate	Judgment: Impulsive	Thought Process: Disorganized and tangential
Mood: Anxious	Serial Sevens: Accurate	Insight: Poor	Delusions: Paranoid Hallucinations: Auditory
Attitude: Guarded	Immediate Memory: Intact	Intelligence: Low to average	
Affect: Blunted/flat Speech: Guarded	Remote Memory: Intact		
Motor Activity: Restless	General Knowledge: Mostly accurate		
Orientation: Fully oriented	Proverb Interpretation: Refused		
	Similarities/Differences: Refused		

interview, a complete mental status exam was conducted. Basic information related to Jacob's presentation, mental functioning, and higher-order abilities and thought form and content was gathered. (See Table 5.1 for an example of a mental status description.)

At the initial interview, Jacob's symptoms seemed consistent with four negative symptoms that are important for determining and influencing the intervention process (Woo & Keatinge, 2008). The first consideration is that Jacob appeared to be suffering from associative disturbances that were related directly to how he interacts within the environmental context. Very often he is unsure of the best way to relate to others, as evidenced by his behaviors with his new friends. To win their friendship, he would either try to buy their allegiance or withdraw from all social contact. He also would not allow his mother or father to touch or hug him and, according to his father he would often think nothing of getting up in their faces when he wanted something. Talking with Jacob's family makes it understandable how disturbing these behaviors seem. Jacob's behaviors have become so dysfunctional that they clearly disturb his social and occupational functioning and have resulted in his isolation from others within his environmental context.

The second associated feature relative to Jacob's assessment is related to affective disturbances. Jacob often exhibits unpredictable moods and emotions, and at times he appears to have a splitting of affect. In this type of splitting, Jacob exhibits polarities in showing his emotions. Although his overall mood appears depressed, he can be angry one minute and laughing the next. The incongruence between the emotions Jacob is exhibiting and the actual situation alarms his family and friends. This unpredictability of actions led to Jacob's eventual hospitalization and his parents' reluctance to let him live with them in their home.

The third associated feature, in addition to associative and affective disturbances, is that Jacob also suffered from autistic-like symptoms—a separation or lack of responsiveness to the reality surrounding him. This makes it difficult to communicate with him and to determine exactly how much he is able to comprehend. Jacob's father describes him as being in a world of his own; he cannot communicate with Jacob or get him to respond appropriately to conversation or requests needed to facilitate his personal care.

Jacob also appeared extremely ambivalent, with a great deal of difficulty in making decisions or adhering to structure in terms of completing his own activities of daily living. During administration of the WHODAS, however, he was able to maintain conversation and contact for approximately 5 minutes. Similar to when he requested to try the WHODAS, he consistently expressed willingness to do something but moments later changed his mind and refused to go somewhere or participate in an activity. For Jacob, simple tasks, such as dressing himself or deciding whether to go outside, appeared to be daunting. He also repeatedly changed his mind about taking his medicine, getting out of bed, or where to walk in the yard.

For Jacob, the delusions he experienced included many beliefs that he felt were true despite evidence to the contrary. He was so convinced that people were out to get him that this belief clearly disturbed his daily functioning ability. Jacob believed that the police, his family, and his friends were against him and he could never trust any of them, often refusing their efforts to help him. Jacob also appeared to be having auditory hallucinations, as evidenced by his talking to himself. He suffered from what are often referred to as delusions of reference. In this type of paranoid delusional thinking, he was convinced that others were out to get him—even his mother, who he believed tried to poison him. It is important to differentiate the delusions of reference, so common in schizophrenic conditions, from ideas of reference as experienced in some of the personality disorders. For example, in the schizotypal personality disorder, there is often social withdrawal from family and friends, accompanied by ideas of reference.

An idea of reference is different from a delusion of reference in that the idea of reference is much more individualized. An idea of reference often refers to a specific, individual event or item that can be surrounded by magical thinking or involve a certain degree of exaggerated importance. An example of an idea of reference is the client who believes that because his father had a heart attack, he will also have one, regardless of his state of health. However, other areas of the client's life are not affected by such beliefs. This is very different from the more extensive condition known as schizophrenia, in which the client can exhibit delusions of reference. Jacob, in the case example, suffered from delusions of reference: Police, family, and friends were all out to get him. Delusions of reference are much more pervasive and affect almost every part of the client's life.

Most often medications are used to help clients gain control of this aspect of the illness, and it is important to determine how long Jacob had not been taking his antipsychotic medications. In schizophrenia, it appears that auditory hallucinations (e.g., inaccurately hearing spoken speech or voices) are the most common, almost 70% of all reported hallucinatory symptoms (Hoffman, 2000). This means that Jacob often struggles with addressing these auditory hallucinations and how the voices relate to what he is experiencing. Jacob did not report being commanded by these voices to engage in certain behaviors, but this area needs further assessment.

Many clients like Jacob report experiencing disturbances in motor behavior, such as bizarre posturing, catalepsy (a state of stupor), and waxy flexibility. For example, in waxy flexibility, a client may appear somewhat rigid and may seem to be stuck in certain positions or stay frozen in these positions for a long time. Waxy flexibility and catalepsy are both characterized by a state of continual and unusual muscle tension (Moore & Jefferson, 1997). Clients in this position appear to be stuck and unable to move on their own. This type of behavior can frighten inexperienced mental health practitioners, family, or friends.

The bizarre nature of the behavior often results in the client posturing and being unable to respond. This may be so fear-provoking to family members that they withdraw support. When this occurs, it is essential to educate the client, his or her family, and professionals about the condition of schizophrenia, the possible signs and symptoms, and the interventions that work best to address them.

For Jacob and so many other individuals who suffer from schizophrenia, the symptoms tend to be so arbitrary and susceptible to change that the course of the illness can remain unpredictable. The mental health practitioner must be aware of current and past symptoms and anticipate changes in symptoms that may develop during the intervention process, as well as in the future course of the illness. This understanding of schizophrenia becomes particularly important when a practitioner is gaining an increased knowledge about the disease process and the mechanisms that lead to development of difficulties (Flaum, 1995).

CASE APPLICATION OF THE DIAGNOSTIC ASSESSMENT

Given the behaviors that Jacob has exhibited and his past history, as well as the symptoms that he is now experiencing, Jacob's diagnosis, according to the *DSM-5,* similar to *DSM-IV,* continues to be schizophrenia. Because the subtype paranoid type has been dropped, his principal diagnosis and reason for visit is now:

Schizophrenia (reason for visit)
295.90 (ICD-9CM) or F20.9 (ICD-10CM)

The assignment of schizophrenia is supported by the long chronic history of positive and negative symptoms. These symptoms have lasted for a period of at least 6 months and have been clearly displayed for approximately 1 month unless Jacob was given antipsychotic medication (APA, 2000). Of the two or more symptoms needed for criterion A, Jacob has delusions, hallucinations, and disorganized speech. He also has negative symptoms including diminished emotional expression and avolition (a lack of goal-directed behavior). Criterion B is met, as he is clearly having difficulties with interpersonal relations and self-care. He has had signs of the disturbance since his diagnosis in his middle 20s, initially met the minimal criteria for the diagnosis, and since its onset has had periodic episodes of the disorder ever since (criterion C). From gathering his history and listening to his father, he has no reported history of depressive episodes or manic ones, which would rule out schizoaffective disorder and depressive or bipolar disorder (criterion D). Although he has been using substances such as marijuana, it appears this usage may be limited, and he tested negative for any drugs, including cannabis, on a recent drug screen (criterion E). He does not have a history of autism spectrum disorder (criterion F). It appears that Jacob clearly meets the criteria for schizophrenia as his principal diagnosis.

Although in *DSM-5* there are no subtypes for the disorder, multiple specifiers can be utilized. The next step is to examine whether he qualifies for a specifier and, if so, what ones. Starting with the first group of specifiers related to the course of the illness, the variability of the symptoms displayed that are characteristic of the disorder makes selecting the appropriate specifier essential. In Jacob's situation, this is not the first manifestation of the disorder, and he has had multiple admissions related to this problem. In looking back over the past year to help identify the course of the illness, it appears that Jacob is having an acute episode, as he is now actively displaying the full symptoms of the disorder once again. Since he has had multiple episodes and is having a series of acute episodes in which the criteria for the disorder are met, the following specifier is selected:

***Specify* if: Multiple episodes, currently in acute phase**

It appears that an additional specifier related to whether the symptoms remain constant should also be used. In Jacob's case, although it is possible that he has had periods of remission, it appears that the course is continuous in nature.

***Specify* if: Continuous**

In schizophrenia, there is also the possibility of specifying whether he has catatonia. As described earlier, catatonia by itself is not a diagnosis, but regardless he does not appear to have the symptoms required nor is there a medical disorder that needs to be accounted for. Because many of the symptoms of catatonia can overlap, the diagnosis of decreased motor activity and decreased engagement is not enough to place the diagnosis.

Similar to the other disorders in this section, the rating of the symptoms and the severity is important to support the proper diagnosis. Given the variable course of this disorder, the Clinician-Rated Dimensions of Psychosis Severity scale mentioned earlier is used. The initial assessment using the scale is completed with the expectation it will be done again in 7 days to measure progress and any changes.

This scale can help identify the positive symptoms Jacob is experiencing, as well as the frequency and intensity of symptoms such as hallucinations, delusions, disorganized speech, and abnormal psychomotor behavior. For example, the most common form of hallucinations in the schizophrenia spectrum disorders is auditory, and this is what Jacob is experiencing. He reports the auditory hallucinations are of the persecutory and command nature, telling him he will not be successful. He states that he wishes the voices would stop. Using the rating scale from 0 (not present) to 4 (present with severe pressure to respond to the voices that cannot be avoided) on domain I, Jacob is given a 4. He is also experiencing delusional thinking, as he believes Elvis is his brother and so forth. This area (domain II) is also given a 4. Domain III relates to disorganized speech. At times during the interview, it was hard to understand Jacob as his speech was rambling and disorganized. This was given a 2. He did not display any abnormal psychomotor behaviors (domain IV). On domain V, which outlines the presence of negative symptoms such as restricted emotional expression and avolition, this was present at the mild level; although he showed decreased facial expressions and self-initiated behavior, he was able to control it and regain the conversation most of the time, with semiappropriate affect to the conversation. This domain was rated as present but mild and given a 2. Domain VI relates to impaired cognition. He did appear to have some of these symptoms, as evidenced by his inability to process basic thoughts and link them to appropriate actions. This level was also given a 2, noting the symptoms were present but mild, as he could relate when needed. Domain VII is related to depression, which did not seem present, nor was mania, so both were rated as 0 (not present). Jacob's total score was 14, scoring the highest on hallucinations and delusions, which were impairing his ability to function.

This scale may help to identify the window of symptom presence and the intensity essential to identifying the active phase of a disorder. It is expected the scale will be given every 7 days for as long as possible while Jacob is at the facility and upon discharge follow-up to monitor changes. To establish the meaning of this score, Jacob's age and socioeconomic status (SES) can be taken into account. Once age and SES are addressed, his functioning is compared with what would be considered average and the degree to which it goes outside the normal range of variation and deviates from the average (mean) level of functioning.

Clinician-Rated Dimensions of Severity Scale Rating:

Severe, hallucinations and delusions highest scores.

The clinician-rated dimensions of severity scale seems particularly relevant to the measures of the positive symptoms but more limited in terms of the negative ones. To measure the negative symptoms, other scales may be considered. One recent scale that shows promise is the Scale for the Assessment of Negative Symptoms (SANS) (Lyne et al., 2013). This scale measures the most common negative symptoms in the disorder, such as affect flattening, alogia, avolition, anhedonia, and asociality, as well as attention.

In terms of other diagnoses in addition to the principal diagnosis, the diagnosis of posttraumatic stress disorder (PTSD) could be given provisionally, but there does not appear to be enough information to determine whether some of his behaviors may be related to stressors that originally surfaced from his military experiences or just life experiences in general. In speaking with the client, Jacob said that he had never been diagnosed with or treated for PTSD, nor has he had any actual combat-related experience. It is possible, however, that although Jacob presents with symptoms that seem indicative of schizophrenia, some of the symptoms he is experiencing could be heightened by his military experiences. Due to the lack of information related to this disorder, it was decided not to list it as a second diagnosis or as a provisional diagnosis at this time.

There is concern noted that he is drinking wine with his friends, although he and his father both deny that alcohol or marijuana is a problem. He has had several negative drug screens, and if he was smoking marijuana, it would most likely have shown up in at least one of his drug screens either at the jail or in the unit. Jacob and his father both say that when Jacob buys wine, his friends generally drink it, not him, which appears likely based on his behavioral patterns. Jacob reports the wine could be poisoned, and he generally will not eat or drink anything that his father has not prepared. Based on this information, indicators of substance abuse for alcohol and/or marijuana is not warranted at this time. It does not appear that Jacob has any medical problems, and he has recently had a physical exam that did not reveal any significant results, so none are recorded.

His psychosocial stressors include problems with primary support (strained family relations), problems related to the social environment (recent arrest for vagrancy, fighting, and resisting arrest), housing problems (recent eviction), and economic problems (inability to manage disability income). These stressors need to be listed as other conditions that may be the focus of clinical attention. These were previously addressed on Axis IV of the *DSM-IV,* and this specific designation was eliminated; careful and comprehensive assessment should not overlook the need for their continued use. For inclusion, they should be added as supportive information.

After examining Chapter 22 of the *DSM-5* and the other conditions that may be a focus of clinical attention, the following were selected for inclusion.

A significant problem for Jacob is strained family relations and lack of family support. It is not that the family—in this case, Jacob's father—does not care about Jacob; rather, it appears he is tired and frustrated with Jacob's repeated problems and his unsuccessful attempts to help in the past. Also, his father has his own medical conditions and is unable to provide any more support than he already has. In looking at the relational problems identified in this section, none appears to clearly represent Jacob's situation. Jacob is not a child but in many ways behaves as one in terms of the supervision and oversight he needs to complete his daily activities. Unfortunately, the lack of options in this revised chapter of the *DSM* limits the coding possible to better explain Jacob's situation in regard to his family. In the absence of a stronger, more relevant category related to family relationships, the category *other circumstances of personal history,* with the subcategory o*ther personal risk factors,* is identified. No description applies for this category, so clarification of its use is delineated by Jacob's lack of family support and lack of a current support network that can help him better meet his own independent and social needs. Counseling involving his father will be recommended, as there appears to be a definite, although markedly strained, bond between the two. In addition, Jacob will need help in building other healthy social relationships, particularly learning to recognize and avoid befriending people who have taken advantage of him in the past.

Other Circumstances of Personal History

V69.9 (Z72.9) Problem Related to Lifestyle

Jacob was arrested for problems related to his mental disorder and does not appear to have any other criminal history or intent. He does now, however, have involvement with the legal system and has recently been incarcerated for his unsupervised behaviors and his actions while homeless. Jacob has little insight into his role in the incarceration and will need support to ensure that he has a more supervised environment where he is better able to meet his own needs. Consequences of his behavior will need to be examined to avoid any future problems with the legal system.

Problems Related to Crime or Interaction with the Legal System

V62.5 (Z65.2) Problems Related to Other Legal Circumstances

(Recent arrest for vagrancy, fighting, and resisting arrest)

Jacob has had previous problems living in a residential facility. Most of these problems revolve around his inability to manage his own affairs or let others he can trust do it for him. He has been homeless in the past and is now homeless again. Efforts to secure adequate housing are central to further treatment and discharge planning. If adequate housing is not secured, regardless of the treatment plan successes that result, Jacob will again find himself in a similar situation. He also has a lack of family support; as his father ages, he has become frailer and is now legally blind and reports he cannot handle his son anymore. The father feels he needs to concentrate on his own medical needs and at his doctor's request is no longer capable or willing to assist in managing Jacob's finances. Exploring supervised placement options will allow Jacob the maximum level of independence possible. Because these types of placement options may be limited, advance planning in this area has to be addressed early in the treatment phase. He will also need some type of assistance to manage his disability income. With reports of his being taken advantage of in the past when he has managed his own affairs, addressing his resistance to helping efforts will be approached in the treatment planning process. Efforts to help him learn to manage his money better are needed, as well as learning to accept help and supervision from others in regard to his financial planning.

Housing and Economic Problems (recent eviction)

V60.0 (Z56.82) Homelessness

V60.1 (Z56.9) Other Problem Related to Employment

Economic Problems (inability to manage disability income)

V60.9 Unspecified Housing or Economic Problem

(Has difficulty managing his own funds and budgeting)

Specifically concerning Jacob's independent functioning and disability level, a global measure of disability, the WHO Disability Assessment Schedule (WHODAS, version 2.0), was considered. This instrument replaced the GAF utilized in *DSM-IV-TR*. The WHODAS is based on the International Classification of Functioning, Disability and Cognitive Health (ICF) and can be used with adults and (in a separate version) with caregivers. For Jacob, the adult version, a 36-item, self-administered measure for those age 18 and older, is most appropriate. It can measure disability across six domains.

The expectation was to complete the caregiver version, but Jacob seemed interested in completing the self-administered one. Because Jacob does not have a caregiver who could complete this scale and measure his performance over the past 30 days, the social worker decided to give it a try and offered to help him with it. Jacob stated he was capable; however, he asked the social worker to provide assistance in examining each domain. Discussing these domains might provide fertile ground for the treatment plan to follow, as well as establish the client's level of insight and awareness of his own behaviors.

In the first domain, six questions related to understanding and communicating are designed to measure an individual's cognitive domain. The questions can be rated from none to so extreme that at its most severe point, cognitive functioning can prohibit performance.

When reviewing these questions with the social worker, Jacob rated all those that explore concentrating, remembering, analyzing, understanding, and maintaining conversations as severe (rating 4). He did not, however, see his learning a new task as problematic and gave it a 2. He cited being able to work with the social worker in using this scale as an example and smiled.

The second domain of the scale has five questions on how well Jacob can get around and complete tasks. It follows a similar scoring format with questions that assess for problems with standing, moving, or walking inside and outside the home. He does not see any of these areas as a problem in terms of standing for long periods, standing up, moving, getting out, or walking a long distance. Neither did the social worker, so he rated them as none. He did state that "he gets around good" but "trouble always finds me." When this was discussed, he stated that he was "innocent of any wrongdoing and falsely accused." He also complained that the voices in his head often interfere and tell him where to go, even if he does not want to.

The third domain is performance of self-care and how capable Jacob is with basic skills required for grooming, such as washing and dressing, and the degree to which self-feeding is possible. Jacob is in the acute phase, and all of the scores in this area are in the severe range. Jacob, however, did not see them as problematic and listed them as none (scored as 0) stating that "people need to just leave me alone as I can self-clean internally with the push of a button."

The fourth domain involves getting along with people and how Jacob interacts with people in his support system, as well as how he makes new friends and interacts with people he does not know. At this point, Jacob began to get distracted. It was obvious to the social worker that he was losing attention, and she did not press him to continue the report instrument any further.

The social worker hopes to use this instrument again with Jacob when he starts to feel better, as it would be a good way to discuss some of the problems Jacob is having with interactions. The fifth domain on the scale involves completion of household tasks, how the individual feels about addressing these tasks, and perceived ability, as well as school and work, gathering information related to the appropriate life situation.

In the last domain are eight questions on how the individual sees his or her role in society, along with any concerns or preoccupations with health.

For Jacob, using this scale proved interesting. It started discussions and provided information for the treatment plan. However, after giving it a good try Jacob was unable to continue after completing and discussing the first few sections. On this first attempt, completion of the WHODAS self-administered version was not possible. The scale on the first attempt was noted as inability to complete, but it will be tried again prior to discharge and after discharge to examine changes in individual perceptions and functioning. For this inpatient evaluation, the caregiver version was used to measure the behaviors he was able to complete on the unit.

WHODAS Score: Unable to Complete

TREATMENT PLANNING AND INTERVENTION STRATEGY

Once the initial assessment is complete and the diagnostic assessment is formulated, assigning either the principal or a provisional diagnosis, the next step involves the treatment planning to follow. To start the process, a general statement of Jacob's goals and objectives for the treatment process are outlined in Quick Reference 5.4. With the information gathered during the diagnostic assessment, these goals and objectives provide the starting point for treatment, including the intervention plan that allows for application. As part of the intervention process, problem behaviors are clearly identified and related directly to the stated goals and objectives. Treatment should be provided in a continuum of care that allows flexible application of modalities based on a cohesive treatment plan. In developing the treatment plan for Jacob, the practitioner will need to gather a comprehensive history, including information about medical conditions. Because Jacob has difficulty recalling his treatment history, supplemental information is needed from family and others in his immediate support system. Information about whether Jacob has had a recent medical exam is vital because he does not appear motivated for self-care. It is not known whether he is eating and sleeping; Jacob's overall nutritional status is questionable. In addition, a referral for a blood test should be considered to detect use or abuse of drugs or hormonal problems.

For individuals diagnosed with schizophrenia, planned and early intervention can offer the client a better chance for considerable improvement. Often intervention with individuals diagnosed with this mental disorder requires a comprehensive approach that combines individual therapy, case management, family support, and medication management.

Acute Treatment Plan and Intervention

To best assist a client diagnosed with schizophrenia such as Jacob, two treatment plans are

QUICK REFERENCE 5.4

JACOB'S IDENTIFIED GOALS

To help Jacob stabilize with a plan that allows him to return to the most appropriate and least restrictive environment possible.

Objectives

To help Jacob reduce his feelings of agitation and paranoia.

To help Jacob get control of his behaviors and independently complete his own activities of daily living (ADL).

To help Jacob find an appropriate place to live upon discharge.

To help Jacob manage his own affairs.

recommended. The first is an acute care plan, and the second is to assist with the client's transitional or continued care needs. In the acute care plan, the primary goal is stabilization. The initial acute care plan will serve as the transitional plan for the client when he or she is discharged. Some type of long-term supervised care or community case management that assists the client with necessary linkages for a successful return to the community should follow this. At discharge, the decrease in or elimination of the client's agitation, paranoia, and incoherence needs to be documented. Also, as the client stabilizes (before discharge), the mental health practitioner needs to meet with the client to discuss discharge plans and to plan the transition care part of the treatment plan (see Sample Treatment Plans 5.1 and 5.2).

Transition Care, Treatment Planning, and Strategy for Jacob

With his permission, while Jacob was still hospitalized, the mental health practitioner began to make telephone calls to family members and various assisted living facilities. After an honest and comprehensive presentation of Jacob's case to the representative of the potential services, Jacob was accepted into a community-based program provided by the mental health center in his area. This program offered a stepwise approach designed to assist individuals with chronic mental health problems, allowing the client to return to the community. In this program, clients such as Jacob start out in a more restrictive atmosphere and go through stages of training that allow for less restrictive facilities until they end up in apartments, either alone or with a roommate, operated by the center. If Jacob fails to meet the goals for a particular level of care, he will remain at the best one that he can achieve until he is ready to progress further. It is highly recommended that the client and his family make arrangements to visit the program. Jacob's father agreed to visit him and to lend support while Jacob is in the program.

General Considerations for Chronic Care Treatment Planning and Practice Strategy

Treatment planning for people with schizophrenia requires a combination of medication, psychosocial intervention, and development of adequate social support (Grohol, 2006). Bola (2006) suggests, however, that before immediately starting a course of medication therapy, especially in acute early-episode psychotic disorders such as schizophrenia, developing and implementing a psychosocial treatment might provide a safe alternative to medication intervention. When the disorder progresses and the client needs more supervised placement, other facilities that offer more supportive and intensive levels of care may need to be considered. When a client is placed in these more restrictive residential settings, a case manager is expected to monitor the client once a month. By the time the client is on the last level, the case manager is helping with only minimal problems, such as medication monitoring and facilitating community linkage. If Jacob's medication compliance is still a problem, an injectable medication with a longer-lasting effect would be suggested. In addition, medication monitoring would include suggesting adjustments or changes if the client is not receiving the desired effect. The client would be monitored for medication-related conditions, such as tardive dyskinesia, as well as side effects, such as dystonia and akathisia. If these conditions are present, newer antipsychotic medications would be considered, and an evaluation for PTSD would be recommended. A referral to attend Alcoholics Anonymous (AA) or Narcotics Anonymous (NA) may also be considered if the drinking or substance use becomes increasingly problematic.

SAMPLE TREATMENT PLAN 5.1

Sample Acute Care Goals and Intervention Provided

Goal

To stabilize Jacob for discharge to the least restrictive environment.

Objectives

- To help Jacob reduce agitation and paranoia.
- To help Jacob get control of his behaviors and activities of daily living (ADL).
- To help Jacob find an appropriate place to live upon discharge.
- To help Jacob manage his own affairs and the course of the symptoms he is experiencing to the best of his ability.

Treatment Provided

- Psychiatric evaluation and consultation.
- Prescribed medication and monitoring for mental status and side effects. Nursing assessment and ongoing nursing care.
- Contacts with clinician for counseling to address skill building.
- Participation in therapeutic and psychoeducational group meetings as scheduled.
- Observation and, as needed, other care by the treatment team.

Sample Application of Acute Plan

- Medication compliance.
  Objective: Monitor and evaluate medication effectiveness, side effects, and compliance, and report observations to social worker once a month.
- Stabilization of schizophrenia.
  Objective: As client moves up the levels in the program, he will take progressively more responsibility for making sure that he takes his medication.
- Linkage with community resources.
  Objective: During the next month, the client will phone a self-help group for individuals suffering from schizophrenia in the area and inquire about meetings. He will report back to the social worker on this task when they meet.
- Development of a support system.
  Objective: The client will phone and inquire about a day treatment program run by the facility and decide if he wants to participate in the program (1-month time frame).
- Education about medications.
  Objective: The client will attend all psychoeducational group meetings at the facility and meet with his social worker once a month for counseling.
  Objective: The client will be prepared to discuss with the social worker these objectives and the progress he has made during the month.

Continual assessment for suicidal thoughts and ideation is necessary. Although this was not a direct consideration for Jacob, suicide is the leading cause of death in schizophrenia (Walker et al., 2008). The media provide a disservice when they present mentally ill persons as dangerous individuals; in reality, people without such illnesses commit 95% of all homicides

SAMPLE TREATMENT PLAN 5.2

Treatment Plan Development Topic: Schizophrenia

Definition: Two or more characteristic symptoms (delusions, hallucinations, disorganized speech, grossly disorganized or negative symptoms) with at least one of the first three required. The symptoms must persist for at least 6 months, 1 month of which must include the characteristic symptoms, and the person must experience a decline in two or more areas of functioning. Symptoms may not be associated with a general medical condition, schizo-affective, mood disorder, substance abuse, or withdrawal. If a pervasive developmental disorder exists, a diagnosis of schizophrenia can be made only if the symptoms are prominent and are present for at least 1 month (and last more than 6 months).

Signs and Symptoms

- Delusions.
- Hallucinations.
- Disorganized speech.
- Grossly disorganized behavior or catatonic behavior.
- Negative symptoms (diminished emotional expression or avolition).
- One or more areas of functioning are disturbed (self-care activities, work, social, and academic).
- Inappropriate affect.

Goals

1. Client will not pose danger to self or others.
2. Client will independently perform self-care activities.
3. Client will maintain prescribed medication regimen after discharge.
4. Client will increase adaptive functioning.

Objectives	Interventions
1. Identify and control symptoms of psychosis (hallucinations, delusions, and disorganized speech), as measured by observations of psychiatric staff and self-reports by client, during the course of treatment and after release.	Psychiatric staff to record behaviors associated with hallucinations or delusions in chart every day.
2. Increase cooperation (with taking prescribed medications) from zero compliance before hospitalization (self and family reported) to full cooperation (taking medications as prescribed), as reported by hospital staff in client's chart.	Client will take his medication as prescribed each day.
3. Increase performance of self-care activities from 0 per day to 5 per day, as measured by staff behavior count, by the end of treatment.	Clinician to contract with client specific self-care behaviors to be learned and performed daily. Clinician to apply a cognitive-behavioral approach to teach/train client to perform self-care activities (brushing teeth, combing hair, bathing, dressing, etc.).

(continued)

SAMPLE TREATMENT PLAN 5.2 (Continued)

	Clinician will work with client and family of client to reinforce, maintain, and expand on self-care activities when client is released from the hospital.
4. Maintain taking prescribed meds after discharge, as evidenced by record of full compliance in case management record and family reports (indefinitely).	Case manager will monitor client's compliance with medication protocol through two times/week contact with client and family members.
5. Increase social functioning from a score of 15 at pretest to a score of 55 by the end of treatment on the Social Adjustment Scale for Self-Report (SAS-SR).	Client will receive positive reinforcement from family members and clinician for behaving in a socially positive way. Client will participate in at least 12 weeks of social skills classes.
6. Family members will show an increase in adaptive functioning, as measured by a score of 55 to a posttest score of 250 by the end of treatment on the Social Behavior and Adjustment Scale (SBAS).	Client's family will participate in a 6-week educational program about schizophrenia. Client's family will network with other families who share similar stressors.
7. Family of client will increase existing household income by $500/month through SS Disability to help care for client in the home, within 6 months.	Family of client will be assisted in filing for SS Disability for client's special needs.

(Ferriman, 2000). Those with schizophrenia are more likely to harm themselves than someone else. Furthermore, this tendency to harm themselves may be based in the guilt many clients feel for the burdens they put on their family; many clients blame themselves for their illness. The negative portrayal by the media has only recently started to change (Frese, Knight, & Saks, 2009).

Generally, the individual treatment provided for people who suffer from schizophrenia is supportive in nature. Other methods, however, are being tried and explored. For example, Lukoff (2007) advocates a spiritually focused recovery model to empower persons with schizophrenia to manage their own rehabilitation plan and attempt to achieve their treatment goals. Other programs have focused on intensive treatment milieus with minimal use of medications (Bola & Mosher, 2002; Calton & Spandler, 2009; Ciompi & Hoffman, 2004). The Soteria project sponsored two programs in the United States (Bola & Mosher, 2002) and one program in Switzerland (Ciompi & Hoffman, 2004) with significant results at the 2-year follow-up. Participants in the Soteria program demonstrated significant improvement in global psychopathology; combination outcomes including social functioning, employment, and independent living; and fewer readmissions to inpatient settings when compared with the control group (Bola & Mosher, 2003).

Other alternative therapies suggested to treat schizophrenia include acupuncture, magnetic field therapy, naturopathic medicine, sound therapy, and traditional Chinese medicine (Chopra, 1994). In addition to those of Lukoff (2007), other approaches to the treatment of schizophrenia incorporate spirituality and religion in treatment (Huguelet, Mohr, & Borras, 2009). An aspect of spirituality and religion is the cultural lens through which clients understand illness or disease, and the way the client responds often follows this cultural expectation. None of the alternative therapy methods described should be attempted without the supervision and specification of a licensed health practitioner.

Family and Support Systems

Special attention and emphasis should always be given to building the client's family and community support systems. Schizophrenia is a disease that can cause its victims to feel lonely and isolated, and on account of its unpredictable course, this chronic illness can manifest behaviors that alienate family and friends. It is important to ensure that the family does not burn out or withdraw support from the client. Support groups can help family members see that they are not alone and that others are also struggling. Family members need to be educated that the condition of schizophrenia is real and that their loved one is not just making it up to gain attention. Learning to identify the unusual behaviors associated with this condition may help family members better understand and accept their loved one's behaviors (NIMH, 2009c). In addition, myths about schizophrenia in which persons with this illness are portrayed as menacing figures also need to be addressed, because these depictions are often violent and may lead to the belief that all individuals suffering from schizophrenia are violent (Long, 2000). One factor that is associated with violence among persons diagnosed with schizophrenia is substance abuse comorbidity; however, the risk factor for those with substance abuse comorbidity is similar to the substance-abusing population who are not diagnosed with psychosis (Fazel, Gulati, Linsell, Geddes, & Grann, 2009; Tracker, 2009).

Family members must be encouraged to remain part of the support system, and strategies should be used to keep the family involved (e.g., case management support, community residential placement). Most of the therapeutic interventions used with individuals suffering from schizophrenia are intended to be supportive. For example, in the case of Jacob, most of the practitioner's goals were directed toward helping him develop and sustain his social support system. Supportive therapy may provide the client with friendship and encouragement; it may also give the client practical advice about how to access community resources, information on how to develop a more active social life, vocational counseling, suggestions for minimizing friction with family members, and, above all, hope that his or her life circumstance will improve (Long, 2000).

Medication as a Treatment Modality

Over the years, treatment for the individual who suffers from schizophrenia has been primarily supportive therapy, family and community supports, and psychopharmacology. In schizophrenia, the mystery surrounding what the disease entails has led to its being treated by trial and error with a variety of supposed remedies that can assist to control behaviors and alter body states (Lehmann & Ban, 1997). For the most part, medications used as the primary treatment modality for individuals who suffer from schizophrenia focus on controlling symptoms.

Older Typical Neuroleptic Medications The primary medications used for this condition were first introduced in 1952. One of the first documented cases was how the medication chlorpromazine (Thorazine) was used accidentally as an antipsychotic (neuroleptic) medication (Bishara & Taylor, 2009). This medication is a combination of narcotic, sedative, and hypnotic drugs and was used with a client suffering from schizophrenia in Paris (Lehmann & Ban, 1997). Often referred to as the typical antipsychotic medications, this older group of drugs was labeled neuroleptics because of the side effects on the nervous system. Chlorpromazine (Thorazine)

QUICK REFERENCE 5.5

OLDER OR TYPICAL ANTIPSYCHOTIC MEDICATIONS IN SCHIZOPHRENIA

Medications Used With the Psychotic Disorders

Antipsychotic Drugs (Neuroleptic Drugs)

Used to treat severe psychotic disorders (e.g., schizophrenia). Generally, symptoms include hallucinations, delusions, psychotic behaviors, and a depressed, flat affect. Peak concentrations occur between 2 and 4 hours. Generally, two antipsychotic medications are not prescribed at the same time. After discharge, wait approximately 3 to 6 months before considering changing the medication to ensure that the client has gotten the full affect.

Old or Typical Antipsychotic Medications

Chlorpromazine/Thorazine

Thioridazine/Mellaril

Trifluoperazine/Stelazine

Fluphenazine/Prolixin

Haloperidol/Haldol

Loxapine/Loxitane

Thiothixene/Navane

was followed by the development of other neuroleptics, such as trifluoperazine (Stelazine), haloperidol (Haldol), fluphenazine (Prolixin), thiothixene (Navane), and thioridazine (Mellaril) (WebMD, 2009). As the first medications introduced in this area, these traditional or typical antipsychotics became the state of practice. These medications worked directly as dopamine inhibitors that block other neurotransmitters, including acetylcholine, histamine, and norepinephrine. After 30-plus years of use, this group of older neuroleptic drugs started to fall from favor, and today they are no longer considered the first line of treatment for schizophrenia and the psychotic disorders. The primary reason that these medications lost their favor within the medical community was the complicated side effect profiles and feelings of tiredness. These pervasive side effects often disturbed client performance, motivation, or emotional responsiveness (WebMD, 2009). (See Quick Reference 5.5.)

Extrapyramidal symptoms (EPS), which affect the motor system, are a common side effect with these medications. *Dystonia,* characterized by sudden and painful muscle stiffness (National Alliance on Mental Illness [NAMI], 2003), may present as grimacing, difficulty with speech or swallowing, oculogyric crisis (upward rotation of the eyeballs), muscle spasms of the neck and throat, and extensor rigidity of the back muscles (Carpenter et al., 1998). These reactions often occur within the first few days of treatment. *Akathisia* is less obvious than dystonia, although it is the most common form of EPS. It is an extreme form of motor restlessness that may be mistaken for agitation (NAMI, 2003). The individual feels compelled to a constant state of movement, and many times clients report an inner restlessness, evidenced by a shaking leg or constant pacing. During assessment, these clients cannot sit still and often exhibit restless legs or uncontrollable foot tapping.

Another form of EPS, which results from long-term treatment with these older antipsychotic medications, is tardive dyskinesia (TD). This condition involves pronounced involuntary movements of any group of muscles, most commonly the mouth and tongue (NIMH, 2009d). This syndrome generally occurs with elderly individuals, especially women (NIMH, 2009c). It is a negative consequence of long-term use of conventional antipsychotic medications, with intervention duration the primary developmental factor (Carpenter et al., 1998). Awareness of the development of TD is particularly important because preventing it is far more desirable than treating it; it can be irreversible (NAMI, 2003). One way to address this issue is to prescribe the medication in lower doses, but for chronic schizophrenia, this may not be an option. (See Quick Reference 5.6.)

These typical, older antipsychotics tend to have a high potential for developing EPS side effects (Lambert, 1998). The medications often prescribed to decrease or control movement-related side effects are referred to as *anti-Parkinson medications*. When a client is receiving a traditional or typical antipsychotic medicine, it is critical to determine if another medication has been prescribed to assist and counter the side effects that might result. (See Quick Reference 5.7.) Special care should be taken, as some clients might consider selling these medications on the streets, particularly benztropine and trihexyphenidyl, which may have a high potential for abuse. When the potential for abuse is suspected, the practitioner needs to share this information with the treatment team or the prescriber and consider an over-the-counter medication, such as diphenhydramine, to help control the symptoms of EPS.

Newer Atypical Neuroleptic Medications The 1990s saw the development of several new drugs to treat schizophrenia and other psychotic disorders. These are known as atypical or nontraditional antipsychotic medications (NIMH, 2009c). These medications have gained popularity because they appear to have lower side effect profiles than the traditional antipsychotic medications. Also, they clearly helped clients feel less sleepy while assisting with thought clarity and interpreting emotion more

QUICK REFERENCE 5.6

General Conditions and Side Effects with Antipsychotic Medications

Most common side effect with the older antipsychotic medications is drowsiness or sleepiness.

General Conditions Related to Medication Use

Parkinsonian or Extrapyramidal Symptoms (EPS) Include:

Dystonia—Acute contractions of the tongue (stiff or thick tongue).

Akathisia—Most common form of EPS (e.g., inner restlessness).

Tardive dyskinesia—A permanent neurological condition that can result from using the older antipsychotic medications and not taking anything to help control the EPS side effects.

QUICK REFERENCE 5.7

Selected Anti-Parkinson Medications

Generic Name (Brand Name)

Benztropine (Cogentin)

Biperiden (Akineton)

Diphenhydramine (Benadryl)

Trihexyphenidyl (Artane)

accurately (Lambert, 1998). For these reasons, they are often used as the first line of treatment. (See Quick Reference 5.8.)

The oldest medication in this category is known by the brand name Clozaril (clozapine). Because of documented deaths attributed to infections secondary to clozapine-induced agranulocytosis, this medication was at one time withdrawn from unrestricted use (Davis & Casper, 1977). This unfortunate side effect caused a severe reduction in the number of granulocytes, a type of white blood cell. Without these granulocytes, the body is unable to fight life-threatening infections. Today, when this medication is used, strict monitoring is required to be sure this condition does not develop. This medication is primarily used for treatment-resistant schizophrenia, and this strict monitoring of blood levels has been required since the Food and Drug Administration (FDA) approved it for use in the United States in 1990 (NIMH, 2009a). Other atypical antipsychotic medications that soon followed include risperidone (Risperdal), olanzapine (Zyprexa), quetiapine (Seroquel), ziprasidone (Geodon), aripiprazole (Abilify), and paliperidone (Invega).

Risperidone (Risperdal) was introduced as one of the first official atypical antipsychotic medications in 1992 (Schulz, 2000). In studies, risperidone seemed more effective in reducing positive and negative symptoms than older, more traditional medications such as Haldol (Armenteros, 1997). Risperidone has been used with schizotypal personality disorder to decrease

QUICK REFERENCE 5.8

Newer or Atypical Antipsychotic Medications

Clozapine (Clozaril)

Risperidone (Risperdal)

Olanzapine (Zyprexa)

Quetiapine (Seroquel)

Ziprasidone (Geodon)

Aripiprazole (Abilify)

Paliperidone (Invega) Generic Namers are listed first.

the psychotic-like, or positive, symptoms of the condition as well as negative symptoms, such as cognitive impairment (Saklad, 2000). Another atypical antipsychotic, olanzapine (Zyprexa), appears to be well tolerated and readily accepted by clients, especially because of its low incidence of EPS and its ability to address the negative symptoms of schizophrenia when given at higher doses. All practitioners should be aware, however, that olanzapine and any of the other newer atypicals may increase blood glucose levels in individuals with diabetes (*Physicians' Desk Reference,* 2009). Quetiapine (Seroquel) is an atypical antipsychotic medication that was introduced in the United States in 1998. It has fewer side effects than some of the other antipsychotic medications but does cause considerable sedation in the early stages of treatment (Schulz, 2000). Newer atypicals include ziprasidone (Geodon), aripiprazole (Abilify), and paliperidone (Invega). Two additional medications in this area approved by the FDA in 2009 are iloperidone (Fanapt) and asenapine (Saphris) (Drugs.com, 2009a). The side effects associated with iloperidone include dizziness, dry mouth, fatigue, nasal congestion, a sudden decrease in blood pressure (orthostatic hypotension), sleepiness, rapid heart rate (tachycardia), and weight increase. The side effects for asenapine include the inability to sit motionless (akathisia), a decrease in oral sensitivity (oral hypoesthesia), and drowsiness (somnolence) (Drugs.com, 2009a, 2009b).

The FDA has issued a public health advisory regarding an increased incidence of death with elderly individuals who suffer from dementia. Therefore, these medications are to be prescribed with caution to elderly clients who have problematic behavioral symptoms and dementia (NIMH, 2009d).

Discussion of all the medications used to treat the psychotic disorders is beyond the scope of this chapter; for a more comprehensive review, see Dziegielewski (2006, 2010). For the most part, these medications enable people to stabilize symptoms, return to their homes, and live within their community of origin (WebMD, 2009).

Mental health practitioners must educate clients and their family members that taking these medicines will not result in a quick fix. Depending on the specific medication, peak concentrations in the system can vary, resulting in varied time periods before therapeutic effects can be detected. Also, the relief gained from the use of antipsychotic medications does not cure but only helps to control the symptoms. Further, although the side effect profiles associated with these medications show a lower incidence of EPS, there can be other disturbing side effects. Medications play a prominent role in management of psychosis, and it is beyond the scope of this chapter to cover all the potential medications used and their side effect profiles. Dziegielewski (2010) presents psychopharmacological information to the nonmedically trained practitioner.

SPECIAL TOPICS

Deletion of Shared Psychotic Disorder From DSM-5

Many experienced practitioners familiar with *DSM-IV* and *DSM-IV-TR* may wonder what happened to the diagnosis shared psychotic disorder that was removed in *DSM-5.* Historically, shared psychotic disorder was presumed to be extremely rare. The disorder was once called induced psychotic disorder, double insanity, or folie à deux (French for "madness of two"). Shared psychotic disorder was dramatic and inherently interesting because it usually involved two people sharing the same delusional system. In addition, it was believed that as many as four people or an entire family, generally living in close proximity or the same household, could be involved (Oshodi, Bangaru, & Benbow, 2005). It was believed this diagnosis developed within families, although it was unclear whether there was a genetic connection.

It was believed that shared psychotic disorder appeared to develop in clients with a history of social isolation. These individuals slowly disconnected from family, friends, and anyone who may threaten or challenge the nonbizarre delusions that were present and guided their daily routines. In individuals who shared this disorder, the delusional system of one individual influenced the other party, such that the other person would grow to share the primary individual's delusional beliefs. In such cases, one individual grows in prominence and power within the relationship and is said to be primary or the leader, and the other individual increasingly takes on a secondary role. The primary individual leads the secondary; often the secondary does not originally believe the delusional themes of the primary. Eventually, however, the secondary compromises and accepts it as an accurate perception. Often the secondary has some form of cognitive impairment or may simply become vulnerable to repeated, unchallenged, delusional themes that later result in acceptance and compromise (Woo & Keatinge, 2008). If the secondary is removed from the situation, he or she may be able to remit the delusional thinking patterns and recover. The primary has a much harder time in treatment because the convictions are so much more pronounced (Munro, 1999).

This nonbizarre delusional system was believed to protect the individuals and keep them in isolation. An example might be two sisters living alone, one of whom believes that the neighbors and the landlord are sneaking into the house when they leave it and are touching and rearranging things. The primary continually tells the other sister (the secondary) that this is happening. At first, the secondary disputes the claims; then later she slowly and progressively begins to accept them as real. Eventually, the sister in the secondary role compromises and accepts this is happening. To avoid it happening again, they must barricade their home to keep out all intruders who may sneak in during the night. To protect themselves, they isolate themselves inside the home.

Aside from the delusions, the thoughts and behaviors of those with shared psychotic disorder are usually quite normal. This normalcy in some areas may confuse others regarding the seriousness of the situation. The cause of shared psychotic disorder has yet to be identified, but stress appears to play a key role. Being in and maintaining isolation can also contribute to the development of this disorder. People who have shared psychotic disorder simply grow to share the same delusional system. These delusions are not the result of any other mental health disorder, a medical condition, or drug taking (either prescribed or illegal) (First, 2014). It was believed that these delusions and patterns of coping behavior would grow and strengthen and these individuals would rarely seek treatment because they do not see their behavior as problematic. In examining this behavior and clarifying the criteria in *DSM-5,* early discussions of the revisions focused on deleting this diagnosis (Cardinal & Bullmore, 2011). With the publication of *DSM-5,* this disorder was eliminated and some of the criteria related to the delusional content was maintained in other diagnoses in the chapter.

SUMMARY AND FUTURE DIRECTIONS

Although great strides are being made in understanding the psychotic disorders, particularly schizophrenia, we are only at the beginning of what can be learned. Schizophrenia spectrum and the psychotic disorders present a varied course that often means chronic and disabling illnesses that separate the individual from reality, and treating the symptoms holds little promise for cure. Management of clients suffering from the psychotic disorders generally includes psychopharmacological and psychosocial approaches. These types of treatments need to provide a broad array of services addressing housing and other social support needs. Looking specifically at females with the diagnosis, Landgraf, Blumenauer, Osterheider, and Eisenbarth (2013) believe such services may also help clients avoid legal difficulties and incarceration. Furthermore, many clients suffering from psychotic symptoms get limited relief. When medication and counseling together are not enough, clients suffering from these disorders are often termed partial responders (Dziegielewski, 2010). Unfortunately, many individuals are not helped substantially by the traditional courses of supportive therapy or medication intervention.

In mental health practice, the debate continues as to what constitutes relief or good outcomes for the client who suffers from a psychotic disorder. The ultimate goal of intervention when treating any of the psychotic disorders is to free the client from the usual debilitating problems that accompany symptom occurrence. In addition, intervention is designed to help the client feel better and be more productive in dealing with life expectations and tasks. The skills of the mental health practitioner need to be directed toward helping clients gain some semblance of control over life events and tasks. In addition to improvements in medication use, recent developments in the treatment of psychotic symptoms have led to a sincere interest in using diagnostic information to assist both professionals and family members in understanding these often-devastating conditions. Despite the advent of new medications and the greater understanding of how these disorders can affect the individual, there is still much to be learned. The role of mental health practitioners is essential in ensuring that quality-of-life issues are considered; their primary duties cannot be focused on how to measure and cut costs.

When working with individuals who suffer from any of the psychotic disorders, especially schizophrenia, practitioners need to directly confront the stigma often associated with this illness. According to Krajewski, Burazeri, and Brand (2013), the stigma can be both an attribute and a cause of the disease. In turn, this negative perception could be perceived as a second disorder. Practitioners can help clients and their families avoid the negative stereotypes associated with the schizophrenia spectrum and the psychotic disorders by addressing the problematic life circumstances that surround relapse. Education with the avoidance of blame-seeking behavior can support making productive life changes that form the basis of the intervention provided.

REFERENCES

Altschule, M. D., Bigelow, L. B., Bliss, E. L., Cancro, R., Cohen, G., Gjessing, L. R., . . . Snyder, S., (1976). The genetics of schizophrenia. In S. Wolf (Ed.), *The biology of the schizophrenic process*. New York, NY: Plenum Press.

American Psychiatric Association. (1952). *Diagnostic and statistical manual of mental disorders*. Washington, DC: Author.

American Psychiatric Association. (1987). *Diagnostic and statistical manual of mental disorders* (3rd ed., rev.). Washington, DC: Author.

American Psychiatric Association. (1994). *Diagnostic and statistical manual of mental disorders* (4th ed.). Washington, DC: Author.

American Psychiatric Association. (2000). *Diagnostic and statistical manual of mental disorders* (4th ed., text rev.). Washington, DC: Author.

American Psychiatric Association. (2004). Practice guidelines for the treatment of patients with schizophrenia (2nd ed.). *American Journal of Psychiatry*, *161*, 1–56.

American Psychiatric Association. (2013). *Diagnostic and statistical manual of mental disorders* (5th ed.). Arlington, VA: American Psychiatric Publishing.

Armenteros, J. L. (1997). Risperidone in adolescents with schizophrenia: An open pilot study. *Journal of the American Academy of Child & Adolescent Psychiatry, 36*, 694–697.

Ayuso-Gutierrez, J. L., & del Rio Vega, J. M. (1997). Factors influencing relapse in the long term course of schizophrenia. *Schizophrenia Research, 28*, 199–206.

Baron, M., Gruen, R., Rainer, J. D., Kane, J., Asnis, L., & Lord, A. A. (1985). A family study of schizophrenia and normal control probands: Implication for the spectrum concept of schizophrenia. *American Journal of Psychiatry, 142*(4), 447–455.

Bishara, D., & Taylor, D. (2009). Asenapine monotherapy in the acute treatment of both schizophrenia and bipolar I disorder. *Neuropsychiatric Disease and Treatment, 5*, 483–490.

Bola, J. R. (2006). Psychosocial acute treatment in early-episode schizophrenia disorders. *Research on Social Work Practice, 16*(3), 263–275.

Bola, J. R., & Mosher, L. R. (2002). Predicting drug-free treatment response in acute psychosis from the Soteria project. *Schizophrenia Bulletin, 38*, 559–575.

Bola, J. R., & Mosher, L. R. (2003). Treatment of acute psychosis without narcoleptics. *Two-year outcomes from the Soteria project. Journal of Nervous and Mental Disease, 191*, 219–229.

Brzustowicz, L., Hodgkinson, K., Chow, E., Honer, W., & Bassett, A. (2000, April 28). Location of major susceptibility locus for familial schizophrenia on chromosome 1g21-q22. *Science, 288*, 682–687.

Calton, T., & Spandler, H. (2009). Minimal-medication approaches to treating schizophrenia. *Advances in Psychiatric Treatment, 15*, 209–217.

Cardinal, R. N., & Bullmore, E. T. (2011). *The diagnosis of psychosis.* New York, NY: Cambridge University Press.

Carpenter, W. T., Conley, R. R., & Buchanan, R. W. (1998). Schizophrenia. In S. J. Enna & J. T. Coyle (Eds.), *Pharmacological management of neurological and psychiatric disorders* (pp. 27–52). New York, NY: McGraw-Hill.

Chopra, D. (1994). *Alternative medicine: The definitive guide.* Fife, WA: Future Medicine.

Ciompi, L., & Hoffman, H. (2004). Soteria Berne. An innovative milieu therapeutic approach to acute schizophrenia based on the concept of affect-logic. *World Psychiatry, 3*, 140–146.

Clark, A. F. (2006). Schizophrenia and schizophrenia-like disorders. In C. Gillberg, R. Harrington, & C. Steinhausen (Eds.), *A clinicians handbook of child and adolescent psychiatry* (pp. 79–110). New York, NY: Cambridge University Press.

Cohen, A., Patel, V., Thara, R., & Gureje, O. (2008). Questioning an axiom: Better prognosis for schizophrenia in the developing world? *Schizophrenia Bulletin, 34*(2), 229–244.

Crow, T. J., Chance, S. A., Priddle, T. H., Radua, J., & James, A. C. (2013). Laterality interacts with sex across the schizophrenia/bipolarity continuum: An interpretation of meta-analyses of structural MRI. *Psychiatry Research, 210*, 1232–1244.

Dassori, A. M., Miller, A. L., Velligan, D., Saldana, D., Diamond, P., & Mahurin, R. (1998). Ethnicity and negative symptoms in patients with schizophrenia. *Cultural Diversity and Mental Health, 4*(1), 65–69.

Davis, J. M., & Casper, R. (1977). Antipsychotic drugs: Clinical pharmacology and therapeutic use. *Drugs, 12*, 260–282.

Drugs.com. (2009a). *New drug approvals.* Retrieved from http://www.drugs.com/newdrugs.html

Drugs.com. (2009b). *FDA approves Fanapt.* Retrieved from http://www.drugs.com/history/fanapt.html

Dutta, R., Greene, T., Addington. J., McKenzie, K., Phillips., M., & Murray. R. M. (2007). Biological, life course, and cross-cultural studies all point toward the value of dimensional and developmental ratings in the classification of psychosis. *Schizophrenia Bulletin, 33*(4), 868–876.

Dziegielewski, S. F. (2006). *Psychopharmacology for the non-medically trained.* New York, NY: Norton.

Dziegielewski, S. F. (2007). *Issues in schizophrenia: The social worker's role in optimizing adherence.* Special Report, December 31, 2007, 1–12. Available for CEU credit on line from CEZone.com. Peer-reviewed by Ralph Aquila, M.D.

Dziegielewski, S. F. (2008). Brief and intermittent approaches to practice: The state of practice. *Journal of Brief Treatment and Crisis Intervention, 8*(2), 147–163.

Dziegielewski, S. F. (2010). *Psychopharmacology and social work practice: A person-in-environment approach* (2nd ed.). New York, NY: Springer.

Easing the emotional cost of schizophrenia. (1997). *Journal of Psychosocial Nursing, 35*(2), 6.

Fazel, S., Gulati, G., Linsell, L., Geddes, J. R., & Grann, M. (2009). Schizophrenia and violence: Systematic review and meta-analysis. *PLoS Medicine, 6*(8), e1000120. doi: 10.1371/journal.pmed.1000120

Ferriman, A. (2000). The stigma of schizophrenia. *British Medical Journal, 320*(8), 522.

First, M. B. (2014). *DSM-5 Handbook of differential diagnosis.* Washington, DC: American Psychiatric Publishing.

Flaum, M. (1995). Schizophrenia. In C. L. Shriqui & H. A. Nasrallah (Eds.), *Contemporary issues in the treatment of schizophrenia* (pp. 83–108). Washington, DC: American Psychiatric Press.

Frese, F. J., III Knight, E. L., & Saks, E. (2009). Recovery from schizophrenia: With views of psychiatrists, psychologists, and others diagnosed with this disorder. *Schizophrenia Bulletin, 35*(2), 370–380.

Glick, I. (2005). *New schizophrenia treatments*. Presentation at the Schizophrenia and Bioplar Education day. Stanford University, Palo Alto, CA.

Gottesman, I. I. (1991). *Schizophrenia genesis: The origins of madness*. New York, NY: Freeman.

Green, A. I. (2007). Substance abuse and schizophrenia: Pharmacological approaches. *Journal of Dual Diagnosis, 3*(2), 63–72.

Grigorenko, E. L. (2009). *Multicultural psychoeducational assessment*. New York, NY: Springer.

Grohol, J. M. (2006). *Schizophrenia treatment*. Retrieved from http://www.psychcentral.com/disorders/sx31t.htm

Guilmatre, A., Dubourg, C., Mosca, A. L., Legallic, S., Goldenberg, A., Drouin-Garraud, V., . . . Campion, D. (2009). Recurrent rearrangements in synaptic and neurodevelopmental genes and shared biological pathways in schizophrenia, autism, and mental retardation. *Archives of General Psychiatry, 66*(9), 947–956.

Gur, R. E., & Pearlson, G. D. (1993). Neuroimaging for schizophrenia research. *Schizophrenia Bulletin, 19*(2), 337–353.

Hoffman, R. E. (2000). Transcranial magnetic stimulation and auditory hallucinations in schizophrenia. *Lancet, 355*, 1073–1076.

Hollis, C. (1995). Child and adolescent (juvenile onset) schizophrenia. A case controls study of premorbid developmental impairments. *British Journal of Psychiatry, 166*, 489–495.

Hong, C. J., Lee, Y. L., Sim, C. B., & Hwu, H. G. (1997). Dopamine D4 receptor variants in Chinese sporadic and familial schizophrenics. *American Journal of Medical Genetics (Neuropsychiatric Genetics), 74*, 412–415.

Huguelet, P., Mohr, S., & Borras, L. (2009). Recovery, spirituality and religiousness in schizophrenia. *Clinical Schizophrenia & Related Psychoses, 2*(4), 307–316.

Kendler, K. S., & Diehl, S. R. (1993). The genetics of schizophrenia: A current, genetic epidemiological perspective. *Schizophrenia Bulletin, 19*(2), 261–286.

Kendler, K. S., Gruenberg, A. M., & Tsuang, M. T. (1985). Psychiatric illness in first degree relatives of schizophrenic and surgical control patients: A family study using *DSM-III* criteria. *Archives of General Psychiatry, 42*(8), 770–779.

Kendler, K. S., McGuire, M., Gruengerg, A. M., O'Hare, A., Spellman, M., & Walsh, D. (1993). The Roscommo family study. 1: Methods, diagnosis of probands and risk of schizophrenia in relatives. *Archives of General Psychiatry, 50*(7), 527–540.

Keshavan, M., Marshall, W., Shazly, M., & Paki, M. (1988). Neuroendocrine dysfunction in schizophrenia: A familial perspective. *Psychiatry Research, 23*(5), 345–348.

Keshavan, M. S., Montrose, D. M., Pierri, J. N., Dick, E. L., Rosenberg, D., Talagala, L., & Sweeney, J. A. (1997). Magnetic resonance imaging and spectroscopy in offspring at risk for schizophrenia: Preliminary studies. *Progressions in Neuro-Psychopharmacological and Biological Psychiatry, 21*, 1285–1295.

Kessler, R. C., Heeringa, S., Lakoma, M. D., Petukhova, M., Schoenbaum, M., Wang, P. S., & Zaslavsky, A. M. (2008). Individual and societal effects of mental disorders on earnings in the United States: Results from the national comorbidity survey replication. *American Journal of Psychiatry, 165*(6), 703–711.

Krajewski, C., Burazeri, G., & Brand, H. (2013). Self-stigma, perceived discrimination and empowerment among people with a mental illness in six countries: Pan European. *Psychiatry Research, 210*, 1136–1146.

Lambert, L. (1998). New medications aid cognition in schizophrenia. *Journal of the American Medical Association, 280*(11), 953.

Landgraf, S., Blumenauer, K., Osterheider, M., & Eisenbarth, H. (2013). A clinical and demographic comparison between a forensic sample of female patients with schizophrenia. *Psychiatry Research, 210*, 1176–1183.

Laurens, I., Hodgins, B., Maughan, R., Rutter, M., & Taylor, E. (2009). Community screening for psychotic-like experiences and other putative antecedents of schizophrenia in children aged 9–12 years. *Schizophrenia Research, 90*(1), 130–146.

Lawrie, S. M., & Abukmeil, S. S. (1998). Brain abnormality in schizophrenia: A systematic and quantitative review of volumetric magnetic resonance imaging studies. *British Journal of Psychiatry, 172*, 110–120.

Lehmann, H. E., & Ban, T. A. (1997). The history of the psychopharmacology of schizophrenia. *Canadian Journal of Psychiatry, 42*(2), 152–162.

Lieberman, J. A., Ma, J., Alvir, J. M. J., Woerner, M., Degreef, G., Bilder, R. M., . . . Kane, J. M., (1992). Prospective study of psychobiology in first-episode schizophrenia at Hillside Hospital. *Schizophrenia Bulletin, 18*(3), 351–371.

Lewandowski, K. E., DePaola, J., Casmari, G. B., Cohen, B. M., & Ongur, D. (2009). Tactile, olfactory, and gustatory hallucinations in psychotic disorders: A descriptive study. *Annals of the Academy of Medicine Singapore, 38*(5), 383–385.

Locke, D. C., & Bailey, D. F. (2014). *Increasing multicultural understanding* (3rd ed.). Thousand Oaks, CA: Sage.

Long, P. W. (2000). *Schizophrenia: A handbook for families: Schizophrenia youth's greatest disaster.* Retrieved from http://www.mentalhealth.com/dis/p20-ps01.html

Lukoff, D. (2007). Spirituality in the recovery from persistent mental disorders. *Southern Medical Journal, 100*(6), 642–646.

Lum, D. (Ed.). (2011). *Culturally competent practice: A framework for understanding diverse groups and justice issues* (4th ed.). Pacific Grove, CA: Brooks/Cole, Thomson Learning.

Lyne, J., Renwick, L., Grant, T., Kinsella, A., McCarthy, P., Malone, K., . . . Clarke, M. (2013). Scale for the assessment of negative symptoms structure in first episode of psychosis. *Psychiatry Research, 210*, 1191–1197.

Maier, W., Hallmeyer, J., Minges, J., & Lichtermann, D. (1990). Morbid risks in relatives of affective, schizo affective, and schizophrenic patients: Results of a family study. In A. Maneros & M. T. Tsuang (Eds.), *Affective and schizoaffective disorders: Similarities and differences* (pp. 201–207). New York, NY: Springer-Verlag.

Malhotra, A. K., Pinsky, D. A., & Breier, A. (1996). Future antipsychotic agents: Clinical implications. In A. Breier (Ed.), *The new pharmacotherapy of schizophrenia* (pp. 41–56). Washington, DC: American Psychiatric Press.

Menezes, N. M., Arenovich, T., & Zipursky, R. B. (2006). A systematic review of longitudinal outcome studies of first-episode psychosis. *Psychological Medicine, 36*(10), 1349–1362.

Mental Health America. (2009). *Factsheet: Schizophrenia in children.* Retrieved from http://www.mentalhealthamerica.net/conditions/schizophrenia

Moore, D. P., & Jefferson, J. W. (1997). *Handbook of medical psychiatry.* St. Louis, MO: Mosby.

Munro, A. (1999). *Delusional disorder: Paranoia and related illnesses.* New York, NY: Cambridge University Press.

Munro, A., & Mok, H. (2006). An overview of treatment in paranoia/delusional disorder. *Canadian Journal of Psychiatry, 40*, 616–622.

National Alliance on Mental Illness. (2003). Tardive dyskinesia. Retrieved from http://www.nami.org/Content/ContentGroups/Helpline1/Tardive_Dyskinesia.htm

National Institute of Mental Health. (2009a). *How is bipolar disorder treated?* Retrieved from http://www.nimh.nih.gov/health/publications/bipolar-disorder/how-is-bipolar-disorder-treated.shtml

National Institute of Mental Health. (2009b). *Post-traumatic stress disorder (PTSD).* Retrieved from http://www.nimh.nih.gov/health/topics/post-traumatic-stress-disorder-ptsd/index.shtml

National Institute of Mental Health. (2009c). *Schizophrenia.* Retrieved from http://www.nimh.nih.gov/health/publications/schizophrenia/index.shtml

National Institute of Mental Health. (2009d). Mental health medications. Retrieved from, http://www.nimh.nih.gov/health/publications/mental-health-medications/index.shtml?utm_source=twitterfeed&utm_medium=twitter

Nauert, R. (Ed.). (2007). New genetic link for schizophrenia. Retrieved from http://psychcentral.com/news/2008/02/28/new-genetic-link-to-schizophrenia/1977.html

Organista, K. C. (2007). *Solving Latino psychosocial and health problems: Theory, practice and populations.* Belmont. CA: Wiley.

Oshodi, A., Bangaru, R., & Benbow, J. (2005). A paranoid migrant family: Folie a famille. *Irish Journal of Psychological Medicine, 22*, 26–29.

Paniagua, F. A. (2014). *Assessing and treating culturally diverse clients: A practical guide* (4th ed.). Los Angeles, CA: Sage.

Physicians' desk reference (63rd ed.). (2009). Montvale, NJ: Medical Economics.

Qiu, A., Wang, L., Younes, L., Harms, M. P., Ratnanather, T. J., Miller, M. I., & Csernansky, J. G. (2009). Neuroanatomical asymmetry patterns in individuals with schizophrenia and their non-psychotic siblings. *NeuroImage, 47*(4), 1221–1229.

Raz, S., & Raz, N. (1990). Structural brain abnormalities in the major psychosis: A quantitative review of the evidence from computerized imaging. *Psychological Bulletin, 108*(1), 93–108.

Rusch, N., Heekeren, K., Theodoridou, A., Dvorsky, D., Muller, M., Paust, T., . . . Rossler, W. (2013). Attitudes toward help-seeking and stigma among young people at risk for psychosis. *Psychiatry Research, 210*, 1313–1315.

Saklad, S. R. (2000). APA studies focus on side effects, efficacy of antipsychotics. *Psychopharmacology Update, 11*(1), 1.

Schmidt, N. B., Norr, A. M., & Korte, K. J. (2014). Panic disorder and agoraphobia: Considerations for *DSM-V. Research on Social Work Practice, 24*(1), 57–66.

Schore, A. N. (2014). Introduction. In J. J. Magnavita & J. C. Anchin (Eds.), *Unifying psychotherapy: Principles, methods, evidence from clinical science* (pp. xxi–xliv). New York, NY: Springer.

Schulz, S. C. (2000). New antipsychotic medications: More than old wine and new bottles. *Bulletin of the Menninger Clinic, 64*(1), 60–75.

Siris, S. G. (2000). Management of depression in schizophrenia. *Psychiatric Annals, 30*(1), 13–17.

Soni, A. (2009). The five most costly conditions, 1996 and 2006: Estimates for the U. S. civilian noninstitutionalized population [Statistical Brief #248]. Agency for Healthcare Research and Quality, Rockville, MD. Retrieved from http://www.meps.ahrq.gov/mepsweb/data_files/publications/st248/stat248.pdf

Tandon, R. (2012), Getting ready for DSM-5: Psychotic disorders. *Current Psychiatry, 11*(4), E1–E4. Retrieved from http://www.currentpsychiatry.com/index.php?id=22161&cHash=071010&tx_ttnews[tt_news]=176766

Tracker, C. M. E. (2009). Violence in schizophrenia rare in the absence of substance abuse. *JAMA, 301*, 2016.

Tsuang, D. (2004). Rates of schizophrenia among relatives of schizophrenic patients. Retrieved from http://schizophrenia.com/research/hereditygen.htm

Walker, E., Mitial, V., Tessner, K., & Trotman, H. (2008). Schizophrenia and the psychotic spectrum. In W. E. Craighead, D. J. Miklowitz, & L. W. Craighead (Eds.), *Psychopathology: History, diagnosis, and empirical foundations* (pp. 402–434). Hoboken, NJ: Wiley.

WebMD. (2009). Schizophrenia medications. Retrieved from http://www.webmd.com/schizophrenia/guide/schizophrenia-medications

Weiner, I. B. (1987). Identifying schizophrenia in adolescents. *Journal of Adolescent Health Care, 8*(4), 336–343.

Weisman, A. G. (1997). Understanding cross-cultural prognostic variability for schizophrenia. *Cultural Diversity and Mental Health, 3*(1), 23–35.

Wong, S. E. (2013). A critique of the diagnostic construct schizophrenia. *Research on Social Work Practice.* doi: 10.1177/1049731513505152

Woo, S. M., & Keatinge, C. (Eds.). (2008). *Diagnosis and treatment of mental disorders across the lifetime.* Hoboken, NJ: Wiley.

Woods, S. W., & McGlashan, T. H. (2011). The risk–benefit ratio of the proposed DSM-5 attenuated psychosis syndrome. *American Journal of Psychiatry, 168*(12), 1338.

CHAPTER 6

Bipolar and Related Disorders

SOPHIA F. DZIEGIELEWSKI AND OLGA MOLINA

INTRODUCTION

Families and communities pay a heavy toll when a disorder involving an individual's mood is not recognized and treated. For so many individuals who suffer from bipolar and the related disorders, the mood swings can create problems with family relations and support systems. There is also an increased potential for suicide. Children, adolescents, and adults who suffer from a bipolar disorder often incur employment or school difficulties that have devastating effects on the individual and his or her family, with the eventual involvement of the judicial system. Promptly recognizing the signs and symptoms of a bipolar disorder in children, adolescents, and adults is imperative. Furthermore, no single medicine, treatment, or therapy holds the key to success, and all options should be used to assist this population.

This chapter presents a brief overview of the bipolar and related disorders listed in the *Diagnostic and Statistical Manual of Mental Disorders*, Fifth Edition (*DSM-5*; American Psychiatric Association [APA], 2013), including bipolar I disorder, bipolar II disorder, cyclothymic disorder, substance/medication-induced bipolar and related disorder, bipolar disorder due to another medical condition, and other specified and unspecified bipolar and the related disorders. Specific attention is given to bipolar disorders in adults. Discussion of the bipolar disorders from a community and societal perspective identifies how critical it is for mental health practitioners to complete a thorough diagnostic assessment, treatment plan, and practice strategy. Effective treatment of the bipolar and related disorders in children and adults requires attempting to reduce the magnitude of disturbances these disorders can have on the individual and his or her support system.

Starting with a comprehensive diagnostic assessment is the key to identifying the symptoms required to place the diagnosis. The focus of this chapter is that fluctuating mood disturbances remain difficult to define and that not just one method of treatment works for all clients. Knowledge of multiple methods allows the most comprehensive treatment. An individualized diagnostic assessment, treatment plan, and implementation of the practice strategy are essential for improving an individual's functioning in society and helping that person to once again become able to enjoy life.

TOWARD A BASIC UNDERSTANDING OF THE BIPOLAR AND RELATED DISORDERS

Bipolar disorder, the most common of the bipolar and other disorders, is sometimes referred to as manic-depressive illness. When characterized in lay terms, it can be referred to as mood swings in which the individual suffers from repeated ups and downs. These mood fluctuations, however, are not consistent with everyday responses and are severe mood shifts. According to the National Institutes of Health (NIH) (n.d.), there is no single cause for this illness, and many factors, when present and acting together, increase the risk of developing this illness.

Two significant factors in a better understanding of the disorder are genetics and brain structure and functioning. Concerning genetics, cognitive dysfunction may be a core feature related to the strong genetic component (Samame, 2013). This genetic link is similar to the depressive and the schizophrenia spectrum disorders in that the mental disorder is most likely to also occur in a parent or sibling. Although the exact genetic connection or linkage remains unknown, searches for a similar hot spot that could better explain these complex disorders, taking into account environmental factors, provide fertile ground for present and future research (NIH, n.d.).

The second factor is brain structure and functioning, and the newer brain-imaging tools, such as functional magnetic resonance imaging (fMRI) and positron emission tomography (PET), bring us much closer to understanding this connection (see Quick Reference 6.1). These advanced radiological techniques can help identify changes in the brain (Arden & Linford, 2009). Thus, actual changes in the brain exist, and similarities between schizophrenia spectrum disorders and the bipolar disorders have been identified (Crow, Chance, Priddle, Radau, & James, 2013). Although helpful, however, these imaging studies can represent a client only at a particular point in time (Childress, 2006). As a supplement to the diagnostic assessment, these procedures should be considered. Unfortunately, the cost of these imaging studies, regardless of the information they contribute, can be prohibitive. In the diagnostic assessment, utilizing tests like these can assist in what is sometimes referred to as defensive medicine, designed to firm the diagnosis and protect both the client and the prescriber (Titolo, 2008).

In the United States alone, 10 million individuals are estimated to be affected by the bipolar disorders (Torpy, 2009). The symptoms characteristic of the disorder may be especially frustrating because the complaints reported generally result in negative medical workups. Thus, addressing these multifaceted disorders creates misunderstandings and frustration on the part of both health care providers and their clients

QUICK REFERENCE 6.1

Neuroimaging

Functional magnetic resonance imaging (fMRI) is a specialized type of MRI; this form of neuroimaging has gained in popularity since the 1990s because it is less invasive and has less radiation exposure than previous versions. This technique examines neuronal activity within the brain influenced by increased blood flow to the local vasculature. It provides the ability to observe structures within the brain, helping to identify which structures are actually related to what function.

Positron emission tomography (PET), which was introduced in the mid-1970s, is used to monitor neuronal activity by utilizing radioactive injected tracers that enter the brain.

Source: Definitions summarized from Dziegielewski (2010).

(National Institute of Mental Health [NIMH], 2000). To further complicate this scenario, about 90% of individuals with bipolar disorder experience recurrences during their lifetimes, often within 2 years of an initial episode, and the consequences of recurrent illness for individuals are substantial (Perlis et al., 2006).

UNDERSTANDING INDIVIDUALS WHO SUFFER FROM BIPOLAR AND RELATED DISORDERS

The diagnostic assessment of an individual suffering from any type of bipolar disorder shows the presence of two primary symptoms: a depressed mood and an elevated mood. Displaying both symptoms can confuse both families and practitioners. When clients report the symptoms of depression, it may lack clarity, and there may be problems in semantics related to defining what is experienced. When they experience a bipolar episode and the energy returns, optimism may rise, only to have it extinguished as the lift in mood becomes uncontrollable and destructive to the expected purpose.

With fluctuations in mood, feelings of depression or mania can frequently be overstated or understated. These feelings can also be influenced by the definition and normalcy standards set within an individual's unique social and environmental context. For many individuals, depression can mean feeling sad, blue, or down in the dumps; for others, it can involve anger and agitation that reflect consistent patterns, signs, and symptoms relative to the bipolar episode. Furthermore, mood changes are expected, and some form of depression (also referred to as dysphoric mood) characteristic of the mood disorders is present in almost all mental health conditions, with the only possible exceptions being some forms of mania, schizophrenia, and dementia (Klap, Unroe, & Unutzer, 2003).

Adults with bipolar disorder seem in some ways more unfortunate than those who suffer from recurrent major depression because more than 90% of those who have one manic episode go on to have further episodes (APA, 2000). Overall, the probabilities of full recovery for bipolar and unipolar disorder are equally discouraging; about 60% of individuals experience another manic episode within 2 years after an acute episode, and at least 50% experience significant interepisode symptoms (Miklowitz, George, Richards, Simoneau, & Suddath, 2003).

To better understand the bipolar and related disorders, the first step is becoming aware of the different mood episodes that characterize the disorders. One major source of confusion for beginning professionals has been the assumption that the mood episodes actually constitute a mental disorder, although they do not. In the *DSM-IV* and the *DSM-IV-TR*, like *DSM-5*, the mood episodes are not considered diagnostic conditions. A simple way to think of these episodes is that they are the basic ingredients or the building blocks for the disorders that follow.

Bipolar Disorders: The Episodes and the Specifiers

A thorough understanding starts with defining the mood episodes that are the ingredients of the bipolar and related disorders. The types of mood episodes that make up the mood disorders are manic, hypomanic, and major depressive episodes (APA, 2013). (See Quick Reference 6.2.)

Manic Episode

In a manic episode, the client's mood is persistently elevated, expansive, and irritable, but the predominant mood disturbance is irritability, especially when others do not fulfill the client's wishes or meet his or her expectations.

QUICK REFERENCE 6.2

Types of Mood Episodes

Manic episode: Present mood is persistently elevated, irritable, and expansive, with severe mood disturbance, and leading to impaired functioning. There must be at least three of these symptoms: pressured speech, increased psychomotor agitation, flight of ideas, decreased need for sleep, increased involvement in goal-oriented activities, distractibility, and inflated self-esteem or grandiosity. There is also excessive involvement in pleasurable activities, which have the potential for high risk and negative consequences. The time frame for the episode is at least 1 week. If hospitalization to control or address behaviors occurs, the 1-week time frame is not needed.

Hypomanic episode: Similar to manic, but all features and symptoms are less severe, although they still interfere with functioning. Criteria for hypomanic include a distinct period of persistently expansive, irritable, elevated mood that lasts at least 4 days but less than 1 week. There must be present at least three symptoms (whereas four symptoms are required if there is predominantly an irritable mood): pressured speech, increased involvement in goal-oriented activities, psychomotor agitation, distractibility, decreased need for sleep, and inflated self-esteem or grandiosity. There is also excessive involvement in pleasurable activities, which have the potential for high risk and negative consequences.

Major depressive episode: Depressed mood for at least 2 weeks or a loss of interest or pleasure in nearly all activities, plus at least five additional symptoms experienced by the client almost daily for the same 2-week period. Associated features include sleeping and appetite disturbances (very common symptoms); fatigue or decreased energy; changes in sleep; changes in psychomotor activity; reduced ability to think, concentrate, or make decisions; feelings of worthlessness or guilt; morbid ideation or suicidal ideation, plans, or attempts; and irritable mood.

Source: Summarized criteria from the *Diagnostic and Statistical Manual of Mental Disorders*, Fifth Edition, Copyright 2013 by the American Psychiatric Association.

According to *DSM-5* the manic episode requires 4 specific criteria be examined (A-D). Criterion A outlines the time frame of the disorder along with the frequency and intensity. In this criterion assessment involves clearly identifying changes in behavior that result in persistently elevated mood, energy levels with increased goal-directed behavior which often may not be socially or occupationally productive. The active time frame should last at least one week. One exception to this criterion is if the individual is hospitalized and when this is the case no time frame is required. Frequency and intensity information is documented when the individual reports feeling for at least a week, increased activity and energy nearly every day almost all day.

Criterion B, during the active phase of one week along with elevated mood, the client must also exhibit at least three or more of the seven identified symptoms: inflated self-esteem and grandiosity; a decreased need for sleep and can sleep as few as 3 hours a night and not feel the need for more; increased or pressured speech with an intense desire to keep talking; distractibility, difficulty concentrating and easily directed and redirected making it difficult to follow patterned and sequenced thought; increased goal-related activities and psychomotor agitation; and preoccupation and subsequent involvement in completing tasks that constitute high risk behaviors that could have harmful results or painful consequences. When the client presents primarily with irritable mood at least four of the seven symptoms are required to adequately meet the criterion (APA, 2013, p. 124). When documenting the behaviors consistent with this disorder a client in this active phase often shows little restraint and may exceed the limits on their credit cards, spending extravagantly. They may show little regard for the safety of others and drive recklessly. They may also act indiscriminately, engaging in sexually promiscuous behaviors and perhaps unsafe sexual practices. In documenting criterion B, these types of problematic behaviors should be listed.

In criterion C, the behaviors must be clinically severe and impair social and occupational functioning. For those suffering from this disorder the severity can easily result in hospitalization to control the excessive behaviors and to ensure no harm to others or personal safety. In this active phase the individual may also experience psychotic-like behaviors that further impair the interpretation of events and how they communicate and respond to others around them. In criterion D, it needs to be clear that the episode being suffered is not related directly to another mental or medical condition, nor is it related to substance or other types of drug-induced responses.

Hypomanic Episode

In a hypomanic episode, the symptoms initially may appear similar to the manic episode, as it involves persistently elevated, expansive, or irritable mood. In a hypomanic episode, the client's mood is persistently elevated, expansive, and irritable, but the predominant mood disturbance is irritability, especially when frustrated with activities of daily living or social or occupational tasks. According to *DSM-5* the hypomanic episode requires 6 specific criteria be examined (A-F). Criterion A outlines the time frame of the disorder along with the frequency and intensity. Utilizing criterion A requires clearly identifying changes in behavior that result in persistently elevated and expansive mood, with energy levels and increased goal-directed behavior that are often not socially or occupationally productive. The active time frame should last at least 4 days with individuals reporting increased activity nearly every day almost all day.

In criterion B[1], over the 4-day period along with elevated mood, the client must also exhibit at least three or more of seven potential symptoms: inflated self-esteem and grandiosity; a decreased need for sleep and can sleep as few as 3 hours a night and not feel the need for more; increased or pressured speech with an intense desire to keep talking; distractibility, difficulty concentrating and easily directed and redirected making it difficult to follow patterned and sequenced thought; increased goal-related a ctivities and psychomotor agitation; and preoccupation and subsequent involvement in completing tasks that constitute high risk behaviors that could have harmful results or painful consequences. When the client presents primarily with irritable mood at least four of these symptoms are required to adequately meet the criterion. When documenting the behaviors consistent with this disorder a client in this active

[1] Although criterion B is not a direct quote, it is summarized from the *DSM-5* dimensional criteria. For complete and abbreviated listing of the criteria, see the appropriate section of the *DSM-5*. To assist the reader, page numbers are provided in this text.

phase often shows little restraint and may exceed the limits on their credit cards, spending extravagantly. They may show little regard for the safety of others and drive recklessly. They may also act indiscriminately, engaging in sexually promiscuous behaviors and perhaps unsafe sexual practices.

In criterion C, the behaviors are clearly uncharacteristic of the individual. Criterion D outlines how others who are familiar with the individual clearly see this as not normal behavior for that person and express that it constitutes a clear change in previous types of behaviors and functioning. In criterion E, the behaviors and the resulting mood disturbance can impair functioning but are not nearly as severe as those occurring in the manic phase. If in this hypomanic phase the behaviors are severe enough to be hospitalized, it would not constitute a hypomanic episode. In criterion F, it needs to be clear that the episode being suffered is not related directly to a substance or other types of drug-induced responses (APA, 2013, pp. 124–125).

In summary, this period of abnormal mood is accompanied by a minimum of three additional symptoms from a selected list: nondelusional grandiosity, inflated self-esteem, pressured speech, a flight of ideas, and increased involvement in goal-directed activities or psychomotor agitation (APA, 2013). There is often a decreased need for sleep, and the individual reports trouble either falling or staying asleep. These individuals may take on projects and tasks that keep them very busy, although they may become distracted and not finish the commitments originally made. Similar to the manic episode, during a hypomanic episode the individual also may engage in high-risk behaviors that he or she finds pleasurable while ignoring the potential harmful consequences. Clients often report experiencing a euphoric mood. Although some interactions may involve sarcasm, overall the individuals appear cheerful. Often while in the hypomanic episode, individuals may report feeling self-confident and good.

The time period for this mood episode to last is approximately 4 days, and during this time it is clear that the individual is exhibiting signs that are uncharacteristic of previous levels of functioning. Individuals experiencing a hypomanic mood episode would not need to be hospitalized; although the symptoms may impair functioning, and marked impairment is not noted. What differentiates the hypomanic episode from the manic episode is the absence of sophisticated and pronounced delusional thinking. Furthermore, individuals experiencing a hypomanic episode do not show evidence of psychotic features, even though others interacting with them are aware that the behaviors they are exhibiting are uncharacteristic.

Major Depressive Episode

According to the *DSM-5*, criteria for the diagnosis of the third type of mood episode, the major depressive episode, requires three characteristic criteria (A-C). Criteria A involves five or more signs, in addition to the first sign of depressed mood or loss of pleasure and interest. In this episode one or the other must be present in addition to the five or more additional signs. Depressed mood involves feelings of sadness or hopelessness that cannot be controlled or avoided. In addition, there may also be a clear loss of interest or pleasure in nearly all activities. Like many other mental disorders, the diagnostic criterion of depressed mood and loss of interest must be significant enough to interfere with individual functioning and his or her performance of usual activities. In addition, criterion A requires that five or more additional symptoms must be present. There are nine symptoms that need to be considered of which five are required to meet the criterion A. The first of the nine symptoms includes documented incidents relevant to depressed mood. It must be clear how often these episodes occur, denoting the frequency and intensity to be evident daily happening almost all of the time. This depressed mood will need to be substantiated by self-report where the individual states he or she is expressing feelings of sadness, haplessness, and hopelessness. Or if the individual cannot communicate his or her feelings the depressed mood can be observed and noted by others. Others may report that the individual has no energy, cannot complete previously capable tasks, or is tearful most of the time. Of important note is that depression in children and adolescents can often manifest itself differently from adults and the resultant picture can be quite different than the depressed, quiet, and subdued adult. Oftentimes when children and adolescents are depressed they get openly angry, and frustration is how they display their sadness and discontent.

In the second potential symptom the individual shows a lack of interest or pleasure in almost all activities that he or she previously found pleasurable. When there is a markedly diminished interest or pleasure in activities that are usually pleasurable it is referred to as anhedonia. The third potential symptom involves appetite. Often individuals suffering from a major depressive episode report appetite disturbances that occur on almost a daily basis. At times these eating patterns involve consuming too much food, resulting in weight gain (5% of body weight in 1 month); if they involve eating too little, they may result in weight loss. The weight loss has to be significant, and a specific amount is outlined. To facilitate the assessment of this symptom, these questions are suggested: Has the client gained or lost weight recently (focusing on the last month)? If so, how much weight has been lost or gained? The answers to these questions help the practitioner determine if the client is suffering from anorexia (eating less) or hyperphagia (overeating) to cope with the depressive feelings. The fourth area is related to sleep disturbance, where the individual is either sleeping too much (hypersomnia) or experiencing an inability to sleep or disturbed sleep patterns (insomnia). This pattern of sleep disturbance needs to happen nearly every day. To facilitate the assessment of this symptom, these questions are suggested: Is the client sleeping at night? If so, for how long? How does the client feel when he or she wakes up? Does he or she report feeling refreshed? When the third and fourth potential symptom exist, these disturbances in eating and sleeping, which are common in this disorder, are often assessed first. Eating and sleeping are considered basic for survival. Referring specifically to insomnia and the loss of appetite, the term used to describe these symptoms is *vegetative*. When it involves oversleeping (hypersomnia) and overeating (hyperphagia), it is referred to as *reversed vegetative symptoms*.

The fifth symptom results in psychomotor agitation (uncontrolled restlessness) or retardation (slowed and feeling exhausted), where the individual cannot seem to escape these feelings and behavioral manifestations as they occur almost every day, and do not appear to subside even for a short period of time. The sixth symptom results in inescapable fatigue and energy depletion, where it is not uncommon for the individual to feel as if the energy has been "sucked out." The seventh symptom involves feelings related to disturbances in mood where the individual reports excessive and unfounded feelings of guilt blaming the self for the illness experienced or the inability to escape feelings of dread and doom. Cognitive disturbances are outlined in symptom eight where there is a decreased ability to think and concentrate. Similar to the other symptoms in the list, this one as well seems to occur every day almost all day, making planning the simplest of cognitive tasks almost impossible. Lastly is the possibility for recurrent thoughts related to death and dying. These thoughts can preoccupy the individual and often suicidal ideations (the idea to kill oneself) become prominent. This symptom can be very dangerous as the individual may actually develop and formulate a plan to commit suicide (suicidal intent). When this symptom is present a clear plan to assess and plan for any subsequent intervention needs to be clear and direct.

Criterion B, requires that the symptoms displayed cause clinically significant distress that impair social and occupational functioning. Criterion C requires that the symptoms displayed and the diagnosis placed not be attributable to another medical condition or the effects related to substance use, intoxication, or withdrawal (APA, 2013, p. 125).

In summary, those suffering from a major depressive episode will often experience daily bouts of depressed mood, psychomotor agitation or changes in psychomotor activity, agitation or retardation nearly every day, fatigue or loss of energy, feelings of worthlessness or guilt, and difficulty thinking, concentrating, or making decisions. Because there are so many different characteristics that can affect mood and result in depression, it is important to assess for the possibility of a grief reaction, especially when related to the death or loss of a loved one. In these cases the practitioner needs to gather a comprehensive picture, and when assessing for the presence of each of the nine symptoms, be sure to also gather a through history taking into account recent situational events as well as social and cultural mores and expectations.

Although it is beyond the scope of this chapter to discuss all the signs and characteristic symptoms of all the bipolar disorders, the societal context and a brief overview of the most common ones are presented. For specific word-for-word criteria the reader is referred to the *DSM-5*, pages 123-126, which provide a list of specific criterion for each episode.

Specifiers for Bipolar and Related Disorders

Making a diagnostic impression related to the bipolar and other disorders involves assessing whether a mental disorder exists by gathering information from collateral sources such as family and friends. When this is coupled with a strong and dynamic relationship between the practitioner and the patient, the best types of therapeutic assessments result (Frances, 2013). In the bipolar and related disorders, similar to most of the other disorders, in the *DSM-5*, a disorder may not clearly fit into distinct diagnostic categories (Garland & Howard, 2014), or the bipolar or related disorder tends to follow a similar or recognized pattern. In cases such as this, a *subtype* or *course specifier* may be warranted.

In the *DSM-5*, for the bipolar disorders there are no subtypes to clarify a diagnosis where the phenomenological criteria are mutually exclusive and exhaustive (APA, 2013). A subtype is used, however, for the diagnosis of schizoaffective disorder (discussed in Chapter 5). The reason a subtype is used in that disorder is its close relationship with the bipolar and related disorders. A subtype qualifier is used to outline homogeneous groupings of disorders, such as that seen in schizoaffective disorder. In schizoaffective disorder, documenting a subtype is always easy to recognize because it is coded as *specify* whether. Therefore, in schizoaffective disorder, it can be characterized with the subtype *bipolar type* to indicate that the criteria required for the manic episode and possibly a depressive episode may also occur during the course of the schizoaffective disorder. There is also a second subtype, the depressive type. Like the other subtype for schizoaffective disorder, the depressive type applies to the criteria being met for the schizoaffective disorder while also displaying symptoms equivalent to a major depressive episode.

In the bipolar and related disorders, diagnostic categories and course specifiers are used to show how criteria that are similar within this diagnostic category can lead to homogeneous (or similar) subgroupings that highlight certain shared features. To examine the specifiers in this category, nine specifiers are outlined that, when indicated, may be applied across each of the diagnoses: with anxious distress, with mixed features, with rapid cycling, with melancholic features, with atypical features, with psychotic features, with catatonic features, with peripartum features, and with seasonal pattern.

With Anxious Distress Often an individual with a bipolar disorder presents with significant features related to anxiety. Using the specifier, coded *specify if*, with anxious distress allows the crosscutting of core anxiety-related symptoms characteristic of the episode of mania, hypomania, or depression. When this specifier is used, two or more of the symptoms—feeling keyed up, unusually restless, difficulty concentrating because of worry, fear something awful might happen, and feeling the loss of control—must occur most days when the client is also experiencing the mood episode.

With Mixed Features Another specifier for this category of disorders is with mixed features. Mixed features can be further divided into two types: *manic or hypomanic episode with mixed features* and *depressive episode with mixed features*. Those familiar with the term *mixed* as related to these disorders may be reminded of the mixed episode that was previously listed and described in *DSM-IV* and *DSM-IV-TR*. In *DSM-5*, the mixed episode was deleted as a type of episode and modified to represent mixed features. The manic or hypomanic episode with mixed features is designed to address a series of mood-related features that can happen during the manic, hypomanic, or the mixed episode. Outlined are six characteristic symptoms, and the individual must suffer from at least three of them during the last time period when the criteria were also met for the manic or hypomanic episode. With mixed features, the individual may appear to suffer from dysphoria or depressed mood most evident by others reporting that the individual is crying and reporting feeling sad or lost and noting how uncharacteristic these behaviors are. This is especially noteworthy as onlookers are also seeing symptoms of the manic or hypomanic mood. In addition, the remaining seven characteristics further describe depressive features such as diminished interest, psychomotor retardation, loss of energy, feelings of worthlessness, and recurrent thoughts of death, all superimposed on the manic or hypomanic episode, where such features stand in direct contrast. When a mixed features qualifier is added, it must be indicative of a direct change from the person's mood and be unusual, inconsistent behavior noted by others viewing it. It is essential to ensure that these strange symptoms are not caused by a substance or a medical disorder, so a clear history and physical as well as laboratory tests are always suggested.

The second type of specifier denoted as mixed feature is the *depressive episode with mixed features*. In this specifier, the full criteria for the major depressive episode are met, although the individual presents with at least three of the seven outlined criteria that are characteristic of a manic or hypomanic episode: elevated and expansive mood, grandiosity and inflated self-esteem, pressured speech, flight of ideas, increased energy, and decreased need for sleep. The individual may also engage in uncharacteristic and high-risk behaviors that could easily lead to the onset of interpersonal troubles, disruptions among family and friends, and other social, occupational, and/or legal difficulties. All of these symptoms are very uncharacteristic of the depressive episode and to onlookers would seem mood-incongruent.

With Rapid Cycling Another specifier for this category of disorders is with rapid cycling, which can be used for both bipolar I and bipolar II disorder. Rapid cycling is the switch to an opposite episode, for example, from a major depressive episode to a manic episode. There needs to have been at least four mood episodes within the past 12 months. These episodes need to meet the same criteria of duration and symptom numbers as the criteria for a major depressive, manic, or hypomanic episode and be either in a period of remission or a switch to an opposite episode. The only difference between rapid cycling and other episodes is the frequency of the episodes. To distinguish rapid cycling from episodes caused by a substance, a medical history, laboratory tests, and a physical are suggested.

With Melancholic Features The specifier with melancholic features is characterized by a loss of pleasure in activities previously considered pleasurable. The loss or lack of pleasure needs to be present during the most severe period of the episode. In addition, three or more of the following six symptoms must be present: a distinct depressed mood or empty mood, depression that is worse in the mornings, early-morning awakening (at least 2 hours earlier than usual), psychomotor retardation or agitation, significant weight loss or anorexia, and excessive guilt. Melancholic features are noted at the most severe stage of the episode, where there is almost a complete absence of pleasure, and even in positive circumstances, the mood does not improve. These features are seen most frequently in the inpatient setting because of the severe loss of pleasure in almost all activities. The numbness often experienced is more characteristic of the most severe stages of the disorder and is more likely in individuals with psychotic features.

With Atypical Features Another specifier is with atypical features, which is more common than the name implies. With atypical features, the mood is brightened with the occurrence of positive events. In addition to this characteristic, at least two of the following symptoms are necessary: significant weight gain or increase in appetite, hypersomnia (increase in sleep), leaden paralysis (heavy feelings in arms or legs), and sensitivity to interpersonal rejection that affects social or occupational functioning. With atypical features, the mood may remain brightened for an extended period if events are favorable. There can be an increase in food intake that leads to weight gain. There may also be leaden paralysis, which is characterized by a heavy sensation in the arms or legs. Sensitivity to rejection from others is present even when the client is not in a depressed episode.

With Psychotic Features The specifier with psychotic features is characterized by delusions or hallucinations during the episode. There are two types: mood-congruent and mood-incongruent features. With *mood-congruent*, the content of the delusions and hallucinations is consistent with the manic episode of grandiosity and invulnerability and may also include paranoia. With *mood-incongruent* features, the content of the delusions and hallucinations is inconsistent with the themes of the episode, or there is a mixture of mood-congruent and mood-incongruent features.

With Catatonic Features The specifier with catatonic features can be present in either a manic or depressive episode. The criteria for catatonic features are in Chapter 5.

With Peripartum Feature The specifier with peripartum onset is applied if symptoms occur during pregnancy or 4 weeks postdelivery. This specifier is used for manic, hypomanic, or major depressive episodes in both bipolar I and bipolar II disorders. An estimated 3% to 6% of women experience the onset of a major depressive episode during pregnancy or during the weeks following delivery. There are severe symptoms of anxiety and sometimes panic attacks during this period.

The peripartum specifier can be with or without psychotic features. One of the psychotic features can be infanticide, a hallucination women experience commanding them to kill the infant or delusions that the infant is possessed. Women with a prior history of depressive or bipolar disorders are at an increased risk of a postpartum episode with psychotic features. Once there has been a postpartum episode with psychotic features, the risk of recurrence is between 30% and 50% for future deliveries.

With Seasonal Pattern One last specifier for this type of disorder is with seasonal pattern. This feature is characterized by a recurring seasonal pattern of at least one type of manic, hypomanic, or depressive episode. If a depressive episode occurs during the winter months, it does not mean that a manic or hypomanic episode will also occur seasonally. This specifier applies only for bipolar I and bipolar II disorder. Seasonal mood patterns should always be distinguished from a psychosocial stressor that occurs regularly at the same time of the year (e.g., summer unemployment), which would not be proper use of this specifier.

The seasonal pattern episodes commonly begin in the fall and last to the spring. Summer episodes are less common, and in either case, the pattern of onset needs to be present for at least a 2-year period, without any non-seasonal episodes during this time frame. Symptoms that are common during major depressive episodes with seasonal pattern are hypersomnia, overeating, weight gain, and craving for carbohydrates. A seasonal pattern appears more likely in bipolar II disorder than in bipolar I disorder.

Specifiers Related to Remission and Current Severity

In the bipolar and related disorders, the coding allows specifying if there is partial remission or full remission. The term *remission* is particularly useful to the practitioner when the criteria for a past disorder are not currently met, yet the practitioner's clinical judgment is that the criteria will shortly be met and the condition is dormant but still there and could soon match what has occurred before. With the bipolar and related disorders, this specifier requires that symptoms of the manic, hypomanic, or depressive episode are present but full criteria are not met, or there is a period of less than 2 months without significant symptoms of mania, hypomania, or depressive episode. In full remission, no significant symptoms are present. The use of *specify current symptoms* can be further quantified and listed after the diagnosis with severity, such as mild, moderate, and severe.

In mild, there are few symptoms, if any, and the symptoms create only a minor social or occupational impairment. In moderate, the number and intensity of the symptoms are between mild and severe and have a moderate impact on social or occupational functioning. In severe, the number of symptoms is substantial, and they markedly interfere with social or occupational functioning.

When applying any of the additional qualifiers or specifiers, the practitioner needs to make sure the application is related to the current level of problem behavior and must clearly document the frequency, intensity, and duration of why the specifier was noted. Diagnostic codes, usually three to five digits, are often utilized to report statistical information and to facilitate retrieval of information. The fourth and fifth digits of the code can be assigned to the subtype. Careful coding of these specifiers is noted.

OVERVIEW OF THE BIPOLAR AND RELATED DISORDERS

Bipolar disorder is a severe, recurrent psychiatric illness characterized by extreme fluctuations in mood with vacillating episodes of major depression and mania (Basco, Ladd, Myers, & Tyler, 2007). Bipolar disorder was often referred to as *manic depression* or *bipolar affective disorder.* In *DSM-IV* and *DSM-IV-TR*, the combined chapter termed the mood disorders was eliminated. In *DSM-5*, the information previously in this chapter is now divided into two chapters that separate the bipolar disorders from the depressive disorders. Actually, the placement of these disorders is quite deliberate in that schizophrenia spectrum, bipolar disorder, and the depressive and anxiety disorders are listed next to each other to create a bridge between the disorders.

The *DSM-5* is unique over the previous versions as the chapter sequencing now allows noting overlapping symptoms, as well as cross-cutting, where symptoms from one disorder are also relevant for another. For the most part in *DSM-5*, the criteria for the bipolar disorders episodes remained unchanged, with the only exception being the mixed episode, which was replaced with a specifier to address rapid cycling. The bipolar disorders continue to consist of several primary disorders.

According to Leahy (2007), the bipolar disorders afflict 3% to 5% of the U.S. population. What particularly concerns mental health professionals is that the rates for completed suicide for persons suffering from bipolar disorder are 60 times higher than in the general population, making bipolar disorder a chronic, devastating, and often underdiagnosed mental health disorder (Leahy, 2007).

When suffering from one of the bipolar disorders, clients can experience recurrent psychiatric episodes with high levels of hospitalization, long-term morbidity, comorbidity, and disability (Baldessarini, Perry, & Pike, 2007). Multitudes of symptoms can occur in quick succession (Farrelly, Dibben, & Hunt, 2006). Despite the availability of psychotropic medications and increased research supporting treatment efficacy, the majority of people with bipolar disorder are not able to maintain long-term remission (Vieta et al., 2008). Even with good medication maintenance, 75% of people with bipolar disorder are estimated to relapse within 5 years (Williams et al., 2008). There may also be an increase in dangerous behaviors. These high-risk behaviors can result in car accidents and other tragic events, making individuals who suffer from bipolar disorder a major concern for public safety and law enforcement as well as the health care system (Baldessarini et al., 2007). A further complication is that controlling the symptoms can be difficult, and those who suffer from the bipolar disorders are responsible for 5% to 15% of new and longer psychiatric hospitalizations (Miasso, Cassiani, & Pedrao, 2008).

In all of the bipolar disorders, individuals suffering from them have at least one symptom related to mania or hypomania, in contrast to those who suffer from the depressive or unipolar disorders. The episodes, as stated earlier, are classified as depressive, manic, or mixed, coinciding with the predominant features. Even when a client initially presents with only manic or hypomanic symptoms, it is assumed that if a bipolar disorder exists, the depressive episode will eventually occur.

The symptoms of the depressive form of bipolar disorder are usually clinically indistinguishable from those exhibited in the major depressive disorders, although psychomotor retardation and hypersomnia may also occur in the depressed phase of bipolar disorder. The essential difference between the depressive disorders and the bipolar and related disorders is that the depressive episodes have only a depressive component (thus the term *unipolar*), whereas the bipolar disorder has both phases (thus the term *bipolar*). Manic or hypomanic episodes either immediately precede or immediately follow a depressive episode. In some cases, the manic and depressive episodes are separated by intervals of relatively normal functioning (APA, 2000). Harel and Levkovitz (2008) state that "although abnormal mood elevation is the cardinal diagnostic feature that distinguishes bipolar disorder from recurrent major depressive disorder, depression more than mania is the leading cause of impairment and death among patients" suffering from a bipolar disorder (p. 121).

According to the *DSM-5*, there are seven primary types of bipolar and related disorders: bipolar I disorder, bipolar II disorder, cyclothymic disorder, substance/medication-induced bipolar and related disorder, bipolar and related disorder due to another medical condition, unspecified bipolar and related disorder, and unspecified bipolar disorder. (See Quick Reference 6.3).

The *DSM*-5 identifies seven subgroups of bipolar and related disorders. Each of these subgroups includes criteria to determine if a client is experiencing a single manic episode or hypomanic episode, along with the depressive episodes, and starts with highlighting the most recent episode. In addition, there are specifiers that mental health practitioners can use to describe the episode recurrence. Each diagnosis has its own group of potential specifiers and is

QUICK REFERENCE 6.3

DESCRIPTION OF BIPOLAR MOOD DISORDERS

Bipolar I Disorder: This disorder is considered the most severe and is characterized by at least one manic episode and a history of hypomanic or a depressive episode. Specific criteria for the number of symptoms required for each manic, hypomanic, or depressive episode must be met.

Bipolar II Disorder: This disorder is characterized by one or more depressive episodes with at least one hypomanic episode: a period of elevated or irritable mood with increased activity, lasting at least 4 consecutive days and present throughout each day most of the time.

Cyclothymic Disorder: This disorder is characterized by a persistent mood disturbance lasting at least 2 years (1 year in children and adolescents), and the individual must not be without the symptoms for 2 months. This disorder, although considered more chronic because of the duration of the symptoms, is less severe because the symptoms experienced do not meet the criteria for either the full hypomanic or depressive episodes.

Substance/Medication-Induced Bipolar and Related Disorder: This disorder is characterized by a disturbance in mood that clinically predominates and includes symptoms of elevated or irritable mood, with or without depressed mood, or diminished interest or pleasure in all or most activities. A physical exam and laboratory tests are needed to confirm that the symptoms developed during or soon after substance intoxication or withdrawal or after taking a medication as evidence that the substance/medication produces the mood symptoms. The disorder is not better explained by a bipolar or related disorder that is not induced by substances/medications, does not occur only during a delirium, and causes significant impairment in social, occupational, or other areas of functioning. Categories of the substances include alcohol, phencyclidine, other hallucinogen, sedative, hypnotic or anxiolytic, amphetamine or other stimulant, cocaine, other, or unknown substance.

Bipolar and Related Disorder Due to Another Medical Condition: This disorder is characterized by a period of elevated or irritable mood with abnormally increased activity or energy that is presented clinically. Results from laboratory tests and physical exams show evidence of another medical disorder. The disturbance is not explained by another mental disorder and does not occur exclusively during a delirium. The disorder must cause significant impairment in social, occupational, or other areas of functioning to meet this diagnosis. It is indicated to specify with manic features, with manic or hypomanic features, or with mixed features.

Other Specified Bipolar and Related Disorder: This disorder is characterized by impairment in social, occupational, or other significant areas of functioning but does not meet full criteria for any of the other categories of bipolar and related disorders. This diagnostic category can apply to the following four clinical presentations: short-duration hypomanic episodes (2–3 days) and major episodes, hypomanic episodes with insufficient symptoms and major depressive episodes, hypomanic episode without prior major depressive episode, and short-duration cyclothymia (less than 24 months).

Unspecified Bipolar and Related Disorder: This disorder presents with symptoms characteristic of bipolar and related disorder but does not meet the full criteria for any of the bipolar and related disorder category. The unspecified bipolar disorder category used when there is insufficient information to place a more formal diagnosis and may be used in settings such as emergency rooms.

Source: Summarized criteria from the *Diagnostic and Statistical Manual of Mental Disorders*, Fifth Edition. Copyright 2013 by the American Psychiatric Association.

listed earlier in this chapter and individually with each diagnosis. (See Quick Reference 6.4.)

Bipolar I Disorder

Bipolar I disorder can involve depressive, hypomanic, or manic episodes (Maxmen, Ward, & Kilgus, 2009). The expected course results in a clearly defined manic episode that comes as the first episode and it can be followed by hypomanic or depressive episodes (APA, 2013). To diagnosis bipolar I disorder, however, according to *DSM-5* there are two criteria that must be met (A-B). Criterion A requires that at least one manic episode be present. See earlier in this chapter for the specific criteria relative to the manic episode. In criterion B, the potential for hypomanic and depressive episodes exists, but the full criteria for the manic and major depressive episodes must be met and are not better explained by another mental disorder such as selected schizophrenia spectrum and the psychotic disorders (APA, 2013).

QUICK REFERENCE 6.4

Four Subgroups of Bipolar I Disorder

1. Bipolar I Disorder, Most Recent Episode Manic (Mild, 296.41), (Moderate, 296.42), (Severe, 296.43). With psychotic features (296.44), In partial remission (296.45), In full remission (296.46), Unspecified (296.40).
   Currently (or most recently) in a manic episode.
   There has previously been at least one major depressive episode.
2. Bipolar I Disorder, Most Recent Episode Hypomanic (296.40, for cases not in remission). Severity and psychotic specifiers do not apply. With psychotic features (NA). In partial remission (296.5). In full remission (296.46), Unspecified (296.40).
   Currently (or most recently) in a hypomanic episode.
   There has previously been at least one manic episode or mixed episode.
3. Bipolar I Disorder, Most Recent Episode Depressed (Mild 296.51), (Moderate, 296.52), (Severe, 296.53). With psychotic features (296.54), In partial remission (296.55), In full remission (296.56), Unspecified (296.50).
   Currently (or most recently) in a major depressive episode.
   There has previously been at least one manic episode or mixed episode.
4. Bipolar I Disorder, Most Recent Episode Unspecified 296.7 (Severity, psychotic, and remission specifiers do not apply).
   Criteria, except for duration, are currently (or most recently) met for a manic, hypomanic, or major depressive episode.
   There has previously been at least one manic episode or mixed episode.

In addition to these subgroups, practitioners should also write as many of the following specifiers as apply to the current or most recent episode (these do not have codes):

With anxious distress

With mixed features

With rapid cycling

With melancholic features

With atypical features

With mood-congruent psychotic features

With mood-incongruent psychotic features

With catatonia

With peripartum onset

With seasonal pattern

Source: Summarized criteria from the *Diagnostic and Statistical Manual of Mental Disorders*, Fifth Edition. Copyright 2013 by the American Psychiatric Association.

Since the manic episode must be documented by history or must exist at the present time, be sure to note the time frame and whether it has lasted at least 1 week, and is present almost every day. The exact time frame is not given in *DSM-5* as to what constitutes almost all day, every day but approximately 75% to 100% of the time appears to be a safe estimate. Criterion A for the hypomanic disorder is similar in terms of the frequency and intensity; however the time frame is at least 4 consecutive days. In criterion B, for both the manic and the hypomanic episodes three or more (or four or more if the mood is noted as irritable) of the characteristic symptoms need to be present. For both episodes criterion B involves inflated self-esteem or grandiosity, decreased need for sleep, increased talkativeness or pressured speech, flight of ideas, distractibility, increased goal-directed activity or psychomotor activity, and excessive involvement in activities that have a high potential for painful consequences, such as unrestrained buying sprees (APA, 2013). Subsequent criteria for the manic episode extend from criteria A-D, whereas the hypomanic episode requires fulfillment of criteria A-E. The depressive episode, defined earlier in this chapter, requires experiencing criteria A-C, involving a longer time frame of at least 2 weeks and a clear change from previous mood exhibiting either depressed mood or a loss of interest or pleasure in what was previously considered pleasurable (APA, 2013).

When working with clients in the active phase the mood in a manic or hypomanic episode can be characterized as euphoric and cheerful or it can turn to agitated and angry. Therefore, usually a persistent irritable mood can quickly turn into an elevated one. Regardless of the mood of the initial presentation the resultant ideas and behaviors are usually excessive and may involve increased sexual promiscuity and unsafe, unrestricted sexual activity. Individuals engage in multiple projects with the increased energy level they have at this time. There may also be a preoccupation with religious activities.

When identifying three or more of the following symptoms (or four if the mood is only irritable) the following may be evident and represent a change from their usual behavior: (1) Self-esteem is typically inflated, and individuals can have delusions of grandeur, thinking they are famous or wealthy; (2) commonly, individuals have a decreased need for sleep, waking up several hours earlier than they usually do and feeling rested and energetic; the onset of a manic episode is often this decreased need for sleep; (3) individuals are increasingly talkative, often interrupting others when they speak and engaging in conversations with strangers; speech may be rapid, pressured, and loud; (4) flight of ideas or racing thoughts that cannot be expressed through speech and are characterized by accelerated speech changing from topic to topic; (5) a high level of distractibility where things such as background conversations may make it difficult for an individual to stay focused; (6) an increase in goal-directed activity, including sexual, occupational, political, or religious; (7) a marked impairment in judgment leading to buying sprees on credit cards, unplanned trips, reckless driving, and poor investments. Usually a manic episode results in a hospitalization to prevent harm to self or to others.

Practitioners should keep in mind that clients with bipolar I disorders frequently report depressive episodes as well as symptoms such as agitation and hyperactivity that often are associated with it. Between episodes, 20% to 30% of clients continue to suffer from labile mood (mood lability or fluctuations) that is significant enough to disturb interpersonal or occupational relations. In some cases, psychotic features may develop. When this happens, subsequent manic episodes are more likely to have psychotic features.

The manic episodes characteristic of bipolar I disorder, when compared to the hypomanic ones, tend to be extreme, with a significant impairment of occupational and social functioning. A person who experiences a manic episode has a marked elevated, euphoric, and expansive mood, frequently interrupted by outbursts of irritability or even violence, particularly when others refuse to go along with the manic person's antics and schemes. For a manic episode to exist, the mood must persist for at least 1 week. In addition, three of these symptoms must also occur in the same time period.

1. There is a notable increase in goal-directed activity, which sometimes may appear to be a nonrelievable restlessness.
2. Thoughts and mental activity may appear to speed up, so that the individual appears to exhibit a flight of ideas or thoughts that race through the brain.
3. Distractibility, high levels of verbal output in speech or in writing, and a severely decreased need for sleep may also occur.
4. Inflated self-esteem is common and, when severe, becomes delusional, so that the person harbors feelings of enormous grandeur and power.
5. Personal and cultural inhibitions loosen, and the person may indulge in activities with a high potential for painful consequences, such as foolish business ventures, major spending sprees, and sexual indiscretions (APA, 2013).

Bipolar II

In bipolar II, a clinical course is characterized by a current or past major depressive episode, accompanied by at least one hypomanic episode. The presence of a manic episode precludes the diagnosis of bipolar II disorder. The presence of the hypomanic episode as opposed to the manic episode is a critical factor for differentiating between these two conditions.

Bipolar II disorder is generally characterized by one or more depressive episodes with at least one hypomanic episode that generally lasts approximately 4 days. Similar to bipolar I, it also requires three (or four for those with irritable mood) of the seven symptoms: inflated self-esteem or grandiosity, decreased need for sleep, more talkative than usual, flight of ideas (racing thoughts), distractibility (to external stimuli), psychomotor agitation, and excessive involvement in activities with a high potential for painful consequences (shopping sprees, sexual promiscuity).

In bipolar II, the symptoms must cause clinically significant distress or impairment in social, educational, or occupational functioning, although in some cases the hypomanic episodes themselves do not cause impairment. Often this impairment results from major depressive episodes or from chronic patterns of unpredictable mood. According to the *DSM-5*, bipolar II disorder, which was previously thought to be gender-related, now based on new research evidence appears mixed. The occurrence of the disorder also reports mixed results when comparing women and men; however, women may be at risk of developing subsequent episodes related to postpartum hypomania. (See Quick Reference 6.5.)

What bipolar I and bipolar II disorders have in common is the presence of the major depressive episode with the same associated five symptoms from the list of nine. Persistent depressed mood, loss of interest in activities, poor concentration, feelings of hopelessness, and changes in eating and sleeping patterns characterize the depressive phase. In contrast, the hypomanic client usually exhibits increased levels of energy, irritability, decreased need for sleep, changes in eating patterns, increases in activities (including spending), and increases in pressured verbalization. Because

QUICK REFERENCE 6.5

Diagnostic Criteria for Bipolar II Disorder (296.89)

- Presence (or history) of one or more major depressive episodes.
- Presence (or history) of at least one hypomanic episode.
- There has never been a manic episode.
- The mood symptoms in Criteria A and B are not better accounted for by schizoaffective disorder and are not superimposed on schizophrenia, schizophreniform disorder, delusional disorder, or other specified or unspecified schizophrenia spectrum and other psychotic disorders.
- The symptoms cause clinically significant distress or impairment in social, occupational, or other significant areas of functioning.

Specify current or most recent episode:

Hypomanic or Depressed.

Specify if:

With anxious distress

With mixed features

With rapid cycling

With mood-congruent psychotic features

With mood-incongruent psychotic features

With catatonia

With peripartum onset

With seasonal pattern

Specify course if full criteria for a mood episode are not currently met:

In partial remission or in full remission.

Specify severity if full criteria for a mood episode are currently met:

Mild, Moderate, or Severe.

Source: Summarized criteria from the *Diagnostic and Statistical Manual of Mental Disorders*, Fifth Edition. Copyright 2013 by the American Psychiatric Association.

of the increase in energy and activities, many individuals become quite creative during these spurts and later experience the depressive trend. Individuals with bipolar II disorder are at higher risk for suicide and usually have a strong family history of bipolar or depressive disorders (Oquendo, Currier, & Mann, 2006).

Cyclothymic Disorder

According to the *DSM-5*, clients with a diagnosis of cyclothymic disorder have milder symptoms than those who suffer from the other types of bipolar disorders, although the symptoms are more consistent and last for approximately 2 years. According to the *DSM-5*, criterion A-F must be met to place this diagnosis (APA, 2013). To meet the criteria for cyclothymic disorder, criterion A and B require that the symptoms be continuous, and the individual suffering from this disorder cannot be without hypomanic and depressive symptoms for a period of 2 months (APA, 2013). Within this time frame there will be times when the disorder does not meet the criteria for the full hypomanic or major depressive episode and at least half of the time period the symptoms are displayed. This is why although this is a milder type of a bipolar disorder, Austrian (2005) referred to it as chronic. What makes this disorder different from bipolar II is that according to criterion C the full criteria of the three episodes consistent with these disorders (manic, hypomanic, and depressive) have never been met. Furthermore, in criterion D it cannot be better attributed by another disorder such schizophrenia spectrum and other psychotic disorders. Criterion E suggests that a complete medical work-up be conducted to rule out medical conditions such as hyperthyroidism that can clearly mimic the symptoms of these disorders as well as the effects of substance experience, subsequent use, intoxication, and withdrawal. In criterion F, the cycling and the mood changes that occur must be severe enough to cause social and occupational problems that affect daily functioning and productivity levels.

Lastly, if an individual experiences only a clear major depressive episode without a hypomanic one, this diagnosis should not be used. In the diagnostic assessment, the time frame is reduced to 1 year in children and adolescents rather than 2, as needed in adults. Also, in children and adolescents the presentation of depression does not always match that of adults and the child and the adolescent may show the feelings of depression in an agitated state. When working with children and adolescents examining the criteria for DMDD, listed earlier in this chapter, may be of most help.

Substance/Medication-Induced Bipolar and Related Disorder

In substance/medication-induced bipolar and related disorder that is characterized by elevated or expansive mood, there may or may not be evidence of a depressive mood episode. In this disorder, it must be clear that the disorder-related symptoms appeared after the client ingested the substance or during intoxication or withdrawal. This category also covers the substances of abuse, prescribed medications, and possible medical conditions that can produce maniclike symptoms. The symptoms cause clinically significant distress or impairment in social, occupational, or other important areas of functioning.

Bipolar and Related Disorder Due to Another Medical Condition

In bipolar and related disorder due to another medical condition, the linkage to the medical illness causing this disorder must be clear, and thus the symptoms displayed must easily be connected back to the illness. In this condition, the disturbance the client is experiencing cannot be better explained by another mental disorder and does not occur during the course of a delirium. Similar to all diagnoses, the symptoms must cause clinically significant distress or impairment in social, occupational, or other principal areas of functioning. In addition, the disturbance may necessitate hospitalization to prevent harm to self or others and may include psychotic features. In coding the disorder, it can be specified as: with manic features, with manic- or hypomanic-like episode, or with mixed features. Bipolar Disorder NOS was replaced with unspecified bipolar disorder.

Other Specified Bipolar and Related Disorder

In this disorder, there are symptoms of bipolar and related disorders that cause impairment in social, occupational, or other significant areas of functioning but do not meet full criteria for any of the other categories of bipolar and related disorders. This category can apply to the following four clinical presentations:

1. Short-duration hypomanic episodes (2–3 days) and major depressive episodes. In this clinical presentation, individuals present with two or more episodes of hypomania that last only 2 or 3 days.
2. Hypomanic episodes with insufficient symptoms and major depressive episodes. In this clinical presentation, the individual experiences one or more episodes of hypomania but does not meet the criteria of at least 4 consecutive days of elevated mood and at least two other symptoms of a hypomanic episode.
3. Hypomanic episode without prior major depressive episode. In this clinical presentation, one or more hypomanic episodes have never met the full criteria for a major depressive or manic episode.
4. Short-duration cyclothymia (less than 24 months), where multiple hypomanic symptoms do not meet the full criteria for hypomanic episode and major depressive episode that lasts less than 24 months (less than 12 months for children and adolescents). The hypomanic or depressive symptoms last at least 2 months at a time and cause significant impairment in functioning.

Unspecified Bipolar-Related Disorder

This disorder presents with symptoms characteristic of bipolar and related disorders but does not meet the full criteria for any disorder in the bipolar and related disorder category. The unspecified bipolar disorder category is used when there is insufficient information for a more specific diagnosis, such as in emergency rooms. It can also be used if the practitioner decides not to place the reason the disorder does not meet the criteria, which could include a multitude of reasons. When this disorder is given, however, it is expected that the symptomatology present will be monitored so the symptoms indicative of the diagnostic category can be identified.

SUMMARY OF BIPOLAR DISORDERS

The most helpful aspect of the updates made to *DSM-5* criteria for the bipolar and related disorders is recognition that anxiety can occur in multiple mental health disorders. The crosscutting and the wide array of specifiers outlined earlier in this chapter for each diagnosis allow the inclusion of anxiety, mixed features, with rapid cycling and other specifiers and documenting not only the presence of these features but also the severity. Anxiety can be measured as it relates to the symptoms exhibited by the client regardless of the diagnostic category. This allows each disorder that is accompanied by some type of anxiety dimension to rate the symptoms of anxiety from 0 (no anxiety) to 4 (severely anxious with five symptoms and motor agitation). The ranking for the dimension of anxiety follows the traditional scale listed earlier.

In addition, the dimensional assessment and the crosscutting of symptoms encourage the rating of suicide potential, especially as it relates to the substance use dimension. Each disorder category also lists the conditions that may be comorbid with it. For example, in bipolar I disorder, it is common to assess for possible comorbidity with the anxiety disorders, ADHD and the disruptive impulse control disorders, and alcohol use disorder, especially since half of all patients diagnosed with bipolar disorder also have a substance use disorder that can complicate any treatment provided. It also lists medical conditions; for example, in bipolar I disorder, there is a high indication of metabolic syndrome and migraines, whereas in bipolar II, there is a higher prevalence of the eating disorders, such as binge eating disorder (BED), as well as cyclothymic disorder and the substance and sleep-related disorders. Paris (2013) states that the new *DSM-5* and recognition of overlapping symptoms allows further definition of the bipolar disorders and the linkage that can be made to schizoaffective disorder, recognizing the overlap of symptoms resulting in each.

In terms of treatment, since bipolar disorder may worsen over time, the treatment plans must remain as flexible as the disorder. Treating the symptoms needs to take into account the vast array of psychosocial domains and the problems that can occur with fluctuating moods and vacillating energy levels.

DIAGNOSTIC ASSESSMENT IN ADULTS WITH BIPOLAR DISORDER

Regardless of the type of bipolar disorder, remember that variability in the client's behavior and actions is expected and that these changes in behavior and energy level can occur gradually or quite suddenly. One factor to consider during the assessment phase is whether the client is experiencing uncharacteristic behaviors that require the addition of a specifier such as rapid cycling. Some clients with bipolar disorder may show symptoms of mixed features that may qualify for either the manic or hypomanic mixed or the depressed mood specifier that is indicative of uncharacteristic concurrent depressive, manic, or hypomanic symptoms. For those individuals who have mixed-state presentations, rapid cycling can be prominent and affect approximately 33% of people with bipolar II. Rapid cycling is a risk factor for recurrence, suicidal behavior, comorbidity, poor outcome, decreased functioning, and resistance to lithium treatment (Hajeka et al., 2008).

When a diagnosis of bipolar disorder is confirmed using the *DSM-5* criteria (APA, 2013), attention focuses almost immediately on determining whether the client meets the criteria for depressive, manic, or hypomanic episodes. In addition, every mental health practitioner should assess for critical symptoms that could reflect other mental health problems and how these exogenous factors can influence the resulting episode. The complex and multifaceted symptoms can be complicated with other psychiatric problems that also require attention and treatment. For example, priority is given to identifying substance-related disorders important during the assessment phase and continuing through the treatment phase. When there is a history of alcohol and drug use, special attention must be paid to prescribing medications for treatment of this disorder. Failure to obtain substance use information at the point of assessment can become harmful if the client uses medications while taking these substances.

Once the diagnosis has been confirmed, assessments include suicide potential, history and risk of violence, psychotic symptoms, risk-taking behaviors that can include sexual acting out, and substance and alcohol abuse (Sublette et al., 2009). Suicide assessment is critical, as the risk for suicide is 37 times higher when the client is in the combined mixed state followed by the depressive state and 18 times higher when the client is in the depressed state (Valtonen et al., 2008). For example, in their study of 176 individuals with bipolar disorders I and II, Valtonen et al. (2008) found that over an 18-month period, females were more than twice more likely to attempt suicide than males. In addition, those with bipolar disorder II were twice as likely to attempt suicide as those with bipolar I. Other risk factors related to increased suicide were anxiety disorders and comorbid personality disorders. Because research has demonstrated that depressive episodes usually follow manic phases (Mitchell & Malhi, 2004), watching for this trend can lessen the high risk of suicidal thoughts and attempts at suicide. Clients who already rely on alcohol and drugs have easy access to substances that can be used in a suicide attempt.

The immediate plan for the bipolar client who appears to be a danger to self or others should be to assess rapidly what appears to be occurring, to protect the client from harm, to begin a medication regimen, and to stabilize the dangerous symptoms. Hospitalization is usually recommended because it ensures an environment where these objectives can be met and where the client can continue therapeutic work. Furthermore, allowing time to adjust medications in a supervised setting may contribute to continued medication compliance and management upon discharge to a less restrictive environment. The period of hospitalization can also serve as a time when clients and family members become educated about the nature of the illness and the treatment alternatives. Having family understanding and support can facilitate discharge.

To facilitate and provide direct application of the diagnostic assessment with an adult, an in-depth biopsychosocial analysis of a case involving a male client with bipolar disorder is presented. (See the following Case Example.) Issues critical for the diagnostic assessment are outlined that examine the best way to elicit key factors that affect treatment planning and intervention strategy.

CASE EXAMPLE - CASE OF DAN

Dan, a 50-year-old White male who owns his own landscaping business, was brought to a crisis assessment unit by the police because he was found naked in a neighbor's yard. When the police questioned him as to what he was doing, he told them "he was God and fertilizing the ground." Per the police report, it was documented that Dan was found planting a tree in his neighbor's yard, without permission, at midnight, under a spotlight in the nude. The neighbor's adult daughter also told police that from the window she saw him masturbating in the hole he had dug to plant the tree. When the police arrived on the scene, the neighbor told them that he did not want to press charges and that Dan was a nice guy most of the time. He and his family just wanted to see him get help. The police stated that Dan did not resist arrest, and his bizarre ramblings led them to believe he needed mental health treatment rather than being arrested and sent to jail.

At his interview in the crisis unit, Dan reported that he felt great and his neighbor had contracted with him to plant some trees for him earlier in the week. His speech would start out coherent, and then he would begin rambling. The content of his speech was pressured as he started to describe how he was Johnny Appleseed and then begin to talk about time factors and other hard-to-follow irrelevant information. At times, he would make jokes, laugh at them, and be very surprised that the social worker doing the interview was not laughing, too. He became easily distracted by the slightest noise in the hallway, and these distractions disturbed his train of thought. When the social worker completing the initial assessment tried to bring him back on task, he became irritated and asked bluntly, "Do you have a brain?" He reported no suicidal ideation or intent, but his judgment and insight were impaired. When asked what he would do when he left the unit, he said he would plant more trees as he wanted to take care of the world and make it a better place. When asked about his previous behavior, he stated that he saw nothing wrong with spreading a little love seed with his love tool. He then asked the social worker if she wanted to see it. She said, "No, thank you" and told him that

(continued)

CASE EXAMPLE - CASE OF DAN (CONTINUED)

was unacceptable behavior. He replied with "Sorry, just trying to loosen you up a little as you are way too serious." When told that hospitalization was recommended and asked if he would sign himself in voluntarily, he agreed and said he would just have to bring his cheer to the inpatient unit. The social worker phoned the psychiatrist on call, and Dan was admitted to the unit, with a plan to stabilize him again on lithium.

Several weeks later, Dan was brought to the unit again but this time by his brother. His brother said that he was very concerned about Dan as he had refused to eat for the past 2 days and was not willing to get out of bed. He said his brother's employees from the nursery called and told him to check on Dan. The employees stated that just the week before, Dan opened the nursery store and started giving away plants, telling customers their purchases were on the house. After he gave away numerous expensive plants and refused to take money that was offered, his employees questioned his behavior. He threatened to fire them if they interfered. Later in the same day, he offered them early Christmas bonuses because business was improving so much. Further, after staying at work for a couple of hours that day, he told them all to take the day off and celebrate life. They had not seen him since, and that was a week ago. An employee who often ran the nursery went by to check on him and noticed his car was at his home but no one answered the door. He reported this to Dan's brother and asked him to check on Dan. When his brother went to the house and knocked on the door, no one answered. Dan lives alone, but his brother had a key. When he opened the door and entered the house, Dan was sitting on the floor with his head in his hands. He was surrounded by boxes of seeds and other packages of items he must have purchased at a local store. His brother was frustrated as he described the situation to the intake social worker, stating that he has no idea how his brother is going to pay his credit card bills and commenting that he had unopened boxes for six (on-sale) brand-new electric can openers.

This time in the clinical interview, Dan presented a very different picture. His mood was clearly depressed, his affect was flat, and he suffered from alogia (poverty of speech). He made no eye contact and refused to respond to questions from the social worker or his brother. He muttered very softly in a low, monotone voice, "I wish I was dead . . . I wish I was dead." When asked if he would harm himself, he said yes, he would shoot himself if he had a gun. When asked if he had a gun at home, he said no, but when his brother was asked outside the individual interview with Dan, his brother said that Dan had several guns. The social worker explained to the brother that she was going call the psychiatrist for an assessment and medication evaluation, get the on-staff nurse practitioner to provide a medical clearance, and seek inpatient admission for his brother. In addition, the social worker told the brother to make sure that the inpatient unit mental health practitioner was aware that his brother had guns at home so this could be addressed at discharge. The social worker would be sure to also pass this information along in her report and ask that the client be placed on suicide watch and precautions be taken for his safety upon admission to the unit.

Completion of the Diagnostic Assessment for Dan

A complete understanding of the biological, psychological, and sociocultural perspectives is required in the assessment. As with any disorder, basic facts to obtain and consider about the individual include age, culture, gender, socio-economic status, marital status, family history, developmental or childhood history, incidence

QUICK REFERENCE 6.6

Mental Status Description

Presentation *Disheveled* *Unkempt*	Mental Functioning *Average intelligence*	Higher-Order Abilities *Some difficulty with abstracts*	General Knowledge: *Mostly accurate*
Mood: *depressed*	Affect: *flat*	Judgment: *impaired*	Insight: *poor*
Motor Activity: *Somewhat restless*	Thought, Form, & Content *Distractible and preoccupied*	Delusions: *Not at present time* Hallucinations: *None*	Speech: *hesitant* Clarity: *normal*
Attitude: *guarded*	Immediate Memory: *Intact*	Remote Memory: *Intact*	Intelligence: *average*
Serial Sevens: *Accurate*	Simple Calculations: *Mostly accurate*	Proverb Interpretation: *Confused, frustrated*	Orientation: *Fully oriented*

of abuse or neglect (including domestic violence), and educational status. Level of motivation for starting treatment is an important factor because it sets the stage for what is to come. Other factors to assess include attitudes of family and others, recreational activities, composition of social circle, availability of substances, mental health disorders issues (e.g., depression, anxiety, disability), medical issues, possible substance-related issues, and how these relate to mental status (e.g., orientation to person, place, time, and situation). There are no apparent personality disorders or intellectual disabilities present. There are no other medical conditions noted on this assessment or during his past psychiatric hospitalization. The psychosocial stressors include problems with primary support (strained family and employee/work relations), problems related to the social environment (recent incidents with the police), and occupational problems, as he is the boss with his employees. To start the diagnostic assessment, a mental status exam is conducted. (See Quick Reference 6.6.)

Given the behaviors that Dan exhibited on intake at the crisis unit, hospitalization became necessary. For Dan, his principal diagnosis is:

Bipolar I Disorder, Current and Most Recent Episode Depressed.

With the elimination of the multiaxial diagnosis used in *DSM-IV* and *DSM-IV-TR*, the information previously provided on Axis IV and Axis V is no longer a requirement. Elimination of these axes, however, should not result in the exclusion of essential supportive information. When including this information, pay special attention to Chapters 21 and 22 of the *DSM-5*. Chapter 21, The Medication-Induced Movement Disorders and Other Adverse Effects of Medication, and Chapter 22, Other Conditions That May Be a Focus of Clinical Intervention, are not mental disorders. Rather, they are conditions that may assist in outlining and further documenting the supportive information central to the diagnosis.

In the case of Dan, the information provided in Chapter 22 may be of the most help. There are several supportive factors that need to be taken into account that can support the diagnostic assessment. The first are the biopsychosocial stressors (especially those related to the family situation and key relationships). It is clear that Dan has impaired insight and does not see his role in many of the problems that are facing him. He has isolated himself from his employees, family, and mostly his brother, who seems to be his strongest supporter. His financial problems are building because of his mismanagement of his funds.

Dan clearly has strained family relationships. Unfortunately, the revised conditions updated in *DSM-5* do not appear comprehensive enough to describe Dan's particular situation and how it can affect his diagnosis. This makes documenting a specific code to match the supporting information difficult. Dan and his brother's relationship remains strained and since there is no specific coding the general term is used to describe the situation:

Other Problems Related to Primary Support Group: No Specific Category

Dan is having problems with his business, which is his employment. The closest of the other conditions that may be a focus of clinical attention that can be coded to represent his situation is:

V62.29 (Z56.9) Other Problem Related to Employment

In summary, Dan denies any problems with his medications, and to further assess his medical condition, a history, a physical, and a medication evaluation referral is planned. When making this diagnostic impression, it appeared that there was at least one manic episode documented 2 weeks earlier by the same social worker at the crisis unit. This previous episode also resulted in hospital admission. In gathering history from his brother, it does not appear that Dan has a history of schizophrenia or any other psychotic disorder. Per his brother, only during these episodes of bizarre behavior is he most concerned. His brother states that for the most part, Dan is a solid businessman and his employees really like him. His brother says sometimes he can go a year or more and be normal, even when he knows his brother is functioning without his lithium, and then something will happen. He is not sure what triggers it; it could be a call from his ex-wife or visiting his biological adult son, who is diagnosed with bipolar II disorder.

When Dan started to feel better, a more extensive history was gathered. At that time, Dan reported that for the past 10 years he has been admitted several times to the inpatient unit and stabilized upon discharge. He has a regular psychiatrist and reports taking lithium "only when he has to as it makes him too thirsty." He states that his moods can change, and sometimes he feels as if he is going to fall off the edge of the earth and prefers his previous elevated mood to his more depressed ones. When asked about treatment and if he is taking medications to help with his reported feelings of highs and lows, he says that he has a medicine cabinet full of medications. He states that he prefers exercise to medications and therapy. Dan reports that he does not take his medications regularly because of various side effects and an inability to tolerate many of the medications prescribed. According to Dan, it appears that many of the antipsychotics and mood stabilizers sedate him and make him so depressed he has no energy. He keeps repeating how good he felt last week and really does not want to take anything to change that. He said one time when he was given a selective serotonin reuptake inhibitor by his general medicine physician, he became very excited. He is convinced he triggered his own manic episode.

When Dan feels extremely energetic, the mania has manifested itself with delusions, compulsions, argumentative behavior, paranoia, dissociation, anxiety, and obsessions. Dan reports that the first severe symptoms presented at around age 30; this is confirmed in his documented medical history. Medications that have been prescribed that have not stabilized him include lithium (which he still takes), valproic acid (Depakote), amitriptyline (Elavil), quetiapine (Seroquel), citalopram (Celexa), fluoxetine (Prozac), paroxetine hydrochloride (Paxil), sertaline (Zoloft), nefazodone hydrochloride (Serzone), mirtazapine (Remeron), bupropin hydrocholoride (Wellbutrin), gabapentin (Neurontin), alprazolam (Xanax), and zolpidem (Ambien) (for sleep).

Once the initial information about the client's symptoms has been obtained, it should guide the diagnostic assessment process. When completing an assessment with clients who suffer from a mood disorder, special attention needs to be given to identifying the mood episodes that are being exhibited. Once the mood episode is established, the criteria are later applied to the existence of a mood disorder. When determining whether the criteria for a mood episode are met, the disturbance in mood must be severe enough to affect many areas of an individual's functioning. Current and past behaviors must be considered when identifying a mood episode.

While the *DSM-5* provides technical definitions of manic and hypomanic episodes, it is helpful for the practitioner to know the kinds of symptoms such clients regularly present. During the assessment process, to confirm the presence of a manic or hypomanic episode, the mental health practitioner should elicit information about changes in these areas: sleeping and eating habits/patterns, levels of energy and restlessness, increase in activities (especially those considered risk taking or destructive), problems concentrating, and when the client becomes easily distracted. Mood changes include instances of extreme feelings of happiness and laughing inappropriately (usually accompanied with agitation). The client may become very talkative, and speech takes on a pressured quality, with racing thoughts; the client reports that he or she cannot keep up with the influx of ideas. Other factors include assessing for impaired judgment, grandiose thinking, inflated self-esteem, increased irritability and impatience with others, easy excitability, and indications of violent behavior. Disorientation, incoherent speech, and bizarre hallucinations are not uncommon, and often individuals have impaired social relationships characterized by a lack of interest.

For clients with a poor history of treatment compliance, a history of substance abuse may further complicate the diagnostic or intervention process. Always ask the client what substances are used and the date of first and most recent use. In this case, Dan denied any and all substance use or experimentation besides experimentation with marijuana and sporadic use of alcohol. A sample chart may help to organize this information (see Quick Reference 6.7).

In the diagnostic assessment, it is critical to get a complete medical and medication history. Ask the client questions about health conditions, as well as using medical records and previous history and physicals to substantiate information received. When gathering the medical history, ask if clients have any specific allergies and write them down so you can alert the team.

For his socialization and support system resources, Dan states he has very few friends, and his employees do not associate with him outside work. He reports numerous relationships with women, but these relationships never last; he believes they use him for his money. He reports that he has an undeserved reputation of being deceitful and misleading and as a result has difficulty keeping and maintaining relationships with others. Dan reports that he feels dumped by his last four relationships. He is unable to identify any social or recreational interests. When discussing sociable manners and involvement with others, it became clear that Dan frequently feels inferior when socializing with people, except for his brother. It is also clear that Dan's inappropriate delusional behavior during the manic episodes

QUICK REFERENCE 6.7

SUBSTANCE USE/ABUSE FOR DAN

Drug Substance	Age of First Use	Frequency	Usual Amount	Date of Last Use
Marijuana	13	Occasionally	One to two joints	12/2013
Alcohol	12	One to two times per week	One to two wine coolers/ beer	1/27/2014
Hallucinogens	17	Once		2008
Amphetamine	19	Once		2005
Cocaine	NA			
Ecstasy	22	Once		2010
Nicotine	12	Weekly	Pack a week	Regular

and suicidal thoughts during the depressive episodes create stressors in social situations. Dan appears very suspicious of different social circumstances and is unwilling to enter into situations where friendships can result. When asked about excessive spending, Dan agrees that he compulsively goes on shopping binges, which frequently prevent him from paying his bills. Dan's legal history involves being arrested once for writing a check with insufficient funds that was settled with the receiver and the bank without legal involvement, and no other arrests thus far. Law enforcement, however, has been called numerous times to his home over the years due to reports of bizarre behavior. The police in his neighborhood all know him for that reason, but he has never become violent to self or others.

Because of the instability of the client's moods, a suicide assessment is needed. At the last interview, when Dan started to feel better, he reported that he was currently not feeling suicidal. On this admission, however, he admitted suicidal ideation and probable intent. As part of the discharge plan, the mental health practitioner needs to inquire whether he has access to weapons, and if he does, a safety plan needs to be put in place. As a result, Dan may agree to give the weapons for safekeeping to a trusted family member or friend prior to returning home. Since Dan has a very good relationship with his brother, permission from Dan will be obtained to invite his brother to participate in any available family-group support sessions.

Upon discharge, it is documented that his appetite has increased and he has gained several pounds while in the hospital. He states he has had problems with insomnia for years. The mental status exam revealed that Dan is aware of his name (orientation to person), where he is (orientation to place: city, state, name of the facility), what day and time it is (orientation to time: time, day, day of week, month, year), and spatial or situational orientation (his current situation, serial sevens, spell word backward, medications taken, age, year born, last meal, count backward from 10, three-object recall, etc.). He was thus oriented times four (oriented x4). His eye contact strayed often and was fair. On this third assessment prior to discharge, his motor activity was normal, and he denied suicidal ideation and intent. Speech was still somewhat pressured but more goal-directed. There was no abnormality of thought content, ideas of reference, or obsessions/compulsions. His concentration is adequate to the interview. In general, his insight still appears to be poor.

Treatment Planning and Intervention Strategy for Dan

A complete treatment plan for Dan with goals, objectives, and practice strategy is shown in Sample Treatment Plan 6.1. With the information gathered during the diagnostic assessment as the basis of treatment, the intervention plan allows for application. As part of the intervention process, problem behaviors must be clearly identified and related directly to the stated goals and objectives. Treatment should be provided in a continuum of care that allows flexible application of modalities based on a cohesive treatment plan. In developing the treatment plan for Dan, the practitioner needs to gather a comprehensive history, which includes information about how he feels during the manic episode and the depressive episodes (see Quick Reference 6.8). Once treatment planning is complete, options for counseling strategy will be outlined, taking into account these identified factors (see Quick Reference 6.9).

Since Dan has difficulty recalling his treatment history, supplemental information is needed from family and others in his immediate support system. Information about whether Dan has had a recent medical exam is important, especially since upon this admission he does not appear motivated for self-care. It is not

SAMPLE TREATMENT PLAN 6.1

Bipolar I Disorder, Most Recent Episode Depressed-Moderate

Definition of the Disorder:

This disorder is considered the most severe and is characterized by at least one manic episode and a history of hypomanic or depressive episode. Specific criteria for the number of symptoms required for each manic, hypomanic, or depressive episode must be met.

Signs and Symptoms to Note in the Record

- Inflated self-esteem or grandiosity when in the manic episode.
- Decreased need for sleep when in the manic and the depressed episodes.
- Pressured speech in the manic episode; alogia in the depressed.
- Flight of ideas or racing thoughts in the manic episode.
- Distractibility in both the manic and the depressed episodes.
- Psychomotor agitation in the manic episode; retarded and delayed in the depressed.
- Excessive involvement in pleasurable activities that may have harmful consequences, such as sexual promiscuity or impulse buying in the manic episode and severe depressed response to this behavior when in the depressed phase.

Goals

1. Help client become aware of triggers for the manic episode, thereby allowing a return to a normal activity level; increase good judgment.
2. Reduce agitation, impulsive behaviors, and pressured speech, and increase sensitivity to consequences of behaviors.
3. Cope with underlying feelings of low self-esteem and fears of rejection or abandonment.
4. Increase controlled behavior, achieve a more stable mood, and develop more deliberate speech and thought processes.

(continued)

SAMPLE TREATMENT PLAN 6.1 (*Continued*)

Objectives	Efforts and Interventions by Practitioner
1. Cooperate with a psychiatric evaluation and ongoing treatment, and take medications as prescribed.	Arrange for a psychiatric evaluation for psychotropic medications and follow-up to monitor client's reaction to the medication.
2. Reduce impulsive behaviors, and establish a clear safety plan to reduce the potential for harm to self or others.	Develop a clear no-harm, no-risk agreement and safety plan. This will involve the client as well as others in his support system with a focus on recognizing triggers that will require psychiatric support and follow-up, as well as inpatient admission.
3. Decrease grandiosity and express self more realistically.	Confront the client's grandiosity through supportive counseling, and reinforce more realistic self-statements.
4. Discuss behaviors and recognize triggers for the start of a mood episode.	Discuss with client triggers that lead to expansive behaviors and what to do when this occurs.
5. Speak more slowly and maintain focus on one subject at a time.	Provide structure for the client's thought processes and actions by directing the course of the conversation and developing plans for the client's behaviors. Plan will be simple and focus on identifying triggers and calling for help when triggers occur. In this case, client will call brother first as agreed on by both.
6. Address feelings of low self-esteem and fear of rejection with an effort to expand his support system.	Psychotherapy to explore the psychosocial stressors that are precipitating the client's manic behaviors.

QUICK REFERENCE 6.8

CHARACTERIZATIONS, SYMPTOMS, AND BEHAVIORS FOR DAN

During periods of manic episodes, Dan has shown the following symptoms:

- Inflated self-esteem and delusional behavior.
- Periods of decreased need for sleep, difficulty falling asleep, and other times has inexhaustible energy and goes without sleep for several days (evidenced by his delusional activity at night).
- Periods of being more talkative than usual with a need to keep talking. Inappropriate conversations with pressured speech and irrelevant joking.
- During communications with others, there is flight of ideas, and his speech becomes disorganized and incoherent.
- Easily distracted and does not take into account rules and social expectations, evidenced by his bizarre behaviors.
- Increase in bizarre goal-related activities at work and at home.

- Excessive involvement in pleasurable activities with high potential for painful consequences.
- Frequently does not accept responsibility for his behaviors or see a problem with exhibiting them; lack of insight.
- Sexual interest is excessive with poor impulse control, resulting in public and private masturbation attempts.
- No medical conditions noted that influence behavior.

During depressive episodes, Dan has shown the following symptoms:

- Depressed all day, nearly every day, as evidenced by reports of feelings of sadness and observed by others.
- Marked diminished interest or pleasure in all, or almost all, activities most of the day, as evidenced by inability to answer his door or perform basic activities of daily living (ADLs).
- Insomnia or hypersomnia nearly every day.
- Experiences fatigue and loss of energy every day.
- Experiences feeling worthless with suicidal ideation on admission.
- Diminished ability to think or concentrate and is indecisive.
- Suicidal ideation with possible intent and guns at home. Denies danger to others.

QUICK REFERENCE 6.9

Counseling Strategies for Cognitive Therapy for Dan

- Identify with Dan the cognitive distortions that occur in the manic and depressive phases and are factors for his development and maintenance of mood disorders.
- Examine mania-related behaviors, especially those that trigger delusional thinking and inappropriate sexual acting out.
- Discuss negative distortions related to expectations of the environment, self, and future that contribute to depression.
- Examine Dan's perceptions of the environment and activities that are seen as unsatisfying or unrealistic. Review work- and social-related behaviors, identifying why they are problematic and developing a plan to address them.
- Identify dysfunctional patterns of thinking and behaving, and guide the client to evidence and logic that test the validity of the dysfunctional thinking.
- Assist Dan in understanding automatic thoughts that occur spontaneously and contribute to the distorted affect (e.g., personalizing, all or nothing, mind reading, discounting negatives), looking specifically at situations, thoughts, and consequences. If this technique is not helpful or does not work for Dan, help him to understand and explore other possibilities.
- Help Dan use "I" statements in identifying feelings and reactions.

(continued)

QUICK REFERENCE 6.9 (*Continued*)

Peer Support Group Therapy

- This type of therapy will help Dan develop social relationships and provide a format for learning how to better communicate and increase social interaction.
- Also, this group will help Dan in discussing medication-related issues and serve as an avenue for promoting education related to the affective disorder and its treatment. Dan often stops taking his medications and does not like the side effects; discussion regarding the danger and the consequences of this behavior can be outlined.

Family Therapy for Depression and Mania

- Involve Dan's brother in treatment planning designed to formulate a therapeutic plan to resolve symptoms and restore or create adaptive family- and work-related function.
- Build an alliance with the client and the family members. It is important to establish a positive working relationship between the client and his family.
- Provide education on using both psychotherapy and pharmacotherapy. This is especially important because of the variable and small therapeutic window of effectiveness with lithium use.
- Obtain the brother's view of the situation and specify problems; clarify each individual's needs and desires. Allow family members to vent about the chronic burden they have experienced and problem-solve ways to address this.
- Decrease the use of coercion and blaming.
- Increase cooperative problem solving.
- Increase each member's ability to express feeling clearly and directly and to hear others accurately.

known whether he is eating and sleeping, and Dan's overall nutritional status is questionable. In addition, a referral for a blood test should be considered to detect use or abuse of drugs and monitor his lithium levels. Careful evaluation of the medications he is taking and has taken in the past needs to be ongoing.

GENERAL INTERVENTION STRATEGIES: MODELS AND TREATMENT MODALITIES FOR THE BIPOLAR DISORDERS

Bipolar disorder generally worsens over time, and as a chronic illness, the severity and frequency of episodes can increase. Individuals with bipolar disorder potentially lose 14 years of effective living and die 9 years early (Jones, Sellwood, & McGovern, 2005). The bipolar disorders present with a variety of symptoms that often cause major functioning problems across a vast array of psychosocial domains. This leads to frustration for the individual, the family, and other support systems (Jones, 2004). Clients with this disorder are often overwhelmed by the symptoms associated with their fluctuating moods, vacillating energy levels, and repeated disruptions when trying to complete the tasks of daily living. The client who suffers from bipolar disorder is faced with the challenge of understanding and tracking two separate sets of symptoms within one illness: those that arise during a manic state and those reflected in the depressive phase (Jones et al., 2005).

For many clients with bipolar disorders, the challenge is learning how to determine whether their cheery disposition or depressed states are within normal limits or indicative of a manic swing or a depressive downtrend. The client may not be able to depend on his or her own assessment to detect the changes in mood, but relatives and friends can be very helpful in identifying the mild mood fluctuations and changes that appear to represent an unusual state for the client. Although support systems can become taxed by these behaviors, collateral supporting reports are always helpful. These clients commonly become resistant to seeking and maintaining treatment, especially those who are in the manic or elevated high states of the illness. There is a high degree of comorbid disorders, such as personality disorder, generalized anxiety, panic disorder, and substance abuse (Leahy, 2007). In a study of 429 individuals with bipolar disorder, 32.9% reported having discontinued all medications for the disorder at some point in the past without informing the physician (Baldessarini et al., 2007). Clients in the manic phase of the illness often avoid or refuse support. When social workers understand the differences that can occur in mood states and the specific criteria that characterize each of the bipolar disorders, they are in a better position to assist clients and their families in accepting, monitoring, and treating this form of mental illness. Understanding and managing this symptomatology medically can be difficult for clients, their relatives, and other support systems.

A thorough assessment that leads to an accurate diagnosis is only the beginning phase of the intervention. It can be difficult to convince a client with a bipolar disorder that he or she is in fact experiencing serious changes in mood states and that help is necessary. Other reasons for treatment nonadherence include psychiatric and substance abuse use comorbidities and the client's attitudes toward the treatments and medications (Sajatovic, Valenstein, Blow, Ganoczy, & Ignacio, 2007). Miasso et al. (2008) report that nonadherence can be directly related to how clients perceive taking medication and the social stigma, as well as the side effects of the medications that can affect their overall performance.

Prescription Medications and Other Psychotherapeutic Agents: Lithium

In both children and adults, the main goal of psychological and psychopharmacological treatment is to prevent relapse and improve psychosocial functioning. Medications are frequently utilized as either the sole treatment strategy or as a supplemental treatment strategy for the bipolar disorders in adults, adolescents, and children. The same medications are often used for the disorder regardless of a client's age. Miklowitz (2008) warns, however, that "despite significant strides in pharmacological treatment of bipolar disorder, most bipolar patients cannot be maintained on drug treatments alone" (p. 1408).

Of the bipolar disorders, bipolar I is recognized as the easiest to treat with medications; the other types of the disorder present a much greater challenge for health care providers (Fountoulakis, 2008). Individuals with bipolar disorder experience significantly greater impairment from depressive episodes and take longer to recover than from manic episodes. Due to the limited efficacy of pharmacotherapy, adjunctive psychosocial treatments are often utilized (Miklowitz et al., 2007).

Because bipolar disorders are recurring illnesses with remissions and relapses or recurrences of both depressive and manic or hypomanic episodes, clients often require an ongoing regimen of medication. Most people with bipolar disorder may have to take medications throughout their life. The goal of medication therapy is to (a) stabilize the depressive or manic symptoms, (b) prevent relapse of depressive or manic episodes, (c) reduce subthreshold symptoms, (d) decrease suicide risk, (e) reduce cycling frequency, and (f) improve overall functioning (Usery, Lobo, & Self, 2008). Various categories of psychotropic medications are used in the treatment of bipolar disorders, yet the majority of individuals with bipolar disorder need to be monitored carefully, as many are not able to maintain remission in the long term (Vieta et al., 2008).

The medications used to treat bipolar disorder fall into four groups: (1) mood stabilizers, (2) atypical antipsychotics, (3) anticonvulsants, and (4) antidepressants. Of these medications, the most common are mood stabilizers (Dulcan, 2006), yet their efficacy can be limited, and they often produce side effects. The oldest of the mood stabilizers and still the most commonly prescribed is lithium (Eskalith or Lithobid). The antipsychotic medication risperidone (Risperdal) for the treatment of acute mania in children and adolescents with bipolar disorder appears to hold promise (Haas et al., 2009). It is beyond the capacity of this chapter to discuss all of these medications categories; for a more comprehensive review for the nonmedically trained, see Dziegielewski (2006, 2010).

Lithium is used with all ages; however, caution is stressed when used with children and adolescents. Dulcan (2006) recommends a course of only up to 2 years. Over the last few years, this medication has been used with children and adolescents to control behavioral outbursts or rage. When it is used for this purpose, the medication is generally prescribed only until more appropriate ways to control the child's anger (such as problem-solving and coping skills or a safer medication) can be found (Dulcan, 2006).

Lithium can assist the client by providing symptomatic control of both the manic and depressive phases of bipolar disorder and in long-term prophylaxis against condition recurrence (Culver, Arnow, & Ketter, 2007). Lithium is less effective in treatment of acute depressive episodes than for manic episodes (Keck, 2005). Despite the side effects, lithium remains among the most widely used medications, along with antidepressants, for depression. Lithium can reduce impulsivity and aggression, thus reducing suicidal behavior. It is established as having efficacy against recurrent manic or depressive episodes (Goldberg, 2007). Although lithium should diminish manic symptoms in 5 to 14 days, it may take months before the condition is fully controlled (Dulcan, 2006). Because lithium has a short half-life, it is rapidly excreted from the system. Caution should be used, as the drug is highly toxic and must be monitored regularly by medically trained professionals. Furthermore, with its high toxicity and excretion rate, lithium can be particularly problematic in older people (Physicians' Desk Reference [PDR], 2009), who should take it only if they have normal sodium intake and normal heart and kidney function. Since the therapeutic range for lithium is limited, there is a fine line between the therapeutic dose and a toxic one (Usery et al., 2008). Maintaining a safe and therapeutic dose requires routine monitoring of lithium levels and at minimum an established baseline between other recommended tests (white blood cell, calcium, kidney function, thyroid function, etc.) (Dulcan, 2006). It is beyond the scope of this chapter to describe all the side effects of this medication; the National Institute of Mental Health (2009) gives a very comprehensive and simple-to-understand summary.

With lithium, as with any medication routine, a complete medical history needs to be taken to ensure that other factors, such as potential thyroid or renal problems and possible pregnancy, have been assessed (NIMH, 2009). Concerning women of childbearing years, Einarson (2009) believes many psychotropic drugs are generally safe; however, he states strongly that a woman with a serious psychiatric disorder should always be considered high risk, and both she and the fetus should be monitored carefully during and after pregnancy. In addition, there should be monitoring of potential problems every 2 to 3 months while a client is taking lithium. Overdosing with lithium can be fatal (PDR, 2009), and the need to properly educate clients and family members to the dangers of using this medication cannot be overemphasized.

Counseling Strategy

Several types of counseling are frequently considered for working with individuals who suffer from the mood disorders. A complete diagnostic assessment can help the mental health practitioner decide what problem behaviors are most prominent and how to address what is identified. Leahy (2007) recommended eight lessons essential for clinicians working with clients who suffer from bipolar disorder:

1. Learn to adequately diagnose hypomania and mania prior to the client taking medications.
2. Bipolar has a high genetic component, which helps to medicalize the problem, normalize the use of medication, and reduce moralization.
3. Realize that psychological therapy involves recognizing and treating the specific episode while working toward treatment maintenance over the long term.
4. Pharmacological treatment can assist with the mood swings for the individual suffering from bipolar disorder.
5. A psychoeducational component is necessary so the client understands the illness.
6. Mental health practitioners should work closely with the prescribing psychiatrist in identifying and addressing the specific problems of the current episode.
7. Despite the strong genetic component to bipolar disorder, life events, coping skills, and family environment may play a part in the expression of depressive and manic episodes.
8. Cognitive therapy can help clients understand aspects of both their depressive and manic episodes.

Electroconvulsive Therapy for Depression and Mania

Electroconvulsive therapy (ECT) is a form of treatment for depression and other mental illnesses that involves the introduction of a series of brain seizures in the patient (Pandya, Pozuelo, & Malone, 2007; West, Prado, & Krystal, 1999). The fact that ECT has such an undeservedly bad reputation can deter its use as an effective treatment for a number of mental health disorders (Pandya et al., 2007). To date, there is no definitive explanation as to how or why ECT works. Yet there have been more than 100 theories, including neurochemical, neuroendocrine, and neurophysiologic reasons, concerning this matter during the 70 years ECT has been available (Payne & Prudic, 2009). It is known that it is not the electrical shock that causes the therapeutic effect but rather the resulting seizure, which is a rapid firing of neurons in the brain (Fischer, 2000).

An estimated 1 million ECT treatments are performed globally each year. In the United States, the number of treatments is estimated at 300,000 annually (McCall, 2001). Usage has increased during the past two decades because of its efficiency and the resulting shorter hospital stay (Payne & Prudic, 2009). However, society's stigma against ECT has inhibited its use. Not only do many public and rural hospitals not offer it as a treatment but also many doctors are never taught how to perform the procedure. As a result, ECT is considered a treatment of last resort.

The ECT procedure is not without its risks, and, similar to medications, side effects are possible. There are no absolute contraindications for ECT; however, a complete medical workup is always indicated. "The cardiovascular, central nervous, and pulmonary systems carry the highest risk from general anesthesia and the induction of generalized seizure activity" (Pandya et al., 2007, p. 680). According to Payne & Prudic (2009), adverse effects of ECT may include apprehension or fear, headache, muscle soreness, nausea, cardiovascular dysfunction, prolonged apnea, prolonged seizures, and emergent mania. The most troubling of these affects is cognitive dysfunction, which often entails memory loss for a period of time before and after the procedure. This memory loss frequently lasts several weeks but can extend up to 6 months. In some cases, the memory loss persists longer. Research has shown that the cognitive dysfunction caused by ECT does not adversely affect functions not associated with memory, such as intelligence and judgment, in any lasting way. According to Payne & Prudic (2009), approximately 80% of patients report side effects; memory impairment is the most frequent, with a range of responses including fear, humiliation, increased compliance, failure, worthlessness, betrayal, lack of confidence, and degradation, as well as a sense of having been abused and assaulted.

According to McCall (2001), despite all the controversy surrounding ECT, the APA has determined that ECT is an effective treatment option for people suffering from the mood disorders, as well as several of the psychotic disorders. It can also be used with affective disorders and psychotic depression, which is seldom responsive to medications. In addition, ECT can lead to significant improvement of patients with severe affective disorders. Reid, Keller, Leatherman, and Mason (1998) found that 90% of all patients they reviewed who had undergone ECT had been diagnosed with a severe mood disorder and the remaining 10% had schizophrenia. With the research supporting the effectiveness of ECT for mood disorders, specifically bipolar disorder and depression, ECT can be viewed as an appropriate treatment option (Fischer, 2000).

The ECT procedure is effective with clients who are acutely suicidal and in the treatment of severe depression, particularly in those clients who are also experiencing psychotic symptoms and those with psychomotor retardation in sleep, appetite, and energy. It is often considered for treatment only after a trial of therapy with antidepressant medication has proved ineffective (Griswold & Pessar, 2000). Although ECT is still considered an effective treatment for the mood disorders, other neuromodulatory treatment techniques are being explored. Pandya et al. (2007) report that the popularity of several other treatments used in this area is increasing, but these treatments are often not considered unless several unsuccessful trials with an antidepressant medication have been used. Promising treatments on the horizon include vagus nerve stimulation (an implanted pacemaker-like device that stimulates the vagus nerve), deep brain stimulation (electrodes implanted in precise areas of the brain), and repetitive transcranial magnetic stimulation (uses an induction coil delivered in brief daily sessions). For a brief description and further information regarding the future of these treatments, see Pandya et al. (2007).

SPECIAL TOPICS

Bipolar Disorder in Childhood and Adolescence

Following the developmental perspective outlined in *DSM-5,* childhood disorders are always listed first in each chapter. Given the prevalence of the disorder, however, this chapter lists the bipolar and related disorders in adults first. The number of children and adolescents with this disorder is growing.

Between 10% and 15% of adolescents with recurrent major depressive episodes may later develop bipolar disorder. With the average age of 20 for the onset for bipolar disorder, a client can have a differential diagnosis of attention-deficit hyperactivity disorder (ADHD), conduct disorder, and schizophrenia. Also, bipolar symptoms may be easily misunderstood if there are no distinguishing symptoms of risk-taking behavior from the reckless nature of manic symptoms of the adolescent. If agitation is prominent in bipolar disorder, hypomanic symptoms may be misunderstood as reflecting an anxiety state (APA, 2000). When the diagnosis of bipolar disorder in children is presented, careful attention to more common conditions, such as ADHD or conduct disorder, can present with similar symptoms (Rowland, Lesesne, & Abramowitz, 2002). For additional information on existing co-conditions and complications, see Chapter 3.

The existence of the mania episode of bipolar in children and adolescents remains controversial. In the data that are available, bipolar disorder resembling the adult form of the illness is rare in prepubertal children, yet if an expanded phenotype is accepted, this disorder may be more common. Until these questions are answered or resolved, identifying bipolar in children will remain controversial (Faedda, Baldessarini, Glovinsky, & Austin, 2004). Recent research on bipolar disorders in children and adolescents appears to support an increased prevalence of this disorder. In several studies, most adults diagnosed with bipolar disorders in the United States experienced the onset of illness in their teen years or before. Bipolar disorder has frequently been misdiagnosed as ADHD or oppositional defiant disorder (ODD), conduct disorder (CD), or depression. Until recently, a diagnosis of bipolar disorder was rare in childhood, yet the best chance for children with emerging bipolar symptoms is early identification and intervention (NIMH, 2000).

Although the *DSM-5* (APA, 2013) does not indicate separate criteria for diagnosing bipolar disorder in children and adolescents, it considers developmental parameters when using the adult criteria of the disorder in children (Kronenberger & Meyer, 1996; Netherton, Holmes, & Walker, 1999). For example, Kronenberger and Meyer (1996) state that "mixed episodes occur when a child meets the criteria for a manic episode and a major depressive episode 'nearly every day' for 1 week or more, with marked impairment in functioning" (p. 156). When working with children and adolescents, Fountoulakis (2008) warns that a diagnosis is often difficult because the symptoms they experience can manifest periodically. When the symptoms of the disorder constitute repeated occurrences and result in obvious decline, however, bipolarity should be suspected. Symptoms often exhibited in this population include marked decline in school performance; restlessness; pulling or rubbing hair, skin, and clothes; excessive complaining and shouting; crying; aggressive outbursts; and antisocial behaviors.

Adults and children may both present with grandiosity, but the way these symptoms present can differ. For example, adults often engage in behaviors like excessive spending, inflated self-esteem, and inappropriate attire. Children and adolescents who are grandiose may exhibit these symptoms by being argumentative and bossy and showing attitudes of superiority to other children and adults (Hamrin & Pachler, 2007). Furthermore, according to Fountoulakis (2008), these children may initially present as quite personable and well liked by friends despite the grandiose and overconfident behaviors.

Generally, adolescents over the age of 13 are more commonly diagnosed with bipolar disorders (Axelson et al., 2006). In a study of 255 children and adolescents with bipolar disorder, Axelson et al. (2006) found that the mean age of onset was 12.9 years. For adults, the median age of onset has been documented as approximately 18 years, with a range from 18 to 22.7 years of age (Colom et al., 2005; Goldberg & Garno, 2009). Nevertheless, there has been a 40-fold increase in pediatric diagnosis of bipolar disorder (Baroni, Lunsford, Luckenbaugh, Towbin, & Leibenluft, 2009). Furthermore, consistent with a person-in-situation stance, social workers should ensure that a diagnosis is not reached too quickly, that it is not based solely on behaviors exhibited in isolation, and that the behaviors are not more extreme variations of symptoms associated with ADHD, conduct disorder, anxiety, or aggression. An accurate diagnostic impression is critical because if a child or adolescent is misdiagnosed with ADHD instead of bipolar disorder and a stimulant is given, the clinical picture might worsen considerably (Fountoulakis, 2008).

SUMMARY AND FUTURE DIRECTIONS

Dealing with any form of mental illness is a major challenge for clients, mental health practitioners, and family members. Bipolar disorders, with their varying changes in mood, present a unique challenge because the symptoms experienced may not be addressed until clients reach acute episodes of mania. In addition, clients with this disorder often present with coexisting psychiatric disorders that require concurrent attention. The assessment process in diagnosing bipolar disorder is an essential component of treatment. Assessing the client for critical or harmful problems such as suicidal ideation during a depressive episode may require addressing these problems first as a way of securing the client's safety. Assessment also includes the appropriate use of the criteria provided by the *DSM-5* and the inclusion of medication as the first priority in treatment strategy.

Mental health practitioners need to be well versed in the signs and symptoms identified in the *DSM-5* and be able to use this manual to facilitate the diagnostic assessment, treatment planning, and intervention that follow. If a mental health practitioner suspects that any client, regardless of age, may suffer from bipolar disorder, it is critical to confirm this diagnosis using the *DSM-5* criteria (APA, 2013). Doing this requires determining that the client meets the criteria for one of the mood states of bipolar disorder. In other words, does the client meet criteria for depressive, manic, or hypomanic episodes? In addition, every practitioner should also assess for critical symptoms reflective of other mental health problems that a client can exhibit; these overlapping symptoms can confuse the diagnostic impression.

Given the unique and different presentations of the disorder, the bipolar disorders in particular can be complex and difficult to assess and treat. More research is needed to establish the best evidence-based practices. Also, with the changes in the *DSM-5* and elimination of the multiaxial system, particularly Axis IV, the assessment of supporting information remains limited. With the development of these disorders and the suspected linkage to supportive/environmental circumstances (NIH, n.d.), it is clear that a more comprehensive diagnostic system will be needed; *DSM-5* now falls short in addressing this important aspect of mental health diagnosis, assessment, and treatment. In addition, more research is needed in the area of children and adolescents. Accurate measurements of problem behaviors and social problems provide fuel for the most comprehensive approaches to high-quality client care.

Mental health practitioners are in a unique position not only to provide services to those with bipolar disorders but also to advocate for the needs of the client that are going unmet. Families with an individual suffering from bipolar and related disorders need the support of the community, physicians, and mental health organizations. Support groups for both client and family can provide low-cost assistance. The legal justice system and medical society red tape need to be removed or simplified to expedite aid and assistance to clients with bipolar and related disorders. Finally, in the diagnostic assessment, mood variability makes it imperative to teach individuals in the client's support system to be aware of suicidal indications. Mental health practitioners spend a great deal of time with clients; it is critical that they understand the intricate nature of mood disorders as they teach clients and their families about the disorder and help clients accept intervention efforts.

REFERENCES

American Psychiatric Association. (2000). *Diagnostic and statistical manual of mental disorders* (4th ed., text rev.). Washington, DC: Author.

American Psychiatric Association. (2013). *Diagnostic and statistical manual of mental disorders* (5th ed.). Arlington, VA: American Psychiatric Publishing.

Arden, J. B., & Linford, L. (2009). *Brain-based therapy with adults: Evidence-based treatment for everyday practice.* Hoboken, NJ: Wiley.

Austrian, S. G. (2005). *Mental disorders, medications, and clinical social work* (3rd ed.). New York, NY: Columbia University Press.

Axelson, D., Birmaher, B., Strober, M., Gill, M. K., Valeri, S., Chiappetta, L., . . . Keller, M. (2006). Phenomenology of children and adolescents with bipolar spectrum disorders. *Archives of General Psychiatry, 63*(10), 1139–1148. doi: 10.1001/archpsyc.63.10.1139

Baldessarini, R. J., Perry, R., & Pike, J. (2007). Factors associated with treatment non-adherence among U.S. bipolar disorder patients. *Human Psychopharmacology Clinical Experience, 23*(2), 95–105.

Baroni, A., Lunsford, J. R., Luckenbaugh, D. A., Towbin, K. E., & Leibenluft, E. (2009). Practitioner review: The assessment of bipolar disorder in children and adolescents. *Journal of Child Psychology and Psychiatry, 50*(3), 203–215. doi: 10.1111/j.1469-7610.2008.01953.x

Basco, M. R., Ladd, G., Myers, D. S., & Tyler, D. (2007). Combining medication treatment and cognitive-behavior therapy for bipolar disorder. *Journal of Cognitive Psychotherapy: An International Quarterly, 21*(1), 7–15.

Childress, A. R. (2006). What can human brain imaging tell us about vulnerability to addiction and relapse? In W. R. Miller & K. M. Carroll (Eds.), *Rethinking substance abuse: What the science shows, and what we should do about it* (pp. 46–60). New York, NY: Guilford Press.

Colom, F., Vieta, E., Sanchez-Moreno, J., Martinez-Aran, A., Reinares, M., Goikolea, J. M., & Scott, J. (2005). Stabilizing the stabilizer: Group psychoeducation enhances the stability of serum lithium levels. *Bipolar Disorders,* 7(Supplement 5), 32–36.

Crow, T. J., Chance, S. A., Priddle, T. H., Radua, J., & James, A. C. (2013). Laterality interacts with sex across the schizophrenia/bipolarity continuum: An interpretation of meta-analyses of structural MRI. *Psychiatry Research, 210*(3), 1232–1244. doi: 10.1016/j.psychres.2013.07.043

Culver, J. L., Arnow, B. A., & Ketter, T. A. (2007). Bipolar disorder: Improving diagnosis and optimizing integrated care. *Journal of Clinical Psychology, 63*(1), 73–92. doi: 10.1002/jclp.20333

Dulcan, M. K. (2006). *Helping parents, youth, and teachers understand medications for behavioral and emotional problems* (3rd ed.). Washington, DC: American Psychiatric Publishing.

Dziegielewski, S. F. (2006). *Psychopharmacology for the non-medically trained.* New York, NY: Norton.

Dziegielewski, S. F. (2010). *Social work practice and psychopharmacology: A person-in-environment approach* (2nd ed.). New York, NY: Springer.

Einarson, A. (2009). Risks/safety of psychotropic medication use during pregnancy. *Canadian Journal of Clinical Pharmacology, 16*(1), e58–e65.

Faedda, G. L., Baldessarini, R. J., Glovinsky, I. P., & Austin, N. B. (2004). Treatment-emergent mania in pediatric bipolar disorder: A retrospective case review. *Journal of Affective Disorders, 82*(1), 149–158.

Farrelly, N., Dibben, C., & Hunt, N. (2006). Current management of bipolar affective disorder: Is it reflective of the BAP guidelines? *Journal of Psychopharmacology, 20*(1), 128–131.

Fischer, J. S. (2000). Taking the shock out of electroshock. *U.S. News & World Report, 128*(3), 46.

Fountoulakis, K. N. (2008). The contemporary face of bipolar illness: Complex diagnostic and therapeutic challenges. *International Journal of Neuropsychiatric Medicine: CNS Spectrums, 13*(9), 763–774, 777–779.

Frances, A. (2013). *Essentials of psychiatric diagnosis: Responding to the challenge of* DSM-5. New York, NY: Guilford Press.

Garland, E. L., & Howard, M. O. (2014). A transdiagnostic perspective on cognitive, affective, neurobiological processes underlying human suffering. *Research on Social Work Practice, 24*(1), 142–151.

Goldberg, J. F. (2007). What psychotherapists should know about pharmacotherapies for bipolar disorder. *Journal of Clinical Psychology: In Session, 63*(5), 475–490.

Goldberg, J. F., & Garno, J. L. (2009). Age at onset of bipolar disorder and risk for comorbid borderline personality disorder. *Bipolar Disorders, 11*(2), 205–208.

Griswold, K. S., & Pessar, L. F. (2000). Management of bipolar disorder. *Family Physician, 62*(6) 1343–1353, 1357–1358.

Haas, M., Delbello, M. P., Padina, G., Kushner, S., Van Hove, I., Augustyns, I., . . . Kusumakar, V. (2009). Risperidone for the treatment of acute mania in children and adolescents with bipolar disorder: A randomized, double-blind, placebo-controlled study. *Bipolar Disorders, 11*(7), 687–700. doi: 10.1111/j.1399-5618.2009.00750.x

Hajeka, T., Hahn, M., Slaney, C., Garnham, J., Green, J., Ruzickova, M., . . . Alda, M. (2008). Rapid cycling bipolar disorders in primary and tertiary care treated patients. *Bipolar Disorders, 10*(4), 495–502. doi: 10.1111/j.1399-5618.2008.00587.x

Hamrin, V., & Pachler, M. (2007). Pediatric bipolar disorder: Evidence-based psychopharmacological treatments. *Journal of Child and Adolescent Psychiatric Nursing, 20*(1), 40–58.

Harel, E. V., & Levkovitz, Y. (2008). Effectiveness and safety of adjunctive antidepressants in the treatment of bipolar depression: A review. *Israel Journal of Psychiatry and Related Sciences, 45*(2), 121–128.

Jones, S. (2004). Psychotherapy of bipolar disorder: A review. *Journal of Affective Disorders, 80*(2–3), 101–114.

Jones, S. H., Sellwood, W., & McGovern, J. (2005). Psychological therapies for bipolar disorder: The role of model driven approaches to therapy integration. *Bipolar Disorders*, 7(1), 22–32. doi: 10.1111/j.1399-5618.2004.00157.x

Keck, P. E. (2005). Bipolar depression: A new role for atypical antipsychotics? *Bipolar Disorders*, 7(Supplement 4), 34–40. doi: 10.1111/j.1399-5618.2005.00213.x

Klap, R., Unroe, K. T., & Unutzer, J. (2003). Caring for mental illness in the United States: A focus on older adults. *The American Journal of Geriatric Psychiatry, 11*(5), 517–524.

Kronenberger, W. G., & Meyer, R. G. (1996). *The child clinician's handbook.* Needham Heights, MA: Allyn & Bacon.

Leahy, R. L. (2007). Bipolar disorder: Causes, contexts, and treatments. *Journal of Clinical Psychology: In Session, 63*(5), 417–424. doi: 10.1002/jclp.20360

Maxmen, J. S., Ward, N. G., & Kilgus, M. (2009). *Essential psychopathology and its treatment* (3rd ed.). New York, NY: Norton.

McCall, W. V. (2001). Electroconvulsive therapy in the era of modern psychopharmacology. *International Journal of Neuropsychopharmacology, 4*(3), 315–324.

Miasso, A. I., Cassiani, S. H., & Pedrao, L. J. (2008). Bipolar affective disorder and medication therapy: Identifying barriers. *Revista Latino-Americana De Enfermagem, 16*(4), 739–745.

Miklowitz, D. J. (2008). Adjunctive psychotherapy for bipolar disorder: State of the evidence. *American Journal of Psychiatry, 165*(11), 1408–1419.

Miklowitz, D. J., George, E. L., Richards, J. A., Simoneau, T. L., & Suddath, R. L. (2003). A randomized study of family-focused psychoeducation and pharmacotherapy in the outpatient management of bipolar disorder. *Archives of General Psychiatry, 60*(9), 904–912.

Miklowitz, D. J., Otto, M. W., Frank, E., Reilly-Harrington, N. A., Wisniewski, S. R., Kogan, J. N., . . . Sachs, G. S. (2007). Psychosocial treatments for bipolar depression: A 1-year randomized trial from the systematic treatment enhancement program. *Archives of General Psychiatry, 64*(4), 419–426. doi: 10.1001/archpsyc.64.4.419

Mitchell, P. B., & Malhi, G. S. (2004). Bipolar depression: Phenomenological overview and clinical characteristics. *Bipolar Disorders, 6*(6), 530–539. doi: 10.1111/j.1399-5618.2004.00137.x

National Institute of Health, National Institute of Mental Health. (n.d.). Bipolar Disorder. Retrieved from http://www.nimh.nih.gov/health/topics/bipolar-disorder/index.shtml

National Institute of Mental Health. (2000). *Bipolar disorder research at the National Institute of Mental Health* [NIH Publication NO. 00–4500]. Bethesda, MD: Author.

National Institute of Mental Health. (2009). How is bipolar disorder treated? Retrieved from http://www.nimh.nih.gov/health/publications/bipolar-disorder/how-is-bipolar-disorder-treated.shtml

Netherton, S. D., Holmes, D., & Walker, C. E. (1999). *Child and adolescent psychological disorders: A comprehensive textbook*. New York, NY: Oxford University Press.

Oquendo, M. A., Currier, D., & Mann, J. J. (2006). Prospective studies of suicidal behavior in major depressive and bipolar disorders: What is the evidence for predictive risk factors? *Acta Psychiatrica Scandinavica*, *114*(3), 151–158.

Pandya, M., Pozuelo, L., & Malone, D. (2007). Electroconvulsive therapy: What the internist needs to know. *Cleveland Clinical Journal of Medicine*, *74*(9), 679–685. doi: 10.3949/ccjm.74.9.679

Paris, J. (2013). *The intelligent clinician's guide to the* DSM-5™. New York, NY: Oxford University Press.

Payne, N. A., & Prudic, J. (2009). Electroconvulsive therapy part I: A perspective on the evolution and current practice of ECT. *Journal of Psychiatric Practice*, *15*(5), 346–368. doi: 10.1097/01.pra.0000361277.65468.ef

Perlis, R. H., Ostacher, M. J., Patgel, J. K., Marangell, L. B., Zhang, H., Wisniewski, S. R., . . . Thase, M. E. (2006). Predictors of recurrence in bipolar disorder: Primary outcomes from the systematic treatment enhancement program for bipolar disorder (STEP-BD). *Focus*, *4*(4), 553–561.

Physicians' Desk Reference [PDR]. (2009). *Physicians' desk reference* (63rd ed.). Montvale, NJ: Medical Economics.

Reid, W. H., Keller, S., Leatherman, M., & Mason, M. (1998). ECT in Texas: 19 Months of mandatory reporting. *Journal of Clinical Psychiatry*, *59*(1), 8–13.

Rowland, A. S., Lesesne, C. A., & Abramowitz, A. J. (2002). The epidemiology of attention-deficit/hyperactivity disorder (ADHD): A public health view. *Mental Retardation and Developmental Disabilities Research Reviews*, *8*(3), 162–170.

Sajatovic, M., Valenstein, M., Blow, F., Ganoczy, D., & Ignacio, R. (2007). Treatment adherence with lithium and anticonvulsant medications among patients with bipolar disorder. *Psychiatric Services*, *58*(6), 855–863. doi: 10.1176/appi.ps.58.6.855

Samame, C. (2013). Social cognition throughout the three phases of bipolar disorder: A state-of-art overview. *Psychiatry Research*, *210*(3), 1275–1286. doi: 10.1016/j.psychres.2013.08.012

Sublette, M. E., Carballo, J. J., Moreno, C., Galfalvy, H. C., Brent, D. A., Birmaher, B., . . . Oquendo, M. A. (2009). Substance use disorders and suicide attempts in bipolar subtypes. *Journal of Psychiatric Research*, *43*(3), 230–238.

Titolo, T. R. (2008, March 27). MRI, CT, fMRI, PET, and SPECT neuroimaging [Web blog post]. Retrieved from Titolo Law Group: Brain and spine injury law blog, http://brainandspine.titololawoffice.com/articles/brain-injury/pet-scan

Torpy, J. M. (2009). Bipolar disorder. *Journal of the American Medical Association*, *301*(5), 564. doi: 10.1001/jama.301.5.564

Usery, J. B., Lobo, B., & Self, T. (2008). Pitfalls in prescribing: How to minimized drug therapy risks. *Consultant*, *48*(1).

Valtonen, H. M., Suominen, K., Haukka, J., Mantere, O., Leppamaki, S., Arvilommi, P., & Isometsa, E. T. (2008). Differences in incidence of suicide attempts during phases of bipolar I and II disorders. *Bipolar Disorders*, *10*(5), 588–596. doi: 10.1111/j.1399-5618.2007.00553.x

Vieta, E., Suppes, T., Eggens, I., Persson, I., Paulsson, B., & Brecher, M. (2008). Efficacy and safety of quetiapine in combination with lithium or divalproex for maintenance of patients with bipolar I disorder (international trial 126). *Journal of Affective Disorders*, *109*(3), 251–263.

West, M., Prado, R., & Krystal, A. D. (1999). Evaluation and comparison of EEG traces: Latent structure in nonstationary time series. *Journal of the American Statistical Association*, *94*(446), 375–394.

Williams, J. M. G., Alatiq, Y., Crane, C., Barnhofer, T., Fennell, M. J. V., Duggan, D. S., . . . Goodwin, G. M. (2008). Mindfulness-based cognitive therapy (MBCT) in bipolar disorder: Preliminary evaluation of immediate effect on between-episode functioning. *Journal of Affective Disorders*, *107*(1–3), 275–279. doi:10.1016/j.jad.2007.08.022

CHAPTER 7

Depressive Disorders

SOPHIA F. DZIEGIELEWSKI

INTRODUCTION

The depressive disorders, particularly major depressive disorder, have been referred to as the common cold of mental health (Durbin, 2013). Families and communities pay a heavy toll when a disorder involving an individual's mood is not recognized and treated. For so many individuals who suffer from these disorders, problems with family relations and support systems are common, as well as the potential for suicide. In children, adolescents, and adults who suffer from a depressive disorder, lack of desire to function can lead to employment and school difficulties. These feelings of depressive mood can have devastating effects on the client and his or her family. It is imperative to promptly recognize what would be considered a normal depressive reaction and what constitutes a depressive disorder in children, adolescents, and adults. Furthermore, no single medicine, treatment, or therapy holds the key to success, and all options should be used to assist individuals suffering from these disorders.

This chapter presents a brief overview of the mood disorders listed in the *Diagnostic and Statistical Manual of Mental Disorders, Fifth Edition* (*DSM-5;* American Psychiatric Association [APA], 2013) to better understand and assess these conditions. It is beyond the purpose of this chapter to explore in detail all of the diagnoses in the depressive disorders or the treatments that can be applied. Rather, the purpose of this chapter is to introduce the reader to the primary disorders listed in *DSM-5,* including disruptive mood dysregulation disorder, major depressive disorder, persistent depressive disorder (dysthymia), premenstrual dysphoric disorder, substance/medication-induced depressive disorder, depressive disorder due to another medical condition, other specified depressive disorder, and unspecified depressive disorder.

The application section of this chapter provides a case example of an individual suffering from disruptive mood dysregulation disorder, with specific recommendations for completing the diagnostic assessment and the subsequent treatment plan. The extent, importance, and early predictors of problem behaviors and symptoms are explored. The various aspects of the disorder are presented, with a case application that highlights diagnostic assessment, treatment planning, and evidence-based treatment strategy. In addition, the latest practice methods and newest research findings are highlighted to further the understanding of these often-devastating illnesses. Discussion of the depressive disorders from a community and societal perspective helps to identify how critical it is for mental health practitioners to complete a thorough diagnostic assessment, treatment plan, and practice strategy. Helping individuals also has to take into account the magnitude of disturbances these disorders can have on the individual and his or her support system, and strategies to assist are covered. The focus of this chapter is that depressive disorders can be difficult to define and, once clarified, require professionals to realize that one method of treatment does not work for all clients. Each client and the symptoms he or she experiences require awareness of different methods for developing an individualized treatment plan. These individualized plans need to take into account a client's current situation and support structure to help the client to improve functioning.

TOWARD A BASIC UNDERSTANDING OF THE DISORDERS

According to the *DSM-5*, several disorders fall into this category. The most prominent characteristic shared is the cognitive, somatic, and emotional changes reflecting feelings of extreme sadness or irritability. The duration, timing, and presumed cause of the illness differentiate the disorders. The effects experienced can be so severe that they affect an individual's ability to function (APA, 2013). According to the *Morbidity and Mortality Weekly Report,* a recent survey showed that among 235,067 adults representing 45 states, the District of Columbia, Puerto Rico, and the Virgin Islands, 9.1% met the criteria for depression and reported significant symptoms of depression during the 2 weeks prior to the survey (Centers for Disease Control and Prevention, 2010). An earlier study by the World Health Organization (WHO, 2009) reported that 121 million people worldwide were affected by depression and that the depressive disorders were the leading cause of disability, 33% of those living with a disability. Furthermore, throughout the world, especially in low- and moderate-income countries, mental health services remain limited.

For many mental health practitioners, clients who report symptoms of depression are commonplace and it is often one of the most ambiguous to define (Barnhill, 2014). When these feelings become pervasive and disturb almost every aspect of functioning, clinically depressed mood is noted. In this type of depressive symptomatology, an individual's basic needs are affected, including disturbances in sleeping and eating, loss of interest or pleasure in previously satisfying situations and activities, feelings of guilt, low self-worth, poor concentration, and depressed mood. The term *unipolar* is used to identify the specific mental health conditions that are characterized by occurrences of depressed mood.

Nearly 30 million U.S. adults are affected with major depressive symptoms, with one-third of them classified as severely depressed (Nemeroff, 2007). It is estimated that 16% of the population will suffer from depression at some point in their lives (Capriotti, 2006; Hansen, Gartlehner, Lohr, Gaynes, & Carey, 2005). Depression linked to suicide results in approximately 850,000 lives lost each year worldwide (WHO, 2009).

In terms of onset of the disorder, age is a significant variable that can denote the course and symptomatology of an illness, particularly anxiety and suicide risk (Wikowska-Chmielewska, Szelenberger, & Wojnar, 2013). This stresses the importance of diagnosing this disorder as early in the course as possible. Two percent to 6% of children and adolescents suffer from depression (Whittington et al., 2004). About 25% of people over the age of 65 with a chronic medical illness suffer from depressive symptoms, and 15% suffer from major depressive disorder (Sheikh et al., 2004). Reports of depressive symptoms in older adults range from 10% to 25% in community and primary care settings and 50% in nursing homes and medical settings (Skultety & Zeiss, 2006). Treatment for unipolar illness is lacking. According to WHO (2009), fewer than 25% of those with severe depressive symptoms have proper access to care. Of the clients who seek treatment to address their depression, 50% to 80% go unrecognized or misdiagnosed (Higgins, 1994).

Undetected depression in primary care settings ranges from 30% to 70%; of those whose depression is detected, less than 50% receive adequate treatment (Liu et al., 2006). Yet depression remains a common problem. Research indicates the rate of depression is 5% to 10% for patients with multiple health care issues in primary care and 10% to 14% for patients under general hospital care (Timonen & Liukkonen, 2008). African Americans are one-third less likely to receive medication treatment for depression and anxiety than White Americans (Gonzalez et al., 2008). In males, depressive symptoms can be masked in angry responses, and depression may be assessed as less severe despite serious deficits in functioning.

These clients may be especially frustrating to help because their complaints (generally somatic) usually result in negative medical workups and laboratory tests, leaving those in the medical field at a loss for how to help. Given the prevalence and diverse presentation of symptoms, addressing these multifaceted disorders leads to misunderstandings and frustration on the part of both health care providers and clients (National Institute of Mental Health [NIMH], 2000). To further complicate this scenario, about 70% of the individuals who have suffered from depression once can expect a recurrence (Resnick & Carson, 1996). Therefore, creating a comprehensive assessment involves a delicate balance of clinical judgment and the latest research (Schore, 2014).

IMPORTANT FEATURES RELATED TO THE DEPRESSIVE DISORDERS

When the mental health practitioner is completing the diagnostic assessment of an individual who suffers from a mood disorder, depression is a common symptom that overlaps symptomatology with many other disorders. In addition, when clients report feelings of depression, a lack of clarity and problems in semantics in defining what is actually being experienced in terms of magnitude and frequency can be problematic. Feelings of depression are frequently overstated or understated, influenced by the definition and normalcy standards set within an individual's unique social and environmental context. For many, depression can mean feeling sad, blue, or down in the dumps; for others, it has clearly established criteria with consistent patterns, signs, and symptoms of a mood disorder. Furthermore, some forms of depression (also referred to as dysphoric mood) overlap other mental health conditions. Therefore, in understanding the depressive disorders, the first step is becoming aware of the different types of depressive disorders listed in *DSM-5*.

Problems With Self-Reporting of Symptoms

One reason this lack of proper assessment of symptoms is so problematic is the symptoms that clients self-report. Much of what we know about a client suffering from depression—or any mental health condition, for that matter—comes from self-report. How the client interprets and reports the symptoms being experienced can be misleading because feelings of depression can be easily overstated or understated. The client's subjective experience is being reported; this interpretation reflects the definition and standards of normalcy within his or her social, cultural, and environmental context (Paniagua, 2014).

The symptom of *anhedonia,* a complete loss of pleasure in all activities, may affect self-report. Anhedonia clearly affects how events and symptoms are perceived and expressed. Because depressed individuals often maintain some capacity for experiencing pleasure (Woo & Keatinge, 2008), the degree to which this impression affects self-report can vary. This can make the reporting of symptoms confusing:

Is the individual feeling pleasure from certain activities or not? Is he reporting what he is feeling now or what he remembers feeling in the past? To address this variability in the reporting of symptoms, the first step toward effective treatment is identifying a clear, concise, psychosocial criteria-based diagnostic standard.

Taking into account the influence of life factors on self-report is essential. Reported symptoms are always influenced by many factors, including current or past relationship problems, irritability with the situation, and work-related conflicts. All diagnostic interpretations must be sensitive to the influence of cultural and stress-related environmental and social factors (Paniagua, 2014). Some ethnic minority groups are exposed to tremendous contextual stressors that can affect the presentation in depression, including poverty, poor and rundown neighborhoods, acculturation, and loss associated with "never going home again" (White, Roosa, Weaver, & Nair, 2009). Similarly, the social context of immigrants needs to be assessed, as their depressive symptoms may stem from a conflict of values from their country of origin and American customs and values, problems with speaking the English language, parenting stress, and conflict between children's and parents' beliefs and customs.

Therefore, in assessing depression, the practitioner must consider not only what symptoms a client reports but also the cultural influences and complexities of the client's cultural identity (McGoldrick, Giordano, & Garcia-Preto, 2005). McGoldrick et al. (2005) point out that ethnicity is not the only dimension of culture but it is a necessary component of understanding an immigrant's adjustment to his or her new life and any change or loss experienced in the process. Social workers must also be willing to consider how gender, socioeconomic status, social class, geography, race, religion, and politics influence that adjustment; how important these factors are in accurately assessing depression; and how to best use a client-oriented support system as part of the treatment process (Locke & Bailey, 2014).

Clients suffering from depression can become frustrated with medical providers because the complaints reported are somatic and no physical causes are revealed. In turn, providers can also be frustrated for the same reason. In research on the opinions of general practitioners, Krupinski and Tiller (2001) discovered that assessment was limited to a specific set of symptoms: sleep disturbances, insomnia, early wakening, loss of appetite, overeating, weight changes, depressed mood, hopelessness, and sad and gloomy feelings. Being depressed is characterized by a combination of emotional, somatic and cognitive experiences that can lead to compounded feelings of hopelessness, each as varied as the situation that surrounds it (Garcia & Petrovich, 2011).

In addition, often the subjective problems clients report result in negative findings on the mental status exam. Symptoms such as feeling sad, blue, or down in the dumps are difficult to quantify. From a professional perspective, clearly establishing the criteria that reflect consistent patterns, signs, and symptoms of the mood disorder can be difficult. This is further complicated by the overlapping symptoms of depression present in other mental health conditions with few exceptions (mania, hypomania, and certain forms of schizophrenia and dementia). For these reasons, enhancing self-report is important, requiring clear, concise, psychosocial criteria-based diagnostic standards, as well as gathering collateral information and perceptions of significant others, family, coworkers, and friends (Woo & Keatinge, 2008). This need for additional supportive information to quantify the symptoms experienced can be frustrating for both client and practitioner. Clients may complain about the number of self-report measures utilized. Practitioners can become frustrated with the number of measures and symptom checklists used and question how helpful they are and whether they are the best use of therapeutic time (Rizq, 2012).

ENDOGENOUS AND EXOGENOUS DEPRESSION: MAKING A DISTINCTION

Two types of serious depression are severe forms of depressive illness. The first is often referred to as *endogenous* or *melancholic depression* (Woo & Keatinge, 2008). In this type, symptoms of depressed mood are related directly to internal biologic factors, such as neurotransmitter dysfunction (Sadock & Sadock, 2008). People who experience this type of depression often report a loss of pleasure in almost all their usual activities and symptoms of severe anhedonia, hopelessness, and inappropriate guilt. Suicidal symptoms may become a concern (Woo & Keatinge, 2008). Electroconvulsive therapy (ECT), referred to historically as shock treatment, is often considered an endogenous treatment. It involves direct (biologic) stimulation of the neurotransmission process. Antidepressant medications also are successful in lifting endogenous depression; however, they affect the neurochemical pathways chemically rather than electrically (Maxmen, Ward, & Kilgus, 2009).

In the second type of serious depression, there is a primary relationship between personal character-related factors or neurotic responses and precipitating events. This form of *exogenous* or environmental depression is sometimes referred to as *reactive depression;* the signs and symptoms manifested relate directly to life stressors or other psychosocial factors, such as divorce, unemployment, or injury (Tierney, McPhee, & Papadakis, 1997). Depressive factors such as decreased psychomotor speed, attention, and verbal memory may also be directly related to reactive life circumstances such as unemployment, even when the depressive condition is in remission (Shimizu et al., 2013).

Bettmann (2006) conceptualized understanding by utilizing attachment theory: In response to stressors, clients experience depression through isolating themselves from social contact. They feel unlovable and unworthy and show this insecurity by withdrawing. When a traumatic experience with loss or grief occurs, they do not know how to reach out to others in their support system. For the most part, grief and sadness are normal responses to loss, whereas severe depression is not. In depression, the survivor feels a marked sense of worthlessness and guilt, but with grief, individual self-esteem remains intact. Also, grief reactions and experiences can be relative to a certain culture (Vazquez & Rosa, 2011). Despite some similarities, there are often significant differences that could easily be misinterpreted by a practitioner who is not aware of the client's cultural relationships, mores, and expectations (Paniagua, 2014; Locke & Bailey, 2014). For this reason, Vazquez and Rosa (2011) cautioned mental health practitioners to differentiate between normal symptoms of grief, which at first may resemble a mental disorder, and actual depression symptomatology. To better understand exogenous factors, practitioners need to be skilled in determining what constitutes clinical depression that requires treatment and what is indicative of normal bereavement and grief (Friedman, 2012).

Symptoms include anxiety, chronic nervousness, insomnia, agitation, restlessness, and physical symptoms (Capriotti, 2006), and the signs of depression can be confused with anxiety or bipolar disorder. When physical signs mask depression, assessing depressive factors beyond the anxiety and worry and beyond the headaches, chronic pain, fatigue, and eating problems may uncover the emotions an individual is feeling inside.

Whether depression is *endogenous* (related to internal causes), *exogenous* (related to external or environmental causes), or a combination of both, the first clinical feature usually presented in major depression is *dysphoria* (a disturbance in mood) or *anhedonia* (a loss of pleasure or interest in normally enjoyable activities) (Maxmen et al., 2009). Besides dysphoria or anhedonia, depressed individuals present with a wide range of complaints that include feelings of guilt, inability to concentrate, feelings of worthlessness, somatic complaints, feelings of anxiety, chronic fatigue, and loss of sexual desire (Woo & Keatinge, 2008). As with any mental health problem, an accurate diagnosis of major depressive disorder requires clear documentation of the client's cognitive, behavioral, and somatic complaints. Although it is beyond the scope of this chapter to discuss all the signs and characteristic symptoms of all the mood disorders, the societal context and a brief overview of the most common ones are presented here.

OVERVIEW OF THE DEPRESSIVE DISORDERS

Somatic, cognitive, and emotional concerns identified in the *DSM-5* are the predominant features linking the disorders. In addition, these disorders all share depressed mood with subsequent changes in eating, sleeping, and energy levels; impairments in executive function and attention; and changes in self-awareness and perception. When depressed clients experience a loss of interest or pleasure in activities and difficulty concentrating, these symptoms can lead to problems with performing activities of daily living (ADLs) and making decisions. Although some types of mixed presentations in depression exist, the *DSM-5* focuses primarily on the depressive ones (Koukopoulos, Sani, & Gahaemi, 2013). For a diagnosis, however, these problems must be severe enough to affect occupational and social functioning. When suffering from depressive disorders, all individuals experience some degree of depressive symptoms, although the duration, time frame, and etiology may vary (APA, 2013). (See Quick Reference 7.1.)

Those familiar with *DSM-IV* and *DSM-IV-TR* will note several changes with these disorders, the biggest being separating the depressive disorders into their own chapter. The primary reason for this was to assist with moving away from the categorical response to a more

QUICK REFERENCE 7.1

Depressive Disorders: Brief Definitions

- Disruptive Mood Dysregulation Disorder (DMDD)
  DMDD has 11 specific criteria (ranging from A to K) that must be met. The core feature is irritability that is persistent for at least a year and maintains a severe and continuous course that is not related to a developmental phase. The behaviors are not consistent with the precipitating event and involve either verbal or behavioral manifestations toward people or property. Temper outbursts must be continuous, occurring at least three or more times over a 7-day period. Other criteria are documented in this text.
- Major Depressive Disorder
  There are nine primary symptoms, and the individual must have at least five of them. In addition, the symptoms must all occur during the same 2-week period,

(continued)

QUICK REFERENCE 7.1 (*Continued*)

and the individual who suffers from major depressive disorder must have either a depressed mood or a loss of interest or pleasure in daily activities consistently for the 2-week period. Of the nine symptoms, at least one must be depressed mood or loss of interest or pleasure.

- Persistent Depressive Disorder (dysthymia)
  This is a milder yet more chronic form of the disorder, requiring a 2-year history of depressed mood. The individual suffering from this disorder is not without the symptoms for more than 2 months at a time. The disorder is considered less severe than major depressive disorder but is constant for a period of 2 years, during which the individual experiences some symptoms related to the disorder almost every day.
- Premenstrual Dysphoric Disorder (PMDD)
  This new condition to the *DSM-5* occurs in women who have severe depressive symptoms, irritability, and tension that occur before menstruation.
- Substance/Medication-Induced Depressive Disorder
  Meet the criteria for major depressive disorder and document the substance/medication taken, confirmed by history, physical exam, or lab result. The individual needs to experience the symptoms soon after ingestion or with resultant intoxication or withdrawal from the substance. In addition, that the substance taken is capable of displaying the side effects that resulted has to be confirmed.
- Depressive Disorder Due to Another Medical Condition
  Similar to the criteria for substance/medication-induced disorder, the individual is expected to suffer from a persistent depressed mood, accompanied by diminished interest and pleasure in activities that once were pleasurable. There also needs to be direct evidence from an adequate history, physical exam, or lab result that makes the connection to the medical condition causing it.
- Other Specified Depressive Disorder or Unspecified Depressive Disorder
  The diagnosis of either of these disorders requires the symptoms characteristic of the depressive disorders. The three specifiers are recurrent brief depression, short-duration depressive episode, and depressive episode with insufficient symptoms. The primary difference between the specified and the unspecified disorder is that in the specified disorder, the practitioner documents the reason that it does not meet the criteria.

Source: Summarized criteria from the *Diagnostic and Statistical Manual of Mental Disorders*, Fifth Edition. Copyright 2013 by the American Psychiatric Association.

dimensional one that could note different degrees of severity. It can also better take into account the crosscutting of overlapping symptoms and, in the clearer cases where comorbidity is suspected, related diagnostic criteria for anxiety and mania (Moran, 2013). While there are still overlapping symptoms between the depressive and the bipolar disorders, differences in clinical presentation, history, and treatment can be significantly different and based on this information warranted separation in *DSM-5* into separate chapters (Barnhill, 2014).

Besides adding the specified and unspecified depressive disorders to this chapter, two other new disorders were included. *Disruptive mood dysregulation disorder* is new to the *DSM*, and *premenstrual dysphoric disorder* was taken from the area for further study. All are defined in the next section of this chapter. Therefore, the depressive disorders listed in the *DSM-5* are disruptive mood dysregulation disorder, major depressive disorder, persistent depressive disorder (dysthymia), premenstrual dysphoric disorder, substance/medication-induced depressive disorder, depressive disorder due to another medical condition and other specified depressive disorder, and unspecified depressive disorder.

Disruptive Mood Dysregulation Disorder

Disruptive mood dysregulation disorder (DMDD) is a new diagnosis added to the *DSM-5* that was not listed in the previous edition. It was originally added to this category to address the increased incidence of bipolar disorder in children and adolescents since 2001 (Moran, 2013). This disorder is said to be 40 times more common than it was in the past. To help address this phenomenon, this new diagnosis was created and can be applied to children between the ages of 7 and 18.

The DMDD has very specific criteria, with the core feature being irritability that is persistent, severe, and continuous rather than cyclic. Those that qualify for this diagnosis have persistently irritable and angry mood that transcend age-appropriate temper tantrums (Wood, 2014). In criterion A, taking into account the developmental age of the child, the behaviors exhibited must be significantly out of proportion to the precipitating event and involve either verbal outbursts and rage or behavioral manifestations such as physical aggression toward people or property. The key factor in meeting criterion A is that all resulting behaviors indicative of the diagnosis must be severe and clearly outside of what would be expected relevant to the situation. Crierion B, defines the extent of these outbursts further by relating it directly to the developmental age as well. The events should be documented, and when both verbal and behavioral outbursts occur, both should be noted. In addition, the age of the child must always be compared with what types of behaviors would be considered normal at that age. To determine criterion B, the practitioner needs to be versed in what is considered normal for the age range. The documented behaviors must be inconsistent with the developmental level. In criterion C, the temper outbursts must be continuous and occur at least three or more times over a 7-day period. In addition to the temper outbursts, the angry and irritable mood must be consistent, even when outbursts are not occurring. This angry and irritable mood is so prominent that others notice, and when the practitioner gathers collateral information, parents, teachers, and others close to the child are quick to state the concern related to mood (criterion D).

In criterion E, the time frame is reinforced. The symptoms must be monitored over 12 or more months. Therefore, documentation of the symptoms must be clear, and a history of past behaviors over the past year has to be gathered and verified. Also, in looking back over that year and documenting the agitated behavior, there can be no points of remission that lasted 3 or more months. Documentation of the symptoms must also take into account the settings in which they occur, such as home, school, or with peers. The behaviors must occur in at least two of the three settings to meet criterion F. In terms of age of onset, which outlines criterion G, the diagnosis should not be given prior to age 6 or have a first onset after age 18. To document the disorder, criterion H requires that the symptoms listed previously should occur before age 10. In criterion I, the full conditions for a manic or hypomanic episode should not be met and when symptoms do resemble these episodes it should not last longer than a day. With the overlap of symptoms that can occur, caution needs to be exercised to address the possibility of confusing hypomanic or manic episodes with the chronic verbal or physical outbursts characteristic of this disorder. In criterion J, the symptoms being experienced cannot be better explained by another mental disorder, such as an episode of major depressive disorder. Other related disorders to be ruled out are autism spectrum disorder (ASD), posttraumatic stress disorder (PTSD), separation anxiety disorder, or persistent depressive disorder, previously referred to as dysthymic disorder. In criterion K, the symptoms cannot be better explained by a substance or another medical or neurological condition (APA, 2013, p. 156).

In summary, for the most part, the agitation characteristic of this disorder is continuous. The severe verbal or physical outbursts occur three or more times a week and are grossly out of proportion in intensity and/or duration to the situation. Also, this diagnosis requires that the behaviors and outbursts are not developmentally appropriate. One reason this diagnosis, new to *DSM-5,* is in this chapter, rather than the chapter with the bipolar disorders, is that as individuals with these symptoms age, they are more likely to develop depressive or anxiety disorders rather than bipolar disorders, as originally thought (Barnhill, 2014).

Major Depressive Disorder

According to the *DSM-5,* there are nine primary symptoms, and the individual must have at least five of them. In addition, the symptoms must all occur during the same 2-week period, and the individual who suffers from major depressive disorder must have either a depressed mood or a loss of interest or pleasure in daily activities consistently for the 2-week period as one of the five symptoms noted to meet criterion A (APA, 2013). The criteria must represent a change from the individual's normal mood and be significant enough to be reported by the client and noticed by others close to him or her.

The APA (2013) for major depressive disorders requires identifying five symptoms from the list of nine:

1. *Depressed mood:* Depressed mood most of the day, nearly every day. Clients self-report these symptoms by stating that they are feeling sad, lost, and alone. Often they might appear sad and tearful while discussing simple unassociated events or issues. In children or adolescents, similar to DMDD, the presentation is often angry or irritable, and although still very sad, the presentation can be different.
2. *Markedly diminished interest or pleasure:* When symptomatic, these individuals report markedly diminished interest or pleasure in almost all activities most of the day, nearly every day. Establishing the frequency and intensity of this criterion can be done in two ways: self-report and observation. Documenting behaviors through client self-report is central to the diagnostic assessment, but subjectivity can limit accuracy. Therefore, it is important to supplement self-report with observation, either through direct observation or as reported by collateral contacts. To achieve the most comprehensive report, both self-report and observation are recommended. When gathering collateral contacts, be sure to ask the informant about behaviors specific to the past 2 weeks, along with the actual changes in behavior

that differ from his or her previous level of functioning.

3. *Appetite changes:* Appetite and weight loss or gain may occur. To be considered significant, a clear change in weight is expected while the individual is not actively dieting or trying to gain weight. Over a month's time, a change of more than 5% of body weight should be noted. Eating behaviors and appetite change need to be examined over a 1-month time frame as opposed to the 2 weeks relevant to the condition; therefore, counting this criterion for the diagnosis requires extending the evaluation beyond the 2-week period. To facilitate the assessment of this symptom, these questions are suggested: Has the client gained or lost weight recently (focusing on the past month)? If so, how much weight has been lost or gained? The answers to these questions will help the practitioner determine if the client is suffering from anorexia (eating less) or hyperphagia (overeating) to cope with the depressive feelings.
4. *Sleep disturbance:* Symptoms related to either insomnia or hypersomnia are noted every day. Sleep is an important criterion for any disorder, and in *insomnia,* the individual reports either trouble falling asleep or being unable to obtain uninterrupted sleep. In *hypersomnia,* the individual experiences excessive sleepiness that often occurs during what would be considered awake hours. This is especially problematic when it happens in dangerous situations as while driving a car. Whether insomnia or hypersomnia, sleep difficulties should be clearly documented, along with how functioning is affected. Given the prevalence of sleep problems in the depressive disorders, objective measures of sleep disturbance should be implemented whenever possible (Castro et al., 2013). To facilitate the assessment of these symptoms, the following questions are suggested: Is the client sleeping at night? If sleeping nightly, for how long? How does the client feel when he or she wakes up? Does he or she report feeling refreshed? Disturbances in eating and sleeping are common in this disorder and are often assessed first. Eating and sleeping are basic for survival. Therefore, in referring specifically to insomnia and loss of appetite, the term used to describe these symptoms is *vegetative.* Oversleeping (hypersomnia) and overeating (hyperphagia) are referred to as *reversed vegetative symptoms.*
5. *Psychomotor agitation:* Psychomotor agitation often exhibits as extreme restlessness, and the individual feels he or she cannot calm the self internally. Clients may explain it as their insides are on fire and they just cannot escape their inner feelings of excitement or restlessness. To characterize these internal symptoms of excitement, they should be clearly related to the depressive disorder being evaluated. Careful attention needs to be given to the onset of the disorder and whether it could be substance/medication related or have some other nervous system causative factor.
6. *Fatigue and loss of energy:* This symptom is often evidenced by clients' reports that they just do not have the energy to complete basic tasks. When coupled with a loss of desire or feelings of hopelessness, the symptoms of fatigue and lack of energy can be magnified greatly. The individual is not able to complete even the most basic of tasks required. In

cases such as this, the fatigue or loss of energy needs to be self-reported by the client as constant, lasting most of the day, almost every day over the 2-week period.

7. *Feelings of worthlessness or guilt:* When consistent with major depressive disorder, the guilt-related thoughts and feelings of worthlessness are excessive or inappropriate to the situation. Often these thoughts take on a delusional quality, and the individual holds on to the irrational thought even with clear evidence to the contrary. With delusional thinking, the individual remains convinced that his or her thinking patterns flow logically, even after it is pointed out that the reaction is beyond what would be expected for the current situation. Such guilt and feelings of worthlessness may be so overwhelming that the individual cannot seem to move beyond those feelings. The intrusive thoughts are so severe they interfere with daily routines, causing extreme difficulty in concentrating on anything unrelated to the delusional beliefs. When this excessive preoccupation with delusional thoughts constitute self-blaming, there may be no escape from the feelings that dominate the view, clouding life circumstances and subsequent options.
8. *Diminished concentration and indecisive thoughts:* Thoughts and the resultant behaviors are linked. When an individual can think and function on a certain level and this becomes impaired, there is a constant comparison of what the individual was able to do before and what he or she is capable of doing now. For these symptoms to be relevant, there must be a significant decline in the individual's ability to concentrate and problem-solve. The indecision clearly affects problem-solving ability, and this decline should be evident in self-report as well as by others close to the individual. This makes gathering collaborative communications and input essential to the diagnostic impression to be completed.
9. *Recurrent thoughts of death:* As noted in *DSM-IV* and *DSM-IV-TR,* the depressed individual may often express the idea of self-harm that may or may not be related to a specific plan. If an attempt is noted in the client's past, the circumstances surrounding it, if known, should be documented. In treatment, knowing this information may assist with predicting future risk. Any suicidal ideation (thoughts related to suicide) should be documented. In addition, although not mentioned in the *DSM-5* criteria, humans are social creatures, and almost all suicidal thoughts may be associated in some way with significant other(s). Danger to self can also involve danger to others. When an individual is preoccupied with feelings of his or her own death and death can be seen as a relief, it can be an irrational but consistent reaction to link death to a loved one. In the distorted perception, the individual could see it as helping and a relief to actually harm the loved one. Recurrent thoughts of death can obscure any thoughts of the satisfaction in living, and whether this may relate to other people should always be assessed when this criterion is positive. As discussed later in this chapter, a clear safety plan for all involved is always recommended in the treatment process.

Additional criteria for this disorder are reflected in criterion B, as it must also affect social, occupational, educational, or other important functioning, and the individual must report distress due to this change in mood. For children and adolescents, the mood may be reported as irritable, and the general presentation therefore often differs from what is seen in an adult and may be confused with DMDD. However, in DMDD, the mood is consistently agitated for at least a year and does not take on a cyclic pattern in which the individual seems better, as is the case in major depressive disorder. It should not be diagnosed in young adults older than age 18.

Like the other mental disorders, the depressed mood in this disorder cannot be caused by substances such as drugs, alcohol, or medications (criterion C), and it cannot be caused by or be part of another mental health disorder, such as any of the schizophrenia spectrum and other psychotic disorders such as schizoaffective disorder, schizophreniform disorder, delusional disorder, or other specified or unspecified disorder in this category (criterion D). In addition, there cannot be a documented history of manic or hypomanic episodes. (For a more detailed explanation of manic and hypomanic episodes, see Chapter 6.)

In major depressive disorder, the diagnosis is seen as separate from bipolar disorder or any of the psychotic disorders. Furthermore, careful consideration should be extended when the symptoms are accounted for by bereavement. Bereavement can mimic severe depression but is related directly to the death of a loved one. The *DSM-5* and the changes made to this section have been the subject of a great deal of controversy, especially the deletion of the bereavement exclusion. In *DSM-IV-TR,* the criteria for major depressive episode included a specific criterion (previously criterion E) for exclusion related to bereavement. This criterion stated: "The symptoms are not better accounted for by bereavement" and was summarized to mean that symptoms related to the death of a loved one could be counted only when "the symptoms persist for longer than 2 months or are characterized by marked functional impairment, morbid preoccupation with worthlessness, suicidal ideation, psychotic symptoms, or psychomotor retardation" (APA, 2000, p. 356). Therefore, with the previous criteria, given the death of a loved one and the symptoms of a major depressive episode, the diagnosis of major depressive disorder would most often be postponed till after a 2-month period had lapsed.

Based on the numerous discussions and concerns voiced within work groups and through feedback, there was a clear movement to delete the 2-month waiting period in *DSM-5.* The potential for exclusion of this criteria gained attention on many fronts. When describing those against it, Moran (2013) reported that they felt that it could medicalize bereavement, a normal phase of life transition. Some professionals felt that the course of bereavement was so unpredictable that it could take 1 to 2 years for a response. Other professionals felt that the death could be a trigger for major depressive disorder, and a delayed diagnosis could affect appropriate and timely treatment. Regardless of why the change was made, bereavement is no longer considered relative to the 2-month exclusion criteria. When assessing for major depressive disorder, carefully consider differentiating the presence of the risk factors related to bereavement.

The risk factors associated with major depressive disorder are divided into four areas:

1. **Temporal:** In the temporal domain, how an individual relates to his or her life situation is highlighted. When neuroticism is evidenced by negative affectivity, it becomes a strong risk factor for the development of the disorder, especially when the negativity is the repeated response to life stressors. In negative

affectivity, the individual may have many fears related to being alone, rejection, and self-confidence. Therefore, when life stressors are approached, the fear of abandonment and separation insecurity may be very difficult to overcome.

2. **Environmental:** Childhood experiences—especially exposure to extreme stressors, regardless of the type—can put someone at higher risk for developing the disorder. There is a higher risk of developing depression in families with a biological relative who also has the disorder.
3. **Genetic and Physiological:** The increase is higher for the disorder (approximately 40% higher than the general population) when the biological parents or other first-degree relatives also suffer from it. This increased risk carries over to early-onset and recurrent forms. One primary characteristic that increases the chance is when the individual, similar to the parents, also shows a great deal of neuroticism related to life stressors.
4. **Course Modifiers:** When individuals suffer from any mental disorders and certain medical disorders, especially chronic or debilitating medical conditions, the incidence of major depressive disorder increases.

For documenting major depressive disorder, the *DSM-5* establishes diagnostic codes. In major depressive disorder (single episode or recurrent), this coding scheme is used:

1. For the diagnosis major depressive disorder, the first three digits using *ICD-9-CM* are always 296.xx, and using *ICD-10,* it starts with F3x.x.

   Major Depressive Disorder

   296.xx (*ICD-9-CM*) or F3x.x (*ICD-10-CM*)
2. The fourth digit denotes whether it is a single (denoted with the number 2) or recurrent (denoted with a 3) major depressive episode in *ICD-9-CM,* and it is the second digit in *ICD-10-CM.* For a disorder to be considered recurrent, there must be at least 2 months from the end of one episode to the beginning of another. This means in the period between, the symptoms of the major depressive episode are not met. This would be coded:

   296.2x single/296.3x recurrent for *ICD-9-CM*

   F32.x single/F33.x recurrent for *ICD-10-CM*
3. The fifth digit indicates the severity, presence of psychotic features, and remission status. There are three levels of severity: mild, moderate, and severe. When identifying mild severity, the criteria for the disorder are met, but the impairment that results to social and occupational functioning is considered minimal. When they are more than minimal but not meeting the specifier criteria for severe, it is considered moderate. When the severity specifier severe is used, the criteria for the disorder have been met, and many more symptoms than required cause significant impairment and often require immediate attention. When the severe severity specifier is used, interference with social and occupational functioning is extremely problematic. Although easy to remember, Zimmerman (2012) warns that these specifiers may not be comprehensive or descriptive enough to truly capture the level of severity being experienced. The severity course specifier can also be used to denote whether there

are psychotic features (hallucinations, delusions, and formal thought disorder) present. This specifier would be added and simply written "with psychotic features" when the level of severity is also utilized. Remember in coding that when the symptoms of psychosis are present, always document with psychotic features. This diagnosis also allows the coding of partial, full, or unspecified remission. Keep in mind, however, that remission specifiers can be used only when the full criteria for the major depressive episode are no longer met.

Severity Specifier:

- 296.x1 Mild severity [*ICD-9-CM*] or F3x.0 [*ICD-10-CM*]
- 296.x2 Moderate severity [*ICD-9-CM*] or F3x.1 [*ICD-10-CM*]
- 296.x3 Severe severity [*ICD-9-CM*] or F3x.2 [*ICD-10-CM*]
- 296.x4 With psychotic features [*ICD-9-CM*] or F3x.3 [*ICD-10-CM*]
- 296.x5 In partial remission [*ICD-9-CM*] or F3x.4 [*ICD-10-CM*]
- 296.x6 In full remission [*ICD-9-CM*] or F3x.5 [*ICD-10-CM*]
- 296.x0 Unspecified [*ICD-9-CM*] or F3x.9 [*ICD-10-CM*]

The other specifiers for major depressive disorder—with anxious distress, mixed features, melancholic features, atypical features, with mood congruent or mood incongruent psychotic features, with catatonia (see Chapter 5), with peripartum onset, and with seasonal patterns—cannot be coded within the numbering system. They are to be written out and listed after the official diagnosis and are linked directly to the current episode.

In summary, in completing a diagnostic assessment for an individual suffering from a major depressive disorder, what the disorder actually is needs to be clear. Normal life situations and developmental phases can create feelings of sadness or depressed moods in everyone. A depressed mood becomes pathological only when the magnitude or duration of the experience exceeds normal limits, taking into account the precipitating event. Making the diagnosis relies on examining the nine potential symptoms outlined in criterion A and how they affect the individual's level of functioning. Remember that it is not uncommon for individuals experiencing these symptoms to consider suicide and experience recurrent thoughts of death (morbid ideation) or suicidal ideation, plans, or attempts.

Persistent Depressive Disorder (Dysthymia)

Persistent depressive disorder (dysthymia) is a milder yet chronic form of the disorder that was termed *dysthymia* in *DSM-IV-TR*. In this new edition of the *DSM*, this diagnosis now includes some of the criteria related to dysthymia and some related to major depressive disorder, chronic type from the *DSM-IV-TR*. According to the APA (2013), *DSM-5* criteria for this revised disorder now require a 2-year history of depressed mood, during which the individual suffering from the disorder is not without the symptoms for more than 2 months at a time. The disorder is considered less severe than major depressive disorder but is constant for a period of 2 years, when the individual experiences some symptoms related to the disorder almost every day (criterion A). In this disorder, different criteria for children continue; the 2-year criterion does not apply as long as 1 year for children or adolescents is documented. For the most part, persistent depressive disorder, consistent with its new name, is a depressive mood disorder characterized by a long and chronic course.

For this disorder, criterion B identifies six potential symptoms, at least two of which should be documented during the course of the illness. The first symptom is poor appetite or overeating, and the second is insomnia or hypersomnia. Similar to the nine criteria listed in major depressive disorder, this disorder overlaps some of the same criteria, and these two are perfect examples. Regarding appetite changes for this disorder, the criterion is not nearly as specific as it is for major depressive disorder, nor does the individual have to be influenced by it multiple times daily. Also, although appetite and weight loss or gain may occur, the time frames are not nearly as pronounced. This may be related to the long, chronic nature of the disorder; regardless, eating and appetite changes over the last 2 years should be noted. Therefore, if counting this criterion for the diagnosis in symptom monitoring, information regarding verification of the changes is needed; getting a specific history or asking the client to maintain a food diary is appropriate. The same questions asked for those suffering from major depressive disorder may be of assistance here: Has the client gained or lost weight recently (focusing on the last month)? If so, how much weight has been lost or gained? Since this is over a 2-year period, variations in eating patterns should be noted, as well as the starting and current weight. Once again, the answers to these questions help the practitioner determine if the client is suffering from anorexia (eating less) or hyperphagia (overeating) to cope with the depressive feelings.

The second symptom is disturbed sleep, including insomnia and hypersomnia. Since the body often cannot compensate for disturbed sleep with more sleep at a later time, the chronic nature of this disorder makes sleep quality an important symptom to assess. Disturbed sleep patterns that continue with little relief over a long period can clearly affect the mental health of the individual and the depressive symptoms experienced. In insomnia, the sleep patterns are disturbed, and clients report trouble falling asleep or having uninterrupted sleep. In hypersomnia, the individual experiences excessive sleepiness that often occurs during what would be considered awake hours. It is especially problematic when it happens in dangerous situations, such as while driving a car. Whether insomnia or hypersomnia, sleep difficulties should be clearly documented, along with how they are affecting the individual's functioning.

The other four symptoms for criterion A are low energy or fatigue, low self-esteem, poor concentration and difficulty making decisions, and feelings of hopelessness. When present, these symptoms can affect the individual's ability to complete basic tasks and lead to basic interpersonal as well as social and occupational problems. When there is a lack of self-esteem, the evaluation of one's own worth becomes a constant source of internal debate. To meet criterion C, the pattern must be consistent and not exceed more than 2 symptom-free months. Also, the client needs to be assessed for other disorders that might confuse the symptoms and complicate the diagnosis. For example, in criteria D, E, and F, how long the individual has had the disorder is assessed to rule out major depressive disorder with its overlapping symptoms, and a history is needed of manic, hypomanic, or cyclothymic disorder or schizophrenia spectrum and other psychotic disorders. The time frame for this disorder is essential in differentiating it from any other depressive disorders, as it must interfere with functioning most of the day, on more days than not, for at least 2 years. Also, this disorder's depressive symptoms cannot be due to a medical condition, medication, illegal drug, or psychotic disorder. Accompanying symptoms include disturbances in appetite (lack of appetite or overeating) and sleep (insomnia or hypersomnia), low energy or fatigue, low self-esteem, poor concentration, difficulty in making decisions, and feelings of hopelessness.

In documenting the diagnosis, the following course specifiers may be of help: with anxious distress, with mixed features, with melancholic features, with atypical features, with mood congruent or incongruent psychotic features. It can also be specified as in remission or partial remission and whether onset is early or late. The types of episodes that occurred over the last 2 years based on the most recent one can be coded as with pure dysthymic syndrome, with persistent major depressive episode, with intermittent major depressive episodes, establishing whether it is with current or without the current episode. For more information on how to code these and more comprehensive explanations, see the source of this information, the *DSM-5* (APA, 2013). As in the other disorders, current severity can be specified as mild, moderate, or severe and follows a similar definition to the severity specifiers for the other disorders in this chapter.

Although the symptoms of persistent depressive disorder (dysthymia) have traditionally been considered less severe than major depressive disorder, it can still have grave consequences, including severe functional impairment and increased morbidity from physical disease. The same concerns with major depressive disorder are also noted with dysthymic disorder in terms of an increased risk of suicide.

Persistent depressive disorder can also occur in children. The mood children display, however, usually differs from that of adults. In children suffering from dysthymic disorder, the mood is often irritable and may appear to be an angry depression. Children and adolescents usually exhibit the symptoms differently from the majority of adults with this disorder. The agitated or angry form of depression often seen in children and adolescents coincides with their own feeling of pessimism, low self-esteem, and poor social skills. It is important to distinguish this disorder from DMDD, which displays a constant agitated depression with verbal or physical aggression. The case example in this chapter for DMDD may help the reader differentiate this disorder from chronic depressive disorder.

In assessing for persistent depressive disorder (dysthymia), careful consideration is needed to differentiate the presence of risk factors. Several risk factors associated with this disorder follow:

Temporal: In the temporal domain and how an individual relates to his or her life situation, similar to the major depressive disorder, there is a tendency toward neuroticism (negative affectivity), which becomes a strong risk factor for developing poorer global functioning and developing anxiety-related disorders as well as conduct disorder.

Environmental: Childhood experiences involving parental loss or separation put the individual at higher risk for the disorder.

Genetic and Physiological: The increased risk is higher for the development of the depressive disorders in general, and this one in particular, when a first-degree relative has it.

In summary, the easiest way to think of persistent depressive disorder (dysthymia) is to remember that it is chronic, requires gathering information for a 2-year history (1 year for children or adolescents), where symptom-free periods cannot last longer than 2 months. In the adult, occupational and social functioning are impaired, but in children and adolescents, the primary indicator is impaired school performance and poor social interaction (APA, 2013). Also, if in the first 2 years of this disorder, the depressive symptoms intensify and meet the full criteria for the major depressive episode, the diagnosis is changed to major depressive disorder if the additional criteria and time frames are met. In reviewing the criteria for this disorder, it is easy to see how the changes in *DSM-5* highlight the importance of recognizing how chronicity can affect treatment outcomes. The new name in *DSM-5*, persistent depressive disorder (dysthymia), includes both dysthymic disorder and chronic major depressive disorder (Moran, 2013).

Premenstrual Dysphoric Disorder

Premenstrual dysphoric disorder (PMDD) is a condition in women who have severe depressive symptoms, irritability, and tension before menstruation. This diagnosis is new to *DSM-5;* in *DSM-IV-TR,* it was listed as an area for further study. According to the *DSM-5* (APA, 2013), at least 5 of the 11 symptoms must be present for the disorder to be diagnosed, and these symptoms must occur in the final week before the onset of menses (criteria A and B). In criterion B, the 11 symptoms are divided into two groups. The first group has four criteria, and the second group has seven possible symptoms. Of the five symptoms required for the diagnosis, the female needs to have at least one symptom from both groups. The first four symptoms include documentation of marked affective lability, irritability, depressed mood, and anxiety and tension. The second group of symptoms (criterion C) has depressive symptoms such as decreased interest in usual activities, difficulty concentrating, a lack of energy, changes in appetite, sleep problems, and a sense of being out of control. There may also be physical symptoms, such as breast tenderness, joint or muscle pain, and feeling bloated. The symptoms should be confirmed in at least two previous cycles and cause significant impairment (criteria D and F). For the most part, when displaying these symptoms, the client's responses are severe, and she has extreme reactions and what could be considered mood swings, where the emotion experienced does not correspond to the triggering event. The symptoms should not be attributable to another mental disorder, a medical disorder such as hyperthyroidism, or related to the effects of a substance, drug of abuse, or medication (criteria E and G). As a new disorder in *DSM-5,* it will be interesting to see whether future research continues to support it.

Substance/Medication-Induced Depressive Disorder

When suffering from substance/medication-induced depressive disorder, the individual is expected to experience either depressed mood or markedly diminished interest or pleasure in daily activities that used to be at least somewhat pleasurable before (criterion A). In addition, an adequate history of what substance/medication was taken is needed. In criterion B, this substance/medication taken is to be confirmed by history, physical exam, or lab result. The individual needs to experience the symptoms soon after ingestion or with resultant intoxication or withdrawal from the substance. Once the information is gathered, especially by history or physical exam, it needs to be confirmed that the substance taken is capable of displaying the side effects that resulted. Similar to other diagnoses in this area, it is important to determine that the disorder is not related to another mental health condition such as delirium and that the symptoms are indicative of the substance ingested and not something else (criteria C and D). In addition, as with any diagnosis, the disturbance has to be severe enough to interfere with social, occupational, or other important areas of functioning, resulting in impairment or distress. *DSM-5* outlines specific time frames that should be followed.

In addition, this disorder requires specification of the onset and whether it is during intoxication or during withdrawal. The same symptom severity rating scale recommended for measurement in the other disorders in this chapter is also listed for this one. Also, what constitutes a substance use disorder should be known.

Depressive Disorder Due to Another Medical Condition

Like the criteria for substance/medication-induced disorders, the individual is expected to suffer from a persistent period of depressed mood, accompanied by diminished interest and pleasure in activities that once were pleasurable (criterion A). In addition, there needs to be direct evidence by history, physical exam, or lab result that makes the connection to the medical condition causing it. For any medical condition, the nonmedically trained practitioner needs to work collaboratively and consult with a medically trained practitioner skilled in identifying and addressing the medical condition that is causing the symptoms. Once the information is gathered, especially by history or physical exam, it needs to be confirmed that the medical condition is the cause, that it is not based on a mental health disorder, and that it is not occurring during the course of delirium (criteria C and D). As with any diagnosis, the disturbance has to be severe enough to interfere with social, occupational, or other important areas of functioning, resulting in impairment or distress. The *DSM-5* requires that the name of the medical disorder is documented and that the medical disorder is listed before this particular mental health disorder or any other mental health disorders. This disorder does require determining the relevant specifiers and whether there are clear depressive features, a major depressive-like episode, or mixed features.

Other Specified Depressive Disorder or Unspecified Depressive Disorder

Either of these diagnoses requires that the symptoms characteristic of the disorders are denoted. In the specified or the unspecified depressive disorder, the symptoms characteristic of a depressive disorder are required, and they must cause clinically significant distress in social or occupational functioning. There are three examples given in the *DSM-5* that can make this category warranted. The first is termed *recurrent brief depression,* where along with other criteria, the main difference to be noted is the time frame. This time frame differs from major depressive disorder in that the individual is experiencing at least four symptoms of the disorder for 2 to 13 days as opposed to the 14 days required for the major depressive episode. The *short-duration depressive episode* is from 4 to 13 days as opposed to the 14 days required, and in the last specifier, *depressive episode with insufficient symptoms*, the 14-day period is met, but only one of the eight symptoms of a major depressive episode is present.

Generally, in these disorders there may also be contradictory information or disorders with depressive symptoms that do not fully meet the criteria for any specific disorder. Professionals choose to place these diagnoses when there is inadequate information to fully assign a diagnosis. The primary difference between the specified and the unspecified disorder is that in the specified disorder, the practitioner documents the reason that it does not meet the criteria. Therefore, the unspecified disorder is often used in a crisis situation or emergency room setting or simply if the practitioner does not see the immediate benefit of listing the reason that a formal diagnosis is not to be placed.

THE DEPRESSIVE DISORDERS AND THE DIAGNOSTIC ASSESSMENT

The clinical picture for depression can be complicated because of the subjectivity that is possible in reporting depressive symptoms. Therefore, a clear, succinct diagnosis of unipolar disorder can be challenging. When the reported symptoms are clear and depressed mood is the only sign noted, the diagnosis of a depressive disorder seems most appropriate.

Careful attention should be given to properly assessing any recurrent thoughts of death or suicide. One rule to remember is that an individual is most likely to harm himself or herself not while in the throes of a depressive episode but rather when the feelings of depression begin to lift. The return of energy gives the client the initiative to act on thoughts and feelings expressed. If there is suicidal ideation, watching for the return of energy is critical because now the client may have the energy to act with intent. Like almost all the other mental health diagnoses, the unipolar disorders cannot be attributed to a medical condition, substance use disorder, another mood or mental disorder. The following case example will examine the new depressive diagnosis, DMDD, more closely.

Completion of the Diagnostic Assessment: Joey

In interviewing Joey, examining the criteria presented is important for a comprehensive diagnostic assessment. To start the process and the appropriateness of placing DMDD as the principal diagnosis and reason for visit, the criteria were studied closely. Joey appears to meet the core criteria for the disorder, which is irritability that is persistent, severe, and continuous rather than cyclic. To formalize the diagnostic impression, however, all criteria need to be examined. In criterion A, taking into account Joey's age of 12, the behaviors he is exhibiting appear outside the range of what would be expected with the

CASE EXAMPLE - CASE OF JOEY

Joey, a 12-year-old overweight male, arrived at the clinic with his head down. Although kicking the desk leg repeatedly, he refused to look up for the first 10 minutes of the session. His mother was outside, eagerly waiting for him to be seen. Prior to meeting with Joey, she told the social worker that she was really worried about him and that is why she brought him in. She complained of his constant angry outbursts and said she and Joey's 14-year-old sister could not handle him anymore. Since her divorce from his father became final approximately a year ago, Joey had become increasingly difficult to manage. Joey's mother said he was never an easy child and was always negative about things, but the divorce seemed to worsen his negativity. Joey's father did visit but said he did not want to stay long because he did not know how to deal with Joey's temper tantrums. She stated his teachers were also complaining of his temper tantrums in the classroom. He has not been doing well in school, and his grades are continuing to decline. In addition, Joey's mother said she recently got a phone call from his only friend's mother, stating that Joey was no longer welcome in their home. Apparently the two boys got into an argument about a video game, and Joey ripped it from the player, threw it on the ground, and stomped on it till it broke into pieces. His friend's mother said she did not want that kind of behavior around her own children.

At the beginning of the interview, Joey would not speak. After a minute of silence, the practitioner explained that looking at a person who was speaking was a way of showing courtesy and that he was listening. Joey eventually lifted his head, stopped kicking the desk, and began to talk. Joey explained that he really did not want to be around people, as he did not understand them and would get so frustrated. He said it may not look like he is listening, but he hears every word; he just does not want to respond. Joey reported that people constantly picked on him. He did not want to be angry, but he just would get so frustrated with them and the demands they put on him. When asked what demands he was referring to, he said in a defiant tone to mimic the person talking, "Turn off the radio, turn off the game, do your homework, sit in your chair" and looked at me and said, "Stop kicking my desk." When he was reminded that he had not been asked to stop kicking the desk, he said quickly, "You were thinking it. I just beat you to the punch."

He stated that he has no friends, hates his family, and always feels so sad and empty, and that makes him even angrier. When he discussed his anger, he said it was constant, and the only time he did not feel it for a period of time was when he met his best friend. He described their friendship as good until they got in a fight over the video game. His friend told him he could not play it, as he had to go home because his mother said his dinner was ready.

When he gets angry, sometimes he eats. Since his appetite has increased, he has gained weight, sleeps excessively, feels tired most of the time, and wants to avoid people as much as possible. Joey reports that he has difficulty concentrating, is often bored, and has little interest in school or friends. Although Joey does not admit directly to suicidal thoughts, he states openly he does not like himself or others and many times wishes he were dead. His mother and his sister confirm Joey's self-statements. Fifteen minutes into the session, Joey excused himself for a drink of water and took a bathroom break for 10 minutes. When interviewing his mother, she explained that since the divorce about a year ago, he has become harder to control, and each week he has several tantrums over the "silliest of things." She said that one outburst just yesterday was related to a breakfast waffle. He was so angry that it burned in the toaster that he ripped the cord out of the wall, and when she tried to discipline him, he threw the waffle on the floor and stomped it with his foot. She also explained that in the past year he has been cruel to his older sister, and she is not helping matters; when he gets upset she calls him a psycho, and then his anger escalates even further. His mother stated that during the past year his angry outbursts have been increasing, and she knows he is depressed but he will not admit it. When she tries to talk with him, he just gets angry. She says, "He is just angry all the time." She worries about his irritability, depression, disruptive behaviors, and temper tantrums, and his behavior scares her. His behavior is unexpected and reckless. To support this statement, she described several incidents. The first occurred when she told her son she could not take him to the park because she had to go to the store to get groceries. He was so angry he jumped on the back of her vehicle as she was pulling out of the driveway. Another incident occurred when he was caught walking on the ledge of their house outside his window two stories high. When questioned, she said he replied with "I just needed some fresh air." She explained that at times she feels he is going to be okay and seems to be enjoying a task; however, irritability surfaces quickly when what he wants is refused or things do not go his way. Some days she says he can sleep all day, and others he states he cannot sleep at all. Over the last 2 years, his mother reported multiple episodes of his being unable to complete tasks because he was easily distracted. When asked to do something and he was completing a task he had selected, he would refuse to stop what he was doing and get angry at the interruption. His mother reports that over the past year he started taking her cell phone without permission. With the phone, he would call total strangers, which has resulted in using up her minutes and getting some angry return calls. She says that there have been so many incidents where he has temper outbursts when things do not go his way, she could write a book.

Six months ago, his behaviors resulted in arrest on simple assault for chasing his mother and sister around the house with a fork. His family members have lost patience with his habitual moaning and complaining, as well as his angry outbursts related to events that other family members consider trivial matters. His sister and mother say he will argue, make verbal threats, and show rage for hours over simple things like not getting a glass of milk, a sandwich, or a television program when he wants it. Two weeks ago, he got on a city bus with his sister, put on headphones, and listened to music at top volume, but when he was asked to turn his music down, he became irritable, nasty, and cruel to the passengers. This resulted in another arrest, where he was placed in an inpatient mental health facility for several days. Joey's mother said she will now involve the police in transporting her son to a hospital or residential treatment when there is a physical threat or he becomes irrational. It is obvious his

CASE EXAMPLE - CASE OF JOEY (CONTINUED)

mother is very frustrated and would prefer not to take him home with her unless we can help him control his behaviors. She would prefer that he not take medication for the outbursts, and Joey agrees. Both state that the last time he took an antidepressant, his symptoms appeared worse. They did not know the name of the medicine because he only took it for a short time.

---

precipitating event. For example, what happened with the waffle when he did not get his way was one example. In the short time in the interview, it became clear that Joey was prone to verbal outbursts and rage. He would also destroy property, as evidenced by his behavior at his friend's house when he smashed the video game. The behaviors he is exhibiting are not developmentally appropriate responses for his age. In criterion C, the temper outbursts must be continuing and occur at least three times over a 7-day period. From talking to his mother and watching Joey in the session, this appeared highly possible, although his mother did not say exactly how many outbursts Joey had in the past week. She estimated at least four significant incidents of problematic behavior over the past 2 weeks but did confirm that even when he was not "throwing a tantrum," he was still "snippy and irritable" to all in the family. His mother said she was so tired of his complaining that she just wanted to give him a "happy pill" so she could have a break. His angry, irritable mood was noted by teachers and the parents of his friend. His behavior at the friend's house was so problematic that he is not welcome back. In terms of the time frame, he does appear to be exhibiting this behavior for at least 1 year. Also, in looking back over that year, the agitated and angry depressive feeling seems continuous, with only one brief time of remission, which did not last very long, related to meeting his new friend. He has had problems at school and appears to have engaged in high-risk behaviors, such as walking on a window ledge. In terms of age of onset, according to his mother, the agitation and restlessness has gotten worse since he hit around age 9.

There does not appear to be any cyclic behavior that would rule out either hypomanic or manic episodes. Also, he does not have any other mental disorders. His mother shared that she had asked his teacher if he might have ADHD, and the teacher said, "He is always sarcastic to the other children in his class, and this is why he has so few friends. He does not have a problem with attention; he just gets too frustrated." Other related disorders were ruled out, such as autism spectrum disorder (ASD), posttraumatic stress disorder (PTSD), separation anxiety disorder, and persistent depressive disorder (previously referred to as dysthymic disorder). He does not appear to be using any substances.

Joey does have some traits that are consistent with oppositional defiant disorder, such as angry, irritable mood and argumentative and defiant behavior. In his case, however, the four symptoms required are not severe enough for a separate diagnosis, and regardless, according to *DSM-5,* when these two disorders coexist, the DMDD is to be used. In summary, although it is rare for there to be one diagnosis alone, Joey appears to meet the criteria for DMDD. This is listed as both his principal diagnosis and the reason for visit. He does not have any other mental disorders noted.

Disruptive Mood Dysregulation Disorder
296.99 (F34.8)
(Reason for visit)

During these periods of mood disturbance, he has shown these symptoms:

- Inflated self-esteem as evidenced by his demanding others to do things for him and his inability to express or understand shame/guilt. He often experiences irritability, and if triggered, verbal or physical outbursts can surface rapidly when his wishes and desires go unfulfilled, and he can become volatile.
- Periods where he has a decreased need for sleep, difficulty falling asleep, and at other times sleeps for long periods.
- Easily distracted and frequently leaves those who are around him to tend to unimportant or irrelevant external stimuli. Goal-directed activities can become difficult.
- Increase in goal-directed activities at home/school as evidenced by extensive computer use and playing video games.

Overall, these problematic behaviors are severe enough to cause marked impairment in usual social activities and relationships at home and school. For example, Joey has been arrested for crimes such as assault and battery and disturbing the peace. He displays impaired social interaction related to narcissistic behavior, evidenced by inability to develop satisfying relationships.

Other Conditions That May Be a Focus of Clinical Attention

With the elimination of the multiaxial diagnosis often used in *DSM-IV* and *DSM-IV-TR,* the information previously provided on Axis IV and Axis V is no longer a requirement. Therefore, it is essential that in addition to the principal and the provisional diagnosis, the types of information previously listed there still be included. For practitioners interested in including this information from Section II of the *DSM-5,* Chapters 21 and 22 may be of particular help. Chapter 21 has the medication induced movement disorders and other adverse effects of medication, and Chapter 22 has the other conditions that may be a focus of clinical intervention. In the case of Joey, the information in Chapter 22 may be of the most help. In this chapter, there are several supportive factors that need to be taken into account that can support the diagnostic assessment. The first are the biopsychosocial stressors (especially those related to the family situation and key relationships).

In this case, most of the concerns focus around Joey's temper outbursts and his verbal and at times unpredictable physical responses. His mother is concerned about his returning home, based on his unpredictable behavior. Family relations and discipline patterns are extremely strained. The revised conditions updated in *DSM-5* do not appear comprehensive enough to describe Joey's particular situation and how it can affect his diagnosis. Therefore, this supplemental information is provided, and the code that closest represents his family situation is:

V61-20 (Z62.820) Parent–Child Relational Problem

In addition, Joey is exhibiting problems in school due to poor grades and nonattendance in class. He has failed several important exams and has not met academic markers. The closest of the other conditions that may be a focus of clinical attention that can be coded here is:

V62.3 (Z55.9) Academic or Educational Problem

The last area for supportive attention involves his problems related to crime and the legal system. He has been arrested twice, and his lack of insight into his behavior makes more trouble likely. This will need to be addressed in the treatment planning process, as his impulsive, irresponsible acts could continue to have serious implications within the legal system.

V62.5 (Z65.3) Problems Related to Other Legal Circumstances

Treatment Planning and Documentation: Joey

A treatment plan that highlights the goals and objectives that Joey can achieve needs to be formulated. With the information gathered during the diagnostic assessment as the basis for treatment, the treatment planning addresses the steps needed for the intervention to follow. In the diagnostic assessment, information given by the client and his or her family is supplemented with other resources to confirm history and check out all possible contradictory information and comorbid conditions. Joey will also undergo a complete physical examination, complete blood count and general chemistry screening, a thyroid function test, and if substance abuse was suspected, a test of urine toxicology. In addition, referral for a blood test should be considered to detect use or abuse of drugs or hormonal problems. The client is not taking any medications, but a consult with a medically trained professional may be helpful to explore any medications that can help the agitated depression he is experiencing.

Problem behaviors must be clearly identified in terms of the intervention efforts. A clinical interview is often an adequate method to assess the treatment needs, but rapid assessment instruments may assist the therapist in arriving at a more careful and comprehensive assessment and treatment plan. The Mood Disorder Questionnaire developed by Hirschfeld et al. (2000) offers an overall assessment of the client's symptoms and functioning. The Semantic Differential and Mood Scales (SDFMS) developed by Lorr and Wunderlich (1988) permit a therapist to measure changes on various dimensions of symptoms relevant to depression and mania. The Mood Related Pleasant Events Schedule (MRPES) developed by MacPhillamy and Lewinsohn (1982) can be used to measure changes in the client's perception of life events and provide the clinician with quantifiable data in making modifications to treatment plans. The Family Sense of Coherence (FSOC) and Family Adaption Scales (FAS) used together and designed by Antonovsky and Sourani (1988) can be used to evaluate the family's sense of coherence and adaption, helping the therapist better understand family dynamics and functioning. In addition, the Depression Impairment Scale for Parents (DISP) may be helpful in measuring the impact of Joey's depression on their own mental health (Lewis et al., 2013). See Sample Treatment Plan 7.1.

Transition Care, Treatment Planning, and Practice Strategy

Individuals with depression have internal working models that include cognitive schemata about themselves and the world around them (McBride, Atkinson, Quilty, & Bagby, 2006). The theoretical rationale of using cognitive-behavioral therapy rests on how individuals cognitively structure their view of the world and how their unique patterns of thinking influence their affect and behavior (Hamamci, 2006). In comparing medication with cognitive-behavioral therapy, at 8 weeks patients taking medication had response rates of 50% compared with 43% of individuals who received cognitive-behavioral therapy alone (DeRubeis et al., 2005).

Antidepressant medications also can be used to treat related conditions, such as obsessive-compulsive disorder and symptoms of anxiety, while blocking the symptoms of panic and

SAMPLE TREATMENT PLAN 7.1

Disruptive Mood Dysregulation Disorder (DMDD)

DMDD has 11 specific criteria (ranging from A to K) that must be met. The core feature is irritability that is persistent for at least a year and maintains a severe and continuous course that is not related to a developmental phase. The behaviors are not consistent with the precipitating event and involve either verbal or behavioral manifestations toward people or property. Temper outbursts must be continuous, occurring at least three times over a 7-day period. Other criteria are documented in this text.

Signs and Symptoms to Note in the Record

- Agitated depression, sleep difficulty, distractibility, verbal outbursts (rage)
- Physical outbursts (destruction to people or property), psychomotor agitation
- Impulsivity

Goals

1. Reduce uncontrollable angry outbursts, return to a normal activity level, and increase good judgment.
2. Reduce agitation and impulsive behaviors, and increase sensitivity to consequences of behaviors.
3. Cope with underlying feelings of low self-esteem and fears of rejection or abandonment.
4. Increase controlled behavior, achieve a more stable mood, and develop more deliberate speech and thought processes.
5. Address feelings of angry depression and develop alternative ways of coping.

Objectives	Interventions
1. Cooperate with a psychiatric evaluation and participate in treatment as warranted.	Arrange for a psychiatric evaluation to assist with angry behaviors. Discuss the potential for medication to assist with the depression. Request a no-harm, no-risk safety plan be put in place.
2. Reduce impulsive behaviors.	Behavioral rehearsal and cognitive behavioral strategy to recognize triggers and consequences of behaviors.
3. Express self and desires more realistically.	Help client problem-solve using behavioral rehearsal and individual supportive therapy (psychotherapy), to reinforce more realistic self-statements.
4. Be able to sit calmly for 30 minutes without agitation or distractibility.	Reinforce client's increased control over his energy, and help the client set attainable goals and limits on his agitation and distractibility.
5. Speak more slowly and maintain focus on one subject at a time.	Provide structure for the client's thought processes and actions by directing the course of the conversation and developing plans for the client's behaviors.
6. Identify and process feelings related to angry outbursts and thoughts related to underlying depression.	In supportive therapy, help the client identify two reasons for his angry outbursts, and problem-solve other ways to address his frustrations.

assisting with medical complications, such as rapid heartbeat, terror, dizziness, chest pains, nausea, and breathing problems. Studies seem to support that cognitive therapy with a highly trained therapist can be very effective over using just medications in moderately and mildly depressed individuals (Seligman & Reichenberg, 2007). Cognitive-behavioral therapy focuses on the interaction of the individual's thoughts, emotions, and behaviors (Rude & Bates, 2005). The primary principles of cognitive therapy are teaching clients how to identify their dysfunctional thoughts and beliefs and how they contribute to their depression (Vidair & Gunlicks-Stoessel, 2009).

Seligman and Reichenberg (2007) reported that individual psychotherapy alone is appropriate for mild to moderate uncomplicated forms of depression, and the more severe forms do better utilizing a combination approach of both medication and psychotherapy. Some professionals fear, however, that use of these newer antidepressants will become too familiar, and more change-related behaviors, such as those related to exercise, sleep, and diet, will take second place.

Several types of counseling are frequently considered for working with individuals who suffer from depressive disorders. The following options are suggested for guiding the counseling process.

1. Learn to adequately diagnose the depressive disorder, the time frame, and the actual behaviors that result.
2. Help to educate the client and his or her family about the disorder and the behaviors that can result.
3. Have the client and his or her family participate in the selection of the treatment and the treatment process as much as possible.
4. Regardless of the type of therapy used. it will involve recognizing and treating the specific behaviors while also working on maintenance of the treatment goals and formulating a discharge plan.
5. Always have the client identify problem behaviors and help problem-solve and formulate goals whenever possible.
6. Pharmacological treatment may assist with the depressive mood and the resultant behaviors. Educate clients and family members on questions to ask the medically trained professionals and reasonable expectations for the use of medications. Work collaboratively with a medically trained practitioner to help the client make decisions regarding the use of medications.
7. Use psychoeducational applied problem-solving whenever possible to address problem behaviors.
8. Cognitive-behavioral therapy can help clients understand aspects of the disorder as well as restructure problematic thoughts.

When working with Joey, the following treatment modalities are suggested: peer support group therapy, family therapy, and family support group therapy. (See Quick Reference 7.2.)

Medication as a Treatment Modality

When depression is severe and exercise, sleep adjustments, and diet do not seem to be working, treatment guidelines suggest drug therapy is a possibility. Prior to resorting to medication, however, a complete assessment of factors related to levels of exercise and considerations for achieving restful sleep and controlling diet are always suggested (Dziegielewski, 2010). Once the assessment is complete, medication management is one of the primary treatments for the depressive disorders, and the person who responds best to medication for the treatment of depression is someone who suffers from more than just the blues. A prolonged depressed mood

QUICK REFERENCE 7.2

Counseling Strategies for Joey

Cognitive Therapy

- Help Joey identify cognitive distortions that support the development and maintenance of problematic thoughts and behaviors. Examine unrealistic cognitive distortions related to his agitated depressive outbursts.
- Discuss negative distortions related to expectations of the environment, self, and future that contribute to depression.
- Examine Joey's perceptions of the environment and activities that are seen as unsatisfying or unrealistic.
- Identify dysfunctional patterns of thinking and behaving, and guide Joey to evidence and logic that can test the validity of the dysfunctional thinking.
- Assist in understanding automatic thoughts that occur spontaneously and contribute to the distorted affect (e.g., personalizing, all or nothing, mind reading, discounting negatives), looking specifically at situations, thoughts, and consequences. If this technique is not helpful or does not work for Joey, help him understand and explore other possibilities.
- Help Joey use "I" statements in identifying feelings and reactions.

Peer Support Group Therapy

- Provides clients with a feeling of security when discussing troublesome or embarrassing issues. Also, this group will help Joey in discussing medication-related issues and serve as an avenue for promoting education related to his outbursts and unpredictable behaviors.
- This group will help Joey gain a sense of perspective on his condition and tangibly encourage him to link up with others who have common problems. A sense of hope is conveyed when an individual is able to see that he is not alone or unique in experiencing affective illness.

Family Therapy for Depression

- Work with Joey's family system (mother and sister) to formulate a therapeutic plan to resolve symptoms and restore or create adaptive family function.
- Build an alliance with Joey and the family members, establishing a positive working relationship between the client and his family.
- Combine psychotherapeutic and pharmocotherapeutic treatment education. Discuss realistic expectations of the medications and how they can help in treatment.
- Obtain each family member's view of the situation and specify problems seeking understanding and shared meaning of events among the members. Encourage a nonblaming and accepting therapeutic atmosphere for the client and the family. Assure the family members that they did not cause the condition. Allow family members to ventilate about the chronic burden they have experienced. Help Joey's sister deal with Joey's behaviors, and examine how she may be contributing in some ways to his behavioral outbursts.

(continued)

QUICK REFERENCE 7.2 (*Continued*)

- Review ambient family stress. Examine any objective and subjective burdens the family is experiencing due to observable aspects of the illness and the need to provide caregiving. Look for criticism or emotional overinvolvement of family members in response to Joey's illness.
- Help to redefine the nature of the family's difficulties.
- Encourage recognition of each member's contribution to the discord.
- Recognize and modify communication patterns, rules, and interactional patterns.
- Increase reciprocity through mutual exchange of privileges.
- Decrease the use of coercion and blaming, and increase cooperative problem solving.
- Increase each member's ability to express feelings clearly and directly and to hear others accurately.

Family Support Group Therapy

- Provide an atmosphere for growth and change, and discuss importance of complying with the treatment strategy outlined.
- Provide family members with a feeling of security when discussing troublesome or embarrassing issues. Also, this group will help family members discuss medication-related issues and serve as an avenue for promoting education related to the identified mood disorder and its treatment.
- This group will help family members gain a sense of perspective on Joey's condition and tangibly encourage the family members to link up with others who have common problems. A sense of hope is conveyed when family members are able to see that they are not alone or unique in experiencing affective illness.

Source: Information summarized from Griswold and Pessar (2000).

that does not respond to short-term psychotherapy or crisis intervention and that interferes with a person's family life and mental, physical, job, and social functioning indicates the need for antidepressant medication (Shindul-Rothschild & Rothschild, 1998). Further, most medically trained professionals agree that practice guidelines indicate that when an individual fails to respond to two or more trials on an antidepressant as monotherapy (medications alone) or when clients fail to achieve full remission using medications alone, other types of treatment interventions are suggested (Valenstein et al., 2006).

When depression runs in families, particularly those whose mothers were depressed or when there is a first-generation family history of major depression, drug therapy is often recommended by the medical community (Goodman & Tully, 2006). Antidepressant medications have resulted in $12 billion in annual sales in the United States (Schatzberg, Cole, & Debattista, 2007). The consensus is that depression has been underdiagnosed and inadequately treated in the United States; fewer than 10% of people suffering from major depression are estimated to receive an appropriate therapeutic dose of medication (Capriotti, 2006). Before prescribing an antidepressant, the prescriber needs to take into account factors such as drug side effect profiles, the potential for toxicity or overdose, and other client characteristics, such as presentation of symptoms, other medical conditions, and general health and age (Schatzberg et al., 2007).

Schatzberg et al. (2007) suggest that 50% to 65% of patients are expected to respond to any given trial of an antidepressant. However, not all clients respond to medication. An estimated 29% to 46% of people with major depression fail to respond to antidepressants, and half of those who do not respond to the first antidepressant fail to respond to a second (Corya et al., 2006). Antidepressants work by attempting to normalize naturally occurring brain chemicals called neurotransmitters, specifically serotonin and norepinephrine. Other antidepressants work on the neurotransmitter dopamine (Cheung, Emslie, & Mayes, 2006).

Although classification systems can differ slightly, generally antidepressant drugs are classified into three major groups: (1) tricyclic antidepressants, (2) monoamine oxidase inhibitors, and (3) newer antidepressants such as serotonin-selective reuptake inhibitors (SSRIs) and similar drugs (Brophy, 1991; Tierney et al., 1997; Woo & Keatinge, 2008). The popularity of these medications, especially the newer generation antidepressants, has risen dramatically, which can be seen in recent sales figures and profits for pharmaceutical companies (IMS, 2009).

A multitude of studies have examined the efficacy of antidepressants (Debonnel et al., 2007; Kennedy, Anderson, & Lam, 2005; Segal, Vincent, & Levitt, 2002) and the efficacy of medications on severely depressed individuals (Versiani, Moreno, Ramakers-van Moorsel, & Schutte, 2005). Some studies focus on different age groups, such as the use of antidepressants by elderly persons (Sheikh et al., 2004) and children and adolescents (Cheung et al., 2006; Moreno, Arango, Parellada, Shaffer, & Bird, 2007). Serious concerns have been noted with the use of these medications (particularly the SSRIs) with children and adolescents. The concerns in this area were so severe that in 2004 the Food and Drug Administration instructed manufacturers to include black box warnings about the risks of suicidal thoughts and behaviors on all antidepressants for children and adolescents; in 2006 this warning was extended to include young adults (age 18–24). For more information on this topic, see Dziegielewski (2010) or Jureidini (2009). Additional studies examined the use of medications for depressive symptoms in PTSD (Smajkic et al., 2001) and suicidal patients (Simon & Savarino, 2007).

Utilizing psychopharmacological treatment for depression has three major purposes: (1) to treat an acute episode, (2) to prevent a relapse, and (3) to prevent future episodes (Gitlin, 1996). Depression is often marked by recurrence and chronicity. A general three-phase framework for understanding the treatment of depression is acute, continuation, and maintenance (Hirschfeld et al., 1997). A single client could move through all three phases of treatment under the care of one clinician or three different therapists. In the acute phase, the primary goal is to stabilize symptoms, which could include suicidal ideation, inability to sleep, or other severe symptoms that impair daily functioning. As a rule for practice, when suicidal thoughts are present, a complete assessment and safety plan are always needed and considered the first priority (Seligman & Reichenberg, 2007). At this point, medications such as the SSRIs are used (NIMH, 2009). (See Quick Reference 7.3.)

Once the client is stabilized, the goal in the continuation phase is to sustain the stabilization. At this point, psychotherapy is often combined with pharmacological treatment, and cognitive-behavioral therapy is often the treatment of choice (Rude & Bates, 2005; Vidair & Gunlicks-Stoessel, 2009). The maintenance phase is

QUICK REFERENCE 7.3

SELECTIVE SEROTONIN REUPTAKE INHIBITORS

Drug

fluoxetine (Prozac)

paroxetine hydrochloride (Paxil)

sertraline (Zoloft)

fluvoxamine (Luvox)

citalopram (Celexa)

focused on prevention. In maintenance, the goal is to prevent the client from experiencing another depressive episode (Hirschfeld et al., 1997). Therefore, maintenance treatment is synonymous with prevention.

When medication is used as a primary treatment modality in depression, social workers and other mental health practitioners often serve as part of an interdisciplinary team. Understanding the role of medications in treatment and what is realistic for clients to expect as the benefit is essential. The practitioner often spends the most quality time with clients, increasing the likelihood that he or she is one of the first team members to become aware of regimen problems, possible side effects, or medication reactions (Dziegielewski, 2010). Simple education concerning realistic expectations about what the medications can do to assist with depressed mood is essential. In youth, for example, many believe that if they do not feel good, something is wrong. This expectation allows them to avoid having to deal with uncomfortable feelings that may be a normal part of life experience (Jureidini, 2009). All nonmedically trained practitioners need to understand the antidepressant medications their clients are taking and assist them with realistic impressions of what a medication can or should do, as well as with compliance issues, pharmacy shopping, side effect profiles, and medication insurance coverage. In addition, they must provide education, information, and support (Dziegielewski, 2006, 2010).

SPECIAL TOPICS

Addressing Sexuality

Traditionally, mental health practitioners have used a biopsychosocial approach (Hepworth, Rooney, & Larsen, 2002) to understand the difficulties clients experience and to empower them to take charge of their lives and strive for new and improved levels of health and mental health satisfaction and functioning (Dziegielewski, 2013). When they treat clients with depression, they expand the biopsychosocial model to include assessment of sexuality and spirituality.

To assess the impact of depression on sexuality, careful accumulation of data that are likely to affect sexual response is needed. The factors include age, marital status, religious beliefs, intimate relationships, socioeconomic status, education level of both partners, nature of the marital relationship, functional ability of the male partner, levels of anxiety, type of anorgasmia (primary versus secondary), and gynecological, physiological, and medical conditions (Dziegielewski, Jacinto, Dick, & Resnick-Cortes, 2007). In assessing depression and sexual functioning, the level of sexual performance prior to the current onset of depression is noted to determine changes in arousal, desire, or performance. Distinguishing between loss of libido and a sexual disorder is important. In males, a loss of libido may be attributed to a decrease in testosterone, combined with depression, anxiety, low self-esteem, work-related stress, and relationship problems (Dziegielewski, Turnage, Dick, & Resnick-Cortes, 2007). These combined factors may interact in contributing to a sexual dysfunction; therefore, it is important to determine which came first.

ASSESSMENT OF DANGER TO SELF OR OTHERS

The immediate plan for the client suffering from depression who expresses suicidal ideation or intent is to assess whether there appears to be a danger to self or others. This should be done quickly. Asking direct questions about what appears to be occurring will start the process. As part of the assessment process, precautions should be outlined to protect the client from harm and stabilize dangerous symptoms. When the client has a concrete plan, hospitalization is usually recommended because it can ensure an environment where safety objectives can be met and where the client can continue therapeutic work. Being familiar and comfortable with assessing for danger to self or others is essential and often starts with asking direct questions: Have you ever thought about killing yourself? If so, what would you do? Does the individual have access to the means of harm or a concrete plan? If the client is feeling suicidal, is it possible he or she might try to kill or harm someone else? How would the client do it? What would stop him or her?

If hospitalization is required, allowing time to adjust medications in a supervised setting may contribute to continued medication compliance and management upon discharge to a less restrictive environment. The period of hospitalization can also serve as a time when clients and family members become educated about the nature of the illness and the treatment alternatives. Having family understanding and support can facilitate discharge.

Electroconvulsive Therapy for Depression

Electroconvulsive therapy (ECT) is a form of treatment for depression and other mental illnesses that involves the introduction of a series of brain seizures in the patient (Pandya, Pozuelo, & Malone, 2007; West, Prado, & Krystal, 1999). The fact that ECT has such an undeservedly bad reputation can deter its use as an effective treatment for a number of mental health disorders (Pandya et al., 2007). To date, there is no definitive explanation as to how or why ECT works. Yet there are numerous neurochemical, neuroendocrine, and neurophysiologic hypotheses (Willoughby, Hradek, & Richards, 1997). What is known is that it is not the electrical shock that causes the therapeutic effect but rather the resulting seizure, which is a rapid firing of neurons in the brain (Fischer, 2000).

No nationwide figures show the true frequency of ECT usage, but it is probable that ECT usage has increased during the past two decades because of its efficiency and the resulting shorter hospital stays (Willoughby et al., 1997). Fischer (2000) concluded that more than 100,000 patients receive ECT every year and that it is probably not used more because of the societal stigma. Many public and rural hospitals do not offer it as a treatment; some doctors are never taught or simply prefer not to use the procedure.

As a result, ECT may be considered a treatment of last resort.

It is not without its risks, and, similar to medications, side effects are possible. There are no absolute contraindications to using ECT; however, a complete medical workup is always indicated. "The cardiovascular, central nervous, and pulmonary systems carry the highest risk from general anesthesia and the induction of generalized seizure activity" (Pandya et al., 2007, p. 680). According to Willoughby et al. (1997), "Adverse effects of ECT may include apprehension or fear, headache, muscle soreness, nausea, cardiovascular dysfunction, prolonged apnea, prolonged seizures, and emergent mania" (p. 11). The most troubling of these effects is cognitive dysfunction, which many times entails memory loss for a period before and after the procedure. This memory loss frequently lasts several weeks but can extend up to 6 months. In some cases, the memory loss persists longer. Research has shown that the cognitive dysfunction caused by ECT does not adversely affect functions not associated with memory, such as intelligence and judgment, in any lasting way. According to Johnstone (1999) approximately 80% of patients report some side effects; memory impairment is the most frequent, with a range of responses including fear, humiliation, increased compliance, and feelings of failure, worthlessness, betrayal, lack of confidence, and degradation, as well as a sense of having been abused and assaulted.

According to Willoughby et al. (1997), despite all the controversy surrounding ECT, the APA has determined that ECT is an effective treatment option for people suffering from the depressive disorders as well as several of the bipolar disorders. It can also be used with affective disorders and psychotic depression, which is seldom responsive to medications. In addition, ECT can lead to significant improvement of patients with severe affective disorders. Reid, Keller, Leatherman, and Mason (1998) found that 90% of all patients they reviewed who had undergone ECT had been diagnosed with a severe mood disorder, and the remaining 10% had schizophrenia. With the research supporting the effectiveness of ECT, specifically bipolar disorder and depression, ECT can be viewed as an appropriate treatment option (Fischer, 2000).

Electroconvulsive therapy is effective with clients who are acutely suicidal and in the treatment of severe depression, particularly in those clients who are also experiencing psychotic symptoms and those with psychomotor retardation in sleep, appetite, and energy. It is often considered for treatment only after a trial of therapy with antidepressant medication has proved ineffective (Griswold & Pessar, 2000). Other neuromodulatory treatment techniques are also being explored. Pandya et al. (2007) report that the popularity of several other treatments used in this area is increasing, but these treatments are often not considered until after several unsuccessful trials with an antidepressant medication. Promising treatments on the horizon include vagus nerve stimulation (an implanted pacemaker-like device that stimulates the vagus nerve), deep brain stimulation (electrodes implanted in precise areas of the brain), and repetitive transcranial magnetic stimulation (uses an induction coil delivered in brief daily sessions). For a brief description and further information regarding the future of these treatments, see Pandya et al. (2007).

SUMMARY AND FUTURE DIRECTIONS

Dealing with any form of mental illness is a major challenge for clients, mental health practitioners, and family members. The depressive disorders present a unique challenge: Symptoms may not be addressed because they are confused with the depressive symptoms that are natural to life experiences. In addition, clients suffering from the depressive disorders can often present with coexisting psychiatric disorders that require concurrent attention. In addition, when first diagnosed in childhood such as in DMDD the child or adolescent may continue to be at risk for other mental health disorders related to mood, anxiety or substance (Wood, 2014). The assessment process in diagnosing the depressive disorders is an essential component of treatment. Assessing the client for critical problems such as suicidal ideation during a depressive episode may require addressing these problems first as a way of securing the client's safety. Assessment also includes the appropriate use of the criteria provided by the *DSM-5* and the possible inclusion of medication as the first priority in treatment strategy.

Regardless of the type of depressive disorder a client is suffering from, during assessment, remember the variability that can result in the client's behaviors and actions. Mental health practitioners need to be well versed in the signs and symptoms identified in the *DSM-5* and able to use this manual to facilitate the diagnostic assessment, treatment planning, and intervention that will follow. If a mental health practitioner suspects that any client, regardless of age, may suffer from depressive disorder, confirming this diagnosis using the *DSM-5* criteria (APA, 2013) is critical. In addition, every practitioner should assess for critical symptoms reflective of other mental health problems. Accurate measurements of problem behaviors and social problems provide fuel for the most comprehensive approaches to high-quality client care.

Mental health practitioners are in a unique position not only to provide services to those with depressive disorders but also to advocate for the ongoing needs of clients. Many families struggle with loved ones who suffer from the disorder. Family inclusion in support and intervention is central to providing comprehensive quality care. Finally, in the diagnostic assessment, suicidal ideation and possible intent make it imperative to teach those in the client's support system to be aware of suicidal verbalizations and to participate in safety plans ensuring protection for the client and the family member. Mental health practitioners spend a great deal of time with clients and since they understand the intricate nature of depressive disorders, they are well equipped to teach clients and their families about the disorder and help all involved to participate and accept intervention efforts.

REFERENCES

American Psychiatric Association. (2000). *Diagnostic and statistical manual of mental disorders* (4th ed., text rev.) Washington, DC: Author.

American Psychiatric Association. (2013). *Diagnostic and statistical manual of mental disorders* (5th ed.). Arlington, VA: American Psychiatric Publishing.

Antonovsky, A., & Sourani, T. (1988). Family sense of coherence and family adaption. *Journal of Marriage and Family, 50*(1), 79–92.

Barnhill, J. W. (2014). Depressive disorders: Introduction. In J. W. Barnhill (Ed.), *DSM-5™ clinical cases* (pp. 71–81). Washington, DC: American Psychiatric Publishing.

Bettmann, J. E. (2006). Using attachment theory to understand the treatment of adult depression. *Clinical Social Work Journal, 34*(4), 531–542.

Brophy, J. J. (1991). Psychiatric disorders. In S. A. Schroeder, M. A. Krupp, L. M. Tierney, & S. J. McPhee (Eds.), *Current medical diagnosis and treatment* (pp. 731–786). Norwalk, CT: Appleton & Lange.

Capriotti, T. (2006). Update on depression and antidepressant medications. *MEDSURG Nursing, 15*(4), 241–246.

Castro, L. S., Castro, J., Hoexter, M. Q., Quarantini, L. C., Kauati, A., Mello, L. E, . . . Bittencourt, L. (2013). Depressive symptoms and sleep: A population-based polysomnographic study. *Psychiatry Research, 210*(3), 906–912. doi: 10.1016/j.psychres.2013.08.036

Centers for Disease Control and Prevention. (2010). Current depression among adults–United States, 2006–2008. *Morbidity and Mortality Weekly Report, 59*(38), 1229–1235. Retrieved from http://www.cdc.gov/mmwr/preview/mmwrhtml/mm5938a2.htm?s_cid=mm5938a2_e%0d%0a

Cheung, A. H., Emslie, G. J., & Mayes, T. L. (2006). The use of antidepressant to treat depression in children and adolescents. *Canadian Medial Association Journal, 174*(2), 193–200. doi: 10.1503/cmaj.050855

Corya, S. A., Williamson, D., Sanger, T. M., Briggs, S. D., Case, M., & Tollefson, G. (2006). A randomized, double-blind comparison of olanzapine/fluoxetine combination, olanzapine, fluoxetine, and venlafaxine in treatment-resistant depression. *Depression and Anxiety, 23*(6), 364–372. doi: 10.1002/da.20130

Debonnel, G., Saint-Andre, E., Hebert, C., deMontigny, C., Lavoie, N., & Blier, P. (2007). Differential physiological effects of a low dose and high doses of venlafaxine in major depression. *International Journal of Neuropyschopharmacology, 10*, 51–61.

DeRubeis, R. J., Hollon, S. D., Amsterdam, J. D., Shelton, R. C., Young, P. R., Salomon, R. M., . . . Gallop, R. (2005). Cognitive therapy vs. medications in the treatment of moderate to severe depression. *Archives of General Psychiatry, 62*(4), 409–416. doi: 10.1001/archpsyc.62.4.409

Durbin, E. (2013). *Depression 101*. New York, NY: Springer.

Dziegielewski, S. F. (2006). *Psychopharmacology for the non-medically trained*. New York, NY: Norton.

Dziegielewski, S. F. (2010). *Psychopharmacology and social work practice: A person in environment approach* (2nd ed.). New York, NY: Springer.

Dziegielewski, S. F. (2013). *The changing face of health care social work: Opportunities and challenges for professional practice* (3rd ed.). New York, NY: Springer.

Dziegielewski, S. F., Jacinto, G., Dick, G., & Resnick-Cortes, C. (2007). Orgasmic disorders. In B. Thyer & J. Wodarski (Eds.), *Social work in mental health: An evidence-based approach* (pp. 427–456). Hoboken, NJ: Wiley.

Dziegielewski, S. F., Turnage, B. F., Dick, G., & Resnick-Cortes, C. (2007). Sexual desire and arousal disorders. In B. Thyer & J. Wodarski (Eds.), *Social work in mental health: An evidence-based approach* (pp. 403–426). Hoboken, NJ: Wiley.

Fischer, J. S. (2000). Taking the shock out of electroshock. *U.S. News & World Report, 128*(3), 46.

Friedman, R. A. (2012). Grief, depression, and the *DSM-5*. *New England Journal of Medicine, 366*(20), 1855–1857. doi: 10.1056/NEJMp1201794

Garcia, B., & Petrovich, A. (2011). *Strengthening the DSM: Incorporating resilience and cultural competence*. New York, NY: Springer.

Gitlin, M. J. (1996). *The psychotherapist guide to psychopharmacology* (2nd ed.). New York, NY: Free Press.

Gonzalez, H. M., Croghan, T. W., West, B. T., Tarraf, W., Williams, D. R., Nesse, R., . . . Jackson, J. S. (2008). Antidepressant use among Blacks and Whites in the United States. *Psychiatric Service, 59*(10), 1131–1138. doi: 10.1176/appi.ps.59.10.1131

Goodman, S. H., & Tully, E. (2006). Depression and women who are mothers: An integrative model of risk for the development of psychopathology in their sons and daughters. In C. L. M. Keys & S. H. Goodman (Eds.), *Women and depression: A handbook for the social, behavioral, and biomedical sciences* (pp. 241–280). New York, NY: Cambridge University Press.

Griswold, K. S., & Pessar, L. F. (2000). Management of bipolar disorder. *Family Physician, 62*(6), 1343–1353, 1357–1358.

Hamamci, Z. (2006). Integrating psychodrama and cognitive behavioral therapy to treat moderate depression. *Arts in Psychotherapy, 33*(3), 199–207.

Hansen, R. A., Gartlehner, G., Lohr, K. N., Gaynes, B. N., & Carey, T. S. (2005). Efficacy and safety of second-generation antidepressants in the treatment of major depressive disorder. *Annals of Internal Medicine, 143*(6), 415–426.

Hepworth, D. H., Rooney, R. H., & Larsen, J. (2002). *Direct social work practice: Theory and skills*. Pacific Grove, CA: Brooks/Cole.

Higgins, E. (1994). A review of unrecognized mental illness in primary care: Prevalence, natural history, and efforts to change the course. *Archives of Family Medicine, 3*, 899–907.

Hirschfeld, R. M. A., Keller, M. B., Panico, S., Arons, B. S., Barlow, D., Davidoff, F., . . . Wyatt, R. J. (1997). The National Depressive and Manic-Depressive Association consensus statement on the undertreatment of depression. *Journal of the American Medical Association, 277*(4), 333–340. doi: 10.1001/jama.1997.03540280071036

Hirschfeld, R. M. A., Williams, J. B. W., Spitzer, R. L., Calabrese, J. R., Flynn, L., Keck, P. E., . . . Zajecka, J. (2000). Development and validation of a screening instrument for bipolar spectrum disorder: The mood disorder questionnaire. *American Journal of Psychiatry, 157* (11), 1873–1875. doi: 10.1176/appi.ajp.157.11.1873

IMS. (2009). *IMS Health reports U.S. prescription sales grew 1.3% in 2008 to $291 billion*. Retrieved from http://www.imshealth.com/portal/site/imshealth/menuitem.a46c6d4df3db4b3d88f611019418c22a/?vgnextoid=078ce5b87da10210VgnVCM100000ed152ca2RCRD&vgnextfmt=default

Johnstone, L. (1999). Adverse psychological effects of ECT. *Journal of Mental Health, 8*(1), 69–85. doi: 10.1080/09638239917652

Jureidini, J. (2009). How do we safely treat depression in children, adolescents and young adults? *Drug Safety, 32*(4), 275–282. doi: 10.2165/00002018-200932040-00002

Keller, M. B., Hanks, D. L., & Klein, D. N. (1996). Summary of the mood disorders field trial and issue and overview. *Psychiatric Clinics of North America, 19*(1), 1–28.

Keller, M. B., Klein, D. N., Hirschfeld, R. M., Kocsis, J. H., McCullough, J. P., Miller, I., . . . Marin, D. M. (1995). Results of the *DSM-IV* mood disorders field trial. *American Journal of Psychiatry, 152*(6), 843–849.

Kennedy, S. H., Anderson, H. E., & Lam, R. W. (2005). Efficacy of escitalopram in the treatment of major depressive disorder compared with conventional selective serotonin reuptake inhibitors and venlafaxine XR: A meta-analysis. *Journal of Psychiatry and Neuroscience, 31*(2), 122–131.

Koukopoulos, A., Sani, G., & Gahaemi, S. N. (2013). Mixed features of depression: Why *DSM-5* is wrong (and so was *DSM-IV*) [Editorial]. *The British Journal of Psychiatry, 203*(1), 3–5. doi: 10.1192/bjp.bp.112.124404

Krupinski, J., & Tiller, J. W. G. (2001). The identification and treatment of depression by general practitioners. *Australian and New Zealand Journal of Psychiatry, 35*, 827–832.

Lewis, K., Elam, K., Sellers, R., Rhoades, K., Jones, R. B., Thapar, A., . . . Thapar, A. (2013). The depression impairment scale for parents (DISP): A new scale for the measurement of impairment in depressed parents. *Psychiatry Research, 210*(3), 1184–1190.

Liu, C. F., Campbell, D. G., Chaney, E. F., Li, Y. F., McDonnell, M., & Fihn, S. D. (2006). Depression diagnosis and antidepressant treatment among depressed VA primary care patients. *Administration Policy Mental Health & Mental Health Services Research, 33*, 331–341.

Locke, D. C., & Bailey, D. F. (2014). *Increasing multicultural understanding* (3rd ed.). Thousand Oaks, CA: Sage.

Lorr, M., & Wunderlich, R. A. (1988). A semantic differential mood scale. *Journal of Clinical Psychology, 44*, 33–38.

MacPhillamy, D. J., & Lewinsohn, P. M. (1982). The Pleasant Events Schedule: Studies on reliability, validity and scale intercorrelation. *Journal of Consulting and Clinical Psychology, 50*(3), 363–380. doi: 10.1037/0022-006X.50.3.363

Maxmen, J. S., Ward, N. G., & Kilgus, M. (2009). *Essential psychopathology and its treatment* (3rd ed.). New York, NY: Norton.

McBride, C., Atkinson, L., Quilty, L. C., & Bagby, M. R. (2006). Attachment as moderator of treatment outcome in major depression: A randomized control trial of interpersonal psychotherapy versus cognitive behavior therapy. *Journal of Consulting and Clinical Psychology, 74*(6), 1041–1054.

McGoldrick, M., Giordano, J., & Garcia-Preto, N. (Eds.). (2005). *Ethnicity and family therapy*. New York, NY: Guilford Press.

Moran, M. (2013). *DSM-5* Updates depressive, anxiety, and OCD criteria. *Psychiatric News, 48*(4), 22–43.

Moreno, C., Arango, C., Parellada, M., Shaffer, D., & Bird, H. (2007). Antidepressants in child and adolescent depression: Where are the bugs? *Acta Psychiatrica Scandinavica, 115*(3), 184–195. doi: 10.1111/j.1600-0447.2006.00951

National Institute of Mental Health. (2000). *Bipolar disorder research at the National Institute of Mental Health* (NIH Publication No. 00–4500). Bethesda, MD: Author.

National Institute of Mental Health. (2009). *What medications are used to treat depression?* Retrieved from http://www.nimh.nih.gov/health/publications/mental-health-medications/what-medications-are-used-to-treat-depression.shtml

Nemeroff, C. B. (2007). The burden of severe depression: A review of diagnostic challenges and treatment alternatives. *Journal of Psychiatric Research, 41*, 89–206.

Pandya, M., Pozuelo, L., & Malone, D. (2007). Electroconvulsive therapy: What the internist needs to know. *Cleveland Clinical Journal of Medicine, 74*(9), 679–685.

Paniagua, F. A. (2014), *Assessing and treating culturally diverse clients: A practical guide* (4th ed.). Los Angeles, CA: Sage.

Reid, W. H., Keller, S., Leatherman, M., & Mason, M. (1998). ECT in Texas. *Journal of Clinical Psychiatry, 59*, 5–13.

Resnick, W. M., & Carson, V. B. (1996). The journey colored by mood disorders. In V. B. Carson & E. N. Arnold (Eds.), *Mental health nursing: The nurse patient journey* (pp. 759–792). Philadelphia, PA: Saunders.

Rizq, R. (2012). The perversion of care: Psychological therapies in a time of IAPT. *Psychodynamic practice: Individuals, groups and organizations, 18*(1), 7–24. doi: 10.1080/14753634.2012.640161

Rude, S. S., & Bates, D. (2005). The use of cognitive and experiential techniques to treat depression. *Clinical Case Studies, 4*(4), 363–379. doi: 10.1177/1534650103259749

Sadock, B. J., & Sadock, V. A. (2008). *Kaplan and Sadock's comprehensive textbook of psychiatry*. Baltimore, MD: Lippincott, Williams, & Wilkins.

Schatzberg, A. F., Cole, J. O., & Debattista, C. (2007). *Manual of clinical psychopharmacology* (6th ed.). Washington, DC: American Psychiatric Press.

Schore, A. N. (2014). Introduction. In J. J. Magnavita & J. C. Anchin (Eds.), *Unifying psychotherapy: Principles, methods, evidence from clinical science* (pp. xxi–xlix) New York, NY: Springer.

Segal, Z., Vincent, P., & Levitt, A. (2002). Efficacy of combined, sequential, and crossover psychotherapy and pharmacotherapy in improving outcomes in depression. *Journal of Psychiatry Neuroscience*, *27*(4), 281–290.

Seligman, L., & Reichenberg, L. W. (2007). *Selecting effective treatments: A comprehensive, systematic guide to treating mental disorders* (3rd ed.). Hoboken, NJ: Wiley.

Sheikh, J. I., Cassidy, E. L., Doraiswamy, M. P., Salomon, R. M., Hornig, M., Holland, P. J., . . . Burt, T. (2004). Efficacy, safety, and tolerability of sertraline in patients with late-life depression and comorbid medical illness. *Journal of the American Geriatrics Society*, *52*(1), 86–92.

Shimizu, Y., Kitagawa, N., Mitsui, N., Fujii, Y., Toyomaki, A., Hashimoto, N., . . . Kusumi, I. (2013). Neurocognitive impairments and quality of life in unemployed patients with remitted major depressive disorder. *Psychiatry Research*, *210*(3), 913–918. doi: 10.1016/j.psychres.2013.08.030

Shindul-Rothschild, J. A., & Rothschild, A. J. (1998). Psychotropics in primary care. In L. A. Eisenbauer & M. A. Murphy (Eds.), *Pharmacotherapeutics and advanced nursing practice* (pp. 37–51) New York, NY: McGraw-Hill.

Simon, G. E., & Savarino, J. (2007). Suicide attempts among patients starting depression treatment with medications or psychotherapy. *American Journal of Psychiatry*, *164*(7), 1029–1034. doi: 10.1176/appi.ajp.164.7.1029

Skultety, K. M., & Zeiss, A. (2006). The treatment of depression in older adults in the primary care setting: An evidence-based review. *Health Psychology*, *25*(6), 665–674.

Smajkic, A., Weine, S., Djuric-Bijedic, Z., Boskailo, E., Lewis, J., & Pavkovic, I. (2001). Sertraline, paroxetine, and venlafaxine in refugee posttraumatic stress disorder with depression symptoms. *Journal of Traumatic Stress*, *14*(3), 445–452. doi: 10.1023/A:1011177420069

Tierney, L. M., McPhee, S. J., & Papadakis, M. A. (Eds.). (1997). *Current medical diagnosis and treatment* (36th ed.). Stamford, CT: Appleton & Lange.

Timonen, M., & Liukkonen, T. (2008). Clinical review management of depression in adults. *British Medical Journal*, *336*, 435–439.

Valenstein, M., McCarthy, J. F., Austin, K. L., Greden, J. F., Young, E. A., & Blow, F. C. (2006). What happened to lithium? Antidepressant augmentation in clinical settings. *American Journal of Psychiatry*, *163*(7), 1219–1225. doi: 10.1176/appi.ajp.163.7.1219

Vazquez, C. I., & Rosa, D. (2011). *Grief therapy with Latinos: Integrating culture for clinicians*. New York, NY: Springer.

Versiani, M., Moreno, R., Ramakers–van Moorsel, C. J. A., & Schutte, A. J. (2005). Comparison of the effects of mirtazapine & fluoxetine in severely depressed patients. *CNS Drugs*, *19*(2), 137–146. 10.2165/00023210-200519020-00004

Vidair, H. B., & Gunlicks-Stoessel, M. L. (2009). Innovative child and adolescent treatment research for anxiety and depressive disorders. *Depression and Anxiety*, *26*(4), 307–308.

West, M., Prado, R., & Krystal, A. D. (1999). Evaluation and comparison of EEG traces: Latent structure in nonstationary time series. *Journal of the American Statistical Association*, *94*(446), 375–394.

White, R. M. B., Roosa, M. W., Weaver, S. R., & Nair, R. L. (2009). Cultural and contextual influences on parenting in Mexican American families. *Journal of Marriage and Family*, *71*(1), 61–79.

Whittington, C. J., Kendall, T., Fonagy, P., Cottrell, D., Colgrove, A., & Boddington, E. (2004). Selective serotonin reuptake inhibitors in childhood depression: Systematic review of published versus unpublished data. *Lancet*, *363*, 1341–1345.

Wikowska-Chmielewska, J., Szelenberger, W., & Wojnar, M. (2013). Age-dependent symptomatology of depression in hospitalized patients and its implications for *DSM-5*. *Journal of Affective Disorders*, *150*(1), 142–145.

Willoughby, C. L., Hradek, E. A., & Richards, N. R. (1997). Use of electroconvulsive therapy with children: An overview and case report. *Journal of Child and Adolescent Psychiatric Nursing*, *10*(3), 11–17.

Woo, S. M., & Keatinge, C. (Eds.). (2008). *Diagnosis and treatment of mental disorders across the lifetime*. Hoboken, NJ: Wiley.

Wood, W. C. (2014). Case 4.1: moody and irritable. In J. W. Barnhill (Ed.), *DSM-5 ^{TM} clinical cases* (pp. 73–75). Washington, DC: American Psychiatric Publishing.

World Health Organization. (2009). Depression. Retrieved from http://www.who.int/mental_health/management/depression/definition/en/print.html

Zimmerman, M. (2012). Symptom severity and guideline-based treatment recommendations for depressed patients: Implications for *DSM-5*'s potential recommendation of the PHQ-9 as the measure of choice for depression severity. *Psychotherapy and Psychosomatics*, *81*(6), 329–332.

CHAPTER 8

Obsessive-Compulsive and Related Disorders

SOPHIA F. DZIEGIELEWSKI AND BARBARA F. TURNAGE

INTRODUCTION

Stress is a subjective emotional state, experienced by all, that is a normal part of everyday life. When stress and anxiety occur, an uncomfortable feeling often results that causes a response to the situation, event, or circumstance. When this response becomes excessive, however, it can become problematic, affecting an individual's cognitive, behavioral, physiological, biological, and social responses. The *Diagnostic and Statistical Manual of Mental Disorders*, Fifth Edition (*DSM-5*; American Psychiatric Association [APA], 2013) categorizes these extreme responses as anxiety disorders. Included in these disorders are obsessive-compulsive disorder, body dysmorphic disorder, hoarding disorder, trichotillomania (hair pulling disorder), excoriation (skin picking) disorder, substance/medication-induced obsessive-compulsive and related disorder, obsessive-compulsive and related disorder due to another medical condition, other specified obsessive-compulsive and related disorder, and unspecified obsessive-compulsive and related disorder.

This chapter introduces the *DSM-5* taxonomical classification of the anxiety disorders and provides a concise explanation of the disorders listed under this category. It is beyond the purpose of this chapter to explore in detail all of the diagnoses of the anxiety disorders and the treatment options specific to each. Rather, this chapter introduces the primary disorders listed in *DSM-5*. The various aspects of the disorders are presented, with a case application that highlights the diagnostic assessment, treatment planning, and evidence-based treatment strategy. The extent, importance, and early predictors of problem behaviors and symptoms are explored. In addition, the latest practice methods and newest research and findings are highlighted to further the understanding of these often-devastating illnesses.

TOWARD A BASIC UNDERSTANDING OF THE OBSESSIVE-COMPULSIVE AND RELATED DISORDERS

Obsessive-compulsive disorder (OCD) and the related disorders are characterized by "recurrent obsessions or compulsions that are severe enough to be time consuming or cause marked distress or significant impairment" (APA, 2013, p. 235). The significant impairment occurs in the person's normal routine, occupational functioning, academic functioning, social activities, or relationships (APA, 2000). Obsessions can be defined as recurring and distressing thoughts, images, and urges (APA, 2013). These factors are beyond the control of the individual and are perceived as inappropriate and anxiety provoking (Barnhill, 2014). Some of the most common obsessions are a fear of contamination, a fear of being harmed or harming others, disturbing visions of a sexual or aggressive content, doubting, and unacceptable impulses (Cooper, 1999).

Compulsions are defined as "repetitive behaviors (e.g., hand washing, ordering, checking) or mental acts (e.g., praying, counting, repeating words silently) that the person feels driven to perform in response to an obsession, or according to rules that must be applied rigidly" (APA, 2013, pp. 235, 237). Common compulsions are cleaning (or avoidance of contaminated objects), checking, counting, repeating, hoarding, and putting things in order (Cooper, 1999). The goal of these compulsions is to alleviate the anxiety caused by the mental obsessions (APA, 2013, p. 238). Therefore, there is a relationship between compulsive behaviors and the obsessions that cause them, although completing the behaviors does not relieve the thoughts that drive them. The compulsions are seen to be excessive, and the occurrence of one without the other is rare.

There are a number of suspected causes, including genetic, biological, personality development, and environmental factors. Biological components are thought to include an imbalance in the neurotransmitter serotonin. Research is ongoing to identify genes linked to OCD by exploring family trends of OCD and related disorders. An example of environmental influences is an inordinate emphasis on cleanliness. The lifetime prevalence of OCD in adults has been estimated at 1.1% to 1.8% (APA, 2013). The average age of onset is about 14, with onset after the age of 35 unusual (APA, 2013). Although OCD is more likely to have an earlier age of onset in males during childhood, females are more likely to experience symptoms that surround cleaning (APA, 2013, p. 240). Associated disorders (often referred to as the obsessive-compulsive spectrum disorders) in adults include major depression, anxiety disorders, eating disorders, and personality disorders. In children, OCD is often associated with learning disorders and disruptive behavior disorders (APA, 2013). According to Cooper (1999), alcohol abuse, Tourette's syndrome, epilepsy, and Syderham's chorea have also been frequently seen with OCD.

The treating clinician needs to address multiple issues when working with an individual with OCD. First, the clinician must not diagnose OCD when the obsession or compulsion arises from another mental disorder (APA, 2013). For example, a patient may present with excessive worries that resemble obsessive thinking, but if these worries are realistic to the situation, the diagnostic criteria would not be met.

Also, clinicians have found that patients' fear and embarrassment about their behaviors often make them reluctant to disclose their symptoms. Their concerns may be related to depression and anxiety and not characteristic of the full list of symptoms needed to place the disorder. Therefore, the disorder might not come to the practitioner's attention until the client presents with a secondary physical symptom, such as dry hands due to excessive washing. In this case, the clinician may suspect OCD and explore this possible diagnosis by asking nonthreatening questions. Another problem is family members' inability to understand that the patient can't simply stop the behaviors. This makes family education related to the condition important for treatment success.

Theories related to understanding anxiety disorders provide the underlying mechanisms from which treatment, interventions, and prevention methods are informed. These theoretical approaches help to explain the complex interactions and impacts that can occur among interpersonal, intrapersonal, and environmental relationships. Theories related to the understanding of anxiety disorders are often based in the biological sciences, neuropsychology, cognitive psychology, and social psychology. With the assistance of cognitive and social psychology, the recognition of fear and its subsequent extinction can be understood. Huff, Hernandez, Blanding, and LaBar (2009) point out in their analysis of fear extinction that learning and training of fear can be restructured. With OCD, some clients misattribute meaning to situations and other environmental cues. Furthermore, deficits in memory and executive function impair information processing; consequently, judgment and decision making are impaired, resulting in the attribution of negative messages specific to situations or social circumstances (APA, 2013). In the individual suffering from a type of obsessive-compulsive and related disorder, some disruption in organic brain function has reduced his or her background capacities to process and understand information. The disruption affects the individual's ability to attribute meaning, motivation, and intention to cues. When this occurs, the individual may inappropriately react to perceived threats, resulting in anxiety and maladaptation, especially if the person suffers from a brain lesion or head injury. A perceived threat may cause the onset of panic and social withdrawal. The emotions are constant, but their interpretation is impaired secondary to the organic brain-related processing problems that leave the individual responding with impaired metacognitions.

UNDERSTANDING INDIVIDUALS WHO SUFFER FROM THE OCD SPECTRUM DISORDERS: WHEN URGES BECOME OVERWHELMING

According to the National Institute of Mental Health (NIMH; 2008), anxiety disorders are estimated to affect more than 50 million people over age 18 in the United States. Many have a median onset as early as age 13 (approximately 34 million people). In 2004, the indirect and direct economic costs associated with the treatment of anxiety disorders were $46.6 billion per year—a third of all mental health expenditures allotted for that year. Anxiety disorders can begin with an individual treatment cost of at least $350 per year (NIMH, 2008). For those suffering from an anxiety disorder, the economic impact and social costs incurred are profound.

The unintended social impact of these disorders can prove hazardous. When an individual is socially and situationally bound by thoughts, impaired cognitive processes, and emotions that cause worry, fear, and distress, his or her ability to socialize and meet others is hindered. So is the ability to perform optimally in occupational and educational settings, and overall personal health is compromised. In terms of quality of life, these circumstances result in the individual being unable to form and sustain relationships and can lead to subsequent withdrawal from family and friends. When the anxious feelings are great, the individual may be unable to seek, obtain, or sustain employment. When employed, fear and anxiety can lead to withdrawal and absences from work. Clients may also avoid participation in scholastic pursuits, and all of these can affect the individual's economic standing. Anxiety is a prominent feature in all of the disorders in this chapter and remains reflective in the predominant excessive obsessional thoughts and compulsive behaviors that characterize these disorders (Barnhill, 2014). When consistent and inescapable stress and anxiety can lead to immediate and prolonged health, mental health, and substance abuse concerns that could result in physical deficiencies, other social problems, and possible death.

Unlike other types of anxiety-related disorders, the disorders in this category are often shrouded in a veil of secrecy. The individual often does not initially seek attention and may avoid help-seeking behavior until people close to him or her recommend it. Experiencing the symptoms of anxiety, coupled with a strong mental and physical desire to engage in certain behaviors, can make individuals suffering from these disorders particularly difficult to treat. Often they are not sure what

QUICK REFERENCE 8.1

Presentation of Anxiety

- Clients who are anxious often do not seek the help of a primary care physician unless urged by family members or support system influences, such as emergency responders.
- Clients often cannot control the signs and symptoms experienced and try to address them with repetitive behaviors.
- Clients present with both physical and mental symptoms (e.g., tremors, dyspnea, dizziness, sweating, irritability, restlessness, hyperventilation, pain, heartburn) and when confronted, may back away from help or attention to their concerns.

is causing the problem and take their own actions to solve it. The desire to perform the behavior is both overwhelming and confusing. The individual as well as the practitioner may at first be confused as to whether the symptoms being experienced may be medically related, especially in skin-picking disorder. If the person can be convinced to have a physical exam, usually no medical reason is determined for the symptoms displayed and the activities performed. Family and friends aware of the situation may call police or other emergency responders to convince their loved one to get attention, or the person may be referred first to a mental health practitioner. (See Quick Reference 8.1.).

IMPORTANT FEATURES RELATED TO THE OBSESSIVE-COMPULSIVE AND RELATED DISORDERS

When preparing for the diagnostic assessment and selecting the appropriate diagnosis, the practitioner must first be aware of the key features prevalent in the obsessive-compulsive and related disorders that are used for the diagnosis. Creating any diagnostic impression and the treatment plan to follow requires balancing groundbreaking research, assessment of client history and medical information, and the practitioner's judgment and experience (Schore, 2014). Starting this process calls for familiarity with the characteristics consistent with each of the disorders in this chapter. These characteristics include the presence of obsessions and compulsions (see Quick Reference 8.2). *Obsessions* involve an individual's mental acts—the repetitive thoughts and images that disturb an individual's functioning (APA, 2013). *Compulsions* include both the mental acts that drive the behaviors and the actual behaviors an individual performs to try to avoid or quell the recurring thoughts (APA, 2013). The easiest way to think of an obsession is as the thought that governs the generally repetitive behaviors. Most of the disorders in this category manifest primarily in body-focused behaviors that can result in physical damage, such as skin picking and hair pulling. In all of the obsessive-compulsive and related disorders, there is a desire to stop the resulting behavior, but an inability to do so.

Included in the *DSM-5* classification of the obsessive-compulsive and related disorders are several disorders that share featured characteristics and criteria that specify common metacognitions and physiological responses. Metacognitions involve processing emotional and situational states that provide the basis for an individual's trust and safety assessments. Inappropriate allocation of attentive processing and disordered information

QUICK REFERENCE 8.2

OBSESSIONS AND COMPULSIONS

Obsessions: Persistent, recurring, and distressing intrusive thoughts, images, and urges inappropriate, anxiety provoking, and contrary to the individual's free will.

Compulsions: Persistent repetitive behaviors (e.g., checking and rechecking, collecting, skin picking) or mental acts (e.g., counting) in response to an obsession or to applied rigid rules, and not performed for pleasure or gratification.

processing (e.g., breakdown in adaptive signal-to-noise discrimination) with inappropriate and exaggerated innocuous body sensations are central to understanding the clinical phenomenology of the anxiety disorders (Wise, McFarlane, Clark, & Battersby, 2009). Processing stressful events requires executive functions such as interpretation, attention, and memory, and these functions are applied when threat and danger assessments and responsive actions are formed (as in fight or flight). When excited, the individual then tries to regulate these emotions, invoking compensatory emotions such as fear, worry, distress, terror, or despair. What the individual attributes to the situation provides the basis for anxious responses. If any component of these processes is impaired, then judgment and decision making in these situations become inaccurate. When judgment and interpretation are impaired, the individual believes, assesses, and feels that his or her own perception is accurate. Responses to stress and anxiety, especially severe levels, can include physiological reactions that stimulate the sympathetic and parasympathetic nervous systems, resulting in increased heart rate, trembling, sweating, nausea, shortness of breath, dizziness, headaches, and diarrhea.

When anxiety is involved, it can be the sum total of all of these components; its symptomatology is observed in its frequency and intensity, its excessiveness and unreasonableness, and its intrusiveness and inappropriateness to the domain of the individual's life. These shared components are found in the disorders listed in this taxonomical category. Symptoms of all of these disorders can include, but are not limited to, fear, worry, preoccupation, restlessness, irritability, anger, terror, distress, helplessness, horror, poor concentration, hypervigilance, motor restlessness, disturbed sleep, fatigue, shortness of breath, dizziness, palpitations, trembling, and muscle tension (APA, 2013).

Problems With Self-Reporting of Symptoms

One reason this lack of proper assessment of symptoms is so problematic is that clients self-report the feelings they are experiencing. Much of what we know about a client suffering from obsessive-compulsive and related disorders—or any mental health condition, for that matter—comes from self-report. How the client interprets and reports the symptoms can be misleading because feelings of anxiousness or urges to perform tasks often are overstated or understated. Also, clients with these disorders in particular may tend to hide the symptoms in internal silence and not discuss them with others until they can no longer be hidden. In trying to protect their current state, clients may minimize their subjective experiences. Therefore, the situational events that surround the obsessions and compulsions have to be examined. Once identified, this interpretation has to be compared with the definition and standards of normalcy within an individual's unique social, cultural, environmental context (Paniagua, 2014). The degree to which this impression affects self-report can vary. Therefore, the reporting of symptoms can be confusing: Is the individual feeling pleasure from certain activities or not? Is he reporting what he is feeling now or what he remembers feeling in the past? The first step toward effective treatment is identifying a clear, concise, psychosocial, criteria-based diagnostic standard.

Taking the influence of life factors into account on self-report is essential. Reported symptoms are always influenced by many factors, including current or past relationship problems, irritability with the situation, and work-related conflicts. All diagnostic interpretations must be sensitive to the influence of cultural and stress-related environmental and social factors (Paniagua, 2014). Some ethnic minority groups are exposed to tremendous contextual stressors that figure prominently, including poverty, poor and rundown neighborhoods, acculturation, and the loss associated with "never going home again" (White, Roosa, Weaver, & Nair, 2009). Similarly, the social context needs to be assessed when clients are immigrants, as their depressive symptoms may stem from a conflict between values from their country of origin and American customs and values, problems speaking the English language, parenting stress, and conflict between children's and parents' beliefs and customs. This point may be an important consideration in hoarding disorder, where objects gathered take on particular meanings to the individual that cannot easily be parted with, regardless of the negative health circumstances that may be present.

Therefore, in assessing obsessions and compulsions, consider not only what symptoms a client reports but also the cultural influences and complexities of the client's cultural identity (McGoldrick, Giordano, & Garcia-Preto, 2005). McGoldrick and colleagues point out that ethnicity is not the only dimension of culture, but it is a necessary component in understanding an individual's adjustment to his or her new life and the losses experienced to get there. Social workers must also be willing to consider how gender, socioeconomic status, social class, geography, race, religion, and politics influence that adjustment; how important these factors are in accurately assessing OCD; and how to best use a client-oriented support system as part of the treatment process (Locke & Bailey, 2014).

Clients suffering from obsessions and compulsions can become frustrated with medical providers because the complaints they report are somatic, and no physical causes are revealed. In turn, providers can also be frustrated because, after completion of a medical examination, no physical cause for the problem is revealed. In addition to problems with the subjectivity of clients' reporting and negative medical findings is lack of clarity in identifying the condition the client is suffering from. For these reasons, clear, concise, psychosocial, criteria-based diagnostic standards and gathering collateral information and perceptions from significant others, family, coworkers, and friends are recommended to enhance the self-report (Woo & Keatinge, 2008). Also, clients sometimes complain about the number of self-report measures used. Practitioners can feel this frustration at times, too, and question how helpful self-reports are and whether they are always the best use of therapeutic time (Rizq, 2012).

OVERVIEW OF THE OBSESSIVE-COMPULSIVE AND RELATED DISORDERS

The *DSM-5* provides the standardized classification system for psychiatric disorders across the United States (APA, 2013). Using the criteria for

QUICK REFERENCE 8.3

OVERVIEW OF OBSESSIVE-COMPULSIVE AND RELATED DISORDERS

- Obsessive-compulsive disorder (OCD): OCD has four specific criteria (ranging from A to D) that must be met. The core criterion is the presence of obsessions and/or compulsions.
- Body dysmorphic disorder (BDD): BDD has four specific criteria (ranging from A to D) that must be met. Individuals with this disorder exhibit a "preoccupation with one or more perceived defects or flaws in physical appearance" that may or may not be visible to others.
- Hoarding disorder (HD): HD has six specific criteria (ranging from A to F) that must be met. Individuals with hoarding disorder suffer from an inability to discard possessions that may have significant financial value, emotional value, or no value at all.
- Trichotillomania (hair pulling disorder): Five specific criteria (ranging from A to E) must be met. This disorder consists of hair loss associated with recurrent hair pulling when the individual has tried unsuccessfully to decrease or stop the hair pulling.
- Excoriation (skin picking) disorder: Five specific criteria (ranging from A to E) must be met. The recurrent skin picking results in skin lesions and/or skin infections; there are unsuccessful attempts to stop or decrease the skin picking.
- Substance/medication induced obsessive-compulsive and related disorder: Five specific criteria (ranging from A to E) must be met, along with two components that can be documented based on history and medical examinations (physical exams and laboratory finds).
- Obsessive-compulsive and related disorder due to another medical condition: Five specific criteria (ranging from A to E) must be met. The behaviors related to the disorder dominate the individual's situation. There is evidence based on history and medical tests that the disorder results from another medical condition.
- Other specified obsessive-compulsive and related disorder: The designation of this category requires that the symptoms are characteristic of an obsessive-compulsive and related disorder. This category can be used when there is not enough information to make a full diagnosis or when the symptoms do not fully reach the criteria of the obsessive-compulsive and related disorder.
- Unspecified obsessive-compulsive and related disorder: This diagnosis is used when the symptoms do not fully meet the obsessive-compulsive and related disorder categories and the cause for not meeting the disorder is not listed.

Source: Summarized from the *Diagnostic and Statistical Manual of Mental Disorders*, Fifth Edition. Copyright 2013 by the American Psychiatric Association.

the mental disorders as outlined in the *DSM-5* allows standardization across disorders and quick, effective determinations of individual psychopathology (Schmidt, Norr, & Korte, 2014). (See Quick Reference 8.3.) The characteristic symptoms of obsessive-compulsive and related disorders are the presence of recurrent and consistent thoughts, urges, and images. In an effort to move past these obsessions; the individual participates in behaviors or mental acts. A brief overview of the nine disorders follows.

Obsessive-Compulsive Disorder (OCD)

Obsessive-compulsive disorder (OCD) has four specific criteria (ranging from A to D) that must be met. The core criterion is the presence of obsessions and/or compulsions. Criterion A has two sub-parts, one that describes the obsessions and another that describes the compulsions. The first two criteria under criterion A are related to defining obsessions. First, the obsessions consist of recurrent and persistent thoughts, urges, and images. The intrusive and unwanted thoughts, urges, and images can lead to distress and anxiety. Second, the individual may develop repetitive ritualistic behaviors to ignore and/or suppress the obsessive thoughts, urges, and images. When this happens it is referred to as a compulsion. Once the existence of compulsive behavior is established criterion A further defines two ways in which compulsions are quantified. In the first statement compulsions are referred to as mental acts that constitute repetitive ritualistic behaviors preformed to prevent and/or reduce the distress and anxiety related to the obsessive thoughts, urges, and images. The second sub-criterion describes how a compulsion takes into account an unrealistic perspective where these excessive attempts at reducing anxiety continue to fail to avoid some dreaded event or situation. Based on criterion A it is clear that the compulsions are a direct result of the obsession. In compulsions, the resulting behaviors are repetitive and ritualistic, and the individual needs to perform them to prevent and/or reduce the distress and anxiety related to the obsessive thoughts, urges, and images. Criterion B highlights the time consuming nature of the obsessions and the compulsions. Furthermore, to qualify as an obsession or a compulsion under criterion B, the thoughts, urges, and images, along with the compulsive behaviors used to reduce the anxiety, must take more than 1 hour per day or be time consuming enough to cause significant impairment with distress related to daily functioning. In criterion C, the symptoms cannot be attributable to the physiological effects of a substance and/or a medical condition; and, criterion D, where it cannot meet the criteria for another mental disorder.

In addition to the primary characteristic criteria the disorder can be further classified using specifiers. There are two specifiers for this diagnosis. The first *specify if* category relates to insight. When using OCD, specify if the individual presents with good or fair insight, poor insight, or "absent insight/delusional beliefs" (APA, 2013, p. 237). The individual with good or fair insight recognizes the distorted beliefs but is unable to suppress the unwanted thoughts, urges, images, repetitive behaviors, and/or the mental acts. The individual with poor insight believes that the OCD beliefs are probably true (APA, 2013, p. 237). Individuals with absent insight/delusional beliefs are convinced that the delusional thoughts are true (APA, 2013, p. 237). The insight category helps the practitioner determine treatment protocol. The practitioner must also specify if the disorder is accompanied by either motor or verbal tics. Although a qualifier for tic-related is included if it is believed the individual has a tic disorder, the practitioner must determine which disorder is the primary disorder (APA, 2013).

Body Dysmorphic Disorder (BDD)

Body dysmorphic disorder (BDD) has four specific criteria (ranging from A to D) that must be met. In criterion A, individuals with this disorder exhibit a "preoccupation with one or more perceived defects or flaws in physical appearance that are not observable or appear slight to others" (APA, 2013, p. 243). In criterion B, these perceived defects or flaws that may not be as visible to others become the focus of great attention and this preoccupation results in repetitive behaviors such as mirror checking or seeking reassurance of others when the cause of concern is simply not visible or concerning to others. Because of the individual's preoccupation, he or she may continue to perform repetitive behaviors. The individual may have also participated in mental acts, such as comparing self with others. In criterion C, this preoccupation must be so excessive that the individual experiences clinically significant distress or impairment in social, occupational, or other important areas of functioning. Lastly, in criterion D, an individual who suffers from BDD remains primarily preoccupied with appearance and does not meet the criteria for an eating disorder (APA, 2013).

Two types of specifiers are outlined; one relates to muscle dysmorphia and the other is related to insight. When diagnosing an individual with this disorder, the practitioner must specify whether the individual also has muscle dysmorphia. Individuals who present with muscle dysmorphia perceive their body build as distorted (e.g., "body build is too small or insufficiently muscular") (APA, 2013, p. 243). The practitioner must use this specifier even if the client's perception of his or her body build is distorted in only one part of the body. The second specifier for BDD that constitutes *Specify if*, relates to insight. The practitioner must specify if the individual presents with good or fair insight, poor insight, or if the individual does not understand that the delusions are not true (absent insight/delusional beliefs) (APA, 2013). Individuals with good or fair insight recognize that the distorted beliefs may not be true, and the individual with poor insight believes that the distorted beliefs are probably true.

Hoarding Disorder (HD)

Hoarding disorder (HD) has six specific criteria (ranging from A to F) that must be met. In criterion A, individuals with HD suffer from an inability to discard and/or a desire to save possessions that others might perceive as valueless. Hoarded possessions can range from having significant financial value, emotional value, to no value at all. In criterion B, the primary problem is the extreme desire to save these items as a way of avoiding the distress that it creates. In criterion C, the accumulation of possessions reduces the quality of the individual's living environment as they encroach upon available living space and in extreme cases can directly cause a health hazard. The clinically significant distress resulting from hoarding impacts the individual's social and occupational level of functioning (criterion D). In criteria E and F, the diagnosis of HD is not attributed to symptoms of another mental disorder or medical condition.

There are two specifiers to be used with HD; one involves acquisition and the other OCD spectrum disorder involves insight. The practitioner must use the specifier with excessive acquisition when hoarded items are not needed or there is no space to maintain the hoarded items. The insight specifier is also used when diagnosing HD. Identify is whether the individual with HD has good or fair insight regarding hoarding, poor insight, or "absent insight/delusional beliefs" (APA, 2013, p. 247). Individuals with HD who possess good or fair insight recognize the problematic features of maintaining the hoarded items. Individuals with poor insight don't see the hoarding as a problem. When provided evidence that hoarding the items is problematic, individuals with absent insight/delusional beliefs focus on the necessity of hoarding the items and refuse to believe any information that contradicts their need to hoard.

Trichotillomania (Hair Pulling Disorder)

Trichotillomania (hair pulling disorder) has five specific criteria (ranging from A to E) that must be met. In criterion A, this disorder constitutes hair loss that is associated with recurrent hair pulling. In criterion B, the individual has tried unsuccessfully to decrease or stop the hair pulling but cannot seem to control the urge. The recurrent hair pulling leads the individual to suffer clinically significant distress or impairment in important areas of daily functioning, including social and occupational functioning (Criterion C). In the last two criteria, D and E, the hair pulling is not better explained by a medical condition or another mental disorder. In general, when diagnosing this disorder special attention should always be paid to criteria D and E and whether the individual has a medical condition that manifests in dermatological itching or a substance-related disorder that can cause skin-picking such as methamphetamine. These types of medical or substance-related disorders can cause hair loss and confuse the symptoms being displayed. Lastly, there are no specifiers with this disorder although often this disorder may be comorbid with major depressive disorder or skin picking disorder.

Excoriation (Skin Picking) Disorder

Excoriation (skin picking) disorder has five specific criteria (ranging from A to E) that must be met. Criterion A, outlines how the recurrent skin picking results in skin lesions and/or skin infections. Criterion B, identifies how the individual has made unsuccessful attempts to stop or decrease the skin picking. The clinically significant distress resulting from the skin picking has also impaired the individual socially, occupationally, and in other areas of functioning (Criterion C). Similar to hair picking disorder, criteria D and E, require that the disorder is not better explained by physiological effects of a substance or another mental disorder.

Substance/Medication-Induced Obsessive-Compulsive and Related Disorder

Substance/medication-induced obsessive-compulsive and related disorder has five specific criteria (ranging from A to E) that must be met. The repetitive behaviors and/or symptoms characteristic of the obsessive-compulsive and related disorders are central in formulating the clinical presentation. Criteria B has two components that can be documented based on history and medical examinations (physical exams and laboratory findings); that is, the disorder occurs during or after the exposure to a substance. In criterion C it is essential to rule-out the potential for the disorder to be non-substance related. In these cases the individual suffers from the obsessive compulsive and the related disorder and the substance only complicates the picture. This is most evident when the symptoms persist after the substance has been discontinued for at least one month. The individual may also have a history of the disorder and the substance complicates the clinical presentation. In these cases, this diagnosis should not be used as substance/medication is not considered the cause. Further, in criterion D, the symptoms do not precede usage of the substance or occur during the course of a delirium. The clinically significant distress resulting from the disorder impairs the individual socially, occupationally, and in other areas of functioning (Criterion E). In this diagnosis a central factor when completing the diagnostic assessment is to ensure that the symptoms cannot "be better explained by an obsessive-compulsive and related disorder that is not substance/medication-induced" (APA, 2013, p. 257).

There are three specifiers for this disorder: onset during intoxication, onset during withdrawal, and onset after medication use (APA, 2013). The practitioner uses the specifier onset during intoxication when the disorder occurs during intoxication. The specifier onset during withdrawal is used when the individual experiences the disorder during or shortly after withdrawal from intoxication. The specifier onset after medication use is during or after taking medication. This specifier is also used after a modification in the individual's medication regimen.

Obsessive-Compulsive and Related Disorder Due to Another Medical Condition

Obsessive-compulsive and related disorder due to another medical condition has five specific criteria (ranging from A to E) that must be met. In criterion A, the behaviors related to at least one of the disorders included in this chapter dominate the individual's situation. Criterion B, outlines the importance of a history and physical as well as medical tests conducted to ensure that the symptoms present are not indicative of another medical condition. Criterion C, addresses the importance of ensuring the symptoms are not relevant to another mental disorder related to anxiety or other mental health factors. Criterion D, the mental disorder does not exclusively occur during the course of a delirium. Lastly, criterion E stresses the importance of identifying the clinically significant distress that results from the disorder and how it impairs the individual socially, occupationally, and in other areas of functioning.

The specifiers for this disorder include obsessive-compulsive disorder-like symptoms, appearance preoccupations, hoarding symptoms, hair-pulling symptoms, and skin-picking symptoms. Use obsessive-compulsive disorder–like symptoms when these types of "symptoms predominate the clinical presentation" (APA, 2013, p. 261). If the clinical presentation is dominated by appearance preoccupations, hoarding symptoms, hair-pulling symptoms, or skin-picking symptoms, use the symptom that dominates the clinical presentation as the specifier.

Other Specified Obsessive-Compulsive and Related Disorder

Other specified obsessive-compulsive and related disorder and the designation of this category require that the symptoms are characteristic of an obsessive-compulsive and related disorder. Additionally, due to the symptoms manifested, the individual experiences clinically significant distress "in social and occupational functioning, and other important areas of functioning" (APA, 2013, p. 263). This category can be used in emergency situations when the practitioner may not have enough time to make a full diagnosis. Also, this category can be used when the symptoms do not fully reach the criteria of the obsessive-compulsive and related disorder. At this time, there are no specifiers for this disorder.

Unspecified Obsessive-Compulsive and Related Disorder

Unspecified obsessive-compulsive and related disorder is used when the symptoms do not fully meet the obsessive-compulsive and related disorder categories. The symptoms presented cause clinically significant distress. There is also impairment of social, occupational, or other important areas of functioning. To qualify as an obsession or a compulsion, the thoughts, urges, and images, along with the compulsive behaviors used to reduce the anxiety, must take more than 1 hour per day. Symptoms cannot be attributable to physiological effects of a substance and/or a medical condition. At this time, there are no specifiers for this disorder.

TOWARD A BETTER UNDERSTANDING OF OBSESSIVE-COMPULSIVE DISORDER

Often OCD results in recurrent obsessions or compulsions that remain so severe that they consume an inordinate amount of the individual's time. Included in the *DSM-5* criteria for OCD is the individual's recognition of the excessiveness and unreasonableness of the obsessions and compulsions, not accounted for by a medical condition or the physiological effects of a substance. The obsession and compulsion must take longer than 1 hour a day to complete. In obsessional thinking, the individual acknowledges that thoughts are a product of his or her own mind and are not imposed from another source, such as thought insertion. This impairment must be severe enough to interfere with an individual's ability to perform daily activities, to impair occupational and academic functioning, and to disrupt relationships.

Repeated fears of contamination or of being harmed or of harming others, disturbing visions of a sexual or aggressive content, doubting, need to have things in a particular order, and unacceptable impulses are present (APA, 2013; Cooper, 1999). Because the thoughts and worries are not simply about real-life problems, the individual attempts to ignore, suppress, or neutralize them with some other thought or action. The cognitive bias in OCD attributes the maintenance of obsessive thoughts and compulsive actions to the distress experienced from the actions themselves (e.g., their moral aspect); consequently, thinking these thoughts increases the likelihood of an event occurring (with subsequent behaviors to neutralize thoughts related to the catastrophic consequences) (Abramowitz, Whiteside, Lynam, & Kalsy, 2003).

Fears resulting in behaviors employed in the absence of objective danger or contamination, applied in a nonjudicious manner, result in the common features of anxiety disorders such as OCD (Deacon & Maack, 2008). The particular aim of OCD is to prevent or reduce distress of a dreaded event or situation in response to these thoughts (Pietrefesa & Coles, 2009). These avoidance behaviors are defined as compulsions in OCD and as repetitive behaviors or mental acts preventing or reducing anxiety or distress rather than for pleasure or gratification (e.g., hand washing, ordering, checking, praying, counting, or repeating words silently) (APA, 2013; Deacon & Maack, 2008; Pietrefesa & Coles, 2009). Common compulsions include cleaning (or avoidance of contaminated objects), checking, counting, repeating, requesting or demanding assurances, hoarding, and putting things in order (APA, 2000; Cooper, 1999). Compulsive acts are excessive, such as repeated visits to physicians to seek assurance; heavy use of alcohol or sedative, hypnotic, or anxiolytic medications; avoiding public restrooms; and avoiding shaking hands with strangers.

The selective neuropsychological deficits in executive function, nonverbal memory, motor speed, and visuospatial and visuoconstructional skills (Simpson et al., 2006; van den Heuvel et al., 2005) can explain the misattribution, impaired judgment, emotional response, and inhibited behaviors. Noteworthy is the misattribution of safety behaviors that erroneously are thought to avoid the feared catastrophe (Abramowitz et al., 2003; Deacon & Maack, 2008). The individual engages in excess preventive measures where the presence of the fear does not exist. This unintentionally causes a negative feedback loop, whereby the thought of the safety behavior and subsequent action increases and substitutes the thoughts and behaviors misattributed to danger. It has been postulated that the obsessions and compulsions in individuals with OCD may also be in response to two underlying dimensions of harm avoidance and incompleteness, characterized by pathological doubt, perfection, and a high degree for control (Pietrefesa & Coles, 2009). In neuropsychological studies of individuals with OCD, van den Heuvel et al. (2005) noted that such individuals spent more time generating alternative solutions or checking next responses when a mistake is made (i.e., the increased performance-monitoring characteristic of the critical self-evaluation of performance, leading to self-correction and repetitive behavior).

Associated disorders in adults include other anxiety disorders (e.g., phobias, panic disorders, generalized anxiety disorder), major depression, eating disorders, substance use disorders, learning disorders, disruptive behavior disorders, and personality disorders (obsessive-compulsive personality disorder, avoidant personality disorder, and dependent personality disorder) (APA, 2013). Although recurrent or intrusive thoughts may be shared in the criteria for all of these disorders, the differentiation is made in that these cognitive concerns cannot be related primarily to the symptoms captured within another disorder, and the presence of these disorders should be compared closely to the criteria and risk factors related to the disorder.

Risk Factors Associated With Obsessive-Compulsive Disorder

An estimated 2.2 million people in the United States age 18 and older have been diagnosed with obsessive-compulsive disorder (NIMH, 2008). Risk factors associated with developing and triggering OCD include genetic/environmental factors, neurobiological factors, infections, and stressful life events. These factors should be taken into consideration when assessing for OCD during the diagnostic evaluation.

Genetic/Environmental Factors Parents or family members with OCD give individuals a high risk of developing the disorder (APA, 2013; Mayo Clinic, 2013; Steinhausen, Bisgaard, Munk-Jørgensen, & Helenius, 2013). Heredity in the development of OCD has been found in concordance for obsessive-compulsive symptoms, subclinical OCD, in first-degree relatives, and in twin studies (APA, 2013; do Rosario-Campos et al., 2005; Nestadt et al., 2000). Genetic factors should be considered when assessing for the presence of OCD.

Neurobiological Factors The role of brain dysfunction in striatal functions (e.g., striato-pallido-nigral and subthalamic), altered gene expressions, and basal ganglia determines motor function, abnormalities in memory, visuospatial processing, and executive functions affecting timing and motor speed in obsessive-compulsive disorder (Saint-Cyr, 2003; Simpson et al., 2006; van den Heuvel et al., 2005). Abnormalities found in the orbitofrontal-striatal function have been related to OCD (van den Heuvel et al., 2005). Hypothalamic-pituitary-adrenal axis impairment increases emotional reactivity, including blushing, increased substance abuse, behavioral inhibition, social incompetence, and disruption of affiliation found in obsessive-compulsive disorders and other types of anxiety disorders (Mathew, Coplan, & Gorman, 2001; van den Heuvel et al., 2005). The disruption to synaptic and cellular processes in anxiety disorders, with impairment to the basal ganglia associated with implicit learning and memory storing of fear episodes, accentuates the role of organ function in the disorder. Brain dysfunction is a risk factor for the development of OCD. The evaluation should consider assessing for cognitive impairments (e.g., changes in mental status), head injury, and head trauma to evaluate the presence of organic deficits contributing to the disorder.

Stressful Life Events Stressful life events have been associated with the intensification of ritualistic behaviors, increasing the risk of

OCD. These events include important life transitions and mourning, where intrusive thoughts trigger these rituals to alleviate the emotional distress characteristic of obsessive-compulsive disorder (APA, 2013; Mayo Clinic, 2013). Events can include pregnancy (as a major life transition) or an unexpected death, particularly if the death has been complicated. Focus on general stress in nonclinical populations has found increased intrusive thoughts in response to stressful and aversive stimuli, highlighting the impact of the environment in inducing obsessive impulses and the link to stress and OCD (stressful life events and traumatic stress events) (Cromer, Schmidt, & Murphy, 2007). The presence of stressful life events should always be assessed in clients suffering from OCD.

Infections Hemolytic streptococcal infection (e.g., scarlet fever and strep throat) is a risk factor in the development of OCD (APA, 2013; Mayo Clinic, 2013; Hofmeijer-Sevink et al., 2013). Streptococcal infections related to pediatric autoimmune neuropsychiatric disorders (PANDAS) can trigger symptoms and neurological abnormalities. Risk of OCD is increased when this is accompanied by the abrupt onset of symptoms and when the individual carries the particular gene set also found in relatives with PANDAS (APA, 2013; Mell, Davis, & Owens, 2005). As in genetic and environmental factors, the presence of these infections should be assessed in the diagnostic evaluation to differentiate diagnoses.

OBSESSIVE-COMPULSIVE DISORDERS AND THE FACTORS FOR CONSIDERATION IN THE DIAGNOSTIC ASSESSMENT

In starting the diagnostic assessment for this disorder, two factors must be clearly understood:

1. *Anxiety and depressive symptoms can overlap with other disorders.* In professional practice, mental health practitioners quickly realize that the client with a single problem does not exist, nor does the client who clearly and concisely fits perfectly into an identified diagnostic category. Clients often have multiple problems that require a multifaceted approach to intervention. The same can be said for clients with OCD who have multiple anxiety-related mental health problems and difficulties (Dziegielewski, 2010; Hofmeijer-Sevink et al., 2013). Some of these problems can easily overlap other mental health conditions, such as anxiety disorders and trauma- and stressor-related disorders, as well as the mood disorders such as bipolar and the depressive disorders. Because the etiology of OCD is not yet fully understood, the use of medications to control anxiety and the obsessive thoughts can take into account the little we do understand. As the understanding of the causes and origins of OCD increases, so will the ability of mental health professionals to treat these disorders.

2. *Cultural considerations:* Because the diagnostic assessment will serve as the foundation for intervention with an individual who has OCD, it is imperative to consider the cultural background and experiences of the client and how the client's culture may influence or affect subsequent behavior (Locke & Bailey, 2014). Furthermore, some theorists have postulated that cultural factors can be directly involved in acculturation and adjusting to a new culture (Locke & Bailey, 2014). For the obsessions and compulsions common in OCD, understanding ethnic group identity, religion, and spirituality can help to establish culturally sanctioned behaviors that appear to be different from behaviors demonstrated in the dominant culture. For the practitioner, Lum (2011) notes that taking into account the cultural context or knowledge of the cultural environment is a critical factor in determining how one evolves as a cultural being. Furthermore, Locke

and Bailey (2014), although referring to African Americans, could be referring to all cultural groups in that all individuals need to be taught that deviations from what is considered normal by the dominant culture does not indicate that what he or she believes is abnormal. This makes use of the Cultural Formulation Interview (CFI), as described earlier in this text, very important. This interview format enables evaluation of the way the individual approaches and responds to situations from a clear cultural perspective. In addition, the practitioner may find in Appendix 3 of the *DSM-5* some of the best studied culturally related syndromes and idioms of distress that may be encountered in clinical practice. Being aware of these idioms of distress can help the practitioner be inclusive of the culture as well as identify what could be considered problematic behaviors identified or communicated in more understandable cultural terms.

Especially when clients report problems with persistent intrusive and unwanted thoughts, urges, or images; repetitive behaviors such as excessive hand washing; or mental acts such as repeating words silently, unwarranted labeling of pathology could be avoided if the behaviors experienced were explored in relation to norms of the client's cultural reference group. As times change and cultures become more blended, ethnic differences may eventually do the same. Standard definitions will continue to be questioned; Paniagua (2014) suggests eliminating the term *minority* altogether. Regardless of the current definition, to provide a comprehensive assessment, cultural factors are important in both the diagnostic assessment and the intervention plan. Cultural factors always need to be identified and taken into account in working with clients.

Use of the Dimensional Assessment

One essential part of the *DSM-5* is the switch from a categorical diagnostic assessment to a dimensional one. In these disorders, the hope of introducing crosscutting of symptoms and the dimensional assessment rests on the fact that OCD is complicated; therefore, complete assessment of the current symptoms an individual is experiencing is essential. In introducing the dimensional assessment, the hope is to get a better understanding of the conditions across this spectrum and to better differentiate them. The diagnostic criteria presented for each diagnosis make clear that the criteria to make the diagnosis have been tightened up. For example, in OCD, four symptoms identified in the criteria must be present more than 1 hour per day. Firming up the criteria for each of the diagnoses, coupled with the specifiers, defines distinct stages and dimensions of the illnesses described (Tandon, 2012). In addition, clarity in formulating the diagnostic assessment assists in developing the symptom-specific treatment that the practitioner will need to follow.

Additional Measurement Scales

Various scales can be used to assess for obsessive-compulsive behavior, including self-report measures that can establish the duration, intensity, and frequency of presenting symptomatology. They also assess the presence of metacognitions, attributions, harm reduction, tolerance level, and behavioral responses associated with OCD. They can establish the basis for differential diagnosis and set a baseline for treatment planning and interventions. This section describes screening instruments to assess mental status and comorbidity in these disorders (e.g., depression and anxiety).

The Obsessional Beliefs Questionnaire is an 87-item, 7-point, Likert-based questionnaire that assesses beliefs considered characteristics of obsessive thinking (Moretz & McKay, 2008). Individual subscales represent the domains of cognitions related to OCD: control thoughts

(14 items), importance of thoughts (14 items), responsibility (16 items), intolerance of uncertainty (13 items), and perfectionism (16 items). Higher scores are indicative of the presence of OCD.

The Contamination Cognitions Scale (CCS) assesses the overestimation of threat from potentially contaminated objects, listing 13 common objects associated with germs (e.g., door handles, toilet seats) and asks clients to rate the likelihood and severity of contamination if they were to touch each object and refrain from washing their hands (Deacon & Maack, 2008).

The Obsessive-Compulsive Inventory is a 42-item self-report measure of the frequency of OCD symptoms and the distress experienced from them in the past month (Moretz & McKay, 2008; Pietrefesa & Coles, 2009). A total score of 168 is possible, and a score of 42 or more indicates the presence of OCD. Seven subscales, utilizing a 5-point Likert scale, measure constructs of OCD (washing, checking, ordering, doubting, obsessing, hoarding, and mental neutralizing) (Moretz & McKay, 2008).

The Obsessive-Compulsive Trait Core Dimensions Questionnaire is a 20-item self-report measure that assesses compulsive behaviors in OCD—harm avoidance and incompleteness (Pietrafesa & Coles, 2009). Each of the two subscales has 10 items rated on a 5-point Likert scale. The scale demonstrates good internal consistency for each subscale.

The Yale-Brown Obsessive-Compulsive Scale is a 10-item, 5-point Likert scale measuring the severity and frequency of obsessions and compulsions experienced during a day. It has two subscales, obsessions and compulsions, with a score range from zero (no symptoms) to 40 (extreme symptoms), demarcating the level of severity associated with symptoms by focusing on time spent, interference, distress, resistance from the obsessions and compulsions, and level of control over them (Goodman et al., 1989).

The Vancouver Obsessional Compulsive Inventory is a 55-item scale with six subscales measuring cognitive and behavioral constructs of OCD: contamination, checking, obsessions, hoarding, just right, and indecisiveness (Moretz & McKay, 2008).

To establish mental state and areas of cognitive functioning, the Folstein Mini Mental State Examination contains questions assessing orientation to time, place, attention, and memory. This measure is dependent on age and educational background and is sensitive to individuals who may not be familiar with the information presented on these tests, such as names of presidents, geographic locations, and important dates and events; it also takes into account the different conceptualization of place and location with respect to an individual's background (Adler, 2007; APA, 2000; Amin, Kuhle, & Fitzpatrick, 2003; Insel & Badger, 2002). It addresses task completion as related to attention and memory through engaging actions of writing, copying, and observation.

Because of the shared phenomenology of anxiety disorders with other *DSM* disorders, scales that assess both anxiety and depression have been used to assess for the severity of anxiety present. Scales such as the Cognitive-Somatic Anxiety Questionnaire (CSAQ) created by Schwartz, Davidson, and Goleman (1978) may be helpful in starting this process. The CSAQ is a 14-item instrument that focuses thoughts and somatic modes of trait anxiety and is used to assess the presence of general anxiety in situations. The CSAQ has a score ranging between 7 and 35; the higher the score, the higher the level of cognitive and somatic complaints. The Beck Depression Inventory is a 21-item, self-report, multiple-choice questionnaire that measures the presence of depression with items particular to anxiety (Center for Psychological Studies, 2008). It describes a specific behavioral manifestation of depression evaluated through four self-evaluative statements with ordinal measurement to assess for severity of symptoms. Hudson's (1977) Generalized Contentment Scale (GCS) is a 25-item scale measuring the severity of nonpsychotic depression. It produces a score from zero to 100, with higher scores indicating greater depression (Hudson, 1992; Hudson & Proctor, 1977). The GCS has three cutoff points: 30, 50, and 70 (all ±5). Scores below 30 indicate the absence of a clinically significant depression; scores above 50 indicate some suicidal ideation; and scores above 70 nearly always indicate severe stress and suicidal tendencies. (See Fischer and Corcoran, 2007, for a copy of the scale and scoring information).

These scales are useful in determining the onset, frequency, and severity of OCD. They can also specify the types of thoughts and behaviors that cause the most distress and emotional reactions and responses to the obsessions and compulsions in OCD. They can be used to establish the diagnosis and the level of function.

Beginning the Diagnostic Assessment

To better understand OCD, it is necessary to examine the risk factors and symptoms, the diagnostic criteria, the problems identifying the disorder, and the interventions that have been used to treat persons with this disorder. The case example and the rest of this section focus specifically on OCD from a personal, community, and societal perspective. Based on this information, a treatment plan and practice strategy are developed to embrace, identify, and effectively treat individuals who suffer from OCD. The practitioner should always ensure that a physical exam has ruled out any recognizable medical illness or substance use that can account for the obsessive and compulsive symptoms. Working collaboratively with a medically trained professional is always recommended.

CASE EXAMPLE - CASE OF KURT

Kurt is a 45-year-old White male of average height and weight, appearing his stated age, who was referred by his family physician for a mental health assessment. The client reports experiencing morbid ideation, intense stress and worry, thought intrusions, inability to sleep, difficulty leaving his house, and hypervigilance. He described his problems as "worrying about everything and not being able to relax." He reports that these symptoms have been present for more than 6 months, with worsening symptoms in the past month. His weight loss is slightly over 10 pounds in the past month, and he has had difficulties with his personal and family life secondary to employment concerns and difficulties in completing his daily tasks. He is accompanied to the mental health assessment by his wife and daughters.

Kurt states he has difficulties with intrusive thoughts and behaviors, which he reports are "necessary." When asked to define the nature of these thoughts, Kurt states he is experiencing disturbing images of disease and how its presence could harm him and his family. These images cause him to experience intense disgust and alarm, as he can "see" the presence of these images all around. When asked what occurs when he experiences these thoughts, he replies that he has to clean the bathrooms, bedrooms, and kitchen that family members had used. He also described how this morning when he pulled out of the driveway, he noticed a piece of litter on the curb. He pulled back into the driveway, picked up the litter, and went into the house to throw it away. He then reports having to clean his pathway in the kitchen and is preoccupied with germs, viruses, and bacteria all around him. He is worried that illness will come and cause death. He reports that when these thoughts are present, he must clean to relieve them. When asked what occurs when he does not clean, he reports that he is unable to stop cleaning. Kurt reports that in the past month he has been increasingly concerned about the possibility of death and harm and worrying about the possibility of someone breaking into his house. He states he is constantly checking and rechecking everything to make sure the house is secure. He often locks and relocks the door just to verify that it had been locked correctly. He reports thoughts of horrific images of what could transpire if the checking and cleaning routines are not kept, which cause him to feel terror. He is afraid of having his residence robbed, although he is living in a middle-income family neighborhood and has not suffered any criminally related behavior. When asked to describe what occurs in response to these thoughts, he reports repeated checking and rechecking that the door is locked and germ-free. When he cannot complete his ritual of checking the door, he feels petrified with fear. He reports knowing that his current concerns are causing him harm and reports frustration, anger, and a sense of worthlessness regarding his inability to control his thoughts and emotions. When asked how these thoughts and behaviors have affected other areas of his life, he reports that he often forgets to shower or bathe due to constant worry. Similar concerns existed in his last employment setting, and these ritualistic behaviors have caused strain in his relationships and personal life.

Kurt reports that he was employed as a manager for more than 5 years. As a manager, he was under a lot of pressure to make sure things were done correctly and reports a strong sense of control and need for perfection, which he states was demanded in his job. He feels he did not have difficulties with past employers and that they were pleased with his performance, and losing this job has added to his stress. When describing his job, he states that internal problems forced him to increasingly check and recheck his reports and figures, and he demanded more of his employees. He found it increasingly difficult to leave his office. His high need for order has become increasingly more rigid. He reports that his thoughts about disease escalated during this time, and their pressure conflicted with his ability to carry out tasks. He reports that he was released from his employment duties a month ago.

He denies any medical concerns at this time and denies taking medication. He denies any allergies to medications. He reports that he was a "social drinker" and has no past history of illicit drug use. He denies a history of treatment for substance abuse and denies any past treatment for mental health–related concerns at the time of this interview.

Kurt reports strain in his relationships due to his intrusive thoughts and behaviors. He reports that his wife has become increasingly angry with him, yelling at him when he requests reassurance regarding his thoughts. He reports also feeling concerned about the impact this will have on the quality of their relationship. His intense desires for cleanliness while neglecting his own personal hygiene has not improved matters related to intimacy with his wife. He states that he loves his wife but is unable to stop his presenting problems. He is also concerned that his relationship with his daughters has been affected. He denies feeling suicidal and states he has no plan and would not harm himself because of the loss this would cause for his family.

Completion of the Diagnostic Assessment for Kurt

The diagnostic assessment starts with an initial interview, where the initial symptoms of a client are assessed and evaluated. To facilitate the interview, a complete mental status exam was conducted. Basic information related to his presentation, mental functioning, and higher order abilities and thought form and content were gathered. (See Quick Reference 8.4.)

QUICK REFERENCE 8.4

Mental Status Description

Presentation	Mental Functioning	Higher Order Abilities	Thought Form/Content
Appearance: Unkempt	Simple Calculations: Mostly accurate	Judgment: Limited	Thought Process: Obsessive
Mood: Anxious	Serial Sevens: Accurate	Insight: Good or Fair	
Attitude: Guarded	Immediate Memory: Intact	Intelligence: Average	General Knowledge: Mostly accurate
Affect: Blunted/flat Speech: Guarded	Remote Memory: Intact		
Motor Activity: Restless	Orientation: Fully oriented	Similarities/ Differences: Intact	
		Proverb Interpretation: Refused	

The assessment of OCD should take into consideration all criteria specified under the *DSM 5* and subsequent risk factors. The assessment should include all of the demographic information available, physical examinations, current and past history (medical and mental), and specific background features that contribute to understanding presenting symptoms specified in the *DSM 5* and in this book. There are no laboratory examinations to establish OCD, but dermatologic problems offer clues to the severity of symptoms present (e.g., excessive hand washing) (APA, 2013). Based on the information provided, he meets the criteria for the principal diagnosis, which in this case is also termed the reason for visit of OCD. There is no evidence of tic-related symptoms, so there are no specifiers applied.

Obsessive Compulsive Disorder (reason for visit)

Coding 300.3 (*ICD-9-CM*) or F(42) (*ICD-10-CM*)

Kurt was referred by his primary care physician for a mental health assessment. He reports intrusive and obsessive thoughts regarding contamination (germs, disease, bacteria, and viruses) and voices concerns about harm to himself and his family. He reports engaging in compulsive behaviors such as cleaning, checking, and ordering to avoid thinking about his problems. The intrusive thoughts have been present for more than 6 months, with a worsening of symptoms in the past month. He currently reports morbid ideation, insomnia, agoraphobia, intrusive thoughts, excessive behaviors, stress, worry, and difficulty in completing and maintaining daily functions. He identifies being stressed related to his loss of employment, marital discord, and relationship concerns with his daughters. He has poor personal hygiene and states he has no medical concerns at the time of this interview. He denies any suicidal and/or homicidal ideation and having any auditory, visual, gustatory, olfactory, or tactile hallucinations. His motor function appears within normal limits. Judgment and decision making are limited.

The presenting clinical features of Kurt's symptoms are obsessions and compulsion. These include Kurt's report that he experiences intrusive thoughts related to contamination—that is, he reports thinking of ways of reducing the germs, bacteria, and viruses that he sees all around. These thoughts are further exacerbated by his concern related to reports of germs "in the news" and how they cause death. He reports increased intrusion of thoughts of being harmed and/or his family being harmed with onset in the past month, related to the increased stress and pressure he is currently experiencing secondary to his loss of employment. He reports that, secondary to these intrusions, he engages in excessive safety and preventive behaviors to reduce the emotions he experiences, such as worry, fear, terror, and disgust. He states that in general he has a high need for control, perfectionism, and orderliness, and the onset of pressure increased his symptom severity. Due to his current symptoms, he reports marital strain, as his constant requests for reassurance are frustrating and angering his wife. This concern causes him further stress, which exacerbates his presenting problem.

He is cognizant of the excessive nature of his thoughts and behaviors. When he attempts to cease these repetitive behaviors, he experiences strong negative emotions, which prompt him to reengage in compulsions. He is cognizant of the effect of stress exacerbating his symptoms. Delusions and/or hallucinations are not present, and his mental state is within normal limits, so a diagnosis of schizophrenia or a psychotic disorder is not applicable for his condition. He does not present with substance use problems or a medical condition, so anxiety disorders related to these can also be ruled out. With the high score of distress symptoms on his Obsessive-Compulsive Inventory scale, there appears to be a strong presence of OCD, and given his presenting problem and symptom duration, Kurt is given the diagnosis of obsessive-compulsive disorder.

Kurt's report of morbid ideation is in response to his symptoms and current stressors. He reports a weight loss of slightly more than 10 pounds in the past month, secondary to his loss of employment and onset of new intrusive symptoms. He reports difficulty sleeping secondary to his fear, terror, worry, and stress and reports that his symptoms are affecting all facets of his life (e.g., employment, relationships, personal satisfaction). Kurt's current morbid thoughts are related to feeling frustrated, angry, and emotionally weak at his inability to control his intrusive thoughts. He does not ruminate about "being worthless" or engage in persistent brooding, as found in major depression. Because of his present actions, he reports evading illness and reducing potential threats to him and his family, indicative of mood congruency with obsessions rather than of major depression. Because of his presenting features, the diagnosis of major depression is not applicable at the time of this interview.

Intelligence testing should be addressed when his presenting symptoms are stabilized or it appears that they are related to issues of an organic nature, including assessment of defense mechanism and personality disorders. During the interview, Kurt was given the Obsessive-Compulsive Inventory Scale to measure the frequency and distress experienced from symptoms within the past month. Kurt scored 122 of 168, which indicates the presence of OCD, with a mean score of distress higher than 2.5 in the subscales of washing, checking, doubting, ordering, and obsessions. His overall mean score of distress is 2.9, suggesting moderate to severe distress related to his symptoms. He was also given the Folstein Mini Mental State Examination to assess his mental state. He is oriented and demonstrates no impairment with recall, attention and calculation are intact, and he demonstrates no impairments in language, reading, writing, or copying.

Kurt denies any medical concerns at the time of the interview. He denies any allergies to any medications, and this should be written in all caps to alert other providers in his integrated care.

Other Conditions That May Be a Focus of Clinical Attention

With the elimination of the multiaxial diagnosis often used in *DSM-IV* and *DSM-IV-TR*, the information previously provided on Axis IV and Axis V is no longer a requirement. Therefore, in addition to the principal and provisional diagnoses, the types of information previously listed there should still be included. For practitioners interested in including this information from Section II of the *DSM-5*, Chapters 21 and 22 may be of particular help. Chapter 21 has the medication-induced movement disorders and other adverse effects of medication, and Chapter 22 has the other conditions that may be a focus of clinical intervention. In the case of Kurt, the information in Chapter 22 may be of the most help outlining several supporting factors. The first are the biopsychosocial stressors (especially those related to the family situation and key relationships).

Various social stressors are currently affecting Kurt, and these stressors will also be indirectly applicable to establishing his overall level of functioning. He is currently unemployed, having lost his job in the past month. Financial concerns are placing more stress on his current condition. He reports marital strain and relationship problems with his daughters related to his compulsive behaviors. His psychosocial stressors should be addressed:

- Loss of employment
- Financial concerns
- Marital concerns
- Family dynamics and interpersonal relationship concerns

Clinical attention must also address the severity of his obsessive symptoms and how they affect his daily functioning. Kurt does not present with suicidal ideation but does express morbid ideation. He has obsessive rituals, which are the nature of his presenting problem. These rituals affect his daily and occupational functioning. He was able to maintain employment for the past 5 years until the stress at his employment setting worsened his present symptoms, resulting in his employment loss last month. His mental state is within normal limits, and his impairments are not infused with delusions or hallucinations. Kurt denies any medical concerns and stated he is not taking any medications at this time, and he has no known allergies. Kurt voiced his inability to sleep and a recent weight loss. He identified himself as a social drinker. He reported no history of illicit drug use. He also denied past treatment for substance use and mental health issues. He has serious impairments to his personal and occupational functioning. (See Quick Reference 8.5.)

Treatment Planning and Intervention Strategy

Creating a treatment plan starts with identifying problematic behaviors and how to best address them (see Sample Treatment Plan 8.1). To start

QUICK REFERENCE 8.5

Identify Primary and Presenting Problems for Kurt

Primary problem:	Obsessive thoughts and compulsive behaviors.
Presenting problems:	Current unemployment and strained personal and family relations. Difficulty in completing activities of daily living.

treatment planning, cognitive and behavioral concerns are identified. Issues in OCD are determined by the severity and intensity of the obsessions and compulsions and what the client believes about them. In OCD, clients are cognizant that their reactions to these obsessions and compulsions are beyond reason and in excess but cannot stop them. Individuals with OCD frequently present to outpatient settings rather than inpatient settings, unless the obsessions are related to themes of hurting others and cause severe distress. Assessment for the presence of these obsessions and subsequent care should be implemented. In OCD, the ability to complete tasks is present, although inhibitions are noted. Under certain conditions, the hindered visuospatial capacities and inhibitions hamper clients' ability to effectively problem-solve when under intense stress or perceived negative criticisms. It is appropriate to assess under what conditions the symptoms worsen in severity and intensity. This information can be useful in treatment planning and implementation.

The obsessions and compulsions are usually attributed to a negative feedback loop whereby clients see and experience some relief from performing the behaviors. Also, clients might believe that performing these behaviors protects them from worsening symptoms. Cognitive restructuring can be used to modify the obsessions connected to the compulsion. In restructuring these thoughts, behaviors related to them have to be extinguished. Doing this requires clients to learn new ways of processing information and regulating emotions related to the thoughts and behaviors experienced. Changing a ritualized behavior is never easy; effort and patience are required for clients to implement a more constructive pattern of behavior. Treatment should address the application of extinction of behaviors and thoughts performed in response to the stressors.

Desensitizing the client from the emotions and thoughts experienced is attributed to positive and longer-lasting responses for addressing problematic behaviors. In OCD, this desensitizing may require repeated sessions where clients are requested to hold an item that they are told is infected with germs and to restrain impulses and emotions prior to using a sanitizer. Clients can learn coping skills that can be applied and generalized to other areas, such as doorknobs, until the obsessions and compulsions are stabilized. The treatment plan must include addressing the obsessions and compulsions, the symptoms causing the most distress. Treatment plans should include a long-term objective that focuses on developing beliefs and patterns that increase functioning and reduce distress. Short-term objectives can focus on education, cognitive restructuring, training, and systematic desensitization.

Deep breathing and relaxation can soothe emotions associated with thoughts and actions. With their intense emotions and difficulty in sleeping, individuals with OCD experience difficulty in managing the impact of their emotions and are subject to muscle tension. Learning to tune in to the physiological reactions of OCD can increase recognition and self-regulation. Ways to regulate physiological reactions (e.g., breathing exercises, massages, tension and release exercises, and general physical exercise) should be included in the treatment planning and utilized to improve other areas disturbed in clients' lives. Included in the long-term objective of achieving self-regulation, and in relation to short-term objectives, the addition of breathing exercises and massage sessions between a couple could improve daily functioning affected by the OCD.

Accurate assessment of the pressure and stress is critical to a successful outcome, as this component of added stress for the client is also a source of frustration for family members. Often these stressors include ignorance regarding OCD, family dynamics dysfunction, communication difficulties, and associated social problems that result from these stressors. Family education is important in working with individuals suffering from OCD. Areas of focus include improving communication; providing a forum for frustrations, concerns, and problem solving; engaging support groups; and improving the quality of relationships among family members. Objectives regarding education and maximizing healthy communication patterns should be included in the treatment plan. The quality of intimate relationships can be addressed through marital counseling. The long-term goal is to improve clients' ability to engage in activities of daily living (see Sample Treatment Plan 8.1).

Like all disorders in this book, the record-keeping focus in OCD needs to be problem-oriented. Documenting behavioral responses needs to be linked to measurable results in treatment planning. Specific information related to observable behaviors is necessary in the documentation of OCD, and the greater the specificity of the presenting problem, the greater the success in treatment implementation. Making a connection between the thoughts and resulting behavior is critical in the problem-oriented record documentation. The thoughts, as observed through behaviors, can be addressed in the treatment plan. Documentation of concrete examples of symptoms, such as motor tension (restlessness, tiredness, shakiness, or muscle tension), autonomic hyperactivity (palpitations, shortness of breath, dry mouth, trouble swallowing, nausea, or diarrhea), or symptoms of hypervigilance should be included. Once this behavior is identified and outlined, a measurable treatment plan can be established.

Intervention strategies for OCD and all of the anxiety disorders are addressed later in this chapter, as they share common underlying principles and treatments. The treatment plan should assess criteria defined for OCD; establish a baseline for frequency, duration, and intensity of symptoms.

He has several psychosocial stressors currently affecting him. Kurt's current mental health issues have affected his relationships with his wife and daughters. K is also experiencing employment concerns; he lost his job because of difficulties in completing his daily tasks.

Kurt's client record should reflect the impact of his psychosocial stressors and current symptoms. He is socially isolated except for the contact he has with his family. He has no friends to offer support. His work performance was affected by his difficulties with concentration and follow-through. His symptoms are serious because of the disturbing and intrusive nature of the thoughts, urges, and images he sees. He also reports an inability to sleep and feeling detached. K appears to have "good to fair insight"; he reported feeling frustrated and angry, with a sense of worthlessness regarding his inability to control his thoughts and emotions.

General Considerations for Practice Strategy

The intervention strategies discussed are applicable to all of the OCD diagnoses in this chapter. Models to treat OCD generally utilize multiple approaches designed to target different components of the disorder. In general, more than one psychotherapeutic approach is used in combination with other interventions. Some require more intense application, but all are geared to target thoughts, behaviors, and emotions in response to misattributions, erroneous information processing, and environmental factors. Regardless of what intervention is used, all seek to better understand, address, and recognize triggers and identify ways of reattributing and refocusing problematic behaviors.

Focusing specifically on the individual psychosocial interventions has to address metacognitions, emotion regulation, physiological responses, and the corresponding behaviors

SAMPLE TREATMENT PLAN 8.1

Obsessive-Compulsive Disorder (OCD)

OCD has four specific criteria (ranging from A to D) that must be met. The core features are obsessive thoughts, urges, and images that are recurrent and persistent. In response to these thoughts, urges, and images, the person performs repetitive behaviors or mental acts. A criterion of these obsessions and compulsions is that they are time-consuming and cause impairment in the individual's daily functioning. The thoughts, urges, and images, along with the behavioral and mental acts to control them, are not better explained by a medical or substance cause. Symptoms have been present for 6 months, worsening in the past month.

Signs and Symptoms to Note in the Record

- Morbid ideation
- Intense stress and worry
- Thought intrusions
- Inability to sleep
- Difficulty completing tasks due to obsessions and compulsions
- Hypervigilance
- Weight loss
- Interpersonal difficulty with family and significant others

Long-Term Goals

1. Develop cognitive beliefs and behavioral patterns to control, alleviate, and reduce the frequency, intensity, and duration of OCD symptoms.
2. Increase capacity to self-regulate.
3. Increase abilities to strengthen relationships with wife and daughters.

Short-Term Goals

1. Reduce morbid ideation.
2. Reduce stress and worry.
3. Cope with underlying feelings related to leaving his home.
4. Decrease hypervigilance, increase controlled behavior, achieve a more stable mood, and develop more deliberate thought processes.
5. Address interpersonal relationships with wife and daughters.

Short-Term Goals and Objectives	Interventions
1. Cooperate with a psychiatric evaluation and participate in treatment as warranted.	Arrange for a psychiatric evaluation to assist with morbid ideation. Discuss the potential for medication to assist with morbid ideation. Request a no-harm, no-risk safety plan be put in place.
2. Identify intrusive thoughts and reduce stress, worry, and intrusive thoughts.	Psychotherapy to address recognizing triggers and destressing activities.
3. Express concerns about leaving his home.	Help client problem-solve using behavioral rehearsal and individual psychotherapy to reinforce leaving home for planned activities.

(continued)

SAMPLE TREATMENT PLAN 8.1 (*Continued*)

4. Be able to sit calmly for 30 minutes without agitation or distractibility.	Reinforce client's increased control over his energy, and help the client set attainable goals and limits to reduce his hypervigilance.
5. Process how feelings related to thoughts, urges, and behaviors affect relationships with members of the family (wife and daughters).	Provide structure for the client's thought processes and actions by directing the course of the conversation and developing plans for the client's behaviors. In psychotherapy, provide opportunities for client's wife and daughters to speak with him one-on-one to repair their relationships.
6. Take medications as prescribed by physician.	Assess needs for OCD medications and arrange for prescription if needed.
7. Identify anxiety-causing and/or anxiety-producing cognitive mechanisms.	Provide education to client about OCD, including but not limited to psychological and physiological symptoms. Encourage client to identify anxiety-producing cognitions, feelings, and emotions and distress level associated with them. Reality-test cognitions, assisting to differentiate between functional and dysfunctional thoughts.
8. Identify behaviors in response to cognitions.	Engage client in thought-stopping exercises paired with anxiety-producing cognitions. Encourage client to identify and verbalize feelings and emotions in response to and when not in response to anxiety-producing thoughts, urges, and images. Provide education on systematic desensitization, its mechanisms, and its applications.
9. Implement self-relaxation techniques when anxiety-producing situations recur.	Assist client to sustain negative emotions, feelings, and physical symptoms in response to not engaging in compulsive actions. Educate client about self-relaxation techniques to alleviate fear, worry, terror, and/or stress.
10. Engage support systems.	Provide education to family regarding OCD. Provide family sessions for family to voice concerns, frustrations, and thoughts regarding treatment. Provide family sessions to address communication patterns that facilitate healthy dynamics. Provide family sessions to address marital discord.

associated with OCD. These interventions can involve multiple treatment modalities (e.g., individual, group, family, and through technology), all designed to increase cognitive, behavioral, and psychosocial functioning. The psychosocial interventions listed have been cited as most effective in treating OCD. Often individuals with OCD do not seek treatment because they are opposed to psychological therapies or because medication only or medication and therapies are not appealing (Layard, Clark, Knapp, & Mayraz, 2007). Most professionals agree that psychosocial interventions are considered best practices (with or without medications) at targeting the behavioral and problematic components of OCD.

One popular approach for treating OCD spectrum disorders remains cognitive-behavior therapy (CBT) because of its demonstrable results and cost-effectiveness. The emphasis is on expanding the client's sense of self-efficacy, independence, participation, self-monitoring, and control in treatment. It can be utilized in various treatment modalities (individual, groups, couples, families, Internet). All psychosocial interventions need to take into account the restrictions by managed care organizations and insurance plans in their billing and reimbursements. The CBT interventions complement other treatment modalities in an integrated approach and are equally as effective on their own to address OCD and related disorders. The techniques utilized in CBT are ideal for working with obsessive-compulsive problems because they allow mental health practitioners to be relatively confrontational yet respectful of the client. "Specifically, difficulties in safety, trust, power and control, self-esteem, and intimacy are targeted [cognitive component of CBT]" (Keane, Marshall, & Taft, 2006, p. 180). This relationship is essential for promoting client independence and positive self-regard.

Particularly for OCD, focusing on thoughts and their impact on emotional regulation and reactions is suited where information processing is impaired (Fruzzetti, Crook, Erikson, Lee, & Worrall, 2008). The application of the cognitive model helps to identify thoughts and the precipitation of physiological and cognitive reactions; if not identified, it creates a self-perpetuating cycle that intensifies anxiety (McEvoy & Perini, 2009; Siev & Chambless, 2007). A useful component of CBT is that it addresses the misperception of threat and danger assessments (real or imagined) and the activation of fear, terror, rage, and worry common in OCD. The CBT model utilizes components to address obsessive-compulsive thoughts, urges, images, and actions (self-monitoring, cognitive restructuring including evaluating and reconsidering interpretive and predictive cognitions, relaxation training, and rehearsal and coping skills) (Siev & Chambless, 2007). It is a present-based therapy that reinforces the client's focus on the now and increases reality testing to sustain functioning while increasing coping capabilities and restructuring thoughts and behaviors.

A second individualized approach in addition to cognitive-behavioral therapy is contemporary behavior therapy. It can be used to provide the active implementation of behaviors to extinguish emotions, thoughts, and behaviors that affect individuals. It is often rehearsed in sessions and applied through imagery, modeling, and computer models to create a response in a safe setting with the actual application of the individual exposing himself or herself to the perceived threat or source of distress. Exposure therapies (e.g., systematic desensitization, also known as in vivo exposure therapy, and/or eye movement desensitization and reprocessing [EMDR]) are particularly useful for individuals suffering from OCD; these interventions can be therapist guided or self-guided. The exposure therapies that use flooding involve gradual or prolonged exposure to the focus stimuli that create the fear or anxiety reaction (Zoellner, Abramowitz, Moore, & Slagle, 2008). Relaxation training is also a behavior-based therapy; learning to control muscle tension through taught relaxation techniques reduces obsessive thoughts, urges, and images and compulsive responses.

Self-help interventions are cost-effective and target individuals who are reluctant to enter or unsure of entering treatment or who seek affiliation (e.g., books, self-help groups). The CBT interventions are increasingly applied to novel therapeutic situations utilizing Internet-based services that generate automatic decision making (Andersson, 2009). These interventions assess individuals' decision making and provide educational protocols and support to increase awareness and motivation. Utilizing Internet-accessible self-help materials and computer-based live group exposure sessions, an identified therapist provides support, encouragement, and occasionally direct therapeutic activities via e-mail (Andersson, 2009). In particular, computer-based therapies target individuals with OCD who do not actively seek or who have reservations about treatment. Included in these interventions are panic disorder, social anxiety disorder, posttraumatic stress disorder, mood disorders, substance use disorders, and other health-related problems (Andersson, 2009; Walker, Roffman, Picciano, & Stephens, 2007).

For the most part, regardless of the intervention, taking into account the support system and participating in couples or family therapy is always recommended. It allows family members to verbalize thoughts, emotions, and concerns related to any mental disorder. Family members can experience difficulties secondary to rituals, fears, inability to perform functions, neglect, and violence. Codependency occurs and leaves family members feeling hopeless in making life manageable. Families need education and support to learn coping skills and receive help in understanding their loved one's behavior. Family therapy can offer support, education, and a forum to vent feelings and problem-solve. The family as a whole needs assistance in strengthening its own support systems.

In summary, for any treatment strategy to be successful, an integrated approach is needed that focuses on evidence-based practices. Market-based principles applied to service delivery have shifted health care to a specialization of services that emphasize quality assurance and cost-effectiveness. This model of health care practice dominates all aspects and types of treatment availability, emphasizing evidence and best practices, with a feedback loop between billing and reimbursement. Utilizing an integrated approach allows expediency in treatment, through rapid identification, safety control measures among providers, and intervention techniques that reduce harm. The resultant approach stresses demonstrated effectiveness while encouraging client participation. The mechanisms for the allocation of services specify not just specialization but integration as a quality-control measure. Because of its multifactorial aspects, OCD requires the integrated specialization of professionals. This is already evident in the pharmacological intervention services, counseling, and screening for medication side effects and hazardous effects. The integrated approach facilitates the integration of family and a supportive system of care to achieve more successful outcomes, reducing harm and increasing sustainability. Internet-based OCD interventions may also be helpful for targeting individuals who are reluctant to engage in treatment or need the convenience it affords. These methods offer measures that help to identify the presence of anxiety disorders, can assess intrusive obsessive thoughts, and help to relabel and reattribute them.

Self-Regulatory Executive Function Model

The self-regulatory executive function model (S-REF) is particularly useful in addressing metacognitive beliefs associated with OCD. According to this model, attentional control and inflexibility, such as an inability to shift, are contributing factors in emotional disorders (McEvoy & Perini, 2009). It addresses beliefs that increase the likelihood of selecting coping strategies that promote self-focused attention (threat monitoring, thought suppression, worry, and rumination) and maintain emotional disorders (McEvoy & Perini, 2009). "The model differentiates three levels of processing: automatic, low-level processing of external and internal stimuli; controlled processing directed toward the control of action and thought; and a permanent store of self beliefs" (Matthews & Wells, 2000, p. 83). The model's treatment aim is to increase attention shifting externally, increase flexibility and control, and employ the application of cognitive-behavioral therapy and attention training. Self-knowledge driving the maladaptive responses is examined, as are metacognitive beliefs influencing thoughts that maintain dysfunction, and processing schemata are modified to provide alternative processing to problematic stimuli (Matthews & Wells, 2000). Intervention focuses on three phases of attention training: selective attention, attention switching, and divided attention. These techniques require that individuals focus on one particular sound to the exclusion of others for 30 seconds. Once complete attention is shifted to another sound, it is then shifted to another approximately every 5 seconds—thus dividing attention simultaneously—and focused on as many sounds as possible for approximately 15 seconds (Matthews & Wells, 2000; McEvoy & Perini, 2009). The model's CBT and attention training serve as a supplemental component and have demonstrated improvements in increased attention, self-control, and disengaging from obsessive thoughts, urges, and images.

Medication as a Treatment Modality

Pharmacological advances are available to address aspects of brain-related dysfunction associated with OCD. This mode of intervention is effective but not without controversy. Excessive availability and inadequate regulation have increased the consumption of psychotherapeutic drugs through prescriptions, illegal street vendors, and the Internet. Increased use of benzodiazepines and other anxiolytics has contributed to an estimated 15% to 44% of chronic benzodiazepine users becoming addicted and experiencing discontinuance problems. Upon cessation, these individuals experience severe withdrawal symptoms, including emergent anxiety and depressive symptoms (Hood, O'Neil, & Hulse, 2009). Benzodiazepines—for example, clonazepam (Klonopin), temazepam (Restoril), and alprazolam (Xanax)—have little effect on OCD symptoms (Spoormaker & Montgomery, 2008). Benzodiazepine and prescription antianxiety medications, excluding nonbenzodiazepine antianxiety agents (e.g., hypnotics, sedatives, and anxiolytics), can be misused and abused by individuals with OCD, which creates further problems of withdrawal and dependence (World Health Organization, 2009).

In certain types of OCD, pharmacotherapy may be less effective when using traditional selective serotonin reuptake inhibitors (SSRIs) (Pietrefesa & Coles, 2009). The SSRIs approved by the Food and Drug Administration to treat OCD include sertraline (Zoloft), fluoxetine (Prozac), and paroxetine (Paxil), which may exhibit modest effectiveness in treating OCD (Keane et al., 2006; Spoormaker & Montgomery, 2008). Tricyclic antidepressants are used less often because of side effects and potential toxicity, specifically imipramine (Tofranil) and amitriptyline (Elavil). Efficacy of the monoamine oxidase inhibitors (MAOIs), such as phenelzine (Nardil) and brofaromine (Consonar), is not supported for certain types of OCD and used as a last resort based on the problematic side effects and dietary restrictions (Keane et al., 2006). Other psychotherapeutic medications include antipsychotic agents, such as nefaxodone (Serzone), trazodone (Desyrel), and mirtazapine (Remeron), to treat insomnia and in rare circumstances hallucinations. Other sleep agents, such as cyproheptadine (Periactin), slightly worsened nightmares and symptom severity in some cases of OCD (Spoormaker & Montgomery, 2008).

Antiadrenergic agents are changing the future direction of pharmacological treatment in OCD, as these agents target specific neurobiological components relative to the clinical presentation. The association between noradrenergic hyperactivity and pharmacological agents targeting specific adrenergic receptors (associated with hyperarousal and hypervigilance) might be more applicable and efficient and provide better clinical and treatment outcomes than traditional psychotherapeutic drugs, such as prazosin (Minipress) (Keane et al., 2006; Strawn & Geracioti, 2007). Pharmacological interventions that target neurobiological and organic mechanisms related to the clinical presentation of OCD may also prove safer, relevant, and more appropriate than the types of pharmacological treatments currently available.

SUMMARY AND FUTURE DIRECTIONS

The obsessive-compulsive and related disorders share common features such as compulsions and repetitive behaviors as well as anxiety-related behaviors. These disorders also share altered neurological disturbances, cognitive alterations, and behavioral disruptions. A breakdown in attention and information processing that results in physiological responses and inappropriate threat-meaning assignments remains central to the clinical phenomenology. The disorders in this category include obsessive-compulsive disorder, body dysmorphic disorder, hoarding disorder, trichotillomania (hair pulling disorder), excoriation (skin picking) disorder, substance/medication induced obsessive-compulsive and related disorder, obsessive-compulsive and related disorder due to another medical condition, other specified obsessive-compulsive and related disorder, and unspecified obsessive-compulsive and related disorder. Despite their common features, their clinical presentations vary in specificity of cognitive and behavioral responses, with intensity and excessive and inappropriate responses found in all.

These disorders require a comprehensive analysis of the multifactorial basis of how these disorders evolve and using this information to support the application of specific problem-behavior-focused interventions. Treatments and intervention practices to address the constructs of these disorders, particularly OCD, focus on cognitive restructuring, training executive functions in new ways to process information, learned physiological responses, desensitization, and extinction of behaviors. These methods focus on the neuropsychological deficits in cognition and emphasize reducing emotional reactions that accompany these disorders, such as fear, terror, anxiety, distress, and worry. Treatment needs to take into account associated risk factors and diagnostic measurements. Future directions should include research in information processing and attributions related to emotional and behavioral reactivity, accuracy in constructs of diagnostic assessments, technological models and applications, and preventive measures to reduce the onset and impact of stress responses and their progress.

REFERENCES

Abramowitz, J. S., Whiteside, S., Lynam, D., & Kalsy, S. (2003). Is thought–action fusion specific to obsessive-compulsive disorder?: A mediating role of negative affect. *Behaviour Research and Therapy, 41*(9), 1069–1079.

Adler, G. (2007). Intervention approaches to driving with dementia. *Health and Social Work, 32*(1), 75–79.

American Psychiatric Association. (2000). *Diagnostic and statistical manual of mental disorders* (4th ed., text rev.). Washington, DC: American Psychiatric Press.

American Psychiatric Association. (2013). *Diagnostic and statistical manual of mental disorder* (5th ed.). Arlington, VA: American Psychiatric Publishing.

Amin, S., Kuhle, C., & Fitzpatrick, L. (2003). Comprehensive evaluation of the older woman. *Mayo Clinic Proceedings, 78*(9), 1157–1185.

Andersson, G. (2009). Using the Internet to provide cognitive behavior therapy. *Behaviour Research and Therapy, 47*, 175–180.

Barnhill, J. W. (2014). Obsessive-compulsive and related disorders: Introduction. In J. W. Barnhill (Ed.),

DSM-5™ clinical cases (pp. 125–129). Washington, DC: American Psychiatric Publishing.

Center for Psychological Studies. (2008). *Beck Depression Inventory Scale*. Retrieved from Nova Southeastern University: http://www.cps.nova.edu/~cpphelp/BDI.html

Cooper, M. (1999). Treatment of persons and families with obsessive compulsive disorder: A review article. *Crisis Intervention, 5*, 25–36.

Cromer, K. R., Schmidt, N. B., & Murphy, D. L. (2007). An investigation of traumatic life events and obsessive-compulsive disorder. *Behavior Research and Therapy, 45*(7), 1683–1691.

Deacon, B., & Maack, D. J. (2008). The effects of safety behaviors on the fear of contamination: An experimental investigation. *Behaviour Research and Therapy, 46*(4), 537–547.

Do Rosario-Campos, M. C., Leckman, J. F., Curi, M., Quatrano, S., Katsovitch, L., Miguel, E. C., & Pauls, D. L. (2005). A family study of early onset obsessive compulsive disorder. *American Journal of Medical Genetics (Neuropsychiatric Genetics Part B), 136B*(1), 92–97. doi: 10.1002/ajmg.b.30149

Dziegielewski, S. F. (2010). *Psychopharmacology and social work practice: A person in environment approach* (2nd ed.). New York, NY: Springer.

Fischer, J., & Corcoran, K. (2007). *Measures for clinical practice: A source book. Volume 2: Adults* (4th ed.). New York, NY: Oxford University Press.

Fruzzetti, A. E., Crook, W., Erikson, K. M., Lee, J. E., & Worrall, J. M. (2008). Emotion regulation. In W. T. O'Donohue & J. E. Fisher (Eds.), *Cognitive behavior therapy: Applying empirically supported techniques in your practice* (pp. 174–186). Hoboken, NJ: Wiley.

Goodman, W. K., Price, L. H., Rasmussen, S. A., Mazure, C., Fleischmann, R. L., Hill, C. L., . . . Charney, D. S. (1989). Yale–Brown obsessive compulsive scale. 1. Development, use, and reliability. *Archives of General Psychiatry, 46*(11), 1006–1011.

Hofmeijer-Sevink, M. K., van Oppen, P., van Megen, H. J., Batelaan, N. M., Cath, D. C., van der Wee, N. J., . . . van Balkom, A. J. (2013). Clinical relevance of comorbidity in obsessive compulsive disorder: The Netherlands OCD Association study. *Journal of Affective Disorders, 150*(3), 847–854. doi:10.1016/j.jad.2013.03.014.

Hood, S., O'Neil, G., & Hulse, G. (2009). The role of flumazeil in the treatment of benzodiazepine dependence: Physiological and psychological profiles. *Journal of Psychopharmacology, 23*(4), 401–409.

Hudson, W. W. (1992). *The WALMYR Assessment Scale scoring manual*. Tempe, AZ: WALMYR.

Hudson, W. W., & Proctor, E. K. (1977). Assessment of depressive affect in clinical practice. *Journal of Consulting and Clinical Practice, 45*(6), 1206–1207.

Huff, N. C., Hernandez, J. A., Blanding, N. Q., & LaBar, K. S. (2009). Delayed extinction attenuates conditioned fear renewal and spontaneous recovery in humans. *Behavioral Neuroscience, 123*(4), 834–843.

Insel, K., & Badger, T. (2002). Deciphering the 4 D's: Cognitive decline, delirium, depression, and dementia—a review. *Journal of Advanced Nursing, 38*(4), 360–368.

Keane, T. M., Marshall, A. D., & Taft, C. T. (2006). Posttraumatic stress disorders: Etiology, epidemiology, and treatment outcome. *Annual Review of Clinical Psychology, 2*, 161–197.

Layard, R., Clark, D., Knapp, M., & Mayraz, G. (2007). Cost–benefit analysis of psychological therapy. *National Institute Economic Review, 202*, 90–98.

Locke, D. C. & Bailey, D. F. (2014). *Increasing cultural understanding* (3rd ed.). Los Angeles, CA: Sage.

Lum, D. (Ed.). (2011). *Culturally competent practice: A framework for understanding diverse groups and justice issues* (4th ed.). Pacific Grove, CA: Brooks/Cole, Thomson Learning.

Mathew, S. J., Coplan, J. D., & Gorman, J. M. (2001). Neurobiological mechanisms of social anxiety disorder. *American Journal of Psychiatry, 158*(10), 1558–1567.

Matthews, G., & Wells, A. (2000). Attention, automaticity, and affective disorder. *Behavior Modification, 24*(1), 69–93.

Mayo Clinic. (2013). *Obsessive compulsive disorders: Risk factors*. Retrieved from http://www.mayoclinic.org/diseases-conditions/ocd/basics/risk-factors/con-20027827

McEvoy, P. M., & Perini, S. J. (2009). Cognitive behavioral group therapy for social phobia with or without attention training: A controlled trial. *Journal of Anxiety Disorders, 23*, 519–528.

McGoldrick, M., Giordano, J., & Garcia-Preto, N. (Eds.). (2005). *Ethnicity and family therapy*. New York, NY: Guilford Press.

Mell, L. K., Davis, R. L., & Owens, D. (2005). Association between streptococcal infection and obsessive compulsive disorder, Tourette's syndrome, and tic disorder. *Pediatrics, 116*(1), 56–60.

Moretz, M., & McKay, D. (2008). Disgust sensitivity as a predictor of obsessive-compulsive contamination symptoms and associated cognitions. *Journal of Anxiety Disorders, 22*(4), 707–715.

National Institute of Mental Health. (2008). *The numbers count: Mental disorders in America*. Retrieved from http://www.nimh.nih.gov/health/publications/the-numbers-count-mental-disorders-in-america/index.shtml

Nestadt, G., Samuels, J., Riddle, M., Bienvenue, O. J. 3rd., Liang, K. Y., LaBuda, M., . . . Hoehn-Saric, R. (2000). A family study of obsessive compulsive disorder. *Archives of General Psychiatry, 57*(4), 358–363.

Paniagua, F. A. (2014). *Assessing and treating culturally diverse clients: A practical guide* (4th ed.). Los Angeles, CA: Sage.

Pietrefesa, A. S., & Coles, M. E. (2009). Moving beyond an exclusive focus on harm avoidance in obsessive-compulsive disorder: Behavioral validation for the separability of harm avoidance and incompleteness. *Behavior Therapy, 40*(3), 251–259.

Rizq, R. (2012) The perversion of care: Psychological therapies in a time of IAPT. *Psychodynamic Practice: Individuals, Groups and Organisations, 18*(1), 7–24. doi: 10.1080/14753634.2012.640161

Saint-Cyr, J. A. (2003). Frontal-striatal circuit functions: Context, sequence, and consequence. *Journal of the International Neuropsychological Society, 9*(1), 103–127.

Schmidt, N. B., Norr, A. M., & Korte, K. J. (2014). Panic disorder and agoraphobia: Considerations for *DSM-V*. *Research on Social Work Practice, 24*(1), 57–66.

Schore, A. N. (2014). Introduction. In J. J. Magnavita & J. C. Anchin (Eds.), *Unifying psychotherapy: Principles, methods, evidence from clinical science* (pp. xxi–xliv). New York, NY: Springer.

Schwartz, G. E., Davidson, R. J., & Goleman, D. J. (1978). Patterning of cognitive and somatic processes in self-regulation of anxiety: Effects of meditation versus exercise. *Psychosomatic Medicine, 40*(1), 321–328.

Siev, J., & Chambless, D. L. (2007). Specificity of treatment effects: Cognitive therapy and relaxation for generalized anxiety and panic disorder. *Journal of Consulting and Clinical Psychology, 75*(4), 513–522.

Simpson, H. B., Rosen, W., Huppert, J. D., Lin, S., Foa, E. B., & Liebowitz, M. R. (2006). Are there reliable neuropsychological deficits in obsessive-compulsive disorder? *Journal of Psychiatric Research, 40*(3), 247–257.

Spoormaker, V. I., & Montgomery, P. (2008). Disturbed sleep in post-traumatic stress disorder: Secondary symptom of core feature? *Sleep Medicine Reviews, 12*(3), 169–184.

Steinhausen, H., Bisgaard, C., Munk-Jørgensen, P., & Helenius, D. (2013). Family aggregation and risk factors of obsessive–compulsive disorders in a nationwide three-generation study. *Depression and Anxiety, 30*(12), 1177–1184. doi: 10.1002/da.22163

Strawn, J. R., & Geracioti, T. D., Jr. (2007). The treatment of generalized anxiety disorder with pregabalin, an atypical anxiolytic. *Neuropsychiatric Disease and Treatment, 3*(2), 237–243.

Tandon, R. (2012). Getting ready for DSM-5: Psychotic disorders. *Current Psychiatry, 11*(4), E1–E4. Retrieved from http://www.currentpsychiatry.com/articles/evidence-based-reviews/article/getting-ready-for-dsm-5-psychotic-disorders/a92f94271661c41feb5a4-c5e9e56c659.html

Van den Heuvel, O. A., Veltman, D. J., Groenewegen, H. J., Cath, D. C., van Balkom, A. J., van Hartskamp, J., . . . van Dyck, R. (2005). Frontal-striatal dysfunction during planning in obsessive-compulsive disorder. *Archives of General Psychiatry, 62*(3), 301–309.

Walker, D., Roffman, R., Picciano, J., & Stephens, R. (2007). The check-up: In-person, computerized, and telephone adaptations of motivational enhancement treatment to elicit voluntary participation by the contemplator. *Substance Abuse Treatment, Prevention, and Policy, 2*, 1–10.

White, R. M. B., Roosa, M. W., Weaver, S. R., & Nair, R. L. (2009). Cultural and contextual influences on parenting in Mexican American families. *Journal of Marriage and Family, 71*(1), 61–79.

Wise, V., McFarlane, A. C., Clark, C. R., & Battersby, M. (2009). Event-related potential and autonomic signs of maladaptive information processing during an auditory oddball task in panic disorder. *International Journal of Psychophysiology, 74*(1), 34–44. doi: 10.1016/j.ijpsycho.2009.07.001

Woo, S. M., & Keatinge, C. (Eds.). (2008). *Diagnosis and treatment of mental disorders across the lifetime*. Hoboken, NJ: Wiley.

World Health Organization. (2009). *Organization for Economic Co-operation and Development health working papers No. 42—Policies for healthy aging: An overview*. Paris: Organization for Economic Co-operation and Development.

Zoellner, L. A., Abramowitz, J. S., Moore, S. A., & Slagle, D. M. (2008). Flooding. In W. T. O'Donohue & J. E. Fisher (Eds.), *Cognitive behavior therapy: Applying empirically supported techniques in your practice* (pp. 202–210). Hoboken, NJ: Wiley.

CHAPTER 9

Trauma- and Stressor-Related Disorders

Sophia F. Dziegielewski and Barbara F. Turnage

INTRODUCTION

Stress and stressful situations create a subjective emotional state that can become a normal part of everyday life. When stress and anxiety occur, precipitated by a traumatic or stressful event, uncomfortable feelings often result that cause a response to the situation, event, or circumstance. When the response to traumatic or stressful events becomes excessive, problematic responses can affect every aspect of an individual's cognitive, behavioral, physiological, biological, and social responses. The *Diagnostic and Statistical Manual of Mental Disorders,* Fifth Edition (*DSM-5;* American Psychiatric Association [APA], 2013) categorizes these extreme responses as *trauma- and stressor-related disorders*. These disorders are reactive attachment disorder (RAD), disinhibited social engagement disorder (DSED), posttraumatic stress disorder (PTSD), acute stress disorder (ASD), adjustment disorders, other specified trauma- and stressor-related disorders, and unspecified trauma- and stressor-related disorder.

This chapter introduces the *DSM-5* taxonomical classification of the trauma- and stressor-related disorders and discusses how important it is to build resilience in the emersion of trauma (Pack, 2014). It is beyond the purpose of this chapter to explore in detail all of the diagnoses for trauma-and stressor-related disorders and the treatment options specific to each. Rather, it is to introduce the primary disorders as listed in *DSM-5,* with posttraumatic stress disorder as the focus. The extent, importance, and early predictors of problem behaviors and symptoms are explored. The various aspects of the disorder are presented with a case application that highlights the diagnostic assessment, treatment planning, and best-practices treatment strategy. In addition, the latest practice methods and newest research and findings are highlighted.

TOWARD A BASIC UNDERSTANDING OF TRAUMA- AND STRESSOR-RELATED DISORDERS

Trauma can be defined as the occurrence of emotionally traumatic events that overwhelm an individual. All of the disorders presented in this chapter require identification of a triggering event (Barnhill, 2014). This triggering event does not have to be isolated; it can be a multitude of events that are repeated and ongoing. Although much of the current research has focused on major catastrophes and people's reactions to them, each individual may respond to trauma differently. For some, the event teaches resilience and to push forward beyond what is generally expected. In *normative stress reactions* the aftermath of the trauma may last two to three days (Friedman, 2014). Yet, when

Special thanks to Jennifer Loflin and Carol (Jan) Vaughn for the earlier version of this chapter and to Carmen Chang Arriata for earlier versions and contributions to this topic and previous chapters.

the reaction becomes too extensive and the individual cannot function or regroup, a disorder may result. What all of the disorders listed in this chapter of the *DSM* share is exposure to a traumatic event. For reactive attachment disorder and disinhibited social engagement disorder, this early trauma can include social neglect.

Theories related to understanding trauma- and stressor-related disorders provide the underlying mechanisms on which treatment and prevention methods are based. Reactions to trauma vary considerably (APA, 2013), and theoretical approaches to better understanding often have their basis in anxiety. In the trauma- and stressor-related disorders, however, anxiety may or may not be present. Theories on understanding stressor-related disorders are often based in the biological sciences, neuropsychology, cognitive psychology, and social psychology. Stressor-related reactions can be complex and involve complex interactions affecting interpersonal, intrapersonal, and environmental relationships. In learning and retaining important information, impaired responses in the medial prefrontal cortex can result in impairment to metacognitions, which are critical to forming impressions about people and events (Sripada et al., 2009). Metacognitions include mental processes that provide the basis for trust and safety assessments. Because basic emotions are hardwired and recognized among all humans and animals, emotions are displayed that allow adaptation to the social environment. Recognizing and interpreting emotions such as happiness, sadness, anger, fear, joy, rage, terror, love, despair, and disgust also help the individual identify a threat and act correspondingly (fight or flight). These emotional reactions often occur after the stressful event and are considered a normal stress reaction. In addition, cognitive reactions and problems with interpretation may also occur. These can include feelings of disassociation, disorientation, and difficulty concentrating (Friedman, 2014). Cognitive and social theories help us better understand mental states and the resulting interactions, creating the basis for the communication and development of emotional schemata that provide a blueprint of memories. Influenced by these preprogrammed types of memories, a stimulus occurs, and the result is a learned response or prewired action. When feeling anxious after being exposed to a traumatic event, the individual often reacts to avoid harm and seek safety. When meaning is misattributed to a particular situation, another reaction may be triggered, even after safety has been secured. In addition, deficits in memory and executive function can impair information processing; consequently, judgment and decision making can also be impaired. Furthermore, the disruption affects the individual's ability to attribute meaning, motivation, and intention to cues. When this occurs, the individual may inappropriately react to perceived threats, resulting in anxiety and maladaptation.

UNDERSTANDING INDIVIDUALS WHO SUFFER FROM THE TRAUMA- AND STRESSOR-RELATED DISORDERS

Trauma and stress can affect people differently. When most people experience anxiety, they have an adequate set of background capacities and can attribute meaning, motivation, and intention. Extreme circumstances, especially over a period of time or in the formative years, including repeated social and emotional neglect or situational factors such as acts of betrayal, malevolence, and deceit (e.g., war, torture), can be especially difficult to process. The way these life circumstances and events are interpreted can create problematic blueprints that once seemed functional but do not serve the individual well at different times and under different circumstances. For example, during certain developmental periods or repeatedly over time, exposure to cruelty, perversion, or betrayal may lead to a greater sense of threat or fear. The threat of emotional or physical injury may also create a breakdown of social norms, as well as the "sense of safety associated with being a member of rule-guided community" (Charuvastra & Cloitre, 2008, p. 305). Impairment in this cognitive process alters the individual's schema and brain function, resulting in anxiety or feelings of disassociation. The onset of panic and social withdrawal remains, but the interpretation is impaired, secondary to past experiences and impaired metacognitions. In working with these clients, the issue becomes how to restructure the metacognition and processing of novel information to reduce the anxiety or to respond to the situation in a more productive way than escape or an immediate defensive response.

Attention, recall, recognition, problem solving, strategizing, visualizing, set shifting, and generativity are basic human abilities. The actions individuals use to respond is guided by these processes, whether in response to fear, terror, disgust, anger, or love. In the trauma- and stressor-related disorders, recognition of these prewired responses can provide the key to best practices, treatment, and interventions and enable practitioners to understand human interaction, at its best and worst, and how disorders related to anxiety or disassociation can be prevented. Since individuals can react differently to the same traumatic event clear individual interpretation of the symptoms experienced particular to the individual will constitute the central focus for the formulation of the diagnostic assessment (Friedman, 2014).

IMPORTANT FEATURES RELATED TO THE TRAUMA- AND STRESSOR-RELATED DISORDERS

When preparing for the diagnostic assessment and placing the appropriate diagnosis, the practitioner must first be aware of the key features prevalent in the trauma- and stressor-related disorders that constitute the diagnosis. Any diagnostic impression and the treatment plan to follow always require a balance of groundbreaking research and the practitioner's judgment and experience (Schore, 2014). For the trauma- and stressor-related disorders, starting this process requires familiarity with the intensity that comes when feelings related to stressful life situations and events are overwhelming. An individual's extreme reaction to dread or fear can result in excessive anxiety or fear. The individual seeks escape as thoughts related to the situation create so much fear and panic that flight is viewed as the only means of response. If flight is not possible, the body adjusts to survive, and whether the threat is perceived or real, the prewired response to the threat of emotional or physical harm results. When an anxious reaction accentuates the interaction between situational and cognitive factors, and escape is not possible, a friend or companion may be able to help the individual. If insight is intact, the individual worries about his or her responses to situations and may avoid, become numb, or restrict potential interactions to avoid the occurrence or recurrence and protect the self.

When people experience anxiety in response to stressors, the features related to panic-like attacks and the fear of being unable to escape may seem overwhelming and confusing. Not sure what is causing the problem, many individuals seek medical attention for answers. The individual as well as the practitioner may at first be confused as to whether the symptoms are medically related (see Quick Reference 9.1). When a physical exam has been completed and no medical reason can be determined for the symptoms displayed, a referral to a mental health practitioner is often made.

QUICK REFERENCE 9.1

Presentation of Anxiety

- Clients who are anxious often seek the help of a primary care physician before seeing a mental health practitioner.
- Physical reactions such as tension, fatigue, racing pulse, and rapid breathing can easily be misinterpreted for medical symptoms.
- Emotional reactions such as fear, grief, and anger and avoidance can often be attributed to medical factors. Interpersonal reactions such as irritability, withdrawal, and isolation, along with feelings of abandonment that are not typical to past social connections create an uncomfortable social situation, where the individual often seeks answers attributing it to medical causes which appear "more acceptable" than interpersonal ones.

Since clients present with both physical and mental symptoms (e.g., tremors, dyspnea, dizziness, sweating, irritability, restlessness, hyperventilation, pain, heartburn, and disassociation or numbness related to the physical symptoms being experienced), confusion or attribution to medical causes is often at the forefront of seeking intervention.

Problems With Self-Reporting of Symptoms

One reason this lack of proper assessment of symptoms is so problematic is the symptoms that individuals self-report. When in treatment, much of what we know about a client suffering from a traumatic event—or any mental health condition, for that matter—comes from self-report (Watts et al., 2014). For example, in PTSD, several studies have examined veterans and the variation in their self-reports of the trauma experienced (Mott, Hundt, Sansgiry, Mignogna, & Cully, 2014; Rosendal, Mortensen, Andersen, & Heir, 2014; Watts et al., 2014). For all individuals experiencing trauma, how the client interprets and reports symptoms can be misleading because feelings related to the traumatic event can vary, change over time, or simply be overstated. In addition, the client's subjective experience is being reported, and this interpretation has to reflect the definition and standards of normalcy within the client's unique social, cultural, environmental context (Paniagua, 2014). Living in high-trauma environments where safety is not expected can lead to a culture of expectation very different from what others unfamiliar with that environment might expect. When added to the different interpretation some individuals report after experiencing the same event it is easy to see how interpretation and standardization for setting the tone for crisis treatment can be diffuclt.

For these reasons, gathering clear, concise, psychosocial criteria-based diagnostic standards, as well as collateral information and perceptions of significant others, family, coworkers, and friends, is recommended (Woo & Keatinge, 2008). Anxious clients may be uncomfortable filling out assessment measures, so go slowly and be sensitive to this issue (Rizq, 2012). When someone is actively in crisis nothing has to be immediate and a slow client-sensitive progression is always recommended.

OVERVIEW OF THE TRAUMA- AND STRESSOR-RELATED DISORDERS

The *DSM-5* provides the standardized classification system for psychiatric disorders across the United States. Using the criteria for the mental disorders as outlined in the *DSM-5* allows standardization across disorders and quick, standardized determinations of individual psychopathology (Schmidt, Norr, & Korte, 2014).

The disorders in this section involve trauma that is experienced either directly or indirectly (APA, 2013). Stressful life events include important life transitions, whether positive or negative, such as pregnancy (a major life transition) or an unexpected death, particularly where death has been complicated. Focus on general stress in nonclinical populations has found increased intrusive thoughts in response to stressful and aversive stimuli. Included in the *DSM-5* classification of trauma- and stressor-related disorders are several that share featured characteristics and criteria that specify common metacognitions and physiological responses (APA, 2013). Metacognitions involve the processing of emotional and situational states that provide the basis for an individual's trust and safety assessments. Inappropriate allocation of attentive processing and disordered information processing (e.g., breakdown in adaptive signal-to-noise discrimination), with inappropriate and exaggerated innocuous body sensations, are central to understanding the clinical phenomenology of stress and anxiety reactions (Wise, McFarlane, Clark, & Battersby, 2009).

Processing stressful events requires executive functions such as interpretation, attention, and memory, and these functions are applied when threat and danger assessments and responsive actions are formed (as in fight or flight). When excited, the individual then tries to regulate these emotions, invoking compensatory emotions such as fear, worry, distress, terror, or despair. What the individual attributes to the situation provides the basis for anxious responses. If any component of these processes is impaired, then judgment and decision making in these situations becomes inaccurate. When judgment and interpretation of a situation are impaired, the individual believes, assesses, and feels that his or her own perception is accurate. Responses to stress and anxiety, especially when severe, can include physiological reactions that stimulate the sympathetic and parasympathetic nervous system, resulting in increased heart rate, trembling, sweating, nausea, shortness of breath, dizziness, headaches, and diarrhea.

Reactive Attachment Disorder

Disorders in the *DSM-5* are listed in each chapter in developmental order, and the ones most likely to occur in childhood are listed first. The first in this chapter is reactive attachment disorder (RAD). In *DSM-IV* and *DSM-IV-TR,* RAD was listed as one diagnosis with two clear subtypes: the emotionally withdrawn/inhibited and the indiscriminately social/disinhibited. In *DSM-5,* this distinction was dropped; research determined that RAD was actually two separate disorders. This modification resulted in both a title change, introducing a second disorder termed disinhibited social engagement disorder, and changes to the criteria for RAD, which maintained the same title. For those familiar with the previous classification in the *DSM,* keeping the same title but changing the criteria may be confusing at first.

In *DSM-5,* the current definition of RAD is a disorder in infancy or early childhood that involves difficulty in responding to a caregiver for comfort or attention (APA, 2013). This early bonding is believed to be necessary to develop many of the important social skills required later in life for forming attachments. Seven specific criteria (ranging from A to G) must be met. In criterion A, outlines the importance of attachment to the caregiver and the consistent pattern of inhibition and emotional withdrawal that occurs. Often the child not only avoids comfort from the caregiver but also, when it is provided, responds minimally and may appear distressed after receiving it (APA, 2013). Criterion B is the response the child gives socially to others. In this social response, the child shows minimal response and has a limited positive response with either flat or blunted affect, and the child may have unpredictable bouts of anxiety, sadness, or irritability when the situation does not warrant it. For diagnostic purposes, of the three types listed, the child must complete at least two to qualify for the diagnosis.

In criterion C, it is clear that in the past the child has not received adequate caregiving and response to needs. This lack of attention may include a persistent lack of social attention, not showing affection to the child, or avoiding meeting the child's requests for attention with affection or support. It may also be related to repeated environmental changes where the caregiver has changed consistently or individual bonding related to one primary caregiver has not been possible. This may be seen when children are placed in repeated foster care homes or simply bounced back and forth between different caregivers with little bonding occurring with the transitions. Criterion C can also involve rearing in settings such as institutions or large care homes where individual attention is simply not possible (APA, 2013). To place the diagnosis, at least one of these three circumstances must be present. In criterion D, this lack of connection has led to the child's difficulty in bonding and social interaction with the caregiver or significant others. In criteria E, because this disorder has some similar traits to autistic spectrum disorder (ASD). Criterion F, requires that the practitioner identify whether the symptoms were present and affecting functioning back in the early child-rearing environment (with onset prior to age 5), especially when it involves social interaction and communication difficulties. Lastly, in criterion G, to avoid confusion with what may be considered normal developmental milestones, the diagnosis should not be placed until the infant is at least 9 months old (APA, 2013, p. 266). The primary symptoms of this disorder are that the child presents with disturbed interactional patterns with significant others that are developmentally inappropriate, and even when comfort responses are provided, the child seems unable to respond. This frustrates the caregiver who is trying to be nurturing and is disregarded.

Disinhibited Social Engagement Disorder (DSED)

This disorder is similar to RAD in that it requires a developmental onset age of at least 9 months, is a childhood disorder, and involves some form of extreme or insufficient care that resulted in the behaviors exhibited. This is where the similarities end. In disinhibited social engagement disorder (DSED), five specific criteria (ranging from A to E) must be met. Criterion A is at the opposite pole of RAD. The child actively contacts and interacts with many adults, including ones he or she is not familiar with. Some degree of reluctance or fear of unfamiliar individuals is consistent with normal development. In children with this disorder, fear and discretion are either reduced or absent when approaching unfamiliar adults. The child does not show fear and may be so friendly that the adult stranger feels uncomfortable. This extreme friendliness may go beyond what is considered socially and culturally appropriate and put the child at risk; he or she may go off with an unfamiliar adult at the adult's request or ask an adult to take them home. For a child to meet criterion A, at least one of these behaviors must be present. This disorder must be distinguished from attention-deficit/

hyperactivity disorder (ADHD), where the resultant behaviors are related to inattentiveness or impulsivity. For these children, criterion B requires that the behavior be developmentally related to caregiving and rest within a pattern of socially disinhibited behavior. Like RAD, criterion C is insufficient care or caregiving and requires at least one of the following related to social neglect: repeated changes in primary caregivers and unusual child-rearing settings such as institutions where the caregiver-to-child ratio is insufficient and attention and bonding to the child is limited. These patterns of behavior with over-interactions may be the result of a persistent lack of social attention, where the child has not received adequate attention by the caregiver in meeting his or her needs. It may also be related to consistently changing caregivers, such as placement in repeated foster care homes. Or criterion C can involve experiencing limited child rearing in settings such as institutions or large care homes where individual attention is simply not possible. In criterion D, it is expected that this lack of connection has led to the child's difficulty in differentiating between appropriate interpersonal bonding and social response. Lastly, in criterion E, to avoid confusion with what may be considered normal developmental milestones, the diagnosis should not be placed until the infant is at least 9 months old (criterion E; APA, 2013, p. 269). This childhood disorder's primary characteristic is display of overly familiar interactions with strangers in excess of what would be expected with familiar interactions and social and cultural norms.

Posttraumatic Stress Disorder (PTSD)

In posttraumatic stress disorder, the person has been exposed to a traumatic stressor involving direct personal experience, witnessing, or learning about events and situations involving actual or threatened death, serious injury, or a threat to one's physical integrity (APA, 2013; Charuvastra & Cloitre, 2008). It has a prevalence of 7.7 million people age 18 and above in the United States and can be found in any age group, with a median onset at age 23 (National Institute of Mental Health [NIMH], 2008). Prevalence is highest among survivors of rape, military combat and captivity, and ethnically or politically motivated internment and genocide (APA, 2013). Included in the *DSM* are the defined traumatic events associated with PTSD. Traumatic injuries caused by human design (e.g., manmade disasters, crimes, torture, rape) are most likely to increase the incidence of PTSD in relation to the intensity and physical proximity of the stressor (APA, 2000; Charuvastra & Cloitre, 2008).

In *DSM-5,* PTSD is broken down into two populations: older than age six and under the age of six. For individuals age six and older, the specific criteria for the diagnosis are eight problematic areas (criteria A to H). Of four factors related to exposure to the trauma, one or more must be present. The first and second are either directly experiencing the traumatic event or watching it occur to a family member or close friend. If the exposure was not direct, it could be learning about the traumatic event, although this event occurring to someone close to the individual would have to be particularly violent or unexpected and accidental. The last area related to the event is what might be seen by first responders and those who work in emergency situations who are repeatedly exposed to traumatic, horrific events and suffer a type of secondary trauma- or stress-related response.

Criterion B requires at least one of five symptoms associated with the event. The first symptom is the presence of recurrent unwanted memories. These distressing involuntary memories highlight one or more elements associated with the event. Second are distressing recurrent dreams about the event or with content surrounding the event. Third, the individual might experience dissociative periods with flashbacks when involved with people or situations that remind him or her of the event or of individuals involved in the event. As dissociative experience can occur on a continuum, the individual may or may not be aware of the dissociative episode. In children age six and above, a dissociative episode may be relived during play. The fourth symptom is experiencing an intense psychological distress that is triggered by exposure to events, people, or things that remind the individual of the traumatic event. The fifth symptom for criterion B is when exposed to cues that resemble the traumatic event the presence of marked psychological reactions (internal or external) may develop.

After the traumatic event, the individual may avoid people, places, and situations associated with the event (criterion C). The symptoms associated with criterion C are the avoidance of anything associated with the traumatic event, including efforts to control thoughts, feelings, individuals, places, memories, and things associated with the event. After the traumatic event, the individual may forget key aspects of it (criterion D). That is, the individual may experience dissociative amnesia and thereby forget who was involved in the event, as well as other key factors about the event. This distorted memory of the event is not due to substance usage or a medical condition. The individual's view of self may become distorted as the individual works to sort through what happened. The individual's distorted thinking about the event may alter feelings toward self and others and result in feelings of fear, anger, guilt, and shame. The individual's interest in others and events may be reduced because of the event, and he or she may also feel detached from loved ones. A final symptom of criterion D is an inability to experience joy, love, happiness, and other positive emotions. Criterion E is an inability to engage in social activities. The symptoms are the client's irritability and angry outbursts. These irritable, angry outbursts may occur without provocation. The individual may also participate in reckless and/or self-destructive behaviors. Another symptom in this criterion is hypervigilance. When startled, the individual's response may be exaggerated. The individual may also have problems when trying to concentrate.

For the disturbance that is reflected in criteria B through E, the symptoms last more than one month (criterion F). Additionally, the disturbance causes the individual significant distress in school, home, work, and elsewhere (criterion G). The practitioner must make sure when diagnosing PTSD that the symptoms cannot be better explained by substance use or a medical condition (criterion H).

When diagnosing PTSD with clients age six and older, the practitioner must specify when depersonalization or derealization is present. Depersonalization is when clients experience moments when they are outside of their bodies. Derealization is when clients perceive the world around them as unreal or they feel like they are experiencing a dreamlike state while they are awake. Before these subtypes can be used, the practitioner must make sure that the client's experiences are not due to the use of a substance or a medical condition. The practitioner must specify if full criteria for PTSD were not met until 6 months after the event.

In diagnosing PTSD specifically for individuals age six and younger, the specific criteria for the diagnosis involve seven problematic areas (criteria A to G). Criterion A starts by outlining three factors related to exposure to the trauma requiring actual or threatened exposure (APA, 2013). The child may have directly experienced the traumatic event or watched it occur to a family member or close friend. Witnessing the traumatic event does not include seeing someone hurt via television, video games, or movies. The third way criterion A can be met is if the child learned about a traumatic event that happened to a parent or caregiver.

In criterion B, at least one of five symptoms associated with the event is required. The first symptom is recurrent unwanted memories. The child may express these spontaneous, distressing, involuntary memories via play. Second, the child may experience distressing recurrent dreams related to the event. These dreams may not be directly about the event and instead feature content surrounding the event, or it may be hard to tell what the dreams are about. Third, the child may experience dissociative periods with flashbacks involving people related to or involved in the event (APA, 2013). The child may not be able to remember what happened during the dissociative experience. In children age six and younger, a dissociative episode may be relived during play. Fourth, when the child is reminded of the event, intense psychological distress may occur. The fifth symptom for criterion B is the presence of biological reactions (internal or external) when the child is exposed to stimuli associated with the traumatic event. One biological symptom is children wetting themselves when they see something or someone associated with the event.

The child may attempt to avoid people, places, and situations that are associated with the event (criterion C), and the child's efforts to control thoughts, feelings, individuals, places, memories, and things associated with the event are more pronounced after the event occurred (APA, 2013). Children might even avoid objects that remind them of the event. Since the event, the child's ability to enjoy play and activities with significant others has been reduced. The child appears to be sad, fearful, and confused. When someone brings up a positive memory that is indirectly associated with the event, the child may withdraw from the person speaking to avoid discussing anything associated with the event. The child's overall play activities as well as interest in other activities may be diminished after the event. The child's ability to show positive emotions has also been dampened by the event.

After the event, the child may have a difficult time becoming interested in previous joyful activities, events, and people (criterion D). The child may easily become agitated and irritable, display angry outbursts, and become aggressive toward animate and inanimate objects. The child's emotional outbursts may be temper tantrums that are efforts to verbally express emotions. The child may become hypervigilant, watching for cues that the event is happening or will happen again. When startled, the child's response may be exaggerated. The child may also have problems with concentrating and sleeping.

The symptoms the child experiences must last more than one month (criterion E; APA, 2013). Additionally, the disturbance causes the client significant distress at school, home, and elsewhere (criterion F). The practitioner must make sure when diagnosing PTSD that the symptoms cannot be better explained by substance use or a medical condition (criterion G).

When diagnosing PTSD in a child age six or younger, the practitioner is required to specify whether depersonalization or derealization is present (APA, 2013). Depersonalization is when children experience moments when they are outside their bodies; derealization is when children perceive the world around them as unreal or they feel like they are experiencing a dreamlike state when they are awake. Before these subtypes can be used, the practitioner must make sure that the child's experiences are not due to the use of a substance or a medical condition. The practitioner must also specify if the criteria for PTSD were not fully met until six months after the event occurred.

Characteristic features of PTSD include persistent re-experiencing, avoidance, and hyperarousal in response to stimuli associated with the traumatic event (APA, 2013). Re-experiencing the event, as recollections or distressing dreams in which the event is remembered, is specified in the *DSM-5;* in some circumstances, dissociation occurs, and the person behaves as if the event is re-experienced (flashbacks). When these flashbacks occur, the client may attempt to avoid reliving these experiences. These attempts include avoiding thoughts, feelings, conversations, activities, situations, people, and reminders of the traumatic event. These circumstances are associated with intense physiological responses and psychological distress; the person then tries to avoid any stimuli related to the trauma (APA, 2013; Spoormaker & Montgomery, 2008). Associated responses are intense emotions of fear, helplessness, horror, distress, anxiety, irritability, and anger (APA, 2013). Associated symptoms of psychological distress include, but are not limited to, impaired memory; impaired executive functions; impaired affect regulation; self-destructive and impulsive behavior; feelings of ineffectiveness, shame, despair, and hopelessness; insomnia; nightmares; a loss of previously held beliefs; social withdrawal; and impaired relationships with others.

The *DSM-5* notes that pretraumatic factors may be associated with the development of PTSD, such as childhood emotional problems. Children with an emotional problem prior to experiencing the traumatic event are more likely to develop PTSD. Individuals from poor environments may be more prone to PTSD because of violence present in their neighborhoods. Individuals in ethnic minority groups may be prone to PTSD because of the barriers they face. Other contributing factors are a history of depression and/or PTSD in a first-degree relative, childhood adversities, education level, and cognitive ability (APA, 2013; Keane, Marshall, & Taft, 2006; Mayo Clinic, 2009). Low cortisol levels among groups of trauma survivors and in familial transmission indicate that the hypothalamic-pituitary-adrenal axis has become resistant to the effects of cortisol. This leaves the system consistent with the increased reactivity and hyperarousal to explicit and implicit trauma reminders in trauma survivors found in PTSD (Keane et al., 2006; Yehuda et al., 2000). The presence of these symptoms increases the risk of PTSD and should be assessed in the evaluation.

Peritraumatic factors, such as military personnel and immigrants from areas of social unrest and civil conflict, also should be considered. The practitioner should note the severity of the event, the threat level of the event, the severity and types of injury, and interpersonal violence. In non-Western and developing countries, PTSD is observed at higher rates (APA, 2013; Keane et al., 2006). Regional and world location in the risk for PTSD has to be considered in the assessment.

Posttraumatic factors for developing PTSD include temperament and environment. At least 50% of individuals suffering from ACD develop PTSD (APA, 2013, p. 284). Other temperamental factors for developing PTSD include inadequate coping strategies and negative evaluation of self. Environmental factors include repeated exposure to information, people, or artifacts associated with the event. Having a strong support system aids in avoiding these posttraumatic factors.

There is no association of age with PTSD. The disorder can begin at any age, but the median onset is 23 (NIMH, 2008). There is an association, however, between the development of PTSD and gender according to type of trauma experienced. Men have a higher rate of PTSD secondary to life span issues and age of entry into combat; women have a higher rate of trauma related to sexual assault (APA, 2013; Keane et al., 2006). When controlling for gender and type of trauma, there is little difference in the overall prevalence rate between men and women and the development of PTSD.

Stressors that increase the risk of PTSD include dealing with extra stress after the event (loss of a loved one, pain and injury, loss of a job or home) (NIMH, 2009). Partial or complete loss of emotional support after the event increases the risk of developing PTSD. Marital status is not significantly associated with PTSD but can confer a protective factor for exposure to a traumatic event (Keane et al., 2006). Unhealthy relationships and domestic violence are risk factors for the development of PTSD.

The type, intensity, and duration of a traumatic event increase the associated risk of developing PTSD (APA, 2013; Mayo Clinic, 2009). Types of traumatic events include combat exposure; terroristic attacks; seeing people hurt, killed, or tortured; and other life-threatening events such as kidnapping, muggings and robberies, natural disasters, plane crashes, car accidents, rape, childhood neglect and abuse, and life-threatening medical diagnoses (APA, 2013; Mayo Clinic, 2009; NIMH, 2009). The type of trauma should always be clearly identified and assessed as a risk factor in the development of PTSD.

Ten diagnoses can overlap with PTSD and should be considered for differential diagnosis: adjustment disorder, other posttraumatic disorders and conditions, acute stress disorder, anxiety disorders and obsessive-compulsive disorder, major depressive disorder, personality disorders, dissociative disorders, conversion disorder (functional neurological symptom disorder), psychotic disorders, and traumatic brain injury (TBI). The diagnosis of each of these disorders is made when the client's symptoms do not fully meet the criteria for PTSD or another one of these disorders better explains the client's symptoms. For example, adjustment disorder is used when the traumatic event does not meet the criteria for PTSD. The diagnosis of other posttraumatic disorders and conditions is used when a specifier condition warrants separate diagnosis. The major difference between ASD and PTSD is the time frame for the onset of symptoms. With ASD, if the symptoms last longer than one month, the practitioner needs to reassess the diagnosis. If the client's intrusive thoughts are not in reference to an actual event, the practitioner should consider anxiety disorders and OCD. Clients with major depressive disorder do not present with symptoms that meet all of the criteria for PTSD; that is, their symptoms do not meet criteria B or C or all of criteria D and E. When a client's interpersonal difficulty precedes the traumatic event, the client may be better served by a diagnosis of personality disorder, with PTSD as a specifier. When a client presents with dissociative symptoms and also meets the full criteria for PTSD, the practitioner should diagnosis PTSD with dissociative symptoms (APA, 2013, p. 279).

A client who has a neurological disorder may experience a traumatic event. When this occurs, the practitioner should consider diagnosing and treating the PTSD instead of the neurological disorder. When a client reports flashbacks, the practitioner must check to see if the client suffers from a psychotic disorder. Treatment should be based on the most pressing symptoms before deciding to focus on the PTSD. The practitioner must be aware that TBI can result from a traumatic event such as a car accident. When symptoms can be separated from experiencing the event and symptoms related to the injury, the practitioner must decide if the diagnosis of PTSD with TBI-related neurocognitive symptoms is appropriate. This diagnosis helps to determine and direct treatment.

Regarding comorbidity for PTSD, "individuals with PTSD are 80% more likely . . . to meet the criteria for at least one other mental disorder" (APA, 2013, p. 280). In particular, combat military personnel are at a great risk of developing PTSD along with major depressive disorder and an anxiety disorder (Mott et al., 2014).

Acute Stress Disorder (ASD)

The onset of acute stress disorder (ASD) is characterized by exposure to an extreme traumatic stressor and development of recurrent anxiety, dissociative, and other symptoms; reminders of the stressor are avoided subsequent to the hyperarousal experienced (APA, 2013). These symptoms are present 3 days after the exposure up to 1 month later. The individual also experiences nine of 14 symptoms: 4 intrusion symptoms, one negative mood symptom, two dissociative symptoms, two avoidance symptoms, and five arousal symptoms (APA, 2013, pp. 280–281). These symptoms of ASD—also found in PTSD—can include difficulty in sleeping, irritability, poor concentration, hypervigilance, and motor restlessness. Included in the *DSM*-5 criteria for ASD is experiencing a traumatic event, with the individual re-experiencing a minimum of three dissociative symptoms lasting from 3 days to a maximum of one month after the event. For example, the individual may suffer a subjective sense of numbing, detachment (emotional and physical), absence of emotional awareness of his or her surroundings, derealization, depersonalization, or dissociative amnesia.

This disorder occurs in people exposed to trauma. Risk factors for developing ASD include temperamental, environmental, genetic, and physiological factors. In reference to temperament, individuals with a "high level of negative affectivity, greater perceived severity of the traumatic event, and an avoidant coping style" are at greater risk of developing ASD after a traumatic event (APA, 2013, p. 284). Environmental factors for ASD include a history of trauma, including being involved in, witnessing, or learning about a traumatic event. Genetic factors related to developing ASD include being female. Physiological factors include response patterns to stressful events. The individual's culture as related to a cultural response pattern must be considered in diagnosing. Disorders that must be ruled out are adjustment disorders, panic disorder, dissociative disorders, PTSD, OCD, psychotic disorder, and TBI. Comorbidity with other disorders is present, as are medical conditions resulting from trauma (e.g., head injury) (APA, 2013; Bryant, Moulds, Guthrie, & Nixon, 2003). Although ASD does not lead to an automatic diagnosis of PTSD, if symptoms are present longer than one month, the *DSM* suggests that PTSD should be considered.

Acute stress disorder and PTSD share the circumstances of a traumatic stressor. The type of stressor can vary and be the result of floods, hurricanes, war, rape, or other types of individualized, severely traumatic experiences. Clients either experienced the stressor directly or watched it be experienced by others. In *DSM-5,* the symptoms and stressors related to these disorders are similar, except the duration of the symptoms. In ASD, the symptoms occur in three days to one month after the stressor, whereas in PTSD, the symptoms must occur for more than 1 month. Because not all individuals experience the same traumatic event in the same way, careful evaluation of the condition and supportive information is required. Another difference between PTSD and ASD is that the signs and symptoms related to the stressor may not manifest immediately and may take much longer. In summary, with ASD, five specific criteria (ranging from A to E) must be met. Although these symptoms are similar to those of PTSD, for ASD, clients must develop the disorder 3 days to 1 month after "exposure to one or more traumatic events" (APA, 2013, p. 281).

Adjustment Disorders

The adjustment disorders occur in relation to an identifiable stressor. Onset occurs within 3 months of encountering the stressor. This diagnosis is used when the individual's response to the stressor does not match the intensity of the stressor. Cultural factors and the context of the stressor are considered before determining if the response is out of proportion. This disorder is diagnosed when the individual's symptoms do not meet the criteria for another disorder. Care must be taken to determine if the individual's response represents normal bereavement. Another criterion of this diagnosis is that after the cessation of the stressor, the individual's symptoms do not last past 6 months. There are six features to specify when using this diagnosis. If the individual presents with "low mood, tearfulness, or feelings of hopelessness," the specifier with depressed mood is used (APA, 2013, p. 287). The specifier with anxiety is used if the individual presents with "nervousness, worry, jitteriness, or separation anxiety" (APA, 2013, p. 287). If the individual presents with a combination of symptoms (depression and anxiety), the specifier with mixed anxiety and depression is used. If one of the symptoms is problematic conduct, the specifier used is with disturbance of conduct (APA, 2013, p. 287). If the predominate symptoms are mixed, the specifier used is with mixed disturbance of emotion and conduct (APA, 2013, p. 287). When an individual presents with maladaptive symptoms, the specifier used is unspecified. The time frame for the onset of this disorder is 3 months after exposure to the stressor; if the individual experiences symptoms after 6 months, the practitioner should reconsider the diagnosis. When making the diagnosis, the practitioner must consider the individual's environment as well as the individual's culture. Differential diagnosis disorders to rule out include major depressive disorder, PTSD and ASD, personality disorders, psychological factor affecting other medical conditions, and normative stress reaction.

Other Trauma- and Stressor-Related Disorder and Unspecified Trauma- and Stressor-Related Disorder

These disorders are applied to an individual whose symptoms do not meet the full criteria for the other trauma- and stressor-related disorders. In the specified disorder, the practitioner states the reason it does not meet the criteria, and in the unspecified disorder, it is not stated. Although the individual's symptoms cause considerable stress in significant areas of the individual's life, the symptoms do not meet the full criteria for one of the other stress-related disorders. The practitioner can use this disorder when diagnosing adjustment-like disorders that have a delayed onset or a longer duration. Other trauma- and stressor-related disorder can be used when diagnosing culturally specific stress disorders. Another example of when to use this disorder is when an individual's grief is considered persistent complex bereavement (APA, 2013, p. 289). In the unspecified, the reason is not stated. The unspecified could occur in emergency rooms or in situations where the reason is not openly stated.

BEGINNING THE DIAGNOSTIC ASSESSMENT

Cultural considerations should be clearly examined and understood in the diagnostic assessment for the trauma- and stressor-related disorders. Ethnic group identity, religion, and spirituality can help to establish culturally sanctioned behaviors that appear to be different from behaviors in the dominant culture. The results of experiencing a stressor or trauma may be interpreted very differently based on cultural expectations and mores. For example, recent literature has begun to accept and respect the incidence of historical trauma suffered by minority populations through reliving experiences of our ancestors such as colonialism, slavery, natural disasters, and war (Derezotes, 2014).

When cultural factors can influence trauma, the Cultural Formulation Interview (CFI) may be of assistance. This instrument allows a clear evaluation of how the individual approaches and responds to his or her own problems, taking into account potential cultural influences. The practitioner may also find helpful the description of the best-studied culturally related idioms of distress in the *DSM-5* appendix. Awareness of these idioms of distress can help the practitioner be inclusive of the culture, identify problematic behaviors, and communicate strategy with more culturally sensitive terms. These measurements may be especially helpful when clients report problems with nerves, being possessed by spirits, multiple somatic complaints, or a sense of inexplicable misfortune. In these cases, unwarranted labeling of pathology can be avoided, and the behaviors experienced can be explored in relation to norms of the client's cultural reference group.

As times change and cultures blend, ethnic differences may do the same. Standard definitions will continue to be questioned, as evidenced by Paniagua (2014), who suggested eliminating the term *minority* altogether. Nevertheless, cultural factors are important in both the diagnostic assessment and the intervention plan and must always be identified and taken into account. The CFI may be particularly helpful in formulating a concrete measure to explore the definition of the problem, as well as past and current helping strategies. The ways cultural factors can affect or contribute to problematic behavior should not be underestimated. Grigorenko (2009) provides an excellent edited resource for making culturally sensitive assessments.

Supporting the Dimensional Assessment

One essential part of the *DSM-5* is the switch from a categorical diagnostic assessment to a dimensional one. With the trauma- and stressor-related disorders, crosscutting of symptoms can be used to differentiate disorders with overlapping symptoms. In addition, various scales can be used during the assessment process, including self-report measures that can establish the duration, intensity, and frequency of presenting symptomatology. Measurement instruments that facilitate the mental status exam include the Folstein Mini Mental State Examination (MMSE), which contains questions assessing orientation to time, place, attention, and memory. This measure is dependent on age and educational background and is sensitive to individuals who may not be familiar with the information presented on these tests, such as names of presidents, geographic locations, and important dates and events. It also takes into account the different conceptualization of place and location with respect to an individual's background (Adler, 2007; Amin, Kuhle, & Fitzpatrick, 2003; Insel & Badger, 2002). It addresses task completion as related to attention and memory through engaging actions of writing, copying, and observation.

Other measurements can help with assessing the presence of metacognitions, attributions, harm reduction, tolerance level, and behavioral responses associated with anxiety levels that result from trauma exposure. Because of the shared phenomenology where some individuals experience anxiety and depression, scales that assess both clinical features can be used to assess the severity of anxiety present. Scales such as the Cognitive-Somatic Anxiety Questionnaire (CSAQ) created by Schwartz, Davidson, and Goleman (1978) may be helpful in starting this process. The CSAQ is a 14-item instrument that focuses on the thoughts and somatic modes of trait anxiety and is used to assess the presence of general anxiety. The CSAQ has a score between 7 and 35; the higher the score, the higher the level of cognitive and somatic complaints. When looking specifically at depressive symptoms, the Beck Depression Inventory, a 21-item, self-report, multiple-choice questionnaire, may be of particular help. It measures the presence of depression with items particular to anxiety (Center for Psychological Studies, 2008). It describes a specific behavioral manifestation of depression through four self-evaluative statements, with ordinal measurement to assess for severity of symptoms.

Another scale with a focus on nonpsychotic depression is Hudson's (1992) Generalized Contentment Scale (GCS). This 25-item scale measures the severity of nonpsychotic depression. It produces a score of zero to 100, with higher scores indicating greater depression. The GCS has three cutoff points: 30, 50, and 70 (all ±5). Scores below 30 indicate the absence of clinically significant depression, scores above 50 indicate some suicidal ideation, and scores above 70 nearly always indicate severe stress and suicidal tendencies (see Fischer & Cocoran, 2007 for a copy of the scale and related information for use).

The Penn Inventory for Posttraumatic Stress Disorder (PI-PTSD) is a 26-item, 3-point Likert, self-report measurement that assesses symptoms of PTSD for multiple traumatic experiences (U.S. Department of Veteran Affairs, 2009a). Included are items related to anxiety, such as self-knowledge (Matthews & Wells, 2000). A score range of zero to 78 reflects the severity of PTSD present (higher scores reflect severity). Because it is not specific to a type of trauma, the PI-PTSD can assess the presence of multiple traumatic experiences and their effects.

The Los Angeles Symptom Checklist (LASC) is a 43-item, 5-point Likert, self-report measure associated with 17 symptoms embedded in the scale measuring general distress (U.S. Department of Veteran Affairs, 2009b). Each item is rated, and a score of 2 or higher is a symptom counted toward the diagnosis. The sum of all 43 items provides a global index of distress and adjustment problems (higher scores reflect greater distress and adjustment problems). In establishing a diagnosis, this scale can assist in identifying the presence and criteria of PTSD.

The Screen for Posttraumatic Stress Symptoms (SPTSS) is a 17-item, 11-point Likert, self-report measure used to assess symptoms of PTSD (U.S. Department of Veteran Affairs, 2009c). Item scores can determine symptoms and criteria for the diagnosis of PTSD, and the scale is particularly useful for those with multiple traumatic events and an unknown trauma history. Like the LASC, this scale is useful in establishing the presence and criteria for the disorder. The Impact of Events Scale measures intrusion and avoidance indirectly related to traumatic events (i.e., thoughts and images, distressing dreams, waves of feelings, repetitive and inhibited behaviors) (Sundin & Horowitz, 2002). This scale can be used with other measurements and provides an assessment of the presence of symptoms associated with traumatic impact.

In summary, this type of rapid assessment instrument can be used to evaluate the level of distress and its effect on daily functioning. These brief measurements provide good assessments and diagnosis. They assist in providing a more comprehensive analysis of the severity of the condition, differential diagnosis, and establishing criteria for PTSD (e.g., duration of deterioration, onset of condition). The case example and the rest of this section focus specifically on the condition of PTSD. Based on this information, a treatment plan and practice strategy are developed that can efficiently embrace, identify, and effectively treat individuals who suffer from this type of trauma- and stressor-related disorder.

Completion of the Diagnostic Assessment: Marmarie

The diagnostic assessment takes into consideration all risk factors and criteria specified in the

CASE EXAMPLE - CASE OF MARMARIE

Marmarie is a 32-year-old Hispanic female, of average height and weight, appearing her stated age. She was referred by her family physician for a mental health assessment. Marmarie's clothing is clean and appropriate for her age, weight, and height. Although she shows some anxiousness, she openly discusses her concerns with the practitioner. Marmarie recently started experiencing what she describes as uncontrollable bouts of anxiety that are serious enough to stop her from completing tasks or finishing projects she has started. She reports experiencing morbid ideation, intense stress and worry, thought intrusions, and a pronounced inability to sleep. When she does sleep, she has very intense dreams and often wakes up in a cold sweat but cannot always remember her dreams. Approximately 9 months ago, Marmarie's home was broken into, and the intruder raped her after stabbing her in the arm and chest. She has recovered from her wounds and thought she was doing much better. At first, she was afraid to be alone at home. This seemed to subside, and now it appears to be happening again.

Marmarie describes an incident when she was walking back to her apartment and the lights were dim; she could see her attacker coming toward her. Knowing he was in jail, at first she questioned herself and whether this could be real. As he continued to draw closer, she could feel her heart race. She stopped and did not run because she was so consumed with fear. She said she kept speaking to herself in her mind, telling herself to run, but her legs would not move. As he got closer, it appeared as if his face shifted to someone else. Finally, she was able to move and ran as fast as she could up the stairs to her apartment. She locked the door and fell to the floor in tears.

Since this incident, she reports feeling preoccupied with seeing or running into the man who had brutally attacked and stabbed her. She states she wishes she could turn off her thoughts. Just thinking about the event causes her breathing to quicken and she can feel her pulse racing. She said she remembers that night well and how secure she felt in her apartment prior to the attack. Now she constantly has difficulty leaving her apartment, often feels hypervigilant, and is always looking around. She states that at times when she thinks about the trauma, the events seem to fade and feel unreal, as if she is in a bubble for protection, or others are on a different channel or distorted.

Her symptoms have been present for more than 6 months, with worsening symptoms in the past month. There is weight loss of slightly more than 10 pounds in the past month, and difficulties with her personal and family life secondary to employment concerns and difficulties in completing her daily tasks. She denies any medical concerns at present and denies taking medication. She reports she has no known allergies. She states she is a "social drinker" and denies any past history of illicit drug use. She denies a history of treatment for substance abuse and denies any past treatment for mental health concerns at the time of this interview.

DSM-5. To be comprehensive, it includes all demographic information available, physical examinations, current and past history (medical and mental), geographic location, immigration status, type of trauma experienced, and specific background features. For Marmarie, the type of trauma experienced can be related directly to the attack and rape that occurred 9 months ago. Since the attack, she has had periods when she thought she was better, but these periods did not last very long. She recently had a physical exam, and no medical concerns were noted. She is not taking any medications to control her anxiety. The stab wounds left permanent scars, but

QUICK REFERENCE 9.2

Mental Status Description

Presentation	Mental Functioning	Higher-Order Abilities	Thought Form/Content
Appearance: Well groomed	Simple Calculations: Accurate	Judgment: Accurate, some confusion related to interpreting previous and current events	Thought Process: Organized but difficulty concentrating, unwanted memories
Mood: Anxious and fearful when discussing the traumatic event, feels hopelessness and helpless	Serial Sevens: Accurate	Insight: Adequate, show signs of self-blame for unwanted memories	Delusions: None Hallucinations: None
Attitude: Open, expresses confusion related to event, distant, at times angry with uncontrolled emotions	Immediate Memory: Intact	Intelligence: Average	
Affect: Blunted/flat, fearful expressions Speech: Guarded	Remote Memory: Intact	Proverb Interpretation: Accurate	
Motor Activity: Restless	General Knowledge: Mostly accurate	Similarities/ Differences: Accurate	
Orientation: Fully oriented, startle reactions magnified			

luckily no damage was noted to any vital organs. She does report, however, that sometimes when she touches her scars from the stabbing, they seem hot to her touch and become painful. When examined, by her physician, however, no medical conditions relative to these reported symptoms could be determined.

The diagnostic assessment starts with a comprehensive mental status exam. Basic information related to her presentation, mental functioning, and higher order abilities and thought form and content were gathered. (See Quick Reference 9.2.)

Once the mental status exam is complete, the next phase starts with identifying the presenting problems and how they relate to the problems reported. (See Quick Reference 9.3.)

In describing the symptoms Marmarie was experiencing, she reported that the traumatic event occurred 9 months ago, when she was beaten, raped, and stabbed (criterion A). She also reports being required to testify in court against her attacker. She states that was the hardest thing she ever had to do because the man looked to her to be pure evil. She stated she could feel his eyes

QUICK REFERENCE 9.3

IDENTIFY PRIMARY AND PRESENTING PROBLEMS FOR MARMARIE

Primary problem:	Intrusive thoughts related to the previous trauma.
Presenting problems:	Complaints of inability to control thoughts related to home invasion and sexual assault.

on her in the courtroom as she testified. When he was sentenced to 20 years in prison, she said she did not feel much relief, and the decision was not as satisfying, nor did it bring closure for her, as the lawyer suggested and she had hoped. Related to criterion B, she reports several problematic responses since the attack. She reports that she cannot stop herself from thinking about the traumatic event and wishes she could turn off her mind. She does not report any troubling dreams but does report difficulty in falling asleep or achieving restful sleep. She states she also is having problems with recurring thoughts that are problematic; she mentioned the time she mistook someone else for her attacker, ran to her apartment, and locked the door in fear. She stated she plans to move from her apartment because at times she can feel the event around her, and certain things trigger the event in her mind. For example, the other day she reported she was making a cup of tea and heard a noise in the bedroom. Her immediate fear response was overwhelming, and it was all she could do not to run from the apartment. When it happened, she called her friend who was able to calm her, but she did spend the night at her friend's. She states she will not go to a support group, as suggested; she simply does not want to think or talk about the event (criterion C). She states that she just wants to put it away on a shelf, locked in a box, and never deal with it again.

For criterion D, she suffers from two or more of the symptoms related to problematic cognitions after the event. For example, she stated that at times she blames herself and has these recurring thoughts and ideas about "what if": What if I had just locked the window and not had the screen down? What if I had gone to church regularly? God may have protected me. What if I was a better person? This would not have happened to me. And so on. Under criterion E, two symptoms are required, and she has sleep disturbance and hypervigilance, as well as an exaggerated startle response. She has clearly been experiencing the symptoms for more than 1 month, and she is not taking any substances. The experience is causing her such distress she feels she cannot date anyone, and the thought of intimacy brings back too many memories and makes her fearful and anxious (criteria F to H).

It appears that Marmarie meets the criteria for the principal diagnosis of PTSD, which also is the reason for the visit.

> Posttraumatic Stress Disorder (reason for the visit)
> 398.81 (*ICD-9-CM*) and F43.10 (*ICD-10-CM*)

The use of subtypes and course specifiers is encouraged in utilizing the *DSM-5*. The subtype related to PTSD helps to clarify phenomenological criteria that are mutually exclusive and exhaustive (APA, 2013). The homogeneous grouping for Marmarie and her symptoms is *derealization*. This subtype was selected because she reports thinking about the trauma and then events seem to fade and seem unreal. At times she feels like she is in a bubble walking in a dreamlike state, and events and discussions happening around her "are on a different channel" or distorted.

Posttraumatic Stress Disorder (reason for the visit)
398.81 (*ICD-9-CM*) and F43.10 (*ICD-10-CM*)
specify whether: With dissociative symptoms–derealization

A specifier referred to as delayed expression relates directly to the full diagnostic criteria not being met until approximately 6 months after the traumatic event. For Marmarie, use of this specifier does not seem to fit because she began experiencing the full criteria for the disorder soon after the occurrence. After the traumatic event, the symptoms developed, and when she was exposed to certain environmental or situational triggers, the symptoms become more pronounced.

With the elimination of the multiaxial diagnosis often used in *DSM-IV* and *DSM-IV-TR*, the information previously provided on Axis IV and Axis V is no longer a requirement. Therefore, in addition to the principal diagnosis, any supportive information relative to the client's situation that can affect the diagnosis should be reported. For practitioners interested in including this information, Chapters 21 and 22 in the *DSM-5* may be of particular help. Chapter 21 has medication-induced movement disorders and other adverse effects of medication, and Chapter 22 has other conditions that may be a focus of clinical intervention. In Marmarie's case, Chapter 22 may be of the most help. Several supportive factors need to be taken into account that can support the diagnostic assessment. The first are the biopsychosocial stressors (especially those related to the family situation and key relationships).

Various social stressors are currently affecting Marmarie, and these stressors are also indirectly applicable to establishing treatment. She is currently employed, although her symptoms are affecting the quality of her work. Fear of losing her job because of her symptoms is placing more stress on her. She reports no relationship problems with her biological family or her friends. Her psychosocial stressors are:

- Impact of symptoms on employment
- Being home alone especially at night
- Running into the perpetrator
- Disruptive ability to walk alone in neighborhood in low light

None of the conditions listed in the chapter clearly explains the circumstances Marmarie is experiencing; however, the conditions that come closest are listed next. The other condition that best explains the supporting information for Marmarie is adult abuse by nonspouse or partner. The rape and subsequent assault can be documented as:

Adult Physical Abuse by Nonspouse or Nonpartner, Confirmed
995.81 (T74.11XA)
Adult Sexual Abuse by Nonspouse or Nonpartner, Confirmed
995.83 (T76.21XD)

In general, Marmarie appears on the outside to those who do not know her to be functioning adequately, but there is clear impairment in her social functioning and daily functioning. She does not present with suicidal ideation but does express morbid ideation. She does not have obsessive rituals and is able to maintain employment. However, she remains concerned that increased symptoms would have an impact on her employment. Her mental state is within normal limits, although she does have serious impairments to her personal and occupational functioning. The application of the taxonomical classification can help to establish a baseline for the frequency, duration, and intensity of symptoms.

Treatment Planning and Intervention Strategy: Marmarie

Positive and longer-lasting responses to problematic behaviors are attributed to desensitizing the client to emotions and thoughts. In PTSD cases, in particular Marmarie's case, this desensitizing may require repeated sessions when she is asked to select a time period for sitting alone in her home. She needs to start with a short period and gradually increase the time. By mastering this task, Marmarie can gradually become comfortable in her home. This desensitizing exercise can be extended to becoming comfortable in other parts of her home. The treatment plan must include addressing the thoughts and dreams Marmarie experiences, which are the symptoms causing her the most distress. Treatment plans should include a long-term objective that focuses on developing beliefs and patterns that increase functioning and reduce distress. Short-term objectives can focus on the application of education, cognitive restructuring, training, and systematic desensitization.

Deep breathing and relaxation can soothe emotions associated with thoughts and actions. Individuals with PTSD experience difficulty in managing the impact of their emotions and are subject to muscle tension. Learning to tune in to the physiological reactions of PTSD can help clients increase recognition and self-regulation. Ways to regulate physiological reactions include breathing exercises, massages, tension and release exercises, and general physical exercise. They should be included in treatment planning and used to improve other disturbed areas in clients' lives.

Accurate assessment of the pressure and stress is critical to a successful outcome. Often these stressors include ignorance regarding PTSD, family dynamics dysfunction, communication difficulties, and social problems that result from these stressors. Family education can be important in working with individuals suffering from PTSD. Areas of focus include improving communication, providing a forum to vent frustrations and concerns and do problem solving, engaging in support groups, and improving the quality of relationships among family members. Objectives regarding education and maximizing healthy communication patterns should be included in the treatment plan. The long-term goal is to improve clients' ability to engage in activities of daily living. (See Sample Treatment Plan 9.1.)

The recording format with PTSD is problem-oriented and directly related to documenting the problem area and providing measurable results. Specific information related to observable behaviors is necessary in the documentation of PTSD, and the greater the specificity of the presenting problem, the greater the success in treatment implementation. Making a connection between thoughts and resulting behavior is critical in problem-oriented recording. The thoughts, as observed through behaviors, can be addressed in the treatment plan. Documentation of concrete examples of symptoms, such as motor tension (restlessness, tiredness, shakiness, or muscle tension), autonomic hyperactivity (palpitations, shortness of breath, dry mouth, trouble swallowing, nausea, or diarrhea), and hypervigilance, should be included. Once behaviors are clearly outlined, a measurable treatment plan can be established.

General Considerations for Treatment Planning and Practice Strategy

Treating the trauma- and stressor-related disorders and treatment planning methods are diverse

SAMPLE TREATMENT PLAN 9.1

Posttraumatic Stress Disorder (PTSD)

The development of fear, helplessness, or horror in response to an event, including actual life-threatening events or threatened death for self and others, the witnessing of an event involving the death or threat of harm to another, or learning of the death or threat of injury to a family member or friend.

Signs and Symptoms to Note in the Record

- Continuous avoidance of persons, places, things, emotions, and feelings associated with the traumatic event.
- Physiological responses when exposed to stimuli associated with traumatic event.
- Difficulty in sleeping and possible nightmares.
- Difficulty in concentrating.
- Incidents of stressful responses.
- Distressing dreams.
- Distressing events.
- Experiences related to the tragic event.
- Persistent re-experiencing of the traumatic event—flashbacks.
- Incidents of hypervigilance.
- Avoidance behaviors.
- Reckless self-destructive behavior.
- Medically related symptoms: motor tension (restlessness, tiredness, shakiness, or muscle tension), autonomic hyperactivity (palpitations, shortness of breath, dry mouth, trouble swallowing, nausea, or diarrhea), hypervigilance.

Goals

1. Reduce uncontrollable thoughts related to the traumatic event in order to return to a normal activity level and complete daily tasks.
2. Reduce morbid ideation and feelings of intense stress and worry while approaching daily activities.
3. Learn to identify triggers for flashbacks and begin relaxation to calm overwhelming feelings of impending victimization.
4. Increase controlled behavior, while confronting painful memories.
5. Develop cognitive beliefs and behavioral patterns to control, alleviate, and reduce the frequency, intensity, and duration of anxiety symptoms and avoidance behavior.

Long-Term Goals

1. Return to previous level of functioning prior to traumatic event.
2. Learn to use coping skills to assist in initiating and maintaining close relationships.
3. Cognitively re-experience the traumatic event without a physiological response.
4. Exhibit acceptance of the traumatic event.

(continued)

SAMPLE TREATMENT PLAN 9.1 (*Continued*)

Objectives	Interventions
1. Identify and confront threatening situations and thoughts.	Provide education about PTSD, including but not limited to psychological and physiological symptoms. Address painful memories and discuss how to confront them realistically and in a relaxed state. Help client problem-solve using behavioral rehearsal and individual psychotherapy, and reinforce more realistic self-statements. Encourage client to identify anxiety-producing cognitions, feelings, and emotions and the distress level associated with them.
2. Examine the meaning of the event and how it is affecting current relationships.	Psychotherapy to address recognizing triggers and consequences related to intrusive thoughts and behaviors.
3. Psychiatric consult and possible medication evaluation.	Provide supportive discussion related to medication evaluation. Assess needs for antianxiety medications, and arrange for prescription evaluation if needed. Help client problem-solve questions for the psychiatrist regarding concerns related to medication use.
4. Express self-desires more realistically.	Reinforce client's increased control over her energy, and help the client set attainable goals and limits to address fears. Reality-test cognitions, assisting to differentiate between functional and dysfunctional thoughts.
5. Process feelings related to the traumatic event, and identify patterns of self-blame and avoidance.	In psychotherapy, help client identify two reasons for her fears related to the event, and problem-solve other ways to address her concerns.
6. Implement self-relaxation techniques.	Educate client about self-relaxation techniques to alleviate fear, worry, terror, and/or stress.
7. Engage support systems.	If requested, provide education to family regarding PTSD. If requested, provide family sessions to address communication patterns that facilitate healthy dynamics.

and complex, and a multitude of treatment interventions can be utilized. Marinchak & Morgan (2012) suggest six factors to take into account when addressing any type of behavioral treatment (p. 138):

1. Treatment, regardless of the type utilized, has to involve a collaborative relationship between the client and the practitioner. If goals and objectives are not mutually negotiated, the treatment will be limited in success.
2. The client has to commit to participate and actively address the problem behaviors identified, both in and outside the therapy session.
3. Complete a functional analysis to clearly identify the problems the client is experiencing and which ones need immediate attention.
4. Work with the client to develop treatment goals and the strategy for implementation. An adequate knowledge of different treatment strategies allows the

practitioner to individualize the plan of intervention to follow.

5. Have a clear plan and indicators to evaluate treatment progress, success, and follow-up.
6. In working with substance disorders and PTSD in particular, relapse is always a significant concern. Providing information on long-term recovery strategies and specific practice strategy related to relapse is always recommended.

A brief summary of several popular approaches follows.

Cognitive-Behavioral Therapy

Cognitive-behavioral therapy (CBT) has demonstrated efficacious, cost-effective results in the treatment of anxiety disorders and other disorders included in the *DSM-5*. The emphasis is on expanding the client's sense of self-efficacy, independence, participation, self-monitoring, and control in treatment. It can be utilized in various treatment modalities (individual, groups, couples, families, Internet). All psychosocial interventions need to take into account the restrictions placed by coordinated care organizations and insurance plans in their billing and reimbursements. The CBT interventions complement other treatment modalities in an integrated approach and are equally as effective on their own in addressing anxiety disorders. The techniques utilized in CBT are ideal for working with anxiety problems because they allow mental health practitioners to be relatively confrontational yet respectful of the client. "Specifically, difficulties in safety, trust, power and control, self-esteem, and intimacy are targeted [cognitive component of CBT]" (Keane et al., 2006, p. 180). This relationship is essential for promoting client independence and positive self-regard.

Particularly for addressing trauma- and stress-related anxiety, focusing on thoughts and their impact on emotional regulation and reactions is important when information processing is impaired (Fruzzetti, Crook, Erikson, Lee, & Worrall, 2008). The cognitive model helps to identify thoughts and the precipitation of physiological and cognitive reaction; if not identified, it creates a self-perpetuating cycle that intensifies anxiety (McEvoy & Perini, 2009; Siev & Chambless, 2007). A useful component of CBT is that it addresses the misperception of threat and danger assessments (real or imagined) and the activation of fear, terror, rage, and worry that is common in anxiety disorders. The CBT model has components to address anxiety (self-monitoring, cognitive restructuring [including evaluating and reconsidering interpretive and predictive cognitions], relaxation training, and rehearsal and coping skills) (Siev & Chambless, 2007). It is a present-based therapy that reinforces the client's focus on the now and increases reality testing that sustains functioning while addressing and increasing coping capabilities and restructuring thoughts and behaviors.

One cognitive-behavior–based intervention is Albert Ellis's rational emotive behavior therapy (REBT) (Ellis, 2008; Ellis & Grieger, 1977). It is particularly helpful for clients' catastrophizing, personalizing, or imagining the worst case, where they are responsible for identifying the catastrophic outcome. It focuses on clients' irrational and unrealistic thoughts. Internal rules are identified and replaced with more functional and adaptive alternatives (Ellis & Grieger, 1977). The A-B-C-D-E format provides the structure for the analysis of cognitions.

A is the activating event (real or imagined).

B is the belief that the person has about A (rational or irrational belief, functional or dysfunctional).

C is the consequence (emotional, behavioral, or both).
D is the disputation of the distorted beliefs (provide evidence for belief).
E is the new effect or philosophy that evolves out of the rational belief replacing the faulty belief (Ellis, 2008; Ellis & Grieger, 1977).

Clients are taught that an irrational or faulty belief they have about A causes C. They learn that everyone, including themselves, is a fallible and imperfect human being. Thus REBT teaches clients to develop unconditional self-acceptance and unconditional acceptance of others. It employs active-directive techniques, such as role playing, assertiveness training, and conditioning and counterconditioning procedures (Ellis, 1971).

Self-Regulatory Executive Function Model

The self-regulatory executive function (S-REF) model is particularly useful in addressing metacognitive beliefs associated with rumination, major depression, panic disorder, social phobia, hypochondriasis, obsessive-compulsive symptoms, and worry. According to this model, attentional control and inflexibility, such as an inability to shift, are contributing factors in emotional disorders (McEvoy & Perini, 2009). It addresses beliefs that increase the likelihood of selecting coping strategies that promote self-focused attention (threat monitoring, thought suppression, worry, and rumination) and maintain emotional disorders (McEvoy & Perini, 2009). "The model differentiates three levels of processing: automatic, low-level processing of external and internal stimuli; controlled processing directed toward the control of action and thought; and a permanent store of self beliefs" (Matthews & Wells, 2000, p. 83). The model's treatment aim is to increase attention shifting externally, increase flexibility and control, and employ cognitive-behavioral therapy and attention training. Self-knowledge driving the maladaptive responses is examined, as are metacognitive beliefs influencing thoughts that maintain dysfunction, and processing schemata are modified to provide alternative processing to problematic stimuli (Matthews & Wells, 2000). Intervention focuses on three phases of attention training: selective attention, attention switching, and divided attention. These require that individuals focus on one particular sound to the exclusion of others for 30 seconds. Once complete attention is shifted to another sound, it is then shifted to another approximately every 5 seconds—thus dividing attention simultaneously—and focused on as many sounds as possible for approximately 15 seconds (Matthews & Wells, 2000; McEvoy & Perini, 2009). The model's CBT and attention training serve as a supplemental component and have demonstrated improvements in increased attention, self-control, and disengagement from threats in panic disorders and social phobia.

Computer-Based Treatments

Self-help interventions are cost-effective and target individuals who are reluctant to enter treatment or who seek affiliation (e.g., books, self-help groups). The CBT interventions are increasingly applied to novel therapeutic situations utilizing Internet-based services where automatic decision making is generated (Andersson, 2009). These interventions assess individuals' decision making and provide educational protocols and support to increase awareness and motivation. Utilizing Internet-accessible self-help materials and computer-based live group exposure sessions, an identified therapist provides support, encouragement, and occasionally direct therapeutic activities via e-mail (Andersson, 2009). In particular, computer-based therapies are used to target individuals with panic disorder, social anxiety disorder, and posttraumatic stress disorder who do not actively seek or who have reservations about treatment. Included in these interventions are mood disorders, substance use disorders, and other health-related problems (Andersson, 2009; Walker, Roffman, Picciano, & Stephens, 2007).

Behavior Therapies

Contemporary behavior therapies work to extinguish negative emotions, thoughts, and behaviors. They are often rehearsed in sessions and applied through imagery, modeling, and computer models to create a response in a safe setting with the actual application of clients exposing themselves to the perceived threat or source of distress. Exposure therapies (e.g., systematic desensitization, also known as in vivo exposure therapy and/or eye movement desensitization and reprocessing [EMDR]) are particularly useful for individuals suffering from phobias, separation anxiety, PTSD, and OCD; these interventions can be therapist- or self-guided. Exposure therapies that use flooding involve gradual or prolonged exposure to the focus stimuli that create the fear or anxiety reaction (Zoellner, Abramowitz, Moore, & Slagle, 2008). Behavior therapies are particularly effective when executive functions are disturbed and clients have difficulty imagining events or situations that can trigger fear. "*In vivo exposure* generally involves returning to the site of the traumatic event to reduce avoidance and promote mastery over the associated trauma cues" (Keane et al., 2006). *Relaxation training* is also a behavior-based therapy. Learning to control muscle tension through taught relaxation techniques reduces anxiety and physiological responses.

Family Therapy

Family therapy allows family members to verbalize thoughts, emotions, and concerns related to any mental disorder. Family members can experience difficulties secondary to rituals, fears, inability to perform functions, neglect, and violence. Codependency is a dynamic that leaves family members feeling hopeless in making life manageable. Families need education and support to learn coping skills and understand their loved one's behavior. Family therapy can also offer a forum to vent feelings and problem-solve. It is important that the family as a whole receive assistance in strengthening its own support systems.

PULLING IT ALL TOGETHER: AN INTEGRATED APPROACH

The current approach to health care service delivery is the integrated approach, and the emphasis is on evidence-based practices (Youngner, Gerardi, & Rothbaum, 2013). Market-based principles and application to service delivery have shifted health care to a specialization of services that emphasizes quality assurance and cost-effectiveness. This model of health care practice dominates all aspects and types of treatment availability, emphasizing evidence and best practices, with a feedback loop between billing and reimbursement. An integrated approach allows expediency in treatment through rapid identification, safety control measures among providers, and intervention techniques that reduce harm. The resultant approach stresses demonstrated effectiveness while encouraging client participation. The mechanisms for the allocation of services specify not just specialization but integration as a quality-control measure. All treatment is under scrutiny for reimbursement despite the implementation of the Wellstone–Domenici Mental Health and Addiction Parity Act of 2008 that emphasizes the integration of effectiveness, efficiency, need, and demonstrable results for continuation of services (More, 2008).

Because of their multifactorial aspects, trauma-related and other anxiety disorders require the integrated specialization of professionals. This is already evident in the pharmacological intervention services, counseling, and screening for medication side effects and hazardous effects. The integrated approach facilitates the integration of family and a supportive system of care to achieve more successful outcomes, reduce harm, and increase sustainability.

Internet-based anxiety disorder interventions are beneficial in targeting individuals who are reluctant to engage in treatment and/or do not desire the restrictions to acquire treatment. These methods offer some potential advances to identify unmet needs and integrate services through a novel application of interventions that applies best practices to address diagnostic components related to a disorder. Measures that help to identify the presence of anxiety disorders should be integrated into care to facilitate treatment acquisition, demonstrate evidence, and facilitate communication among interdisciplinary providers.

Models to treat anxiety disorders utilize a component of multiple approaches to target different components of the disorder (Youngner et al., 2013). In general, more than one psychotherapeutic approach is used in combination with other interventions.

Medication as a Treatment Modality

Pharmacological advances are available to address aspects of brain-related dysfunction associated with the trauma- and stressor-related disorders. This mode of intervention is effective but not without controversy. Excessive availability and inadequate regulation have increased the consumption of psychotherapeutic drugs through prescriptions, illegal street vendors, and the Internet. Increased use of benzodiazepines and other anxiolytics has contributed to an estimated 15% to 44% of chronic benzodiazepine users becoming addicted and experiencing discontinuance problems. Upon cessation, these individuals experience severe withdrawal symptoms, including emergent anxiety and depressive symptoms (Hood, O'Neil, & Hulse, 2009). Benzodiazepines—for example, clonazepam (Klonopin), temazepam (Restoril), and alprazolam (Xanax)—have little effect on PTSD symptoms (Spoormaker & Montgomery, 2008). Benzodiazepine and prescription antianxiety medications, excluding nonbenzodiazepine antianxiety agents (e.g., hypnotics, sedatives, and anxiolytics), can be misused and abused by individuals with anxiety disorders, which creates further problems of withdrawal and dependence (World Health Organization, 2009).

In certain types of anxiety disorders, pharmacotherapy may be less effective when using traditional selective serotonin reuptake inhibitors (SSRIs) (Pietrefesa & Coles, 2009). The SSRIs approved by the Food and Drug Administration to treat anxiety include sertraline (Zoloft), fluoxetine (Prozac), and paroxetine (Paxil), which may be modestly effective in treating PTSD (Keane et al., 2006; Spoormaker & Montgomery, 2008). Tricyclic antidepressants, specifically imipramine (Tofranil) and amitriptyline (Elavil), are used less often because of side effects and potential toxicity. Efficacy of the monoamine oxidase inhibitors (MAOIs), such as phenelzine (Nardil) and brofaromine (Consonar), is not supported for certain types of anxiety disorders and used as a last resort, based on the problematic side effects and dietary restrictions (Keane et al., 2006). Other psychotherapeutic medications include antipsychotic agents, such as nefaxodone (Serzone), trazodone (Desyrel), and mirtazapine (Remeron), to treat insomnia and, in rare circumstances, hallucinations. Other sleep agents, such as cyproheptadine (Periactin), slightly worsened nightmares and symptom severity in anxiety disorders such as PTSD (Spoormaker & Montgomery, 2008).

Antiadrenergic agents are changing the future direction of pharmacological treatment of the anxiety disorders because they target specific neurobiological components relative to the clinical presentation. The association between noradrenergic hyperactivity and pharmacological agents targeting specific adrenergic receptors (associated with hyperarousal and hypervigilance) might be more applicable and efficient and provide better clinical and treatment outcomes than traditional psychotherapeutic drugs, such as prazosin (Minipress) (Keane et al., 2006; Strawn & Geracioti, 2007). Pharmacological interventions that target neurobiological and organic mechanisms related to the clinical presentation of anxiety disorders may also prove safer, more relevant, and more appropriate than the types of pharmacological treatments currently available.

SUMMARY AND FUTURE DIRECTIONS

The trauma- and stressor-related disorders in the *DSM-5* share common features and criteria that focus on metacognitions and physiological responses. The disorders in this chapter share a basis in altered physiological organ function, neurological disturbances, cognitive alterations, and behavioral disruptions. A breakdown in attention and information processing leads to serious problems in functioning and responses that are inappropriate to the situation at hand. Despite their common features, their clinical presentations and cognitive and behavioral responses can vary.

Treatments and intervention practices to address the constructs of these stress-related disorders focus on cognitive restructuring, training executive functions in new ways to process information, learned physiological responses, desensitization, and extinction of behaviors. These methods focus on the neuropsychological deficits in cognition and emphasize reducing emotional reactions that accompany these disorders, such as fear, terror, anxiety, and worry. Treatment has to take into account associated risk factors and diagnostic measurements. Future directions should include research information related to emotional and behavioral reactivity, accuracy of diagnostic assessments, and preventive measures to reduce the onset and impact of stress responses.

REFERENCES

Adler, G. (2007). Intervention approaches to driving with dementia. *Health and Social Work, 32*(1), 75–79.

American Psychiatric Association. (2000). *Diagnostic and statistical manual of mental disorders* (4th ed., text rev.). Washington, DC: Author.

American Psychiatric Association. (2013). *Diagnostic and statistical manual of mental disorders* (5th ed.). Arlington, VA: American Psychiatric Publishing.

Amin, S., Kuhle, C. & Fitzpatrick, L. (2003). Comprehensive evaluation of the older woman. *Mayo Clinic Proceedings, 78*(9), 1157–1185.

Andersson, G. (2009). Using the Internet to provide cognitive behavior therapy. *Behaviour Research and Therapy, 47*, 175–180.

Barnhill, J. W. (2014). Trauma-and stressor-related disorders: Introduction. In J. W. Barnhill (Ed.), *DSM-5™ clinical cases* (pp. 141–142). Washington, DC: American Psychiatric Publishing.

Bryant, R. A., Moulds, M., Guthrie, R., & Nixon, R. D. (2003). Treating acute stress disorder following mild traumatic brain injury. *American Journal of Psychiatry, 160*, 585–587.

Center for Psychological Studies. (2008). *Beck Depression Inventory Scale*. Retrieved from Nova Southeastern University: http://www.cps.nova.edu/~cpphelp/BDI.html

Charuvastra, A., & Cloitre, M. (2008). Social bonds and posttraumatic stress disorder. *Annual Review of Psychology, 59*, 301–328.

Derezotes, D. S. (2014). *Transforming historical trauma through dialogue*. Los Angeles: CA: Sage.

Ellis, A. (1971). *Growth through reason*. Palo Alto, CA: Science and Behavior Books.

Ellis, A. (2008). Cognitive restructuring of the disputing of irrational beliefs. In W. T. O'Donohue & J. E. Fisher

(Eds.), *Cognitive behavior therapy: Applying empirically supported techniques in your practice* (pp. 91–95). Hoboken, NJ: Wiley.

Ellis, A., & Grieger, R. (Eds.). (1977). *Handbook of rational-emotive therapy*. New York, NY: Springer.

Fischer, J., & Corcoran, K. (2007). *Measures for clinical practice: A source book. Volume 2: Adults* (4th ed.). New York, NY: Oxford University Press.

Friedman, M. J. (2014). Two reactions to trauma. In J. W. Barnhill (Ed.), *DSM-5™ clinical cases* (pp. 146–148). Washington, DC: American Psychiatric Publishing.

Fruzzetti, A. E., Crook, W., Erikson, K. M., Lee, J. E., & Worrall, J. M. (2008). Emotion regulation. In W. T. O'Donohue & J. E. Fisher (Eds.), *Cognitive behavior therapy: Applying empirically supported techniques in your practice* (pp. 174–186). Hoboken, NJ: Wiley.

Grigorenko, E. L. (2009). *Multicultural psychoeducational assessment*. New York, NY: Springer.

Hood, S., O'Neil, G., & Hulse, G. (2009). The role of flumazeil in the treatment of benzodiazepine dependence: Physiological and psychological profiles. *Journal of Psychopharmacology, 23*(4), 401–409.

Hudson, W. W., & Proctor, E. K. (1977). Assessment of depressive affect in clinical practice. *Journal of Consulting and Clinical Practice, 45*(6), 1206–1207.

Hudson, W. W. (1990). *The WALMYR Assessment Scale scoring manual*. Tempe, AZ: WALMYR.

Insel, K., & Badger, T. (2002). Deciphering the 4 D's: Cognitive decline, delirium, depression, and dementia—a review. *Journal of Advanced Nursing, 38*(4), 360–368.

Keane, T. M., Marshall, A. D., & Taft, C. T. (2006). Posttraumatic stress disorders: Etiology, epidemiology, and treatment outcome. *Annual Review of Clinical Psychology, 2*, 161–197.

Marinchak, J. S., & Morgan, T. J. (2012). Behavioral treatment techniques for psychoactive substance disorders. In S. W. Walters & F. Rotgers (Eds.), *Treating substance abuse: Theory and techniques* (3rd ed., pp. 138–166). New York, NY: Guilford Press.

Matthews, G., & Wells, A. (2000). Attention, automaticity, and affective disorder. *Behavior Modification, 24*(1), 69–93.

Mayo Clinic. (2009). *Post-traumatic stress disorder (PTSD): Risk factors*. Retrieved from http://www.mayoclinic.com/health/post-traumatic-stress-disorder/DS00246/DSECTION=risk-factors

McEvoy, P. M., & Perini, S. J. (2009). Cognitive behavioral group therapy for social phobia with or without attention training: A controlled trial. *Journal of Anxiety Disorders, 23*, 519–528.

More, J. (2008). *Wellstone–Pete Domenici Mental Health Parity and Addiction Equity Act of 2008: Explained in brief.* Retrieved from http://www.treatmentsolutionsnetwork.com/blog/index.php/2008/12/16/wellstone-pete-domenici-mental-health-parity-and-addiction-equity-act-of-2008-explained-in-brief/

Mott, J. M., Hundt, N. E., Sansgiry, S., Mignogna, J., & Cully, J. A. (2014). Changes in psychotherapy utilization among veterans with depression, anxiety, and PTSD. *Psychiatric Services in Advance, 11*(3), 106–112.

National Institute of Mental Health. (2008). *The numbers count: Mental disorders in America*. Retrieved from http://www.nimh.nih.gov/health/publications/the-numbers-count-mental-disorders-in-america/index.shtml

National Institute of Mental Health. (2009). *Post-traumatic stress disorder (PTSD)*. Retrieved from http://www.nimh.nih.gov/health/topics/post-traumatic-stress-disorder-ptsd/index.shtml

Pack, M. (2014). Vicarious resilience: A multilayered model of stress and trauma. *Affilia, 29*(1), 18–29. doi: 10.1177/0886109913510088

Paniagua, F. A. (2014). *Assessing and treating culturally diverse clients: A practical guide* (4th ed.). Los Angeles, CA: Sage.

Pietrefesa, A. S., & Coles, M. E. (2009). Moving beyond an exclusive focus on harm avoidance in obsessive-compulsive disorder: Behavioral validation for the separability of harm avoidance and incompleteness. *Behavior Therapy, 40*(3), 251–259.

Rosendal, S., Mortensen, E. L., Andersen, H. S., & Heir, T. (2014). Use of health care services before and after a natural disaster among survivors with and without PTSD. *Psychiatric Services in Advance, 11*(3), 91–97.

Rizq, R. (2012) The perversion of care: Psychological therapies in a time of IAPT. *Psychodynamic Practice: Individuals, Groups and Organisations, 18*(1), 7–24. doi: 10.1080/14753634.2012.640161

Schmidt, N. B., Norr, A. M. & Korte, K. J. (2014). Panic disorder and agoraphobia: Considerations for DSM-V. *Research on Social Work Practice, 24*(1), 57–66.

Schore, A. N. (2014). Introduction. In J. J. Magnavita & J. C. Anchin, *Unifying psychotherapy: Principles, methods, evidence from clinical science* (pp. xxi–xliv). New York, NY: Springer.

Schwartz, G. E., Davidson, R. J., & Goleman, D. J. (1978). Patterning of cognitive and somatic processes in self-regulation of anxiety: Effects of meditation versus exercise. *Psychosomatic Medicine, 40*(1), 321–328.

Siev, J., & Chambless, D. L. (2007). Specificity of treatment effects: Cognitive therapy and relaxation for generalized anxiety and panic disorder. *Journal of Consulting and Clinical Psychology, 75*(4), 513–522.

Spoormaker, V. I., & Montgomery, P. (2008). Disturbed sleep in post-traumatic stress disorder: Secondary symptom or core feature? *Sleep Medicine Reviews, 12*(3), 169–184.

Sripada, C. S., Angstadt, M., Banks, S., Nathan, P. J., Liberzon, I., & Phan, K. L. (2009). Functional neuroimaging of mentalizing during the trust game in social anxiety. *NeuroReport, 20*(11), 984–989. doi: 10.1097/WNR.0b013e32832d0a67

Strawn, J. R., & Geracioti, T. D., Jr. (2007). The treatment of generalized anxiety disorder with pregabalin, an atypical anxiolytic. *Neuropsychiatric Disease and Treatment, 3*(2), 237–243.

Sundin, E. C., & Horowitz, M. J. (2002). Impact of event scale: Psychometric properties. *British Journal of Psychiatry, 180*, 205–209.

U.S. Department of Veterans Affairs. (2009a). *Penn Inventory for Posttraumatic Stress Disorder*. Retrieved from U.S. Department of Veterans Affairs: National Center for PTSD: http://www.ptsd.va.gov/professional/assessment/adult-sr/penn-inventory-ptsd.asp

U.S. Department of Veteran Affairs. (2009b). *Los Angeles Symptom Checklist (LASC)*. Retrieved from U.S. Department of Veterans Affairs: National Center for PTSD: http://www.ptsd.va.gov/professional/assessment/adult-sr/lasc.asp

U.S. Department of Veteran Affairs. (2009c). *Screen for Posttraumatic Stress Symptoms (SPTSS)*. Retrieved from US Department of Veteran Affairs: National Center for PTSD: http://www.ptsd.va.gov/professional/assessment/adult-sr/sptss.asp

Walker, D., Roffman, R., Picciano, J., & Stephens, R. (2007). The check-up: In-person, computerized, and telephone adaptations of motivational enhancement treatment to elicit voluntary participation by the contemplator. *Substance Abuse Treatment, Prevention, and Policy, 2*, 1–10.

Watts, B. V., Shiner, B., Zubkoff, L., Carpenter-Song, E., Ronconi, J. M., & Coldwell, C. M. (2014). Implementation of evidence-based psychotherapies for posttraumatic stress disorder in VA specialty clinics. *Psychiatric Services in Advance, 11*(3), 1–6. doi: 10.1176/appi.ps.201300176

Wise, V., McFarlane, A. C., Clark, C. R., & Battersby, M. (2009). Event-related potential and autonomic signs of maladaptive information processing during an auditory oddball task in panic disorder. *International Journal of Psychophysiology, 74*(1), 34–44.

Woo, S. M., & Keatinge, C. (Eds.). (2008). *Diagnosis and treatment of mental disorders across the lifetime*. Hoboken, NJ: Wiley.

World Health Organization. (2009). *Organization for Economic Co-operation and Development health working papers no. 42—Policies for healthy aging: An overview*. Paris, France: Organisation for Economic Co-operation and Development.

Yehuda, R., Bierer, L. M., Schmeidler, J., Aferiat, D. H., Breslau, I., & Dolan, S. (2000). Low cortisol and risk for PTSD in adult offspring of holocaust survivors. *American Journal of Psychiatry, 157*, 1252–1259.

Youngner, C. G., Gerardi, M., & Rothbaum, B. O. (2013). PTSD: Evidence-based psychotherapy and emerging treatment approaches *FOCUS, 11*(3), 307–314. doi: 10.1176/appi.focus.11.3.307

Zoellner, L. A., Abramowitz, J. S., Moore, S. A., & Slagle, D. M. (2008). Flooding. In W. T. O'Donohue & J. E. Fisher (Eds.), *Cognitive behavior therapy: Applying empirically supported techniques in your practice* (pp. 202–210). Hoboken, NJ: Wiley.

CHAPTER 10 Sexual Dysfunctions

Sophia F. Dziegielewski and Joshua Kirven

INTRODUCTION

As individuals progress through the life cycle and seek to join sexually with a mate, problems can occur, and these problems need to be acknowledged and discussed. Many individuals suffering from sexual problems are uncomfortable and uneducated on what actually is normal performance (Buehler, 2014). Sexual health can be further complicated by previous sexual experiences that include sexual abuse, sexual behaviors, and parental attitudes toward sex, as well as other environmental factors that can greatly affect individuals. If ignored, these varied factors can lead to the development of sexual disorders, where an individual is unable to participate in a sexual relationship as he or she wishes (Meston & Rellini, 2008). Because sexual development is often misunderstood, neglected, or abused within the society, individuals who suffer from sexual problems may not know how to address them. They may also not be comfortable discussing concerns and expressing problems related to sexual activity and performance; to engage in such talk is often considered taboo.

This chapter explores the most common sexual disorders: Delayed ejaculation (DE), erectile disorder (ED), female orgasmic disorder (FOD), female interest/arousal disorder, genito-pelvic pain/penetration disorder, male hypoactive sexual desire disorder, premature (early) ejaculation (PE), substance/medication-induced sexual dysfunction, other specified sexual dysfunction, and unspecified sexual dysfunction. Basic criteria are listed for completing the diagnostic assessment and treatment plan to follow. It is beyond the purpose of this chapter to address all aspects of the sexual disorders; therefore, selected disorders covered in this chapter include those outlined in the fifth edition of the *Diagnostic and Statistical Manual of Mental Disorders* (*DSM-5*; American Psychiatric Association [APA], 2013). The application section of this chapter provides a case example of the sexual dysfunctions with specific recommendations for completing the diagnostic assessment and the subsequent treatment plan. Various aspects of the disorder are presented, highlighting the diagnostic assessment, treatment planning, and evidence-based treatment strategy. In addition, the latest practice methods and newest research and findings are noted to further the understanding of these stressful, often emotionally devastating illnesses.

TOWARD A BASIC UNDERSTANDING OF THE SEXUAL DYSFUNCTIONS

In the human life cycle, each individual develops into a sexual being with certain needs, desires, and expectations. The similarities as well as the differences that occur in development can be pronounced. This complex interchange of

Special thanks to Gary Dick, PhD, for his contributions to the previous edition of this chapter.

human sexual behavior is influenced by a complex interaction among physiological, behavioral, psychosocial, political, and cultural factors (Buehler, 2014; Lipsith, McCann, & Goldmeier, 2003). This fact makes understanding and becoming adaptable through awareness of one's sexuality a central component of productive, normal human growth and development (Dziegielewski, Jacinto, Dick, & Resnick-Cortes, 2007).

This development is never easy, as sexual development and expression is considered a unique and private affair. Often individuals have trouble discussing sexual issues with their own intimate partners; even more difficult is sharing this information with professional strangers. In turn, practitioners may not have formal training and education in this area and may also feel uncomfortable identifying and discussing the problems a client is experiencing (Buehler, 2014).

According to social learning theory, individuals acquire much of their sexual behavior in large part according to socially acceptable (i.e., reinforced) or unacceptable (i.e., punished) codes of expression (i.e., contingencies). For example, rarely is intimate sexual expression ever modeled, given this high degree of secrecy and privacy. Furthermore, the traditional modes of education are not often utilized. Schools are leery about providing this type of education and view much of it as the responsibility of the parent. Yet parents feel unprepared and uncomfortable in approaching this subject (Burgess, Dziegielewski, & Green, 2005). Not only is there no parental modeling or social influence but also, as result of this privatization of sexuality, children can receive inaccurate, inappropriate, or exploitive information. In adolescence, sexually active teens who are not properly educated and aware can make uninformed decisions leading to teenage pregnancy, health concerns, gender confusion, and long-term consequences (Kirven, 2014). These one-time decisions can further lead to mistakes such as unwanted teenage pregnancy (Kirven, 2014; Patel & Sen, 2012). Accurate and honest information at this level is essential because from this starting point, all expectations will be modeled.

When there is a general attempt to avoid sharing sexual information or simply neglect during this phase of human development, gaps in learning are created. There are few appropriate channels for obtaining information considered unknown, embarrassing, or forbidden. This lack of attention to the development of human sexuality can have serious, long-term effects that cause adults to struggle with unrealistic expectations or lack the proper coping skills to deal with sexual behaviors throughout their lives (Horton, 1995). Acceptance of sexual needs, desires, and expectations can be highly variable, complicating the definition of what is normal sexual behavior and what is related to a sexual problem (Nicolson & Burr, 2003).

Sexual disorders occur in both men and women. The sexual response of both men and women varies over time and across the life cycle. Multiple factors need to be considered in diagnosing lack of or diminished sexual desire and arousal problems, including the relationship with the sexual partner, prior sexual abuse and past negative sexual experiences, poor sexual body image (small breast size for women and small penis size for men), internalized negative emotions about sexuality, life stress, fatigue, mental health issues such as anxiety and depression, and medication or medical conditions. In addition, because so many individuals may not have had high-quality sex education on what is normal and what is not, for both men and women, the practitioner needs to inquire about the effect of the aging process on sexual desire and arousal.

With all sexual dysfunctions, to be considered a sexual disorder, the lack of desire must be viewed as a problem that is persistent and recurrent. According to the *DSM-5*, for all of the sexual disorders, except substance/medication induced disorder, experiencing the problems for a minimum of six months is expected (Barnhill, 2014). It cannot be related exclusively to another major clinical diagnosis (such as major depression or an adjustment disorder), caused by substance abuse, or be related to a general medical condition, and it must cause marked distress or interpersonal difficulty (APA, 2013).

Once the definition and diagnostic criteria of a sexual disorder have been reached, the application and relevance of this definition for each individual must be explored. Special consideration always needs to be given to what constitutes a sexual desire or arousal problem. Therefore, the problem of assessing *normal* and *abnormal* sexual behavior continues to be complicated. According to Knopf and Seiler (1990), the average couple generally has sexual intercourse two to three times a week; however, this number is highly dependent on the individual couple's preferences and needs. Simply stated, the number of times couples have or do not have sexual intercourse is not considered a problem—unless it is deemed so by the participating couple (Dziegielewski, Jacinto, et al., 2007). The frequency of sexual behavior in a relationship is only one factor to be explored in the determination of a sexual disorder. An individual's perceptions about sexual desire and arousal can be swayed by a multitude of factors, such as personal beliefs and expectations, societal attitudes and mores, cultural pressure, parental influence, spiritual and religious teaching, socioeconomic status, and education level (Stuntz, Falk, Hiken, & Carson, 1996).

INDIVIDUALS WHO SUFFER FROM A SEXUAL DYSFUNCTION

Sexual response is an outcome of how an individual feels toward the self, as well as how he or she sexually responds toward others. Both males and females have the same embryonic tissue, and in terms of orgasmic response difficulties, the differences are not that great (Redelman, 2006). The terminology and the resulting diagnosis to describe these dysfunctions may differ. For example, in *DSM-5*, males and females can experience orgasmic difficulties; however, different diagnoses can result. In males, the diagnosis can also result in either delayed or premature ejaculation whereas in women, it could result in a new diagnosis to *DSM-5* termed genito-pelvic pain/penetration disorder (Barnhill, 2014). Because expression of human sexuality is influenced by previous sexual experiences, internal needs and desires, conflict between socialization and desire, and the relationship with the partner, it has cognitive, affective, and physiological components (Rowland, Tai, & Slob, 2003). When assessing an individual for any of the sexual dysfunctions related to reaction, special attention should always be given to factors related to the human sexual response. These multidimensional factors can influence physiological, cognitive, affective, social, religious, situational, and environmental factors (Rowland et al., 2003). Situational and environmental factors, such as societal mores as they relate to sexual roles and expectations, family attitudes, sex education or lack of it, and religious beliefs, can all affect the ability to achieve orgasm (Dziegielewski, Jacinto, et al., 2007).

Individuals who suffer from a sexual dysfunction may also have lessened physiologic sexual responses. For example, some studies suggest that individuals suffering from a sexual disorder may actually experience less sexual arousal or are simply less attentive to their own physiological cues than are sexually functional individuals (Borello-France et al., 2004; Hofman et al., 2004). These individuals may, in turn, also have difficulty labeling physiological genital cues relating to their own sexual arousal. However, the results from studies conducted in this area have been conflicting, and more research is required to establish this as a predictor for understanding sexual responses.

Having a sexual dysfunction can affect quality of life and self-esteem and lead to depression and anxiety. Individuals' lack of access to information regarding the origins and treatment of sexual problems and the professional practitioner's reluctance to discuss human sexuality can further contribute to the secrecy that surrounds problems with sexual functioning and sexual suffering (Dziegielewski, Turnage, Dick, & Resnick-Cotes, 2007). Reasons can include reluctance on the part of the practitioner and/or the couple or individual to talk about the problems because of embarrassment and/or shame. Also, at times couples may not be comfortable talking about such issues in front of each other and more may be shared in individual sessions (Graham, 2014). For a diagnosis of a sexual dysfunction an individual must report distress over a period of time and report what would be considered to be clinically significant disturbances in his or her ability to respond to sexual pleasure. Acknowledging and approaching these types of problems is the first step, regardless of the treatment to follow (Meston & Rellini, 2008).

IMPORTANT FEATURES AND TERMS RELATED TO THE SEXUAL DYSFUNCTIONS

When completing the diagnostic assessment with an individual who suffers from a sexual dysfunction, defining what constitutes normal behavior and reasonable expectations can be difficult. This is further complicated by individuals' lack of knowledge of normal response. Feelings of inadequacy can be overstated or understated and thereby influenced by the definition and normalcy standards set within an individual's unique social and environmental context. Understanding the sexual disorders starts with reviewing some basic and important terms.

Phases of the Sexual Response Cycle

Understanding the sexual response cycle can provide valuable information to the practitioner working with individuals who suffer from a sexual dysfunction. From this perspective, the sexual response cycle is divided into four phases: *desire phase* (desires and fantasies about sex), *excitement phase* (subjective interpretations and actual physiologic changes), *orgasm phase* (generalized muscular tension and contractions in the sex organs), and *resolution phase* (general sense of relaxation and release of the previously created muscular tension) (WebMD, 2012). Concerning specifically the disorders referred to as sexual dysfunctions, achieving orgasm is an important aspect in identifying the disorder and shaping the treatment to follow. In some disorders, male and female, the orgasm is delayed or absent following a normal excitement phase, or the opposite reaction, which results in premature ejaculation when the orgasm comes too quickly in males (Maxmen, Ward, & Kilgus, 2009).

Subtypes: Occurrence, Generalized Versus Situational

When diagnosing the sexual dysfunctions there are several subtypes that should always be taken into account. According to the *DSM-5* (APA, 2013) a subtype is both mutually exclusive and exhaustive and is coded as:

Specify whether:

Generalized: Not limited to certain situations, partners, or types of stimulation

Situational: Occurs only with certain situations, partners, or types of stimulation

When present, specifying whether these subtypes exist can help to quantify the course of the disorder and the types of situations where it occurs. In the first subtype, the problem may be *generalized*, throughout all an individual's sexual experiences, or *situational*, with a specific type of stimulation, partner, or circumstance. The disorder is also distinguished by whether it is lifelong or acquired. In the past the terms primary or secondary were utilized. Generally, the term *primary*, currently referred to as lifelong, is applied to individuals who have never been able to achieve sexual satisfaction through any means. The term *secondary*, currently referred to as *situational*, is applied to individuals who have been able to achieve sexual satisfaction in the past but for whatever reason are currently anorgasmic. Situational sexual dysfunctions may vary in degree, type, or situation. Problems may occur with a specific partner or certain partners only, a prior history of satisfaction but only under certain types of stimulation such as masturbation, or in certain situations and particular contexts. In *DSM-5*, the disorders that involve orgasm, such as female orgasmic disorder (FOD), allow this to be addressed further through use of a specifier. In such cases, the practitioner is given the option to outline whether the individual has ever experienced an orgasm, and later this can be applied to the treatment program to follow.

Subtypes: Prevalence, Lifelong or Acquired

In diagnosing the sexual dysfunctions, the practitioner has the ability to also assign an additional subtype related to the prevalence of the disorder and whether it is *lifelong* or *acquired*.

When diagnosing the sexual dysfunctions, according to the *DSM-5* (APA, 2013) these subtypes are documented as:

Specify whether:

Lifelong: The sexual problems and concerns have always been present through all sexual activity.

Acquired: The sexual problems and concerns only occurred after a time when satisfactory sexual activity was reported.

In many individuals with sexual dysfunctions, the subtypes help to define the time of onset and how that may indicate different etiologies and interventions. *Lifelong* refers to a sexual problem that has been present from the client's first sexual experiences, and *acquired* applies to sexual disorders that develop after a period of relatively normal sexual function. *Generalized* refers to sexual difficulties that are not limited to certain types of stimulation, situations, or partners, and *situational* refers to sexual difficulties that occur with only certain types of arousal, stimulation, conditions, and partners. When looking specifically at situational factors, examine the degree to which the dysfunction causes subjective distress and interpersonal difficulty. Often situational factors can have multiple etiologies, and a number of causal factors can contribute to the onset of these problems in women and men (Dziegielewski, Jacinto, et al., 2007). For example, an individual may suffer from the side effects of medications, such as antidepressants and other types of medications used for chronic conditions. Other causes include situational factors, such as relationship conflict, traumatic experience (e.g., rape), sexual and physical abuse, menopause, surgery, hysterectomy, removal of ovaries, and incontinence surgery. In both men and women, a detailed psychological, relational, social, and medical history is important (McCabe, 2009).

When assessing whether a dysfuntion is lifelong or situational, clinical judgment about the diagnosis of sexual dysfunction should always take into account cultural factors. Cultural factors may influence expectations or reflect gender prohibitions about the experience of sexual pleasure. In addition, natural aging may be associated with a normative decrease in sexual response. Clinical judgment should be used to determine if the sexual difficulties are the result of inadequate stimulation; in these cases, there may still be a need for care, but it may or may not be limited to circumstances in which lack of knowledge about effective stimulation prevents the experience of arousal or orgasm. These subtypes can assist in designating the onset of the difficulty, which can be related to the assessment as well as the treatment goals to follow.

Specifying Severity

In *DSM-5*, several disorders are further specified by whether the severity level is *mild, moderate,* or *severe*. Throughout the *DSM,* each diagnosis is broken down into characteristics that must be considered to support a diagnosis. Generally, criterion A is most relevant to the specific characteristics needed for the diagnosis; therefore, this criterion is almost always the most relevant specifying current severity. When the term *mild* is used, it means that there is evidence that the symptoms outlined in criterion A (the specific criteria required) cause mild distress. In *moderate* distress, the symptoms meet the criteria of the disorder and affect the development of the disorder, causing stress noted in almost all the potential characteristics of a diagnosis. The specifier for *severe* indicates that the symptoms cause significant distress that can be linked to almost all of the criteria that need to be identified for the disorder from those listed under criterion A.

Unfortunately, the *DSM-5* does not quantify what dictates mild, moderate, or severe, so this is up to the practitioner. The key is using measurement instruments to assist in quantifying behaviors, as well as self-report and partner perceptions of the severity of the disorder. Regardless of the specifier used, always keep in mind that regardless of the level of severity, the minimum criteria for the disorder have to be met. For example, if applying this qualifier to FOD, mild symptoms meet the minimum criteria for the disorder, in which the symptoms of either marked delay in frequency or absence of orgasm and/or marked reduced intensity of the orgasm have to occur in almost all experiences at least 75% of the time.

OVERVIEW OF THE SEXUAL DYSFUNCTIONS

When an individual believes that he or she has encountered difficulties that cause significant disturbance in the sexual relationship, these resulting conditions are often termed *sexual dysfunctions*. In an attempt to understand problems that can develop within the human sexual response cycle, the *DSM-5* lists the essential feature of sexual dysfunction as clinically significant difficulty in either responding to or experiencing sexual pleasure. The sexual dysfunctions characterized in the *DSM-5* are delayed ejaculation, erectile disorder, female orgasmic disorder, female interest/arousal disorder, genitopelvic pain/penetration disorder, male hypoactive sexual desire disorder, premature (early) ejaculation, substance/medication-induced sexual dysfunction, other specified sexual dysfunction, and unspecified sexual dysfunction.

The types of disorders in this category are a mixed and diversified group. For problems to be considered a sexual dysfunction, the symptoms experienced are typically characterized as causing a clinically significant disturbance in a person's ability to respond sexually or to experience sexual gratification. This is further complicated by the fact that an individual may have several sexual dysfunctions at the same time. When this occurs, the types of difficulties need to be documented; when severe enough to meet the criteria for an independent diagnosis, it should be documented as such. To further improve precision regarding duration and severity criteria and to reduce the likelihood of overdiagnosis, all *DSM-5* sexual dysfunctions (except substance/

QUICK REFERENCE 10.1

Sexual Dysfunctions as Categorized in the DSM-5: Brief Descriptions

Delayed Ejaculation: There is a marked delay or the inability to achieve ejaculation, when engaging in partnered sexual activity, despite the presence of adequate sexual stimulation and the desire to ejaculate.

Erectile Disorder: Failure to obtain or maintain erections during partnered sexual activities.

Female Orgasmic Disorder: Difficulty experiencing orgasm and/or markedly reduced intensity of orgasmic sensations.

Female Interest/Arousal Disorder: Lower desire for sexual activity than her partner with absence or reduced frequency or intensity of at least three of six indicators for a minimum duration of approximately 6 months.

Genito-Pelvic Pain/Penetration Disorder: Four commonly comorbid symptom dimensions: (1) difficulty having intercourse, (2) genito-pelvic pain, (3) fear of pain or vaginal penetration, and (4) tension of the pelvic floor muscles.

Male Hypoactive Sexual Desire Disorder: Both low/absent desire for sex and deficient/absent sexual thoughts or fantasies are required for a diagnosis of the disorder.

Premature (Early) Ejaculation: Ejaculation that occurs prior to or shortly after vaginal penetration, operationalized by an individual's estimate of ejaculatory latency (i.e., elapsed time before ejaculation) after vaginal penetration.

Substance/Medication-Induced Sexual Dysfunction: Alcohol- or drug-induced sexual problems such as erection or lubrication, difficulty experiencing sexual pleasure, and difficulty reaching orgasm or with ejaculation, which is pronounced and long-lasting.

Other Specified Sexual Dysfunction: Applies when symptoms characteristic of a sexual dysfunction cause clinically significant distress in the individual but do not meet the full criteria for any of the disorders in the sexual dysfunctions diagnostic class. The reason is specified.

Unspecified Sexual Dysfunction: This category applies to presentations in which symptoms characteristic of a sexual dysfunction cause clinically significant distress in the individual but do not meet the full criteria for any of the disorders in the sexual dysfunctions diagnostic class. The reason that the criteria are not met is not documented.

medication-induced sexual dysfunction) now require a minimum duration of approximately 6 months and more precise severity criteria. These changes provide useful thresholds for making a diagnosis and distinguish transient sexual difficulties from more persistent sexual dysfunction. (See Quick Reference 10.1.)

Delayed Ejaculation (DE)

The distinguishing characteristic of delayed ejaculation (DE) is a marked postponement of or inability to achieve ejaculation (APA, 2013). According to *DSM-5*, criteria A-D are needed to confirm the diagnosis. Central to the diagnosis is criterion A which outlines the importance of marked delay or inability to achieve orgasm. This must be found to be problematic and occur frequently (75% to 100% of the time) with partnered sexual activity. In this criterion, the male reports difficulty or inability to ejaculate, despite the presence of adequate sexual stimulation. He has the desire to ejaculate but an inability to achieve adequate stimulation to do so. Diagnosing this disorder generally involves sexual activity with a partner rather than alone. Criterion A, also requires marked postponement or delay in ejaculation. Addressing what qualifies as a delay can be difficult as there is not a clear definition with precise boundaries and this makes exactly what constitutes clinical significance difficult. In most cases, meeting this criterion will be determined by individual's interpretation and self-report. Criterion B requires that the problem be disturbing and prolonged extending for a period of at least 6 months. The disturbance must cause clinically significant distress (criterion C); and in criterion D, the sexual disorder is not better explained by another mental, medical, substance-related, or situational condition.

When assessing whether criterion A-D are met for this dysfunction, attention needs to be given to identifying what constitutes consensus for a reasonable time to reach orgasm. Because this is a partnered activity definitions from both partners is essential. Common concerns may start with reporting prolonged thrusting to achieve orgasm, leading to becoming frustrated to the point of exhaustion or genital discomfort. This unrewarded behavior often results in ceasing further efforts to keep trying. Some men report avoiding sexual activity because of a repetitive pattern of difficulty in ejaculating; others report that their partners feel less sexually attractive because of their inability to ejaculate easily.

Subtypes are utilized, and course specifiers are encouraged. A subtype clarifies a diagnosis where the phenomenological criteria are mutually exclusive and exhaustive (APA, 2013). Subtypes are easy to recognize in documenting because the coding starts with *specify* whether. The subtype qualifiers in DE relate to the time span. This homogeneous grouping allows the subtypes lifelong/acquired and generalized/situational. The second grouping for this diagnostic category is the course specifier. Contrary to the diagnostic subtype, the course specifier is not considered mutually exclusive and exhaustive and is provided to show how criteria that are similar within a diagnostic category can be grouped. There are many examples of specifiers added in *DSM-5*, but not all diagnoses have them. Also, the specifier coded "specify if" should not be confused with "specify current severity," which results in categorizing the diagnosis as mild, moderate, or severe. In mild, the basic criterion is a marked delay in ejaculation or a marked infrequency, with the symptoms causing some distress but not enough to affect all sexual encounters. In moderate distress, the symptoms are more extensive and exhibited in many but not all of the sexual encounters where ejaculatory performance is desired or expected. When the specifier is severe, the criteria for the diagnosis are met, and the individual experiences distress in all sexual encounters, resulting in total avoidance of any such experiences.

In assessing DE, three factors related to the individual and his circumstances should always be considered: (1) individual vulnerability factors (e.g., poor body image, history of sexual or emotional abuse), (2) psychiatric comorbidity (e.g., depression, anxiety), and (3) medical factors relevant to prognosis, course, or treatment. Two additional environmental circumstances need to be assessed: (1) stressors (e.g., job loss, bereavement) and (2) cultural/religious factors (e.g., inhibitions related to prohibitions against sexual activity, attitudes toward sexuality). Because DE by definition involves partnered sexual activity, two aspects of the partner ought to be considered to give the most complete picture of the situational context: (1) partner factors (e.g., partner's sexual problems, partner's health status) and (2) relationship factors (e.g., poor communication, discrepancies in desire for sexual activity). Each factor should be assessed individually; each may contribute differently to the presenting symptoms of males suffering from this disorder.

The *DSM* falls short in identifying these multiple factors and how they relate to the complexity of placing the diagnosis. That the diagnosis requires partnered activity input on this relationship is key to not only whether the characteristics of the disorder are met but also the severity. Of all the sexual dysfunctions, DE is one of the most complicated for completing a comprehensive diagnostic assessment.

Lifelong DE is relatively uncommon in clinical practice. In studies analyzing the distribution of sexual dysfunctions in men, DE always appears as the least expressed sexual complaint. The prevalence in the general male population is 1.5 in 1,000. There may be multiple causes for the disorder, and the disorder should not be caused exclusively by the direct physiologic effects of a substance or a general medical condition. In the past, Waldinger and Schweitzer (2005) criticized this definition for its failure to separate DE and failure of ejaculation (anejaculation) (McMahon et al., 2004). However, Waldinger and Schweitzer (2005) introduced a good practical definition of DE. They diagnose DE when a man finds it difficult or impossible to ejaculate, despite the presence of adequate sexual stimulation, erection, and a conscious desire to achieve orgasm. They support the current definition that the etiology of DE is frequently multidimensional, resulting from the man's biologic set point for ejaculatory latency, as affected by multiple organic and psychogenic factors, in varying combinations during his life (Perelman, 2004; Richardson, Nalabanda, & Goldmeier, 2006).

Evidence-based research on lifelong DE is limited, and currently there is no approved drug treatment for lifelong DE. Researchers have explored the effects of drugs such as yohimbine, cyproheptadine, and bupropion on male ejaculatory function. However, this research has been confined to either animal experiments (Carro-Juareza & Rodriguez-Manzo, 2003; Menendez, Moran, Velasco, & Marin, 1988) or antidepressant-induced DE (Clayton et al., 2004). Bupropion is an atypical antidepressant in the chemical class of aminoketones. It is not only the antidepressant least associated with sexual side effects (Gartlehner et al., 2008; Serretti & Chiesa, 2009) but also one of the drugs of choice for the treatment of antidepressant-induced sexual dysfunction, according to a survey of psychiatrists (Balon & Segraves, 2008; Dording et al., 2002).

Erectile Disorder (ED)

Under normal circumstances, when a man is sexually stimulated, his brain sends a message down the spinal cord and into the nerves of the penis. The nerve endings in the penis release chemical messengers, called neurotransmitters, that signal the arteries that supply blood to the corpora cavernosa (the two spongy rods of tissue that span the length of the penis) to relax and fill with blood. As they expand, the corpora cavernosa close off other veins that would normally drain blood from the penis. As the penis becomes engorged with blood, it enlarges and stiffens, causing an erection. Problems with blood vessels, nerves, or tissues of the penis can interfere with an erection.

The key feature of erectile disorder (ED) is the repeated failure to obtain or maintain erections during partnered sexual activities. As defined in the *DSM-5,* ED requires that criterion A-D be met in order to place the diagnosis. In criterion A, at least one of three symptoms must reportedly occur at least 75% to100% of the time. The first is being unable to obtain the erection during sexual activity. The second is an inability to maintain the erection until the sexual activity has become satisfying to the couple participating in the partnered activity. The third is a marked decrease in erectile rigidity. In criterion B, to firm the diagnostic criteria, a careful sexual history is necessary to ascertain that the problem has been present for at least 6 months and the symptoms cause significant distress with each sexual experience (criterion C). Criterion D requires that the assessment clearly address any possibility of the symptoms being related to another mental, medical, substance disorder or other relationship specific circumstances. If these are present the diagnosis of a sexual dysfunction should not be given. Because symptoms may occur only in specific situations involving certain types of stimulation or partners, or they may occur in a generalized manner in all types of situations, stimulation, or partners, the same subtypes and specifiers can be utilized as in DE.

Up to 30 million American men are estimated to frequently suffer from ED, and it strikes up to half of all men between the ages of 40 and 70. Doctors used to think that most cases of ED were psychological in origin, but they now recognize that, at least in older men, physical causes may play a primary role in 60% or more of all cases. In men over the age of 60, the leading cause is atherosclerosis, or narrowing of the arteries, which can restrict the flow of blood to the penis. Injury or disease of the connective tissue, such as Peyronie's disease, may prevent the corpora cavernosa from completely expanding. Damage to the nerves of the penis from certain types of surgery or neurological conditions, such as Parkinson's disease or multiple sclerosis, may also cause ED. Men with diabetes are especially at risk for erectile dysfunction because of their high risk of both atherosclerosis and diabetic neuropathy.

Some drugs, including certain types of blood pressure medications, antihistamines, tranquilizers (especially before intercourse), and antidepressants known as selective serotonic reuptake inhibitors (SSRIs), can interfere with erections. Smoking, excessive alcohol consumption, and illicit drug use may also contribute. In some cases, low levels of the male hormone testosterone may contribute to erectile failure. Psychological factors, such as stress, guilt, or anxiety, may also play a role, even when the ED is primarily due to organic causes. The potential for medical and substance/medication related causes makes addressing criterion D an important consideration for placing this diagnosis and a complete medical work-up should always be considered if it was not already done.

Diagnosing the underlying cause of erectile dysfunction begins with asking the man questions about when the problem began, whether it happens with only specific sex partners, and whether he ever wakes up with an erection. (Men whose dysfunction occurs only with certain partners or who wake up with erections are more likely to have a psychological cause for their ED.) Sometimes, the man's sex partner is also interviewed. In some cases, domestic discord may be a factor. The nonmedically trained practitioner should always provide a referral for a thorough medical history to find out about past pelvic surgery, diabetes, cardiovascular disease, kidney disease, and any medications the man is taking. The physical examination should include a genital examination, hormone tests, and a glucose test for diabetes. Sometimes blood flow through the penis may be measured.

Female Orgasmic Disorder (FOD)

As outlined in *DSM-5* (APA, 2013), female orgasmic disorder (FOD) is characterized by four specific criteria A-D. In criterion A, the specific criteria central to the disorder are outlined. The woman must suffer from at least one of the two symptoms in criterion A. When referring to the orgasm, she must experience either a marked delay, infrequency, or absence or a markedly reduced intensity of the orgasmic sensations (APA, 2013). Similar to the other sexual dysfunctions, the diagnosis of FOD can show wide variability in the intensity of stimulation that elicits orgasm. Similarly, subjective descriptions of orgasm are extremely varied, suggesting that it is experienced in very different ways, both across women and on different occasions by the same woman. For a diagnosis of FOD criterion B requires that the symptoms must persist for at least six months and cause significant distress in almost all (75-100%) of all sexual encounters (criterion C). In criterion D, symptoms that could be related to another mental, medical, substance disorders or other relationship specific circumstances need to be ruled out as a potential cause.

In addition, FOD can have several specifiers to firm the diagnostic impression. Subtypes include whether the condition is lifelong or acquired, as well as, generalized or situational. This particular diagnosis allows for a separate specifier to denote whether the individual via self-report has ever experienced an orgasmic regardless of the circumstance or situation. Lastly, it allows for a specification as to whether the distress is mild, moderate or severe.

Female Sexual Arousal Disorder (FSAD)

Female sexual arousal disorder (FSAD), which is often referred to as Candace syndrome (McCabe, 2006), is a disorder categorized by the recurrent inability to obtain sexual stimulation and maintain it through sexual activity. This disorder, similar to the other sexual dysfunctions listed in *DSM-5* requires that four criterion be met (Criteria A-D). In criterion A there are six sub-parts and to meet this criterion at least three of the following must be present. All six of these sub-crtieria require that when related directly to sexual interest or arousal reactions clearly must either be absent or reduced. There must be either absent or reduced: interest in sexual activity, erotic thoughts or fantasies, desire and reluctance or refusal of partner attempts at initiation, sexual pleasure or excitement in almost all (75-100%) of encounters, non-sexual encounters and sensations from visual, written, or verbal cues, and during almost all (75-100%) sexual encounters regardless of situation, content or partner (APA, 2013).

For a diagnosis of FSAD, criterion B requires that the symptoms must persist for at least six months, and to meet criterion C must cause significant distress in almost all (75-100%) of all sexual encounters. For this disorder, similar to FOD, criterion D, requires that symptoms not be related to another mental, medical, substance disorders or other relationship specific circumstances.

Specifiers for FSAD include: Subtypes as to whether the condition is lifelong or acquired, as well as, generalized or situational. It also allows for a specification as to whether the distress is mild, moderate, or severe.

In assessing FSAD, interpersonal context must be taken into account. A desire discrepancy, in which a woman has lower desire for sexual activity than her partner, is not sufficient to diagnose FSAD. For the criteria of the disorder to be met, there must be absence or reduced frequency or intensity of at least three of six indicators for a minimum duration of approximately 6 months. There may be different symptom profiles across women, as well as variability in how sexual interest and arousal are expressed. Because sexual desire and arousal frequently coexist and are elicited in response to adequate sexual cues, the criteria for FSAD take into account the differences in desire and arousal that often simultaneously characterize the complaints of women with this order. Short-term changes in sexual interest or arousal are common and may be adaptive responses to events in a woman's life and do not represent a sexual dysfunction.

Difficulties arise with this definition in terms of what constitutes an adequate lubrication-swelling response. There is no gold standard regarding the length of time it should take to become aroused or the level of arousal that should be achieved. These responses may vary from one woman to another and depend on a range of factors, including her general mood when sexual stimulation commences and her partner's skill in stimulating her. There may also be differences in physiological and subjective levels of arousal, with some women reporting no feelings of sexual arousal despite evidence of vaginal vasocongestion and others reporting arousal in the absence of such evidence. The expectations and past experiences of clinicians and clients may also lead them to classify the same symptoms as female sexual arousal disorder in one woman but not in another.

Genito-Pelvic Pain/Penetration Disorder (GPPD)

Genito-pelvic pain/penetration disorder (GPPD) is new to the *DSM-5* and is meant to consolidate the previous diagnoses of vaginismus (sexual pain disorder with painful muscle spasms in the vagina) and dyspareunia (sexual pain disorder in males and females). There are four criteria for GPPD (criteria A-D). Criterion A, refers to four commonly comorbid symptom dimensions causing difficulty with vaginal penetration: (1) having difficulty with direct vaginal penetration, (2) genito-pelvic pain while attempting or during intercourse, (3) anxiety or fear of pain related to vaginal penetration, and (4) tightening or tension of the pelvic floor muscles that causes difficulty in any one of these symptom dimensions sufficient enough to cause clinically significant distress. A diagnosis, however, can be made on the basis of marked difficulty in only one symptom dimension. However, all four symptom dimensions should be assessed, even if a diagnosis can be made on the basis of only one. Genito-pelvic pain/penetration disorder is frequently associated with other sexual dysfunctions, particularly reduced sexual desire and interest. Therefore, to meet criterion A, the individual must suffer from at least one or more of the above four symptoms. Similar to the other disorders in this chapter the duration must be at least 6 months (criterion B), and must cause significant distress for the client (criterion C). GPPD, however, differs from several of the other sexual disorders because this disorder does not clearly state that it has to occur in almost all (75-100%) sexual encounters. Criterion D requires that symptoms not be related to another mental, medical, substance disorder or other relationship specific circumstances such as partner violence.

Specifiers for GPPD include subtypes as to whether the condition is lifelong or acquired. It also allows for a specification as to whether the distress is mild, moderate, or severe.

There are numerous hypotheses for the etiology of genito-pelvic pain/penetration disorder (formerly vaginismus); however, none is supported by empirical data for causation. Weijmar Schultz et al. (2005) concluded that they could "not recommend the specification of a biologic or psychological etiology."

Studies have indicated that genito-pelvic pain/penetration disorder is a conditioned response to fear and association of sexual activity with pain, which can in turn cause anxiety around sexual issues (Butcher, 1999; Leiblum, 2000). Other studies, as reviewed in LoPiccolo and Stock (1986), have shown that fear of pain may also be associated with physical pain that occurs concurrently with other medical issues, such as "hymeneal abnormalities, vaginal atrophy, provoked vestibulodynia, endometriosis, infections, vaginal lesions, and sexually transmitted diseases" (Goldstein, Pukall, & Goldstein, 2009).

Despite hypotheses of a link between genito-pelvic pain/penetration disorder and incidents of sexual abuse, there appears to be limited empirical evidence for causation. One study found that women with genito-pelvic pain/penetration difficulties had a higher rate of childhood sexual abuse than the general population (Reissing, Binik, Khalifé, Cohen, & Amsel, 2003). Another component may be a lack of education about sex and sexuality (Buehler, 2014).

Several measurement instruments may be particularly helpful in identifying symptoms related to this disorder:

- Female Sexual Function Index (FSFI) (Rosen et al., 2000)
- Sexual Interaction System Scale (SISS) (Woody, D'Souza, & Crain, 1994)
- Sexual Desire Conflict Scale for Women (SDCSW) (Kaplan & Harder, 1991)
- Golombok-Rust Inventory of Sexual Satisfaction (GRISS) (Kuileter, Vroege, & van Lankveld, 1993)

Male Hypoactive Sexual Desire Disorder (MHSDD)

According to *DSM-5*, Male Hypoactive Sexual Desire Disorder (MHSDD) requires meeting four specific criteria (A-D). When an assessment for male hypoactive sexual desire disorder is being made, age, interpersonal and the sociocultural must be taken into account. A desire discrepancy, in which a man has lower desire for sexual activity than his partner, is not sufficient to diagnose male hypoactive sexual desire disorder. To meet criterion A, both low/absent desire for sex and deficient/absent sexual thoughts or fantasies are required for a diagnosis of the disorder. The judgment of the deficiency is made by the clinician, taking into account complicating factors than can affect sexual functioning. Similar to the other disorders in this chapter the duration must be for at least 6 months (criterion B), and must cause significant distress for the client (criterion C). Similar to GPPD, this disorder does not specify the level of clinical significance by requiring that it has to occur in almost all (75-100%) of all sexual encounters. Criterion D requires that symptoms not be related to another mental, medical, substance disorder or other relationship circumstances such as severe distress.

Specifiers include subtypes as to whether the condition is lifelong or acquired and generalized or situational. It also allows for a specification as to whether the distress is mild, moderate, or severe.

Historically, male hypoactive sexual desire disorder occurs at the initial (desire) phase of the sexual response cycle. Similar to the past, it continues to be identified as "a deficiency or absence of sexual fantasies and desire for sexual activity" (APA, 1994, p. 496). Leif (1977) termed this condition *inhibited sexual desire,* referring to minimal or no interest in sexual activity. Since the occurrence of the disorder can vary, hypoactive sexual desire should be specified into situational (occurring within a specific context) or generalized (occurring across situations and partners) and whether it is lifelong or acquired. Several measurement instruments can assist with the crosscutting of symptoms for the male hypoactive sexual desire disorder:

- Sexual Interaction System Scale (SISS) (Woody et al., 1994)
- Golombok-Rust Inventory of Sexual Satisfaction (GRISS) (Kuileter et al., 1993)
- Sexual Inhibition (SIS) and Sexual Excitation (SES) Scales I (Janssen, Vorst, Finn, & Bancroft, 2002)
- Sexual Desire Inventory (SDI-2)

Premature (Early) Ejaculation (PE)

Premature ejaculation (PE) centers on the concerns of a male that ejaculation is too early or coming too quickly after vaginal or non-vaginal penetration. According to *DSM-5,* there are 4 specific criteria that must be met before placing this diagnosis (A-D). According to criterion A, PE is manifested by ejaculation prior to or shortly (approximately 1 minute) after vaginal penetration. This release is considered too fast by the individual and before his desire to do so. Although the criteria for PE require that the activity be partnered; it does not have to only include vaginal penetration. Other types of penetration can also be applied to this diagnosis, however, the time frames described may not be relevant due to limited research on this type of activity (APA, 2013).

In most cases, meeting criterion A will be determined by an individual's interpretation and self-report. Criterion B requires that the problem be disturbing and prolonged extending for a period of at least 6 months and occur almost all (75-100%) of the time. In addition, to meet criterion C, the disturbance must cause clinically significant distress. In criterion D, the sexual disorder is not better explained by another mental, medical, substance-related, or situational condition such as severe relationship distress.

When assessing whether criterion A-D are met for this dysfunction, attention needs to be given to the description of the ejaculation period following vaginal penetration and the feelings that result. To better assess the symptoms subtypes are utilized, and course specifiers are encouraged. The two possible subtypes help to identify the phenomenological criteria that are mutually exclusive and exhaustive (APA, 2013). This homogeneous grouping allows the subtypes lifelong/acquired and generalized/situational. This diagnostic category also allows for severity specifiers which rest in the time frame with the start of penetration to ejaculation being less than one minute (60 seconds). Specifiers that focus on the time frame are mild, moderate, or severe. In mild, the basic criterion is ejaculation occurring within 30 seconds to one minute of penetration. In moderate ejaculation occurs within 15-30 seconds of vaginal penetration; and in severe, it occurs within 15 seconds of penetration. As stated previously, other types of penetration can occur other than penile-vaginal and in such cases, the application of the specifiers for mild, moderate, and severe would not be appropriate.

To start the diagnostic assessment, ejaculatory time will need to be quantified by self-report and requires the individual to estimate ejaculatory latency (i.e., elapsed time before ejaculation) after vaginal penetration. Regardless of the exact time elapsed, self-reported estimates of ejaculatory latency are sufficient for diagnostic purposes. Generally, a 60-second intravaginal ejaculatory latency time is considered the appropriate cutoff for premature (early) ejaculation in heterosexual men. No such time frame has been established when the activities are nonvaginal. Remember, that although PE is acknowledged to exist in nonvaginal sexually related activities, the duration criterion needs further study and should not be applied to the severity level. Accordingly, the durational definition may apply to males of varying sexual orientations because ejaculatory latencies appear similar across men of different sexual orientations and across different sexual activities, but the specific time criteria need more flexibility.

Premature (early) ejaculation (rapid, early type) is thought to be the most prevalent male sexual complaint (Waldinger, 2005), and it is often recognized has been recognized as the most common sexual disorder among males (Ralph & Wylie, 2005). In a survey of 815 males (age 50 to 80), 46% reported an ejaculatory disturbance, and of that number, 59% reported being highly concerned about it (Rosen et al., 2003). Hawton, Catalan, and Fagg (1992) found various forms of "erectile dysfunction as the most frequent problem in men presenting to sexual dysfunction clinics" (p. 161). Fertility is a major concern in males, and when combined with a concern about the ejaculatory process, this becomes a significant concern for all males regardless of age (Ralph & Wylie, 2005). In this society, males are generally praised for their ability to perform and are chastised when they experience difficulty. An estimated 75% of men will experience premature ejaculation at some point in their lives (Symonds, Roblin, Hart, & Althof, 2003). In a study conducted by Masters and Johnson (1970), 46% of the males who presented to the sexual dysfunction clinic for treatment had the presenting complaint of PE. It has an impact on a man's life, specifically on self-esteem and relationships, and the inability to maintain control over the ejaculation may lead to anxiety, shame, and embarrassment (Symonds et al., 2003).

Masters and Johnson (1970) defined a man as experiencing premature ejaculation if he could not control his ejaculation for a sufficient length of time to satisfy his partner in at least 50% of their coital connections. Using this perspective, the diagnosis of premature ejaculation was not related to the man but depended on the female partner's sexual performance when some women may require more time for an orgasm (Waldinger, 2005). This definition, however, has been criticized as it inadvertently might feed into the misperception that the longer the sexual encounter lasts, the better perception of satisfaction.

Measurement instruments may be of help:

- Brief Male Sexual Inventory (BMSI) (O'Leary et al., 2003)
- Erectile Quality Scale (EQS) (Wincze et al., 2004)

Substance/Medication-Induced Sexual Dysfunction

Substance/medication-induced sexual dysfunction is the diagnostic name for alcohol- or drug-induced sexual problems. These problems can include excessively reduced sexual desire; problems with sexual arousal, such as problems with erection or lubrication; difficulty experiencing sexual pleasure; and difficulty in reaching orgasm or with ejaculation. Unlike the normal fluctuations in sexual interest and sexual performance that everyone experiences, substance- or medication-induced sexual dysfunction is considerably more pronounced and long-lasting. To diagnose this disorder according to the *DSM-5* there are 5 specific crtieria needed (A–E). Criterion A requires that there be clinically significant disturbances in sexual performance, feelings, or desires that clearly affect an individual's sexual functioning. Criterion B requires that it be clear that the symptoms experienced are related to the substance and resulted soon after exposure to the medication or afterwards as part of tolerance and withdrawal. In addition, the substance must be capable of creating the resultant sexual difficulties. Criterion C, requires that the practitioner examine whether it is clearly substance related. For example, did the symptoms come before the substance/medication was taken? Did the symptoms continue after discontinuing the substance or after the time period for tolerance or withdrawal should have subsided (approximately 1 month)? Is there another non-medication substance sexual disorder present that could be complicating the clinical picture? In criterion D the disorder cannot occur during the course of a delirium and, criterion E it has to cause clinically significant distress as per individual self-report. The specifiers relative to this dysfunction outline three time periods: with onset during intoxication; with onset during withdrawal; and, with the onset of medication use. The specifiers for mild (25–50% of the activity), moderate (50–75% of the activity), and severe (75% or more) are all based on how it affects sexual activity (APA, 2013, p. 447).

Utilizing this diagnosis requires information on how different drugs can affect sexual function in different ways, depending on their mechanism of action. Knowledge of the normal biology of sexual function allows predicting whether a medication might cause sexual problems. Drugs that affect libido usually act centrally and may reduce desire by causing sedation or hormonal disturbance. Drugs that interfere with the autonomic system have negative effects on erectile function, ejaculation, and orgasm. Drugs interfering with hormones (e.g., tamoxifen) also affect vaginal response.

Other Specified and Unspecified Sexual Dysfunction

This category applies to presentations in which symptoms characteristic of a sexual dysfunction that cause clinically significantly distress in the individual predominate but do not meet the full criteria for any of the disorders in the sexual dysfunctions diagnostic class. The other specified sexual dysfunction category is used when the clinician chooses to communicate the specific reason that the presentation does not meet the criteria for any specific sexual dysfunction. This is done by recording "other specified sexual dysfunction," followed by the specific reason (e.g., "sexual aversion").

Unspecified sexual dysfunction applies to presentations in which symptoms characteristic of a sexual dysfunction that cause clinically significant distress in the individual predominate but do not meet the full criteria for any of the disorders in the sexual dysfunctions diagnostic class. The unspecified sexual dysfunction category is used when the clinician chooses not to specify the reason that the criteria are not met for a specific sexual dysfunction, including presentations for which there is insufficient information to make a more specific diagnosis.

SEXUAL DYSFUNCTIONS AND THE DIAGNOSTIC ASSESSMENT

The clinical picture for the sexual dysfunctions can be complicated. A clear, succinct diagnosis of the sexual dysfunction, whether it is lifelong or acquired, takes into account the severity of the symptoms. To gain a full clinical picture, information from collateral sources is needed. Careful assessment of the client's perception of the problem and how it relates to his or her current intimate relationships is essential. People expressing these problems are often extremely uncomfortable; they believe that what is happening is a personal and private failure, and they may be reluctant to share (Buehler, 2014). Like almost all the other mental health diagnoses, whether the sexual dysfunction is related to a medical condition, substance use disorder, or another mental health disorder has to be clarified. Other supportive social and environmental causes, as well as a history of abuse, help to identify the multitude of factors that can affect the presentation of sexual difficulties severe enough to be considered a mental disorder.

Regardless of the type of sexual dysfunction present, all are multifactorial problems with psychological, biological, and social ramifications. As such, a comprehensive assessment requires a holistic approach to achieve adequate resolution of the problem. Sexual dysfunction is a common unwanted effect of many types of drug therapy. Clinicians need to be aware of this, as sexual problems are often difficult for patients to talk about, especially when the original problem is unrelated to sexual function. Many patients suffer in silence unless the issue is discussed with them first.

COMPLETING THE DIAGNOSTIC ASSESSMENT

Proper assessment requires the careful accumulation of data that are likely to affect sexual

CASE EXAMPLE - CASE OF JUSTIN

Justin (age 45) and his wife Tricia (age 38) came to couples counseling, reporting that they were having marital problems. Tricia made the original appointment with the practitioner. Tricia's chief complaint at the initial contact was arguing, financial stressors, and verbal and emotional abuse. When the couple arrived for their first session, Justin appeared overweight, disheveled, angry, and depressed. The practitioner asked Justin how long he had been depressed, at which time he replied, "All my life." He was not on medication at the time because he stated he could not afford it, nor did he believe it could help him. He also reported that he was not aware of suffering from any mental health or medical conditions. He had a routine physical 3 months ago for his employment, and no medical problems were noted.

At this point, the practitioner asked Justin and his wife how things were sexually. He replied, "Not good. I am glad you asked." Throughout the remainder of the interview, when discussing sexual topics, Justin was obviously uncomfortable and often looked toward Tricia for the answers. Four factors emerged within the first few minutes of the interview to indicate that Justin was at risk for erectile dysfunction: depression, overweight, marital dissatisfaction, and numerous life stressors. Tricia reported that Justin was depressed and that his mood seemed to improve in the past when they were able to have sex and he reached orgasm. She was very concerned because when they would try to have intercourse, Justin could not keep his erection long enough, nor could he reach orgasm. She said, "He just could not keep it hard." When asked how often this happens, Tricia said almost every time they try to have intercourse. She said that they sometimes avoid it for fear of failure and the frustration it causes for both of them. Justin stated that he agreed. When asked how often they would like to have sex, they both said together, "Daily." When asked how often they try to have sex, they said it used to be weekly, but now they may try weekly but have not succeeded in at least one of them reaching orgasm in over a year. When asked who generally initiates the activity, Tricia said for the last year or so it is always her. Justin agreed.

When asked how long this has been happening, they both agreed it started after the birth of their second child, who was now 10. The wife reported that she felt responsible for Justin's self-esteem and for lifting his depression and was concerned that his lack of sexual performance might be her fault. She said that she did not feel pretty any longer, and her stretch marks from childbirth were pronounced. Justin immediately stated this is not the reason, he thinks she is beautiful, and it was his entire fault. Tricia stated she believed if they just had sex like they used to, he would be less depressed and cranky. Justin admitted that when they had sex in the past, he did feel better about himself, especially after achieving orgasm. Their current sexual situation was making him feel sick inside.

Another presenting problem was that Justin was upset with his wife because she did not always follow through on what she promised. When the practitioner asked them to explain this further, Tricia reported that during the passion of their lovemaking in the past, she would verbalize her fantasies. According to the couple, she would often moan out, "Do me on the dining room table!" Justin was often upset with his wife because she hesitated to fully follow through on her fantasies, and they had never done it on the dining room table. Now he felt frustrated and related his current performance to her unrealistic fantasy. She said, with two children around the house (ages 10 and 12), this simply was a fantasy and not practical. Clearly, the expectations and the difficulty in performing sent mixed messages, although at times inadvertently, that had apparently been a source of tension for quite some time.

In assessing for sexual arousal disorder, the practitioner inquired about erectile disorder. Justin revealed that he had difficulty maintaining an erection and was taking a medication, Viagra (sildenafil citrate), designed to enhance his performance. Earlier in his marriage, he never had a problem with erectile dysfunction, and its occurrence is considered acquired. There was significant stress within the relationship that contributed to both interpersonal conflict and the arousal disorder. Tricia was having problems on the job and difficulty in arranging her work and home schedule, especially given the sports activities their two sons participated in. The couple both acknowledged concern that sexual troubles were central to ongoing verbal and psychological abuse with each other. The couple reported financial difficulties, and both had to work to maintain their current lifestyle.

When Justin was interviewed privately, he stated that he was able to get an erection and on occasion could reach orgasm when his partner was not involved. He also reported that he makes demands on his wife that he knows she cannot fulfill. He reports not doing this deliberately, but he feels like he has so little control in other areas of his life, making demands on her makes him feel better about himself. Justin reported many job stressors. He states he does not like his supervisor, who constantly brags about how great his marriage is and how happy he is. On one occasion, he overheard his supervisor talking about his work performance. He heard him state that he was not performing adequately and was always defensive when approached on the subject. Justin did not question the supervisor about what he heard and does not want Tricia to know his continued employment may be at risk. He reports he does a good job at work but just does not like to interact with people. Often when he is asked questions, he gives brief two-word answers most of the time, and he thinks this may be interpreted as his not caring. He states the nature of the job is always producing stress for him, and he worries that since he has been there for 10 years, they could replace him with a new worker for less money than he is paid. Justin reports he is fearful of his supervisor and hates criticism. The practitioner was aware that engaging Justin, listening to his concerns, and being nonjudgmental was critical because he reported feelings of inadequacy and fears of rejection. The practitioner also praised Tricia for caring so much for Justin as to bring him to therapy to talk more openly about their relationship.

response: age, marital status, religious beliefs, whether the couple reside together, socioeconomic status, level of education of both partners, motivation for treatment of both partners, nature of the marital relationship, functional ability of the male partner, levels of anxiety, type of anorgasmia (primary versus secondary), the presence of psychosis or depression, drug and alcohol use, and gynecological, physiological, and medical condition (Dziegielewski, Turnage, et al., 2007).

In completing the diagnostic assessment with a sexual disorder, note (a) whether the condition is lifelong or acquired (with or without previously normal functioning), (b) whether it is generalized or situational (with a particular partner), (c) if it is conjunct (with or without a partner) or solitary (as in masturbation), and (d) if it is due to psychological, medical, substance, or combined factors. In clinical assessment, practitioners ought to obtain information on the frequency, intensity, duration, setting, and degree of sexual impairment; the level of subjective distress; and the effects on other areas of functioning (e.g., social or occupational) for each client.

Establishing whether the client has had a recent physical is essential as many medical problems can inhibit orgasmic responses; failure to address them is one of the most common reasons for failure of sexual therapy. Medical conditions that can impede assessment and treatment include neurological disorders such as multiple sclerosis, spinal cord and peripheral nerve damage, endocrine and metabolic disorders, diabetes, and thyroid deficiency. Simon et al. (2005) emphasized that in women with hypoactive sexual disorder in particular, there was a chronic absence of desire in 50% of postoophorectomy (ovarian removal) surgery patients. Furthermore, hormonal influences and imbalances related to normal life experiences such as pregnancy and menopause should always be assessed (Barna, Patel, & Patel, 2008). For men, medical conditions such as diabetes and thyroid dysfunction can be particularly problematic.

During the assessment process, note use of substances that can affect sexual behavior: prescription and nonprescription medications, drugs (certain drugs may interfere with vaginal lubrication), and alcohol (alcohol may result in difficulty in gaining an erection) (Johnson, Phelps, & Cottler, 2004). Persons with medical problems need to recognize the effects of some prescription medications on sexual response.

The psychological aspects that can affect sexual response should be noted. For example, a type of psychological turning off can actively suppress sexual desire (Salonia et al., 2004). In such cases, the individual may actively learn to focus on angry, fearful, or distracting associations that result in the physiological inhibition of desire (Kaplan, 1979). Anxiety, power and control struggles, individual body image, problems with self-esteem, and a history of abuse may also inhibit the sexual response. Postcolostomy and postmastectomy patients have the added complication of possible body image issues (Jensen, Klee, Thranov, & Groenvold, 2004). Fear of intimacy, inability to form commitment, dependency issues, guilt, and conflicts in sexual preference and identification can also influence the sexual response cycle (Hofman et al., 2004; Zippe et al., 2004).

In assessing sexual difficulties, individual factors, environmental and situational issues, and partner-relationship issues are central to a comprehensive exam. Environmental and situational factors to consider in assessing sexual function include life stress (Johnson et al., 2004), which frequently results in decreased sexual interest and arousal. These factors, although difficult to isolate and identify clearly, can be extremely amenable to change, and their contribution to intervention success is critical.

Partner-relationship areas to consider include ways of addressing and relating to intimacy, attraction to the partner, communication problems and means of problem solving, sources of marital conflict and discord, family issues and pressure, the presence of small children, living arrangements, and the sense of security in the relationship. Clearly, the quality and nature of the marital relationship is related to most sexual disorders, particularly sexual desire. The partners' preferred frequency of sexual interaction—defined as the frequency of the wish to have sex—should be determined. This is a critical assessment factor because no criteria for normal sexual desire exist. When couples are comparable in their levels of desire, disorders may not be identified. Sexual differences are recognized as disorders when one partner's desire is significantly different from the other's. As Stuart, Hammond, and Pett (1987, p. 93) stated, "If both partners have a similar level of desire, there is no issue. [However, differences in the couple's] level of [sexual] desire may create a problem."

A critical component is the client's desire for sexual activity, along with the frequency of sexual activity; desire and frequency can differ enormously. A person might desire more sexual activity than current circumstances permit, as parents of young children understand all too clearly. In this instance, a low frequency of sexual activity might not reflect a sexual desire disorder.

In summary, the practitioner's assessment of sexual disorders should always include demographic information; identification of the generalized or situational nature of the problem; lifelong or acquired description of the sexual problem; information about the specificity, intensity, and duration of the presenting problem; the antecedent circumstances at the onset of the problem as well as concurrent factors; a complete sexual history, including desired as well as actual frequency of sexual activity; the motivation for seeking treatment; and relevant environmental and situational factors. Referral for a physical examination is also indicated.

Completion of the Diagnostic Assessment: Justin

Assessing the sexual disorders requires the mental health practitioner to consider the lifelong versus acquired nature of the problem and take into account psychosocial factors, including prior history of sexual abuse as a child, the nature of the relationship with the partner, the partner's ability to adequately perform sexually, any physiological or medical factors, and use of substances or medications. During the interview with Justin, he denies any medical problems or prior history of sexual abuse. He states that he wants his marriage to continue but finds the situation growing increasingly difficult to manage.

To determine the appropriateness of a diagnosis related to the sexual dysfunctions, all criteria for the diagnosis must be examined. For ED, according to criterion A, at least one of the three symptoms must be present. During the interview, Justin and Tricia reported that he was having repeated failures to obtain or maintain erections during partnered sexual activities. Tricia said he has been unable to maintain the erection until the sexual activity has become satisfying to her as well as to him, and he simply loses the erection before he ejaculates. Based on these problems, they meet the requirements for all three criteria. To firm the diagnostic criteria, a careful sexual history was gathered and criteria for B-D were assessed. In criterion B, the 6-month history was established and it was clear the problem had been occurring for more than 6 months. Both partners reported feeling dissatisfied with their sexual relationship and the performance problems surrounding their sexual activities (criterion C). Lastly, there were no other mental, medical, or substance use disorders that could be identified. Since the time frame was confirmed as more than a year, and the problem was occurring in almost all of their sexual encounters, all of the criteria for the disorder were met. Premature ejaculation was not considered, as he was unable to ejaculate except when he was alone with masturbation. Given the behaviors that Justin is exhibiting on intake, his principal diagnosis is:

> Erectile Disorder (Reason for visit)
> Coded 302.72 (*ICD-9-CM*) or F52.21 (*ICD-10-CM*)
> *Specify* whether: Acquired
> *Specify* whether: Generalized
> Specify current severity: Severe

With the elimination of the multiaxial diagnosis used in *DSM-IV* and *DSM-IV-TR,* the information previously provided on Axis IV and Axis V is no longer a requirement. Elimination of these axes, however, should not result in the exclusion of this important supportive information. To include this information, special attention should be given to Chapters 21 and 22 of the *DSM-5.* Chapter 21, the medication-induced movement disorders and other adverse effects of medication, and Chapter 22, other conditions that may be a focus of clinical intervention, are not mental disorders. Rather, they are conditions that may assist in outlining and further documenting the supportive information central to the diagnosis.

Justin reports not taking any medications at this time or in the past several months, which eliminates the potential for medication-induced problems. The information in Chapter 22, however, would be helpful in documenting the supportive information required for treatment, especially that related to the family situation and key relationships. There are two primary concerns in the supportive information: (1) problems with primary support group because Justin and Tricia have general relationship difficulties that are exacerbated by the sexual tension and stress between them and (2) occupational problems in which both Justin and Tricia are experiencing job-related stress.

Justin clearly has a strained partner relationship. The circumstances causing their difficulties seem to extend beyond the sexual difficulties and extend to other areas of the relationship, resulting in anger and verbal abuse toward the partner. Difficulties are also noted in partner neglect and potential for verbal abuse, but they do not appear significant enough for another category, and the category of relationship distress seems to capture the feelings voiced in the session.

Other Problems Related to Primary Support Group: V61.01 (Z63.0) Relationship Distress with Spouse

In addition, Justin's problems at home seem to be causing problems at work. Feelings of inadequacy lead Justin to shy away from others and avoid his supervisor. He and his supervisor are having disagreements that may eventually affect his employment status.

V62.29 (Z56.9) Other Problem Related to Employment

Treatment Planning and Intervention Strategy for Justin

A treatment plan that highlights goals and objectives that Justin can achieve needs to be formulated. In the diagnostic assessment, information given by the client and his partner is supplemented with other resources to confirm history and check out all other possible contradictory information and comorbid conditions. Justin recently had a physical examination, but it was an employment physical, and a more complete one will be recommended with a complete blood count and general chemistry screening, a thyroid function test, detection of hormonal problems, and, if substance abuse was suspected, a test of urine toxicology. The client is not taking any medications, but a consult with a medically trained professional could check if any medications can help him with his agitated depression.

As part of the intervention process, problem behaviors are identified and related directly to the stated goals and objectives. (See Quick Reference 10.2.)

Treatment should be provided in a continuum of care that allows flexible application of modalities based on a cohesive treatment plan. Once treatment planning is complete, options for counseling strategy will be outlined, taking into account these identified factors. (See Sample Treatment Plan 10.1)

OVERVIEW OF TREATMENT METHODS FOR THE SEXUAL DISORDERS

In the treatment of the sexual disorders, any skill training intervention needs to include information designed to build general knowledge of human sexuality. A basic knowledge of the anatomy and physiology of self and partner is essential. What knowledge the client has generally was received sporadically and not learned in a

QUICK REFERENCE 10.2

Treatment Plan Strategy

1. Couples counseling to deal with the relationship issues stemming from the sexual dysfunction.
2. Medical examination to assess testosterone levels.
3. Psychiatric evaluation to assess possible need for medications for depression.
4. Individual counseling to discuss individual concerns and feelings of depression and low self-esteem.

nonthreatening environment. A good basis of sex education knowledge is needed to develop skill in expressing individual needs and desires, intimacy, affectional touching, reciprocity of sexual needs, and general sexual functioning (O'Donohue, Letourneau, & Geer, 1993).

Sexual education has to be more than simply teaching body awareness. Treatment of the sexual dysfunctions must take into account physiological problems that affect sexual functioning and perceptions influencing desire that may have emotional causes, such as stress, hidden anger, resentment, intimacy issues, and family of origin issues. Most of the treatment modalities address a multiplicity of issues pertaining to the sexual disorders, and their methods vary. Some

SAMPLE TREATMENT PLAN 10.1

Erectile Disorder, Acquired Type, Generalized Type

A disorder whose essential feature is a persistent inability to achieve or maintain an adequate erection throughout sexual activity, following a period of normal sexual functioning, not limited to a specific type of stimulation, situation, or partner and not due to another mental health, medical or situational condition.

Signs and Symptoms to Note in the Record

- Recurrent lack of physiological response to sexual intimacy.
- Inability to maintain an erection and/or during the initial stages of sexual activity.
- Loss of rigidity during the act of sexual intercourse.
- Ability to attain an erection and when/where/what activity results in attaining one.
- Avoidance of intimacy.
- Lowered self-confidence.
- Lowered self-esteem.

Goals

1. Achieve an erection in response to sexual activity.
2. Maintain erection throughout sexual intercourse.
3. Engage in pleasure-derived responsiveness to desires during intimate relations with his partner.
4. Increase self-confidence.

(continued)

SAMPLE TREATMENT PLAN 10.1 (*Continued*)

Objectives	Interventions
1. Visit with primary care physician.	Routine physical examination to rule out physical causes of the sexual dysfunction. Use self-reports to assess degree of sexual dysfunction and difficulty performing. When using standardized measures for self-report, encourage client to discuss results of self-report measurements with primary care physician and psychiatrist to coordinate treatment. Assessment and appointment with psychiatrist for medication evaluation related to depressive symptoms that may have been overlooked with a general physical exam. Special attention to avoid any medications that might increase or compound orgasmic delay or the likelihood of ED.
2. Share feelings regarding ED.	Reduce client's feelings of embarrassment via general statements and/or non-threatening questions. Encourage client to share/discuss feelings of shame, depression, and inadequacy. Assist client in connecting these emotions to behaviors that perpetuate relationship problems and social isolation. Provide a conjugate therapeutic session to address open line of communication regarding sex, conflict resolution, and feelings with partner.
3. Identify perceptions of partner's needs and difficulty in satisfying these needs.	Assist client in identifying how these perceptions contribute to increased feelings of inadequacy and ED. Encourage client to share how feelings of inadequacy and low self-esteem have resulted in avoidance of intimacy. Encourage client to share difficulties experienced in relationship due to sexual dysfunction.
4. Engage partner in professional advice and problem-solving process.	Encourage client and partner to share feelings, thoughts, and emotions affecting the relationship due to ED. Encourage client and partner to share needs, difficulties, and desires for each other. Encourage client to share difficulties that are being experienced in joint counseling sessions.
5. Journal sexual fantasies resulting in penile erection.	Focus client on the integration of sexual fantasies and successful attainment of an erection. Encourage client to integrate sexual fantasies into current sexual intimate relationship.
6. Experiment with new and varying types of stimuli during sexual relations.	Encourage client and partner to explore varying positions, types of foreplay, and venues increasing and sustaining the arousal response.
7. Verbalize desire for and enjoyment of sexual activity to partner.	Aid client in expressing to partner his enjoyment of intimate relations to reinforce positive sexual relations. Address reactions and feelings associated with this verbal acknowledgment in individual therapy.
8. Referral for marital therapy and/or participation in couples counseling.	Due to relationship concerns, more time and attention are needed to all problems the couple experience in communication and how it affects all areas of their relationship.

treatments concentrate on recognizing and understanding the physiological influences alone (Chambless, Sultan, & Stern, 1984), others view sexual dysfunction as a problem of faulty early sexual development that must be identified and modified (Ravart & Côté, 1992), still other treatments emphasize cognitive-behavioral influences (Palace, 1995), and many treatments use a combination of physiological, developmental, and emotional components as they relate to sexual arousal.

In general, regardless of the sexual disorder, the strongest evidence relates to the effectiveness of a cognitive-behavioral approach. More research is needed to establish whether the group or the individual format is more successful. The limited number of professionals available to lead sessions and the cost-effectiveness of groups indicate group modalities, but some individuals might not be receptive to or ready to participate in a group format. The results of these studies and the current professional concerns emphasizing group work suggest considering such issues prior to the initiation of treatment. To facilitate problem solving and goal attainment an individual session may be warranted to discuss concerns that the individual is uncomfortable discussing as a couple or in a group format (Graham, 2014).

SELECTED ASSESSMENT SCALES AND METHODS FOR TREATING THE SEXUAL DISORDERS

Self-report assessment techniques include rapid assessment instruments, questionnaires, and behavioral records. Available questionnaires include Thorne's 200-Item Sex Inventory Scale, the Sexual Orientation Method, the Self-Evaluation of Sexual Behavior and Gratification Questionnaire, the Sexual Interest Questionnaire, the Sexual Interaction Inventory, and the Derogatis Sexual Functioning Inventory (Conte, 1986). Additionally, the practitioner can design a rating scale that allows the client to report on any aspect of sexual arousal that is of concern to him or her. Such scales are often useful, especially if the time of day can be recorded and a space to record circumstances leading up to the sexual activity or the lack thereof is provided. Contextual factors and the client's own perceptions of the severity of the problem are highly important. Indeed, the systematic client-reported tracking of sexual activities is essential for ascertaining whether problems exist and whether clients are benefiting from treatment.

Kinzl, Traweger, and Biebl (1995) designed a seven-item scale to measure sexual dysfunction for their study of sexual dysfunction in women who had been sexually abused as children. Items on their scale include persistent or recurrent deficiency or absence of sexual fantasy and desire for sexual activity in adulthood; aversion to and avoidance of genital sexual contact with a partner; delay in, or absence of, orgasm following normal sexual excitation; genital pain before, during, or after sexual intercourse; and a lack of a subjective sense of sexual excitation.

Understanding the relationship dynamics of couples experiencing sexual difficulties is an important component of a comprehensive assessment. Essential aspects are the level of commitment to the relationship, contentment, tension, communication (both general and sexual needs), enjoyment of sexual activity, frequency of sexual activity, frequency of sexual thoughts, and each partner's own desired frequency of sexual activity, along with the projected partner's desired frequency (Hawton, Catalan, & Fagg, 1991).

Increased research into the diagnosis and treatment of the sexual disorders has resulted in instruments designed to diagnose and monitor treatment outcomes (Meston & Derogatis, 2002). These instruments measure several aspects of human sexual dysfunction, including sexual drive, quality of erection, ejaculation, sexual satisfaction, sexual inhibition, sexual excitation, psychological and interpersonal relationship issues resulting from erectile dysfunction, quality of life and erectile dysfunction, and orgasm; all offer valid measures on multiple dimensions of sexual dysfunction. In addition to instruments, a skilled, thorough clinical interview is critical to any assessment. Because many sexual desire disorders present concurrently with arousal and orgasm disorders (Nicolson & Burr, 2003), a proper history is essential to the implementation of the best treatment plan. In fact, Segraves and Segraves (1991) reported that of the 475 women they studied with a diagnosis of hypoactive sexual desire disorder, 41% had at least one other sexual disorder, and 18% had sexual disorders in all three phases of the sexual response cycle (desire, arousal, and orgasm). Gathering an adequate history requires noting all the factors that may have caused, may be related to, and may be maintaining the sexual dysfunction.

Because the etiology of a sexual disorder may be physiological, psychological, environmental, or situational, a physical exam is critical (Borello-France et al., 2004; Salonia et al., 2004; Zippe et al., 2004). It should always be the first line of assessment because so many diseases and physical abnormalities produce or exacerbate sexual dysfunction (age, physical health, depression, stress, and medical conditions such as hormone insufficiency, medical illnesses [e.g., diabetes, renal failure, endocrine disorders, neurological disorders, and psychiatric illnesses]). A multitude of studies have linked sexual arousability to hormonal determinants (Rosen & Leiblum, 1987). Alexander (1993) indicates that estrogen-androgen replacement in postmenopausal women appears to increase sexual desire, arousal, and drive. Research also has suggested that 50% to 60% of men diagnosed with psychogenic impotence may suffer from an organic condition (Conte, 1986). Alexander (1993) presented a comprehensive list of the organic causes of decreased sexual desire. In her review, she delineates both reversible and irreversible organic origins for the pituitary, endocrine, neurological, renal, psychiatric, and pharmacologic determinants.

Sexual Interaction System Scale

The Sexual Interaction System Scale (SISS; Woody et al., 1994) was developed to measure a couple's sexual functioning. This instrument explores the nature of the sexual relationship and interactions, sexual satisfaction, and marital adjustment. The study found strong correlations among these factors. The questionnaire has been tested for its psychometric properties and measures multiple dimensions of sexual dysfunction.

Sexual Desire Conflict Scale for Women

The Sexual Desire Conflict Scale for Women (SDCSW; Kaplan and Harder, 1991) is a 33-item scale for women that measures the subjective discomfort and conflict a woman feels in relation to her sexual arousal and desire. The scale examines the woman's subjective evaluation of her emotional being, as opposed to behavioral factors such as orgasm. Kaplan and Harder's study (1991) found that women who have been sexually abused display the highest scores. Development of a similar scale for men to delineate male sexual desire conflicts was recommended; the authors suggested it could produce important gender differences. These instruments are important not only for the assessment of sexual functioning but also for the development of appropriate interventions.

Quality of Sexual Life Questionnaire (QVS)

The Quality of Sexual Life Questionnaire (QVS; Costa et al., 2003) is a 27-item questionnaire designed to assess the quality of life in men with erectile dysfunction. It has three subscales: sexual life, skills, and psychosocial well-being. The QVS detects men with ED as well as the severity of ED. One of the strengths of this instrument is that men are asked about their perceived achievement, satisfaction, and importance of each item. For example, on the item asking about the client's concerns about the quality of ejaculation, the questions are (a) You think things are going: very badly, fairly badly, neither well nor badly, fairly well, or very well; (2) You are: very dissatisfied, somewhat dissatisfied, indifferent, somewhat satisfied, or very satisfied; and (3) In your life you consider this to be: unimportant, somewhat unimportant, important, or very important.

Brief Male Sexual Inventory

The Brief Male Sexual Inventory (BMSI; O'Leary et al., 2003) is an 11-item questionnaire measuring erectile function, ejaculatory function, sex drive, and overall satisfaction. Regarding sexual function, questions include: Over the past 30 days, when you had erections how often were they firm enough to have sexual intercourse? (Not at all, a few times, fairly often, usually, always). In the past 30 days, to what extent have you considered a lack of sex drive to be a problem? (Big problem, medium problem, small problem, very small problem, no problem). In the validation of the BMSI, there was an age-related decrease in erectile function and sexual functioning in all domains assessed. Men in their 40s reported erections firm enough for intercourse 97% of the time, whereas men in their 80s reported erections firm enough for intercourse 51% of the time.

Erectile Quality Scale

The Erectile Quality Scale (EQS; Wincze et al., 2004) is a 15-item self-administered questionnaire that measures the most important aspects of erectile quality. Definitions were developed from qualitative interviews in a sample of 93 men with and without ED. Erectile quality was defined in their own words, along with their opinions about certain aspects of erectile quality that were important to them. The constructs measured on the EQS, which were the same for both heterosexual and homosexual men, were rigidity/hardness, duration, control/confidence, ease of obtaining/speed of onset, sensitivity/sensation, fast recovery, and appearance of penis. This instrument is useful for assessing outcome following treatment for ED.

Female Sexual Function Index

The Female Sexual Function Index (FSFI; Rosen et al., 2000) is a 19-item self-report measure of female sexual functioning that provides scores on six domains of sexual functioning: desire, arousal, lubrication, orgasm, satisfaction, and pain (Meston & Derogatis, 2002).

Golombok-Rust Inventory of Sexual Satisfaction

The Golombok-Rust Inventory of Sexual Satisfaction (GRISS; Kuileter et al., 1993) is a 56-item (28 items for males and 28 for females) self-report developed to measure both the quality of a heterosexual relationship and each partner's sexual functioning within their relationship (Meston & Derogatis, 2002). The GRISS measures 12 domains of sexual functioning: 5 for females, 5 for males, and 2 common gender domains. The domains measuring female sexuality include anorgasmia, genito-pelvic pain/penetration disorder, avoidance, nonsensuality, and dissatisfaction.

Sexual Inhibition and Sexual Excitation Scales I

The Sexual Inhibition (SIS) and Sexual Excitation (SES) Scales I (Janssen et al., 2002) is a

45-item instrument designed to measure male sexual inhibition and excitation. The SES factor has 20 items and four subscales measuring social interaction with a sexually attractive person, excitation as a result of visual stimuli, ease of arousal when thinking or fantasizing about sex, and excitation that is a result of nonspecific stimuli. The SIS factor has 25 items and six subscales: losing one's arousal and erection easily, inhibition due to concern about sexual interactions with a partner, performance concerns, worries and external sources of distraction, fear about the risk of being caught while performing sexual acts, negative consequences of sex, and physical pain, norms, and values.

SPECIAL TOPICS

Erectile Disorder (ED) Treatment Options

Although the commercial availability of Viagra, Levitra, and Cialis has been useful to many men, prostate cancer patients and ED caused by psychological problems often require alternative treatment. A commonly used alternative consists of a three-drug injection containing alprostadil, papaverine hydrochloride, and phentolamine mesylate. Although it is commonly referred to as the Knoxville formula, apparently for the city of its introduction, a number of slightly varying formulas have been in use around the country. The three-drug preparation is administered by injection into the corpora cavernosa to induce erection.

Other traditional therapies for ED include a vacuum pump, injecting a substance into the penis to enhance blood flow, and a penile implantation device. In rare cases, if narrowed or diseased veins are responsible for ED, surgeons may reroute the blood flow into the corpora cavernosa or remove leaking vessels.

In vacuum pump therapy, a man inserts his penis into a clear plastic cylinder and uses a pump to force air out of the cylinder. This forms a partial vacuum around the penis, which helps to draw blood into the corpora cavernosa. The man then places a special ring over the base of the penis to trap the blood inside it. The only side effect with this type of treatment is occasional bruising if the vacuum is left on too long.

Injection therapy involves injecting a substance into the penis to enhance blood flow and cause an erection. The FDA approved a drug called alprostadil (Caverject) for this purpose in 1995. Alprostadil relaxes smooth muscle tissue to enhance blood flow into the penis. It must be injected shortly before intercourse. A similar drug that is sometimes used is papaverine. Either drug may sometimes cause painful erections or priapism that must be treated with a shot of epinephrine. Alprostadil may also be administered into the urethral opening of the penis. In MUSE (medical urethral system for erection), the man inserts a thin tube the width of a spaghetti into his urethral opening and presses a plunger to deliver a tiny pellet containing alprostadil into his penis. The drug takes about 10 minutes to work, and the erection lasts about an hour. The main side effect is a sensation of pain and burning in the urethra, which can last 5 to 15 minutes. The injection process itself is often painful.

Implantable penile prostheses are usually considered a last resort for treating erectile dysfunction. They are implanted in the corpora cavernosa to make the penis rigid without the need for blood flow. The semirigid type of prosthesis is a pair of flexible silicone rods that can be bent up or down. This type of device has a low failure rate, but it unfortunately causes the penis to always be erect, which can be difficult to conceal under clothing.

The inflatable type of device consists of cylinders that are implanted in the corpora cavernosa, a fluid reservoir implanted in the abdomen, and a pump placed in the scrotum. The man squeezes the pump to move fluid into the cylinders and cause them to become rigid. (He reverses the process by squeezing the pump again.) Although these devices allow intermittent erections, they have a slightly higher malfunction rate than the silicon rods. Men can return to sexual activity 6 to 8 weeks after implantation surgery. Because implants affect the corpora cavernosa, they permanently take away a man's ability to have a natural erection.

Assessment and Treatment of Premature Ejaculation (PE)

The best assessment starts by identifying the burden of the condition from the client's perspective (Sotomayor, 2005). Once the level of stigma and embarrassment is noted, clearly defining the time period surrounding premature orgasm is essential. The majority of men complain of premature ejaculation if they orgasm within 1 minute of exposure to the sexual environment (Waldinger, 2005). Based on this expectation, periods could vary from lasting seconds after penetration to 10 minutes. The range of what could be considered normal, unproblematic latency is quite broad, further complicating the definition (O'Donohue et al., 1993). In assessing the client, understanding what both partners want and identifying factors that can affect the duration of the excitement phase are essential in learning the factors that lead to too-quick or unplanned orgasms.

Another factor to consider is whether the premature ejaculation occurred prior to contact, upon penetration or immediately following penetration, or during female coitus. The practitioner treating the sexual disorder should determine if the ejaculation was against volition and before the male wishes it (Waldinger, 2005). Factors to consider include the age of the male, the novelty of the sexual partner or the situation surrounding the encounter, and the frequency of sexual behavior. However, focusing on just one of the three criteria, such as the time from entry to orgasm, can result in an inaccurate diagnosis, making subsequent treatment problematic and incomplete (Dziegielewski, Jacinto, et al., 2007).

A combination approach including relaxation training, enhancement arousal, pubococcygeus muscle training, and cognitive and behavioral pacing strategies is usually considered the most effective psychosocial treatment for this disorder. Using these strategies with the couple rather than alone is considered optimal (Ralph & Wylie, 2005). For a more detailed explanation and overview of treatment in this area, see Metz and Pryor (2000). As a result of increased understanding of premature ejaculation and improved information on the efficacy of pharmacologic treatments, such as the serotonin reuptake inhibitors (SSRIs), there is more interest treating this disorder with medication (Waldinger & Schweitzer, 2005; Waldinger, Zwinderman, Schweitzer, & Olivier, 2004).

Generally, the most common method used to treat premature ejaculation is sensate focus exercises, incorporating the use of the squeeze technique discussed by Masters and Johnson (1970). This treatment starts with sensate focus exercises, where the couple is expected to touch each other with no expectation of reaching orgasm. This nondemanding touching should last several days, and no direct genital penetration is encouraged. Once the female partner has assisted the male in reaching an erection and he reports feeling as if he will ejaculate, the squeeze technique is introduced.

At this stage in the ejaculatory response, the male feels that he cannot control the orgasmic experience, and he can feel the seminal fluid begin to flow. At that moment, the female partner is instructed to stop massaging the penis and to squeeze the glans, below the head of the penis. This means placing her thumb on the rear side of the shaft (toward the partner's body), opposite the frenulum (directly below the head of the penis); two fingers should be used to apply pressure on the top of the glans for 3 or 4 seconds, or until the male reports that he feels uncomfortable enough to lose the urge to ejaculate. These training sessions should continue for 15 to 20 minutes, alternating between sexual stimulation and squeezing, without ejaculation.

Once control over manually stimulated erections has been achieved (approximately 2 or 3 days later), vaginal penetration is attempted. Generally, the woman assumes the top position so she can control the withdrawal of the penis from the vagina. The female is instructed to insert the penis into her vagina and to move as little as possible. This is to give the male time to think about other things and distract him from the urge to ejaculate. If the male feels the urge to ejaculate, the female is instructed to withdraw the penis and implement the squeeze technique as described earlier. Eventually, thrusting and movement is added to stimulate or maintain the erection. A time span of 15 to 20 minutes is considered desirable for ejaculatory control. Masters and Johnson (1970) caution, however, that the female partner, not the male, should be the one to add the pressure to the penis. Also, this technique should not be used as a sexual game. If it is overused, the male may become so skilled and insensitive that he becomes able to avoid stimulation even when there is no desire to do so.

LoPiccolo and Stock (1986) believe there is little evidence for the efficacy of the squeeze technique when used as a solitary method. Further, Kinder and Curtiss (1988) question the use of this technique alone and urge that before the efficacy of this treatment modality can be measured, more research is needed to compare individuals receiving this technique with a similar control group.

In general, three behavioral treatments are associated with erectile dysfunction: (1) communication technique training (to deal with social and relationship issues), (2) sexual technique training (education and the practice of sexual techniques), and (3) a combination treatment. Kilman et al. (1987) studied 20 couples who were tested to determine the effectiveness of several treatments on secondary erectile dysfunction. Three treatment groups (eight 2-hour sessions) were all designed to enhance the male's sexual functioning: a communication education group that stressed positive communication techniques, a sexual training group designed to enhance positive sexual techniques, and a combination treatment group that stressed both communication and sexual training. A fourth group implemented controls to limit the degree of treatment received, thus constituting a less powerful treatment procedure than that given the other groups. Highly structured lectures were provided without any planned applicability or practice time allotted for individual problem solving. The couples in the no-treatment control group were pretested and waited 5 weeks for treatment to begin. After the posttest, they were provided with the combination treatment.

Several pretest measurement inventories and questionnaires were used, including the Sexual Interaction Inventory (SII; LoPiccolo & Steger, 1974), the Marital Adjustment Test (MAT; Locke & Wallace, 1959), the Sex Anxiety Inventory (SAI; Janda & O'Grady, 1980), and the Sexual Behavior and Attitudes Questionnaire (Sotile & Kilmann, 1978). The results were statistically analyzed; in summary, the study supported the view that each of the treatments for secondary erectile dysfunction has statistically significant effectiveness when compared with no treatment at all. This study supported Eastman's (1993) recommendation that the importance of education, communication, and support should not be underestimated, even when a condition is organically generated.

Goldman and Carroll (1990) highlight the importance of education in treating secondary erectile dysfunction in older couples. In their study, 20 couples were randomly assigned to two groups; 10 completed an education workshop, and 10 were used as controls. The workshop provided a structured educational format that focused on the physiological and psychological changes that occur in the sexual response cycle during aging. Sexual behavior was measured along three dimensions utilizing three standardized scales: (1) frequency of sexual behavior, (2) sexual satisfaction, and (3) knowledge and attitudes toward sex. Pretest and posttest scores were reviewed and analyzed.

Study results suggest that couples who attended the workshop had a significant increase in knowledge levels after completion. A slight increase in sexual behavior was noted for the experimental group, with a slight decline in this behavior for the control group. Overall, the educational workshop was considered a success, with a reported increase in knowledge and positive changes, as well as more realistic attitudes once the etiology of sexual satisfaction and erectile functioning was explained.

Although the literature has stressed education in the treatment of erectile difficulty, the addition of play therapy has also been considered. Shaw (1990) focused on this option in treating men who had inhibited ejaculation. The central premise is that sexuality should be fun and pleasurable, not performance oriented. However, the reality for many men is that their desire to perform becomes extremely anxiety provoking (Barlow, 1986). In play therapy, performance anxiety is addressed, and males are taught to reduce the focus on performance. The intervention helps clients recognize and increase the spontaneous aspects of their personalities. In Shaw's study (1990), participants were expected to create and act on fantasies, participate in sensate focus exercises, and take part in sexual expression board games. Fifteen males (followed over 3 years) were able to successfully ejaculate with their own touch, although they were unable to do so with their partners. Of the 12 men who completed the program, all reported relief within 3 to 22 months of intervention.

APPLYING A CULTURAL COMPETENCE LENS TO DIAGNOSIS

With the increasing diversity of the U.S. population, there is a growing demand for practitioners to provide culturally appropriate assessment, treatment, and preventive services. Practitioners need to be attuned to recognizing the role that culture can play in both expectation and action. In assessing and treating the sexual dysfunctions, this is especially important because it can influence not only the cognitions and individual experiences but also the behavior that results. In addition, media and lack of education can produce unrealistic expectations of performance and prowess that may clearly affect not only the relationship but also what the client is willing to share.

For minority groups in general, mental health treatment is often underutilized, with patients reluctant to seek these services and insurers reluctant to pay for them. Research suggests that fewer than half of people with serious mental illness receive treatment (CDC, 2011). Poverty also has an impact on mental health status. In 2010, adults living below the poverty level were three times more likely to have serious psychological distress than adults over twice the poverty level (CDC, 2012). In general, minorities have less access to and less availability of mental health services (U.S. Surgeon General, 2001). These groups also can have lower aggregate education and income levels and a higher likelihood of not receiving any mental health services and of less adequate treatment than other mental health patients. Now compound these factors with the stigma and cultural

QUICK REFERENCE 10.3

Glossary of Selected Cultural Concepts of Distress

- *Ataque de nervios* (anxiety often related to a trauma [Latino])
- *Nervios* (similar to *ataque de nervios* but chronic [Latino])
- *Dhat* syndrome (discharge and impotence [Southeast Asia])
- *Khyai cap* (windlike attacks [Cambodian])
- *Shenjing shuairuo* (stress related, imbalances [Chinese]

perceptions that can be attached to having a sexual dysfunction.

Furthermore, for some of the disorders, particularly PE and ED, these diagnoses cannot be made alone and require input from the sexual partner because the diagnosis requires partnered sexual activity. This makes use of the Cultural Formulation Interview (CFI), as described in Chapter 3, very important. This interview format enables a clear evaluation of the way the client approaches and responds to the culture. In addition, Appendix 3 of the *DSM-5* has some of the best-studied culturally related syndromes and idioms of distress that may be encountered in clinical practice. Being aware of these idioms of distress can help the practitioner be inclusive of the culture as well as identify what could be considered problematic behaviors identified or communicated in more understandable cultural terms. (See Quick Reference 10.3.) In *DSM-5*, nine cultural concepts of distress that could influence the perception of a mental disorder are identified. For example, *Dhat syndrome* is an idiom of distress in Southeast Asia that occurs typically in young males who exhibit a multitude of symptoms of anxiety and distress, manifested in weight loss and other somatic complaints. These symptoms are generally related to *Dhat*, a white discharge noted on defecation or urination that is believed to be connected to semen loss in these young males; based on this symptom, they become impotent and fearful of engaging in sexual intercourse. These symptoms could easily be misinterpreted as related to a sexual dysfunction, as opposed to the cultural underpinnings that would most accurately describe the symptoms.

The CFI and an awareness of cultural concepts of distress are useful, especially when clients report problems with nerves or have multiple somatic complaints, fostered by a sense of inexplicable misfortune. In these cases, unwarranted labeling of pathology should be avoided, and all behaviors need to be explored in relation to norms of the client's cultural reference group. The CFI may be particularly helpful in formulating a concrete measure for exploring the definition of the problem, as well as past and current helping strategy.

Comprehensive assessment information related to cultural background and experiences may influence or affect subsequent behavior (Locke & Bailey, 2014). For self-reporting of sexual behaviors, take into account ethnic group identity, religion, and spirituality to establish culturally sanctioned behaviors. If these behaviors are different from the dominant culture, expecting them to be part of a treatment plan could limit client acceptance and intervention success. Grigorenko (2009) and Paniagua (2014) provide excellent resources for assisting practitioners in making culturally sensitive assessments.

SUMMARY AND FUTURE DIRECTIONS

The topic of this chapter is assessment of sexual dysfunctions, stressing that these disorders are often overlooked in the diagnostic assessment and treatment of individuals and couples. Focus is needed on assessing the onset, context, and etiology of sexual dysfunction. The nature of its onset includes determining whether it is of the lifelong type, meaning the problem has been present since the start of sexual functioning, or it is acquired, meaning it developed after a period of normal sexual functioning. The assessment needs to determine the situation in which the sexual dysfunction occurs. Does it occur only with certain partners, or in specific situations, or is it associated with specific types of stimulation? This information helps to determine if the etiological factors are psychological or a combination of psychological and medical or substance abuse factors (Dziegielewski, Turnage, et al., 2007). When professionals agree about a consistent definition, the identification of shared meaning and the subsequent risk factors can improve treatment possibilities (Lewis et al., 2004).

To improve assessment and intervention strategy, mental health practitioners must develop a comprehensive assessment (including an extensive sexual history), utilize rapid assessment instruments to determine sexual status, be comfortable incorporating sex therapy to supplement individual and couples therapy, and develop a treatment plan with follow-up, all while maintaining a stepwise open communication style. The inclusion of pharmacotherapy, along with cognitive, educational, and behavioral techniques, remains a crucial element in the complete treatment of individuals suffering from any type of sexual difficulty and should not be forgotten or underestimated. In addition to the need for more behavioral science research in the area of sexual dysfunctions, there is the need for research replication. Many different cognitive and behavioral treatments have been conducted on either an individual or a group basis; however, the question of whether the results from these studies will remain consistent across individuals over time needs further exploration.

Each year new measurement scales and ways to improve treatment success are developed. Staying abreast of these changes is essential in providing evidence-based practice strategy. Clients often are not comfortable discussing problems related to sexual health and performance, and creating an environment of acceptance and comfort for disclosure and discussion may be the most important aspect of ensuring treatment success. Many current social work and behavioral science researchers concur with the need to include a psychosocial component with specific measures to address the marital, social, and personal difficulties an individual may express (Birnbaum, 2003; Goldman & Carroll, 1990; Heiman, 2002; Kaplan, 1990; Shaw, 1990). Cognitive, educational, and behavioral techniques remain crucial in the complete treatment of individuals experiencing any type of sexual difficulty, not just the orgasmic disorders.

Evidence-based treatment options are central to the successful treatment of the sexual disorders. More research is needed to determine exactly what types of cognitive-behavioral treatments work best and if the results remain consistent over time. Today, the lack of evidence-based treatments remains a major issue in practice, particularly in the area of the sexual dysfunctions. Contrary to Szasz's (1980) assertion that "the so called sexual dysfunctions (which are psychogenic in nature) are not medical diseases or problems requiring sex therapy" (p. 13), this belief has been shown to be outdated and dangerous. Although the importance of the psychosocial and psychosexual aspects in understanding sexual dysfunctions is well documented, it is frequently overlooked.

We support this contention and uphold the view that treatment success requires the consideration of relationship problems through a cognitive-behavioral model. If relationship problems are determined to be critical, a complete social, culturally sensitive evaluation should be conducted prior to the initiation of physical or biological treatments. A behavioral and cognitive approach to sex therapy is crucial in the treatment of sexual dysfunctions; thus, the roles of the social worker and the behavioral scientist become pivotal as well.

In helping individuals with sexual difficulties, providing these important services in an educative and culturally sensitive therapeutic setting is essential. Gaining experience in providing services to members of certain communities can help the practitioner become recognized as an expert in working with particular populations. Many practitioners also find it gratifying that, beyond growing their practice, they are providing a valuable service by meeting community needs for mental health and health services. When working with secretive and private topics, taking into account supportive information such as the cultural aspects related to identifying and applying them toward treatment is the most important step for treatment that is culturally relevant and sensitive.

REFERENCES

Alexander, B. (1993). Disorders of sexual desire: Diagnosis and treatment of decreased libido. *American Family Physician*, *47*, 832–838; discussion *49*, 758.

American Psychiatric Association. (1994). *Diagnostic and statistical manual of mental disorders* (4th ed.). Washington, DC: Author.

American Psychiatric Association. (2013). *Diagnostic and statistical manual of mental disorders* (5th ed.). Arlington, VA: American Psychiatric Publishing.

Balon, R., & Segraves, R. T. (2008). Survey of treatment practices for sexual dysfunction(s) associated with antidepressants. *Journal of Sex & Marital Therapy*, *34*, 353–365.

Barlow, D. H. (1986). Causes of sexual dysfunction: The role of anxiety and cognitive interference. *Journal of Consulting and Clinical Psychology*, *54*, 140–148.

Barna, M. M., Patel, R., & Patel, M. (2008). Female sexual dysfunction: From causality to cure. *U.S. Pharmacist*, *33*(11). Retrieved from http://www.uspharmacist.com/content/d/feature/c/11464

Barnhill, J. W. (2014). Sexual dysfunctions: Introduction. In J. W. Barnhill (Ed.), *DSM-5™ clinical cases* (pp. 229–230). Washington, DC: American Psychiatric Publishing.

Birnbaum, G. E. (2003). The meaning of heterosexual intercourse among women with female orgasmic disorder. *Archives of Sexual Behavior*, *32*(1), 61–71.

Borello-France, D., Leng, W., O'Leary, M., Xavier, M., Erickson, J., Chancellor, M. B., & Cannon, T. W. (2004). Bladder and sexual function among women with multiple sclerosis. *Multiple Sclerosis*, *10*(4), 455–461.

Buehler, S. (2014). *What every mental health professional needs to know about sex*. New York, NY: Springer.

Burgess, V., Dziegielewski, S. F., & Green, C. E. (2005). Improving comfort about sex communication between parents and their adolescents: Practice-based research within a teen sexuality group. *Brief Treatment and Crisis Intervention*, *5*(4), 379–390.

Butcher, J. (1999). ABC of sexual health: Female sexual problems II: Sexual pain and sexual fears. *BMJ*, *318*(7176), 110–112.

Carro-Juareza, M., & Rodriguez-Manzo, G. (2003) Yohimbine reverses the exhaustion of the coital reflex in spinal male rats. *Behavioural Brain Research*, *141*, 43–50.

CDC. (2011). *Health United States, 2010*, p. 19. Retrieved from http://www.cdc.gov/nchs/data/hus/hus09.pdf

CDC. (2012). *Health United States, 2011*, p. 38. Retrieved from http://www.cdc.gov/nchs/data/hus/hus11.pdf

Chambless, D. L., Sultan, F. E., & Stern, T. E. (1984). Effect of pubococcygeal exercise on coital orgasm in women. *Journal of Consulting and Clinical Psychology*, *52*, 114–118.

Clayton, A. H., Warnock, J. K., Kornstein, S. G., Pinkerton, R., Sheldon-Keller, A., & McGarvey, E. L. (2004). A placebo-controlled trial of bupropion SR as an antidote for selective serotonin reuptake inhibitor-induced sexual dysfunction. *Journal of Clinical Psychiatry*, *65*(1), 62–67.

Conte, H. R. (1986). Multivariate assessment of sexual dysfunction. *Journal of Consulting and Clinical Psychology*, *54*, 149–157.

Costa, P., Arnould, B., Cour, F., Boyer, P., Marrel, A., Jaudinot, E. O., & Solesse de Gendre, A. (2003). Quality of Sexual Life Questionnaire (QVS): A reliable, sensitive and reproducible instrument to assess quality of life in subjects with erectile dysfunction. *International Journal of Impotence Research, 15*, 173–184. doi: 10.1038/sj.ijir.3900995

Dording, C. M., Mischoulon, D., Petersen, T. J., Kornbluh, R., Gordon, J., Nierenberg, A. A. . . . Fava, M. (2002). The pharmacologic management of SSRI-induced side effects: A survey of psychiatrists. *Annals of Clinical Psychiatry, 14*(3), 143–147.

Dziegielewski, S. F., Jacinto, G., Dick, G., & Resnick-Cortes, C. (2007). Orgasmic disorders. In B. Thyer & J. Wodarski (Eds.), *Social work in mental health: An evidence-based approach* (pp. 427–456). Hoboken, NJ: Wiley.

Dziegielewski, S. F., Turnage, B. F., Dick, G., & Resnick-Cortes, C. (2007). Sexual desire and arousal disorders. In: B. Thyer & J. Wodarski (Eds.), *Social work in mental health: An evidence-based approach* (pp. 403–426). Hoboken, NJ: Wiley.

Eastman, P. (1993, May–June). Washington report: Treating erectile dysfunction. *Geriatric Consultant*, 10–13.

Gartlehner, G., Thieda, P., Hansen, R. A., Gaynes, B. N., DeVeaugh-Geiss, A., Krebs, E. E., & Lohr, K. N. (2008). Comparative risk for harms of second-generation antidepressants: A systematic review and meta-analysis. *Drug Safety, 31*(10), 851–865.

Goldman, A., & Carroll, J. (1990). Educational intervention as an adjunct to treatment of erectile dysfunction in older couples. *Journal of Sex & Marital Therapy, 16*, 127–141.

Goldstein, A., Pukall, C., & Goldstein, I. (2009). *Female sexual pain disorders: Evaluation and management*. Sussex, United Kingdom: Wiley-Blackwell.

Graham, C. A. (2014). Case 13.1: Sexual dysfunction. In J. W. Barnhill (Ed.), *DSM-5™ clinical cases* (pp. 230–233). Washington, DC: American Psychiatric Publishing.

Grigorenko, E. L. (2009). *Multicultural psychoeducational assessment*. New York, NY: Springer.

Hawton, K., Catalan, J., & Fagg, J. (1991). Low sexual desire: Sex therapy results and prognostic factors. *Behaviour Research and Therapy, 29*(3), 217–224.

Hawton, K., Catalan, J., & Fagg, J. (1992). Sex therapy for erectile dysfunction: Characteristics of couples, treatment outcome, and prognostic factors. *Archives of Sexual Behavior, 21*(2), 161–175.

Heiman, J. R. (2002). Psychologic treatments for female sexual dysfunction: Are they effective and do we need them? *Archives of Sexual Behavior, 31*(5), 445–450.

Hofman, M., Morrow, G. R., Roscoe, J. A., Hickok, J. T., Mustian, K. M., Moore, D. F., . . . Fitch, T. R. (2004). Cancer patients' expectations of experiencing treatment-related side effects. *Cancer, 100*(4), 851–857.

Horton, A. L. (1995). Sex related hot-line calls: Types, interventions and guidelines. In A. Justins (Ed.), *Crisis intervention and time limited cognitive treatment* (pp. 290–312). Thousand Oaks, CA: Sage.

Janda, L. H., & O'Grady, K. E. (1980). Development of a sex anxiety inventory. *Journal of Consulting and Clinical Psychology, 48*, 169–175.

Janssen, E., Vorst, H., Finn, P., & Bancroft, J. (2002). The Sexual Inhibition (SIS) and Sexual Excitation (SES) Scales: I. Measuring sexual inhibition and excitation proneness in men. *Journal of Sex Research, 39*(2), 114–126.

Jensen, P. T., Klee, M. C., Thranov, I., & Groenvold, M. (2004). Validation of a questionnaire for self-assessment of sexual function and vaginal changes after gynaecological cancer. *Psycho-Oncology, 13*(8), 577–592.

Johnson, S. D., Phelps, D. L., & Cottler, L. B. (2004). The association of sexual dysfunction and substance use among a community epidemiological sample. *Archives of Sexual Behavior, 33*(1), 55–63.

Kaplan, H. S. (1979). *Disorders of sexual desire*. New York, NY: Simon & Schuster.

Kaplan, H. S. (1990). The combined use of sex therapy and intra-penile injections in the treatment of impotence. *Journal of Sex & Marital Therapy, 16*, 195–207.

Kaplan, L., & Harder, D. W. (1991). The sexual desire conflict scale for women: Construction, internal consistency, and two initial validity tests. *Psychological Reports, 68*, 1275–1282.

Kilman, P. R., Milan, R. J., Boland, J. P., Nankin, H. R., Davidson, E., West, M. O., Devine, J. M. (1987). Group treatment for secondary erectile dysfunction. *Journal of Sex and Marital Therapy, 13*(3), 168–182.

Kinder, B. N., & Curtiss, G. (1988). Specific components in the etiology, assessment, and treatment of male sexual dysfunctions: Controlled outcome studies. *Journal of Sex & Marital Therapy, 14*, 40–48.

Kinzl, J. F., Traweger, C., & Biebl, W. (1995). Sexual dysfunctions: Relationship to childhood sexual abuse and early family experiences in a nonclinical sample. *Child Abuse and Neglect, 19*, 785–792.

Kirven, J. (2014). Maintaining their future after teen pregnancy: Strategies for staying physically and mentally fit. *International Journal of Childbirth Education, 29*(1), 57–61.

Knopf, J., & Seiler, M. (1990). *ISD: Inhibited sexual desire.* New York, NY: Morrow.

Kuileter, M. M., Vroege, J. A., & van Lankveld, J. J. D. M. (1993). *The Golombok-Rust Inventory of Sexual Satisfaction. Nederlandse vertalilng enaapassignnen.* Leiden: Netherlands University Medical Center [Dutch translation and adaption].

Leiblum, S. (2000). Vaginismus: A most perplexing problem. In S. R. Leiblum & R. C. Rosen (Eds.), *Principles and practice of sex therapy* (pp. 181–202). (3rd ed.). New York, NY: Guilford Press.

Leif, H. (1977). What's new in sex research. *Medical Aspects of Human Sexuality*, 7, 94–95.

Lewis, R. W., Fugl-Meyer, K. S., Bosh, R., Fugl-Meyer, A. R., Laumann, E. O., Lizz, E., & Martin-Morales, A. (2004). Epidemiology/risk factors of sexual dysfunction. *Journal of Sexual Medicine, 1*(1), 35–39. doi: 10.1111/j.1743-6109.2004.10106.x

Lipsith, J., McCann, D., & Goldmeier, D. (2003). Male psychogenic sexual dysfunction: The role of masturbation. *Sexual and Relationship Therapy, 18*(4), 447–471.

Locke, D. C., & Bailey, D. F. (2014). *Increasing multicultural understanding* (3rd ed.). Thousand Oaks, CA: Sage.

Locke, H. J., & Wallace, K. M. (1959). Short marital and prediction tests: Their reliability and validity. *Journal of Marriage and Family Living, 21*, 251–255.

LoPiccolo, J., & Steger, J. C. (1974). The Sexual Interaction Inventory: A new instrument for assessment of sexual dysfunction. *Archives of Sexual Behavior, 3*, 585–595.

LoPiccolo, J., & Stock, W. E. (1986). Treatment of sexual dysfunction. *Journal of Consulting and Clinical Psychology, 54*(2), 158–167.

Masters, W. H., & Johnson, V. D. (1970). *Human sexual inadequacy.* Boston, MA: Little, Brown.

Maxmen, J. S., Ward, N. G., & Kilgus, M. (2009). *Essential psychopathology and its treatment* (3rd ed.). New York, NY: Norton.

McCabe, M. P. (2006, May 29). *Female sexual arousal disorder and female orgasmic disorder.* American Medical Network. http://www.health.am/sex/more/female_sexual_dysfunction/

McCabe, M. P. (2009). Anorgasmia in women. *Journal of Family Psychotherapy, 20*(2/3), 177–197. doi: 10.1080/08975350902970055

McMahon, C. G. Abdo, C., Hull, E., Incrocci, L,. Levin, L., & Cheng Xin, Z. (2004). Disorders of orgasm and ejaculation in men. In T. F. Lue, R. Basson, R. C. Rosen, F. Guiliano, S. Khoury, & F. Montsori (Eds.), *Sexual medicine: Sexual dysfunction in men and women* (pp. 409–468). Paris, France: Health Publications.

Menendez, A. E., Moran, V. P., Velasco, P. A., & Marin, B. (1988). Modifications of the sexual activity in male rats following administration of antiserotoninergic drugs. *Behavioural Brain Research, 30*(3), 251–258.

Meston, C. M., & Derogatis, L. R. (2002). Validated instruments for assessing female sexual function. *Journal of Sex and Marital Therapy, 28*, 155–164.

Meston, C. M., & Rellini, A. (2008). Sexual dysfunction. In W. E. Craighead, D. J. Miklowitz, & L. W. Craighead (Eds.), *Psychopathology: History, diagnosis, and empirical foundations* (pp. 1–33). Hoboken, NJ: Wiley.

Metz, M. E., & Pryor, J. L. (2000). Premature ejaculation: A psychophysiological approach for assessment and management. *Journal of Sex and Marital Therapy, 26*, 293–320.

Nicolson, P., & Burr, J. (2003). What is "normal" about women's (hetero) sexual desire and orgasm? A report of an in-depth interview study. *Social Science & Medicine, 57*(9), 1735–1745.

O'Donohue, W., Letourneau, E., & Geer, J. H. (1993). Premature ejaculation. In W. O'Donohue & J. H. Geer (Eds.), *Handbook of sexual dysfunctions: Assessment and treatment* (pp. 303–334). Boston, MA: Allyn & Bacon.

O'Leary, M. P., Rhodes, T., Girman, G. J., Jacobson, D. J., Roberts, R. O., Lieber, M. M., & Jacobsen, S. J. (2003). Distribution of the Brief Male Sexual Inventory in community men. *International Journal of Impotence Research, 15*, 185–191. doi: 10.1038/sj.ijir.3900996

Palace, E. M. (1995). Modification of dysfunctional patterns of sexual response through autonomic arousal and false physiological feedback. *Journal of Consulting and Clinical Psychology, 63*, 604–615.

Paniagua, F. A. (2014). *Assessing and treating culturally diverse clients: A practical guide* (4th ed.). Los Angeles, CA: Sage.

Patel, P., & Sen, B. (2012). Teen motherhood and long-term health consequences. *Maternal & Child Health Journal, 16*(5), 1063–1071.

Perelman, M. A. (2004). Retarded ejaculation. *Current Sexual Health Reports, 1*(3), 95–101.

Ralph, D. J., & Wylie, K. R. (2005). Ejaculatory disorders and sexual fuction. *BJU International, 95*, 1181–1186.

Ravart, M., & Côté, H. (1992). Sexoanalysis: A new insight-oriented treatment approach for sexual disorders. *Journal of Sex and Marital Therapy, 18*, 128–140.

Redelman, M. (2007). A general look at female orgasm and anorgasmia. *Sex Health, 3*(3), 143–153.

Reissing, E. D., Binik, Y. M., Khalifé, S., Cohen, D., & Amsel, R. (2003). Etiological correlates of genito-pelvic pain/penetration disorder: Sexual and physical abuse, sexual knowledge, sexual self-schema, and relationship adjustment. *Journal of Sex & Marital Therapy, 29*(1), 47–59.

Richardson, D., Nalabanda, A., & Goldmeier, D. (2006). Retarded ejaculation—A review. *International Journal of STD & AIDS, 17*, 143–150.

Rosen, R., Altwein, J., Boyle, P., Kirby, R. S., Lukacs, B., Meuleman, E., Giuliano, F. (2003). Lower urinary tract symptoms and male sexual dysfunction: The multinational survey of the aging male (MSAM-7). *European Urology, 44*(6), 637–649.

Rosen, R., Brown, C., Heiman, J., Leiblum, S., Meston, C., Shabsigh, R., . . . D'Agostino, R. (2000). The Female Sexual Function Index (FSFI): A multi-dimensional self-report instrument for the assessment of female sexual function. *Journal of Sex and Marital Therapy, 26*(2), 191–208.

Rosen, R. C., & Leiblum, S. R. (1987). Current approaches to the evaluation of sexual desire disorders. *Journal of Sex Research, 23*, 141–162.

Rowland, D. L., Tai, W. L., & Slob, A. K. (2003). An exploration of emotional response to erotic stimulation in men with premature ejaculation: Effects of treatment with clomipramine. *Journal of Sexual Behavior, 32*(2), 145–153.

Salonia, A., Munarriz, R. M., Naspro, R., Nappi, R. E., Briganti, A., Chionna, R., . . . Montorsi, F. (2004). Women's sexual dysfunction: A pathophysiological review. *BJU International, 93*(8), 1156–1164.

Segraves, R. T., & Segraves, K. B. (1991). Hypoactive sexual desire disorder: Prevalence and comorbidity in 906 subjects. *Journal of Sex and Marital Therapy, 17*, 55–58.

Serretti, A., & Chiesa, A. (2009). Treatment-emergent sexual dysfunction related to antidepressants: A meta-analysis. *Journal of Clinical Psychopharmacology, 29*(3), 259–266.

Shaw, J. (1990). Play therapy with the sexual workhorse: Successful treatment with 12 cases of inhibited ejaculation. *Journal of Sex & Marital Therapy, 16*, 159–164.

Simon, J., Braunstein, G., Nachtigall, L., Utian, W., Katz, M., Miller, S., . . . Davis, S. (2005). Testosterone patch increases sexual activity and desire in surgically menopausal women with hypoactive sexual desire disorder. *Journal of Endocrinology and Metabolism, 90*(9), 5226–5233.

Sotile, W. M., & Kilmann, P. R. (1978). The effects of group systematic desensitization on orgasmic dysfunction. *Archives of Sexual Behavior*, 7, 477–491.

Sotomayor, M. (2005). The burden of premature ejaculation: The patient's perspective. *Journal of Sex Medicine* (Suppl. 2), 110–114.

Spector, I. P., Carey, M. P. & Steinberg, L. (1996). The sexual desire inventory: Development, factor structure, and evidence of reliability. *Journal of Sex and Marital Therapy, 22*, 175–190.

Stuart, F. M., Hammond, D. C., & Pett, M. A. (1987). Inhibited sexual desire in women. *Archives of Sexual Behavior, 16*(2), 91–106.

Stuntz, S. S., Falk, A., Hiken, M., & Carson, V. B. (1996). The journey undermined by psychosexual disorders. In V. B. Carson & E. N. Arnold (Eds.), *Mental health nursing: The nurse patient journey* (pp. 879–895). Philadelphia, PA: W. B. Saunders.

Symonds, T., Roblin, D., Hart, K., & Althof, S. (2003). How does premature ejaculation impact a man's life. *Journal of Sex & Marital Therapy, 29*, 361–370.

Szasz, T. (1980). *Sex by prescription*. New York, NY: Doubleday.

U.S. Surgeon General. (2001). *Mental health care for African Americans*. Retrieved from http://www.ncbi.nlm.nih.gov/books/NBK44251/

Waldinger, M. (2005). Lifelong premature ejaculation: Current debate on definition and treatment. *Journal of Men's Health & Gender, 2*(3), 333–338.

Waldinger, M. D., & Schweitzer, D. H. (2005). Retarded ejaculation in men: An overview of psychological and neurobiological insights. *World Journal of Urology, 23*, 76–81.

Waldinger, M. D., Zwinderman, A. H., Schweitzer, D. H., & Olivier, B. (2004). Relevance of methodological design for the interpretation of efficacy of drug treatment of premature ejaculation: A systematic review and meta-analysis. *International Journal of Impotence Research, 16*, 369–381.

WebMD. (2012). *Sex & relationships*. Retrieved from http://www.webmd.com/sex-relationships/guide/sexual-health-your-guide-to-sexual-response-cycle

Weijmar Schultz, W., Basson, R., Binik, Y., Eschenbach, D., Wesselmann, U., & Van Lankveld, J. (2005).

Women's sexual pain and its management. *Journal of Sexual Medicine, 2*(3), 301–316. doi: 10.1111/j.1743-6109.2005.20347.x

Wincze, J., Rosen, R., Carson, C., Koreman, S., Niederberger, C., Sadovsky, R., . . . Merchant, S. (2004). Erection Quality Scale: Initial scale development and validation. *Adult Urology, 64*(2), 351–356.

Woody, J. D., D'Souza, H. J., & Crain, D. D. (1994). Sexual functioning in clinical couples: Discriminant validity of the sexual interaction scale. *American Journal of Family Therapy, 22*, 291–303.

Zippe, C. D., Raina, R., Shah, A. D., Massanyi, E. Z., Agarwal, A., Ulchaker, J., . . . Klein, E. (2004). Female sexual dysfunction after radical cystectomy: A new outcome measure. *Adult Urology, 63*(6), 1153–1157.

CHAPTER 11 Disruptive Impulse-Control and Conduct Disorders

Sophia F. Dziegielewski and Ana M. Leon

INTRODUCTION

Over the past few years, there has been an increased interest in causes, correlates, and factors related to child and adolescent mental health. This increased attention comes as no surprise, as mental health problems can affect every area of a child or adolescent's functioning, as well as that of the family. When a child or adolescent exhibits disruptions in school and personal and peer-related activities, changes in the family's patterns and routines are likely to follow (Hinshaw, 2008). Once these behaviors occur at home it often spills into the school, affecting multiple areas of social and academic functioning that can require immediate attention. When disruptive behaviors become severe, they can lead to serious problems that affect various aspects of the individual's psychological, social, family, and academic functioning and require multidimensional assessments that carefully examine all aspects of the disruptive disorders (Landy & Bradley, 2014).

In working with children and adolescents who suffer from mental illness, completing proper diagnostic multidimensional assessments that take into account the vulnerable nature of this population and include important information from the school, family, community, and other social contexts is essential. Equally important is the recognition that children and adolescents require developmentally appropriate clinical treatment and interventions for any mental health disorder (Spetie & Arnold, 2007). Most mental health professionals acknowledge a need for increased research that more closely examines the mental health needs of children and adolescents, as well as increased access to mental health services. Fortunately, researchers and clinicians who work with children and adolescents continue to strive to provide more inclusive information on effective mental health strategies (Beauchaine & Hinshaw, 2008).

It is beyond the purpose of this chapter to explore all of the diagnoses commonly applied to children. Rather, it is to introduce the disruptive impulse-control and conduct disorders as outlined in *DSM-5*. All of the disorders in this chapter share the same symptoms, related to problematic self-control of emotions and behaviors, and with the exception of the antisocial personality disorder, are commonly diagnosed in children and adolescents. The chapter includes general discussion on completing the treatment plan and information on intervention strategies. The application section focuses on the most severe and more commonly seen of the disruptive behavior disorders—conduct disorder. The extent, importance, and early predictors of problem behaviors and symptoms are explored. A case application highlights considerations in the diagnostic assessment, treatment planning, and evidence-based treatment strategy phases of working with a conduct-disordered child or adolescent.

LIVING WITH PROBLEMATIC SELF-CONTROL OF EMOTIONS AND BEHAVIOR

When it comes to working with children and adolescents who may have a mental disorder, children should not be assessed as if they are simply small adults. Applying adult-based assessment strategy and theories directly to children or adolescents presents a challenge for many mental health practitioners who recognize that children are physically, cognitively, intellectually, emotionally, socially, and developmentally different from adults (Prout, 2007). The dependence of the child and the influence of the peer and family systems on the child are also different from how those systems affect adults. These differences require comprehensive, developmental, and creative approaches to engaging the child and the family in the diagnostic assessment process and in subsequent therapy (Hudson, 2014). Consequently, each revision of the *DSM* has put forth additional diagnostic criteria that take into account the developmental issues related to child and adolescent mental health (Grills-Taquechel & Ollendick, 2008). In addition, the *DSM-5* emphasizes that clinical attention be given to the avoidance of a diagnosis if the clinician can explain the diagnostic behaviors and symptoms as developmentally appropriate (American Psychiatric Association [APA], 2013). In identifying a diagnosis, careful attention should always be paid to a child's age, gender, family situation, and culture, and how these influences can affect any subsequent diagnosis.

When examining specific individual behaviors and symptoms in children, clinicians are reminded that a child's development and mental health are best understood from the continuing debate over the simultaneous influences of nature and nurture and how both affect child and adolescent behavior (Beauchaine, Hinshaw, & Gatzke-Kopp, 2008). A good comprehensive diagnostic assessment takes into account the mutual interdependence of genetic and environmental factors and their influence on child and adolescence behaviors and mental health. The disruptive behavior disorders typically are diagnoses that contain distinguishing characteristics, such as lack of self-control and, when in a more pronounced state, oppositional defiance and aggressive behaviors. These difficult-to-control emotions and behaviors make these disruptive behaviors the most frequent reason children and adolescents receive mental health services (Woo & Keatinge, 2008).

Kearney, Cook, Wechsler, Haight, and Stowman (2008) believe that a behavioral assessment is a crucial aspect of the evaluation process. The behavioral assessment starts with identifying the types of behavior that can be clearly defined and monitored over time. Characteristically, individuals who suffer from the disruptive, impulse-control, and conduct disorders can have symptoms that overlap other disorders, which may complicate the behavioral assessment and diagnostic impression. Furthermore, other social and family factors that affect child development are ongoing and may confuse the diagnostic picture. One such factor may be the recurrent experience of trauma, such as childhood maltreatment (Wekerle, MacMillan, Leung, & Jamieson, 2008). Maltreatment, especially when chronic and severe in childhood, increases the risk for the development of almost every disorder listed in the *DSM*, especially those related to mood, attention, and stress (Perry, 2008). Completing a behavioral assessment is further complicated by the subjective presentation of the child's behaviors by parents and the subsequent interpretation of those behaviors by the practitioner. Often during the assessment process, parents may not provide information on factors such as child maltreatment or domestic violence that may directly influence or contribute to the child's current behaviors. Countertransference experienced by the practitioner often has a powerful influence on the interpretation of a child's symptoms and behaviors (Rasic, 2010). Practitioners should always be aware of countertransference and a tendency to either over-identify or under-identify with the problems a child is experiencing. Furthermore, could the age of the child complicate the way behaviors are interpreted? For example, what is the level of understanding and comprehension of a younger school-age child? Depending on age, can developmental milestones interfere with the child's ability to clearly convey information that describes behavioral problems or emotional concerns? In those instances, practitioners have a responsibility to understand the child's stage of development during the assessment phase and to identify developmentally appropriate treatment strategies to effectively identify, understand, and address the child's mental health problems (Henderson & Thompson, 2011).

Social factors that can influence a child or adolescent's behavior include peer relations and how others' perceptions within the peer group can sway the child's perception of self and subsequent behavior in response to internal and external circumstances and stressors. For example, a child who already feels inadequate and suffers from low self-esteem experiences increased emotional difficulties when peers respond to this vulnerability and bully that child. In this case, an already fragile internalized sense of self is made worse by a peer's reaction, thus diminishing the child's low self-esteem (Patchin & Hinduja, 2010). Other environmental aspects, such as child abuse or neglect that results in unintentional injury, can affect the child's perception of self or social functioning (Faust & Stewart, 2008; Schwebel & Gaines, 2007; Zielinski & Bradshaw, 2006). Aggression, shyness, and a combination of low self-esteem and poor concentration are some frequently seen behaviors. An additional challenge for practitioners is not recognizing that children may develop coping skills needed for adjustment and adaptation to stressful environments. Practitioners focused on the pathology of children's behaviors and on complaints from parents and school systems may fail to recognize that behaviors that reflect conflict, lack of control, and oppositional patterns may be normal developmental responses the child uses at specific stages of development. However, these are sometimes mistaken for psychopathology by parents, school systems, and mental health professionals (Maxmen, Ward, & Kilgus, 2009). An example is the adolescent who, in efforts to fulfill her developmental mandate to differentiate and seek her own identity, experiments with dyeing her hair an unusual color and wearing clothes that are not in keeping with the family's expectations. Parents and the school system may perceive the adolescent as not compliant with expectations, when she is expressing her individuality and following her developmental trajectory to seek independence.

OVERVIEW OF THE DISRUPTIVE, IMPULSE-CONTROL, AND CONDUCT DISORDERS

The *Diagnostic and Statistical Manual for Mental Disorders* (*DSM-5*) is an important assessment tool used by mental health practitioners. The disorders listed in this newly revised chapter for diagnosing children and adolescents include conduct disorder, oppositional defiant disorder, intermittent explosive disorder, pyromania, kleptomania, and other specified or unspecified disruptive impulse-control and conduct disorders. Older adolescents are sometimes diagnosed with antisocial personality disorder, which is listed in this chapter of the *DSM-5* but described in the chapter on the personality disorders. These disorders were placed together in one chapter because of their common characteristics related to problematic self-control and the fact that their subsequent disruptive nature is generally in conflict with societal, family, academic, and community expectations. Almost all of these disorders begin in childhood and rarely have an onset in the adult years. The age of onset, especially in early onset, can have significant consequences for the treatment to follow (Barry, Golmaryami, Rivera-Hudson, & Frick, 2013).

The changes in the *DSM-5* highlight the many modifications made to this diagnostic category since the *DSM-IV* and *DSM- IV-TR*. One obvious modification is the chapter title change. Several disorders were removed from this section, and all the remaining diagnoses have clear symptom criteria that relate directly to self-control. Also, major characteristics of all the disorders in this chapter include the clear violation of the rights of others: aggressive behaviors and destruction of property. Children, adolescents, and adults who suffer from the disorders in this category often end up in situations that conflict with societal norms and lead to trouble with authority figures such as law enforcement. As with any *DSM-5* diagnosis, the diagnoses in this chapter should be considered when there is a behavior/symptom pattern that meets the criteria and when there is impairment.

Both nature and nurture, and how these two factors influence child and adolescent behavior and subsequent mental health problems, should be considered in the origin of childhood and adolescent disorders (Beauchaine et al., 2008). This discussion was highlighted in the *DSM-5*, especially pertaining to properly classifying attention deficit hyperactivity disorder (ADHD) and where to place that diagnosis within the *DSM-5*. Although most of the criteria remained the same, in the *DSM-5* the diagnosis was determined to belong in the neurodevelopmental disorders chapter. The revised title emphasized the developmental correlates linked to the disorder, as well as the need for reclassification when the section on childhood disorders was eliminated. Specific examples were added for diagnosing the condition across the life span and noting problems such as poorer occupational performance, a higher probability of unemployment, and elevated interpersonal conflicts that could easily be identified in adulthood.

The *DSM-5*, Section III, outlines five personality trait domains that are considered for further study. These traits are explained within this book in Chapter 13. The disruptive, impulse-control, and conduct disorders share three of the five personality traits: disinhibition, excessive constraint, and negative emotionality.

Disinhibition is related directly to the child or adolescent's inability to defer immediate gratification. The individual wants things immediately, and the desire for immediate gratification is so strong that the individual does not consider anything beyond the immediate moment and is not able to examine the consequences of his or her actions. In this process, the individual does not apply learning from past experience or consider social sanctions or what is socially acceptable. The emphasis is on obtaining what is desired in the here and now. The second shared characteristic is just the opposite of disinhibition and is referred to as *excessive constraint* or *rigid perfectionism*. From this perspective, the child or adolescent exhibits rule-governed behavior that is rigid beyond what would be expected in the situation. The rigid perfectionism is severe enough to impair social functioning and cause the individual to actively avoid situations where he or she might lack control. If unable to regulate emotions, the individual may become so frustrated with the lack of emotional management that uncontrolled aggressive behaviors may result, with little forethought for the consequences.

The third trait shared by this diagnostic group is not manifested as strongly but can be problematic and result in *negative emotionality*. Generally, clients experience repeated high levels of negative emotions such as anxiety, depression, guilt, shame, or worry. For those suffering from these disorders, normal daily events are often accompanied by feelings of intense worry. Attention and focus are set on negative effects, with an inability to move beyond repetitive obsessive thoughts. When negative emotionality is present, the thoughts are overwhelming and out of proportion to the actual event.

Oppositional Defiant Disorder (ODD)

According to *DSM-5,* individuals suffering from oppositional defiant disorder (ODD) often exhibit angry, irritable, argumentative, and defiant behaviors and/or vindictiveness. Diagnostic criteria outlined in *DSM-5* require three primary criteria categorized alphabetically (A-C). A dimensional assessment requires that symptoms be assessed separately and that criterion A be subdivided into three sections where documentation of at least four symptoms from any of the three categories is utilized to make the diagnosis. In addition, criterion A requires that the behaviors be present for at least 6 months, and there is evidence that the behaviors occur during interaction with at least one individual who is not a sibling. Minor modifications to the selected criteria can be made, based on the age of the child. If the child is under age 5, the behavior should occur on most days but still last a period of 6 months. However, practitioners are cautioned to integrate developmental information when making this or any other diagnosis. For example, children under the age of 5 are often oppositional; they are engaging in normal developmental trends that require them to seek out self-differentiation and separation. In these instances, the oppositional behaviors may be a function of normal development and not pathological. For children age 5 and older, the behaviors should occur at least once a week for the same 6-month period. The 6-month time frame is consistent among all age groups with the exception of vindictiveness and whether the child has displayed spiteful or vindictive behaviors at least twice within 6 months.

Criterion A, requires that the behaviors present must be displayed across three dimensions: angry/irritable mood, argumentive/defiant behavior and vindictiveness (See Quick Reference 11.1.) Identifying whether a child or adolescent is angry/irritable, argumentative/defiant, or vindictive rests with the clinician, who should identify and document specific behaviors that justify the specific coding. Each of the three diagnostic categories for this disorder (angry/irritable mood, argumentative/defiant behavior, and/or vindictiveness) lists eight potential behaviors. To qualify for a diagnosis, regardless of the severity, four of the eight behaviors across the three categories must be displayed. The four behaviors may come from any combination of the three categories. Of the three behavior possibilities (1–3) for oppositional defiant disorder, for angry and irritable mood are: the client losing his or her temper, being touchy or easily annoyed, and displaying angry and resentful behaviors.

Examples of argumentative and defiant behavior are broken down into four (4–7) potential behaviors. The first two involve arguing and rebellious behaviors with a refusal to comply with authority figures. The second two behaviors involve peers or in social situations where the individual often deliberately annoys others, or blames others for his or her own misdeeds, and avoids recognizing or taking responsibility for his or her own actions. In the third area, vindictiveness, there is only one (number 8) behavioral possibility listed where the resulting problematic behaviors that are both spiteful and vindictive occur at least twice over the 6-month period.

QUICK REFERENCE 11.1

Selected Criteria for Oppositional Defiant Disorder

- Persistent pattern of angry, irritable mood lasting at least 6 months.
- Four symptoms from the categories angry/irritable mood, argumentative/defiant behavior, and vindictiveness.
- Must cause social distress in the individual or others related to his or her behavior.
- Common factors related to this disorder that can complicate the disorder are substance use, depressive disorders such as disruptive mood dysregulation disorder, or the bipolar disorders.
- Specific criteria for severity (absent, subthreshold, mild, moderate, severe); for example, severe shows at least four symptoms in three or more different settings.

Source: Summarized criteria from the *Diagnostic and Statistical Manual of Mental Disorders*, Fifth Edition, by the American Psychiatric Association, 2013, Arlington, VA: American Psychiatric Publishing. Copyright 2013 by the American Psychiatric Association.

With any diagnosis, the behaviors need to be severe enough to cause distress for the individual. This disorder diagnosed in children and adolescents is often manifested in peer relationships, family interactions, and transactions with peers and teachers in the academic setting. Specific information on the contextual setting where the disturbances are evident needs to be documented under criterion B. Under section C, clarify whether there are comorbid diagnoses such as substance use, depressive disorders, or psychotic disorders that can cloud the presence of the current disorder. A new diagnosis added to *DSM-5*, disruptive mood dysregulation disorder (Chapter 7), and its presentation of agitated depression may be particularly difficult to differentiate from ODD.

To complete the diagnostic impression, the current level of severity should be assessed. The level is not based on the number of symptoms but rather the numbers of places the symptoms occur. For example, if it occurs in only one setting such as home, school, or when interacting with peers, the specifier mild is applied; if it occurs in two settings, it is considered moderate; in three or more settings, it is considered severe. For some individuals with the disorder, the symptoms may primarily occur in the home, making relationships with parents, siblings, and other family members extremely problematic. With the severity specifier, the practitioner is able to identify the setting where the behaviors are manifested and consider the specific settings when completing the assessment and applying treatment strategies. For example, a child who is displaying oppositional defiant disorder behaviors only at home may warrant almost exclusively family-focused treatment strategies.

For the most part, oppositional defiant disorder is characterized as problematic interaction patterns exhibited by children or adolescents in one or more settings that may include family, school, community, and society. Children and adolescents with these behavioral interactions often experience difficulties in major areas of their lives, including relationships with peers and adults, academic functioning, familial conflict, and problems in their communities. Pardini, Frick, and Moffitt (2010) examined the criteria added to the *DSM-5* and provided fruitful thought for future comment. They questioned the application of these criteria to females as historically this category has always been more rapidly diagnosed in males. In *DSM-5,* the previously held assumption that children and adolescents eventually develop conduct disorder has been refuted, although developing other conditions in adulthood such as anxiety and depressive disorders may occur (APA, 2013).

Intermittent Explosive Disorder (ID)

In intermittent explosive disorder, the individual experiences outbursts of extreme anger, generally against someone close to the person. The response is out of proportion to what would be considered a reasonable reaction to the circumstances. In *DSM-5,* this disorder is divided into diagnostic criteria that describe the types of behavior exhibited, the course of the disorder, the age of onset, and the importance of distinguishing it from other mental disorders and circumstances. In criterion A, the specific criteria that further describe this disorder are provided. This criterion defines the behavioral outbursts as verbal aggression or physical aggression toward property, animals, or individuals that does not result in damage to individuals or property. It also includes another criterion that includes behaviors that damage individuals or property. The major distinction in criterion A is between aggression that does not harm individuals, animals, or nonliving objects such as property and aggression in which others or property is hurt or damaged. The time frame is clear: at least twice weekly for a 3-month period. If this second criterion is met, and at least three behavioral outbursts occur with damage to property or physical assault toward animals or other people resulting, the time frame requires only that the three documented behaviors happen over a 12-month time frame, not weekly as in the primarily verbal aggression type. The key in terms of the time frame is if the verbal aggression type occurs, it is documented weekly for 3 months, whereas the focus on the three behavioral outbursts in the second type focuses on documenting the resultant physical injury to property, animals, or individuals.

In criterion B, the anger response must be so severe that it goes beyond what is typically expected as a response to the trigger event. The excessive response is not premeditated and often occurs on an impulse. The response itself, as with any mental disorder, whether physical injury occurs or not, must cause significant distress or impairment for the individual.

The age-of-onset criterion is set at after the age of 6, and the aggressive episodes are not better explained by another disorder. Generally, in the course of the disorder, these behaviors become most evident in late childhood and rarely begin in adulthood; therefore, being diagnosed with this disorder for the first time after age 40 is extremely rare.

Conduct Disorder (CD)

According to the *DSM*-5 (APA, 2013), conduct disorder is a diverse cluster of problem behaviors in which age-appropriate and expected rules of conduct are ignored. As in *DSM-IV-TR* (APA, 2000), it continues to involve persistent violations of the rights of others and violations of major social rules (Petitclerc, Boivin, Dionne, Zoccolillo, & Tremblay, 2009). From a dimensional perspective, there are 3 criteria described alphabetically (A–C) that must be met. In criterion A 15 different behaviors are identified and the individual must be documented to have experienced at least three of them over the past 12 months, with at least one happening in the past 6 months. The 15 criteria are divided into four distinct areas, and the level of severity based on these criteria can also be noted. The four distinct problematic areas are: aggression to people and animals, destruction of property, deceitfulness and theft, and serious violations of the rules. The key to establishing criterion A for CD is that 3 of the 15 symptoms must be present, and it does not matter which of the four areas they come from.

In the area aggression to people and animals, the first seven potential behaviors range from bullying and threats toward others to initiating physical fights with weapons, behaviors that result in harm to people or animals, and forcing someone into sexual activity. In the area destruction of property, it is easy to see how fire setting or pyromania is sometimes associated with this disorder. However, the destruction may have nothing to do with fire setting and focus more on the deliberate destruction of property by other means. In the area deceitfulness or theft, there are three behaviors to be considered: theft involving breaking into someone's major property, such as a house, other building, or car; patterns of lying to obtain what the individual wants regardless of the consequences to others; and lying to avoid responsibility and stealing nontrivial items without confronting a victim (not breaking and entering into property but instead like stealing cosmetics from a local store). The last area, serious violations of the rules (numbers 13–15) focuses on school and home behaviors where the child may simply disobey parents and not come home at night or run away from home. These behaviors demonstrate a disregard for age-appropriate parental, academic, or social expectations and often lead to more destructive behaviors and activities that may get the attention of law enforcement. An example of how serious violations of the rules lead to more complicated problems is the adolescent who repeatedly sneaks out at night to meet peers who are drinking and using drugs, drives around town high on substances, steals a car and leaves it in an isolated place where it is later found by law enforcement and linked back to her, and now charges are pending. This spontaneous event devastates her as she will now have a felony charge pending on her record. In this example, the adolescent was expected not to run away from home and not to use substances. Failure to follow the rules complicated her life: She is now an offender in the legal system and this event may clearly affect her chances for success in the future.

In addition to the dimensional criterion A, supplemental diagnostic information from criterion B is needed to document disturbances that are severe enough to cause clinical distress. Also, in criterion C the relationship between antisocial personality disorder and conduct disorder is clarified. Generally, the diagnosis is not expected to continue past age 18 and is used after that age only if the similar criteria for antisocial personality disorder are not met. (See Quick Reference 11.2.)

Once the principal diagnosis and the characteristics indicative of the disorder are present, attention must be directed to coding the diagnosis and identifying any subtypes, specifiers, and/or levels of severity.

In CD, three age-specific subtypes specify whether the onset occurred in childhood, adolescence, or is unspecified in regard to the age of onset. For a more detailed explanation and how to apply and document the subtypes and course specifiers, see Chapter 3 of this text. Using a subtype for disorders such as CD helps to clarify the diagnosis where the phenomenological criteria are mutually exclusive and exhaustive (APA, 2013). In CD, the subtype qualifiers allow homogeneous groupings of disorders based on age and clearly delineate the three types. In the childhood-onset type, the child has to display at least 1 symptom characteristic of the 15 symptoms prior to age 10. In the adolescent-onset type, a diagnostic assessment does not reveal any symptoms characteristic of the disorder prior to age 10. In the unspecified onset, information is lacking, and the practitioner is unable to

QUICK REFERENCE 11.2

CONDUCT DISORDER

Individuals who suffer from conduct disorder (CD) often exhibit a pattern of behavior that violates rights of others.

Symptoms are grouped in four categories:

1. Aggression to people and animals.
2. Destruction of property.
3. Deceitfulness or theft.
4. Serious violations of rules.

- Subtypes based on age of onset: childhood, adolescent, and unspecified (documented onset prior to age 10) are utilized.
- When an adolescent turns 18 and the criteria for antisocial personality disorder are met, the diagnosis is changed accordingly.

Source: Summarized criteria from the *Diagnostic and Statistical Manual of Mental Disorders,* Fifth Edition, by the American Psychiatric Association, 2013, Arlington, VA: American Psychiatric Publishing. Copyright 2013 by the American Psychiatric Association.

document whether the symptoms occurred before age 10. The CD diagnostic subtype specifiers are included after the main diagnostic criteria and are easy to recognize because they start with the phrase *specify whether.*

In CD, the second grouping for diagnostic categories is the course specifier. Contrary to the diagnostic subtype, the course specifier in CD is not considered mutually exclusive and exhaustive. In CD, when limited prosocial behavior exists, it should be documented through the specifiers that address the pattern of the child or adolescent's interpersonal and emotional functioning. To use this specifier, it must be clear that over the past 12 months the child or adolescent has displayed at least 2 of the 15 identified symptoms. The display of these symptoms can be manifested in multiple forms and evidenced through various interactions, such as interpersonal and social relationships. Identifying these symptoms requires information from collateral contacts such as family members, teachers, and other people who interact with the child. These collateral contacts help to provide evidence of the settings where these behaviors occur, as well as the actual problematic behaviors exhibited. In CD, the specifier that examines the pattern of interpersonal and emotional functioning is divided into four characteristics. The first is lack of remorse or guilt. In this specifier, the child or adolescent does not show guilt or remorse about the behaviors and may demonstrate such regret only if facing punishment or a consequence for the behaviors. In CD, this specifier is common, and information from family members, teachers, and other social contacts will validate this characteristic across different contextual settings. A second type of specifier includes the callous—lack of empathy type. In this type, the child or adolescent shows wanton disregard for the effects that his or her behavior has on others' welfare. Regardless of the level of harm directed to others, the individual may not see his or her behavior as problematic and in some cases may shift the blame to another. This specifier can seem very similar to the lack of remorse or guilt mentioned earlier, with one minor difference: In the latter, there is a sincere lack of empathy for the victim. Driven by his or her own wants and desires, the lack of empathy entails the individual's lack of appreciation of what the other individual has experienced or what the other individual may need. The driving force for those with CD is that they get their needs and desires met, and their needs supersede the needs of others.

In the third type of specifier, unconcerned about performance, the child or adolescent does not seem to care about achieving school and academic milestones. Grades are often viewed as an inconvenience, not as essential, and when the individual with CD fails in school, blame is placed on someone else. In the fourth and last specifier, shallow and deficient affect, the clients control their negative emotions to gain acceptance but, once achieved, use this newly gained trust to intimidate others or get their way. Often the emotions may seem shallow or insincere, and, although initially they may seem genuine, the more interactions with the individual, the more others begin to question the child or adolescent's sincerity. This specifier that examines interpersonal and emotional functioning follows the subtype criteria in the *DSM-5,* is easily recognizable, and is coded *specify if.* It should not be confused with the specifier that follows, *specify current severity,* which requires the practitioner to specify the severity of the diagnosis.

In CD, *specify current severity* categorizes the diagnosis as mild, moderate, or severe. In the mild type, the CD diagnosis meets the three required characteristics of the 15 identified, but the conduct is considered minor in relation to the range of behaviors possible. Generally, most of the problem behaviors experienced are discipline related and result in minor harm to others. In the moderate type, the behaviors are more prominent and extend beyond those in the mild type, but generally, severe and harmful behaviors are not predominant. In the severe type, more than the minimum criteria for diagnosing CD are clearly exceeded, and others experience severe consequences as the outcome of the individual's behavior. Danger to others is often noted, and examples of behaviors are crimes involving confrontation, use of a weapon, or forced sex.

When a child or adolescent meets the criteria, and the subtypes and specifiers are noted for CD, the practitioner should be prepared to document the pervasive problems in social and academic functioning. Children with CD tend toward lower achievement and school adjustment than their peers (APA, 2013). Problems with reading disabilities are especially prominent, and symptoms of emotional and behavioral maladjustment often lead to a high degree of overlap between CD and ADHD. Children with CD who have a dual diagnosis display more severe and persistent antisocial behaviors than those with a single diagnosis. Diagnosed children are also more likely than others to have fathers with severe antisocial psychopathology. A significant number of children with CD disorder qualify for a diagnosis of depressive disorder, particularly during adolescence. Children approaching puberty with relatives who suffer from depression are significantly more likely to have higher rates of CD than children without the same family prevalence (Wickramaratne, Greenwald, & Weissman, 2000).

Generally, cognitive and academic behavior problems begin early in life and remain chronic throughout the individual's school career. Children with CD show equally broad problems in their social adjustment. As previously described, the risk factor in conduct problems tends to co-occur with a diverse range of overlapping familial and social-ecological stressors, including poor child management skills, parental psychopathology, child maltreatment, domestic violence, marital distress and discord, poverty, and social isolation (Kim-Cohen et al., 2005).

Children with CD experience high levels of peer rejection when they exhibit aggressive and annoying behaviors. Over time, peers begin to counterattack and provoke these children, thereby creating a negative spiral of aggression and rejection. Children with CD often tend to have poor and nonsupportive relationships with their teachers and many significant individuals in their lives, including parents, relatives and extended family, and school personnel. The adults in the child's life find the continuous acting out and aggressive behaviors to be more than they can handle in the classroom, at home, or in the community. Not surprisingly, parents and school officials often clash over how to best address and deal with the child's behavior problems (Frances & Ross, 1996).

In summary, CD can have devastating consequences for children and adolescents who often behave aggressively toward people and animals. For example, they may initiate frequent fights; bully, intimidate, or threaten others; or torture animals. In some cases, acts of aggression include rape, assault with a deadly weapon, or homicide. Children and adolescents with CD tend to engage in destructive behavior that results in loss or damage to other people's property. These children may vandalize public buildings, set fires, or break furniture in the family home. They may also engage in deceitfulness as evidenced by chronic lying, breaking promises, or stealing.

Children with CD also tend to violate important rules set by parents and school officials; they may stay out late, run away overnight, or repeatedly fail to attend school. Overall, most children with CD tend to lack empathy for others and show poor frustration tolerance and high levels of mood irritability (APA, 2013). The *DSM-5* has specifiers that examine the possibility of limited prosocial behaviors such as lack of remorse or guilt or the lack of empathy for what is done and how he or she sees his or her own role in what has occurred. The serious nature and potential complexity of this diagnosis warrants a case example that demonstrates the diagnostic assessment process with children diagnosed as CD. See the case example for application and treatment plan suggestions.

Antisocial Personality Disorder

Different from past versions of the *DSM,* the antisocial personality disorder (APD), described in Chapter 13 and noted here, is dually listed. The task force developing the *DSM-5* decided to dually list this diagnosis because of the overlap of symptomatology. The close relationship with CD and link with externalizing behaviors made it relevant to this section. The task force also felt listing it here in close proximity to the next chapter on substance use disorders is a more natural flow consistent with co-occurrence and comorbidity.

Pyromania

In pyromania, the primary characteristic is multiple episodes of deliberate and purposeful fire setting. The reason for the fire setting, however, cannot be for social or political purposes but rather to fulfill an intense personal desire. Experiencing the fire, whether actually setting it or just watching, helps the individual avoid or reduce the tension that usually precedes it. Pyromania often produces pleasure and feelings of relief, with a pronounced infatuation with the fire and the aftermath. There is no specific information related to age of onset; these characteristic behaviors tend to be episodic and often wax and wane. Since the relationship between fire setting and personal stressors is unclear, making this diagnosis is difficult. Symptoms related to the fire setting are often impulsive and callous, which makes them easily confused with those relevant to conduct disorder and antisocial personality disorder. Also, fire setting could occur during a manic episode, where judgment and intent are clouded, as well as in response to command auditory hallucinations as seen in schizophrenia. When the fire-setting symptoms appear related to the symptom and diagnostic criteria of another disorder that is evident, then a separate diagnosis of pyromania should not be made.

Kleptomania

Another disorder new to this chapter in *DSM-5* is kleptomania. In *DSM-IV,* it and pyromania were listed under the impulse control disorders not otherwise classified. The basic characteristic of this disorder is stealing without having a need to do so. Similar to pyromania, the individual feels intense anxiety, and to calm these feelings, relief is obtained through stealing objects. These objects may be taken without any real need for the object or regard for the consequences of stealing. The desire to steal is so strong that the individual cannot resist, and the worth of the object pales in comparison with the desire to take it. In this disorder, the object is taken clearly to control anxiety, and many times individuals openly state they had no idea why they took it. Generally this disorder begins in adolescence, but there is no clear age of onset or course for how often it happens or what precipitates the events, other than feelings of tension and anxiety. Even when caught or confronted, the individual continues the behavior. Numerous charges for shoplifting or other legal consequences related to the thefts can result. This disorder differs from shoplifting, where the individual takes the object for its worth and the importance of having it. Also, shoplifting is rather common, whereas kleptomania is rare.

Like pyromania, kleptomania must be differentiated from behaviors that can occur in other disorders such as conduct disorder. In conduct disorder, there are often serious violations of the rules where stealing and shoplifting can occur. Practitioners must also assess for the mental health symptoms of other disorders, such as command auditory hallucinations that may lead to impulsive behaviors or compulsive buying during manic episodes. The diagnosis of kleptomania is rare, so when signs and symptoms resemble this disorder, the practitioner should consider the existence of other disorders such as malingering, where symptoms are purposively contrived by the client seeking other gains.

Other Specified Disruptive Impulse-Control, and Conduct Disorder and Unspecified Disruptive, Impulse-Control and Conduct Disorder

According to the APA (2013), the unspecified categories are often listed at the end of each chapter. They are to be used when the criteria outlined are consistent with the category of disorders but for some reason the specific criteria for the diagnosis are not met. When the reason for not meeting the specific criteria is known, it is referred to as other specified disruptive impulse-control, and conduct disorder. One reason for using this classification is when the practitioner can document that the number of symptoms required for a diagnosis is not evident. For example, a client has not met all the symptoms of a conduct disorder over the 12-month period because only two of the three required criteria from the list of 15 potential indicators have been met. In this case, the practitioner suspects another symptom has also occurred but cannot verify it, or the time frame criteria have not been met yet. When using the other specified diagnosis, the practitioner documents the specific reason the full diagnosis cannot be made. In this case, the practitioner would justify using the other specified diagnosis by indicating that enough symptoms have not been met or the time frame criteria needed cannot be identified.

When using the unspecified disruptive, impulse-control and conduct disorder similar to the other specified disorder, the symptoms occurring also cause clinically significant distress. In these cases, however, the practitioner decides not to state why the criteria are not met. The practitioner may suspect what the criteria are similar to when the disorder is specified but does not document it. There may be many reasons for this decision, and most of the time this diagnosis is used when the client is in a crisis or emergency setting and another specified diagnosis may be premature or unclear. The unspecified disruptive, impulse-control and conduct disorder may also be used when more extensive testing and/or evaluations are forthcoming.

THE DIAGNOSTIC ASSESSMENT: APPLICATION BASICS

In completing the diagnostic assessment on individuals suffering from a disruptive, impulse-control and conduct disorder, certain considerations should always be assessed. The first is that these assessments involve children and adolescents who are experiencing specific developmental stages that must be taken into account. The impact of normal human growth and development must be considered in a diagnosis. The practitioner must assess whether the behaviors being exhibited are continuous and outside of what would be considered normal for the developmental age of the individual being assessed. For example, it is not uncommon for adolescents to be influenced by their peers, and in seeking acceptance, they may engage in shoplifting or bullying to fit in with the crowd. The practitioner must distinguish whether these behaviors are happening as part of the experimental identity formation stages of normal development or are a continuous pattern of behaviors that are creating other difficulties for the child in social, familial, academic, and community settings. Making these distinctions is essential not only for the assessment process that sets the stage for treatment interventions but also for the intervention strategies that will need input from other significant individuals in the child's life. The diagnostic categories applicable to children should be used with caution, and developmentally relevant information should be gathered during the assessment process. Practitioners should be well versed in the stages of development and on developmental theories that explain the dynamics of mental illness in children and adolescents.

Second, a categorical and dimensional approach may fall short as outlined in *DSM-5* if underlying causal factors are not given full attention. This makes the environmental circumstances the child experiences essential to understanding the disorder that results. Goldman (1998) proposed a quick and practical schema to assist the practitioner in applying *DSM* diagnoses to children. He proposed that the clinician first confirm the full criteria in the *DSM*, and while reviewing the criteria, consider these questions:

- Where does the problem originate? Distinguish whether problems are generated within the child and caused by a comorbid mental health disorder such as command hallucinations indicative of schizophrenia, or whether it could be related to problems that originate within the child's environment. Environmental concerns include relationship problems with parents, siblings, peers, or adults in authority; problems related to abuse or neglect; and other conditions, such as antisocial behavior, academic problems, identity problems, acculturation problems, phase-of-life problems, or school-related difficulties.

- Is the child's problem a reaction to a specific and identifiable stressor? Once environmental problems are identified, determine what the stressor is that influences problem occurrence. If the stressor is clear, this information can be used to rule out or defer specific mental health disorders, such as adjustment disorders and posttraumatic stress disorders.
- What are the basic areas affected and impaired by the problem? How does this affect the child's school, home, or social play functioning? Goldman (1998) suggests the practitioner should distinguish among behavioral, mood, and dissociative disorders when answering this question.
- Do the symptoms interfere with functioning, and do they reflect long-standing difficulties? Although many times it is too early to determine if a problematic behavior has the potential to be lifelong, the practitioner still needs to be aware when observing behavioral characteristics that have the potential to continue into adulthood. For example, in CD if these behaviors continue to exist from childhood and beyond the teen years, they may reflect antisocial personality disorder, which is usually diagnosed in young adults (at age 18). Children's diagnoses should be re-evaluated and updated throughout the developmental life span, but it is possible that some diagnoses are lifelong. Practitioners should regularly assess the child's mental health diagnosis and make changes accordingly, recognizing that often a childhood diagnosis is similar to the adult diagnosis the individual is given.

In the final analysis, the advantage of the *DSM-5* diagnostic system is that it helps practitioners determine the most effective evidence-based treatment strategies to use with the child or adolescent.

Maximizing Measurement

Today, health and mental health funding often focus on discovering effective evidence-based practices. For an evidence-based assessment to be successful, the practitioner needs to combine the latest research, causal theories, and the client's own unique family circumstances, values, and beliefs (Barry et al., 2013). For conduct disorder in particular, this can be difficult because of the broad and variable range of the problems identified. The MacArthur Foundation's Child System and Treatment Enhancement Projects (Child STEPs) have funded studies that identify "leverage points for, and barriers to, the adoption and implementation of evidence-based practices" in children's mental health services (Schoenwald, Kelleher, & Weisz, 2008, p. 66). Despite this increased attention, there is still much to be learned about mental health problems, effective counseling strategies, and patterns of medication use of children and adolescents (Dziegielewski, 2010). For example, children may not exhibit signs of depression in the same way as adults. Adults who are depressed might present as tearful and sad, whereas adolescents often appear irritable, angry, and aggressive (Noggle & Dean, 2009). When symptoms are difficult to recognize and treat, practitioners can become frustrated, which may push them toward recommending medications to assist with these angry outbursts. During the past decade, this emphasis on both understanding the childhood psychiatric disorders and developing the evidence-based pharmacological and psychosocial treatments has been a mental health priority (Walkup et al., 2009).

Including the impact of familial, social, and cultural factors is important in diagnosing children and adolescents. Children do not operate in a vacuum and are dependent on their relationships with their parents and family systems. Consequently, parental psychopathology and family challenges may cause or contribute to the child's mental health problems. Treatment efforts for mental health problems should involve active parental and/or family participation designed to help the child reach optimal levels of functioning. Where children are concerned, treatment strategies should always include family involvement (Gopalan et al., 2010). During a comprehensive assessment, the practitioner should ask questions about the mental health well-being of parents and family systems. Similarly, the assessment process should include information on different forms of child maltreatment, exposure to different forms of violence, and ongoing domestic violence (Saxe, Ellis, & Kaplow, 2007). Learning about the child and family's cultural values provides some clinical insights on other psychosocial factors that may influence the child's development and, consequently, behavioral symptoms. In some instances, cultural values prescribe specific ways that children should behave, not taking into account the developmental need the child may have to exert his or her new gross and fine motor skills. Unless the practitioner has gained some insight on the cultural values that dictate this expectation, it may not be obvious that what the parent is describing as problematic is in fact normal development that may be in conflict with a specific cultural paradigm (Leon, 2010).

LeCroy and Okamoto (2009) believe the most critical aspect for completing any child assessment is getting direct information from the child, as well as seeking information from collateral sources in the child's environment. Practitioners can record and interpret the symptoms presented by children and take note of environmental circumstances and how they influence the treatment process. To identify high-risk patterns, it is best to investigate functioning through examination of multiple domains, utilizing multiple levels of analysis (Cicchetti, 2008). To facilitate a comprehensive assessment, practitioners must be aware of the various types of instruments that can assist with interpretation of symptoms and behaviors throughout the helping process.

The increased time pressure—and the emphasis on rapid assessment and treatment—has forced mental health practitioners to shorten biopsychosocial assessments to include only salient information on the child's past and current mental health functioning. This makes the assessment critical and forces practitioners to identify the significant aspects of the child's presenting problems and the specific behaviors and circumstances of his or her impaired functioning. To facilitate the diagnostic assessment process, various self-report or rapid assessment instruments (RAIs) and other diagnostic tools are often used. The number of child-focused assessment and diagnostic instruments continues to grow and contribute to better evidence-based approaches. Shapiro, Friedberg, and Bardenstein (2006, pp. 245–246) compare these techniques to a "palette of colors that clinicians select, combine, and blend to paint their pictures of therapy with individual clients."

The RAIs can assist in all types of therapeutic settings, especially in conjunction with the play therapy experience designed to decrease problematic behaviors (Baggerly, 2009). To support the *DSM-5,* there are already a number of dimensional assessments available that focus on children. The Child Behavior Checklist (CBCL) by Achenbach (2001) and the Generalized Anxiety Disorder Severity Scale (GADSS) by Shear, Belnap, Mazumdar, Houck, and Rollman (2006) are two commonly used examples. Practitioners should also make use of family assessment tools

(Leon & Armantrout, 2007). It is beyond the scope of this chapter to present criteria for using specific measurement instruments with children, but several texts provide more information in this area. See Grigorenko (2009) for multicultural psychoeducational assessment strategy and Shapiro et al. (2006) for general mental health assessment with children and adolescents.

To facilitate an accurate and complete assessment of the child or adolescent's behaviors, specific and behavior-focused information must be recorded. A complete assessment should include the following information:

- The problem presented by the child or adolescent.
- Behaviors that demonstrate the problem.
- The intensity, frequency, duration, and specific environmental/contextual circumstances accompanying the problem.
- Areas of the child's functioning affected by the problem.
- Previous coping skills and problem-solving methods used.
- Any previous and current medication and counseling interventions prescribed for the current problem as well as for other problems experienced in the past.
- A developmental assessment of major milestones, separations, major family changes, and medical problems experienced by the child over various developmental stages.
- An assessment of the child's family system, including past and current problems experienced by the parents and other immediate family members.
- Cultural factors affecting treatment compliance (Dziegielewski, 2010).

Gender Considerations

Gardner, Pajer, Kelleher, Scholle, and Wasserman (2002) reported substantial gender differences in the way primary care professionals diagnose and treat mental disorders in children and adolescents. For example, since boys exhibit more externalized symptoms, they are more readily diagnosed with CD and ODD. Girls often experience gender-based referral biases based on their lack of overt functional impairment, even though both genders require treatment. This lack of recognition could adversely affect girls who suffer from these types of disorders being underdiagnosed or neglected in treatment. Practitioners should therefore not assume that only boys can be diagnosed with CD or ODD and, when assessing girls, should inquire about behaviors and symptoms from these two disorders (Hipwell et al., 2011).

In some instances, depending on the cultural values of the girl's family, the practitioner needs to consider general and specific roles and expectations when developing the best treatment plan for that individual. For instance, Latino girls by nature of the culture are generally expected to remain in specific gender roles. Knowing this, the practitioner needs to carefully integrate that information when developing treatment strategies (Leon, 2010). However, practitioners should also keep in mind that acculturation, parents' generation, and socioeconomic factors influence how strictly a specific family adheres to traditional values—in essence, we cannot assume that all members of a specific cultural, racial, or ethnic group have the same values.

In assessing children, practitioners should pay careful attention and not make general assumptions based on adult guidelines. Gender should always be taken into account in terms of how a child or adolescent presents in the clinical setting. Multiple factors can contribute to differences in symptoms and presenting problems among children, adolescents, and adults in the manifestation of psychological and emotional difficulties. Every child and family system has a unique set of circumstances, values, beliefs, and coping skills. A comprehensive assessment needs to include significant information on the specific behavioral, emotional, and psychological problems presented by children (Landy & Bradley, 2014). Obtaining sufficient accurate information helps the health care team, including the physician prescriber, to determine the nature of the child's mental disorder, the type of treatment needed, and whether medication therapy is warranted.

Inclusion of Collateral Contacts

Another significant factor in the assessment and treatment of children and adolescents is information from collateral contacts, which include parents, the school system, the community, and other informants who can provide vital information pertaining to the child's difficulties and affect the treatment process (Landy & Bradley, 2014). This process necessitates eliciting and incorporating feedback from these individuals to complete a comprehensive assessment of the child in his or her current environment (LeCroy & Okamoto, 2009). Also, the practitioner has to assess parents' knowledge and expectations of normal behaviors for their child, given the child's specific age, abilities, and developmental stage. Some parents may not have sufficient knowledge of the child's unique developmental stage and adhere to unreasonable behavioral and emotional expectations for their child. Ultimately, parents without knowledge of normal development may not understand the treatment process and in some instances negatively influence it (Wodarski & Dziegielewski, 2002).

Taking the Family System Into Account

The family system outside the school setting greatly influences the mental health and subsequent treatment of the child and should be the focus of attention during the assessment and treatment phases (Ingoldsby, 2010). Parents have the responsibility and power to generally determine treatment issues such as the duration and medication intervention. They are also the ones who select, arrange, and pay for the child's treatment experience, thereby making inclusion of parents or primary caretakers essential in any treatment to follow (Bromfield, 2007). Moreover, parents become important members of the treatment team, and unengaged parents do not provide ample opportunities at home for the child to continue practicing what is being learned in the treatment sessions. Parents are the ones in the home environment who must continue the work that the practitioner initiates. They are also the ones directly in touch with the school environment and in a position to work closely with teachers to ensure that all of the child's major environmental settings are working in unison (Boyd-Webb, 2001). Parental influence begins during the assessment phase and continues through the termination phase. Parents who do not fully understand or accept the value of counseling or see immediate changes in their child's behavior can change or terminate services for the child. For this reason, practitioners must include parents or caregivers in the diagnostic assessment and throughout the treatment process to ensure they understand what is being completed during the assessment phase and how those results will be utilized during the treatment phase. For example, if a child's family is not supportive of mental health treatment, the child, loyal to the parent, may also adopt a negative perspective of treatment. Often treatment compliance issues emerge in relation to the parents' own perceptions of the diagnostic label and fears of stigmatizing the child. Furthermore, parents' perceptions of the illness, often influenced by culture and other family members, can affect the level of support provided to the child. When considering medication as part of the treatment, Gau et al. (2006) reported that tense parent–child interactions and conflicts between the parents that are not properly addressed can lead to poor compliance with physician-ordered medication use.

Utilizing a Cultural Lens

Because culture is the lens through which we view children and adolescents, "it provides the framework used to label, categorize and make sense of childhood development and behaviors" (Johnson & Tucker, 2008, p. 789). A lack of culturally competent services can complicate treatment for those who seek mental health support within the context of their family, cultural beliefs, and community (Pumariega, Rogers, & Rothe, 2005). Biham (2013) warns that not taking into account culture can result in unsafe cultural practices. He believed that cultural and ethnic factors can influence the manifestation of symptoms in children, similar to the way they affect adults. This makes identification central to understanding the child's role in the family and how he or she has acculturated to his or her environment and to mainstream society. Assessing acculturation and ethnic-sensitive circumstances and how they relate to symptom formation can be better explained by information in the Cultural Concepts of Distress appendix. The *DSM-5* takes this further by introducing the Cultural Formulation Interview (CFI). See Chapter 2 for a description and application for use of the CFI to ensure culturally relevant practice.

In summary, parental perceptions and contributions to care, as well as cultural factors that influence treatment, can be magnified when combined with other family issues and general life stressors. Divorce and family adjustments can interfere with any treatment strategy, as well as the child's short- and long-term development (Johnston, Roseby, & Kuehnle, 2009). Family changes and stressors can add to what children and adolescents are experiencing, especially when they already present with a rich, complex, and evolving biopsychosocial picture. All professionals have to recognize that these clients are continually growing and changing and understand how these updated developmental and life events can change the presentation of any situation. Children are continuously developing and learning to understand their minds, bodies, emotions, and social patterns (Landy & Bradley, 2014). Often children and adolescents feel they have little control over their lives. Empowering the child with reasonable choices they can make throughout the assessment and treatment process can help the mental health practitioner connect more effectively with the child and start the therapeutic process (Shapiro et al., 2006). When starting the diagnostic interview, for example, simply asking children where they wish to sit and whether they understand the purpose of the visit can help children feel that they are a part of the process.

Case Example Application: Completing the Diagnostic Assessment

The diagnostic assessment began with collection of biological and psychosocial information. Charlie is an 11-year-old boy with a teacher who labeled his behaviors as ADHD since the age of 5. He has exhibited escalating disciplinary problems since age 7. He is the youngest of three brothers and one sister. There is a family history of antisocial disorder and alcoholism, suggestive of a biological basis for ADHD that may place him and his siblings at higher risk for developing CD. Charlie denies the use of any illicit drugs or substances. He is currently in a juvenile detention facility after expulsion from his home, a consequence of hitting his brother over the head with a full can of soda while the brother was sleeping.

CASE EXAMPLE - CASE OF CHARLIE

An 11-year-old White male named Charlie was always in trouble and had been brought to the attention of school authorities since age 7 for truancy, fights, and petty thefts. He is currently staying in a juvenile detention facility after hitting his older brother in the head with a can of soda while he was sleeping. Charlie is the youngest child of three brothers and one sister. His mother and father report that when Charlie attended first grade, they received numerous calls and participated in consultations for disruptive and aggressive behavior, school problems, and difficulties with peer relationships. They report that they are unable to control him. They state that Charlie is a fibber and, when questioned about the truth of his statements, he becomes defiantly irate and walks away. In defiance of his parents' attempt to control his behaviors and actions, Charlie has run away from home. His mother reported that he has run away from home twice after arguments with her and his dad. He deliberately avoids the curfews imposed and on at least two occasions has stayed out with friends without telling his parents where he was going or when he will be back. On several occasions, he simply did not come home and arrived the next day with the explanation that he had been "busy with friends." She also suspects that he has taken money from her purse and his father's wallet on numerous occasions without permission.

According to one of his teachers, Charlie had ADHD in the first grade as evidenced by his school and social disruptions. He also experienced some of the same symptoms at home and reportedly was inattentive, hyperactive, and impulsive. In school, problems such as verbal and physical fights and disruptions in his classrooms became commonplace. His parents were often called and told Charlie was inattentive and displaying yelling, running, and jumping behaviors. He also stabbed another child in the hand with a pencil when he did not get his way. More recently, he was expelled from school when he and two friends were fighting in the school hallway after he and his friends were accused of setting fire to school property. In the second grade, his teacher reported he would often take things from the desks of other children, and when confronted, he either denied taking it or blamed another child. Academic and social difficulties resulted in his being held back 2 years in elementary school, and he is now failing in the fourth grade.

His parents report extreme difficulties at home regarding his schoolwork. He has refused to do homework, stating that schoolwork was boring, and openly preferred to play video games that revolved around violence with "blood and guts." After school on several occasions, he chased classmates who had angered him. One child reported that Charlie grabbed him and proceeded to tightly pull the sweatshirt string across the child's neck. Charlie reports that he often thinks about killing someone, and when he does, he hopes the police will finally take him out of his house. He states that he has little concern for the feelings of others and explains all his behaviors as not his fault since others anger him and deserve what he does for not supporting what he needs or wants.

A series of thefts from neighborhood stores and classmates, fighting in the hallways at school, and the incident in which he and a companion set a fire at school resulted in pending criminal charges. The judge placed him in a juvenile detention facility and ordered a mental health evaluation. In the juvenile detention facility, Charlie originally appeared to befriend other adolescents and several staff members; however, soon the staff reported that he was demanding, manipulative, and volatile. He frequently stormed out of supportive therapeutic groups and care plan meetings when decisions were made that did not go his way. He tried hard to ensure that all activities revolved around him and was enthusiastic about them at first. Later, however, he appeared angry that he was not permitted to monopolize the group activities. The staff described Charlie as a manipulative, angry individual with low self-esteem who seemed focused on finding ways to intimidate the other adolescents in the

(*continued*)

CASE EXAMPLE - CASE OF CHARLIE (CONTINUED)

facility. An example of his low self-esteem provided by a facility staff member involved Charlie being complimented for carrying out a chore efficiently. The staff member reported that Charlie appeared to be in disbelief that someone thought he had done a good job; he became quiet and looked at the floor while being complimented. Like other sources of information, the staff at that facility did not report any overt evidence of depression or any other mood disorder in Charlie.

Charlie slashed his wrist 2 months ago and ended up in the psychiatric ward of the hospital for an attempted suicide. He reported that "no one understands him" and that "his problems are caused by everyone else." He also admitted during the initial intake process at the hospital that he purposely hurt himself as a way of making his parents feel guilty for punishing him. When confronted by hospital staff that his suicidal action caused great concern for his parents, especially his father, Charlie's response was "I don't care what happens to him—actually he deserves to suffer as much as possible." The hospital assessment revealed that he did not wish to die and that, per Charlie's report, his suicidal action was manipulative in nature. He also indicated that he wanted his parents to feel sympathy for him and he wanted his father to suffer. Environmental stresses increased 6 years ago, when Charlie's parents both had to take on extra work to adequately support the family. When Charlie was 5, his father had difficulty keeping employment because of problematic alcohol use. It was not until Charlie was 8 that his father began treatment for the alcohol; he is currently in recovery and has maintained his sobriety. Although Charlie wants to get along with his father, his father finds it difficult to cope with the boy's willfulness and anger. When verbal efforts at discipline fail, his father resorts to harsh corporal punishment, often with a switch. The family is plagued with financial hardships and moved 6 months ago for better-paying jobs and employment opportunities.

Charlie was court-ordered for an evaluation, assessment, and presentation of intervention options to this mental health agency. Once the assessment phase was completed and an intervention plan was established, the judge agreed to order Charlie to engage in and complete counseling while he remains in juvenile justice detention for the remainder of his probation period. Charlie's parents and siblings are fearful of him and no longer trust the boy's unpredictable behavior. They want to discuss out-of-home placement options when he is ready for discharge.

In the assessment process, the principal diagnosis or the reason for visit is based on the dimensional examination of the criteria outlined. The reason for visit is assigned after the diagnostic criteria is met to the diagnosis that best explains the reason for admission and program services. To apply the principal diagnosis, the reason for visit should also be taken into account. In this case, a violent episode initiated treatment and started with Charlie smashing a can of soda on his brother's head while the brother was asleep. Since the reason for the visit is reflective of physical aggression toward others, in starting the diagnostic process, the practitioner must be aware of the symptoms related to CD and what is needed to make that diagnosis. A careful review of all the CD diagnostic criteria must be made to determine if this is a correct principal diagnosis for Charlie.

Principal Diagnosis and Reason for Visit

Charlie is given the principal diagnosis of Conduct Disorder/childhood-onset type, severe

(312.82 *ICD-9-CM* or F91.1 *ICD-10-CM*). As outlined earlier, to diagnose CD, there are four categories in which behaviors fall. The categories list 15 criteria that can be broken down into the four distinct areas. If Charlie has any 3 of the 15 symptoms, he could qualify for the diagnosis. Once the criteria are met, any subtypes for the disorder, specifiers, and the level of severity would be noted.

In examining criterion A, the first of the four categories titled aggression to people and animals has seven potential behaviors that range from bullying and threats toward others to initiating physical fights with weapons, behaviors that result in harm to people or animals, and forcing someone to have sexual activity. In the history presented, cruelty to animals was not evident; however, the incidents related to people are clear. To be sure this area is addressed, the practitioner has the option of eliciting information about Charlie's relationship with animals. When asked, the parents state they have no pets currently, and because of their frequent moves, having pets has not been an option. In terms of aggression toward people, Charlie has multiple incidences, ranging from repeated school experiences involving physical fights to incidents at home culminating with harming his brother. Under aggression to people, Charlie qualifies for three of the seven behaviors and repeated incidents of each behavior can be documented. Without examining the remaining three categories in criterion A, Charlie would already quality for the diagnosis of CD.

Examining this category further, however, can be helpful in outlining the subtypes and severity of the behaviors, as well as in identifying key behaviors that the treatment plan will need to address. The next category involves destruction of property. His recent school suspension for setting a fire to destroy school property meets the criteria. Applied to Charlie's situation, it appears that his destruction of property and fire setting focused on deliberate destruction of school property, and the fighting with his peers that resulted was focused on his getting caught. In regard to all his behaviors, Charlie denies any responsibility. The lack of evidence for meeting criteria related to pyromania eliminates it as a second diagnosis, especially since the fire-setting behavior seems symptomatic of the CD, not pyromania. Charlie now meets the criteria for five characteristic behaviors, and only three are needed to confirm the diagnosis of CD.

In the third diagnostic area, deceitfulness or theft, Charlie clearly meets one of the three criteria related to stealing and conning others to either participate or cover for him. When fighting with his friends about the fire setting, Charlie became extremely angry when his friends would not lie for him. In the area that examines serious violations of the rules, school and home behaviors are highlighted; the case information reveals that Charlie has disobeyed his parents and shown a lack of respect for their authority. He repeatedly runs away from home and often disobeys his parents by not coming home at night. Charlie has disregarded age-appropriate parental, academic, and social expectations and meets the criteria for at least three of the four criteria outlined in this section. In total, Charlie meets eight of the criteria needed to make the diagnosis of CD. The diagnostic information for criterion B is met as the behaviors are clearly severe enough to cause clinical distress. Charlie is too young to be given a diagnosis of antisocial personality disorder, which addresses criterion C; however, if these symptoms persist throughout his development, when he reaches age 18, an assessment of his diagnosis and a change to antisocial personality disorder may be warranted. (See Quick Reference 11.3.)

To complete the diagnosis, the subtype relevant to this disorder must be identified. This subtype clarifies the age of onset from three

QUICK REFERENCE 11.3

IDENTIFY PRINCIPAL DIAGNOSIS/REASON FOR VISIT AND PRESENTING PROBLEM

Principal Diagnosis/Reason for Visit Problem:	Conduct disorder *Specify* whether: Childhood-onset type *Specify* if: With limited prosocial emotions; Callous—lack of empathy
Presenting Problem:	*Specify* current severity: Severe Court-ordered mental health evaluation due to his involvement in thefts and fire setting.

possibilities outlined: childhood-onset type (shows one symptom characteristic of CD prior to the age of 10), adolescent-onset type (does not show characteristics of OD before the age of 10), and unspecified onset (the client meets the criteria for the disorder but the age of onset cannot be determined). In Charlie's case, he displayed symptoms of the disorder prior to the age of 10, meaning the accurate subtype is childhood-onset type. According to *DSM-5,* criteria delineating a subtype based on age should be flexible because sometimes it takes 2 years before the symptoms become prominent enough to be diagnosed. In Charlie's case, the symptoms were clearly documented through his developmental and diagnostic history.

> *Specify* whether: 312.81 (F91.1) Childhood-onset type

The diagnosis of CD also requires identification of a specifier on the presence of limited prosocial emotions. Charlie's parents' information and the history provided by the school and legal system show that Charlie clearly has difficulties relating to interpersonal and emotional situations. The four subgroups under prosocial types of behavior are lack of remorse or guilt, callous—lack of empathy, unconcerned about performance, and shallow or deficient affect. Although Charlie meets some of the criteria for all four, the one that seems to permeate the most is callous—lack of empathy. He often blames others for his problems, and when explaining what he has done, he appears disconnected from his behaviors and focuses primarily on how he is affected. His lack of empathy for others is clear as he describes the events that have occurred and his responsibility for the occurrences. Specifically, his response in the hospital after the suicidal gesture indicates that he has no ability to feel empathy for how his actions affect his parents, especially his father. To document this specifier it is coded as:

> *Specify* if: With limited prosocial emotions: Callous—lack of empathy.

To specify current severity, the clinician has to examine whether the minimum criteria, 4 of the 15 listed, are evident. Once this is established, conduct behaviors in excess of those required to complete the diagnosis are considered. If the symptoms meet the diagnosis but are minimal and result in minor harm to others, it is coded as minimal. The coding continues on to moderate and severe as the behaviors continue to increase. For Charlie, the behaviors fell into the severe level. His behaviors clearly exceed those needed for the diagnosis and have resulted in serious consequences and potential harm to others. To document the current level of severity, it is coded as:

Specify: Severe

In summary, the placement of the principal diagnosis is supported by the fact that in the past 12 months, Charlie has exhibited more than three criteria from the four subgroups outlined in the criteria. During this time, Charlie has produced serious violations of rules by staying out at night; being truant from school; destroying siblings' and family belongings; being physically cruel to people; bullying, threatening, deceiving, and intimidating others; stealing from friends and family; and breaking into homes. Charlie also presented with more than one criterion present in the past 6 months reflective of aggression toward people. He states that he often gets what he wants through threats and intimidation, including initiating verbal and physical fights. He also reports that he is unconcerned and disregards the feelings of others who are subjected to his behavior. He has been caught destroying property, such as deliberately setting fire to school property. Other problematic behaviors include deceitfulness and theft by breaking into homes and the school and stealing from parents.

Other Conditions That May Be a Focus of Clinical Attention

With the elimination of the multiaxial diagnosis often used in *DSM-IV* and *DSM-IV-TR,* the information previously provided on Axis IV and Axis V is no longer required. In addition to the principal and the provisional diagnosis, however, the types of supportive information previously listed still need to be included. Chapters 21 and 22 of the *DSM-5* may be of particular help. Specifically, Chapter 21 considers the medication-induced movement disorders and other adverse effects of medication, and Chapter 22 discusses other conditions that may be a focus of clinical intervention. In the case of Charlie, the information provided in Chapter 22 may be of the most help. Several supportive factors need to be taken into account that can support the diagnostic assessment. The first are the biopsychosocial stressors (especially those related to the family situation and key relationships).

Charlie is having problems in his home environment, and at present his parents have stated that they do not want him back because they fear a continuation of his violent behaviors. Although it may be understandable that they feel this way, they are still his parents and expected to provide a safe environment for him. In this case, there are conflictual family relations and disciplinary patterns currently used and applied in the past that have not been successful. His father admits using harsh discipline but does not see any other way to handle the situation. The most relevant of the other conditions that may be a focus of clinical attention and that can be coded here is:

V61.20 (Z62.820) Parent–Child Relational Problem.

Charlie exhibits education deficits due to school change and nonattendance in class. His grades are poor, and he is constantly failing his exams and refusing to meet academic markers. Another applicable condition that may be a focus of clinical attention that can be coded here is:

V62.3 (Z55.9) Academic or Educational Problem

The last area for supportive attention is his problems related to crime and the legal system. He continually has interpersonal and relationship conflicts due to aggressive and annoying behaviors and peer rejection, along with expulsion from home by judge and parents for brutally hurting his brother. He has also been accused of setting fire to school property and related acts of violence with serious legal implications.

V625 (Z65.1) Imprisonment or Other Incarceration
V62.5 (Z65.3) Problems Related to Other Legal Circumstances

Diagnostic Summary

The identification of a CD diagnosis childhood-onset type, severe completes the diagnosis assessment process for Charlie. During the interview, it was evident that Charlie has a seemingly charming, manipulative personality and from an early age has been unable to follow home, school, or society's rules on a consistent basis. Incorrigibility, delinquency, and school problems such as truancy mark his childhood. Charlie's behavioral problems affect every life area of functioning. Charlie remains aware of his own impulses but misattributes them as justifiable reactions to other persons. Charlie's manipulation and consistent acting-out behaviors make it difficult to ascertain when others might actually have provoked him or caused him problems. There are numerous complaints from parents and school that this client fights, lies, steals, starts fires, cheats, and is abusive and destructive. Charlie casually claims to have guilt feelings, but he does not appear to feel genuine remorse for his behavior. He also clearly shows a lack of empathy for others in the callous ways he describes what he has done and how he has affected others. Charlie complains of multiple somatic problems and has made a suicide attempt that health care providers at the hospital perceived as manipulative. The manipulative nature of all his interactions with others makes it difficult to determine whether any of his complaints are genuine. Charlie has many conduct problems in excess of those required to make the diagnosis of CD, and the conduct problems have caused serious harm to his brother and further strained his parent–child relationships.

In cases like Charlie's, there are usually so many pressing problems to sort out and so many different stressors that not until suicide is actually attempted or sucidal thoughts verbalized do many families, physicians, and other health professionals consider comorbid depression. Recent studies of teenagers who have committed suicide showed that they were about 3 times more likely to have CD and 15 times more likely to abuse substances. Suicide should be an area of concern for children diagnosed with CD and must be a part of treatment planning. In Charlie's case, he has attempted suicide, but because of the manipulative nature of his suicidal attempt and his report that he does not wish to die, the suicidal effort appears to be a part of the diagnosis of CD and not a symptom of depression. In Charlie's case, his suicide attempt was followed by contacting his parents for help. In discussion, he was clear that he would not do that again because it did not get the result he had hoped to obtain, which was to have his parents, especially his father, suffer, as well as hoping he could gain sympathy and attention from his parents. He stated he hoped it would take the pressure off him, but it did not. The current and future potential for the risk of danger to self or others will be reassessed in the treatment-planning phase and continually monitored throughout the treatment process.

Contributing Factors

The family history of antisocial disorder, physical abuse, and alcoholism suggests the possibility of a biological basis for CD for the client. Also, the client has a history of ADHD that was present at age 5. Charlie's family and environmental surroundings are poor. Conflicting punitive measures and the frustration from repeated attempts at trying to help the client in the past have all contributed to a lack of current support, and assistance from parents, teachers, and the legal system complicates Charlie's problems. Charlie has poor frustration tolerance; irritability, temper outbursts, and reckless behaviors are common.

Further Information Needed

School and juvenile records will be requested to further validate the diagnosis and assist in treatment planning. Charlie's previous mental health records will be requested to see whether he has had any past symptoms of depression and whether he really had been diagnosed with ADHD previously. Hospitalization records of the client's admittance to a mental health facility for suicide attempt will be requested. Educational testing and intelligence tests will be requested to rule out pervasive problems in academic function. Parents will be asked to follow through with a referral for a medical exam and blood work for Charlie. It may also be helpful to use some standardized assessment instruments, such as the Parent/Guardian Rated *DSM-5* Level 1 Cross Cutting of symptoms measure available in Section III of the *DSM-5*. For more information on use of this scale, see Chapter 3 of this text. Other rapid assessment instruments may also be used to quantify the behaviors noted.

To engage in therapy designed to build prosocial behaviors, the practitioner will have to obtain additional information on the client and evaluate (a) capacity for attachment, trust, and empathy; (b) tolerance for and discharge of impulses; (c) capacity for showing restraint, accepting responsibility for actions, experiencing guilt, using anger constructively, and acknowledging negative emotions; (d) cognitive functioning; (e) mood, affect, self-esteem, and suicide potential; (f) peer relationships (loner, popular, drug-, crime-, or gang-oriented friends); (g) disturbances of ideation (inappropriate reactions to environment, paranoia, dissociate episodes, and suggestibility); (h) history of early, persistent use of tobacco, alcohol, or other substances; and (i) psychometric self-report instruments.

Charlie's school records will provide a great deal of information, such as his academic functioning (IQ, achievement test data, academic performance, and behavior). Other data may be obtained in person, by phone, or through written reports from appropriate staff, such as school principal, psychologist, juvenile detention personnel, teachers, and school nurse. Any standard parent and teacher rating scales of the client's behavior would be useful. If indicated, the practitioner should also make referrals for IQ, speech and language, and learning disability and neuropsychiatric testing. It may be necessary to look at medical evaluations, particularly any physical examination within the past 12 months (i.e., baseline pulse rate). An important component of the treatment plan is to collaborate with the family doctor, pediatrician, or other health care providers to ensure proper medical checkups that include vision and hearing screenings. As records become available, it is necessary to evaluate medical and neurological conditions (e.g., head injury, seizure disorder, and chronic illnesses). The practitioner will review any urine and blood drug screening, especially when clinical evidence suggests substance abuse that the client denies (Dziegielewski, 2005).

Starting the Treatment Process

The presenting problem is the major focus of the subsequent treatment to follow. In this case, once the principal diagnosis has been established and the presenting problem(s) identified, the first task of the mental health practitioner, especially with this child's history of violence toward self and others, is to complete a risk assessment. The practitioner needs to identify the risk of potential suicide and of violence to others and whether there has been a history of either physical or sexual abuse of Charlie and, if so, whether this

QUICK REFERENCE 11.4

RISK ASSESSMENT

Document and assess suicide risk:	No current evidence, past history
Document and assess violence risk:	Possible but slight as under direct supervision
Document and assess child abuse risk:	Current risk slight, past abuse not determined

could have any influence on current behaviors and the subsequent treatment. These questions are asked in a straightforward and direct manner. Once identified, this information needs to be clearly recorded. (See Quick Reference 11.4.)

The second step for the mental health practitioner is to identify behaviors that contribute to impairment in daily functioning. In addition to assessing problematic behaviors, the practitioner should note strengths exhibited by the client and the family system. Capturing both risk and protective factors is always important when assessing children, and these factors should be integrated into the treatment plan and the subsequent treatment process (Polier, Vloet, Herpertz-Dahlmann, Laurens, & Hodgins, 2012). To start this assessment process, the practitioner should engage in a mental status and observe the client's appearance, mood, attitude, affect, speech, motor activity, and orientation. Generalized subjective assessments need to accompany more formalized procedures. For example, mental functioning should be assessed in terms of the client's ability to complete simple calculations, serial 7s, immediate memory, remote memory, general knowledge, proverb interpretation, and recognition of similarities and differences. Questions regarding higher-order abilities and thought form and content need to be processed. (See Quick Reference 11.5.)

In Charlie's behaviors, he has a history of repetitive and persistent patterns of disturbed peer relationships, disobedience and opposition to authority figures, lying, shoplifting, physical fighting, exhibition fighting, fire setting, stealing, vandalism, and school discipline problems since age 7. These conduct problems impair social and academic functioning, as evidenced by few friends, poor grades, school suspension, and involvement in numerous fights. To determine whether he meets the criteria for a second or third mental health diagnosis, other diagnoses with overlapping conditions should be examined.

For Charlie, examining comorbidity or differential diagnosis would start with assessing his possible depressive symptoms, as he has attempted suicide and his behaviors rapidly escalate when he is frustrated or confronted by authorities after being caught in wrongdoing. His self-esteem may be low, despite the image of toughness he presents to the public. Charlie's depression may, in fact, be manifesting itself in angry outbursts and his concurrent conduct and impulsivity problems. This appears different than disruptive mood dysregulation disorder (DMDD); the agitation is not continuous and seems to surround only events related to his not getting what he wants. Other depressive symptoms that may exist appear related to the family's move, his disturbances in the home, and his statements that he is bored with school and schoolwork. Currently, there are no severe symptoms to meet the criteria for a DMDD or a depressive disorder. Although information on a previous diagnosis of ADHD was included in the

QUICK REFERENCE 11.5

MENTAL STATUS DESCRIPTION

Presentation	Mental Functioning	Higher-Order Abilities	Thought Form/Content
Appearance: Unkempt	Orientation: Fully oriented	Judgment: Impulsive	Thought Process: Logical and organized
	Simple Calculations: Mostly accurate		
	Serial 7s: Accurate	Insight: Impaired Unrealistic interpretation of own behaviors	
Mood: Anxious			Delusions: None
	Immediate Memory: Intact	Intelligence: Average	
Attitude: Guarded	Remote Memory: Intact	Proverb Interpretation: Mostly accurate	Hallucinations: None
Affect: Appropriate		Similarities/ Differences: Mostly accurate	
Speech: Normal			
Motor Activity: Restless			

case, no direct connection can be made between that diagnosis and the current behaviors, and it is not clear whether the diagnosis was officially given based on a diagnostic assessment or by the teacher. For this reason, an additional diagnosis of ADHD will not be included. There are no medical conditions noted, but lacerations of the left wrist are noted from Charlie's attempted suicide 2 months ago, along with his reasoning, which was to punish his parents.

Individual strengths include Charlie's intelligence level, which seems average. He does have the ability to assess a situation and make informed decisions. His judgment and insights as to the outcomes of his behavior are limited, although he is aware of what he could have done differently and is capable of problem solving. He also is capable of getting good grades and connecting with people when it is to his advantage. He possesses many of the important prosocial skills needed and is capable of understanding and applying what he learns in social situations. All of these are important skills needed for moving forward and establishing a treatment plan that the client is cognitively and behaviorally capable of completing.

Treatment Plan and Intervention Components

The most important factor to identify when setting up a treatment plan is clearly stating the presenting problem. This requires using the skills and experience of the practitioner and mixing them with the latest research evidence to arrive at the best treatment strategy (Schore, 2014). In Charlie's case, the presenting problem started with a court-ordered referral for a mental health evaluation and subsequent treatment due to his involvement in thefts and fire setting. In formulating the treatment plan, Charlie and his parents were interviewed together and separately to go over the history and to explore all other possible contradictory information and comorbid conditions. School reports helped to verify truancy, behavior problems, and educational status. The practitioner needs to gather a comprehensive history that includes schoolwork and the perspective of both the child and the parents. As noted earlier, lab tests and X-rays are needed to rule out neurological and/or biological components. The referral for a blood test will detect use or abuse of drugs or hormonal problems. Problem behaviors must be clearly identified, as these are the behaviors that will be addressed through the intervention efforts. Practitioners should target the primary symptoms and behavior problems first.

Treatment time can vary among individuals with CD; however, it is rarely brief because establishing new attitudes and behavior patterns takes time. However, early intervention offers Charlie a better chance for considerable improvement and hope for a more successful future. An eclectic approach might work best for Charlie because it encourages practitioner responses that are based on differential assessments of the client's specific needs and problems (Fischer, 2009). Charlie's treatment will combine individual therapy, group therapy, behavioral therapy, social skills training, family support and family therapy, and, potentially, remedial education. Medications may also be of use and may be included in the treatment plan. Although medication may be an important component of treating Charlie's behavior disorders, especially early on, it will work best as an adjunct to psychotherapy. Individual therapy can help Charlie gain greater self-control and insight into his social conduct and develop more thoughtful and efficient problem-solving strategies. Given the complex and interrelated list of problem behaviors Charlie is experiencing, examining each one individually will help to determine the best course of treatment to follow. (See Quick Reference 11.6.)

In individual or group therapy, Charlie will be given the opportunity to understand and express his feelings with words instead of through behaviors. Charlie's treatment will include behavior modification techniques, such as social skill training, through which he can learn to evaluate social situations and adjust his behavior accordingly. Charlie may need to have some kind of remedial education or special tutoring to compensate for any learning difficulties or to address any reading disorders, learning disabilities, or language delays that may be indicated following testing. Although this does not appear to be a concern in the assessment process, some of the defiant behavior he is experiencing may be related to his inability to complete the tasks assigned. If he is agreeable and cooperative, a battery of personality and educational testing could help to reveal this. Also, at times it is easy to focus on the negatives, but the strengths of the client need to be identified and used in each part of the treatment process. Some of Charlie's strengths include the ability to think clearly, receptive and expressive skills, excellent problem-solving abilities, motivation for change, and sound physical health.

In starting the treatment process, the practitioner should keep an open mind and not assume that any treatment is better than no treatment. All treatments should be selected because they are beneficial, effective, and compatible with the client's abilities, level of understanding, and skills. They should also be geared toward enhancing the client's optimal levels of functioning.

QUICK REFERENCE 11.6

Behavioral Problem Identification

Persistent failure to comply with rules or expectations in the home, school, and community.

Excessive fighting, intimidation of others, cruelty and violence toward people, and deliberate fire setting with intention of causing damage and destruction of school property.

History of stealing from family, classmates, and neighbors.

School adjustment characterized by repeated truancy, disrespectful attitude, and suspensions for misbehavior.

Repeated conflict and confrontation with authority figures at home, school, and in the community.

Failure to consider the consequences of actions, taking inappropriate risks, and engaging in thrill-seeking behaviors.

Numerous attempts to deceive others through lying, conning, or manipulating.

Consistent failure to accept responsibility for misbehavior, accompanied by a pattern of blaming others.

Little or no remorse for past misbehavior.

Lack of sensitivity to the thoughts, feelings, and needs of other people.

GENERAL INTERVENTION STRATEGIES: MODELS AND TREATMENT MODALITIES

Multiple types of treatment can be used to assist Charlie. On an individual level, the most common form will include cognitive restructuring and insight-oriented therapies. From a group perspective, family and peer group therapy may also be beneficial. To improve prosocial behaviors, behavioral interventions such as token economies may be used. This can be supplemented with other behavioral techniques infused with anger management and relaxation training. Supportive maintenance strategies to improve social and family dynamics and further build prosocial responses include parent education, family therapy, social skills training, and social skills building. There may also be a need for pharmacotherapy and medication management therapy.

Of all the treatment modalities available, the strained family relationships make family therapy an important component to treating CD. Family therapy and behavioral therapies, such as parent training programs, address the family stress normally generated by living with a child or adolescent with CD. These treatment modalities provide strategies for managing Charlie's behavior and may help the parents encourage appropriate behaviors in their other children and help parents develop more appropriate and effective disciplinary practices. By involving the entire family, this treatment fosters mutual support, positive reinforcement, direct communication, and more effective problem solving within the family. From a systems perspective, changing one part of a family will also change another (Rivett &

Street, 2009). Many target symptoms that may not have been apparent or acknowledged during the client interview may be discovered during interviews with parents, juvenile detention staff, and teachers. Caregivers, custodians, or even a parent may endorse symptoms that could be better conceptualized as normative manifestations of autonomy assertion and immature self-regulatory skills. Most important, because children act out conflicts in their family systems, when using family therapy, the practitioner has an opportunity to help the family identify challenges within the system itself that cause or contribute to the child's problems and defocus Charlie as the problem (Sydow, Retzlaff, Beher, Haun, & Schweitzer, 2013).

Treatment should be provided in a continuum of care that allows flexible application of modalities by a cohesive treatment plan. Selected outpatient treatment is planned for Charlie, including intervention in the family, school, and peer group. His predominance of externalizing symptoms in multiple domains of functioning requires interpersonal and psychoeducational modalities rather than an exclusive emphasis on intrapsychic treatment. This therapy needs to be provided in addition to psychopharmacological approaches. Because Charlie's CD is severe, it may require extensive treatment and long-term follow-up. In preparing the treatment plan, possible family interventions should be developed, including parent guidance and family therapy to identify and work with parental strengths and parent training to help them establish consistent positive and negative consequences and well-defined expectations and rules. Addressing issues of noncompliance is central to treatment with Charlie and all children with this diagnosis. Addressing noncompliance can yield improvement in all areas of behavior (McMahon, Wells, & Kotler, 2006).

In this case, the practitioner decided to work to eliminate harsh, excessively permissive, and inconsistent behavior management practices. It was arranged for the father to receive individual substance abuse counseling and for Charlie to receive individual, peer support, and family group psychotherapy. Therapy focused on supportive, explorative, cognitive, and other behavioral techniques because of the client's age, processing style, and ability to engage in treatment. Psychosocial skill-building training will be used to supplement therapy, as well as other psychosocial interventions. The use of a peer intervention was chosen to discourage deviant peer association and promote a socially appropriate peer network.

Establishing a school intervention for appropriate placement will promote an alliance between parents and school and promote prosocial peer group contact. Coordination and assistance in juvenile justice system interventions may require the inclusion of court supervision and limit settings, as well as other special programs when available. Social services referrals were needed to help the family to obtain benefits and service providers (e.g., case managers). As discharge nears, there may be a need to consider other community resources, such as Big Brother and Big Sister programs and Friends Outside. There may come a time when out-of-home placement (e.g., crisis shelters, group homes, or residential treatment) may be appropriate. As Charlie becomes older, he may require independent-living skills training.

Psychopharmacology may not be able to address some of the true concerns noted but may help with aggressive tendencies. To address disruptive aggressive behaviors, some prescribers might begin with minimum recommended starting daily doses of atypical neuroleptics (Findling et al., 2000; Schur et al., 2003). There are no medications that are specifically for the treatment of CD, so careful consultation with someone skilled in medication prescriptions and the side effects that may result is always warranted.

It is beyond the scope of this chapter to discuss all of the medications that could be used to treat the symptoms of this disorder. For a description of important information about these medications that could benefit nonmedically trained practitioners, see Dziegielewski (2010). A consultation and referral to a medically trained prescriber familiar with this condition is highly recommended, particularly since the risks and side effects of these neuroleptics may outweigh their usefulness in the treatment of aggression in CD.

Determining the best level of care and the criteria for hospitalization of this client can be complex, although the practitioner will choose the least restrictive level of intervention that fulfills both the short- and long-term needs of the client. When or if there is an imminent risk to self or others, such as suicidal, self-injurious, homicidal, or aggressive behavior, or imminent deterioration in the individual's medical status after completing juvenile detention, clear indications of the need for hospitalization exist. Inpatient, partial hospitalization, and residential treatment were considered: (a) therapeutic milieu, including community processes and structure (e.g., level system, behavior modification), and (b) significant family involvement tailored to the needs of the client (conjoint or without patient present), including parent training and family therapy. Because this is a young client, it is even more critical that the family be involved in the treatment process (Lewinsohn, Striegel-Moore, & Seeley, 2000; Maxmen et al., 2009; Rivett & Street, 2009). (See Sample Treatment Plan.)

In summary, when developing treatment plans for children and adolscents practitioners are encouraged to develop behaviorally specific and measurable objectives that allow the child,

SAMPLE TREATMENT PLAN

Conduct Disorder (CD)

Briefly stated, CD involves a repetitive and persistent pattern of behavior that violates the rights of others. The behaviors often fall into four primary areas: aggression to people and animals, destruction of property, deceitfulness or theft, and serious violations of the rules.

Signs and Symptoms to Note in the Record

- **Aggression to People or Animals:** Bullying, threatening, intimidates others, initiates physical fights, uses weapons that can cause serious harm, physically cruel to people or animals, theft with confrontation of the victim, and forced sexual activity.
- **Destruction of Property:** Engaged in fire setting causing damage and intention to harm and destroy property.
- **Deceitfulness and Theft:** Stays out all night, runs away from home repeatedly and stealing items of value and confronting the victim.
- **Serious Violations of the Rules:** Staying out and disobeying parental rules, running away from home repeatedly and for extended periods, and truant from school.

Long-Term Goals

1. Demonstrate increased honesty, compliance with rules, sensitivity to the feelings and rights of others; develop control over impulses and acceptance of responsibility for his behavior.
2. Comply with rules and expectations in the home, school, and community on a consistent basis.
3. Eliminate problematic behaviors, especially those that are illegal or dangerous to self or others.

(continued)

SAMPLE TREATMENT PLAN (*Continued*)

4. Terminate all acts of violence and cruelty toward people and the destruction of property.
5. Express anger through appropriate verbalizations and healthy physical outlets on a consistent basis.
6. Demonstrate marked improvement in impulse control.
7. Resolve the core conflicts that contribute to the emergence of conduct problems.
8. Demonstrate empathy, concern, and sensitivity for the thoughts, feelings, and needs of others on a regular basis.
9. Parents will establish and maintain appropriate parent–child boundaries, setting firm, consistent limits when the client acts out in an aggressive or rebellious manner.

Short-Term Goals

1. Complete psychological testing.
2. Complete a psychoeducational evaluation.
3. Complete a substance abuse evaluation and comply with the recommendations offered by the evaluation findings.
4. Remain in the juvenile detention facility for the remainder of his probation term.
5. Recognize and verbalize how feelings are connected to misbehavior.
6. Increase the number of statements that reflect the acceptance of responsibility for misbehavior.
7. Decrease the frequency of verbalizations that project the blame for problems onto other people.
8. Express anger through appropriate verbalization and healthy physical outlets.
9. Reduce the frequency and severity of aggressive, destructive, and antisocial behaviors.
10. Increase compliance with rules at home and at the alternative school.
11. Increase the time spent with parents in leisure and school activities.
12. Verbalize an understanding of how current acting-out and aggressive behaviors are associated with past neglect and harsh physical punishment.
13. Identify and verbally express feelings associated with harsh physical abuse.
14. Increase participation in extracurricular activities and positive peer group activities.
15. Identify and verbalize how acting-out behaviors negatively affect others.
16. Increase verbalizations of empathy and concern for other people.
17. Increase communication, intimacy, and consistency when addressing parents.
18. Take medication as prescribed by the physician.
19. The parents will postpone recreational activity (e.g., playing basketball with friends) until homework or chores are completed when Charlie is at home.
20. The parents will establish appropriate boundaries, develop clear rules, and follow through consistently with consequences for misbehavior when Charlie returns to home.
21. The parents will increase the frequency of praise and positive reinforcement to the client.
22. The parents will verbalize appropriate boundaries for discipline to prevent further occurrences of abuse and ensure the safety of the client and his siblings.
23. Client and his parents will cooperate with the recommendations or requirements mandated by the criminal justice system.
24. Client and his parents agree to and follow through with the implementation of a reward system or contingency contract.

SAMPLE TREATMENT PLAN (*Continued*)

Therapeutic Interventions

- The practitioner will give a directive to parents to spend more time with the client in leisure, school, or other activities.
- The practitioner will explore the client's family background for a history of physical, sexual, or substance abuse that may contribute to his behavioral problems.
- The practitioner will conduct a family therapy session in which the client's family members are given a task or problem to solve together (e.g., build a craft), observe family interactions, and process the experience with them afterward.
- The practitioner will assist the client's parents in developing more appropriate discipline methods and to cease immediately any present or future physically abusive or overly punitive methods of discipline.
- Charlie will remain in juvenile detention for the protection of siblings from further abuse until deemed unnecessary.
- The practitioner will encourage and support the client in expressing feelings associated with neglect and harsh punishment.
- The practitioner will utilize the family sculpting technique in which the client defines the roles and behaviors of each family member in a scene of his choosing to assess and reconstruct family dynamics.
- The practitioner will conduct family therapy sessions to explore the dynamics that contribute to the emergence of the client's behavioral problems.
- The practitioner will assign the client's parents reading material and relevant books on how to handle children with behavioral difficulties to be discussed in the sessions.
- The practitioner will encourage the parents to provide frequent praise and positive reinforcement for the client's positive social behaviors and good impulse control.
- The practitioner will design and implement a token economy to increase the client's positive social behaviors and deter impulsive, acting-out behaviors.
- The practitioner will utilize the therapeutic skills and games that highlight "Talking, Feeling, Doing" to increase the client's awareness of his thoughts and feelings.
- The practitioner will arrange for the client to participate in group therapy to improve his social judgment and interpersonal skills.
- The practitioner will assign the client the task of showing empathy, kindness, and sensitivity to the needs of others (e.g., read a bedtime story to a sibling, mow the lawn for a grandmother) after removal from juvenile detention.
- The practitioner will encourage the client to participate in extracurricular or positive peer group activities to provide a healthy outlet for anger, improve social skills, and increase self-esteem.
- The practitioner will explore the client's feelings, irrational beliefs, and unmet needs that contribute to the emergence of sexually promiscuous behaviors.
- The practitioner will arrange for a medication evaluation of the client to improve his impulse control and stabilize moods.
- The practitioner will arrange for a psychoeducational evaluation of the client to rule out the presence of a learning disability that may be contributing to his impulsivity and acting-out behaviors in the school setting.

(*continued*)

SAMPLE TREATMENT PLAN (*Continued*)

- The practitioner will firmly confront the client's antisocial behavior and attitude, pointing out consequences for him and others.
- The practitioner will arrange for psychological testing of the client to assess whether emotional factors or ADHD is contributing to his impulsivity and acting-out behaviors.
- The practitioner, with parental permission, will provide feedback to the client, his parents, school officials, and criminal justice officials regarding psychological and/or psychoeducational testing.
- The practitioner will arrange for substance abuse evaluation for the client.
- The practitioner will consult with criminal justice officials about the appropriate consequences for the client's antisocial behaviors (e.g., pay restitution, community service, and probation).
- The practitioner will encourage and challenge the parents not to protect the client from the legal consequences of his antisocial behaviors.
- The practitioner will assist the client's parents in establishing clearly defined rules, boundaries, and consequences for misbehavior.
- The practitioner will actively build the level of trust with the client in therapy sessions through consistent eye contact, active listening, unconditional positive regard, and warm acceptance to increase his ability to identify and express feelings.
- The practitioner will design a reward system and/or contingency contract for the client to reinforce identified positive behaviors and deter impulsive behaviors.
- The practitioner will assist the client in making a connection between feelings and reactive behaviors.
- The practitioner will confront statements in which the client blames others for his misbehavior and fails to accept responsibility for his actions.
- The practitioner will explore and process the factors that contribute to the client's pattern of blaming others.
- The practitioner will teach meditational and self-control strategies (e.g., relaxation; stop, look, listen, and think) to help the client express anger through appropriate verbalizations and healthy physical outlets.
- The practitioner will encourage the client to use self-monitoring checklists at home and in the alternative school to develop more effective anger and impulse control.
- The practitioner will teach the client effective communication and assertiveness skills to express feelings in a controlled fashion and meet his needs through more constructive actions.
- The practitioner will assist the parents in increasing structure to help the client learn to delay gratification for longer-term goals (e.g., complete homework or chores before playing basketball).
- The practitioner will establish clear rules for the client at home and school and ask him to repeat the rules to demonstrate an understanding of the expectations.

parents, and the practitioner to measure treatment progress. For Charlie, the probability of successful achievement of the treatment goals is fair. The rationale for this probability rating is a poor family economic situation and limited means of family support. When parents are preoccupied with finding employment and finances are tight, mental health treatment is not seen as a priority. This becomes even more complicated when the parents have serious mental health issues of their own, such as Charlie's father's alcohol-related problems. For the intervention to be successful, parental support is needed. The potential for Charlie to be released and engage in illegal substance use remains high. Charlie's motivation to participate in treatment is seen as a strength, as he states that he wants to do whatever is needed to be a better child. He also understands that he needs to continue with extracurricular activities, support groups, and, if needed, medication, even after discharge from this facility.

His mother and father state that they really do not want him home. If they continue to see progress, however, they will at least consider it. They state they love their son and are willing to give him another chance, assuming Charlie changes. Both parents report that they will try their best to assist Charlie in treatment and with improvement would be willing to take Charlie back into the family home. A call to Child Protective Services is made to ensure adequate assessment and follow-up care upon discharge since the parents originally stated they would not take Charlie home. As part of the discharge process, it should be affirmed that Charlie's parents are willing to take him home and provide his basic care and safety needs.

Upon completion of the treatment program, a clear discharge and aftercare plan is essential to help the client maintain current treatment gains. To work on his lack of prosocial skills, he will attend peer support groups and continue with established extracurricular activities. Information for follow-up is essential, and a plan to return for either inpatient or outpatient care needed on an emergency basis should be discussed. In the school setting, attending after-school programs with planned activities will help him to continue to work on goals, make constructive social relationships, and prevent isolation. (See Quick Reference 11.7.)

A limited number of evidence-based programs are currently available for the early predictors of early-onset CD. One potential program, Webster-Stratton Incredible Years Program: Parents, Teachers, and Children Training Series, is an evidence-based comprehensive prevention/intervention program to assist children age 3 to 7. The program is designed to strengthen parent and teacher communication. Findings in four studies show that it effectively increases positive parenting practices and reduces antisocial behavior in children at risk for developing CD (August, Realmuto, Hektner, & Bloomquist, 2001; Barrera et al., 2002; Hutchings et al., 2007). The New York University Child Study Center has developed and continues to study the efficacy of ParentCorps, a program that provides long-needed parent practices and child social competence for low-income families of preschool-age children. Evidence supports this as a promising outreach program for poor urban communities where children are at high risk of conduct problem behaviors and academic problems. A program that can address both of these aspects of the condition is desperately needed for economically disadvantaged children in every state throughout the United States.

Further research is needed to determine the long-term impact of such programs on teaching practices, parenting practices, and parent–school involvement. Behavioral parent training is currently one of the most extensively well-validated interventions for children with aggressive and conduct problems. Inclusion of this type of supportive intervention may prevent the resulting behaviors from becoming severe enough to

QUICK REFERENCE 11.7

Discharge Criteria:

- The client must attend school consistently without resistance.
- The client will conform with limits set by authority figures.
- The client will consistently abstain from mood-altering illicit drugs or alcohol.
- The client will demonstrate age-appropriate social skills.
- The client will demonstrate responsible, consistent medication-taking behavior.
- The client will engage in social interaction with appropriate eye contact and assertiveness.
- The client will have home visits completed without serious maladjustment.
- The client's mood, behavior, and thoughts will be stabilized sufficiently to independently carry out basic self-care.
- The client will have no exhibition of sexually inappropriate behavior.
- The client will have no expression of suicidal ideation.
- The client will have no expression of a threat of physical aggression toward self or others.
- The client will have no violent outbursts of temper.
- The client will resolve conflicts peaceably and without aggression.
- The client will verbalize names of supportive resources that can be contacted if feeling suicidal.
- The client will verbalize plans for seeking continued emotional support after discharge.
- The client will verbalize positive plans for the future.

result in a dual diagnosis, such as ADHD and CD. Sadly, a majority of current intervention programs target school-age children, rather than reaching them at a much earlier age. Imagine what opportunities young children would have if their chances were improved by a parental program geared toward very early childhood for those who may be at risk of chronic disruptive behavior disorders. Early intervention can have more of an impact than interventions at age 5, 10, or in later years, when the behavior has become a way of life.

In the National Comorbidity Survey, replication provided evidence that the prevalence and subtypes of CD for some age groups are well correlated within the *DSM-IV* (Nock, Kazdin, Hiripi, & Kessler, 2007). Despite those correlations, clinicians must be vigilant in the search for the newest findings in research, surveys, and evidence-based interventions and treatment (e.g., biological/psychological/social implications and medical studies). Because of the ever-changing advances in understanding, treating, and preventing developmental disorders, more research is a necessary undertaking. In addition, education should be a priority in maintaining evidence-based practices for the treatment and interventions that will improve services and identify mental health conditions such as CD.

Concluding Thoughts: Medication Use

Over the years, concerns related to child and adolescent mental health treatment focusing on medication as a central component have intensified (Cooper et al., 2006; Noggle & Dean, 2009; Thomas, Conrad, Casler, & Goodman, 2006). It has become increasingly important for all helping professionals who work with children to become aware of the behavioral, cognitive, and physiological effects medications can have on children. It is not uncommon, especially when working in a school setting, to be expected to assist children who are taking medications. When medications are involved, the expectation is for the mental health professional to consult with other professionals and help make decisions about the use of medications or the modification of current medication-based treatment schemes (Dziegielewski, 2010).

Roemmelt (1998) and Woolston (1999) warned that addressing mental health conditions in children and adolescents by depending primarily on medications can disguise what the child is really experiencing and give parents and professionals a false sense of control that limits normal childhood development. Also, there is little information on the subjective experience of these children and adolescents and whether they understand their illness or what the medications are designed to do (Floersch et al., 2009). When medications are used as part of the treatment regimen, tread cautiously when assessing and treating the problems and disorders presented by children and adolescents. Always try to utilize a team approach involving all the systems a child or adolescent is exposed to, including school, family system, and other providers.

SUMMARY AND FUTURE DIRECTIONS

Conduct disorder is a complex problem with many forms. No one intervention can be used for every case, and evidence-based clinical diagnostics, treatment, intervention, and research are crucial. This chapter discussed selected disruptive behavior disorders in children, with a focus on CD. What this chapter confirms is that disruptive behavior disorders can start early in life. As such, early prevention, identification, and treatment are essential in allowing children and adolescents with disruptive behavior disorders to overcome them and reach optimal levels of functioning in all areas of development. Controversies regarding the definition, etiology, and subtypes of the disruptive disorders continue to be researched and discussed, and practitioners benefit from the new knowledge that continuously emerges on this group of disorders.

Practitioners must look carefully at the risk factors and combine these with the protective factors that are evident in the child. Once understood during the diagnostic assessment, the identification of these factors remains a critical aspect of the therapeutic process. As with other mental health disorders, a team approach is necessary in addressing the behaviors presented by children and adolescents who exhibit the disruptive disorders. A person-in-environment focus helps to attend to several interrelated dimensions of the client who suffers from CD, thereby focusing on the biological, intellectual, emotional, social, familial, spiritual, economic, communal, and so on, recognizing the client in relation to the immediate and distant environment.

The exact cause of the disruptive disorders is not known. However, there appears to be a direct link to interactions between nature and nurture. Acknowledging these interactions can result in identifying biological, parental, psychological, behavioral, familial, and social environmental risk factors. These risk factors can, in turn, influence the negative interactions that lead to the disruptive behaviors that, if left untreated, continue through adulthood. Accurate identification of disruptive behaviors that lead to these disorders will benefit millions of children and adolescents. Through an increase in evidence-based programs that focus on early identification of disruptive behaviors in children, very young children, especially those from low-income families, may benefit from early interventions. Additionally, there is a great need to help parents increase their child development knowledge and gain a better understanding of child mental health disorders and treatment. The chapter discussed problem behaviors, symptoms, subtypes, associated conditions, and changes that have occurred in the *DSM* in diagnosing the disruptive behavior disorders. A case study completed a diagnostic assessment that examined supporting information for the diagnosis and other contributing factors and then used this information to develop a treatment plan. All mental health practitioners need to stay informed of up-to-date and evidence-based research on the interventions that can be used to treat clients who suffer from the disruptive behavior disorders. With the increase in managed behavioral care, mental health practitioners must develop research that clearly identifies which treatment or combination of treatments is most cost-effective to ensure that clients continue to receive coverage for the necessary treatments.

A number of changes in the future may improve our understanding of the etiology and nosology of disruptive behavior disorders, especially CD. A plethora of current research has demonstrated that mental health problems, disruptive behaviors, and CD can be identified and exhibit moderate stability as they emerge in children as young as 5 months old (Briggs-Gowan, Carter, Bosson-Heenan, Guyer, & Horwitz, 2006; Romano, Zoccolillo, & Paquette, 2006; Shaw, Gilliom, Ingoldsby, & Nagin, 2003; Skovgaard et al., 2007; Tremblay et al., 2004). Manifestations of early childhood behavior disorders and the future development of standardized methodology for clinically assessing preschool children would enhance not only research but also clinicians' intervention and treatment efforts.

Pottick, Kirk, Hsieh, and Tian (2007) found in a survey of 1,401 experienced psychologists, psychiatrists, and social workers that social workers were the least likely professionals to recognize a client suffering from mental illness. Survey results also indicated that psychologists were three times more likely and psychiatrists five times more likely to see mental illness than social workers. There is a fine line between recognizing mental illness and overdiagnosing it. Supporting information from the environment related to the client's situation is essential to both the diagnosis and the treatment. All mental health practitioners must strive for better education and training while reaching out to clients who want to overcome the persistent and severe symptoms of mental health disorders that keep them from achieving optimal levels of functioning in all areas of life. This requires a comprehensive diagnostic assessment, rich with supportive information that can clearly affect the diagnosis obtained as well as the course of treatment.

REFERENCES

Achenbach, T. M. (2001). *The child behavior checklist manual and revised child behavior profiles.* Burlington, VT: Department of Psychiatry, University of Vermont.

American Psychiatric Association. (2000). *Diagnostic and statistical manual of mental disorders* (4th ed., text rev.). Washington, DC: Author.

American Psychiatric Association. (2013). *Diagnostic and statistical manual of mental disorders* (5th ed.). Washington, DC: Author.

August, G. J., Realmuto, G. M., Hektner, J. M., & Bloomquist, M. L. (2001). An integrated components preventive intervention for aggressive elementary school children: The Early Risers program. *Journal of Consulting and Clinical Psychology, 69*(4), 614–626. doi: 10.1037/0022-006X.69.4.614

Baggerly, J. (2009). Play therapy research: History and current empirical support. In A. A. Drewes (Ed.), *Blending play therapy with cognitive behavioral therapy: Evidence-based and other effective treatments and techniques* (pp. 97–115). Hoboken, NJ: Wiley.

Barrera, M., Jr., Biglan, A., Taylor, T. K., Gunn, B. K., Smolkowski, K., Black, C., . . . Fowler, R. C. (2002). Early elementary school intervention to reduce conduct problems: A randomized trial for Hispanic and non-Hispanic children. *Prevention Science, 3*(2), 83–94.

Barry, C. T., Golmaryami, F. N., Rivera-Hudson, N., & Frick, P. J. (2013). Evidence based assessment of conduct disorder: Current considerations and preparations for *DSM-5*. *Professional Psychology: Research and Practice, 44*(1), 56–63. doi: 10.1037/a0029202

Beauchaine, T. P., & Hinshaw, S. P. (Eds.). (2008). *Child and adolescent psychopathology*. Hoboken, NJ: Wiley.

Beauchaine, T. P., Hinshaw, S. P., & Gatzke-Kopp, L. (2008). Genetic and environmental influences on behavior. In T. P. Beauchaine & S. P. Hinshaw (Eds.), *Child and adolescent psychopathology* (pp. 58–90). Hoboken, NJ: Wiley.

Bilham, S. (2013). Cultural aspects for children and young people. In C. Thurston (Ed.) *Essential nursing care for children and young people: Theory, policy, and practice* (p. 82–96). New York: Routledge.

Boyd-Webb, N. (Ed.). (2001). *Culturally diverse parent–child and family relationships: A guide for social workers and other practitioners*. New York, NY: Columbia University Press.

Briggs-Gowan, M. J., Carter, A. S., Bosson-Heenan, J., Guyer, A. E., & Horwitz, S. M. (2006). Are infant-toddler social-emotional and behavioral problems transient? *Journal of the American Academy of Child & Adolescent Psychiatry, 45*(7), 849–858.

Bromfield, R. (2007). *Doing child & adolescent psychotherapy: Adapting psychodynamic treatment to contemporary practice* (2nd ed.). Hoboken, NJ: Wiley.

Cicchetti, D. (2008). A multiple-levels-of-analysis perspective on research in development and psychopathology. In T. P. Beauchaine & S. P. Hinshaw (Eds.), *Child and adolescent psychopathology* (pp. 27–57). Hoboken, NJ: Wiley.

Cooper, W. O., Arbogast, P. G., Ding, H., Hickson, G. B., Fuchs, D. C., & Ray, W. A. (2006). Trends in prescribing of antipsychotic medications for US children. *Ambulatory Pediatrics, 6*(2), 79–83.

Dziegielewski, S. F. (2005). *Understanding substance addictions: Assessment and intervention*. Chicago, IL: Lyceum.

Dziegielewski, S. F. (2010). *Psychopharmacology and social work practice: A person in environment approach* (2nd ed.). New York, NY: Springer.

Faust, J., & Stewart, L. M. (2008). Impact of child abuse timing and family environment on psychosis. *Journal of Psychological Trauma, 6*(2–3), 65–85. doi: 0.1300/J513v06n02_05

Findling, R. L., McNamara, N. K., Branicky, L. A., Schluchter, M. D., Lemon, E., & Blumer, J. L. (2000). A double-blind pilot study of risperidone in the treatment of conduct disorder. *Journal of the American Academy of Child & Adolescent Psychiatry, 39*(4), 509–516.

Fischer, J. (2009). *Toward evidence-based practice: Variations on a theme*. Chicago, IL: Lyceum.

Floersch, J., Townsend, L., Longhofer, J., Munson, M., Winbush, V., Kranke, D., . . . Findling, R. L. (2009). Adolescent experience of psychotropic treatment. *Transcultural Psychiatry, 46*(1), 157–179. doi: 10.1177/1363461509102292

Frances, A., & Ross, R. (1996). *DSM-IV case studies: A clinical guide to differential diagnosis*. Washington, DC: American Psychiatric Press.

Gardner, W., Pajer, K. A., Kelleher, K. J., Scholle, S. H., & Wasserman, R. C. (2002). Child sex differences in primary care clinicians' mental health care of children and adolescents. *Archives of Pediatric and Adolescent Medicine, 156*(5), 454–459 [Electronic version]. Retrieved from http://archpedi.jamanetwork.com/article.aspx?articleid=191797

Gau, S. S. F., Shen, H., Chou, M., Tang, C., Chiu, Y., & Gau, C. (2006). Determinants of adherence to methylphenidate and the impact of poor adherence on maternal and family measures. *Journal of Child and Adolescent Psychopharmacology, 16*(3), 286–297. doi: 10.1089/cap.2006.16.286

Goldman, S. M. (1998). Preface. In G. P. Koocher, J. C. Norcross, & S. Sam (Eds.), *Psychologists' desk reference* (1–2). New York, NY: Oxford University Press.

Gopalan, G., Goldstein, L., Klingenstein, K., Sicher, C., Blake, C., & McKay, M. M. (2010). Engaging families into child mental health treatment: Updates and special considerations. *Journal of the Canadian Academy of Child & Adolescent Psychiatry, 19*(3), 182–196.

Grigorenko, E. L. (2009). *Multicultural psychoeducational assessment*. New York, NY: Springer.

Grills-Taquechel, A., & Ollendick, T. H. (2008). Diagnostic interviewing. In M. Hersen & A. M. Gross (Eds.), *Handbook of clinical psychology: Children and adolescents* (Vol. 2, pp. 458–479). Hoboken, NJ: Wiley.

Henderson, D. A., & Thompson, C. L. (2011). *Counseling children* (8th ed.). Belmont, CA: Brooks/Cole.

Hinshaw, S. P. (2008). Developmental psychopathology as a scientific discipline: Relevance to behavioral and emotional disorders of childhood and adolescence. In T. P. Beauchaine & S. P. Hinshaw (Eds.), *Child and adolescent psychopathology* (pp. 3–26). Hoboken, NJ: Wiley.

Hipwell, A. E., Stepp, S., Feng, Z., Burke, J., Battista, D. R., Loeber, R., & Keenan, K. (2011). Impact of oppositional defiant disorder dimensions on the temporal ordering of conduct problems and depression across childhood and adolescence in girls. *Journal of Child Psychology and Psychiatry*, *52*(10), 1099–1108.

Hudson, J. P. (2014). *A practical guide to congenital developmental disorders and learning disabilities*. New York: Routledge.

Hutchings, J., Bywater, T., Daley, D., Gardner, F., Whitaker, C., Jones, K., . . . Edwards, R. T. (2007). Parenting intervention in sure start services for children at risk of developing conduct disorder: Pragmatic randomized controlled trial. *British Medical Journal*, *334*, 678–682.

Ingoldsby, E. (2010). Review of interventions to improve family engagement and retention in parent and child mental health programs. *Journal of Child & Family Studies*, *19*(5), 629–645. doi: 10.1007/s10826-009-9350-2

Johnson, L., & Tucker, C. (2008). Cultural issues. In M. Hersen & A. M. Gross (Eds.), *Handbook of clinical psychology: Children and adolescents* (Vol. 2, pp. 789–832). Hoboken, NJ: Wiley.

Johnston, J., Roseby, V., & Kuehnle, K. (2009). *In the name of the child: A developmental approach to understanding and helping children of conflicted and violent divorce* (2nd ed.). New York, NY: Springer.

Kearney, C. A., Cook, L. C., Wechsler, A., Haight, C. M., & Stowman, S. (2008). Behavioral assessment. In M. Hersen & A. M. Gross (Eds.), *Handbook of clinical psychology: Children and adolescents* (Vol. 1, pp. 551–574). Hoboken, NJ: Wiley.

Kim-Cohen, J., Arseneault, L., Caspi, A., Taylor, A., Polo-Tomas, M., & Moffitt, T. E. (2005). Validity of *DSM-IV* conduct disorder in 4.5–5 year old children: A longitudinal epidemiological study. *American Journal of Psychiatry*, *162*, 1108–1117.

Landy, S., & Bradley, S. (2014). *Children with multiple mental health challenges: An integrated approach to intervention*. New York, NY: Springer.

LeCroy, C. W., & Okamoto, S. K. (2009). Guidelines for selecting and using assessment tools with children. In A. Roberts (Ed.), *Social workers desk reference* (2nd ed., pp. 381–389). New York, NY: Oxford University Press.

Leon, A. (2010). Latino cultural values in the United States: Understanding their impact on toddler social and emotional development. *International Journal of Interdisciplinary Social Sciences*, *4*(12), 13–25.

Leon, A. M., & Armantrout, E. (2007). Assessing families and other client systems in community-based programmes: Development of the CALF. *Child & Family Social Work*, *12*(2), 123. doi: 10.1111/j.1365-2206.2006.00450.x

Lewinsohn, P. M., Striegel-Moore, R. H., & Seeley, J. R. (2000). Epidemiology and natural course of eating disorders in young women from adolescence to young adulthood. *Journal of the American Academy of Child & Adolescent Psychiatry*, *39*(10), 1284–1292.

Maxmen, J. S., Ward, N. G., & Kilgus, M. (2009). *Essential psychopathology and its treatment* (3rd ed.). New York, NY: Norton.

McMahon, R. J., Wells, K. C., & Kotler, J. S. (2006). Conduct problems. In E. J. Mash & R. A. Barkley (Eds.), *Treatment of childhood disorders* (3rd ed., pp. 137–270). New York, NY: Guilford Press.

Nock, M. K., Kazdin, A. E., Hiripi, E., & Kessler, R. C. (2007). Lifetime prevalence, correlates, and persistence of oppositional defiant disorder: Results from the national comorbidity survey replication. *Journal of Child Psychology and Psychiatry*, *48*(7), 703–713. doi: 10.1111/j.1469-7610.2007.01733.x

Noggle, C. A., & Dean, R. S. (2009). Use and impact of antidepressants in the school setting. *Psychology in the Schools*, *46*(9), 857–868. doi: 10.1002/pits.20426

Pardini, D. A., Frick, P. J., & Moffitt, T. E. (2010). Building an evidence base for *DSM-5* conceptualizations of oppositional defiant disorder and conduct disorder: Introduction to the special section. *Journal of Abnormal Psychology*, *119*(4), 683–688. doi: 10.1037/a0021441

Patchin, J., & Hinduja, S. (2010). Cyberbullying and self-esteem. *Journal of School Health*, *80*(12), 614–621. doi: 10.1111/j.1746-1561.2010.00548.x

Perry, B. D. (2008). Child maltreatment: A neurodevelopmental perspective on the role of trauma and neglect in psychopathology. In T. P. Beauchaine & S. P. Hinshaw (Eds.), *Child and adolescent psychopathology* (pp. 93–128). Hoboken, NJ: Wiley.

Petitclerc, A., Boivin, M., Dionne, G., Zoccolillo, M., & Tremblay, R. E. (2009). Disregard for rules: The early development and predictors of a specific dimension of disruptive behavior disorders. *Journal of Child Psychology and Psychiatry*, *50*(12), 1477–1484. doi: 10.1111/j.1469-7610.2009.02118.x

Polier, G., Vloet, T., Herpertz-Dahlmann, B., Laurens, K., & Hodgins, S. (2012). Comorbidity of conduct disorder symptoms and internalizing problems in children: Investigating a community and a clinical sample. *European Child & Adolescent Psychiatry*, *21*(1), 31–38. doi: 10.1007/s00787-011-0229-6

Pottick, K. J., Kirk, S. A., Hsieh, D. K., & Tian, X. (2007). Judging mental disorder in youths: Effects of client, clinician, and contextual differences. *Journal of Consulting and Clinical Psychology*, *75*(1), 1–8. doi: 10.1037/0022-006X.75.1.1

Prout, H. T. (2007). Counseling and psychotherapy with children and adolescents: Historical developmental, integrative, and effectiveness perspectives. In H. T. Prout & D. T. Brown (Eds.), *Counseling and psychotherapy with children and adolescents: Theory and practice for school and clinical settings* (4th ed., pp. 1–31). Hoboken, NJ: Wiley.

Pumariega, A. J., Rogers, K., & Rothe, E. (2005). Culturally competent systems of care for children's mental health: Advances and challenges. *Community Mental Health Journal*, *41*(5), 539–555.

Rasic, D. (2010). Countertransference in child and adolescent psychiatry—A forgotten concept? *Journal of the Canadian Academy of Child & Adolescent Psychiatry*, *19* (4), 249–254.

Rivett, M., & Street, E. (2009). *Family therapy: 100 key points and techniques*. New York, NY: Routledge.

Roemmelt, A. F. (1998). *Haunted children: Rethinking medication of common psychological disorders*. Albany: State University of New York Press.

Romano, E., Zoccolillo, M., & Paquette, D. (2006). Histories of child maltreatment and psychiatric disorder in pregnant adolescents. *Journal of the American Academy of Child and Adolescent Psychiatry*, *45*(3), 329–336.

Saxe, G. N., Ellis, B. H., & Kaplow, J. B. (2007). *Collaborative treatment of traumatized children and teens: The trauma systems therapy approach*. New York, NY: Guilford Press.

Schoenwald, S. K., Kelleher, K., & Weisz, J. R. (2008). Building bridges to evidence-based practice: The MacArthur Foundation child system and treatment enhancement projects (Child STEPs). *Administration and Policy in Mental Health and Mental Health Service Research*, *35*(1–2), 66–72.

Schore, A. N. (2014). Introduction. In J. J. Magnavita & J. C. Anchin (Eds.), *Unifying psychotherapy: Principles, methods, evidence from clinical science* (pp. xxi–xliv). New York, NY: Springer.

Schur, S. B., Sikich, L., Findling, R. L., Malone, R. P., Crismon, M. L., Derivan, A., . . . Jensen, P. S. (2003). Treatment recommendations for the use of antipsychotics for aggressive youth (TRAAY). Part I: A review. *Journal of the American Academy of Child & Adolescent Psychiatry*, *42*(2), 132–144.

Schwebel, D., & Gaines, J. (2007). Pediatric unintentional injury: Behavioral risk factors and implications for prevention. *Journal of Developmental and Behavioral Pediatrics*, *38*(3), 245–254.

Shapiro, J. P., Friedberg, R. D., & Bardenstein, K. K. (2006). *Child and adolescent therapy: Science and art*. Hoboken, NJ: Wiley.

Shaw, D. S., Gilliom, M., Ingoldsby, E. M., & Nagin, D. S. (2003). Trajectories leading to school-age conduct problems. *Developmental Psychology*, *39*(2), 189–200. doi: 10.1037/0012-1649.39.2.189

Shear, K., Belnap, B. H., Mazumdar, S., Houck, P., & Rollman, B. L. (2006). Generalized anxiety disorder severity scale (GADSS): A preliminary validation study. *Depression and Anxiety*, *23*(2), 77–82.

Skovgaard, A. M., Houmann, T., Christiansen, E., Landorph, T., Jorgensen, T., CCC 2000 Study Team, . . . Lichtenberg, A. (2007). The prevalence of mental health problems in children $1^1/_2$ years of age—The Copenhagen child cohort 2000. *Journal of Child Psychology and Psychiatry, and Allied Disciplines*, *48*(1), 62–70.

Spetie, L., & Arnold, L. E. (2007). Ethical issues in child psychopharmacology research and practice: Emphasis on preschoolers. *Psychopharmacology*, *191*(1), 15–26.

Sydow, K., Retzlaff, R., Beher, S., Haun, M. W., & Schweitzer, J. (2013). The efficacy of systemic therapy for childhood and adolescent externalizing disorders: A systematic review of 47 RCT. *Family Process*, *52*(4), 576–618. doi: 10.1111/famp.12047

Thomas, C. P., Conrad, P., Casler, R., & Goodman, E. (2006). Trends in the use of psychotropic medications among adolescents, 1994 to 2001. *Psychiatric Services*, *57*(1), 63–69. doi: 10.1176/appi.ps.57.1.63

Tremblay, R. E., Nagin, D. S., Séguin, J. R., Zoccolillo, M., Zelazo, P. D., Boivin, M., . . . Japel, C. (2004). Physical aggression during early childhood: Trajectories and predictors. *Pediatrics*, *114*(1), e43–e50. doi: 10.1542/peds.114.1.e43

Walkup, J., Bernet, W., Bukstein, O., Walter, H., Arnold, V., Benson, R. S., . . . Stock, S. (2009). Practice parameter on the use of psychotropic medication in children and adolescents. *Journal of the American Academy of Child & Adolescent Psychiatry*, *48*(9), 961–973.

Wekerle, C., MacMillan, H. L., Leung, E., & Jamieson, E. (2008). Child maltreatment. In M. Hersen & A. M. Gross (Eds.), *Handbook of clinical psychology: Children and adolescents* (Vol. *2*, pp. 856–903). Hoboken, NJ: Wiley.

Wickramaratne, P. J., Greenwald, S., & Weissman, M. M. (2000). Psychiatric disorders in the relatives of probands with prepubertal-onset or adolescent-onset major depression. *Journal of the American Academy of Child & Adolescent Psychiatry, 39*(11), 1396–1405.

Wodarski, J., & Dziegielewski, S. F. (2002). *Human growth and development: Integrating theory and empirical practice.* New York, NY: Springer.

Woo, S. M., & Keatinge, C. (Eds.). (2008). *Diagnosis and treatment of mental disorders across the lifetime.* Hoboken, NJ: Wiley.

Woolston, J. L. (1999). Combined psychopharmacotherapy: Pitfalls of treatment. *Journal of the American Academy of Child and Adolescent Psychiatry, 38*(11), 1455.

Zielinski, D. S., & Bradshaw, C. P. (2006). Ecological influences on the sequelae of child maltreatment: A review of the literature. *Child Maltreatment, 11*(1), 49–62.

CHAPTER 12

Substance-Related and Addictive Disorders

SOPHIA F. DZIEGIELEWSKI

The psychological, sociological, and economic consequences of the substance-related disorders (SUD) and the addictive disorders (AD) on our society are overwhelming. To complicate this further, individuals suffering from these disorders often experience health and mental health problems, such as feelings of depression and anxiety. These symptoms can become so severe that individuals may become unable to perform necessary activities of daily living (ADLs), like eating and sleeping. These effects can devastate the individual and the entire family system (Lander, Howsare, & Bryne, 2013). The individual suffering from the disorder and the circumstances that surround the disorder can lead to unmet developmental needs. The large number of substances available and the resulting effects can often lead to symptom clusters that make it difficult to diagnose when compared to other mental disorders such as schizophrenia spectrum and psychotic disorders, depressive disorders, bipolar disorders and the anxiety disorders (Avery, 2014). The resulting economic consequences and hardships can have far-reaching consequences. Furthermore, their children can be at increased risk of developing the same disorder (Zimic & Jakie, 2012).

From a sociological perspective, the development of an addictive disorder can lead to loss of productivity or employment for some people, and for others it can lead to increased criminal activity and possible incarceration. From an economic perspective, the costs to society of drug abuse and dependence are great, especially the use of expensive medical resources and (inappropriate) admissions to correctional facilities related to substance-seeking and abusing behaviors. Mental health and addictive disorders are some of the most serious health problems facing the United States today.

This chapter describes the *DSM-5* diagnostic criteria for the taxonomical classification of substance-related and addictive disorders (American Psychiatric Association [APA], 2013). In *DSM-5*, these disorders are termed alcohol-related disorders, caffeine-related disorders, cannabis-related disorders, hallucinogen-related disorders, inhalant-related disorders, opioid-related disorders, sedative-hypnotic- or anxiolytic-related disorders, stimulant-related disorders, tobacco-related disorders, other (or unknown) substance-related disorders, and the non-substance-related disorder, gambling disorder. Although this chapter presents a brief overview of this spectrum of disorders, the diagnosis and treatment of alcohol use disorder is the central focus. The application section of this chapter provides a case example related to an individual suffering from SUD with specific recommendations for completing the diagnostic assessment and the subsequent treatment plan. The extent, importance, and early predictors of problem behaviors and symptoms are explored. The various aspects of the disorder are presented with a case application that

Special thanks to Carmen P. Chang-Arratia for her contributions to the previous version of this chapter.

highlights the diagnostic assessment, treatment planning, and evidence-based treatment strategy. The latest practice methods and newest research and findings are noted to extend the understanding of these often-devastating substance- and addiction-related illnesses.

TOWARD A BASIC UNDERSTANDING OF THE SUBSTANCE-RELATED AND ADDICTIVE DISORDERS

As a public health concern, the misuse of alcohol and other drugs (AOD) poses a serious peril in the form of social, economic, and human welfare costs. The impact and costs to the individual, relationships, community, and society make focusing on this area central for research, intervention, and prevention efforts. The harmful effects of alcohol alone produce 2.5 million deaths each year, according to the World Health Organization (WHO) (2014a). Furthermore, an estimated 15.3 million people worldwide meet the criteria for a disorder related to its usage. In addition, of the number of people with reported drug use disorders, 120 out of 148 countries report concurrent HIV infection secondary to injection drug usage. As for psychoactive substance use across the world, there are an estimated 185 million illicit drug users, and alcohol users alone on top of these numbers are another 2 billion (WHO, 2014b). These estimates may be considered a conservative estimate; substance misuse typically involves more than one substance. These numbers also may be under-reported, as they may not take into account excessive use of dependence-producing prescribed drugs. Yet, only a small fraction of individuals actually seek treatment, and for those who do, the threat of relapse remains strong. For this very reason, the National Institute of Drug Abuse (NIDA) is continually seeking ways to foster collaborative research projects with translational effects that will benefit all disciplines (Michel, Pintello, & Subramaniam, 2013).

In the United States, approximately 8 million people meet the diagnostic criteria for alcohol dependence, with approximately 700,000 in treatment at any given time (Evans, Levin, Brooks, & Garawi, 2007). Determinants of alcohol use, such as demographics and socioeconomic factors, policies, education, and living standards, can affect the frequency of alcohol consumption and influence the type of beverage consumed (Poznyak, Saraceno, & Obot, 2005). These same venues and factors apply to illicit and psychoactive substance use. In developed countries with high mortality rates, the rate of illicit and psychoactive drug use is high. Accounting for earlier loss of life, illicit drug use affects mortality rates before the age of 60. Again, this may be underestimated because it may not address other associated risk factors, such as disease, injuries, and violence (WHO, 2014b). There is limited information overall on the prevalence of illicit drug and alcohol use, but from 2006 to 2007 concurrent use was reported at 5.6%, which is equivalent to 7.1 million people between the ages of 12 and 25 (Substance Abuse and Mental Health Services Administration [SAMHSA], 2009a). In 2000, as in 2008, deaths attributable to psychoactive use remained high in males, with 80% for illicit drug use to 90% for alcohol use worldwide, and in women the numbers also remained significant, with estimates ranging from 9.9% to 6.3% (SAMHSA, 2009a, 2009b; Schulte, Ramo, & Brown, 2009; WHO, 2009b). Furthermore, for psychotherapeutic drug use, similar rates of use are evident between the sexes (2.6% for females and 2.4% for males), which is causing significant alarm as it is indicative of the development of a new trend in disorders (SAMHSA, 2009c).

Findings from the 2008 National Survey of Drug Use and Health estimated that 20.1 million people age 12 and older were illicit drug users at the time of the survey. Of the substances recorded, marijuana use attained the highest prevalence (15.2 million users), followed by psychotherapeutic drugs (6.2 million), cocaine (1.9 million), and hallucinogens (1.1 million). Consumption trends in countries with excessive availability and inadequate regulation of drugs show patterns of increased drug abuse. Other substances of concern for use and dependence include the benzodiazepines and other anxiolytics acquired through prescriptions, illegal street vendors, and the Internet. Legally approved and prescribed medications are being used for nonmedical recreational use. In full-time college students age 18 to 23, Adderall, a prescribed medication for the treatment of attention-deficit hyperactivity disorder and a stimulant, is a concern. The addictive nature of Adderall when combined with alcohol and other drugs can lead to adverse health and safety consequences (SAMHSA, 2009c).

The prevalence of these conditions, intermingled with the medical and mental health aspects, makes service delivery via a collaborative team approach essential (Daley & Feit, 2013). Medically trained and nonmedically trained practitioners alike must work collaboratively, as each has an important skill set to contribute. For the nonmedically trained, lack of awareness of medical factors in assessment, especially when there is potential for withdrawal, can lead to serious consequences. For the medically trained, lack of awareness of interpersonal, social, and family factors can also have devastating effects on the individual and his or her family system, when these factors are ignored. Also, when clients return to a familiar environment with similar cues related to the triggers of SUD or AD, regardless of how good the treatment was, relapse can become imminent.

UNDERSTANDING THE INDIVIDUALS WHO SUFFER FROM THE SUBSTANCE DISORDERS

People with substance-related problems are found in all social classes and cultures, from different demographic backgrounds (e.g., genders, ages, and religious perspectives), in various systems (individuals, couples, families, and groups), and in a variety of settings. Earlier theorists related alcohol use problems with morality, failed duty to self, lack of personal self-control, and lack of will. In the past, an inability to attain role functioning due to substance use was assumed to be not just a sign of a sick person; the individual with substance use problems was thought to benefit from the sick person role. These perspectives began to change in the 1960s, as individuals suffering from alcohol-related disorders started to be viewed as medically ill rather than weak or immoral (Jones, 1969). The realization that substance-induced alterations in the brain could be measured by neuroimaging technologies with certain defining characteristic changes further dispelled the myth that it was an individual, self-controlled behavioral failure (Chung, Ross, Wakhlu, & Adinoff, 2012).

For the substance disorders listed in *DSM-5*, the problems associated with chronic care have been brought to the forefront. Tai and Volkow (2013) believe the Affordable Care Act (ACA) of 2010 can be helpful in addressing the needs of those with SUDs in a multitude of ways. The types of conditions being treated and the medications used can easily bring about symptoms that mimic tolerance and withdrawal, and even when under a prescriber's care may lead to what will be negatively termed addiction. The fear of addiction and concerns about being labeled as suffering from a mental disorder may cause individuals to either not take their medicine or do so in ways that cannot be traced. This second way could easily lead to illegal behavior in trying to supplement a treatment regimen that has grown in desire and intensity.

What has remained consistent over time is that the motivational aspects, personality, traits, and characteristics of individuals who suffer from the SUDs and AD share similarities, especially regarding interpersonal factors related to use. Similarities include feelings of incompleteness, imperfection, and emptiness. Often the individual becomes desperate to find a sense of wholeness and completion. This sense of completion may rest in finding and holding on to an external source, such as a person or an object. Guilt and shame become prominent emotions. To increase coping, a variety of defense mechanisms can be used to control anxiety. Because of the instability and different interpretations of the defense mechanisms, however, these terms have been dropped and are no longer listed in the appendix of the *DSM*.

In summary, the reason for the motivation or the magnetic quality it has for some remains for the most part a combination of factors, if not a simple highjacking of the reward system (Rose & Walters, 2012). What does appear consistent is that current research highlights a strong relationship between personality traits and risk-taking behaviors (Schulte et al., 2009). Furthermore, personality and how temperament relates to problem use may be clinically useful in determining the type of treatment modality (individual, group, or self-help) for those with substance-related problems. In treatment, personality characteristics often remain consistent, but behavioral patterns can change and vary with time (Schulte et al., 2009).

Important Features Related to the Substance-Related Disorders

When preparing for the diagnostic assessment and placing the appropriate diagnosis, the practitioner must first be aware of the key features prevalent in the substance-induced and addictive disorders. Creating the diagnostic impression and the treatment plan to follow always requires a delicate balance of groundbreaking research and the practitioner's judgment and experience (Schore, 2014). Starting this process requires familiarity with information supportive of the diagnosis.

Addiction

In the *DSM-5*, there is no qualifier in the nomenclature for addiction, and the word *addiction* is not part of the classification system. Instead, substance use disorder is now utilized to display the range of the behaviors within the disorder that result in chronic relapsing and compulsive use, regardless of whether it is mild, moderate, or severe. From this perspective, not using the term *addiction* serves to limit the diagnostic confusion between the specifiers in relation to certain substances (Potenza, 2006). The fear was that, if included, the term *addiction* could also include nonsubstance behaviors and disorders (e.g., pathological gambling, obesity). Currently, these nonsubstance behaviors are addressed categorically or separately or are simply not addressed within the *DSM*. Proponents of the replacement of the terminology of addiction stated using this term may unintentionally increase rather than decrease the stigma often associated with the term *addiction* (Nunes & Rounsaville, 2006; Potenza, 2006). In *DSM-5*, due to negative connotations and subjective interpretations to established meanings, the term was not included in the criteria outlined for the substance disorders. The term, however, is still widely used across the disciplines and in practice.

Chronic Conditions and Chronic Pain

For the most part, *DSM-5* is careful to avoid the label *dependence* when compulsive, out-of-control drug use is problematic. There is particular interest in avoiding the potential label of *addict* for those who suffer from chronic pain and are medicated as prescribed, when they experience normal tolerance and withdrawal symptoms. The assumption is that the fear of producing addiction has resulted in withholding adequate doses of opioids for severe pain. People simply are afraid to take them because of the fear of addiction. Therefore, *DSM-5* starts to categorically draw a distinction between what is medically prescribed as part of pain management and what is not. In cases where it is medically prescribed, the presence of tolerance and withdrawal symptoms are not counted for the diagnosis of substance use disorder. To substantiate this, however, the context of appropriate medical treatment with prescribed medications needs to be clearly documented. This increase in the necessity to treat chronic pain most probably provided the foundation for the many changes in this chapter. These modifications also assist with highlighting the addictive nature of substances such as Adderall when combined with alcohol and other drugs and how it can lead to serious adverse health and safety consequences (SAMHSA, 2009c).

Comorbidity

Taking comorbidity into account helps to avoid some of the chronic and debilitating diseases that could result. Comparatively, using prescribed medications for nonmedical and recreational purposes continues to rise. When this illegal usage is coupled with the increased need for such medications by individuals who suffer from chronic conditions, problematic patterns of use and misuse can arise. These differentiations allow for the phenomenological analysis of co-occurrence and comorbidity. Listing and assessing diagnoses, whether mental or medical, can facilitate a comprehensive diagnostic assessment. Because many individuals may meet the criteria for using more than one substance, when present, a second or third diagnosis should be listed accordingly. Making the differential diagnosis and adding other disorders when the criteria are met can help to determine which should be considered primary or independent considerations. This is particularly helpful because it provides clinicians with a tool for making the distinction of whether a mental disorder or a substance-induced disorder precedes in the diagnosis of the presenting condition, its subsequent prognosis, and the type of treatment needed. Care should always be noted not to jump to quickly to assume that the symptoms being exhibited are all substance-related or casued by the substance as the comorbidity of other mental health disorders should be examined carefully before any conclusions are reached (Levounis, 2014).

Drug Testing: Tolerance and Withdrawal

Tolerance is the continued use with an increased amount of consumption of the same substance to achieve prior desired effects. Tolerance can vary among individuals and the substances used. (See Quick Reference 12.1.)

Withdrawal is the physiological, cognitive, and subsequent maladaptive behavioral responses to a decline in amount and consumption of the substance of abuse. Stated simply, in withdrawal, the concentration of the substance in the individual's blood and tissue declines after prolonged heavy use of a substance; this requires taking more of the substance to get the same response.

For gathering a history to determine tolerance and the possibility of withdrawal, verbal history is not adequate; it should always be supported with blood tests and other measures such as laboratory tests. When there are high levels of a substance coupled with little evidence of intoxication, tolerance is likely to be high. There is variability among the several types of laboratory tests that can be used to check for medications. Regardless of the test used, a drug test looks for traces of chemically related substances in the system. Depending on the test and the unique circumstances of the person taking it, the benefits can differ. Drug tests can help to determine what drugs or substances were used,

QUICK REFERENCE 12.1

DSM-5—CLARIFYING IMPORTANT TERMS

Tolerance

- Uses increasingly higher amounts of the drug over time to achieve the same effect.
- Finds that the same amount of the drug has much less effect over time than before.
- After using several different drugs regularly, an individual may find that he or she needs to use at least 50% more of the amount to get the same effect.

Interference with Daily Activities: Related to drug use, there is a reduction in the amount of time spent in recreational activities, social activities, or occupational activities. The individual focuses on using drugs instead of engaging in hobbies, spending time with friends, or going to work.

Inability to Stop Using: Unsuccessfully attempted to cut down or stop using the drugs or persistent desire to stop using. Despite efforts to stop using drugs on weekdays, he or she is unable to do so.

Source: Summarized definitions from the *Diagnostic and Statistical Manual of Mental Disorders*, Fifth Edition, by the American Psychiatric Association, 2013, Arlington, VA: American Psychiatric Publishing. Copyright 2013 by the American Psychiatric Association.

how often, and in some cases the mode of administration (e.g., drunk, smoked, or injected). Most tests start with a positive or negative value. A positive result means that the substance or substances were found in the system. Often, when a positive result is obtained, further testing is initiated to examine the substance or other substances in the system. A negative means that the substance was not found in the system. In a false positive, the individual tested positive and was not taking the drug or, most likely, the test was not sensitive enough to sort out one drug from another and so a positive test resulted.

According to the National Institute of Drug Abuse (NIDA; 2011), the most commonly abused drugs in the United States fall into 10 categories: tobacco, alcohol, cannabinoids, opioids, stimulants, club drugs (MDMA, GHB, flunitrazepam [Rohypnol, forget me pill], dissociative drugs [ketamine, PCP], hallucinogens, other compounds (anabolic steroids, inhalants), and prescription medications (depressants, stimulants). Most drug tests look for the following substances: cannabinoids (marijuana and hashish), cocaine (cocaine, benzoylecognine, cocaethylene) and amphetamines (amphetamine and methamphetamine), opiates (heroin, opium, codeine, and morphine), and in rare cases phencyclidine (PCP). In more comprehensive tests, prescription drugs such as oxycodone, hydrocodone, Valium, Xanax, Klonopin, and Restoril; MDMA (ecstasy); GHB; and other barbiturates may be included. It is possible that testing for hallucinogens may be conducted (mushrooms [psilocybin], LSD, and peyote [mescaline]), but testing for these substances would not be done unless specifically indicated.

There are various types of drug tests. For example, when alcohol is suspected, generally a breath test is used. When using a Breathalyzer, the individual blows into the tube and the alcohol content shows up in a digital display.

For alcohol, this test is said to be equally as good as a urine or blood test and not nearly as invasive. Although blood alcohol levels for men and women differ and the number of drinks is often related to how much a person weighs, estimates for when driving skills are significantly affected start at 0.03 for a 140-pound male and the same for a 140-pound female; legally intoxicated for the same weight starts at 0.16 for males and 0.19 in females; with death possible at the same weight with levels of 0.27 in males and 0.32 in females. For a helpful chart that provides specific levels by weight and gender for the BAC, see Be Responsible About Drinking (http://www.brad21.org/bac_charts.html).

A blood test can be used to detect substances that cannot be detected in other ways. Since this test requires drawing the blood through an arm vein or a finger prick for later analysis in a lab, it is most often used in an inpatient setting. In terms of metabolism in drug testing, most of the substances leave the system in approximately 3 days. Therefore, when a drug is suspected, a drug test is generally done as quickly as possible to reveal the most helpful results. Cost may also be a deterrent for using this type of test, which can cost upwards of $100 to administer and process.

Hair tests can determine drug use for longer than the other standardized tests and can measure patterns of use for some substances over weeks and up to 3 months. They are rarely used, however, because of the expense, which, depending on the facility, can cost upwards of $150.

Oral fluid or saliva tests are gaining popularity in countries other than the United States because the test is simple to administer. The individual is asked to put an absorbent collector in the mouth and allow it to absorb saliva. Although easily administered in the workplace and other areas, like blood tests and hair tests, it has to be sent to a laboratory for analysis. It can be particularly helpful in detecting marijuana (cannabis), where the oral fluid test can be used to detect the THC (the active part of cannabis), and certain stimulants such as methamphetamine, amphetamine, MDS, and ecstasy.

The most common form of testing is a urine drug screen. A clean catch (not contaminated by other bodily excretions) is gathered in a cup and tested with a dipstick or sent to a lab. If the urine tests positive on a basic test, it can be further analyzed for the actual substances present. Cost for this test generally starts at $10 to $50.

Clients are often worried and unclear about what tests can be conducted, what the tests will reveal, and in some cases what can they do to trick it. Not much can be done to trick the tests, unless the drug is metabolized through the system or the test is not sensitive to the drug being taken. Also, metabolism and the way a drug is broken down in the system can vary. This is further complicated when the individual is taking more than one drug; then the body takes longer to metabolize and break down the drug to carry traces of the chemical substance away from the system.

Also, some drugs stay in the system longer than others. For example, THC, the active ingredient in cannabis, stays in the system longer than most drugs. Depending on the source, with repeated use, the substance can stay in the system up to 6 weeks. The reason for this prolonged stay is related to the type of substance and how the active ingredients are stored in the body. For example, the first time an individual smokes marijuana, the substance is metabolized in a couple of hours. The more it is smoked, however, the more the THC substance accumulates in the body's fat cells. This storage makes it harder to break down in the system and results in testing positive for the drug long after any effects of the substance are negligible to the user. In addition, taking more than one drug causes the drugs to take longer to be metabolized, again creating a positive test beyond any effects related to the drug itself.

Assessment of Symptoms Measurements

Measurements that can be used to assist in the assessments include the Alcohol Use Disorders Identification Test (AUDIT), Drug Abuse Screening Test (DAST), Alcohol, Smoking, and Substance Involvement Screening Test (ASSIST), and Cut-Down, Annoyed, Guilt, Eye-Opener (CAGE) (with the inclusion of drugs [CAGE-AID]). These self-report measures (with ASSIST as an interviewer-based measure) can be useful in research and practice to acquire information regarding the level of substance-related dependence or abuse. These instruments take from 15 minutes to an hour to administer. Currently, AUDIT and DAST are primarily utilized for assessment and physician billing for extended or brief interventions for substance abuse. Their popularity has increased since the Wellstone-Domenici Mental Health and Addictions Equity Parity Act of 2008 and the introduction of corresponding new current procedural terminology (CPT) codes. The AUDIT's primary function is to assess problems that can occur from alcohol use; it can be used in conjunction with other measurements. It is available in all major languages and has information supporting its reliability and validity with various populations and cultural groups. It is used widely throughout the world in health screenings and primary brief intervention programs (Foxcroft, Kypri, & Simonite, 2009; Humeniuk et al., 2008; Parker, Marshall, & Ball, 2008). There are 10 Likert-based questions, with a score range of 0 to 40 (two supplemental questions are included but not scored), and a threshold score of 8 or more demonstrates risk for alcohol problems. Each measurement's subscales rate alcohol-related consumption, dependence, and alcohol-related problems requiring further inquiry. The AUDIT is considered superior to other self-report measures such as the CAGE in detecting hazardous and harmful drinking (Parker et al., 2008).

Often used in conjunction with the AUDIT, the DAST measures illicit and psychoactive use, particularly in the general assessment of medical, social, and behavioral events attributed to use (Newcombe, Humeniuk, & Ali, 2005). The DAST is a 28-item, yes-no, nominal-base questionnaire, with a score range of 1 to 28, and a score of 6 or more indicates a substance abuse or dependence problem. A shortened version of the DAST, the DAST-10, is also available for the assessment and measurement of abuse or dependence on illicit and psychoactive drugs.

Because of the success of these measurements, particularly the AUDIT, for health screening and brief intervention programs, the ASSIST was developed to identify people with moderate and severe substance use problems, and any resulting hazardous and risky behaviors. It has also been used to determine appropriate treatment levels secondary to risk (Humeniuk et al., 2008). The ASSIST is an interview-administered measurement of eight Likert-based questions, with scores ranging from 0 to 40. It covers 10 substance areas (tobacco, alcohol, cannabis, cocaine, amphetamine-type stimulants, inhalants, sedatives, hallucinogens, opioids, and other drugs) and assesses frequency of use and associated problems. Each substance is scored separately, with a threshold score for alcohol at 11 to 26 for moderate risk and 4 to 26 for illicit and psychoactive substances. The ASSIST also includes questions about injectable drug use.

The CAGE has been used to briefly assess alcohol dependence concerns, with the introduction of the CAGE-AID to assess illicit and psychoactive drug use. The CAGE scale, however, does not focus on detecting risk or problematic drug use in nondependent people (Newcombe et al., 2005).

When these and other measurements are used in conjunction with the biopsychosocial assessment, they can provide a useful

QUICK REFERENCE 12.2

***DSM-5*—General Categories for the Substance-Related Disorders**

Substance-related disorders (substance use disorders and substance-induced disorders)

Alcohol-related disorders

Caffeine-related disorders

Cannabis-related disorders

Hallucinogen-related disorders

Inhalant-related disorders

Opioid-related disorders

Sedative-hypnotic- or anxiolytic-related disorders

Stimulant-related disorders

Tobacco-related disorders

Other (or unknown) substance-related disorders

Non-substance-related disorders (gambling disorder)

self-reported baseline analysis to address and supplement findings of SUDs.

OVERVIEW OF THE SUBSTANCE-RELATED AND ADDICTIVE DISORDERS

The *DSM-5* provides the standardized classification system for psychiatric disorders across the United States. Using the criteria for the mental disorders as outlined in the *DSM-5* allows standardization across disorders and quick, harmonized, and effective determinations of individual psychopathology (Schmidt, Norr, & Korte, 2014). To better understand *DSM-5* and the diagnostic criteria for the substance-related disorders and addictive disorders, those familiar with the *DSM-IV* and the *DSM-IV-TR* will notice the chapter starts with a change of title (APA, 1994, 2000). The previous title of the chapter included only the substance-related disorders and was titled as such. In *DSM-5*, this chapter has been rearranged and expanded, representative of the new title. (See Quick Reference 12.2.)

Non-Substance-Related Disorders: Gambling Disorder

The reason for adding the addictive disorders to the title of this chapter in the *DSM-5* was to include gambling disorder (GD). Previously, GD was listed under the impulse-control disorders. It was moved to this category based on growing evidence that gambling behaviors can activate the brain reward system similar to the most common drugs of abuse. The criteria for the disorder (A to B) state that there must be impairment or clinically significant distress related to four prominent symptoms displayed over a 12-month period. If an individual has four or five of the nine symptoms, the condition is considered mild; six or seven symptoms are considered moderate; and eight or nine symptoms are considered severe.

The symptoms that surround GD behavior outline the need to gamble that results in extreme consequences. The nine indicators start with the need to gamble with increasing amounts of money to get the desired level of excitement (indicator 1). Restlessness and irritability occur if there is an effort to respond to pressure and cut back or stop gambling (indicator 2). The individual cannot stop the gambling behaviors, and attempts at doing so have been unsuccessful and resulted in failure (indicator 3). There is often a preoccupation where previous behaviors are constantly reanalyzed and the individual focuses on trying to make money with multiple and risky ventures in the hopes it will lead to success in the future (indicator 4). Gambling behaviors help to reduce distress and anxiety, making them difficult to resist (indicator 5). With gambling activities, there is also a pattern of repeated attempts to win even after multiple losses, sometimes referred to as chasing one's losses or getting even. There is often a pattern of pervasive lying to cover up the behaviors until others are needed to help regroup from the desperate financial constraints the disorder has caused (indicators 6 and 7). The strains this behavior places on significant others, family, friends, and employment have resulted in many losses outside the gambling behaviors (indicator 8). This behavior cannot be explained as part of another disorder such as a manic episode and must clinically cause impairment in functioning (indicator 9). It can be classified as either episodic or persistent, establishing a pattern that can last from several months to several years. For the most part, the individual is so preoccupied with the gambling behavior that no risk is too great, and the psychological, social, occupational, and economic consequences are far-reaching.

What some may find unusual about this section of the chapter on the substance-related and addictive disorders is that there is only one addictive disorder in the chapter, yet the title refers to the plural addictive disorders. This is most likely related to the expected inclusion of a second disorder for this section. Although not included in the chapter, Internet gaming is included in Section III, areas for further study. It has similar possible effects to the brain as gambling disorder. This potential disorder involves persistent and recurrent use of the Internet to engage in games, and the resulting impairment has a significant impact on occupational and social functioning.

Substance-Related Disorders

The SUDs are the taxonomical category for disorders that addresses substances (e.g., medications, drugs of abuse, or toxins) and the effects these substances can have on the system. In the *DSM-5*, similar to *DSM-IV-TR*, this category is applied with classifications related to several classes of substances. A change is that *DSM-IV* and *DSM-IV-TR* had 11 classes of substances, and *DSM-5* has only 10. Some of the substances were combined into one area. For example, the area previously referred to as amphetamines is now changed to stimulants and includes amphetamine-type substances, cocaine, and other unspecified stimulants.

In *DSM-5*, the 10 classes of drugs that share similar features are alcohol, caffeine, cannabis, hallucinogens, inhalants, opioids, sedatives, stimulants, tobacco, and other (or unknown) substances. (See Quick Reference 12.3.)

Furthermore, this category is broken down into two sections: the substance use disorders (SUDs) and the substance-induced disorders (SIDs). The primary feature that characterizes the SUDs is a cluster of cognitive, behavioral, and physiological symptoms, and regardless of the negative consequences experienced, the individual continues using the substance. In the SIDs, the key feature that links the disorders is the development of a reversible substance-specific syndrome related to the ingestion of a

QUICK REFERENCE 12.3

COMPARISON OF SUBSTANCE-RELATED DISORDERS BETWEEN *DSM-5* AND *DSM-IV/DSM-IV-TR*

***DSM-5*: 10 Substances**

Alcohol	Caffeine	Cannabis
Hallucinogens	Inhalants	Opioids
Sedatives	Stimulants	Tobacco
Other (or unknown) substances		

***DSM-IV/DSM-IV-TR*: 11 Substances**

Alcohol	Sedatives	Nicotine
Caffeine	Anxiolytics	Phencyclidine (PCP)
Inhalants	Amphetamines	Hypnotics
Opioids	Hallucinogens	

substance. Regardless of whether the disorder is classified as a SUD or a SID, when the substance is known, it should be coded appropriately. For example, if it is a stimulant disorder and the stimulant being misused is amphetamines, it should be labeled amphetamine-type substance (305.70); if the substance is cocaine, it is also labeled as a stimulant use disorder, but it is further specified as and labeled cocaine with the appropriate ICD code such as 305.60 for *ICD-9-CM* or F15.10 in *ICD-10-CM*.

A comprehensive assessment of all substance-related disorders requires confirmatory information related to the substance and checking by laboratory findings, urinalysis, and history to indicate the presence, use, severity, and tolerance of the substance. For the specifications set in *DSM-5*, a thorough assessment includes the client's background information, demographics (context and situation, cultural variations toward substance consumptions, age, gender), route of administration of substance, substance of choice, onset and duration of use, associated and differential medical and/or mental health conditions, impairments to global functioning and health, family patterns of use, and exposure and utilization of medications and toxins.

Substance Use Disorders

The substance use disorders (SUDs) can be applied to all 10 substances except caffeine. Caffeine use disorder, however, was included in Section III, under conditions for further study. When conditions are included in the area of further study, there is sufficient evidence to warrant its inclusion, but more research is needed before it is made a formal diagnosis. Diagnoses are placed in this category to request further research to determine appropriate thresholds. Although this diagnosis is listed in *ICD-10*, concerns are noted that the thresholds should be higher, based on the high rate of habitual, daily, and reportedly nonproblematic use of the substance.

In *DSM-5*, this chapter had major revisions from the previous version, and categories were modified to combine substance abuse and substance dependence into one category called substance use. Although some of the criteria remain the same, this new combined category is quite different from what was before. In the substance-related section of the chapter, the diagnoses are now substance use disorder, accompanied by the criteria for intoxication, withdrawal, substance-induced disorders, and unspecified related disorders (APA, 2013).

Of particular note is the new category, substance use. To diagnose this disorder, 11 criteria must be examined and documented for occurrence. Similar to *DSM-IV-TR*, this category provides the taxonomical category for disorders addressing a substance (e.g., medications, drugs of abuse, or toxins) comprising the side effects, taking of a substance, and the effects and exposures to toxins (APA, 2000). This definition now includes and is applied to all the substance areas except caffeine, as these areas—alcohol-related, cannabis-related, hallucinogen-related, inhalant-related, opioid-related, sedative-hypnotic- or anxiolytic-related disorders, stimulant-related (e.g., amphetamines and cocaine), tobacco-related, other (or unknown) substance-related disorders, and the non-substance-related disorders—all share similar features. (See Quick References 12.4 and 12.5.) An important point to remember regarding criteria 11 and 12 (the pharmacological criteria) is that tolerance and withdrawal symptoms are not counted as symptoms for the diagnosis of substance use disorder when they occur in the context of appropriate medical treatment with prescribed medications.

Substance use disorder is identified as a maladaptive pattern of substance use leading to clinically significant impairment or distress, as manifested by 2 (or more) of the 11 specifiers. These symptoms must occur within a 12-month period. The 11 included for criterion A are grouped in four areas: impaired control (numbers 1–4), social impairment (numbers 5–7), risky use (numbers 8–9), and pharmacological criteria (10–11). (See Quick Reference 12.6.) The substance use must constitute a maladaptive pattern of consumption leading to clinically significant impairment or distress, as manifested in two or more of the areas, occurring within a 12-month period (APA, 2013).

In completing the diagnostic assessment for an individual suffering from a substance use disorder, there are 11 criteria divided into four specific areas that need to be carefully evaluated (APA, 2013). To document impaired control, there are four areas to be examined. The first includes assessing the amount of substance being taken and how long it has been taken. The second is looking at substance usage and

QUICK REFERENCE 12.4

HELPFUL HINTS—*DSM-5*—NEW CATEGORY SUBSTANCE USE DISORDER

- Combines abuse and dependence into one category: substance use disorders.
- This new category has graded clinical severity.
- Eliminates the "legal problems criterion for substance use disorder diagnosis."
- Adds criteria for craving, which is defined as a strong desire for a substance, tending to be present on the severe end of the severity spectrum.
- Includes all 10 substances, *except* caffeine.

QUICK REFERENCE 12.5

Substance Use Disorders and Specifiers

Substance	Substance Use
Alcohol	X Use 2–11 criteria ***Specify* if:** In early remission; in sustained remission; in controlled environment **Course severity:** Mild (2–3 symptoms); moderate (4–5 symptoms); severe (6 or more)
	NA
Cannabis	X Use 2–11 criteria ***Specify* if:** In early remission; in sustained remission; in controlled environment **Course severity:** Mild (2–3 symptoms); moderate (4–5 symptoms); severe (6 or more)
Hallucinogens PCP and other hallucinogen disorder	X Use 2–10 criteria ***Specify* if:** In early remission; in sustained remission; in controlled environment **Course severity:** Mild (2–3 symptoms); moderate (4–5 symptoms); severe (6 or more)
Inhalants	X Use 2–10 criteria ***Specify* if:** In early remission; in sustained remission; in controlled environment **Course severity:** Mild (2–3 symptoms); moderate (4–5 symptoms); severe (6 or more)
Opioids	X Use 2–11 criteria ***Specify* if:** In early remission; in sustained remission; on maintenance therapy; in a controlled environment **Course severity:** Mild (2–3 symptoms); Moderate (4–5 symptoms); Severe (6 or more)
Sedatives, hypnotics, and anxiolytics	X Use 2–11 criteria ***Specify* if:** In early remission; in sustained remission; in a controlled environment **Course severity:** Mild (2–3 symptoms); moderate (4–5 symptoms); severe (6 or more)
Stimulants	X Use 2–11 criteria ***Specify* if:** In early remission; in sustained remission; in a controlled environment **Course severity:** Mild (2–3 symptoms); moderate (4–5 symptoms); severe (6 or more)
Tobacco	X Use 2–11 criteria ***Specify* if:** In early remission; in sustained remission; on maintenance therapy; in a controlled environment

(continued)

QUICK REFERENCE 12.5 (*Continued*)

Substance	Substance Use
	Course severity: Mild (2–3 symptoms); moderate (4–5 symptoms); severe (6 or more)
Other (or unknown)	X Use 2–11 criteria ***Specify* if:** In early remission; in sustained remission; in a controlled environment **Course severity:** Mild (2–3 symptoms); moderate (4–5 symptoms); severe (6 or more)

Source: Table created from summarized information from the *Diagnostic and Statistical Manual of Mental Disorders*, Fifth Edition, by the American Psychiatric Association, 2013, Arlington, VA: American Psychiatric Publishing. Copyright 2013 by the American Psychiatric Association.

documenting any unsuccessful attempts at regulating the behavior, especially attempts to self-regulate and/or discontinue use. The third area involves documenting the time devoted to obtaining the substance, along with the intense desire and preoccupation with getting it, in an attempt to avoid the effects that can come from not having access to the substance. To document severe cases of impaired control, note how the individual is planning his or her daily activities around the substance. There is an intense need for the substance, and the desire to obtain it can override other important activities of living. In cases such as this, relapse is quite common, especially when the individual is exposed to environments where this type of behavior has occurred in the past. Just being in these types of places can trigger an intense desire to again obtain and use the substance (APA, 2013).

QUICK REFERENCE 12.6

DSM-5—*Helpful Hints for the Diagnostic Assessment of Substance Use Disorders*

In the diagnostic assessment, there are four areas to assess: impaired control, social impairment, risky use, and pharmacological criteria.

Each area needs to be examined, and the ways in which the individual meets the criteria need to be identified.

Based on the number of areas involved, the level of severity can be documented. Of the 11 criteria, if two or three are positive, the severity level is mild. If there are four or five, the level is moderate, and if there are six or more, the condition is listed as severe.

Remember, each of the 10 substances listed needs to be addressed individually, especially when addressing a tolerance or withdrawal profile.

Three criteria specifically address the behaviors that are indicative of social impairment. The first involves documentation of recurring events that are relevant to poor performance and not fulfilling major obligations at home or activities outside the home, such as work or school. To document the next criterion in this area, this behavior must occur even though it is clear that this behavior is causing recurrent social and interpersonal problems that can be directly attributed to use of the substance. Finally, the need for the substance is so great that the individual wants to have it, even if it interferes with activities, regardless of whether they are recreational or occupational.

To assess risky use, there are two criteria, and both involve patterns where danger to self or others could occur, such as using the substance when it is physically hazardous or continuing the behavior knowing it is causing physical and/or psychological problems directly related to the substance use.

The last two criteria listed in *DSM-5* for diagnosing a substance use disorder are numbered 11 and 12 and listed as pharmacological criteria. The most important aspect of these two criteria is for the clinician to clearly assess whether medical necessity surrounds the use. The *DSM-5* provides a detailed explanation of tolerance, highlighting the need for increased amounts of the substance and the fact that the effect experienced is diminished, even when the same usage dose and pattern is performed (APA, 2013). This section of the *DSM-5* also clarifies the definition of *withdrawal*, noting the effects that can result from discontinuing use of the substance after developing prolonged and heavy use patterns. This becomes so obvious that it can have clear physical and psychological effects and is noted in the blood or tissue of the individual. Again, these two pharmacological criteria cannot be counted toward the level of severity of the diagnosis if the substances are taken under medical supervision. To avoid the symptoms of withdrawal, it is not uncommon for an individual to desperately seek the substance to address the withdrawal symptoms in the hope it will provide relief.

As stated earlier, major changes were made to the criteria for substance addictions (see Quick Reference 12.7). Other changes to this area include ensuring that each substance is more clearly defined and highlighting the discontinuation syndromes related to TCA and the SSRIs. The term *polysubstance* as defined in *DSM-IV* and *DSM-IV-TR* (see Quick Reference 12.8) no longer seems relevant to *DSM-5*, as now each diagnostic category lists the substance independently. Therefore, polysubstance has been deleted from *DSM-5*.

Substance-Induced Disorders

According to *DSM-5*, the substance-induced disorders (SIDs) are further divided into two categories. One is related to substance intoxication and withdrawal, and the other is related to the substance/medication-induced mental disorders that have a direct relationship to the central nervous system (CNS).

Substance Intoxication and Withdrawal

For the 10 substance categories recognized in the area of substance intoxication and withdrawal, the criteria for each can differ. All substances are not created equally, and the effects on the body differ accordingly. This makes defining the substance-induced disorders and the criteria for each dependent on the substance used. It is beyond the scope of this chapter to explain all of the different substances and the individual results that can occur with intoxication and withdrawal. Instead, a general description of several of the criteria will be outlined as examples throughout the chapter. For specific criteria required for each

QUICK REFERENCE 12.7

DISORDERS NOT COVERED IN *DSM-IV-TR*

Substance-Use Disorders

Alcohol-use disorder
Cannabis-use disorder
Inhalant-use disorder
Opioid-use disorder
Polysubstance-use disorder
Sedative, hypnotic, or anxiolytic-use disorder
Other (or unknown) substance-use disorder
Amphetamine-use disorder
Hallucinogen-use disorder
Nicotine-use disorder
Phencyclidine-use disorder

Substance Withdrawal Disorders

*Cannabis Withdrawal

*Indicates that the disorder was not listed in *DSM-IV* or *DSM-IV-TR*.

QUICK REFERENCE 12.8

DSM-IV-TR SUBSTANCES—POLYSUBSTANCE

- Polysubstance dependence, intoxication, or withdrawal.
- Used at least *three* different classes of substances indiscriminately and does not have a favorite drug that qualifies for dependence alone.
- All three substances used in the same *12-month* period.
- Used only when the pattern of multiple drug use is such that it fails to meet the criteria for dependence on any one class of drug.
- In such settings, the only way to assign a diagnosis of dependence is to consider all the substances the person is taking to complement the other.
- This disorder was deleted from *DSM-5*.

Example of Polysubstance Dependence

An individual for a year or more has the following pattern:
Smokes crack—Illegal sedative use regularly—Smokes several joints a day to level out.

This diagnosis is reserved for the following:

- Used at least three substances indiscriminately together, with no drug of choice, and no drug predominates over the others.
- Met the criteria for substance dependence when substances taken together as a whole but not separately.
- Used over a 12-month period.
- This disorder was deleted from *DSM-5*.

Source: Summarized criteria from the *Diagnostic and Statistical Manual of Mental Disorders*, Fourth Edition, Text Revision, by the American Psychiatric Association, 2000, Washington, DC: Author. Copyright 2000 by the American Psychiatric Association.

substance-induced disorder, refer to the *DSM-5* (see Quick Reference 12.9).

For the most part, *substance intoxication* is the reversible yet recent ingestion of a substance with resulting cognitive and behavioral maladaptive responses, such as belligerence and impaired judgment. Special caution, however, is advised: The symptoms in each of the nine substance-related categories are directly linked to the substance being reviewed. The reason only nine substance areas are listed under intoxication is that for one substance, tobacco, use of the term *intoxication* is not relevant, so there is no such disorder as tobacco intoxication disorder.

To examine the category of intoxication further, the symptoms and the subsequent listing of criteria for each disorder need to be examined, as will the particulars related to that substance.

QUICK REFERENCE 12.9

CATEGORIES OF SUBSTANCES: SUBSTANCE INTOXICATION AND SUBSTANCE WITHDRAWAL

Substance	Substance Intoxication	Substance Withdrawal
Alcohol	X Recent ingestion ***Specifiers:*** None	X Heavy and prolonged use ***Specify* if:** With perceptual disturbances
Caffeine	X 5 of 12 symptoms ***Specifiers:*** None	X 3 of 5 symptoms ***Specifiers:*** None
Cannabis	X Recent use ***Specify* if:** With perceptual disturbances (related to reality testing and hallucinations) For cannabis intoxication: Without perceptual disturbances With perceptual disturbances	X Heavy and prolonged use ***Specifiers:*** None
Hallucinogens PCP and other hallucinogen disorder	X Recent use ***Specifiers:*** None	NA
Inhalants	X Recent use: Note substance ***Specifiers:*** None	NA
Opioids	X Recent use ***Specify* if:** With perceptual disturbances (related to reality testing and hallucinations) For opioid intoxication: Without perceptual disturbances With perceptual disturbances	X Heavy and prolonged use Or opioid antagonist after prolonged use ***Specifiers:*** None

(continued)

QUICK REFERENCE 12.9 (*Continued*)

Substance	Substance Intoxication	Substance Withdrawal
Sedatives, hypnotics, and anxiolytics	X Recent use ***Specifiers:*** None	X Prolonged use ***Specify* if:** With perceptual disturbances
Stimulants	X Recent use ***Specifiers:*** The specific intoxicant With perceptual disturbances	X Cessation or reduction ***Specifiers:*** The specific substance that causes the withdrawal
Tobacco	NA	X Daily use for several weeks ***Specifiers:*** None
Other (or unknown)	X Recent use ***Specifiers:*** None	X Heavy and prolonged use ***Specifiers:*** None

Source: Table created from summarized information from the *Diagnostic and Statistical Manual of Mental Disorders*, Fifth Edition, by the American Psychiatric Association, 2013, Arlington, VA: American Psychiatric Publishing. Copyright 2013 by the American Psychiatric Association.

One common characteristic in all nine of the substance categories is related to the physiological effects of the substance that develop shortly after ingestion. These most probably constitute the criteria responses for criteria A through D. Since the specific criterion is further delineated by the symptoms relevant to a particular substance, criterion C may be different for one substance when compared with another. For example, cannabis intoxication criterion C involves two or more of the following signs or symptoms that develop within 2 hours of the cannabis use: (1) conjunctival injection (when the white part of the eye gets red), (2) increased appetite, (3) dry mouth, and (4) tachycardia. The C criterion for alcohol intoxication is completely different, one or more of the signs and symptoms occurring shortly after alcohol use: (1) slurred speech, (2) incoordination, (3) unsteady gait, (4) nystagmus (rapid involuntary eye movements), (6) impairment in attention and memory, and (7) stupor or coma.

A specific diagnosis should not be given if the cause of the symptoms is related to a different substance than the disorder being addressed and can be better explained by another mental or medical disorder (possibly criterion C or D). For example, in the diagnosis of other (or unknown) substance intoxication, there is no criterion D, but since examining whether the condition is attributable to another mental or medical condition is central to the diagnosis, it is labeled criterion C instead of D. Discrepancies and differences in letter sequencing vary repeatedly, and the easiest way for the practitioner to ensure accuracy is to simply use the specific criteria outlined for the substance.

Three common themes in each of the substance intoxication disorders are (1) a recent exposure to or ingestion of a substance; (2) maladaptive behavioral, physiological, and psychological responses to exposure or ingestion of the substance; and (3) the present symptoms are not accounted for by another medical condition or mental disorder. Because substances are different and the effects they can have on the body differ, the variability among individuals resulting in common changes and disturbances during intoxication can also be different. Intoxication and the resultant behaviors often result in problematic repercussions. These symptoms can include maladaptive induced cognitive and behavioral changes that manifest subsequent risk factors that can affect the individual's interpersonal and social circumstances. The resultant cognitive processes (e.g., impaired and disturbed executive functions) and physical and behavioral processes (e.g., psychomotor retardation) remain dependent on the variability among substances, amount of use, duration of use, situational and environmental context of use, and other associated risk factors (e.g., legal problems, interpersonal conflicts, financial difficulties) (APA, 2013).

In substance withdrawal, the induced behavioral, psychological, and physical changes do not cease after dosing stops. Whereas in intoxication, changes resulting from exposure or ingestion cease after the effect of the substance has worn off, in withdrawal, these changes persist and remain indicative of the severity and duration of use. In the eight substances listed, hallucinogens and inhalants do not constitute a diagnosis related to withdrawal. The three common criteria consistent with all diagnoses related to withdrawal are (1) a behavioral, psychological, and physiological change and response to a reduction in or cessation of substance use; (2) significant impairment to other functional areas that are developed secondary to use; and (3) the symptoms exhibited should not be caused by a medical condition or a related mental disorder (APA, 2013). Furthermore, for accurate diagnostic impression, the *DSM-5* specifies symptoms and ingestion and duration levels for withdrawal from certain groups of substances. See Quick Review 12.9.

Intoxication may have harmful and hazardous complications, but generally it does not have the long-lasting symptoms seen in withdrawal. Withdrawal is the biophysical reaction and syndrome related to the reduction of a chemical stimulus in the body. This reaction requires medical attention by an appropriate provider to rule out complications. A clinical feature and predictor of the presence of withdrawal is a high pulse rate, indicating severity of withdrawal. For example, in alcohol withdrawal, the physiological manifestation of alcohol withdrawal syndrome (or delirium tremens [DTs]) may result. They are characterized by tremors, sweating, anxiety, nausea, vomiting, agitation, insomnia, seizure, tachycardia, and respiratory failure. There may also be a previous history of DTs (Parker et al., 2008). These symptoms may overlap with other clinical presentations and can result in serious and permanent complications.

A second example is Wernicke's encephalopathy, a complication of withdrawal due to chronic alcohol dependence, stemming from a thiamine deficiency that presents with a classic triad of symptoms: confusion, ataxia, and opthalmoplegia (Parker et al., 2008). Other symptoms of Wernicke's encephalopathy include DTs, hypothermia, hypotension, memory disturbance, coma, and unconsciousness. While reversible, if left untreated, Wernicke's encephalopathy causes permanent brain damage (Korsakoff's psychosis), resulting in severe short-term memory loss and functional impairment (Parker et al., 2008). It is not uncommon that the individual experiences a loss of pleasure and desire, almost equivalent to a melancholic depression or similar to the negative symptoms of schizophrenia. Furthermore, alcohol withdrawal can present with auditory and visual hallucinations, disorientation, confusion, anhedonia, clouding of consciousness, impaired attention, autonomic hyperactivity, and psychological alterations (Lee et al., 2005; Pozzi et al., 2008). Care should be exercised to determine whether these symptoms are related to withdrawal as opposed to another mental health or medical condition.

Substance/Medication-Induced Mental Disorders The second area listed under the substance-induced disorders is the substance/medication-induced mental disorders. They are often temporary and result in CNS disorders that are considered the direct result of substances of abuse, medications, and several toxins. These disorders can include all 10 classes of the substances listed in this chapter. Also, every chapter of the *DSM-5* disorders also lists this as a category. Many medications and selected other substances can cause substance-related disorders. For example, anesthetics, muscle relaxants, over-the-counter medications, antidepressants, and corticosteroids can cause substance-related disorders. Other substances such as toxins, including lead, carbon monoxide, and nerve gases, can be directly related to accidental intoxication, and inhalants such as fuel and paint used intentionally for the purpose of becoming intoxicated can cause poisoning.

Basic elements in all of these disorders include the following. First, it meets the criteria for a mental disorder (criterion A). The substance must be capable of creating the symptoms present, and the disorder occurs within 1 month of experiencing either intoxication or withdrawal from the substance (criterion B). Laboratory, history, and physical exam findings that support the presence of the disorder are not better explained by an independent diagnosis and do not occur during the course of delirium (criteria C and D). And last, it causes clinically significant distress.

BEGINNING THE DIAGNOSTIC ASSESSMENT: ALCOHOL-RELATED DISORDERS

A clear understanding of the diagnostic assessment leading to the treatment process is essential. Before starting the diagnostic assessment for this disorder, the following factors should be clearly understood.

The Role of Genetics and the Environment

Alcohol use and resulting dependence are influenced by genetics, with heritability estimates ranging from 50% to 70%, genetic factors accounting for 40% to 56% of variance, and influences remaining fairly constant across adulthood (Pagan et al., 2006). Genetic expression is influenced by environmental agents, and environmental influences rather than just strictly genetic factors play a major role in the decision to initiate substance use. Environmental influences account for 55% to 80% of variance with the initiation of alcohol use, with genetic factors accounting for variance in frequency of use and transition from initiation and experimental alcohol use to regular and problematic use (Pagan et al., 2006). The manifestation and expression of genes in alcohol use increase the propensity and importance of drinking behavior once initiation has begun in response to the environmental stimuli.

In the longitudinal research analysis of twins, Pagan et al. (2006) concluded that shared environmental influences were less important for frequency of use, and the influence of additive genetic factors and unique environmental factors were more influential contributors to the frequency of alcohol use. Genetic factors important at initiation overlapped to a small degree the genetic factors influencing the frequency of use, but there was no overlap of unique environmental factors across stages of use. Genetic factors play the largest role in problematic drinking at age 25 in both men and women, whereas common environmental influences were not significant in both sexes. For both sexes, genetic factors influencing alcohol problems substantially overlapped those influencing frequency of use at age 25, and shared environmental influence on initiation moderately overlapped the relatively small shared environmental influences on frequency of use at 25 (p. 496).

Studies addressing the impact of variants in genes associated with encoding alcohol-metabolizing enzymes (ADH1B, ADH1C, and ALDH2) help to explain variations of alcohol use disorders and risks among different individuals and certain groups (Schulte et al., 2009). Inability to break down alcohol in the body leads to rapid intoxication, which sustains the propensity for dependence. In development of the disorder, few professionals would disagree that genetics is important. In treatment, however, this factor alone is not always a predictor. Some individuals develop the disorder without a genetic history, and others with the history do not (Dallery, Meridith, & Budney, 2012).

Awareness of Problematic Alcohol-Related Misuse

Substance-related disorders can create a cumulative pattern of behaviors that interfere with socialization, relationships, and work. For the alcohol-related disorders, legal consequences resulting from driving while intoxicated and disorderly conduct can present particular problems. Physiologically related ailments result in severe and chronic debilitating conditions; cardiac problems and cirrhosis of the liver are only two of the conditions associated with alcohol misuse. Tracking the true effects of alcohol misuse can be difficult because some individuals seek medical treatment for reasons unrelated to their use and dependence. They can also present with different explanations of the cause related to direct or indirect involvement with the criminal justice system. Consumption of alcohol exceeding the limits of accepted social and cultural norms that also impairs health and social relationships defines an alcohol use disorder.

Family Systems Are Often Strained

Noting disturbed familial patterns is of particular importance, especially poor parental relations, poor parental supervision, harsh parental physical punishment, and parental conflict contributing to the individual coming from a broken home. In the alcohol use disorders, other factors include coming from a family with a large number of children, mothers of a young age, single-parent households, low socioeconomic status, and associated alcohol use disorders within a conflicted family environment (Swendsen et al., 2009; WHO, 2006a). Modeling parental alcohol use has a direct effect on children's alcohol use and misuse. There is a direct relationship between parental monitoring and alcohol use in children; if children are monitored, this protective factor can reduce and control hazardous and harmful drinking behavior patterns (Schulte et al., 2009). Furthermore, there is also a connection between alcohol and substance-related use during pregnancy, which can be related to fetal alcohol spectrum disorders (FASD), learning disabilities, mental retardation, and developmental disabilities (MR/DD). It can also increase the future risk that these individuals will develop an alcohol and substance-related disorder themselves (Huggins, Grant, O'Malley, & Streissguth, 2008; Janikowski, Donnelly, &

Lawrence, 2007; Robertson, Davis, Sneed, Koch, & Boston, 2009).

Recognizing Social Stressors That Surround the Individual

Associations with community and societal factors have been found in alcohol use problems. Social stressors such as gangs, delinquent friends, availability of alcohol, and poor social integration can all be problematic (Swendsen et al., 2009; WHO, 2006b). In affiliations with deviant peer groups, harmful alcohol use increases by modeling alcohol drinking behaviors as a way to cope with stress, especially in individuals who lack or have limited self-regulation to cope with emotional effects (Schulte et al., 2009). This modeling effect has an impact on violence and the availability and consumption of alcohol. When under the influence, a person may experience poor social integration because of the effects alcohol use has on the processing of perceived emotional cues. For example, the processing of emotional facial cues following alcohol consumption may become impaired, causing the individual to misattribute facial cues and thereby increasing the likelihood of inappropriate behavioral responses, such as aggression (Craig, Attwood, Benton, Peton-Voak, & Munafo, 2009). Combining misattributed emotional states and harmful and hazardous drinking when individuals have limited self-regulation can be problematic. When witnessing or experiencing violence is commonplace and culturally sanctioned, this type of stressor can lead to subsequent alcohol use problems and increased risks of developing alcohol-related problems.

More Than One Substance That Does Not Clearly Fit Into the Diagnostic Category

Clients suffering from a substance use disorder never fit perfectly into an identified category, especially when more than one substance is used. Clients often have multiple problems that require a multifaceted approach to intervention. Some of these problems can easily overlap other mental health conditions, such as the affective disorders (bipolar and depression) or the dementia- or delirium-based disorders. Chronic use of a substance can result in long-term damage such as cirrhosis of the liver.

CASE EXAMPLE - CASE OF JACK

Jack is a 60-year-old White male who appears older than his stated age and is of average height and weight. Upon admission to the chemical dependency unit at a hospital, he reports that he is not doing well and needs help. He reports that he wishes he was dead, and if he owned a gun, he would shoot himself. He reports ongoing difficulties with alcohol and substance abuse over the past 10 years, but during the past 2 years, it has increased significantly. He states he feels he could control it if he just had more support from his family and friends. Prior to admission, he admitted having several drinks but not for several hours. Jack was intoxicated at time of admission with a blood alcohol level of 0.23, which constitutes clear legal intoxication, and he tested positive for marijuana. Precipitating factors to the hospitalization included loss of residence, when his wife evicted him from their home. For the past few years, they have constantly fought over Jack's giving priority to purchasing alcohol over groceries. The culminating event related to his eviction came when he promised her he would stop drinking and she found several cans of beer in his workshop in the backyard. Her ultimatum came after he was in an automobile accident and hit a tree. He was alone in the car and denied being under the influence, although he admits to drinking that day.

Jack reports that he lost his job of 20 years after recent warnings about his tardiness resulting from late-night partying with friends. He states that due to his "drinking ways," he was also evicted from his friend's house where he was staying and now has nowhere else to go. He reports feeling depressed, and he smokes marijuana to help with his insomnia. Prior to admission, he reports smoking and drinking all day long and presents as inebriated at the time of interview.

Jack reports a history of outpatient chemical dependency treatments, with multiple (at least three) detoxification admissions. There have been multiple attempts at sobriety with attendance in Alcoholics Anonymous (AA). At the time of the interview, he appears depressed, with vague suicidal ideations but no concrete plan. He denies any past history of suicide attempts. At the time of the interview, he denies having access to a weapon. He denies any visual, auditory, tactile, olfactory, and/or gustatory hallucinations.

He reports regularly drinking alcohol and smoking marijuana. He admits to using cocaine and several other substances but says this use is not regular, and he does not seek it out unless it is given to him for free. He drinks on a daily basis, consuming approximately a case of beer and at least a pint of vodka daily. He smokes pot almost daily, and between the alcohol and other drugs, he is spending in excess of $200 a week. He reports he does not have a problem with marijuana but is worried because when he is not drinking, he experiences "shakes, sweats, and vomiting." He reports there is frequently blood when he vomits. He denies a seizure disorder but received medical treatment for seizures he suffered last year due to his use. He reports he was stabilized but refused treatment for his substance-related concerns at that time. He has difficulty with sleeping secondary to his use. He denies issues of gambling at the time of the interview.

In gathering history information, Jack states that his parents were divorced days after his birth. He has a positive family history for substance-related concerns. Jack's birth father is deceased from liver complications of alcohol use. He had limited contact with his father, citing that his father was absent in his life. Jack states his mother remarried to his stepfather and stayed married for 20 years, but they are now divorced. He has had limited contact with them. Jack's stepfather was in the military, and the family traveled often. He states his childhood was unproblematic and denies any abuse issues. Jack states that he has two half-brothers from his mother and stepfather's union and two half-sisters from his birth father's second marriage. Jack denies contact with his siblings. He states he had a close relationship with his younger half-brother, who recently died of cancer. When asked about family history for substance abuse, he reports only his biological father and his one brother drink excessively. He reports his stepfather was a "social" drinker, as was his mother. Jack denies substance abuse treatment for his brother. Jack denies knowledge of mental illness in his family.

After a recent physical, it was determined that at this point Jack does not show direct signs of cirrhosis of the liver. He admitted being noncompliant with his medical treatment, regardless of whether it is related to his alcohol and illicit drug use. According to the history and physical report and upon observation, he complains of stomach cramping but denies having experienced seizures secondary to his substance use. He has no known allergies.

Divorced from a previous marriage, he has been separated from his second wife on and off for over a year, with frequent fighting and arguing secondary to his drinking. He reports having "pushed" her on a "few occasions," and "I never slapped her" when drinking. He had sexual difficulties in the marriage secondary to his drinking, stating a loss of desire and performance concerns, which further affected his marriage. When his financial problems worsened, his wife "kicked me out."

(*continued*)

CASE EXAMPLE - CASE OF JACK (CONTINUED)

Jack reports a lengthy history of different jobs after having completed military service in the Army. During his time in military service, he worked as an assembler and was last promoted to a higher-rank position in operations management. After his enlistment, he reports completing and acquiring a bachelor's degree and then pursuing a chiropractor degree, which he obtained in 1990. He has been successful in this occupation, including opening his own practice, until his problems with alcohol and other substances worsened. He is currently unemployed, lost his practice, and currently is facing a malpractice suit. He reports sporadic income from working "odd jobs" for friends for cash. He denies actively seeking employment at the time of the interview.

Jack reports extensive legal problems secondary to his substance-related concerns. He is currently facing charges for reckless driving, reckless endangerment, and driving without a license. Due to multiple legal problems, his license was revoked and charges are pending which may result in incarceration. He also suffered a malpractice suit, for which he may also lose his chiropractor's license. Secondary to his legal problems and loss of income, he filed for bankruptcy. He acknowledges that these legal difficulties are the result of his substance use. He reports that he has no income. Jack feels that the strain of these concerns has added enormous pressure on him, which he acknowledges has further increased his drinking and drug use.

Completion of the Diagnostic Assessment

The diagnostic assessment starts with an initial interview, where a client's presenting symptoms are assessed and evaluated. To facilitate the interview, a complete mental status exam is conducted. Basic information related to his presentation, mental functioning, and thought form and content are gathered. In treatment, the first stage is completing the diagnostic assessment. A complete understanding of the biological, psychological, and sociocultural perspectives is important in the assessment. Identifying these factors and using a number of measurement tools can assist the mental health practitioner. As with any disorder, basic facts to obtain and consider about the individual include age, culture, gender, socioeconomic status, marital status, family history, developmental or childhood history, incidence of abuse or neglect (including domestic violence), and educational status. Assessing the level of motivation for starting and participating in treatment is an important factor that significantly influences the treatment options presented and accomplished.

Other factors to assess include age of first use, attitude toward use, honesty about usage, social and occupational functioning while using the substance, amount used, frequency of use, duration of use, changes in use over time, attitudes of family and others toward use, recreational activities, composition of social circle, availability of the substance, mental health disorders issues (e.g., depression, anxiety, disability), medical issues (e.g., withdrawal syndrome symptoms), and how these relate to mental status (orientation to person, place, time, and situation), and drug of choice and/or secondary drugs. (See Quick Reference 12.10.)

QUICK REFERENCE 12.10

Common Effects of Excessive Alcohol Consumption Within the Family

The alcohol-dependent person:

- Denies the alcohol problem, minimizes use, blames others, is forgetful, and employs defense mechanisms to protect the self (ego).
- Receives criticism and loses trust of others and the family.
- Spends money needed on alcohol rather than for necessities.
- Financially irresponsible, prioritizing substance use over bills.
- Is unpredictable and impulsive.
- Resorts to verbal and physical abuse in place of honest and open talk.
- Experiences increased sexual arousal but reduced function.
- May have unpredictable mood swings or suffer from depression, guilt, and shame.

The spouse or partner:

- Often hides and denies the problem of the partner.
- Assumes the user's responsibilities, perpetuating the partner's dependence.
- Takes a job to get away from the problem and/or to maintain financial security.
- Has difficulty being open because of resentment, anger, hurt, and shame.
- Avoids sexual contact, seeking separation or divorce.
- Overprotects children and uses them for emotional support.
- Shows gradual social withdrawal and isolation.
- May lose feelings of self-respect and self-worth.
- May use alcohol or prescription drugs to cope.
- May use alcohol to share a relationship with substance-dependent partner.
- May present to the doctor with anxiety, depression, psychosomatic symptoms, or evidence of domestic violence.

Children:

- Have an increased risk of developing alcohol dependency themselves.
- Increased risk of birth defects (from maternal alcohol use).
- Torn between parental conflicts.
- Deprived of emotional and physical support and nurturing.
- Lacking trust in others.
- Avoids peer group activities out of fear and shame.
- Self-destructive and negative when dealing with problems and getting attention.
- Shortsighted in goals, losing sight of values and standards because of a lack of consistent parental monitoring or harsh discipline.
- Truant or failing in school and possible engaging in criminal activity.
- Suffering from diminishing self-worth and status in the family.
- Presenting with learning difficulties, enuresis, or sleep disorders.

QUICK REFERENCE 12.11

MENTAL STATUS DESCRIPTION

Presentation *Disheveled Unkempt*	Mental Functioning *Average intelligence*	Higher-Order Abilities *Some difficulty with abstracts*	General Knowledge: *Mostly accurate*
Mood: *Anxious, depressed*	Affect: *Blunted/flat*	Judgment: *Impulsive*	Insight: *Poor*
Motor Activity: *Somewhat restless*	Thought, Form, and Content *Distractible and preoccupied*	Delusions: *None* Hallucinations: *None*	Speech: *Hesitant* Clarity: *Normal*
Attitude: *Guarded*	Immediate Memory: *Intact*	Remote Memory: *Intact*	Intelligence: *Average*
Serial Sevens: *Accurate*	Simple Calculations: *Mostly accurate*	Proverb Interpretation: *Confused, frustrated*	Orientation: *Fully oriented*

Case Application of the Diagnostic Assessment: Jack

In interviewing Jack, examining the criteria presented is important for a comprehensive diagnostic assessment. To start the process and determine the appropriateness of placing a substance use disorder, a complete mental status exam should be completed. This process starts with noting his general appearance: At age 60, he appears older than his stated age. At the interview, his accessibility appears at first somewhat cooperative, although at other times his responses to questions related to his current situation seem indifferent. The smell of alcohol is resonating around from his clothes and his skin. His eye contact is indirect, and even when eye contact is made, he often looks away into the distance as he speaks. His affect appears blunted, and his rate of speech is often slow and deliberate. Although able to hold a conversation, he seems sparse on some details and at times circumvents topics that appear to make him uncomfortable. (See Quick Reference 12.11.)

In the past, Jack has had a documented blood alcohol level of 0.436 and currently reports daily use of large quantities of alcohol. Based on the accumulated data, laboratory findings, and completion of the AUDIT, Jack appears to be suffering from alcohol-use disorder. This is his principal diagnosis based on his history of problematic use of alcohol and behaviors that extend back well over a 12-month period. Of the 11 possible indicators relative to diagnosis of alcohol use, two were needed to meet the criteria for the diagnosis. According to the assessment, Jack meets the criteria for 6 of the 11 criteria without assessing for factors related to tolerance and withdrawal. He states he has tried to control his drinking but admits he cannot seem to stop (number 1). He has tried numerous times to control or cut back his drinking, with his last failed attempt resulting in his wife evicting him from their home (number 2). He admits to having a strong desire or urge to consume alcohol and has taken money that should have been used on other important daily living necessities such as groceries, spending it instead on the purchase of alcohol (number 3). He was recently fired from his job for his impaired performance and tardiness related to his admitted partying the night before (number 5). He has had numerous problems related to his drinking that have disrupted his family relationships (number 6). He recently had a car accident, and although it is not confirmed it was alcohol-induced, it is most likely the case (number 8). Significant events include loss of income, bankruptcy, and separation from current wife. Upon expected discharge, he has no place to go and, unless assisted, will be homeless. His suggested diagnosis and specifiers include:

Alcohol Use Disorder (reason for visit)
Specify if: In a controlled environment
Specify current severity: Severe 305.90 (*ICD9-CM*) or F10.20 (*ICD-10*)

This diagnosis is placed as Jack reports multiple failed attempts at sobriety with detoxification, counseling, and AA. His employment, social, and intimate relationships have been impaired secondary to his inability to cease his alcohol use. He continues to engage in compulsive, alcohol-seeking behaviors, despite acknowledging the physical, psychological, and social/occupational consequences his alcohol use continues to cause. Second to alcohol use disorder is occasional use of cannabis. Jack does not report using cannabis over a 12-month period and states he recently started using it to calm himself. He also denies compulsive seeking of cannabis, which would continue to further affect his social and occupational functioning as he presents with his use of alcohol. Taking this information into account, the diagnosis of *cannabis use* is not met at the present time.

Other Conditions That May Be a Focus of Clinical Attention

With the elimination of the multiaxial diagnosis used in *DSM-IV* and *DSM-IV-TR*, the information previously provided on Axis IV and Axis V is no longer a requirement. Elimination of these axes, however, should not result in excluding this important supportive information. When including this information, special attention should be given to Chapters 21 and 22 of the *DSM-5*. Chapter 21, the medication-induced movement disorders and other adverse effects of medication, and Chapter 22, other conditions that may be a focus of clinical intervention, are not mental disorders. Rather, they are conditions that may assist in outlining and further documenting the supportive information central to the diagnosis. In the case of Jack, the information provided in Chapter 22 may be of the most help. In this chapter are several supportive factors that need to be taken into account in supporting the diagnostic assessment. The first are the biopsychosocial stressors (especially those related to the family situation and key relationships). (See Quick Reference 12.12.)

In this case, Jack clearly has strained family relationships. Unfortunately, the revised conditions updated in *DSM-5* do not appear comprehensive enough to describe Jack's particular situation and how it can affect his diagnosis. He is no longer living with his wife, who has thrown him out of their home because of his previous substance-related behaviors. Therefore, this supplemental information is provided and the code that most closely represents his

QUICK REFERENCE 12.12

SUPPORTIVE CONCERNS

General Concerns

Isolation from family and community.

Life events revolving around drinking activities.

Financial problems.

Work-Related Concerns

Impaired job performance and recent termination from employment.

Family concerns.

Disturbed family relations, recent separation.

Estrangement from family and friends.

Partner/Spouse/Family Concerns

Recent separation from spouse due to substance-related behaviors.

Financial strains due to misuse of couple's finances.

problems with his primary support group and family situation is:

V61.03 (Z63.5) Disruption of Family Separation or Divorce

Jack was recently terminated by his employer for reasons related to his substance-related activities and is now unemployed, with no current source of income. The closest of the other conditions that may be a focus of clinical attention that can be coded here is:

V62.29 (Z56.9) Other Problem Related to Employment

The last area for supportive attention is his lack of adequate housing for his return. Upon discharge from the facility, he will have no place to go and will require assistance with housing as part of the discharge plan. Jack has serious impairments to his social and occupational functioning secondary to his own behaviors and that of his peer-using friends and his loss of employment and career. Currently, Jack is being admitted to the chemical-dependency unit.

V60.0 (Z59.0) Homelessness

In summary, prior to his substance use disorder, Jack denies any personal, legal, financial, and/or occupational concerns. While co-occurrence of personality and mood disorders are evident in the phenomenological analysis of substance use disorders, accuracy of personality disorders and traits is assessed when client is in full remission of dependence concerns. A scheduled psychological assessment should be arranged posttreatment and stabilization to rule out disability factors such as developmental delays and learning disorders.

The diagnosis of alcohol liver disease, such as liver cirrhosis, requires that specific criteria are met: heavy drinking for more than 5 years in the amount of more than 40 grams/day in men (more than 20 g/day for women), drinking more than 80 grams/day for 2 weeks, jaundice, weight loss, elevated serum levels, and the exclusion of hepatotropic virus infection and drug-induced and toxic liver injuries to explain abnormal findings (Zeng et al., 2008). Presence of liver cirrhosis is an additionally conclusive sign that the patient has been accurately diagnosed with a substance-induced disorder, and alcohol withdrawal should be considered. After a recent physical exam, no evidence of liver cirrhosis or history of seizures was noted. The possibility of developing these conditions will continue to be monitored, especially if the amount of alcohol Jack is drinking continues. If there are medical conditions present and medications are prescribed, the prescriber will need to take into account the possibility of compromised liver functioning. Monitoring for the potential of seizures by professional staff can further decrease medical errors due to prescriptions.

TREATMENT PLANNING AND INTERVENTION STRATEGY

The information gathered during the diagnostic assessment and the identified goals and objectives provide the starting point for treatment, including the intervention plan. As part of the intervention process, problem behaviors are clearly identified and related directly to the stated goals and objectives. Treatment should be provided in a continuum of care that allows flexible application of modalities based on a cohesive treatment plan.

Effective treatment planning for clients such as Jack and others suffering from substance misuse must take into account situational concerns and all of the information discussed in the assessment. In formulating a treatment plan in this area, the plan of intervention—short-term sample treatment goals—should reflect the client's immediate presenting problems. Longer-term functional goals need to directly address reducing alcohol consumption, obtaining and maintaining sobriety, improving social and coping skills, acquiring employment, and securing a place to live. Goals need to be realistic, match the assessment, and reflect the desires of the client initially and throughout treatment process. Additionally, factors such as strengths, support systems, dual diagnoses, and culture are considered in developing the treatment plan.

Objectives for the alcohol-related disorder should be clear and concise. They should take into account where the client is beginning treatment, immediate needs, and the potential of relapse to support the client's desire of sobriety. This will help him not be set up for failure. (See Sample Treatment Plan 12.1.) Ascertaining

SAMPLE TREATMENT PLAN 12.1

ALCOHOL USE DISORDER

Problematic pattern of alcohol use, over a 12-month period, with at least two documented symptoms. Use causes clinically significant impairment and can result in harmful and hazardous interpersonal and social consequences due to use. It is not indicative of tolerance or withdrawal.

Signs and Symptoms

Describe patterns of impaired control, social impairment, risky use, and pharmacological criteria related to tolerance and withdrawal.

(continued)

SAMPLE TREATMENT PLAN 12.1 (*Continued*)

Specific behaviors can include:

- Taken in larger amounts for a longer period than intended.
- Desire and unsuccessful attempts to control substance usage.
- Time spent trying to obtain the substance, disturbing social and other relationships.
- Risk behaviors due to drinking (e.g., binge drinking).
- Neglected responsibilities.
- Absences from school or work.
- Use with awareness that alcohol is exacerbating problems.
- Relationship problems, violence, verbal and physical fights.
- Use of alcohol in situations where dangerous.
- Financial difficulties and mismanagement of funds.

Goals

1. Abstinence from harmful and hazardous drinking.
2. Medical assessment.
3. Introduce new coping skills and/or build existing coping skills.

Objectives	Interventions
1. Evaluate amount and type of consumption of client's alcohol intake.	Encourage client to self-report drinking patterns (e.g., binge drinking). Encourage client to verbalize beliefs regarding drinking patterns. Provide education to client regarding drinking patterns, use, and consequences. Encourage to connect beliefs and consequences to increase awareness of use and patterns. Assist the client to problem-solve and develop strategies to reduce harmful use.
2. Reduce risk factors associated with problem use.	Encourage client to report behaviors due to use that risk client's well-being, interpersonal relationships, and occupational status. Encourage client to verbalize thoughts, feelings, and emotions in response to risk factors due to use. Provide education to client regarding drinking patterns, use, and consequences. Assist client in developing problem-solving strategies to reduce risk behaviors and ameliorate consequences.
3. Establish a support system to utilize and depend on during recovery.	Develop with the client a list of friends and family members who provide positive support. Contact friends/relatives and ask for input on client's substance use. Contact these people and attempt to meet or speak to them about the importance of recovery for client.
4. A physical examination will be completed by a physician.	Refer client to his primary physician for evaluation.

the client's attitude about treatment is central for engaging the client, assessing level of motivation, and developing a successful plan. Upon the initial formulation of the treatment plan, the first stage of implementation is generally detoxification for alcohol dependence as for any substance-related dependence concern.

Medical evaluation is needed to detect coexisting illness mimicking the withdrawal syndrome and rule out other conditions, such as traumatic brain injury. Often these conditions coexist with alcohol and other substance-related concerns, serving as the primary cause for the initial disability and continuation of use. Yet when not due to substance-related factors, symptoms such as confusion, impaired memory, mood changes, alteration in speech, and gait difficulties are symptoms also evident in other medical conditions (e.g., brain injury, heart conditions).With Jack's permission, while he was still receiving services, the practitioner began to make telephone calls to family members and various halfway houses. After an honest and comprehensive presentation of Jack's case to representatives of the potential services, Jack was accepted into a short-term halfway house provided by the mental health center in his area, with services designed to help him readjust back into the community.

General Considerations for Treatment Planning and Practice Strategy

Treating the substance-related disorders and treatment planning methods are diverse and complex, and a multitude of treatment interventions can be utilized. Marinchak and Morgan (2012) suggest six factors that should always be taken into account when addressing any type of behavioral treatment (p. 138):

1. Treatment, regardless of the type utilized, needs to involve a collaborative relationship between the client and the practitioner. If goals and objectives are not mutually negotiated, the treatment approach will be limited in success.
2. The client needs to commit to participate and actively address the problem behaviors identified both in and outside the therapy session.
3. Complete a functional analysis to clearly identify the problems the client is experiencing and which ones need immediate attention.
4. Work with the client to develop treatment goals and assist with developing the strategy for implementation. An adequate knowledge of different treatment strategies allows the practitioner to individualize the plan of intervention.
5. Have a clear plan and indicators to evaluate treatment progress, success, and follow-up.
6. For substance disorders in particular, relapse is always a significant concern. Providing information on long-term recovery strategies and specific practice strategy related to relapse is always recommended.

A brief summary of several popular approaches follows.

Family System Approach

According to the family system perspective, treatment success for the chemically affected individual requires a multidimensional approach that involves the client, his or her family, and to a lesser extent, the larger social network (McCrady, Ladd, & Hallgren, 2012). The client suffering from alcohol use and dependence is viewed as part of a human system that requires more than one and often a combination of intervention approaches. The family is viewed as a set of interconnected individuals acting together to maintain a homeostatic balance. The basic premise of this model is to allow each member of the family to achieve a higher level of functioning and emotional security (Curtis, 1999; Van Wormer, 2008).

Recognizing family dynamics is essential to accomplishing the intended outcome. The substance user does not exist in a vacuum. Rather, the person and his or her addiction are living, breathing, interacting elements of the environment and the family's environment, and the exclusionary observation of the person without these factors is impossible in this model. From this perspective, the substance being misused is seen as a family disease. Significant others and any other persons close to the individual suffering from substance abuse also need to benefit from treatment. Milkman and Sederer (1990) discussed the need to possibly restructure the family to adjust to the recovery of the family member. The support system is a vital and powerful aspect of the client's ability to recover, and intervention strategies not including the client's family system offer poor prognosis for long-term recovery (Parker et al., 2008; Van Wormer, 2008). In addition, as family systems mature, evolve, and change, identifying the family and the subsequent treatment from a static perspective could fall short in terms of continued intervention success.

Studying a single variable in isolation cannot reveal the information needed about the system as a whole; therefore, treatment modalities that do not include the family system can fall short (McCrady et al., 2012). Duncan, Duncan, and Hops (1998) agreed that a thorough analysis of the cognitive, social, and behavioral aspects of the abuser's drinking behavior needs to occur before the intervention can be undertaken. The observation of the system in the environment and the use of homeostasis in perpetuating addiction are of special consideration to the practitioner using this approach.

Cognitive-Behavioral Therapy

Management of stress reactions, anxiety, tension, panic, worry, and emotional pressure is important in this treatment. Considering the principle that a person's emotional and behavioral reactions are determined by the relationship between his or her cognitions and subsequent behaviors, the cognitive-behavioral approach to treatment continues to be utilized as the primary intervention model. Cognitive-behavioral therapy (CBT) has been proven effective in numerous outcome research studies in problems such as anxiety disorders, sexual problems, psychosis, gerontology, depression, obesity, and substance-related disorders. Treatment rests with education, supportive therapy, and techniques that teach individuals the relationships among thoughts, emotions, and behaviors and how these are interconnected to factors related to problem areas. Individuals learn self-regulation, problem-solving strategies, and coping skills.

Utilizing cognitive therapy methods start with the basic assumption that for the most part "despite evidence of biological or genetic components to human behavior, human behavior, especially at the macro level, is largely learned" (Rotgers, 2012, p. 114). Therefore, intervention from this perspective focuses on the client's stated thoughts, emotions, and goals, without postulating unconscious forces. The diagnosis rests in what the client believes he or she is experiencing and later addresses the possible distortions or limitations in his or her perceptions of the event. From this perspective, a client's strengths are highlighted, rather than pathology. Putting the client's identified strengths to use, the practitioner guides the client into trying selected experiences that may alter his or her inaccurate perceptions. Each client's behavior is shaped by personal goals rather than by universal biological drives. The focus is on helping clients realize that to achieve changes they need to expand this consciousness of self, others, and the world around them.

The first step toward intervention is to help clients become aware of the beliefs that guide the substance-related condition. Once these beliefs are recognized, clients are assisted to recognize the circumstances related to use, while being supported in problem-solving alternatives to these circumstances. Some clients will be successful at integrating lifestyle changes, and others will need more time to acquire awareness to integrate changes related to use. Behavior modification and changes in cognitive processes are effective in achieving these goals. These are really guided self-help steps, and clients must work actively to achieve them, with responsibility for commitment to the goals and taking charge of recovery from the substance-related disorder determining the degree of success.

Negative self-statements, private thoughts, or self-talk that in some manner inhibits client performance and maintains use can be cognitively restructured into positive, constructive statements and combined with a perceptual redefinition of clients' reality in the inhibiting situation. Learning to use positive self-statements increases self-regulation and confidence in reinforcing new behaviors. These are important for clients to achieve self-control and manage the implementation of alternatives to use.

Expectancies play an important role in CBT. The theory proposes that people act in accordance with expected outcomes, rationally selecting one from among a set of options that will gain the most and best results. Expectancies can be positive or negative, and four types of expectancies exist. First, the stimuli associated with the effects of drinking may become cues for seeking out anticipated rewards from alcohol or for avoiding the negative consequences of drinking. Second, physiological withdrawal symptoms become cues for drinking to achieve temporary reduction of aversive physical symptoms. A third influence in outcome expectancies is social environmental factors. For instance, an individual may develop alcohol outcome expectations specific to peer affiliations in a particular context or situation. A fourth source of alcohol outcome expectancies is the beliefs an individual holds about the effects of alcohol and what he or she perceives as a benefit or cost from its use. Cognitive-behavioral theory suggests that people are more likely to abuse alcohol if they lack self-efficacy to enable them to achieve the desired outcome. Social skills training and development and redevelopment of problem-solving strategies are components of restructuring beliefs, attitudes, and actions that the individual will use to achieve the desired effects.

Motivational Enhancement Therapies

DiClemente, Bellino, and Neavins (1999) state that "motivation is an important step toward changing any action or behavior" (p. 86). "Motivation appears to be a critical dimension in influencing patients to seek, comply with, and complete treatment as well as to make successful long term changes in their drinking" (p. 87). Determining the level of motivation involves assessment of internal and external motivators. In the assessment as in practice, each stage of practice intervention allows the provider to assess attitude and level of motivation that will lead to engagement and change. To facilitate the assessment process, DiClemente et al. (1999) identify five stages of an individual's decision-making process in contemplating any change: precontemplation, contemplation, preparation, action, and maintenance.

According to Prochaska and DiClemente (1992) the stages of change model (known also as the transtheoretical model [TTM]) are as follows: In the *precontemplation* stage, the client has no intent to change, is usually pressured to attend treatment, and does not recognize the substance use as a problem. In the *contemplation* phase, the client has begun to become aware of the substance-related problem, still has no intent to change, but is weighing the pros and cons to change. The *preparation* stage signals the client's plans to change the substance-related problem in the near future, with behavioral goals set but no action implemented. The *action* stage implements the client's plans to change, with behavioral goals in place, modifying lifestyle, experiences, and settings associated with substance-related use. In the *maintenance* phase, the client maintains lifestyle changes to prevent relapses or associated risks with substance use. These lifestyle changes are differentiated by the source of the desire to effect change from within the person or from external or environmental sources.

Once the baseline for level of motivation is established through assessment, one of several intervention approaches begins. Brief motivational intervention is educating patients about the negative effects of alcohol abuse to motivate them to stop or reduce drinking. It is indicated for the nondependent alcohol use disorders. The course is generally one to four sessions lasting 10 to 40 minutes each. The setting is generally substance abuse outpatient or primary care offices (DiClemente et al., 1999).

The second approach is motivational interviewing (MI), which has been used with substance-related conditions such as alcohol abuse, illicit drug use, and in the addictive disorders such as gambling disorder (Tooley & Moyers, 2012). The application involves educating clients on the stages of change, and feelings of resistance, denial, and ambivalence are viewed as natural components of these stages. Clients are assisted to work through ambivalence toward sobriety. Taken from social psychology, motivation theory is based on the premise: How can I get someone to do something actively on their own without constraints or duress? This question is important to address because when the person becomes empowered, the changes will be made for and by the client without fear, coercion, or force.

Techniques used include four MI principles: (1) encouraging clients to develop an awareness of the discrepancy between goals and behaviors that obstruct goals, (2) expressing empathy toward clients and their situation, (3) rolling with resistance instead of arguing or confronting clients, and (4) reflective listening. The pros and cons of change are examined with support of clients' self-efficacy and ability to change and overcome difficulty. All behaviors are assessed by charting or behavioral counts, and counselors give feedback on problem behaviors. Last, counselors elicit self-motivational statements or affirmations from patient (Van Wormer, 2008). The length of treatment is undefined and can be as long as needed to effect change. Sessions last from 30 to 60 minutes and are generally once a week (DiClemente et al., 1999).

The third approach in motivational therapy is motivational enhancement therapy (MET). This method was developed as a treatment modality with subcomponents combining motivational interviewing with a less intensive setting. It has three types of modalities: brief intervention, integrated motivational enhancement therapy, and motivational enhancement catalyst (Walker, Roffmann, Picciano, & Stephens, 2007). In MET, enhancing the therapeutic alliance stresses avoidance of confrontational approaches that might lead to a premature focus on the addictive behavior and labeling that force clients to accept labels such as addict or alcoholic. Often in sessions, the counselor asks questions that can be answered with yes or no and tries to avoid the expert trap, where clients are put down rather than collaboratively exchange information (Van Wormer, 2008). Resistance is addressed in a similar manner as rational emotive behavior therapy (REBT) and CBT, treating skepticism and rejection as normal components of self-determination. Clients naturally experience trust concerns regarding the treatment modality, and it is as equally valid for clients to reject therapeutic services that do not meet their needs or concerns or that make them feel worse. Through this approach, a client who engages in change without coercion or mandated means has longer-lasting and more effective changes. Motivational enhancement therapy was found effective and provided treatment success to the extent that the client's social support network supported sobriety. Follow-up studies on subjects found that emotional partner support was a key factor in long-term recovery (Van Wormer, 2008). Applying motivational interviewing techniques, MET is particularly useful with clients whose motivation to change is minimal or changeable (Parker et al., 2008; Walker et al., 2007).

Integrated Motivational Enhancement Therapy

Integrated motivational enhancement therapy (IMET) combines multiple clinical components for individuals with more severe dependency issues. Included in this therapy model is MET, cognitive-behavioral skills training, and case management for nine intervention sessions or more (Walker et al., 2007).

The purpose of motivational enhancement catalyst (MEC) is to induce motivation for change in individuals not ready for treatment. To start this process, individuals are screened. When risk factors are identified, free-standing invitations are given to those who are interested, making them aware that services are available. Contact information is given to learn more about the program and its offerings (Walker et al., 2007). Once requests for services are received, these interventions can be delivered through computerized checkups, where miniassessments with feedback are given. This information can be used to help individuals determine or confirm whether they have a problem severe enough to require intervention. The personalized feedbacks, referred to as personalized feedback reports (PFRs), include normative data, graphics use to enhance self-appraisal, risk-related indices, and identification of the client's anticipated pro or con consequences from changing (Walker et al., 2007). According to Walker et al. (2007), there are five variants to this free-standing MEC approach:

1. *In-Person Driver's Checkup (DCU):* This approach is intended to reach problem drinkers not interested in formal treatment but concerned about having a problem. It provides a voluntary assessment of how alcohol use is influencing different areas of functioning. This integrated approach can involve structured interviews, neuropsychological assessment, and feedback on weekly alcohol consumption with measurement of blood alcohol levels. High-risk behaviors are identified and compared with average drinking and other individual and family-related risk-producing behaviors.
2. *Computer-Based Driver's Checkup (CDCU):* This approach addresses problem drinking via computer. The CDCU is a computerized assessment and feedback session, using measurement instruments where participants complete decision-making modules. These exercises outline the positive and negative aspects of drinking and provide feedback while assessing feelings of ambivalence.
3. *In-Person Marijuana Checkup (MCU):* Like the DCU, the MCU is intended to assess adult users of marijuana. It focuses particularly on users who resist seeking treatment or behavior change but display negative consequences from

its use. This comprehensive assessment provides education about the substance and an opportunity for reflection and behavior-specific feedback.

4. *In-School Teen Marijuana Checkup (TMCU):* Through waivers with parental permission, the TMCU is intended to reach adolescents in school settings. This method identifies ambivalent attitudes and offers support and strategies for change through a computerized and self-administered assessment. Personalized feedback is given with a counselor and teen after the computerized assessment is completed. Education and problem-solving efforts focus on delivering change strategies and tips.
5. *Telephone Delivered Sex Checkup (SCU):* Attempting to attract men seeking men (MSM) and reduce incidences of HIV due to high-risk sexual behaviors, the assessment relies on a telephone intervention that provides the opportunity to talk about ambivalent feelings toward unsafe sexual practices. Participants can enroll anonymously by renting a post office box (for which they are reimbursed). Educational materials are then delivered, with possibilities for a follow-up interview.

These MET interventions reach various populations with varying needs and through different methods. These applications are available to providers to address the needs of alcohol- and substance-related concerns at varying stages of change and need. Four sessions are offered over a 12-week period with initiation after completion of an intensive assessment process. The use of standardized measures occurs at session 1, and clear, concise feedback about the patient's addiction behavior is relayed to the patient in each session. Session 2 is intended to develop a change plan. Session 3 is used for reinforcement and enhancing commitment to motivation and change. Session 4 is termination (DiClemente et al., 1999). In assessing the model, research indicates that each individual intervention approach shows promise for a variety of clients suffering from alcohol abuse. In terms of future interventions, more information on the use of combination therapies, such as cognitive and motivation techniques, is needed.

Traditional Self-Help Approach

The traditional 12-step treatment has been traditionally considered a primary intervention strategy for those suffering from alcohol and other narcotic substances misuse (Wallace, 2012). Two popular 12-step orientation programs are Alcoholics Anonymous (AA) and Narcotics Anonymous (NA). Both center around the concept of the inability and powerlessness of chemically affected persons to control their substance use with the expectation of the commitment to lifelong abstinence from alcohol and other substances of abuse (Marinchak & Morgan, 2012). These approaches, particularly AA, are referred to as the traditional approach. The disease model provided through AA is the major nonmedical support system for alcohol-related concerns. This type of treatment provides emotional support and practical advice from individuals who have been in similar circumstances. Many, but not all, chemically affected individuals may benefit by this type of mutual self-help fellowship. It is an extensive model of mutual peer-to-peer self-help group worldwide (described as horizontal clinical relationship services), with more than 100,000 groups, associated with long-term abstinence (Carroll, 2009; Parker et al., 2008).

The 12-step model (see Quick Reference 12.13) forbids promotion, and anonymity is of paramount importance. "While some addicted

QUICK REFERENCE 12.13

12 Steps to Recovery

1. We admitted we were powerless over alcohol—that our lives had become unmanageable.
2. Came to believe that a power greater than ourselves could restore us to sanity.
3. Made a decision to turn our will, and our lives, over to the care of God as we understood Him.
4. Made a searching and fearless moral inventory of ourselves.
5. Admitted to God, to ourselves, and to another human being the exact nature of our wrongs.
6. Were entirely ready to have God remove all these defects of character.
7. Humbly asked Him to remove our shortcomings.
8. Made a list of all persons we had harmed, and became willing to make amends to them all.
9. Made direct amends to such people wherever possible, except when to do so would injure them or others.
10. Continued to take personal inventory and when we were wrong promptly admit it.
11. Sought through prayer and meditation to improve our conscious contact with God, as we understood Him, praying only for knowledge of His will for us and the power to carry that out.
12. Having had a spiritual awakening as the result of these steps, we tried to carry this message to alcoholics and to practice these principles in all our affairs.

Source: National Institute on Alcohol Abuse and Alcoholism, No. 30 PH 359, October 1995.

individuals, for various reasons, will not accept or engage in self-help programs in a manner that produces a good experience, the great majority of addicted men and women will obtain support, encouragement, information, insight, guidance, friendship, genuine caring, and occasionally a much needed friendly kick-in-the-ass from their self-help programs" (Carroll, 2009, p. 331). Also, AA differentiates religion from spirituality and bases beliefs in a "higher power of one's own understanding." Alcoholics Anonymous also urges participation in Al-Anon for family members. Despite criticisms, many feel strongly that this model of intervention works and this type of fellowship program remains an important component of any type of case management and follow-up.

BRIEF INTERVENTIONS IN PRIMARY CARE SETTINGS

For the substance-related disorders, most specifically alcohol use disorder, in the primary care setting, brief interventions may be of assistance (Barry & Blow, 2012). These methods can assist clients with hazardous and harmful drinking in nondependence alcohol use disorders. These approaches are often used in primary care and accident and emergency settings by general practitioners and nurses, requiring minimal training and lasting anywhere from a few minutes to 20 to 30 minutes or for extended brief interventions lasting for four sessions or more (Parker et al., 2008; Walker et al., 2007). Parker et al. (2008) outline brief interventions that educate clients about the negative effects of alcohol abuse and motivate them to reduce consumption to sensible or less risky levels, provide the tools for change, and indicate underlying problems using a model of intervention termed *frames*. In the frames delivery of intervention: (a) *feedback* is respectfully given that outlines the concerns of the client that will provide structure and reduce harm; (b) emphasis is placed on the client's accepting *responsibility* for change; (c) clear *advice* is given to make a change in drinking; (d) discuss a *menu* of options for making change; (e) listen and express *empathy* and be nonjudgmental; and (f) reinforce the patient's *self-efficacy*, stressing that positive change is possible and, when made, that it will be beneficial (p. 498).

Detoxification and Withdrawal

In substance use, entry to the treatment setting often starts with detoxification, although it is not a stand-alone treatment (Zweben, 2012). Detoxification is the medically assisted process during which the client removes all substances and toxins from his or her system. Completion of this phase usually occurs in an inpatient hospital (Henderson, Landry, Phillips, & Shuman, 1994). The risk associated with detoxification of alcohol can lead to dangerous withdrawal syndromes, leaving the client in critical need of immediate medical attention (Fuller & Hiller-Sturmhofel, 1999; Wesson, 1995). In addition to alcohol, the opioids, sedatives, and hypnotics can also result in substantial physical withdrawal symptoms (Carroll & Kiluk, 2012). Generally, benzodiazepines, which can be extremely addicting, remain the standard of care to reduce the symptoms of withdrawal. These withdrawal syndromes are characterized by a continuum of signs and symptoms usually beginning 12 to 48 hours after cessation of intake. The milder symptoms of withdrawal syndrome include tremor, weakness, sweating, hyperreflexia, and gastrointestinal symptoms. Some patients have generalized tonic-clonic seizures (alcoholic epilepsy or rum fits), usually not more than two in short succession (Mattoo et al., 2009; Wesson, 1995).

Medication as a Treatment Modality

Medications in the detoxification and ongoing treatment of substance disorders particularly alcohol and the opiates have continued to emerge as a prominent treatment approach (Carroll & Kiluk, 2012). Although mental health practitioners cannot prescribe medications, it would be a noticeable deficit if they were uneducated in this approach (Dziegielewski, 2010). Recent advances in neuroimaging show actual changes to the brain of individuals suffering from the addictive disorders. This *medicalization* of the substance use disorders can help to make others aware of the neurobiological basis of substance abuse, thereby diminishing societal stigma related to personal failure (Chung et al., 2012). Once we are aware of the genetic and biologic profile of an individual, we can better select and modify medication treatments that maximize safety and efficacy.

The brain consists of multiple neurotransmitter systems that modulate various bodily functions, including opioids such as glutamate, serotonin (5HT), and dopamine (Johnson & Ait-Daoud, 1999). It is beyond the scope of this chapter to describe the neurobiology of substance use; however, awareness of the neurotransmitter dopamine is of particular interest (Chung et al., 2012). Dopamine plays an important role, particularly in how dopamine-rich cells can influence reward responses. In addition, opioids are pain blockers, with effects similar to morphine or heroin occurring naturally in the brain.

In alcohol use, these pain blockers appear to increase the sense of rewarding effects when alcohol is consumed. The GABA (gamma-amino butyric acid) inhibited responses are a key component in aversive pharmacological treatments. Growing evidence demonstrates that the modulation of glutamatergic neurotransmission receptor agonists with *N*-methyl-D-aspartate (NMDA) to inhibit GABA attenuate operant responding for alcohol and prevent alcohol dependence (Evans et al., 2007). When combined to block GABA and decrease NMDA, these blockers provide a decreased response to cravings for alcohol. Glutamate is an excitatory transmitter that works with brain receptor sites, increasing the effects of intoxication, cognitive impairment, and some symptoms of withdrawal in alcohol consumption. Serotonin affects bodily functioning in varied psychological and physiological ways, including cognition, mood, sleep, and appetite. Dopamine is linked to higher brain functioning and organization of thought and perception (Johnson & Ait-Daud, 1999).

Three medications approved by the FDA to treat alcohol dependence are disulfiram (Antabuse), naltrexone (Revia), and acamprosate (Campral); the longest-standing medication used in treatment to prevent relapse from alcohol use is disulfiram (Chung et al., 2012). Disulfiram, often known in the lay community as Antabuse, is referred to as aversive because it produces unpleasant reactions to alcohol when consumed (Evans et al., 2007; Parker et al., 2008). This medication can cause negative physiological reactions, including nausea, vomiting, and increased blood pressure and heart rate, as well as dissociation, cognitive disturbances, and memory impairments (Evans et al., 2007). However, problems with poor compliance decrease the medication's effectiveness. Safety concerns regarding contraindications for people with cardiovascular disease, a history of cardiovascular accident (CVA), hypertension, pregnancy, or psychosis have resulted in reduced use of disulfiram (Evans et al., 2007; Parker et al., 2008).

Naltrexone and acamprosate are considered safer than disulfiram and produce the same effects with minimal contraindications. Naltrexone is an opiate-blocking agent, and acamprosate modulates GABA/glutamate (Bonn, 1999; Petrakis & Krystal, 1997). Memantine (known as Namenda) is used in Europe to treat alcohol dependence; it was approved by the Food and Drug Administration (FDA) in 2003 and also results in decreased craving. It is reported that with memantine, the aversive response is not as severe as the other pharmacological treatments, yet comparison of the same positive response warrants further study (Evans et al., 2007).

Some pharmacological treatments used to treat alcohol withdrawal are central nervous system depressants, also known as psychotherapeutics (e.g., benzodiazepines) (Carroll & Kiluk, 2012). They reduce the signs and symptoms of withdrawal; longer-acting benzodiazepines (e.g., chlordiazepoxide [Librium], diazepam [Valium]) may assist with preventing seizures, and shorter-acting benzodiazepines (e.g., lorazepam [Ativan], oxazepam [Serax]) may assist with preventing significant liver disease (Parker et al., 2008). The main problem with using benzodiazepines in all areas of the substance-related disorders is that these medications can also produce intoxication, dependence, and withdrawal, creating a secondary further addiction problem (Hood, O'Neil, & Hulse, 2009; Miller & Gold, 1998; Myrick & Anton, 1998). Medication-assisted therapy (MAT), which utilizes medications such as methadone and buprenorphine, is designed to assist with withdrawal and reduce the cravings related to substance dependence; however, this medication-focused treatment alone does not create a lifestyle supportive of recovery, and supplemental approaches may be indicated (Rabinowitz, 2009).

TOPICS OF INTEREST

Alcohol: Differences in Age

Variations of drinking patterns emerge in the transition from adolescence to adulthood. Experimentation is a normal developmental pattern in adolescence but can lead to problem drinking into adulthood if onset of drinking begins at earlier ages. Early age of first use is a significant predictor of subsequent transitions from alcohol (or drug use) to dependence (Pagan et al., 2006; Swendsen et al., 2009). Divergence from experimentation to problem use may be attributed to developmental biological changes and environmental factors influencing use, including hormone fluctuations that affect alcohol sensitivities and neurocognitive development. Alcohol sensitivity increases with age, which accounts for the intense and quick sedation that occurs in adults and not in adolescents and causes adults to stop drinking after shorter periods than adolescents (Schulte et al., 2009). This may also explain the increased tolerance developed with earlier-age drinking, leading to dependence into adulthood.

Alcohol: Gender Differences

Prevalence rates for alcohol use disorders remain higher in males than in females. Attributable deaths due to alcohol use also remain higher in males at 90% for alcohol use worldwide and 9.9% to 6.3% in women (SAMHSA, 2009a, 2009b; Schulte et al., 2009). Biological differences in gender allow differences in alcohol reactivity and how these relate to problem drinking. Alcohol sensitivity in drinking affects women nonlinearly, more in the realm of negative motor and cognitive deficits than men, with women suffering greater task completion impairment than men at similar levels of alcohol concentration (Schulte et al., 2009; Sohrabji, 2003). This difference may explain why men develop higher rates of alcohol use disorders than women. Generally, men consume more alcohol than women to achieve the same effects that result in alcohol intoxication. These greater amounts of consumption increase their level of tolerance and consequently the development of dependence. From the standpoint of volume of alcohol consumed and the effects of alcohol sensitivity to cognition in men and women, when 0.5 liter is consumed (three drinks or less), cognitive abilities improved for both compared with those not drinking, whereas drinking 1 liter (six or more drinks) impaired cognitive ability in both sexes. When the volume of alcohol is within the range of 0.5 to 1 liter, however, cognitive ability improves for men but not for women, resulting in susceptibility to alcohol-related cognitive dementia (Sohrabji, 2003).

Physiological gender differences in body mass ratio also may explain protective differences to the effects of alcohol. Greater body fat in women and hormonal changes reduce water levels in the body, increasing sensitivity to alcohol and thus increasing blood alcohol concentrations compared with males with proportional body weight (Schulte et al., 2009). As this sensitivity is higher in women than men, it decreases women's propensity for dependence. This is attributed to differences in metabolic rates; females have slower elimination rates of alcohol than males because of enzymes and hormone fluctuations during reproductive cycles.

Alcohol is metabolized earlier in men because the enzymes of dehydrogenase needed to break down acetaldehyde are higher in men than in women; alcohol metabolism is further affected in women by the presence of estrogen during the reproductive cycle—a hormone not present in males (Sohrabji, 2003). Because of the low elimination rates, secondary conditions related to alcohol consumption in women can lead to breast cancer, loss of bone density (osteoporosis), and Alzheimer's disease. These differences should be considered in assessing for substance-related disorders and subsequent treatment. Yet despite these differences, disparities in treatment and access to care are more pronounced in gender. This situation can be attributed to the difference in rates of stigma between the sexes when addressing alcohol-related concerns.

Substance Disorders and Disabilities

Certain conditions that result in disability, such as learning disorders, sensory impairments (e.g., blindness and deafness), developmental disabilities, mental retardation, and postinjury disabilities (e.g., brain injury or spinal cord injury), increase the risk for substance-related disorders. Of these conditions, learning disabilities account for 40% to 60% prevalence rates of AOD, sensory impairments account for 35% to 50%, postinjury disabilities account for 25% to 75%, mental retardation accounts for approximately 10%, with an unidentified estimate of prevalence rates for individuals with other coexisting disabilities, such as borderline intellectual functioning and developmental disabilities (Janikowski et al., 2007; Robertson et al., 2009). Fifty percent of traumatic brain injury and spinal injuries are related to alcohol-related circumstances, and many of these individuals may return to alcohol use poststabilization. When abstinence is achieved, negative physical circumstances (e.g., seizures) may lead to the need for residential treatment care. Facilities to assist these individuals in recovery are limited, especially when there is a coexisting mental health condition and alcohol and other substance-related conditions (Huggins et al., 2008; Janikowski et al., 2007; Robertson et al., 2009).

Some of the disabilities individuals present with also have a history of alcohol- and substance-related concerns within the family system, and this pattern of behavior can have a lifelong course; for example, prenatal substance abuse and FASD, learning disorders, intellectual disabilities, neurodevelopmental deficits, limited and/or impairment in a triad of function impairment (e.g., executive functions, communication, and behaviors), and limited social interactions place a higher stress on emotion regulation already limited in those with these impairments. Paradoxically, these limitations require prescribed treatment and management for alcohol and substance-related abstinence, including finding alternatives to lifestyle (a limitation in the life domain and occupation), alternatives through problem solving (a cognitive deficit), and substituting peer using and places of use (and emotional difficulty for those with already limited social interactions) (Janikowski et al., 2007).

Taken advantage of and exploited because of their learning differential, functional limitations, and communication barriers, individuals with certain neurodevelopmental disorders and neurophysiological disabilities present with challenges in clinical presentation but require assessment and treatment due to the risk factors involved. Although treatment can be initiated at any stage, because of the severe medical complications resulting from this illness, the goal is to intervene in the early progression to prevent permanent brain damage or death. (See Quick Reference 12.14.)

Integrated Approach: Implications for Practice

Substance use is a multifaceted problem that results from elements of conditioning and of social learning, as well as from neurobiological processes, genetics, cognitive processes, and influences from family systems, society, and

QUICK REFERENCE 12.14

EARLY RECOGNITION OF ALCOHOL-RELATED PROBLEMS

Early Indicators

- ☐ Heavy drinking (more than 6 drinks per day (i.e., greater than 60 grams per day of ethanol for men) and more than 4 drinks per day for women (i.e., greater than 40 grams of ethanol).
- ☐ Concern about drinking by self, family, or both.
- ☐ Intellectual impairment, especially in the abstracting, planning, organizing, and adaptive skills.
- ☐ Eating lightly or skipping meals.
- ☐ Drinking alcohol rapidly.
- ☐ Increased tolerance to alcohol.

Psychosocial Factors

- ☐ Accidents and injuries related to drinking.
- ☐ Absence from work related to drinking.
- ☐ Majority of friends and acquaintances are heavy drinkers; most leisure activities and sports center on drinking.
- ☐ Attempts to cut down on drinking have had limited success.
- ☐ Frequent use of alcohol to deal with stressful situations.
- ☐ Frequent drinking during the workday, especially at lunch break.
- ☐ Heavy smoking.

Investigation Factors

- ☐ Macrocytosis (MCV of red cells more than 100) in the absence of anemia.
- ☐ An elevated GGT (gamma-glutamyl transpeptidase).
- ☐ Elevated serum uric acid level.
- ☐ Elevated high-density lipoprotein.
- ☐ Random blood alcohol level (BAC) greater than 0.05 g %.

Clinical Symptoms and Signs

- ☐ Trauma
- ☐ Scars unrelated to surgery
- ☐ Elevated pulse
- ☐ Hand tremor and sweating
- ☐ Psoriasis
- ☐ Alcohol smell on breath during the day
- ☐ Dyspepsia
- ☐ Morning nausea and vomiting
- ☐ Recurring diarrhea
- ☐ Pancreatitis
- ☐ Hepatomegaly
- ☐ Impotence
- ☐ Palpitations
- ☐ Hypertension
- ☐ Insomnia
- ☐ Nightmares

culture (Lam, O'Farrell, & Birchler, 2012; Latorre, 2000). Turner (1996) explains that for "too long we have labored under an impression that adherence to one approach to practice by definition excluded others; there was some component of disloyalty or some quality of Machiavellian manipulation to attempt to move from one approach to another depending on the situation" (p. 709). When separating these perspectives for practice, each intervention strategy has its own strengths and limitations. For example, the best plan of cognitive-behavioral intervention can easily go astray if environmental agents and family supports are ignored. Incorporating the ideas from systems theory as part of the intervention process allows the practitioner to acknowledge the importance of the situational context, taking into account the whole picture. Intervention needs to include more than just the individual and always involves the systems that will affect family behavior change strategy.

A popular intervention strategy, with current emphasis on evidence-based practices, is the harm reduction approach. In harm reduction, substance-related concerns are addressed from a public health model of care. Harm reduction seeks to decrease problems (harm) incurred from use without denying services or care based on continued substance-related use. From this perspective, services are targeted at the individual's stage of change, and efforts are made to increase the client's motivation for continued changes. Services included in the harm reduction model are needle exchange programs for intravenous (IV) drug users, teaching IV drug injectors how to clean needles, methadone maintenance programs, providing condoms to sexually active clients, providing psychotropic medications for those with co-occurring disorders, and facilitating access and opportunity to treatment to anyone seeking it (Carroll, 2009).

Harm reduction rests on five assumptions, as described by MacMaster (2004):

1. Focus on reducing drug-related harm rather than focus on drug use reduction.
2. Abstinence is effective at reducing substance-related harms, but there are other possible services and objectives to address that can reduce substance-related harm.
3. Substance abuse and dependence are harmful, but some of their more harmful consequences (e.g., HIV/AIDS, hepatitis) can be eliminated without having to achieve complete abstinence.
4. Services for substance-related problems need to be relevant to substance-related concerns and be user friendly to be most effective at minimizing harm.
5. Substance abuse and dependence should be understood from a broad perspective rather than focusing on the problem as an individual act, shifting substance-related solutions away from coercive practices and a criminal justice system.

The harm reduction framework and approach to treatment utilizes the stage-based model of treatment (e.g., motivational enhancement therapies), providing assessment of clients' motivational states and gearing interventions according to their level of motivation and readiness. From this perspective, individuals are supported during the decision-making process, receiving all substance-related services despite active use. This approach is central to integrated care and integrated team treatment and is used with concurrent integrated approaches to public health. Because of its emphasis on effective measures, quality of care, and cost-effective measures, harm reduction is favored by insurance companies and managed care organizations. Likewise, with the Wellstone-Domenici Mental Health and Addiction Equity Parity Act of 2008, in principle, the harm reduction model also integrates rather than differentiates medical from mental health and substance abuse services.

Harm reduction, however, is not without criticism. Programs known as abstinence-based programs are at odds with the harm reduction model. Abstinence-based programs require clients to abstain from use, and if the client has been unable to achieve abstinence, then it is thought best that the client hit rock bottom before he or she can begin to accept and recognize the need for change (Van Wormer, 2008). Others contest this approach by citing that these programs do not discharge or drop out nonabstinent clients. Rather, abstinence-based programs require clients to remain abstinent while in treatment; if they relapse while in treatment, they are transferred to other care options (Carroll, 2009).

In addressing harm reduction, the position of care is that demanding abstinence is an unrealistic position that fails to understand the severity and complications of a substance-related disorder, while acknowledging the *DSM* definition. In contrast, abstinence-based programs take the position that substance use is a problem, and according to the *DSM* definition of a substance use problem, abstinence is the means to achieve control because moderation cannot be achieved. What these two approaches share is that their focus is identifying and treating problematic use. The abstinence-based approach implies that each failed opportunity is a learning experience, which should motivate the client more quickly to desire abstinence (often due to the consequences suffered with each learning experience). The abstinence-based approach focuses solely on individual acts and effects of use on the individual and immediate social relations but does not actively intervene in these acts. The harm reduction approach implies that motivation to change can be enacted at any point without having to fail to achieve the desired result; it supports clients who already suffer from the experience of abuse and dependence without applying further consequences. This focuses on individual acts and social relations and unrelated extended social relations affected by substance-related use. In harm reduction programs, needle exchanges are implemented as a preventive measure (e.g., decrease the incidence of HIV/AIDS, staph infections, and other communicable diseases).

With respect to integrated care and the integration of services, the changes to a market-based delivery of services has continued to shift health and allied professional services to specialized care (attributed to insurance and managed care billing and reimbursement requirements and restrictions). This places a greater demand on provider professional education and training requirements to provide outcome-based services in substance-related programs. The harm reduction-based programs emphasize these stipulations in their approaches and implementation of service provision. Providers from abstinence-based programs sometimes use peer-to-peer providers who provide counseling but do not have the educational requirements of a trained professional. This has caused providers of abstinence programs who formerly did not require educational training to provide substance-use services to now require counselors to acquire specialized training and certifications (e.g., Credentialed Alcohol and Substance Abuse Counseling Programs [CASAC]) so the facility can seek reimbursement for the services provided.

For practitioners, the client has to be viewed as a system, and treatment strategy needs to be customized with a multidimensional approach that addresses the problems identified. Regardless of what approach is used, the role of the practitioner is primarily that of an educator who expects clients to set their own standards, monitor their own performance, and reward or reinforce themselves appropriately. In this respect, the practitioner strives to self-empower clients to become active change agents. An integrated approach that involves family education and support combined with self-help groups is particularly important to patients in treatment.

Significant others and any other persons close to the client with a substance-related disorder typically also benefit from treatment. The family and the client's support system are a vital and powerful aspect of his or her ability to recover. If the intervention strategy does not include the client's family system, the prognosis for long-term recovery from the illness is greatly decreased. From the traditional perspective, AA urges participation in Al-Anon for family members.

Among the tasks of the practitioner are (a) helping the client and the family accept that alcoholism is the primary problem, (b) recommending treatment options, and (c) instilling hope for recovery. Therapeutic alternatives are the use of Antabuse, individual therapy, family therapy, and AA. Relapses, when properly handled, can help the individual with substance abuse accept his or her powerlessness over alcohol. Treatment manuals free to the public for working with specialized populations are listed next. All are available from the U.S. Department of Health and Human Services, Center for Substance Abuse, 1 Choke Cherry Road, Rockville, MD 20857 (http://www.samhsa.gov).

- *Detoxification and substance abuse treatment: A treatment improvement protocol* (TIP). (2006). N. S. Miller and S. S. Kipnis.
- *A provider's introduction to substance abuse treatment for lesbian, gay, bisexual and transgender individuals.* (2009).
- *Substance abuse treatment for persons with HIV and AIDS: Treatment improvement protocol series* (37). (2008). S. L. Batki and P. A. Selwyn, Consensus Panel Co-Chairs.

MISUSE OF PRESCRIPTION MEDICATIONS

Psychotherapeutic drug use has developed into a new trend in substance-related disorders, accounting for 6.2 million people in the United States in the age bracket of 12 and above with abuse and dependence problems (SAMHSA, 2009b; WHO, 2009a). It is the second-highest substance use problem after marijuana use. Excessive availability and inadequate regulation have increased the consumption of psychotherapeutic drugs through prescriptions, illegal street vendors, and the Internet. These modes of acquisition have led to an increased use of benzodiazepines and other anxiolytics. It is estimated that 15% to 44% of chronic benzodiazepine users become addicted and, upon cessation, experience severe withdrawal symptoms, including emergent anxiety and depressive symptoms (Hood et al., 2009).

The *DSM-5* identifies sedatives-hypnotic-anxiolytic-related disorders under the 10 classes of substances in the classification for substance-related disorders (APA, 2013). Included in this category are medications such as the benzodiazepines (e.g., diazepam [Valium] and clonazepam [Klonopin]), carbamates (e.g., gluthethimide) barbiturates (e.g., secobarbital), and barbiturate-like hypnotics, including all prescription sleeping medications (e.g., eszopiclone [Lunesta], zolpidem [Ambien]) and almost all prescription antianxiety medications, excluding nonbenzodiazepine antianxiety agents (e.g., buspirone [Buspar], gepirone) as this group is not generally related to misuse (APA, 2013, p. 552). When used properly, psychotherapeutic medications can alleviate suffering associated with symptoms of mental disorders and/or neurological disorders for those who truly suffer from them. Long-term use of these drugs prescribed for psychosocial stressors rather than for mental disorders has created problems, including dependence. Moreover, nonmedical use of psychotherapeutic drugs has also increased for recreational purposes in youths using stimulants rather than for intended use (e.g., amphetamine and dextroamphetamine [Adderall] and methylphenidate [Ritalin]).

There are three reasons this area has become so controversial.

1. The use and misuse of psychotherapeutic medications have caused major shifts in the structure and delivery of services for mental disorders. The restructuring in the system of care has resulted in a changing of the epistemological basis of the *DSM*. Subsequently, this change has led to modifications to the ontological understanding of mental disorders and classifications, as well as the treatments. To state that these drugs were instrumental in providing solutions to alter an entire structural system is an understatement. The increased availability and unmonitored consumption is an unintended and unexpected consequence.
2. The social sanctioning of psychotherapeutic medications (unlike illicit drugs) leads people to believe that these medications, approved by trusted institutions (such as the FDA), are safe. These medications are seen as cures rather than causes of a social ill. Yet because of the concerns and the large number of people who use psychotherapeutic drugs, their safety and efficacy has become a subject of great discussion. The FDA has authorized label revisions for antidepressants that list stimulant effects, as too many providers are unaware of some adverse and intoxicating effects of these medications (especially the newer psychotherapeutics) (Breggin, 2006).
3. Limited emphasis is placed on the addiction, dependence, and withdrawal that can result from the use of prescription medications. Often, intoxication and dependence are associated primarily with street drugs and alcohol, not with prescription medications. Public perceptions of prescriptions are associated with cures; illicit drugs and alcohol are not—even though their composition and effects are quite similar if not the same. The majority of people who take prescribed psychotherapeutic medications have no prior experience with the intoxicating effects of these drugs, nor do their families and friends, but most can easily recognize the intoxicating effects of alcohol or other types of drug use (e.g., slurred speech, gait disturbance) (Breggin, 2006).

Practitioners working with clients using substances (legally or illegally) need to collaborate with both nonmedically and medically trained personnel to ensure adequate awareness of the medications taken, especially when there is a history of substance misuse. The presumption that medications (whether OTC or prescription) are safe is false and minimizes the likelihood of problematic misuse that could lead to intoxication and withdrawal. The role of the practitioner in helping clients understand, communicate, monitor, and document issues surrounding the use of prescription and nonprescription medications is important. When a client appears to be using a prescription or nonprescription drug improperly and dependence may result, a medical exam must determine the degree of intervention needed. In addition, a comprehensive medication history helps the intervention team prescribe appropriate treatment protocols. It should include past substance abuse history and all drugs used by the client (including OTC prescriptions, herbal remedies, and prescribed medications) (Dziegielewski, 2010). The benefits of psychotherapeutic medications can be far-reaching, and so can their misuse.

SUMMARY AND FUTURE DIRECTIONS

The individual suffering from a substance-related and addictive disorder can experience severe social, psychological, and physical consequences. These disorders can also have a profound impact on individuals, their families, and society. The causes of substance addiction are often as diverse as those afflicted. The etiology of this varied group of disorders can be attributed to genetics and the environment, social stressors, and family systems, with associated risk factors of age, gender, and disability. Yet, intervention that is initiated early can minimize cognitive and biological deterioration, especially with the substances that can lead to withdrawal. In addition, involving the family is central. As Lander et al. (2013) stated so eloquently, treating the individual without the family falls short in two basic areas: It ignores the devastating impact the disorder can have on the family and leaves the family system untreated and unsure how to cope and regroup.

Individuals with substance use disorders and addictive disorders such as gambling disorder who recover continue to need peer, family, and community support. Theories from sociology and psychology related to substance use provide the foundation for the models, practice, treatment interventions, and prevention efforts to follow. Depending on the substance, various treatment modalities can assist clients at various stages of the recovery process (e.g., medically assisted detoxification and pharmacology). These approaches can teach clients to change maladaptive, harmful, hazardous substance use patterns to adaptive alternatives. Models such as cognitive-behavioral therapy, motivational enhancement therapy, and self-help groups can assist. Current approaches utilizing harm reduction versus abstinence-based approaches are available to help the counselor determine which can best serve a client. Regardless of the treatment approach selected, one aspect remains clear. The presence of SUDs is so great in the general population, whether trained to recognize these disorders or not, they will be confronted in practice. One cardinal rule is to always make sure that confidentiality is given the utmost priority and discussed openly with the client (Lander et al., 2013). All practitioners must possess knowledge about substance-related disorders, processes, and the impacts substances can have on both the individual and his or her support system; this information is imperative for effective practice and service.

REFERENCES

American Psychiatric Association. (1994). *Diagnostic and statistical manual of mental disorders* (4th ed., rev). Washington, DC: Author.

American Psychiatric Association. (2000). *Diagnostic and statistical manual of mental disorders* (4th ed., text rev.). Washington, DC: Author.

American Psychiatric Association. (2013). *Diagnostic and statistical manual of mental disorders* (5th ed.). Arlington, VA: American Psychiatric Publishing.

Avery, J. (2014). Substance-related and addictive disorders: Introduction. In J. W. Barnhill (Ed.), *DSM-5™ clinical cases* (pp. 251–252). Washington, DC: American Psychiatric Publishing.

Barry, K. L., & Blow, F. C. (2012). Addressing substance abuse in primary care settings. In S. W. Walters & F. Rotgers (Eds.), *Treating substance abuse: Theory and techniques* (3rd ed., pp. 355–375). New York, NY: Guilford Press.

Bonn, D. (1999). New treatments for alcohol dependency better than old (News). *The Lancet, 353*(9148), 213. doi: 10.1016/S0140-6736(99)00012-4

BRAD. (n.d.). *B.R.A.D.: Be Responsible about Drinking.* Retrieved from http://www.brad21.org/bac_charts.html

Breggin, P. R. (2006). Intoxication anosognosia: The spellbinding effect of psychiatric drugs. *Ethical Human Psychology and Psychiatry, 893*, 201–215.

Carroll, J. F. X. (2009). Concerns about aspects of harm reduction and the overselling of evidence-based practices in the treatment of alcohol/other drug problems. *Alcoholism Treatment Quarterly, 27*(3), 329–337.

Carroll, K. M., & Kiluk, B. D. (2012). Integrating psychotherapy and pharmacotherapy in substance abuse treatment. In S. W. Walters & F. Rotgers (Eds.), *Treating substance abuse: Theory and techniques* (3rd ed., pp. 319–354). New York, NY: Guilford Press.

Chung, P. H., Ross, J. D., Wakhlu, S., & Adinoff, B. (2012). Neurobiological bases of addiction treatment. In S. W. Walters & F. Rotgers (Eds.), *Treating substance abuse: Theory and techniques* (3rd ed., pp. 231–318). New York, NY: Guilford Press.

Craig, L. C., Attwood, A. S., Benton, C. P., Penton-Voak, I. S., & Munafo, M. R. (2009). Effects of acute alcohol consumption and alcohol expectancy on processing of perceptual cues of emotional expression. *Journal of Psychopharmacology, 23*(3), 258–265.

Curtis, O. (1999). *Chemical dependency: A family affair.* Pacific Grove, CA: Brooks/Cole.

Daley. D. C., & Feit, M. D. (2013). The many roles of social workers in the prevention and treatment of alcohol and drug addiction: A major health and social problem affecting individuals, families and society. *Social Work in Public Health, 28*(3–4), 159–164.

Dallery, J., Meredith, S. E., & Budney, A. J. (2012). Contingency management in substance abuse treatment. In S. W. Walters & F. Rotgers (Eds.), *Treating substance abuse: Theory and techniques* (3rd ed., pp. 81–112). New York, NY: Guilford Press.

DiClemente, C. C., Bellino, L. E., & Neavins, T. M. (1999). Motivation for change and alcohol treatment. *Alcohol Research and Health, 23*(2), 86–92.

Duncan, T. E., Duncan, S. C., & Hops, H. (1998). Latent variable modeling of longitudinal and multilevel alcohol use data. *Journal of Studies on Alcohol, 59*(4), 399–409.

Dziegielewski, S. F. (2010). *Psychopharmacology and social work practice: A person in environment approach* (2nd ed.). New York, NY: Springer.

Evans, S. M., Levin, F. R., Brooks, D. J., & Garawi, F. (2007). A pilot double-blind treatment trial of memantine for alcohol dependence. *Alcoholism: Clinical and Experimental Research, 31*(5), 775–782. doi: 10.1111/j.1530-0277.2007.00360

Foxcroft, D. R., Kypri, K., & Simonite, V. (2009). Bayes' theorem to estimate population prevalence from alcohol use disorders identification test (AUDIT) scores. *Addiction, 104*(7), 1132–1137. doi: 10.1111/j.1360-0443.2009.02574.x

Fuller, R. K., & Hiller-Sturmhofel, S. (1999). Alcoholism treatment in the United States: An overview. *Alcohol Research and Health, 23*(2), 69–77.

Henderson, R., Landry, M., Phillips, C., & Shuman, D. (1994). *Intensive outpatient treatment for alcohol and other drug abuse: Treatment improvement protocol (TIP)* (Series No. 8, Publication No. SMA 94B2077). Rockville, MD: U.S. Department of Health and Human Services.

Hood, S., O'Neil, G., & Hulse, G. (2009). The role of flumazeil in the treatment of benzodiazepine dependence: Physiological and psychological profiles. *Journal of Psychopharmacology, 23*(4), 401–409. doi: 10.1177/0269881108100322

Huggins, J. E., Grant, T., O'Malley, K., & Streissguth, A. P. (2008). Suicide attempts among adults with fetal alcohol spectrum disorders: Clinical considerations. *Mental Health Aspects of Developmental Disabilities, 11*(2), 33–41.

Humeniuk, R., Ali, R., Babor, T. F., Farrell, M., Formigoni, M. L., Jittiwutikarn, J., . . . Simon, S. (2008). Validation of the alcohol, smoking and substance involvement screening test (ASSIST). *Addiction, 103*(6), 1039–1047. doi: 10.1111/j.1360-0443.2007.02114.x

Janikowski, T. P., Donnelly, J. P., & Lawrence, J. (2007). The functional limitations of clients with co-existing disabilities. *Journal of Rehabilitation, 73*(4), 15–22.

Johnson, B. A., & Ait-Daoud, N. (1999). Medications to treat alcoholism. *Alcohol Research and Health, 23*(2), 99–106.

Jones, K. (1969). *Drugs and alcohol.* New York, NY: Harper & Row.

Lam, W. K., O'Farrell, T. J., & Birchler, G. R. (2012). Family therapy techniques for substance abuse treatment. In S. W. Walters & F. Rotgers (Eds.), *Treating substance abuse: Theory and techniques* (3rd ed., pp. 256–280). New York, NY: Guilford Press.

Lander, L., Howsare, J., & Byrne, M. (2013). The impact of substance use disorders on families and children: From theory to practice. *Social Work in Public Health, 28*, 194–205. doi: 10.1080/19371918.2013.759005

Latorre, M. A. (2000). A holistic view of psychotherapy: Connecting mind, body, and spirit. *Perspectives in Psychiatric Care, 36*(2), 67–68. doi: 10.1111/j.1744-6163.2000.tb00693

Lee, J., Jang, M., Lee, J., Kim, S., Kim, K., Park, J., . . . Yoo, J. (2005). Clinical predictors for delirium tremens in alcohol dependence. *Journal of Gastroenterology and Hepatology, 20*(12), 1833–1837. doi: 10.1111/j.1440-1746.2005.03932.x

Levounis, P. Addiction. In J. W. Barnhill (Ed.), *DSM-5^{TM} Clinical cases* (pp. 257–259). Washington, DC: American Psychiatric Publishing.

MacMaster, S. A. (2004). Harm reduction: A new perspective on substance abuse services. *Social Work, 49*(3), 356–363.

Marinchak, J. S., & Morgan, T. J. (2012). Behavioral treatment techniques for psychoactive substance disorders. In S. W. Walters & F. Rotgers (Eds.), *Treating substance abuse: Theory and techniques* (3rd ed., pp. 138–166). New York, NY: Guilford Press.

Mattoo, S. K., Singh, S. M., Bhardwaj, R., Kumar, S., Basu, D., & Kulhara, P. (2009). Prevalence and correlates of epileptic seizure in substance-abusing subjects. *Psychiatry and Clinical Neuroscience, 63*(4), 580–582. doi: 10.1111/j.1440-1819.2009.01980.x

McCrady, B. S., Ladd, B. O., & Hallgren, K. A. (2012). Theoretical bases of family approaches to substance abuse treatment. In S. W. Walters & F. Rotgers (Eds.). *Treating substance abuse: Theory and techniques* (3rd ed., pp. 224–255). New York, NY: Guilford Press.

Michel, M. E., Pintello, D. A., & Subramaniam, G. (2013). Blending research and practice: An evolving dissemination strategy in substance abuse. *Social Work in Public Health, 28*(3–4), 302–312. doi: 10.1080/19371918.2013.774660

Milkman, H., & Sederer, L. (1990). *Treatment choices for alcoholism and drug abuse.* New York, NY: Lexington Books.

Miller, N. S., & Gold, M. S. (1998). Management of withdrawal syndromes and relapse prevention in drug and alcohol dependence. *American Family Physician, 58*(1), 139–147.

Myrick, H., & Anton, R. F. (1998). Treatment of alcohol withdrawal. *Alcohol Health and Research World, 22*(1), 38–44.

National Institute of Drug Abuse (NIDA). (2011). *Commonly abused drug chart.* Retrieved from http://www.drugabuse.gov/drugs-abuse/commonly-abused-drugs/commonly-abused-drugs-chart

Newcombe, D., Humeniuk, R., & Ali, R. (2005). Validation of the World Health Organization alcohol, smoking and substance involvement screening test (ASSIST): Report of results from the Australian site. *Drug and Alcohol Review, 24*(3), 217–226. doi: 10.1080/09595230500170266

Nunes, E. V., & Rounsaville, B. J. (2006). Comorbidity of substance use with depression and other mental disorders: From Diagnostic and Statistical Manual of Mental Disorders, fourth edition (*DSM-IV*) to *DSM-V. Addiction, 101*(Suppl. 1), 89–96.

Pagan, J., Rose, R., Viken, R., Pulkkinen, L., Kaprio, J., & Dick, D. (2006). Genetic and environmental influences on stages of alcohol use across adolescence and into young adulthood. *Behavior Genetics, 36*, 483–497.

Parker, A., Marshall, E., & Ball, D. (2008). Diagnosis and management of alcohol use disorders. *British Medical Journal, 336*, 496–501. doi: 10.1136/bmj.39483.457708.80

Petrakis, I., & Krystal, J. (1997). Neuroscience: Implications for treatment. *Alcohol Health and Research World, 21*(2), 157–161.

Potenza, M. N. (2006). Should addictive disorders include non-substance-related conditions? *Addiction, 100* (Suppl. 1), 142–151.

Poznyak, V., Saraceno, B., & Obot, I. (2005). Breaking the vicious circle of determinants and consequences of harmful alcohol use. *Bulletin of the World Health Organization, 83*(11), 803–804.

Pozzi, G., Martinotti, G., Reina, D., Dario, T., Frustaci, A., Janiri, L., & Bria, P. (2008). The assessment of post-detoxification anhedonia: Influence of clinical and psychosocial variables. *Substance Use & Misuse, 43*(5), 722–732.

Prochaska, J. O., & DiClemente, C. C. (1992). Stages of change in the modification of problem behaviors. In M. Hersen, R. M. Eisler, & P. M. Miller (Eds.), *Progress on behavior modification* (pp. 184–214). Sycamore, IL: Sycamore Press.

Rabinowitz, A. (2009). Enhancing medication-assisted treatment: Success beyond harm reduction. *Journal of Social Work Practice in the Addictions, 9*(2), 240–243. doi: 10.1080/15332560902858745

Robertson, S. L., Davis, S. J., Sneed, Z., Koch, D. S., & Boston, Q. (2009). Competency issues for alcohol/other drug abuse counselors. *Alcoholism Treatment Quarterly, 27*(3), 265–279. doi: 10.1080/07347320903014347

Rose, G. W. & Walters, S. T. (2012). Theories of motivation and addictive behavior. In S. T. Walters & F. Rotgers (Eds.), *Treating substance abuse: Theory and application* (3rd ed., pp. 9–27). New York: Guilford.

Rotgers, F. (2012). Cognitive-behavioral theories of substance abuse. In S. W. Walters & F. Rotgers (Eds.), *Treating substance abuse: Theory and techniques* (3rd ed., pp. 113–137). New York, NY: Guilford Press.

Schmidt, N. B., Norr, A. M., & Korte, K. J. (2014). Panic disorder and agoraphobia: Considerations for DSM-V. *Research on Social Work Practice, 24*(1), 57–66.

Schore, A. N. (2014). Introduction. In J. J Magnavita & J. C. Anchin (Eds.), *Unifying psychotherapy: Principles, methods, evidence from clinical science* (pp. xxi–xliv). New York, NY: Springer.

Schulte, M., Ramo, D., & Brown, S. (2009). Gender differences in factors influencing alcohol use and drinking progression among adolescents. *Clinical Psychology Reviews, 29*(6), 535–547. doi: 10.1016/j.cpr.2009.06.003

Sohrabji, F. (2003). Neurodegeneration in women. *Alcohol Research & Health, 26*(4), 316–318.

Substance Abuse and Mental Health Services Administration. (2009a). *The NSDUH report: Concurrent illicit drug and alcohol use*. Research Triangle Park, NC: Office of Applied Studies and Substance Abuse and Mental Health Services Administration.

Substance Abuse and Mental Health Services Administration. (2009b). *Results from the 2008 National Survey on Drug Use and Health: National findings*. Research Triangle Park, NC: Office of Applied Studies and Substance Abuse and Mental Health Services Administration.

Substance Abuse and Mental Health Services Administration. (2009c). *The NSDUH Report: Nonmedical use of Adderall among full-time college students*. Research Triangle Park, MD: Office of Applied Studies and Substance Abuse and Mental Health Services Administration.

Swendsen, J., Conway, K. P., Degenhardt, L., Dierker, L., Glantz, M., Jin, R., . . . Kessler, R. C. (2009). Sociodemographic risk factors for alcohol and drug dependence: The 10-year follow-up of the National Comorbidity Survey. *Addiction, 104*(8), 1346–1355. doi: 10.1111/j.1360-0443.2009.02622.x

Tai, B., & Volkow, N. D. (2013). Treatment for substance use disorder: Opportunities and challenges under the Affordable Care Act. *Social Work in Public Health, 28*(3–4), 165–174.

Tooley, E. M., & Moyers, T. B. (2012). Motivational interviewing in practice. S. W. Walters & F. Rotgers (Eds.), *Treating substance abuse: Theory and techniques* (3rd ed., pp. 319–354). New York, NY: Guilford Press.

Turner, F. J. (Ed.). (1996). *Social work treatment: Interlocking theoretical approaches* (4th ed.). New York, NY: Free Press.

Van Wormer, K. (2008). Counseling family members of addicts/alcoholics: The states of change model. *Journal of Family Social Work, 11*(2), 202–221. doi: 10.1080/10522150802174319

Walker, D. D., Roffman, R. A., Picciano, J. F., & Stephens, R. S. (2007). The check-up: In-person, computerized, and telephone adaptations of motivational enhancement treatment to elicit voluntary participation by the contemplator. *Substance Abuse Treatment, Prevention, and Policy, 2*(2), 1–10. doi: 10.1186/1747-597X-2-2

Wallace, J. (2012). Theory of 12-step-oriented treatment. In S. W. Walters & F. Rotgers (Eds.), *Treating substance abuse: Theory and techniques* (3rd ed., pp. 319–354). New York, NY: Guilford Press.

Wesson, D. R. (1995). *Detoxification from alcohol and other drugs* (Publication No. SMA 95-3046). Rockville, MD: Department of Health and Human Services.

World Health Organization. (2006a). *Interpersonal violence and alcohol*. Geneva, Switzerland: Author.

World Health Organization. (2006b). *Youth violence and alcohol*. Geneva, Switzerland: Author.

World Health Organization. (2009a). *Depression*. Retrieved from http://www.who.int/mental_health/management/depression/definition/en/print.html

World Health Organization. (2009b). *Other psychoactive substances*. Retrieved from http://www.who.int/substance_abuse/facts/psychoactives/en/index.html

World Health Organization. (2014a). *Facts and figures*. Retrieved from http://www.who.int/substance_abuse/facts/en

World Health Organization. (2014b). *The global burden*. Retrieved from http://www.who.int/substance_abuse/facts/global_burden/en/index.html

Zeng, M. D., Li, Y. M., Chen, C. W., Lu, L. G., Fan, J. G., Wang, B. Y., & Mao, Y. M. (2008). Guidelines for the diagnosis and treatment of alcohol liver disease. *Journal of Digestive Diseases, 9*(2), 113–116. doi: 10.1111/j.1751-2980.2008.00332.x

Zimic, J. I., & Jakic, V. (2012). Familial risk factors favoring drug addiction onset. *Journal of Psychoactive Drugs, 44*(2), 173–185.

Zweben, A. (2012). Case management in substance abuse treatment. In S. W. Walters & F. Rotgers (Eds.), *Treating substance abuse: Theory and techniques* (3rd ed., pp. 403–418). New York, NY: Guilford Press.

CHAPTER 13 Personality Disorders

Sophia F. Dziegielewski and George A. Jacinto

INTRODUCTION

This chapter provides information about adults who suffer from the mental disorders known as the personality disorders. Several epidemiological studies in the United States and abroad with different populations provide consistent estimations of persons diagnosed with a personality disorder (cited by Lenzenweger, 2008). The mean prevalence rate for any personality disorder is estimated at 10.56% (Lenzenweger, 2008). This figure suggests that 1 in 10 people have a diagnosable personality disorder, but the actual criteria and treatment options remain controversial. These illnesses relate directly to an individual's personality, which defines the basic core of his or her self-identity, and how the world is interpreted, influencing all interactions that result. Our personality creates the basic defining characteristic from which all responses and behaviors result (Barnhill, 2014). When inflexible and pervasive, these enduring patterns of behavior can cause troubled and disturbed relations that touch every aspect of a person's life. Personality functioning affects the development of individual talents and responses, as well as close relationships with others. The link between developing these disorders and how exhibiting these problematic behaviors affect the family system is not well known. As individuals develop, there does appear to be a correlation with early separation and loss, parental neglect, and other types of family dysfunction, although most professionals agree this factor alone could not account for the development of personality disorders (Sherry, Lyddon, & Henson, 2007). There also appears to be a strong correlation between substance use and personality disorders, so much so that some practitioners believe that when a personality disorder is assessed, so should the possibility of a substance-related disorder (McMain & Ellery, 2008).

This chapter has a brief overview of each disorder and a case example that provides specific treatment planning and intervention-related applications. A lack of understanding of the symptoms related to having a loved one who suffers from a personality disorder can disturb family relationships and thereby alienate support systems critical to enhanced functioning. This chapter highlights the guidelines for using the *Diagnostic and Statistical Manual of Mental Disorders*, Fifth Edition (*DSM-5*; American Psychiatric Association [APA], 2013), to better understand and assess these conditions. The *DSM-5* (2013) dedicates one chapter to the 13 different personality disorders, which are broken down into four areas. Cluster A includes paranoid personality disorder, schizoid personality disorder, and schizotypal personality disorder (described in this chapter but also listed as part of the schizophrenia spectrum and the other psychotic disorders); cluster B is antisocial personality disorder (described in this chapter but listed in the chapter on the disruptive, impulse-control, and conduct disorders), borderline personality disorder, narcissistic personality disorder, and histrionic personality disorder; and cluster C is avoidant personality disorder, dependent personality disorder, and obsessive compulsive personality disorder. In addition, three other types of personality disorders are listed as personality change due to another medical condition, other specified personality disorder, and unspecified personality disorder.

It is beyond the purpose of this chapter to explore in depth all of the diagnoses in the personality disorders and the treatment options specific to each. Rather, this chapter introduces the primary disorders as listed in *DSM-5*. The application section of this chapter provides a case example of an individual suffering from borderline personality disorder. The extent, importance, and early predictors of problem behaviors and symptoms are explored. The various aspects of the disorder are presented with a case application that highlights diagnostic assessment, treatment planning, and evidence-based treatment strategy. In addition, the latest practice methods and newest research and findings are here to further the understanding of these often-devastating illnesses.

The *DSM-5* provides an alternative model in the area for further study that is designed to better understand the traits that characterize the personality disorders. In conceptualizing personality disorders, it focuses on personality functioning and personality traits and is included as an emerging measure for current consideration or future use. The foci of this chapter are to discuss the description of personality disorders listed in the *DSM-5* (2013) and provide an overview of the alternative model to be used for further study in Section III.

TOWARD A BASIC UNDERSTANDING OF THE PERSONALITY DISORDERS

The personality of each individual mediates environmental, cognitive, emotional, spiritual, physical, and interpersonal events. When disturbed, it can negatively affect the individual's way of understanding the self and virtually all interactions in the world in which he or she lives. The notion of personality disorders dates back to the ancient Egyptians; allusion to the disorders is contained in the Ebers Papyrus (Okasha & Okasha, 2000). The ancient Greeks described their god Achilles as antisocial (Walling, 2002); accounts of Alcibiades, a Greek general, describe him as having had the traits of antisocial personality disorder with narcissistic features (Evans, 2006). In addition, whether the condition runs in families is not certain; however, individuals suffering from a personality disorder may also experience a genetic predisposition to developing a disorder similar to that diagnosed previously for a first-degree relative. Research on family members and how best to treat individuals within the family system is gaining interest (Hoffman, Buteau, & Fruzzetti, 2007).

The *DSM-5* (2013) has some minor revisions of the *DSM-IV-TR* (APA, 2000) categories of personality disorders. However, the *DSM-5* also presents an alternative model from which to construe personality disorders, which suggests that an understanding of the disorders is shifting. The APA Board of Trustees decided to include both models to establish continuity between current clinical practice and further study of the alternative approach.

UNDERSTANDING INDIVIDUALS SUFFERING FROM A PERSONALITY DISORDER

Individuals who suffer from a personality disorder often report significant distress or impairment in social functioning (APA, 2013). The personality disorders are placed in three clusters. Each cluster has behavioral symptoms that can impair social functioning, and behaviors can take many forms, from odd-eccentric to dramatic-emotional to anxious-fearful. Furthermore, these unusual symptoms can affect interactions with family members, functioning at school or work, and other areas of an individual's life situation.

Cluster A personality disorders may appear odd and eccentric. Individuals with schizoid and schizotypal characteristics avoid social contact and find it difficult to place themselves in situations where they need to interact with others. Often they may seem odd and threatening to individuals who do not know them. Individuals who suffer from paranoid and schizotypal personality disorders often present as suspicious and guarded, and when communication is compromised, others may avoid them because of their suspicious and threatening presentation.

In the cluster B grouping, individuals present as dramatic-emotional. Antisocial individuals may violate others' rights and might also have the potential to inflict physical harm on others or lie and steal and otherwise con people. Those with borderline personality traits may appear at first to be close and admiring and then, once a relationship is formed, become angry and critical. Their intense anger may result in arguments and physical fights. This erratic and intense behavior makes it difficult for them to develop lasting associations with others. The histrionic and narcissistic personality disorders share the theme of dramatic attention-seeking behavior that gets in the way of developing friendships or romantic relationships. They often do not understand why others avoid them.

Cluster C individuals have characteristics that focus around anxiety and fear and thereby often exhibit anxious and fearful behaviors. Avoidant individuals shun social interaction because they see themselves as inadequate and fear negative responses from others. Dependent individuals experience fear of separation and cling to others, wanting others to make decisions for them. They can appear burdensome to others even in superficial social settings. Those with obsessive-compulsive disorder focus on control of their environment, and their perfectionism can be offensive to others.

Social interaction on all levels can often lead to emotional and sometimes physical injury to those with a personality disorder. Individuals suffering from a personality disorder often feel isolated and negatively judged because of their problematic social interactions; they may also be difficult to work with because they lack insight into their own conduct as well as subsequent willingness to engage in treatment to address problematic behaviors.

History of the Personality Disorder and the DSM

Over the past 50 years, the number and types of personality disorders listed in the *DSM* have changed with each new edition. The *DSM-I* (APA, 1952) had 17 categories of personality "disturbance," as well as "transient situational personality disorders," four of which were labeled as "adjustment reactions." (See Quick Reference 13.1.)

The *DSM-II* (APA, 1965) is similar to the listing of the disorders in *DSM-I* (1952). Its several modifications include deletion of inadequate personality pattern disturbance, emotionally unstable personality pattern disturbance, and dyssocial reaction under the sociopathic personality disturbance, and it removes the special symptoms reactions from the listing. The term *personality disorder* appears to have replaced personality pattern disturbances, personality trait disturbance, and sociopathic personality disturbance. The *DSM-II* (1965) retained the sexual deviations listing and added a description of specific conditions in this section.

The *DSM-III* (1980) and *DSM-III-R* (1987) removed the sexual deviations and substance-

QUICK REFERENCE 13.1

PERSONALITY DISORDERS AS LISTED IN EACH EDITION OF THE *DSM*

DSM-I (1952)	*DSM-II* (1965)	*DSM-III* (1980) *DSM-III-R* (1987)	*DSM-IV* (1994) *DSM-IV-TR* (2000)	**DSM-5* (2013)
Personality Pattern Disturbance (PPD) ■ Inadequate PPD ■ Schizoid PPD ■ Cyclothymic PPD ■ Paranoid PPD **Personality Trait Disturbance** (PTD) ■ Emotionally unstable PTD ■ Passive-aggressive PTD ■ Compulsive PTD ■ PTD, Other **Sociopathic Personality Disturbance** ■ Antisocial reaction ■ Dyssocial reaction ■ Sexual deviation: Specify term ■ Addiction Alcoholism Drug addiction **Special Symptoms/ Reactions** ■ Learning disturbance ■ Speech disturbance ■ Enuresis ■ Somnambulism ■ Other	**Personality Disorders** (PD) ■ Paranoid PD Cyclothymic PD Schizoid PD Explosive PD Obsessive compulsive PD ■ Hysterical PD ■ Asthenic PD ■ Antisocial PD ■ Passive-aggressive PD ■ Inadequate PD ■ Other PD NOS ■ Unspecified PD **Sexual Deviations** ■ Homosexuality ■ Fetishism ■ Pedophilia ■ Transvestitism ■ Exhibitionism ■ Voyeurism ■ Sadism ■ Masochism ■ Other sexual deviation ■ Unspecified sexual deviation **Alcoholism** **Drug Dependence**	***Cluster A*** ■ 301.00 Paranoid ■ 301.20 Schizoid ■ 301.22 Schizotypal ***Cluster B*** ■ 301.70 Antisocial ■ 301.83 Borderline ■ 301.50 Histrionic ■ 301.81 Narcissistic ***Cluster C*** ■ 301.82 Avoidant ■ 301.60 Dependent ■ 301.40 Obsessive compulsive ■ 301.84 Passive aggressive ■ 301.90 Personality disorder NOS **Note:** 301.89 Atypical, mixed or other personality disorder was listed in the *DSM-III* and changed in the *DSM-III-R* to 301.90 Personality Disorder NOS	***Cluster A*** (odd-eccentric) 301.0 Paranoid PD 301.20 Schizoid PD 301.22 Schizotypal PD ***Cluster B*** (dramatic-emotional) 301.7 Antisocial 301.83 Borderline 301.50 Histrionic 301.81 Narcissistic ***Cluster C*** (anxious-fearful) 301.82 Avoidant 301.6 Dependent 301.4 Obsessive-compulsive 301.9 Personality disorder NOS **Note:** 301.84 Passive Aggressive Personality Disorder (listed in the *DSM-III-R*) was removed from the Personality Disorders in the *DSM-IV* and placed in the section titled Criteria Sets and Axes Provided for Further Study.	***General Personality Disorder*** ***Cluster A*** (odd-eccentric) 301.0 Paranoid PD 301.20 Schizoid PD 301.22 Schizotypal PD ***Cluster B*** (dramatic-emotional) 301.7 Antisocial 301.83 Borderline 301.50 Histrionic 301.81 Narcissistic ***Cluster C*** (anxious-fearful) 301.82 Avoidant 301.6 Dependent 301.4 Obsessive-compulsive **Note:** NOS was changed to three diagnostic categories. 310.1 Personality change due to another medical condition 301.89 Other specified personality disorder and unspecified PD 301.9 Unspecified Personality Disorder

**DSM-5* lists *ICD-9-CM* codes in this table; *DSM-5* also lists *ICD-10-CM* codes.

related disorders (alcoholism and drug dependence) sections from the listings under personality disorders. In the *DSM-III-R* (1987), the three clusters of disorders were introduced. Cluster A was disorders with odd or eccentric behaviors. Cluster B included disorders that had dramatic, emotional, or erratic behaviors. Cluster C included those disorders characterized by anxiousness and fear.

In the *DSM-IV-TR* (2000), the personality disorders were grouped into three clusters similar to what was previously described in the *DSM-III-R* (1987). The *DSM III-R* cluster C disorder labeled passive-aggressive personality disorder was removed from the list of personality disorders and does not appear in the *DSM-IV-TR* (2000). Because the symptoms can still be problematic, it has been added to the potential list of defense mechanisms outlined in that version.

In the *DSM-5* (2013), the NOS category was deleted and changed to include three diagnostic labels: personality change due to another medical condition, other specified personality disorder, and unspecified personality disorder. In addition, an alternate model for personality disorders was presented in Section III. The APA Board of Trustees included the alternate model for further study (Kreuger & Markon, 2014).

WHAT IS A PERSONALITY DISORDER?

The development and usage of current criteria for a personality disorder in the *DSM* provide a definition with a clear listing of criteria, thereby making an accurate diagnosis of a specific personality disorder. The general personality disorder criteria involve a long-term pattern of inner experience and behavior that differs strikingly from the expectations of the individual's culture. The pattern is demonstrated by two of the following areas outlined in criterion A: (1) cognitive functioning such as ways of observing and understanding self, others, and events: (2) affective response that includes the range, intensity, mood fluctuation, and proper emotional reaction; (3) social functioning, and (4) impulse control.

Criterion B includes an ongoing pattern that is rigid across a range of personal and social circumstances. Criterion C states that the ongoing pattern results in clinically significant distress or damage in social, occupational, or other significant areas of functioning. Criterion D requires that the onset began in adolescence or early adulthood and is a long-term, stable pattern of behavior. Criterion E states that the long-term pattern is not better accounted for as a distinct element or consequence of another mental disorder. Criterion F requires that the long-term pattern not be the result of physiological effects of a substance of abuse or prescription medication or another medical condition, such as traumatic brain injury.

When assessing for symptoms relevant to the diagnosis, the practitioner needs to first review for the presence of minimal levels of the criteria for a personality disorder. Once the symptoms are identified, the predominance of certain symptoms that form clusters of behavior is noted. To facilitate this process, a brief discussion of the personality disorders organized under clusters A, B, and C is presented with the diagnostic criteria outlined by the *DSM-5* (2013) for the disorder. In addition, for each personality disorder, a brief case example clearly identifies how the behavior meets the criteria. Because the behaviors exhibited are often less severe, although enduring, a brief case scenario clearly outlines the occurrence of the problematic behaviors. After the criteria for the personality disorder are described, each case scenario highlights how these behaviors relate to the diagnostic assessment.

CLUSTER A PERSONALITY DISORDERS

The cluster A personality disorders include paranoid personality disorder, schizoid personality disorder, and schizotypal personality disorder. Each of these personality disorders shares the common theme of odd or eccentric behavior. When diagnosed in this cluster, individuals have trouble relating to others. Others might comment openly or privately that the person with a cluster A personality disorder acts strangely, and people often are uncomfortable around them. Often they appear to others as odd and eccentric, which causes them to be loners, or others avoid them as they say they make them feel uncomfortable.

Paranoid Personality Disorder (PPD) [301.0 (F60.0)]

Paranoid personality disorder (PPD) is characterized by a pattern of distrust and suspiciousness of others, whose motives and intentions are perceived as malicious. These perceptions begin in early adulthood and are present in a number of situations. Those with PPD assume the ill intent of others and believe that others might exploit, harm, or deceive them. At times, they may believe others have seriously injured them when there is no evidence that an injury has taken place (APA, 2013). These individuals and the suspicious nature of their interactions can be so frustrating for others that often they are avoided. It is most often diagnosed in males.

According to the *DSM-5*, there are two primary criteria for the disorder (A-B). Of the seven characteristics of the disorder that constitute criterion A, the individual must have at least four. Generally, individuals suffering from paranoid personality disorder exhibit a pervasive attitude of distrust, and when they interact, they consider others' motivations vindictive or malevolent. This pattern is often so pronounced that the individual avoids others at times because of suspicion of their motives, often questioning their true loyality, trustworthiness, and intent. These patterns of behavior are usually noted as beginning by early adulthood and present in a variety of contexts.

To place the diagnosis, criterion A requires four of the seven characteristic symptoms are required: (A-1) The individual suspects and distrusts others without sufficient basis and believes others are exploiting him or her. He or she may also believe others are trying to cause harm and are deceiving in regard to true intensions. (A-2) The client is preoccupied with unjustified doubts about the loyalty or trustworthiness of friends or associates. (A-3) Often individuals with paranoid personality disorder remain reluctant to confide in others. They do not share because of an unwarranted fear that the information will be maliciously used against them. (A-4) In general conversations, others' remarks are believed to have hidden meanings, even when it is clear no harm was intended. (A-5) Relationships with them are often strained because the client bears a grudge and remains unforgiving, even if the injury or insult was unintended. (A-6) The individual is often on the defensive, feels he or she is under attack, and responds with a counterattack that may appear out of proportion to the event. (A-7) Intimate relationships are strained as the individual is convinced that a partner is having an affair and questions fidelity without cause. In criterion B, other mental disorders that could be causing the characteristic symptoms should be assessed, such as schizophrenia, a bipolar disorder or depressive disorder with psychotic features, or another psychotic disorder, and it is not attributable to the physiological effects of a general medical condition (APA, 2013). If the criteria are met prior to the onset of schizophrenia, the term *premorbid* should be added and documented as paranoid personality disorder (premorbid). The following case example shows the characteristics of the disorder.

CASE EXAMPLE - CASE OF LEON

Leon has gotten up late this morning and suspects that someone who was meaning him harm interfered with his alarm clock so that he would be late for work (Criterion A1). He thinks it is Morgan at work, who he believes wants to make him look bad before his boss so that he will be fired (A6). When he arrives an hour late at work, he is greeted by the receptionist, Mary, who says, "Good morning, Leon" (A4). She was trying to be friendly, but Leon thinks she is trying to get him in trouble with the boss by making a scene so the boss will know he is late. Morgan, who believes she is a good friend of Leon, greets him. He ignores Morgan and goes to his workstation. He is thinking of how disloyal Morgan has been (A2). Leon notices his boss, Jacob, and Morgan were whispering about something. He believes they are discussing his tardiness this morning and plotting to write him up (A1 and A2). He cannot contain himself any longer and confronts his boss about his conversation with Morgan. The boss tells him they were planning a surprise for a coworker who was celebrating her 50th birthday. Leon does not believe his boss. This incident adds to his grudge against Morgan, whom he cannot forgive for meddling with his alarm clock (A5).

In reviewing this case, Leon meets five of the diagnostic criteria (A1, A2, A4, A5, and A6) for a diagnosis of PPD. People with PPD commonly blame others for their own failures. Cultural considerations in diagnosing this disorder may have to do with immigrant groups who do not understand the dominant culture, may experience language barriers, or may not understand rules and regulations of the new country. Several ethnic groups may also display behaviors that might be incorrectly misinterpreted as paranoia (APA, 2013). Persons with PPD can be very difficult to treat in psychotherapy because of their chronic suspiciousness and perception of attacks on their character (Dobbert, 2007).

Schizoid Personality Disorder (SPD) [301.20 (F60.1)]

Schizoid personality disorder (SPD) is characterized by detachment from social contact and a limited range of emotional expression in settings that require interpersonal exchange. Individuals with SPD do not seek or want to develop intimate relationships and do not seek romantic sexual relationships with others. They do not desire to be part of a social group and prefer to be alone. They prefer to work with mechanical or abstract tasks and find little pleasure in hobbies or the activities of life. When others socialize, these individuals prefer to be alone. They do not connect well with others and avoid social contact whenever possible.

According to the *DSM-5*, seven characteristics of the disorder in criterion A, require that an individual must have a minimum of four. People diagnosed with this disorder are characterized by disconnection from social relationships and constrained emotional expression in social settings. They shun human interaction and are loners who prefer solitude and activities that do not include associating with others. Often those diagnosed with this disorder do not have close friends, except possibly a close relative (*DSM-5*).

To fit the diagnostic picture, criterion A requires four of the seven characteristic symptoms: (A-1) The client does not seek close relationships, including association with members of the family of origin. (A-2) The client prefers solitary activities to the exclusion of time spent with others. (A-3) The client lacks interest in experiencing sexual activity with another person. (A-4) The client has few, if any, activities that bring him or her pleasure. (A-5) The client does not develop close friendships to confide in, other than close relatives. (A-6) The client does

CASE EXAMPLE - CASE OF SAL

Sal has just gotten off work as a night watchman at a warehouse, where he is the only employee during the graveyard shift. Sal meets his brother for breakfast and tells him that he chose this job because it allows him to spend a good amount of time alone (Criterion A2). He has never dated and has lived alone in a one-bedroom apartment for 28 years. He is not interested in a sexual relationship, even though his brother has attempted to set him up with dates over the years (A3). He goes from home to work and, on rare occasion, to his brother's home for dinner. He does not desire any acquaintances or friends; he just does not like being around other people (A1). He simply prefers to be alone. He has told his brother on several occasions that he does not like people. Since he entered school, he has never sought to have friends, and he contacts his brother only when he needs something and cannot figure out how to meet his need on his own (A5). Three weeks ago, he was honored for 15 years' service to his company. His boss showered him with praise for keeping the company free of break-ins and stated he was one of the finest employees any employer would want to have as part of the team. After the ceremony, Sal told his boss that he did not know what the ruckus was about and that he did not desire or deserve the recognition (A6). Sal made it clear to his boss he was just doing his job and nothing more and would prefer not to be subjected to another ceremony of this type again in the future.

Sal meets five of the diagnostic criteria (A1, A2, A3, A5, and A6) for a diagnosis of SPD. Persons with SPD do not see themselves as having a problem and are happy with being left alone. Some individuals who come from a variety of cultural backgrounds may display defensive behaviors, avoid social contact, and be misinterpreted as schizoid. For example, a person moving from a rural environment to New York City may react with shock at the different, stressfully charged milieu of the city. An individual may appear to be cold, hostile, and distant, preferring to stay to himself or herself (APA, 2013). When the patterned behavior is related to the disorder, it would not occur to them that they might benefit from psychotherapy. If a person with SPD were to see a therapist, it would be due to a referral from a health professional or relative. Psychotherapy is generally contraindicated for people with SPD because of their intense resistance to change their way of life.

---

not respond to praise or criticism from others. (A-7) The client presents with cold affect, indifference, and flattened affect. In criterion B, other mental disorders that could be causing the characteristic symptoms should be assessed, such as schizophrenia, a bipolar disorder or depressive disorder with psychotic features, or another psychotic disorder or autism spectrum disorder, and it is not attributable to the physiological effects of a general medical condition (APA, 2013). If the criteria are met prior to the onset of schizophrenia, the term *premorbid* should be added and documented as schizoid personality disorder (premorbid). The case example of Sal shows the characteristics of the disorder.

Schizotypal Personality Disorder (STPD) [301.22 (F21)]

Schizotypal personality disorder (STPD) is characterized by significant discomfort with social interaction and close personal relationships and a lack of interest in developing enduring friendships. Additionally, the person with schizotypal personality disorder has cognitive misrepresentations and eccentric behavior. These experiences begin in early adulthood and are present in a number of situations. This personality disorder, although not equivalent to schizophrenia, is sometimes referred to as the most similar to schizophrenia. One reason is the experience of ideas of reference versus delusions. Those diagnosed with STPD often experience ideas of reference that result from attaching meaning to casual events specific to the individual. The person focuses on the paranormal or entertains superstitions that are not within the norms of his or her cultural milieu. This is similar to schizophrenia, where individuals have a more pronounced form of delusional thinking called delusions of reference. In the personality disorder, the ideas of reference are not as pronounced and usually are related to a specific idea or item as opposed to a general theme that pervades every aspect of a person's life. In assessing for this disorder, the cultural context, including beliefs and practices, need to be considered. Many religious rituals, beliefs, and practices may appear to meet criteria for STPD. For instance, shamanism, speaking and singing in tongues, magical beliefs, voodoo ritual, seeing and talking with dead relatives, and the evil eye related to mental health and physical illness are experiences that are common in many cultures. With regard to etiology of the disorder, when compared with the general population, there appears to be a familial predisposition for development of STPD when first-degree biological relatives are diagnosed with schizophrenia. The child may observe the behaviors of a relative with schizophrenia and copy the behaviors (APA, 2013; Dobbert, 2007).

According to the *DSM-5*, of the nine characteristics for Criterion A, an individual must have a minimum of five. Individuals diagnosed with this disorder are characterized by strong anxiety and limited ability to develop close relationships. They also experience cognitive misinterpretation of reality and peculiar behavior. Often those diagnosed with this disorder demonstrate ideas of reference, which should be distinguished from delusions of reference. In addition, they may be preoccupied with the paranormal or superstitious beliefs that are not commonly held by others of their cultural background. To fit the diagnostic picture, five of the nine characteristic symptoms are required: (A-1) The individual reports ideas of reference, not including delusions of reference. (A-2) The client is preoccupied with odd thinking or magical beliefs that affect behavior and do not fit within the individual's cultural context. (A-3) The client experiences physical illusions or odd perceptions. (A-4) The client's peculiar speech and thought process may include metaphorical thinking and expression. (A-5) The individual is suspicious of others or may experience paranoid thoughts. (A-6) There is unsuitable or constrained emotional impact on the individual's reality perception. (A-7) The client presents with eccentric behavior or as strange. (A-8) The client does not develop intimate friendships with others to confide in, other than close relatives. (A-9) The client experiences high levels of social anxiety that is not reduced by familiarity and is related to mistrustful fears instead of negative beliefs about self. In criterion B, other mental disorders that could be causing the symptoms should be assessed, such as schizophrenia, a bipolar disorder or depressive disorder with psychotic features, or another psychotic disorder or autism spectrum disorder (APA, 2013). If the criteria are met prior to the onset of schizophrenia, the term *premorbid* should be added and documented as schizotypal personality disorder (premorbid). The case example of Marge shows the characteristics of the disorder.

CLUSTER B PERSONALITY DISORDERS

The cluster B personality disorders are antisocial, borderline, histrionic, and narcissistic personality disorders. The majority of people who suffer

CASE EXAMPLE - CASE OF MARGE

Marge has lived alone during her adult life. She wears clothes that would have been popular in the 1920s, and her makeup causes her to stand out when she is in public (Criterion A7). She is currently suspicious of her neighbor, who she thinks is watching her (A5). The neighbor has left his apartment the same time Marge has for the past 2 weeks, and she thinks he is plotting to take advantage of her (A1). Marge has no friends and says she fears people, even those she has known casually for a long time (A8). She thinks acquaintances may one day snap and take advantage of her (A9). She has three large dogs in her backyard that she says are there for protection and to keep people away from her. Marge has been known to hold odd beliefs as reported by her acquaintances (A2). She believes she is clairvoyant and makes predictions about the future that are not accurate, according to her coworkers. She recently went to a priest to discuss her psychic gifts but was vague and circumstantial when the priest pressed her for a clear explanation of how her psychic abilities work (A2). She was unsatisfied with her consult with the parish priest. She states openly that she does not date and does not want to have any children as she is not sure she could love a child.

Marge meets six of the diagnostic criteria (A1, A2, A4, A5, A7, and A9) for a diagnosis of STPD. Marge is uncomfortable with interpersonal relationships, entertains perceptual distortions, and appears eccentric to those around her. Treatment options for Marge depend on what she is willing to tolerate. Psychotherapy, especially if resistive, is not always considered the treatment of choice and can be contraindicated for individuals who are diagnosed with STPD (Dobbert, 2007).

from a personality disorder fall in the cluster B group (Caligar, 2006). Each of these personality disorders shares the common theme of dramatic and emotional behavior. Often individuals have intense relationships with family and friends that quickly become strained. This frustrates those in their support system, and it is not uncommon for family and friends to say that they simply cannot take the intensity and drama that typically surround relationships with a person with this type of personality disorder. Caregivers in particular may find these behavioral traits extremely frustrating (Scheirs & Bok, 2007).

Antisocial Personality Disorder (APD) [301.7 (60.2)]

Antisocial personality disorder (APD) is characterized by a history of disregarding others and violating others' rights, beginning in childhood or early adolescence and continuing into adulthood (APA, 2013). Key elements of APD include deceit, manipulation of others, and failure to adhere to social norms. To be given a diagnosis of APD, a person has to have a history of conduct disorder symptoms prior to age 15 (APA, 2000). Somatic marker and social cognition models explain APD. Both models include the cortical (prefrontal cortex) and limbic (amygdalae) structures of the brain as integral to the underlying process in the development of APD (Sinclair & Gansler, 2006). Environmental factors may also contribute to the development of APD. Growing up in a home where parents demonstrate antisocial behavior, including domestic violence, separation, divorce, and living in foster care, can deprive children of an emotional bond that may contribute to APD (Black, 2006). Confusing discipline regimens, child abuse, and inadequate supervision have been associated with development of APD (Black, 2006). There is a potential for association with others who are also aggressive, and they may become gang members (Black, 2006). There may also be intense relationship problems and domestic violence related to and complicated by substance abuse, extreme jealousy, and violent responses (Costa & Babcock, 2008). The key to understanding the individual who suffers from APD (the old term is *psychopath*) is watching for evidence of behavioral deviations from the norm (Federman, Holmes, & Jacob, 2009). The diagnosis of APD is more common in males than in females.

According to the *DSM-5*, of the seven characteristics of the disorder for criterion A, an individual must have a minimum of three. Individuals diagnosed with this disorder are characterized by a pattern of violating the rights of others that begins in childhood or adolescence and persists into adulthood. These individuals are often diagnosed with conduct disorder. Principal features of the diagnosis are deceit and manipulation of others. Those diagnosed with antisocial personality disorder must be at least 18 years old and have a history of some of the symptoms of conduct disorder prior to age 15.

To fit the diagnostic picture, three of the seven characteristic symptoms are required to meet criterion A: (A-1) The client repeatedly has difficulties with the law and engages in risky behaviors without regard for the legal consequences; (A-2) The client has little regard to the feelings or rights of others and often puts his/her wishes first, conning the individual into doing what the client wants regardless of the benefit to the other individual; (A-3) The client is impulsive and often acts before any thought is given to the consequences that result; (A-4) The client wants his or her own way and thinks

CASE EXAMPLE - CASE OF DAVID

David is 14 years old and has had lifelong problems conforming to societal rules and has had repeated incidents involving the legal system (criterion A1). As an adolescent, he regularly stole from parents and stores (A1). When confronted about stealing, he lied and blamed someone else (A2). He cut the family dog with a knife when he was 14 years old; shortly thereafter, he was diagnosed with conduct disorder, which is usually a precursor to the diagnosis of antisocial personality disorder. David has little control over his impulses; for instance, when he wants something, if he does not have the money, he just steals it (A3). When caught, he said he just focused on what he wanted and not on the consequences of his stealing and breaking the law. Because of his low impulse control, he had a history of starting fights in school until he was finally expelled (A4). When he stole a car, he raced the vehicle over 100 mph, placing himself and others in danger (A5). When confronted with his law violations, he never showed remorse for the harm he brought to others (A7). He simply dismissed his wrongdoings as someone else's fault.

David meets six of the diagnostic criteria (A1, A2, A3, A4, A5, and A7) for antisocial personality disorder. Persons diagnosed with APD do not learn from experience. This coincides with the social cognition and somatic marker models that try to explain the development of APD. It appears to be related to urban settings and low socioeconomic status. Practitioners should be careful not to diagnose APD if a person lives in a hostile environment and antisocial behavior is seen as a protective survival tactic. Often persons with APD are arrested for the same crime many times. Due to their lack of insight, individuals with APD may respond best to specific goal-directed treatments with clear goals and objectives that are linked directly to behavioral consequences.

little of hurting others resulting in fights or assaultive behavior to secure what he or she wants from others; (A-5) The client has a wanton disregard for the safety or security of others; (A-6) The client is consistently self-rewarding and often does maintain financial or occupations responsibilities; (A-7) The client presents with a clear lack of remorse and often rationalizes his or her behavior as necessary to obtain what is needed. Consequences for such intrusive behavior are often seen as an inconvenience rather than a problematic consequence. In criterion B, the individual must be 18 years old. Criterion C requires that onset of conduct disorder be prior to the age of 15. Criterion D requires that the occurrence of antisocial behavior in not entirely during incidence of schizophrenia or bipolar disorder (APA, 2013).

Borderline Personality Disorder (BPD) [301.83(F60.3)]

Borderline personality disorder (BPD) is characterized as "an instability of interpersonal relationships, self-image, and affects, and marked by impulsivity that begins by early adulthood and is present in a variety of contexts" (APA, 2013, p. 663). It is diagnosed more frequently in females (75%) than in males. It begins in early adulthood and manifests with symptoms of instability in interpersonal relationships, problems with self-image, unstable affect, and notable impulsivity (APA, 2013, p. 666). It is present in the many person-in-environment circumstances in which a person participates. Circumstances in which BPD symptoms are exacerbated include emotional instability, existential dilemmas, uncertainty, anxiety-provoking choices, conflicts about sexual orientation, and competing social pressures to decide on careers (APA, 2013, pp. 665–666). Difficulties are often noted in setting and establishing boundaries. Crisis situations may be generated to avoid boundaries, and these types of behavior can be very frustrating to family and friends.

According to the *DSM-5*, the criteria for this personality disorder differs from the others in that the criteria are not divided into similar lettered steps. This disorder simply lists the criterion in numerical order. When using the assessment scheme outlined individuals must have nine characteristics of the disorder, clearly experiencing a minimum of five. Individuals diagnosed with this disorder are characterized by a persistent pattern of unstable social relationships, self-image, emotion, and impulsive behavior, the onset of which is during early adulthood. The disorder exists in a number of contexts. Often those diagnosed with this disorder fear abandonment and make every effort to avoid such a situation. In addition, they have intense and unstable social relationships.

To fit the diagnostic picture, five of the nine characteristic symptoms are required: (1) extreme efforts to avoid abandonment that is either real or envisioned; (2) history of unstable and intense interpersonal relationships that alternate between idealization and devaluation of the other person; (3) persistent unstable identity disturbance that manifests with one's self-image or sense of the self; (4) two specific situations need to be identified where self-damaging situations and impulsive behaviors can result, such as reckless driving, excessive spending, substance abuse, binge eating, and unsafe sexual activity; (5) continual self-injury, gestures and threats, or suicidal behavior; (6) emotional instability resulting from a noticeable reactive mood response to life circumstances; (7) persistent feelings of emptiness; (8) difficulty in controlling anger or experiencing unacceptable intense rage; and (9) extreme dissociative symptoms or temporary, stress-related paranoid thoughts with possible separation (through disassociation) from the event (APA, 2013).

CASE STUDY - CASE OF SARAH

Sarah was chronically unemployed because of her difficulty in controlling her anger (criterion 8) and her development of intense and unstable relationships at work (2). She has been seeing a psychotherapist for 10 years. In therapy, she is working on her feelings of emptiness (7), abandonment issues (1), and unstable pattern of relationships, both romantic and nonromantic (2). While in therapy, she has attempted suicide four times (5) and states her partner is to blame for her insecurity. She deliberately planned to be unavailable and not respond to requests by her therapist. She refused to answer the phone when her therapist tried to contact her to check on her well-being. She cut her wrist (self-mutilating behavior), and when she saw the psychotherapist at her next appointment, she said she felt such intense emotional pain she wanted to feel it physically on her body as well (5). She had numerous surface cuts to her arm from previous attempts at suicide. To hide these marks, she would often wear a long-sleeve shirt. When she met with her therapist, however, she often folded up her sleeves to expose the scarring on her arms. She often demonstrates her unstable relationship patterns with her therapist. At times, she reports that she idealizes the therapist and, on other days, devalues her contributions (2). She has been addicted to prescription medication for several years. She doctor-shops so she will always have a sufficient supply of medications, and she smokes marijuana (4).

Sarah meets six of the diagnostic criteria (1, 2, 4, 5,7, and 8) for BPD, which is five times more common among first-degree relatives diagnosed with the disorder than in the general population. The research about the genetic association of families and BPD is mixed in its results. Dobbert (2007) reports that there appears to be an inverse relationship between the neurochemical serotonin and impulsivity. Additional research suggests that it is possible that exposure to abuse as a child suppresses the level of serotonin, and life situations such as this can play an important role in developing BPD (Dobbert, 2007). Symptoms are reported to decline with advancing age, appropriate medication, and psychotherapy. Although BPD is chronic in nature, most people with BPD successfully emerge from psychotherapy and experience a remission of symptoms (Dobbert, 2007).

Histrionic Personality Disorder (HPD) [301.50 (F60.4)]

Histrionic personality disorder (HPD) is characterized by "excessive expression of conditions and attention-seeking behavior. This pattern begins by early adulthood and is present in a variety of contexts" (APA, 2013, p. 667). Often persons diagnosed with HPD have a dramatic flair in their self-presentation to others. They are happy being the center of attention and become uneasy and feel unappreciated when they are not the focus of their environment. While they command the position of life of the party, they are often inappropriately attired in sexually provocative dress and behave in a seductive manner. Although they may present in a dramatic manner, they are often vague about details and extremely impressionistic. Persons with HPD are exceedingly trusting of authority figures and can be highly suggestible.

According to the *DSM-5*, of the eight characteristics of the disorder, an individual must have a minimum of five. Similar to several other personality disorders listed in this section, this disorder also does not use the traditional alphabetical coding. Individuals diagnosed with this disorder are characterized by extreme emotional responses to life events, with a significant focus on attention-seeking behavior. When not the center of attention in social settings, these individuals are awkward and perceive that others do not appreciate them. Because their affectivity is dramatic and engaging, they can charm new associates by their passion, sincerity, and playfulness. In addition, they are often inappropriately sexually solicitous and aggressive.

To fit the diagnostic picture, five of the eight characteristic symptoms are required: (1) experiences discomfort when not the center of attention; (2) when relating to others, often engages in sexually solicitous or offensive behavior; (3) emotional expression is rapidly shifting and shallow; (4) draws attention to self by regularly adjusting physical appearance; (5) presents with excessively impressionistic style of speech that is lacking in specificity; (6) excessive emotional expression characterized by dramatic performance; (7) highly suggestible and effortlessly influenced by others or life situation; and (8) believes relationships are more intimate than they are (APA, 2013). The case of Celeste shows examples of the characteristics of the disorder.

Narcissistic Personality Disorder (NPD) [301.81 (F60.81)]

Narcissistic personality disorder (NPD) is characterized by a grandiose sense of self-importance, need to be affirmed, and lack of empathy that emerges in early adulthood and is present in a number of situations (APA, 2013, p. 670). Individuals with NPD are boastful and pretentious and exaggerate their accomplishments to impress others. They present with a "grandiose sense of self-importance . . . and overestimate their abilities and inflate their accomplishments" (APA, 2013, p. 670). A common feature of a person with NPD is emotional coldness and absence of reciprocal interests with others.

According to the *DSM-5*, of the nine characteristics of the disorder, an individual must have a minimum of five. Individuals diagnosed with this disorder are characterized by lack of empathy, excessive pattern of pretentiousness, and need for admiration. Often they overrate

CASE STUDY - CASE OF CELESTE

Celeste presents herself to her vocational rehabilitation counselor, having been referred by her psychiatrist. She is 42 years old, weighs 350 pounds, and is about 5 feet, 10 inches tall. She is dressed in a provocative outfit: short shorts and a blouse that accentuates her large breasts (criterion 4). She privately states she seeks a job in an environment where she can be the focus of attention (1). She reports that her life is very chaotic and there is a great deal of drama in her relationships and within her life situation (6). While there is a lot of volume and excitement in her conversation, it lacks content. Her flamboyant hyperverbal style lacks details and is quite impressionistic (5). She talks quickly, and her emotions rapidly fluctuate back and forth and appear to be shallow and incongruent (3). As the counselor conducts the assessment, Celeste seems overly familiar, blinking her eyes and touching the counselor on the shoulder in response to a question he asks her (2). When told this behavior is not appropriate, she shrugs her shoulders and smiles. When it happens again and she is confronted directly with this inappropriate behavior, she denies she has violated boundaries. She states that she now believes there is a special connection and that her relationship with her counselor is growing closer. She does not respond easily when boundaries are set and continues to be more intimate than is appropriate, given the professional relationship (8). Celeste meets seven of the diagnostic criteria (1, 2, 3, 4, 5, 6, and 8) for a diagnosis of HPD. In evaluating a person for the diagnosis of HPD, whether the disorder is causing clinically significant impairment is important. Some studies suggest that HPD is of similar prevalence for males and females.

their capabilities, overstate their successes, and appear pretentious and self-important. These individuals require disproportionate admiration and are preoccupied with how positively others regard them. To fit the diagnostic picture, five of the nine characteristic symptoms are required: (1) exhibits a pompous sense of worth, for instance, expecting to be viewed as exceptional without commensurate accomplishments; (2) preoccupied with notions of great success, power, genius, physical attractiveness, and love; (3) believes that one should associate with prominent people (or institutions), because of being special and exceptional; (4) insists on disproportionate admiration; (5) exhibits a feeling of entitlement (e.g., overinflated expectations of positive treatment or reflexive compliance with personal expectations); (6) exploits others to accomplish own ends; (7) lacks ability to empathize with others; (8) exhibits envy of others and believes others are envious of him or her; and (9) demonstrates arrogant, conceited behaviors or viewpoints (APA, 2013).

CASE STUDY - CASE OF GARY

Gary reports to family and friends that he has joined Mensa because he believes he is of high status and prefers to be around geniuses (criterion 1). He does not tell anyone how he actually became a member of Mensa. His friend is sworn to keep confidence and not reveal that to get into Mensa, Gary had his friend take the qualifying test to join the organization. In all settings, he talks about his brilliance and ability to innovate. He also discusses his fantasies with family members about becoming wealthy and powerful (2). He travels in a crowd that pays him attention for his faux successes and alleged brilliance (3). The thing he enjoys most is the attention and admiration of others who believe his story (4). He has a strong sense of entitlement and believes he deserves fame, fortune, and others' compliance in following his wishes (5). When he does not get his way, he becomes belligerent and demands to get his way (9). At work, he uses people to advance in the ranks (6). He has caused two of his supervisors over the past 4 years to be fired, and he assumed their positions. He coldly talks about them and shares his disgust of them as human beings. On a recent occasion at the market, he met one of his former supervisors. He had actually supported the supervisor's termination of employment. The previous supervisor told Gary that he had been unemployed for 3 years since he was terminated from the job where Gary still works. The man said he was in a desperate financial situation and asked if Gary could be of any help getting him back in the agency from which he was terminated. Gary shook his head no and demonstrated no empathy for his situation (7). He coldly dismissed the former supervisor and passed him by, stating openly to him that this was not his problem.

Gary meets eight of the diagnostic criteria (1, 2, 3, 4, 5, 6, 7, and 9) for a diagnosis of NPD. Note that adolescents display narcissistic traits; however, that does not mean that they will become adults diagnosed with NPD. People with NPD may have particular difficulty adjusting to the aging process in that age limits both physical and occupational functioning (APA, 2013, p. 671). There is no consensus about the etiology of NPD. The prevalence of NPD is higher in persons who have first-degree biological relatives diagnosed with NPD (Dobbert, 2007). Therapy can be successful with those diagnosed with NPD who are seriously committed to changing their behavior. Dobbert (2007) asserts that "a consistently applied system of rewards and punishments is more effective" (p. 103).

CLUSTER C PERSONALITY DISORDERS

The cluster C personality disorders are avoidant, dependent, and obsessive-compulsive personality disorders. Each of these personality disorders shares the common theme of anxious and fearful behavior. For all three in this section alphabetical designations are not used for the criteria and only numerical coding is provided.

Avoidant Personality Disorder (AVPD) [301.82 (F60.6)]

Avoidant personality disorder (AVPD) is characterized by "social inhibition, feelings of inadequacy, and hypersensitivity to negative evaluation that begins by early adulthood and is present in a variety of contexts" (APA, 2013, p. 673). Individuals with AVPD avoid contact with others out of fear they may be criticized, rejected, or meet with disapproval. They avoid people as much as possible because if they engage in interaction, the fear of being embarrassed or rejected is too great to confront (CRS-Behavioral Health Advisor, 2009). They do not attempt to make new acquaintances unless they can be sure they will meet with approval and be liked without criticism. They are observed to be shy and inhibited and to stay in the background, seemingly invisible, since they fear being degraded or rejected. Adults with AVPD report less involvement in extracurricular activities and, when compared with other mental disorders, such as major depressive disorder, are often considered less popular (Rettew, 2006). Because they have a limited support network due to isolation, they have few resources to work through a crisis.

According to the *DSM-5*, of the seven characteristics of the disorder, an individual must have a minimum of four. Individuals diagnosed with this disorder are characterized by a history of social inhibition, feeling inadequate, and displaying hypersensitive responses to others' assessment that is perceived as negative. Because these individuals are fearful of disapproval, criticism, and rejection, they avoid work activity that includes interpersonal relating. Often they exaggerate the likelihood of danger in normal daily experience; their protective lifestyle is associated with their need for security and assurance. To fit the diagnostic picture, four of the seven characteristic symptoms are required: (1) exhibit fear of disapproval, criticism, and rejection so they avoid work activities; (2) must be assured that they will be liked to get involved with other people; (3) fear shame and derision from others and this fear of rejection can limit their involvement in intimate relationships; (4) demonstrate anxiety about being criticized or scorned in social interactions; (5) feels inadequate around others and avoids new interpersonal situations such as making new friends; (6) perceive self as incompetent, personally unattractive, or of lower status than others; and (7) fear embarrassment and hesitate to take personal chances or participate in new activities (APA, 2013). The case of Linda shows examples of the characteristics of the disorder.

Dependent Personality Disorder (DPD) [301.6 (F60.7)]

Dependent personality disorder (DPD) is characterized by "a pervasive excessive need to be taken care of that leads to submissive and clinging behavior and fears of separation" (APA, 2013, p. 675). This set of behaviors starts in early adulthood and is experienced in a number of settings. The person with DPD experiences great difficulty in making basic decisions, such as what to wear or what to eat, and needs strong direction and reassurance from others. Individuals with DPD require parents or spouses to make all of the decisions for them. They have great difficulty in getting angry with those they depend on out of fear they may estrange them. When a close

CASE STUDY - CASE OF LINDA

Linda is a 30-year-old British American woman who has worked in a New York garment factory for 12 years. She likes her work setting, and upon arriving at work, she immediately goes to her workstation without engaging in conversation (criterion 1). She stays to herself at break time, even when others invite her to join a conversation (5). Several of her coworkers are part of groups that socialize after work hours. She has been invited to join a card club, a sewing circle, and a service club that helps elderly persons. She says she did not join any of those groups because she was not sure the members would like her if they really got to know her (2). She also was concerned that with more than three people in a group, several members of the group would make fun of her (4). A coworker tried to set her up for a date with Sam, a popular employee who was handsome and kind. Linda said she could not meet Sam for a date because she was afraid she would say something that might cause him to ridicule her (3). She recently started seeing a psychotherapist because she would like to feel more confident and make some real friends. She reports to the therapist that she sees herself as unappealing, feels inferior to others (6), and fears she will be embarrassed if she tries to begin new activities, such as joining the service club that serves elderly persons (7). She is hopeful that she can make some positive changes with the help of her therapist.

Linda meets seven of the diagnostic criteria (1, 2, 3, 4, 5, 6, and 7) for a diagnosis of AVPD. People with AVPD may be disposed to the disorder if they have grown up in a home with overly anxious parents who may have been diagnosed with social phobia or AVPD. However, genetic predisposition and the impact of environmental factors have not been clearly associated with the development of AVPD (Tillfors, Furmak, Ekselius, & Fredrikson, 2001). Cultural practices may consider avoidant behaviors appropriate; conversely, avoidant behavior could be the result of acculturation following immigration to the United States. For instance, language barriers may contribute to isolation and fear of criticism when a person attempts to communicate, which may add difficulty to social situations.

relationship ends, they frantically seek another relationship to replace the previous one.

According to the *DSM-5*, of the eight characteristics of the disorder, an individual must have a minimum of four. Individuals diagnosed with this disorder are characterized by an extreme and enduring need to be cared for that may lead to submissive and clinging conduct due to separation anxiety. Individuals with this diagnosis have difficulty in making the simplest everyday decisions without others' input. They experience strong fears of abandonment and see themselves as completely dependent on the counsel and help of others they perceive as important in their lives.

To fit the diagnostic picture, five of the eight characteristic symptoms are required: (1) difficulty in decision making, requiring excessive levels of advice and reassurance from others; (2) requires others to take responsibility for most important areas of life; (3) fears loss of support or approval and experiences strain when expressing disagreement with others (note that this does not include accurate fears of revenge); (4) experiences strain when starting projects or working alone (due to limited self-confidence in decision-making or capabilities rather than lack of motivation or energy); (5) will go to extreme behaviors to receive nurturance and reinforcement from others and volunteer to perform unpleasant tasks to receive such attention; (6) due to extreme fear of not being able to care for self, experiences feelings of discomfort or helplessness when alone; (7) when a close relationship ends, immediately

CASE STUDY - CASE OF MARK

Mark is a 33-year-old unemployed man who has always lived at home. His parents are in their late 60s and have supported him since birth. Over the years, he has depended on his mother to manage his social and financial affairs (criterion 2). The parents are of modest means and have tried to get Mark to work toward independence with no success. His mother has gotten tired of Mark's dependence and no longer wants to make small, everyday decisions without having to shower Mark with reassurance (1). Mark's uncle owns a survey company, and he has been supportive of Mark over the years. To receive support and nurture from his uncle, Mark has agreed to work on a project where he will have to go into murky swamp water up to his knees to place survey markers. Mark says he does not like going in that water because there are poisonous snakes there, but he wants to make his uncle happy (5). Mark has recently been referred to a therapist by his mother. He shares with the therapist that his greatest fear is being left alone when his parents die (8) and that he fears he will have to care for himself one day and not be able to do so. He does not know who he will turn to for help when his parents die.

Mark meets six of the diagnostic criteria (1, 2, 4, 5, 6, and 8) for a diagnosis of DPD. Individuals with first-degree relatives who have a diagnosis of AVPD are at significantly higher risk of developing DPD (Dobbert, 2007). It has been hypothesized that a father who is dependent on the mother models dependent traits learned by a child who is observing the parents' relationship (Dobbert, 2007). Psychotherapy with persons diagnosed with DPD is extraordinarily challenging because the client can easily transfer dependence onto the therapist.

seeks another relationship for care and support; and (8) experiences an unrealistic worry of being left to care for self.

Obsessive-Compulsive Personality Disorder (OCPD) [301.4 (F60.5)]

Obsessive-compulsive personality disorder (OCPD) is characterized as "a preoccupation with orderliness, perfectionism, and mental and interpersonal control, at the expense of flexibility, openness, and efficiency. The pattern begins by early adulthood and is present in variety of contexts" (APA, 2013, p. 679). Individuals with OCPD are focused on control of their environment. They are preoccupied with orderliness, perfectionism, and control of the mental and interpersonal aspects of their lives. Their sense of control leads to excessive attention to rules, important details, making lists, and following procedures exactly, such that they forget the major reason for completing the activity. Individuals with OCPD often leave important tasks to the last minute because of poor time management. Their perfectionist approach to life and unrealistic performance expectations cause them significant stress, leading to dysfunctional behavior.

According to the *DSM-5*, a numerical listing of the eight characteristics of the disorder is utilized and an individual must have a minimum of four. Individuals diagnosed with this disorder have a history of focusing on orderliness, perfectionistic behavior, and control at the price of efficient, open, and flexible behavior. They may become so involved in a project that they seek perfection in each aspect of the end product, and the project is never completed.

To fit the diagnostic picture, four of the eight characteristic symptoms are required: (1) obsession with details, rules, lists, order, organization, or schedules to the point that the main focus of the activity is forgotten; (2) perfectionistic behavior that obstructs task completion (e.g., due to strict rules, is unable to complete a project); (3) excessive devotion to work to the omission of leisure activities and friendships (not due to economic need); (4) scrupulous, rigid, and overly conscientious ideas regarding matters of morality, ethics, or values, not as a result of cultural or religious affiliation; (5) inability to throw away worn-out or valueless possessions, even when they have no emotional value; (6) unwillingness to assign tasks or work with others unless they agree to do things precisely his or her way; (7) stingy spending approach toward self and others, as money is to be hoarded for future misfortunes; and (8) rigid and stubborn behavior. The case of Ray shows examples of the characteristics of the disorder.

OTHER PERSONALITY DISORDERS

Three disorders that are not part of the A, B, or C clusters are included in this group. These disorders replace the not otherwise specified category in the *DSM-IV-TR* (2000). The diagnostic labels are personality change due to another medical condition, other specified personality disorder, and unspecified personality disorder (*DSM-5*). The first disorder is associated with a medical condition that precipitates personality changes that may meet criteria for one or more personality disorders. Other specified personality disorder is used when the full criteria are not met for a specified personality disorder and the person is experiencing clinically significant distress or impairment in social, occupational, or other functioning (*DSM-5*, 2013, p. 684).

CASE STUDY - CASE OF RAY

Ray is a middle-age Italian American who lives in Chicago. He has lived in his condominium for the past 28 years. He has difficulty getting around his home because he has never thrown away anything he has brought home, except food (criterion 5). He has difficulty from time to time at work because of his rigidity and stubbornness (8). His boss recently asked Ray to change the plans for a piece of furniture he was building. Ray refused to change the design, saying it had to be constructed that way. He was written up for being stubborn and insubordinate. Despite Ray's rigidity, his boss likes the results of his perfectionism (2) and his workaholic traits, which are evident in his high levels of productivity (3). Ray works at least 12 hours a day because he is so fixed on details he has to get perfect, such as organizing his work space and meeting impending tight deadlines that he self-imposes (1). He rarely complains about working overtime but does find fault in the way others do the same or similar jobs in that they do not always do it the way he thinks is best. Ray always volunteers to work on holidays; he says his work is his life (3).

Ray meets five of the diagnostic criteria (1, 2, 3, 5, and 8) for a diagnosis of OCPD, which is diagnosed twice as often in males as in females. A practitioner ought to assess the client's cultural and religious background to exclude behaviors reflecting customs, practices, habits, or interpersonal manners that are culturally sanctioned by the client's group. Although successful psychotherapeutic interventions are complicated by rigidity and stubbornness (Dobbert, 2007), a combination of cognitive-behavioral therapy and selective serotonin reuptake inhibitors (e.g., fluoxetine [Prozac]) may be effective in treating OCPD (Greist & Jefferson, 2007).

Personality Change Due to Another Medical Condition [310.1 (F07.0)]

Individuals with this disorder display (A) an ongoing personality disorder that is at a reduced level of functioning compared with the preinjury pattern of functioning. (B) There is evidence from a medical workup that the disturbance is the result of a direct pathophysiological result of another medical condition. (C) The disorder cannot be explained by another medical diagnosis (including another mental disorder resulting from a different medical condition). (D) The disorder does not happen during the course of a delirium. (E) The disorder causes clinically significant suffering or impairs social, occupational, or other significant areas of functioning. There are six subtypes of specifiers for the disorder: labile, disinhibited, aggressive, apathetic, paranoid, other, combined and unspecified types. The *DSM-5* (2013) also includes a coding note that the other medical condition should be separately coded and listed before the personality change due to another medical condition.

Other Specified Personality Disorder [301.89 (F60.89)]

This label applies to symptoms that do not meet the full criteria for any of the cluster A, B, or C personality disorders; however, the client experiences clinically significant distress or impairment in social, occupational, or other aspects of functioning. This category is used when the clinician wishes to convey the specific reason that the client symptoms do not meet criteria for any specific personality disorder. The clinician would record other specified personality disorder and then indicate the specific reason (e.g., mixed personality features).

Unspecified Personality Disorder [301.9 (F60.9)]

This diagnostic label is used for individuals who do not meet the full criteria for any of the personality disorders yet presents with symptoms typical of a personality disorder. This label is used when the clinician decides not to specify the reason that criteria do not meet the particular

CASE STUDY - CASE OF PETER

Peter is a 60-year-old engineer who has been married for 40 years. He sustained a major vascular neurocognitive disorder, with behavioral disturbance (*ICD-9*–290.40 [F01.51], criterion B). He was referred to an outpatient vocational group and was angry because he was unable to recognize his cognitive processing deficits (criterion E). Recently he went to the market with his wife and proceeded to fondle her breasts in the produce section of the store (criterion A, disinhibited behavior). His wife reports he is labile and his mood vacillates from one of depression to one of optimism. His symptoms are not explained by a preexisting mental disorder (criterion C). During treatment, Peter has not experienced a course of delirium (criterion D). Peter meets five of the diagnostic criteria for a diagnosis of:

290.40 [F01.51] Major vascular neurocognitive disorder, combined type

310.1 [F07.0] Personality change due to major vascular neurocognitive disorder combined type.

personality disorder and includes the appearance in which there is not sufficient information to render a specific diagnosis.

SUMMARY OF THE PERSONALITY DISORDERS

When assessing individuals for a diagnosis of personality disorder, practitioners need to collect as much information as possible about them. Understanding the dynamics in the family of origin, the environment in which the person grew up and currently resides, religious and cultural practices, current physical and mental health, recent events that may cause stress or past life experiences that continue to affect the individual in the conduct of daily affairs, interpersonal style, and currency of the person's social support system are all critical pieces in the assessment process. A more detailed case example follows, including the assessment, diagnosis, and intervention planning for a client who suffers from borderline personality disorder. This case example provides an overview of the multiple factors involved in the diagnostic assessment of a client diagnosed with this type of personality disorder.

BORDERLINE PERSONALITY DISORDER (BPD)

Borderline personality disorder (BPD) is a mental illness with a chronic, fluctuating course. The disorder can be challenging to diagnose as the symptoms displayed can overlap other conditions, such as mood disorders. This commonality is referred to as crosscutting of symptoms in the *DSM-5* (Biskin & Paris, 2012). The diagnosis is common in both psychiatric and general practice settings, with BPD diagnosed in 10% of psychiatric outpatients, 20% of psychiatric inpatients, and 6% of general medical practice patients. In clinical settings, women account for 70% of the patients (Biskin & Paris, 2012). Overall, this type of personality disorder is said to affect an estimated 10 million Americans or approximately 2% to 3% of the population (Gershon, 2007; Goodman, Jeong, & Triebwasser, 2009). Of all the personality disorders, BPD can be considered one of the most devastating, and the diagnosis has begun to serve as a catchall phrase. The behaviors characteristic of this disorder can start with simple threats and extend as far as verbal and physical aggressiveness, as well as suicidal threats and acts (Sieleni, 2007).

Like the other personality disorders, BPD is generally indicative of a lifelong pattern of behavior. Therefore, when an individual is diagnosed with a personality disorder such as this one, numerous things must be considered, and intervention options can vary. This section discusses one of the most common and severe forms of personality disorders known. To reduce the magnitude of disturbances BPD can have on the individual, the family, and society, practitioners must complete a thorough diagnostic assessment, treatment plan, and practice strategy that can efficiently identify and effectively treat individuals who suffer from BPD.

Overview of Borderline Personality Disorder

Borderline personality disorder was first diagnosed in 1938 by Adolph Stern, describing individuals whose conditions tended to worsen during therapeutic intervention and who demonstrated masochistic behavior and psychic rigidity (Biskin & Paris, 2012). Generally, personality disorders develop in childhood or adolescence and become apparent by young adulthood (Grim, 2000). In BPD, individuals suffer with numerous problem behaviors that impair current occupational and social functioning. The exact cause of this disorder, however, remains unknown. One study suggests that a significant number of abused and/or neglected children demonstrate the criteria for BPD during adulthood (Widom, Czaja, & Paris, 2009). It can be particularly frustrating in treatment as a chronic mental illness that historically has not responded well to therapeutic or medicinal interventions.

DSM-5 *and the Diagnostic System*

According to the *DSM-5*, individuals with BPD have a pervasive pattern of instability of interpersonal relationships, self-image, and affects and marked impulsivity beginning by early adulthood (APA, 2013). These individuals make frantic efforts to avoid real or imagined abandonment, sometimes resulting in a suicide attempt or self-mutilation. Additional characteristics of BPD include frequent mood changes, recurrent suicidal or self-mutilating behavior or both, chronic feelings of emptiness, and difficulty controlling inappropriate anger (Dobbert, 2007).

For individuals who suffer from BPD, the criteria outlined are prominent, diagnostic criteria according to the *DSM-5* requires at least five of these nine behavioral patterns exhibited (APA, 2013).

1. Individuals often make frantic efforts to avoid real or imagined abandonment. When this happens regularly, it can become difficult for family and friends to maintain long-term relationships because often everyday relationship fluctuations or upsets are thought of as catastrophic.
2. Relationship patterns often become unstable because of the intense responses and constant demands the individual places on relationships. These intense relationships are often characterized by unstable and intense moods that alternate between the client expressing idealization and devaluation. When utilizing the defense mechanism of idealization, the individual deals with emotional conflict or internal or external stressors by attributing exaggerated positive qualities to others. In devaluation, the individual deals with emotional conflict or internal or external stressors by attributing exaggerated negative qualities to self or others. Constant use of these types of defense mechanisms can easily strain the most caring relationships.
3. These individuals often experience identity disturbances in which they are markedly unable to understand the relationship of the self to others. Patterns of behavior remain persistently unstable, and self-image or the sense of self is often impaired. To get control over these ambivalent feelings, the individual is often seen as compulsive in at least two areas, and the impulsivity is often unpredictable and self-damaging. At times, these individuals have recurrent suicidal attempts and gestures or threats, as well as self-mutilating behavior. Fears of abandonment are often articulated, and cases of domestic violence can be exacerbated (Costa & Babcock, 2008).
4. Self-damaging and self-destructive behaviors need to be documented in at least two situations. It is not uncommon for individuals with BPD to engage in these types of impulsive dangerous behaviors. Careful attention needs to be given to providing specific incidences relevant to the criteria. For example, does the client have repeated tickets for reckless driving or tickets for parking illegally with the reasoning that they were in a hurry? Does the individual talk about excessive spending

and shopping trips where the "must haves" put the budget over the limit? Does the individual discuss incidents of unpredictable behavior where substance use was impulsive and the resulting consequences could have been dangerous? Documenting these types of behaviors are essential to the diagnosis and can provide the basis for goal acquisition and the treatment planning to follow.

5. One of the most frustrating and confusing aspects of treating an individual with BPD is the continual gestures and threats related to self-injury. The individual may also state that he or she is going to commit suicide. And often these claims are made in retaliation for what is perceived as neglect or lack of concern for what the individual considers important. Threats of suicide, especially with a history of para-suicide (previous attempts) should always be taken seriously. Unfortunately, one essential part of treatment with this condition is setting boundaries. When a crisis occurs, either naturally or deliberately created by the client, boundary setting becomes second to ensuring safety and security.
6. Assessing mood and affect are essential to clinical diagnosis. With clients suffering from BPD the affective disturbances that are often subject to extreme responses related to routine life stressors can be exhausting for family and friends and those that interact with the client daily. Although the client may not be aware of how extreme these behaviors and reactions appear to be, the difficulty for maintaining long term relationships becomes pronounced.
7. Oftentimes those suffering from BPD report that whether in a committed relationship or not, they often feel persistent feelings of emptiness. The individual may mention the need to fill a void that always seems to drain their energy while creating doubt in terms of the strength and duration of current relationships. The strain this places on the individual, family, and those that intimately relate to the individual is sincere.
8. The fear of abandonment is often so strong that individuals with BPD have extreme difficulty in controlling anger. This desperate need to control can lead to unacceptable intense rage. These frequent displays of temper can result in physical fights or become so disruptive legal consequences can occur.
9. The last possible criterion relates to experiencing paranoid ideations that are often transient and intense. For long term and intimate relationships this can be very difficult, causing partners and family members to simply end the relationship or discussion to escape. This escape only further feeds feelings of abandonment, creating a vicious circle of intensity. Some clients may also report experiencing dissociative symptoms. When severe these symptoms can result in the client separting his or her self from the situation and entering a surreal state where they do not connect to the event or situation as being real. One client explained it as watching a movie, only you are the lead actor.

In reviewing these nine potential criteria it is easy to see how individuals with BPD often suffer from moods that are unstable, and individuals often complain of chronic feelings of emptiness that are reflected in inappropriate episodes of intense anger or difficulty controlling their actions, based on the fear of abandonment.

At times, the fears and desperation to control the situation may become so severe that these individuals report transient, stress-related paranoid ideation or severe dissociative symptoms. When this occurs, the individual believes people are plotting to destroy his or her relationships (e.g., paranoid ideation) or that he or she is mentally separated from the relationship when reality testing remains intact (e.g., dissociative symptoms).

The core symptom evidenced by the individual who suffers from BPD is emotion dysregulation, an emotional response system that is oversensitive and overreactive to normal life-course events. The individual is unable to modulate the strong emotions and actions associated with the feelings experienced. In addition, the developmental circumstance that produces emotional dysregulation is an invalidating environment in which individuals fail to label and modulate arousal, tolerate distress, and trust emotional responses as valid interpretations of what is happening around them (Linehan, 1993). Up to 75% of individuals with BPD experienced some sort of sexual abuse in childhood, yet the exact relationship between being a victim of abuse and development of the disorder is unclear. Parent–child relationships are important to examine in the diagnostic assessment (Widom et al., 2009). Overall, those who suffer from BPD often have a chronic, fluctuating course that significantly impairs social and occupational functioning (Maxmen, Ward, & Kilgus, 2009).

The chronic nature of progression of BPD mandates exploring alternative forms of treatment. This population has a high rate of use of psychiatric services and emergency room visits. For these individuals, mental health utilization costs are great, treatment dropout rates are high, and estimated rates of completed suicide average approximately 5% (Paris, 2002). In addition, for individuals with BPD, medication noncompliance is common, and the rate of substance abuse is great (Koerner & Linehan, 2000; Stefansson & Hesse, 2008). Individuals with BPD may also use defense mechanisms to deal with their intense feelings. Common defense mechanisms used to control anxiety in BPD include acting out, passive aggression, projection, projective identification, and splitting (Zanarini, Weingeroff, & Frankenburg, 2009).

Measurement Instruments and the Diagnostic Assessment

To facilitate the diagnostic assessment for individuals suffering from BPD, several clinical scales can be used. The overall assumption for using these scales in the self-harm risk assessment is that many negative thoughts coupled with few positive thoughts indicate a risk of suicide (Fischer, 1999). Furthermore, these measurement scales help to identify symptoms, evaluate client progress, and determine the direction of the therapeutic intervention. To facilitate the immediate risk assessment, scales used with individuals with BPD should address parasuicidal behavior, depression, and anxiety. In addition, scales that focus on sexual abuse can help the clinician determine a possible history and the impact of the event on the client's current level of functioning.

One such scale, Reasons for Living Inventory (RFL), is designed to assist with measuring suicide potential by looking at the adaptive characteristics of suicide (Linehan, Goodstein, Nielsen, & Chiles, 1983). The RFL is based on cognitive-behavioral theory, which asserts that cognitive patterns influence suicidal behavior. The scale looks at the topic of suicide from the absent adaptive coping skills in the client. See Fischer and Corcoran (2007a, 2007b) for a more complete list of scales that could be of benefit in this area.

Numerous scales measure level of depression. Differentiating chronic depression from a personality disorder is clinically important, especially from dysthymic disorder, with its long and consistent history (Farabaugh, Fava, & Alpert, 2007). These depression scales may assist with this differentiation. The Self-Rating Scale can provide the practitioner with an easy-to-complete short scale (Zung, 1965). The items on the measurement scale were selected to look at depressive symptoms and include cognitive, affective, psychomotor, somatic, and social-interpersonal items. As many individuals with BPD suffer from anxiety, appropriate scales that address this symptom are imperative. Zung also developed the Self-Rating Anxiety Scale (SAS), which assesses anxiety as a clinical disorder and quantifies the symptoms of anxiety.

The majority of individuals diagnosed with BPD may have been victims of child abuse (Widom et al., 2009). To measure a client's beliefs associated with sexual abuse, the Beliefs Associated with Childhood Sexual Abuse (BACSA) was developed (Jehu, Klassen, & Gazan, 1986). This scale helps to depict changes in clients who are receiving cognitive therapy and identifies distorted beliefs. (See Case Example.)

CASE EXAMPLE - CASE OF CARA

Cara is a 27-year-old White woman who currently lives with her husband and three children in their own home. Cara recently applied for and was approved for Social Security Disability and receives $488 a month. She has a medical problem related to her hip, and her mobility is limited. Her husband is employed as a long-distance truck driver who is generally away for brief periods while contracting cross-country loads. Cara reports a history of emotional problems in the form of anxiety and depression. She reports that she has excessive worry about a number of events in her life. She worries about her children, her mother, her husband, and herself. She often finds these symptoms hard to control and reports restlessness or feeling on edge, irritability, and difficulty in concentrating, but most of all, she fears that she will do something wrong and "everyone" close to her will leave her. She gets so concerned about this that when her husband comes off the road, they often fight. He carries a cell phone, but most times he does not answer it when she calls. She reports that she finds this extremely frustrating—what if something was wrong with the children?—so she calls him repeatedly. He tells her he does not answer the cell phone for safety reasons, but she is not sure she believes this. When describing her husband, she states that she loves him because he is a wonderful father. Other times, she states he cannot be trusted and expects so much from her and their relationship. She seems very conflicted about their relationship; sometimes she blames him for many of their problems, and alternately she blames herself. She also talks similarly about the relationship she has with her mother and states her mother "may not be the best but she is all I have."

She stated that she first had these problems with feelings of anxiety and abandonment when she was a child, with a recurrence of more pronounced symptoms approximately 3 years ago. Cara first received mental health services at age 12. She also received outpatient psychiatric treatment when 23 or 24 years old. She stated that she was admitted after telling her husband she believed her thoughts had power and had made her son sick. She was also fearful of being home alone as others were watching her movements. She said she will never share that type of information with her husband again and she does not currently have any such thoughts. In addition, she participated in a 2-month partial hospitalization program 3 months ago. She is currently receiving outpatient treatment,

(continued)

CASE EXAMPLE - CASE OF CARA (CONTINUED)

occasionally attends a weekly anxiety support group, and sees a psychiatrist every 2 months and a case manager monthly. The psychiatrist currently prescribes her the medication Paxil, and she takes it daily.

Cara was born in a rural town and is one of twin sisters. They were born 2-and-a-half months premature, and she had to stay in an incubator for 4 to 6 months following delivery. Cara's sister died soon after birth. Cara believes many of her problems in infancy are related to the fact that her mother took drugs and smoked during her pregnancy, but she states that she is learning to forgive her but this is often a topic of contention when they fight. The client has eight older biological siblings. Her mother left her family when the client was 2 years old. Cara subsequently lived with grandparents, her father, her mother, and in several foster group homes. She stated that she keeps in regular contact with her mother, who has also suffered from several emotional breakdowns. She does not keep in touch with other family members, although she states she has tried. She states the relationships always start out good, but for some reason they do not return her calls and efforts to communicate. Cara also reported physical, emotional, and sexual abuse during her childhood. She has addressed the abuse in individual therapy, but states that she continues to experience nightmares, flashbacks, and problems with sexual relations.

Cara attended mainstream classes in school and never had to repeat any grades. She graduated from high school in 2004 as an average student. She began a medical secretarial program 1 year after graduation but quit after only 6 weeks. Cara's employment history is sporadic. She was a waitress in the past and reports she lost the job due to her panic attacks.

Cara was married in May 2007 at age 19. After 2 years of marriage, she gave birth to a healthy boy. She has another son, age 2, and a daughter, age 4, with the same man. She currently lives with her husband and their three children. Cara takes care of her personal hygiene except when very depressed. She does some household chores, such as cooking and cleaning, only when absolutely necessary. She enjoys taking care of her children, watching TV, and listening to music. She does not have any hobbies. Cara forces herself to walk once or twice a week for exercise. She has no friends locally despite her attempts to make some. She states she does not understand why her family is not nicer to her given she has a "bona fide social security disability." She stated that "people must think I am boring or screwed up." Cara does not belong to any clubs and does not attend church. She has a valid driver's license but drives only when she has to. She is not able to shop by herself due to panic attacks.

Cara reported first drinking alcohol when she was 16. She admitted drinking heavily on weekends for a while after high school with friends, but she denied having a problem with alcohol abuse and denies current use. She first tried marijuana a few times when she was 16 but denies current use. Cara reported taking powder cocaine once when she was 22. She has never been in any formal substance abuse or 12-step program. Cara denies any current alcohol or drug use. She smokes one pack of cigarettes daily.

Cara reported two incidents of trouble with the law for domestic violence when she was in her early 20s, although the charges were dropped the following day. Cara reported that her husband had become verbally and physically abusive in the past. He refuses to participate in marital therapy. He has told her and this social worker that the "drama" surrounding his wife and her problems is just too much at times. Although he loves her and his children, he needs a break and actually looks forward to taking extended trips in his truck just to get away.

Completion of the Diagnostic Assessment for Cara

The diagnostic assessment began with the collection of psychosocial information. Cara was born as one of twin sisters (the other twin died in infancy), and she has eight older biological siblings. Her mother left her family when the client was 2 years old. Cara subsequently had an unstable living situation growing up, having lived in several places with different people (grandparents, father, mother, foster group homes). She stated that her mother has suffered several emotional breakdowns. Cara also reported extensive physical, emotional, and sexual abuse during childhood. In terms of her emotional development, problems related to emotional instability can be related to experiences in her household while she was growing up. Unfortunately, these circumstances can complicate the diagnosis as, for many survivors of abuse, chronic anxiety and depression may persist into adult life. Cara clearly has difficulty in forming stable relationships. Ordinary interpersonal conflicts may provoke intense anxiety, depression, or rage. She has many arguments with her husband, for which she rotates between blaming herself and blaming him. She grew up in a turbulent relationship, hungers for protection, and is haunted by fear of abandonment. She was unable to protect herself from her father during her childhood and now has trouble being assertive in protecting herself in her current relationships. A desperate longing for nurturance and care makes it difficult to establish safe and appropriate boundaries with others. Further, she has no close friends and does not trust easily, always fearing abandonment. Effective interpersonal relationships depend on both a stable sense of self and appropriate emotional expression, and Cara seems to struggle with problems in this area.

Cara's presenting problems include difficulty with relationships and a strained marital relationship. She reports domestic violence concerns with her current husband and says he threatens to harm her physically when he is angry. She denies that he has hit her but fears he might. Cara reports that the domestic violence is generally emotional abuse, but she fears that when the fighting escalates, it might turn into mutual physical abuse. She does appear to be very concerned about her children, although all look healthy and appear to be well fed and cared for. She has a history of sexual and physical abuse and anxiety. She does not believe her partner would hurt their children.

Overall, Cara has a poor self-image, which is not uncommon for individuals who have suffered abuse. (See Quick Reference 13.2.) Like other adult survivors who have escaped from abusive situations, Cara has a poor self-image and views herself with contempt, shame, and guilt. Although Cara states that she has escaped the abuse from her father and brothers, her present relationship with her husband has the potential to also become abusive. She states, "I escaped an abusive home life, only to fall into another abusive relationship where I once again have to struggle for survival and control."

Once the primary and presenting problems have been identified, the first task of the mental health practitioner, especially with the client history and potential engagement in impulsive activities that could lead to self-harm or suicide attempts, is to complete a risk assessment for Cara. Key questions need to identify the potential for suicide risk, risk of violence to others, and the risk of her impulsive behavior and how it might lead to incidents of abuse toward her children. These questions are asked in a straightforward and direct manner, and this information needs to be clearly recorded. Cara states she is not suicidal and would not harm herself because of her children but shows evidence of lacerations to her wrist from a previous attempt years ago. This happened when her husband told her he was leaving

QUICK REFERENCE 13.2

MENTAL STATUS DESCRIPTION

Presentation	Mental Functioning	Higher-Order Abilities	Thought Form/Content
Appearance: Appropriate	Simple Calculations: Mostly accurate	Judgment: Impulsive	Thought process: Logical and organized
Mood: Anxious	Serial 7s: Accurate	Insight: Impaired	Delusions: None
Attitude: Guarded	Intelligence: Average	General Knowledge: Accurate	Proverb Interpretation: Mostly accurate
Speech: Normal	Remote Memory: Intact	Immediate Memory: Intact	
Motor Activity: Restless	Orientation: Fully oriented	Similarities/Differences: Mostly accurate	

her. She also reports that she would not harm her children in any way. Although she appears impulsive to action, she has no history of hurting them when angry or irritated. Cara also states that there is no current physical abuse in her marriage but the relationship and the fighting get so intense she feels there could be. She states that when they fight, her husband verbally abuses her by calling her names and telling her she is crazy.

The second step for the mental health practitioner is to identify client strengths and the behaviors that contribute to impairment in daily functioning. In addition, the clinician should observe the client's appearance, mood, attitude, affect, speech, motor activity, and orientation. Mental functioning needs to be assessed in terms of the client's ability to complete simple calculations, serial 7s, immediate memory, remote memory, general knowledge, proverb interpretation, and recognition of similarities and differences. In addition, questions concerning higher-order abilities, thought form, and content need to be processed.

The primary problem for Cara is her difficulty in establishing and maintaining healthy relationships. Her current relationships are all intense, unstable, and chaotic. She and her husband battle when he comes off the road, and she fears he will leave her if this pattern continues. Her mother provides some support; however, she reports that she and her mother "like each other one day and the next day they become sworn enemies."

Application of the Diagnostic System

Cara is given two provisional diagnoses. Her primary diagnosis is generalized anxiety disorder (GAD), as her behaviors are characterized by anxiety, worry, restlessness, or feeling on edge, as well as difficulty in concentrating and irritability (see Quick Reference 13.3). However, it is unclear if the anxiety-related symptoms she is experiencing are related to the anxiety disorder or better explained along with her relationship difficulties that are characteristic of the diagnosis BPD. Because she has a documented history of anxiety-related problems that impair social and occupational functioning, previous treatment, and medications, it appears prudent to list it as a possibility for further exploration. Furthermore, at this time it is difficult to tell whether

QUICK REFERENCE 13.3

Identify Primary and Presenting Problem

Principal diagnosis:	Borderline personality disorder
Primary problem:	Thoughts, feelings, and behaviors related to the symptoms of the diagnosis.
Presenting problems:	Difficulty with relationships, poor self-image

the symptoms of GAD are severe enough to warrant such a diagnosis. A risk assessment related to the mood disturbance is required (see Quick Reference 13.4). Of the nine general criteria for BPD, Cara clearly meets five of them supporting this as the principal diagnosis and reason for visit. Her repeated phone calls to her husband are reflective of criterion 1 as she has fears of abandonment. It is clear she has relationship difficulties and meets criterion 2. She shows a pattern of unstable interpersonal communication with her spouse which he summed up as "too much drama." She has poor self-esteem as evidenced by her inability to make and keep friends (criterion 3) and her desperate attempts to keep control of the relationships she has with her spouse (4). Her fear of abandonment is characterized by her chronic feelings of emptiness (criterion 7). Her recent hospitalization was related to paranoid ideations after her son at gotten ill and she believed she had indirectly caused his illness.

In addition, a second provisional diagnosis and the potential for posttraumatic stress disorder (PTSD) will be explored further. This diagnosis is characterized by an extremely traumatic event accompanied by symptoms of increased arousal and by avoidance of stimuli associated with the trauma, which is directly related to her history of child physical and sexual abuse. Cara reports that she often has an intense fear of having sexual relations with her husband and fears that he will leave her, blaming her for the problems they are having. She says that she experiences intense distress when she hears about child abuse or thinks about what happened to her. She begins to relive the incidents in her mind. Based on this reliving of the experience, she detaches from her husband in an attempt to escape the possibility of it happening again. Although it is possible that this client meets the criteria for PTSD, it remains unclear whether the symptoms she is experiencing relate directly to the diagnosis of PTSD or to her primary diagnosis of BPD.

QUICK REFERENCE 13.4

Risk Assessment

Document and assess suicide risk:	No evidence at present time; past attempt
Document and assess violence risk:	Slight with no previous history
Document and assess child abuse risk to her children:	Slight with no previous history

It appears that Cara's emotional development may be limited because of the emotional instability of her household while she was growing up. Her feelings of chronic anxiety and depression may be related primarily to her difficulty in forming stable relationships. For Cara, ordinary interpersonal conflicts may provoke intense anxiety, depression, or rage. Regardless, these two diagnoses are listed as provisional and warrant further exploration and attention in the terms of treatment planning and intervention.

Cara's principal diagnosis and the reason for visit is BPD. Characteristics of BPD include a pattern of unstable, intense relationships; unstable self-image or sense of self; impulsivity; frequent mood changes; chronic feelings of emptiness; and difficulty in controlling anger or inappropriate anger. For Cara, this disorder is clearly related to a history of early abandonment and physical and sexual abuse. Maintaining a firm sense of who she is or how she contributes positively or negatively in a relationship is difficult for her. Individuals with personality disorders live within a system of internal defense mechanisms on which they rely to avoid or overcome feelings. Although these defense mechanisms can cause a great deal of difficulty, clients like Cara utilize them as the only way to deal with problems.

Defense mechanisms include idealization and devaluation. Cara deals with emotional conflict and internal and external stressors through idealization, where she attributes exaggerated positive qualities to family members and all relationships. She also practices devaluation, in which she deals with emotional conflict or internal or external stressors by attributing exaggerated negative qualities to her own actions. For example, Cara has difficulty in establishing and maintaining healthy relationships, and it is understandable that she develops chaotic relationships. There are no current medical conditions that need immediate attention, although there is evidence of lacerations of the right wrist from an attempted suicide years ago. She also has had hip replacement surgery in the past and is on disability. She does report some routine problems with mobility but feels her medical care is adequate.

Supporting circumstances and stressors include relationship conflicts due to aggressive behaviors between her and her spouse (potential for domestic violence) and social environmental pressures due to low income and a poor living environment. She has many arguments with her husband, for which she blames herself. She justifies his violent behavior by willingly faulting herself. Gregory (2008) asserts that "from our earliest recollections, we come to expect only abandonment and abuse" (p. 4). Related to her inability to protect herself from her father during her childhood, Cara has difficulty in protecting herself in her current relationships. She is so desperate for love and attention that it is difficult for her to establish safe and appropriate boundaries with others.

Application of the Principal and Provisional Diagnosis

Borderline personality disorder (reason for visit)
Generalized anxiety disorder (provisional)
Posttraumatic stress disorder (provisional)

Other Conditions That May Be a Focus of Clinical Intervention

Parent–child relational problem (in childhood)
Upbringing away from parents
Personal history of sexual abuse in childhood
Other problem related to psychosocial circumstances

Treatment Planning Considerations

Treatment of BPD is difficult, and the best approaches to practice remain a subject of debate. Psychiatrists commonly recognize bipolar disorder (BD) symptoms and BPD, which causes a dilemma in the diagnosis of the disorder

(American Psychiatric Association as cited by Johnson, Gentile, & Correll, 2010). Further, few treatments have been accepted as designed primarily for the client suffering from BPD (Bateman, Ryle, Fonagy, & Kerr, 2007). One approach gaining popularity is mentalization-based therapy (MBT). In this model, the concepts relative to cognitive psychology (contingency theory) are highlighted and combined with developments in attachment theory. This model was first developed in the context of prolonged inpatient therapy. It disregards the psychoanalytic tenets of the unconscious and focuses on the linkages with neurophysiology (Bateman et al., 2007). Another popular treatment method is cognitive analytic therapy (CAT), which seeks to reintroduce key psychoanalytic object relations theoretical concepts (e.g., separation and individuation) into the treatment setting, along with recognizing the cognitive aspects within the treatment environment. The preferred treatment for BPD continues to be psychotherapy (Marcinko & Vuksan-Cusa, as cited in Johnson et al., 2010).

Although the treatments designed specifically for this population are limited, research in this area is increasing. Recently a study evaluated three treatment approaches for BPD: a transference-focused approach, a dialectical behavioral approach, and a supportive approach. When compared, the structure dynamic approach labeled transference-focused psychotherapy resulted in clients experiencing change in six domains; dialectical behavior therapy and supportive treatment were linked to fewer changes among clients (Clarkin, Levy, Lenzenweger, & Kernberg, 2007). Clarkin et al. (2007) and the research they present suggest that individualized treatments may be the most beneficial. Additional research is needed to explore the specific mechanisms of change in the application of these treatment approaches. In the "Intervention Strategy" section of this chapter, dialectical behavior therapy is discussed in greater detail.

Regardless of the method used, the most important techniques still revolve around developing a stable, trusting relationship with a mental health practitioner. The practitioner should not respond punitively to provocative acts and should actively participate in therapy while providing assurance of the therapist's interest and concern. The negative effects of self-destructive behavior should be outlined. Borderline personality disorder is a lifelong disorder in which a pervasive pattern of disregard for and violation of others' rights occurs that is generally noted as beginning in adolescence. The first step for the mental health practitioner is to clearly define the behaviors that the client is experiencing. Once defined, a treatment plan for how to best address these behaviors is developed. (See Sample Treatment Plan 13.1.)

The goals in therapy are to decrease or eliminate these behaviors and improve the client's adaptation to change (see Quick Reference 13.5). Many clinicians refuse to see these patients or limit the number of individuals with BPD in their practice to only one or two, as such clients are often seen as provocateurs and expert manipulators (Perry, 1997). Individuals with this disorder have reputations for being difficult, noncompliant with treatment, and manipulative. Despite these barriers to treatment, research indicates positive directions for the future and a good prognosis for these individuals (APA, 2000).

The numerous problems identified make it difficult to conclude that any one form of treatment will consistently demonstrate the greatest success (Perry, Tarrier, Morriss, McCarthy, & Limb, 1999). However, combination treatment that includes the possibility of medications and therapy seems to offer promise. Dobbert (2007) asserts that manipulation of serotonin levels and therefore the use of an antidepressant medication along with therapy could assist with reducing aggressive behavior. See Quick Reference 13.6.

QUICK REFERENCE 13.5

IDENTIFICATION OF PROBLEMATIC BEHAVIORS

- Identify problems related to impulse control (e.g., unsafe sex, substance use, or driving recklessly).
- Identify behavioral outcomes or the problems that result when impulses are not controlled.
- Assess for history and use of substances.
- Identify episodes when explosive temper outbursts or threats based in aggression are most likely to occur.
- Identify concrete examples of low self-esteem and unstable self-image.
- Identify feelings of abandonment and attempts to diminish this feeling.
- Identify the potential for lethality or the possibility of danger to self or others.

QUICK REFERENCE 13.6

THERAPEUTIC GOALS

- Assess for suicide risk and stabilize.
- Develop and demonstrate coping skills to deal with mood swings.
- Develop the ability to control impulses.
- Develop and demonstrate anger management skills.
- Learn and practice interpersonal relationship skills.
- Reduce self-damaging behaviors.

SAMPLE TREATMENT PLAN 13.1

BORDERLINE PERSONALITY DISORDER

A pervasive pattern of instability of interpersonal relationships, self-image, and affects, and marked impulsivity beginning by early adulthood and present in a variety of contexts.

Signs and Symptoms

- Frantic efforts to avoid real or imagined abandonment.
- Pattern of unstable and intense relationships characterized by alternating between extremes of idealization and devaluation.
- Identity disturbance—unstable self-image.
- Impulsivity in at least two areas of functioning: spending, sex, substance abuse, reckless driving.
- Recurrent suicidal behavior, gestures or threats, or self-mutilating behavior.
- Affective instability due to a marked reactivity of mood.
- Chronic feelings of emptiness.
- Inappropriate anger, difficulty in controlling anger.
- Stress-related paranoid ideation or severe dissociative symptoms.

Goals

1. Client will stop self-injurious behaviors.
2. Client will maintain prescribed medication regimen.
3. Client will learn to regulate her emotions.
4. Client will learn to express emotions appropriately.
5. Client's family will increase knowledge about BPD.

Objectives	Tasks/Interventions
1. Cease self-injurious behaviors (cutting self, suicide attempts) as measured by client's self-report.	Practitioner will establish a no-harm, no-risk agreement with client as part of a safety plan designed to prohibit her from cutting self or attempting suicide.
2. Continue taking prescribed medications as recorded by client in daily journal.	Client to take medications as prescribed. Client to record in daily journal each time she takes her medication.
3. Identify ways to better regulate emotions, as measured by an average score of 5 at baseline to an average of 2 at the end of treatment on the daily report of emotional intensity.	Practitioner to use technique called dialectical behavior therapy twice per week with client.
4. Identify and learn to express emotions appropriately as measured by an average score of 2 at baseline to an average score of 15 at the end of treatment on clinician-developed behavior count of appropriate behaviors used during sessions.	Practitioner to facilitate client awareness of appropriate behaviors to express emotion. Client to evaluate the intensity of her emotions on clinician/client-developed scale three times per day during treatment Practitioner to evaluate client progress on clinician-developed behavior count of appropriate behaviors at the end of each session.
5. Increase education and problem-solve problems related to having a loved one with borderline personality disorder, as evidenced by scores of pretest and posttest measures relative to information about the disease.	Client's family will participate in 6-week educational program about BPD. Client's family will network with others who have family members with BPD.

Intervention Strategy

The most effective interventions for individuals with BPD appear to include intensive outpatient individual and group psychotherapy. In addition, antidepressants, mood stabilizers, and atypical antipsychotics are often prescribed for individuals with BPD (National Institute of Mental Health [NIMH], 2009). Therefore, the ideal treatment modality for individuals with BPD is most likely a combination approach of extended individual and group therapy, with psychiatric services available to those with more severe symptoms. In addition, best practice with clients diagnosed with BPD addresses suicidal and self-mutilating behavior, depression, anxiety, and issues revolving around childhood sexual abuse. Involving family members, if available, is imperative.

Doing this helps to build a support system for the client and to maximize the quality of interpersonal relationships. As individuals with BPD have intense, chaotic, and emotional relationships, teaching them skills to regulate their emotions is essential (Linehan, 1993).

STRATEGIES FOR INDIVIDUAL THERAPY AND INTERVENTION

Yen, Johnson, Costello, and Simpson (2009) reported that a 5-day dialectical behavior therapy (DBT) partial hospital program demonstrated that improvement continued over a 3-month period. Although this program had a decreased length of inpatient hospitalization days, the combined hospital and community-based model helped these individuals improve their overall level of functioning. Chronic maladaptive relational and behavioral patterns were addressed through intense inpatient group and individual counseling.

Bateman and Fonagy (1999) evaluated the effectiveness of partial hospitalization in the treatment of BPD by comparing the effectiveness of a psychoanalytically oriented partial hospitalization program with standard psychiatric care for individuals diagnosed with BPD. Group psychoanalytic psychotherapy within a structured, flexible, consistent, limit-setting, and reliable partial hospitalization program was evaluated. In this study, individuals with BPD in a partial hospitalization program improved dramatically compared with those in standard psychiatric care. The number of suicide attempts, inpatient days of hospitalization, level of anxiety and depression, and self-mutilation acts all decreased following their participation in the partial hospitalization program. Because BPD is a chronic mental illness that requires intensive psychiatric care, long-term follow-up treatment is imperative. Those who received intensive group and individual treatment did better when community supports were included. The type of therapy most effective with individuals with BPD is a combination of individual psychotherapy and skills training. The goal of skills training is acquisition of adaptive skills. The goal of individual therapy is getting clients to use the skills in place of maladaptive behaviors (Linehan, 1993).

A popular type of intervention for the individual with BPD is DBT, a broad-based cognitive-behavioral treatment that has diversified over time (Fruzzetti & Fruzzetti, 2009). It was originally developed for individuals with BPD. Through controlled clinical trials, it remains effective with this disorder (Feigenbaum, 2007). "The primary dialectic in psychotherapy is that of acceptance and change" (Fruzzetti & Fruzetti, 2009, p. 230). The dialectical perspective contains three main characteristics, each of which is important in understanding BPD and the development of change behaviors.

1. Dialectics directs the client's attention to the immediate and larger contexts of behavior, as well as to the interrelatedness of individual behavior patterns. Change is considered an ongoing process, and recognizing the need for change is central to the treatment process. Change is expected to occur in the client, in the therapy, and within the therapist (Fruzzetti & Fruzzetti, 2009).
2. Reality is a fundamental process of change, and recognizing the synthesis of internal opposing forces will evolve, contradicting and replacing problematic thinking with a new set of opposing forces (Linehan, 1993). The identification of problematic thoughts includes extreme thinking, behavior, and emotions that make progress difficult.
3. It is assumed that the individual and the environment are undergoing continuous transition. This belief aims to assist

the client in becoming more comfortable with change.

Because the core disorder in BPD is emotion dysregulation, this type of therapy creates emotional regulation by teaching the client to label and modulate arousal, to tolerate distress, and to trust his or her own emotional responses as valid interpretations and apply this awareness to events (Linehan, 1993). Therapy tries to reframe dysfunctional behaviors as part of the client's learned problem-solving skills and engages both the practitioner and the client in active problem solving. At the same time, emphasis is placed on understanding the client's current emotional, cognitive, and behavioral responses. In this method, the mental health practitioner is expected to address all of the client's problematic behaviors in a systematic manner. Doing this includes conducting a collaborative behavioral analysis, formulating hypotheses about possible variables influencing the problem, generating possible changes, and trying out and evaluating solutions. This intervention emphasizes the necessity of teaching clients to accept themselves and their life situation as they are in the moment.

Furthermore, the criteria for BPD reflect a pattern of behavioral, emotional, and cognitive instability and dysregulation. Based on this premise, Linehan (1993) outlines four specific skills-training modules aimed at treating these difficulties. In the first module, teaching core mindfulness involves learning emotional regulation skills. In the second module, the client learns interpersonal effectiveness skills to deal with chaotic and difficult relationships. The third module teaches the client emotion regulation skills. The fourth skills-training module teaches the client distress tolerance skills, helping him or her to learn to consciously experience and observe surrounding events.

Dialectical behavior therapy can form the foundation of a sound practice model to follow when establishing a treatment plan for individuals with BPD. Even if the mental health practitioner is unable to engage the client in long-term therapeutic ventures utilizing the treatment methods, DBT may help by improving the client's overall level of functioning. In summary, it appears that no intervention is perfect for all disorders.

According to Fruzzetti and Fruzzetti (2009), when dealing with the personality disorders, especially BPD, a dialectical approach may be most useful when:

- Change-oriented or acceptance-oriented therapy is not successful on its own.
- The treatment reaches a plateau short of its targets for improvement.
- Clients and therapists get stuck in power struggles.
- For multiproblem clients in general (p. 231).

Psychopharmacological Interventions

Psychotropic medication may be helpful as part of the treatment plan for an individual with BPD. The wide range of symptoms apparent in individuals with this illness mandates that every avenue of treatment be explored, including mixing therapy and medication. Although medication has been shown to be effective, medication alone is not considered adequate (Dobbert, 2007; NIMH, 2009).

For individuals with BPD, the treatment dropout rates are high, medication noncompliance is common, and the rate of substance abuse is great (Koerner & Linehan, 2000). Practitioners must stress the need for clients to comply with all aspects of treatment and to help monitor the client's progress, especially the potential of substance abuse. Linking the client to Alcoholics Anonymous groups, substance abuse treatment centers, or both will help them develop a support system that revolves around abstinence.

In terms of specific medications for use with this disorder, attention has been given to certain mood stabilizers and the atypical antipsychotics (Lehmann, 2003). Psychotic symptoms in these individuals include paranoia, delusions, referential thinking, and dissociations. For this reason, medication such as clozapine (Clozaril), an antipsychotic given to people with severe schizophrenia who have failed to respond to standard treatments, has been utilized in an attempt to reduce the episodes of severe self-mutilation and aggression in psychotic patients with BPD (Chengappa, Elbeling, Kang, Levine, & Parepally, 1999). Psychotic symptoms generally increase when the individual is under a great deal of stress. The symptoms related to dissociation include depersonalization, analgesia, derealization, and altered sensory perceptions, and these individuals often experience flashbacks. Research supports that flashbacks in people with PTSD were reduced (Bohus et al., 1999) with naltrexone (Revia). The study concluded that since increased activity of the opioid system contributes to dissociative symptoms, including flashbacks, that these symptoms may respond to treatments with other opiate antagonists. The one area not influenced by naltrexone was the level of tension clients experienced.

Although medication management of BPD is controversial, it warrants further investigation due to the chronicity of the illness. Further research is needed in the treatment of BPD. Central to the presentations of this chronic personality disorder are unpredictability of behaviors and variations in symptomatology. As many psychotherapeutic interventions are researched, medication treatment as a supplement for individuals suffering from borderline personality disorder needs further evaluation to be sure that usage extends beyond just treating the symptoms.

SECTION III: ALTERNATIVE *DSM-5* MODEL FOR THE PERSONALITY DISORDERS

In Section III of the *DSM-5*, an alternative model for personality disorders is presented. In conceptualizing personality disorders, the alternative approach focuses on personality functioning and personality traits. The alternative approach adds the label personality disorder-trait specified (PD-TS) to embrace those who meet criteria for a personality disorder but the criteria for a particular disorder are not present. The PD-TS diagnosis is in response to the NOS category of the *DSM-IV-TR* (2000). The Personality Inventory for *DSM-5* (PID-5) has been developed to use in the assessment of clients with personality disorders (Krueger, Derringer, Markon, Watson, & Skodol, 2012; Krueger et al., 2011).

This alternative model was originally planned to replace the current nomenclature for the personality disorders. Prior to formalizing the final revisions, concerns were voiced about the change, and based on feedback from reviewers, it was not changed after all. The general consensus was that the alternative model would have changed the method of diagnosis, and the feedback received suggested that this drastic a change was too extreme (http://www.DSM5.org). This proposed alternative model, however, did warrant sufficient interest and was included in *DSM-5* in Section III, under the area for further study. The intention was to allow further study outlining how the method may be used by clinicians for firming up assessment and diagnosis (Krueger & Markon, 2014).

This alternative approach included in the area for further study posits 25 personality traits, five domains, and seven personality disorders. Three of the current disorders (schizotypal, antisocial, and borderline) were not included in this model (Hopwood, Schade, Krueger, Wright, &

Markon, 2013). One of the biggest concerns noted with the trait typology proposed is that it lacks empirical evidence to support the critical features of the disorders (Livesley, 2012).

Concerning the personality disorders as well as usage in general, there has been significant controversy around the current *DSM-5* revisions. Some professionals contend that it is scientifically unsubstantiated and improperly tested, and its use could be potentially harmful to clients. In addition, some professionals feel the revisions have raised questions about the integrity of the work (Frances & Jones, 2014). The major concern with the alternative model proposed is that it posits impairment in personality *functioning* and personality *traits* that are considered pathological. In addition, it falls short in identifying supportive information such as environmental concerns and other factors such as poverty. These life circumstances may create unusual behavior that is diagnosed as a personality disorder but is associated with survival, and such behaviors may be changed by educational opportunities and not a negative label (Gambrill, 2014).

SUMMARY AND FUTURE DIRECTIONS

Of all the mental disorders, the personality disorders can have the most distinct impact on day-to-day functioning, often making daily functioning difficult but severe enough to stop it completely. In particular, BPD is a chronic mental illness that historically has not responded to therapeutic or medicinal interventions. According to the *DSM*, the essential feature of BPD is a pervasive pattern of instability with interpersonal relationships, self-image, affects, and marked impulsivity (APA, 2013). Individuals diagnosed with any of the personality disorders often have reputations for being difficult, noncompliant with treatment, and manipulative. Despite these barriers to treatment, research indicates positive directions for the future and a good prognosis for these individuals.

n terms of the diagnostic assessment, once the type of personality disorder is identified, a comprehensive risk assessment is needed that can support the chronic nature of this category of disorders. Often individuals with a personality disorder end up in treatment, but it is not specifically related to the personality disorder symptoms alone. Individual approaches such as dialectical behavior therapy and other psychosocial individual and group therapy approaches can assist in improving a client's overall general and interpersonal adjustment (Fruzzetti & Fruzzetti, 2009). Although some clients suffering from a personality disorder may be resistant to treatment at first, these treatments can be beneficial in improving levels of functioning, enhancing their social relationships, and preventing self-damaging suicidal and self-mutilating behavior.

Additional research needs to be completed in several areas to assess adequate treatment interventions. For BPD specifically, more studies are needed to determine which components of DBT contribute to the positive outcomes. In addition, longitudinal follow-up studies are needed to determine suicide rates and maintenance of long-term treatment gains. Particularly for BPD, the development of a treatment regimen needs to involve follow-up care and community support. Many individuals with this disorder are frequent consumers of inpatient psychiatric services. As a result, their chronic maladaptive relational and behavior patterns may initially need to be addressed in an inpatient setting. Outpatient follow-up treatment helps the client reestablish his or her social network and work on the behaviors that precipitated the admission. The key to best assisting individuals who suffer from the personality disorders, especially BPD, is helping to prevent a relapse.

REFERENCES

American Psychiatric Association. (1952). *Diagnostic and statistical manual of mental disorders.* Washington, DC: Author.

American Psychiatric Association. (1965). *Diagnostic and statistical manual of mental disorders* (2nd ed.). Washington, DC: Author.

American Psychiatric Association. (1980). *Diagnostic and statistical manual of mental disorders* (3rd ed.). Washington, DC: Author.

American Psychiatric Association. (1987). *Diagnostic and statistical manual of mental disorders* (3rd ed., rev.). Washington, DC: Author.

American Psychiatric Association. (2000). *Diagnostic and statistical manual of mental disorders* (4th ed., text rev.). Washington, DC: Author.

American Psychiatric Association. (2013). *Diagnostic and statistical manual of mental disorders* (5th ed.). Arlington, VA: American Psychiatric Publishing.

Barnhill, J. W. (2014). Personality disorders: Introduction. In J. W. Barnhill (Ed.), *DSM-5^{TM} clinical cases* (pp. 297–300). Washington, DC: American Psychiatric Publishing.

Bateman, A., & Fonagy, P. (1999). Effectiveness of partial hospitalization in the treatment of borderline personality disorder: A randomized controlled trial. *American Journal of Psychiatry, 156*(10), 1563–1569.

Bateman, A. W., Ryle, A., Fonagy, P., & Kerr, I. B. (2007). Psychotherapy for borderline personality disorder: Mentalization-based therapy and cognitive analytic therapy compared. *International Review of Psychiatry, 19*(1), 51–62.

Biskin, R. S., & Paris, J. (2012). Diagnosing borderline personality disorder. *Canadian Medical Association Journal, 184*(16), 1789–1794.

Black, D. (2006). *What causes antisocial personality disorder?* Retrieved from http://www.psychcentral.com/lib/2006/what-causes-antisocial-personality-disorder/

Bohus, M. J., Landwehrmeyer, G. B., Stiglmayr, C. E., Limberger, M. F., Bohme, R., & Schmahl, C. G. (1999). Naltrexone in the treatment of dissociative symptoms in patients with borderline personality disorder: An open-label trial. *Journal of Clinical Psychiatry, 60*(9), 598–603.

Caligar, E. (2006). Personality disorders: Psychodynamic treatments. *Psychiatric Times, 23*(8), 12, 17–18.

Chengappa, K. N., Elbeling, T., Kang, J. S., Levine, J., & Parepally, H. (1999). Clozapine reduces severe self-mutilation and aggression in psychotic patients with borderline personality disorder. *Journal of Clinical Psychiatry, 60*(7), 477–484.

Clarkin, J. F., Levy, K. N., Lenzenweger, M. F., & Kernberg, O. F. (2007). Evaluating three treatments for borderline personality disorder: A multiwave study. *American Journal of Psychiatry, 164*(6), 922–928. doi: 10.1176/appi.ajp.164.6.922

Costa, D. M., & Babcock, J. C. (2008). Articulated thoughts of intimate partner abusive men during anger arousal: Correlates with personality disorder features. *Journal of Family Violence, 23*(6), 395–402. doi: 10.1007/s10896-008-9163-x

CRS-Behavioral Health Advisor. (2009, January 1). Avoidant personality disorder. *Health Source: Consumer Edition*, 1.

Dobbert, D. L. (2007). *Understanding personality disorders: An introduction.* Westport, CT: Praeger.

Evans, K. (2006). Alcibiades: Ancient Greek aristocratic idea or antisocial personality disorder? Proceedings of the Fourth International Conference on New Directions in the Humanities, Tunis, Tunisia. July 3–6.

Farabaugh, A., Fava, M., & Alpert, J. (2007). Differentiating chronic depression from personality disorders. *Psychiatric Times, 24*(6), 64–68.

Federman, C., Holmes, D., & Jacob, J. D. (2009). Deconstructing the psychopath: A critical discursive analysis. *Cultural Critique, 72*, 36–65.

Feigenbaum, J. (2007). Dialectical behaviour therapy: An increasing evidence base. *Journal of Mental Health, 16*(1), 51–68. doi: 10.1080/09638230601182094

Fischer, J. (Ed.). (1999). *Measures for clinical practice: A sourcebook* (3rd ed., Vol. 2). New York, NY: Free Press.

Fischer, J., & Corcoran, K. (2007a). *Measures for clinical practice: A source book. Volume 1: Couples, families, and children* (4th ed.). New York, NY: Oxford University Press.

Fischer, J., & Corcoran, K. (2007b). *Measures for clinical practice: A source book. Volume 2: Adults* (4th ed.). New York, NY: Oxford University Press.

Frances, A., & Jones, K. D. (2014). Should social workers use *Diagnostic and Statistical Manual of Mental Diorders-5*? *Research on Social Work Practice, 24*(1), 11–12.

Fruzzetti, A. R., & Fruzzetti, A. E. (2009). Dialectics in cognitive and behavior therapy. In W. T. O'Donohue & J. E. Fisher (Eds.), *General principles and empirically supported techniques of cognitive behavior therapy* (pp. 230–239). Hoboken, NJ: Wiley.

Gambrill, E. (2014). The *Diagnostic and Statistical Manual of Mental Disorders* as a major form of dehumanization in the modern world. *Research on Social Work, 24*(1), 13–36.

Greist, J. H. & Jefferson, J. W. (2007, Summer). Obsessive compulsive disorders. *The Journal of Lifelong Learning in Psychiatry, 5*(3), 283–298.

Gershon, J. (2007, May 1). The hidden diagnosis. *USA Today, 135*, 72–74.

Goodman, M., Jeong, J. Y., & Triebwasser, J. (2009). Borderline personality disorder and bipolar disorder distinguishing features of clinical diagnosis and treatment. *Psychiatric Times, 26*(7), 55–59.

Gregory, D. (2008). *Broken bones, broken lives: Adult recovery from childhood abuse*. Bloomington, IN: AuthorHouse.

Grim, P. (2000, July). Cut to the quick. *Discover*, 21, 38.

Hoffman, P. D., Buteau, E., & Fruzzetti, A. E. (2007). Borderline personality disorder: Neo-Personality inventory ratings of patients and their family members. *International Journal of Social Psychiatry, 53*(3), 204–215.

Hopwood, C. J., Schade, N., Kreuger, R. F., Wright, A. G. C., & Markon, K. E. (2013). Connecting *DSM-5* personality traits and pathological beliefs: Toward a unifying model. *Journal of Psychopathology and Behavioral Assessment, 35*(2), 167–172. doi: 10.1007/s10862-012-9332-3

Jehu, D., Klassen, C., & Gazan, M. (1986). Cognitive restructuring of distorted beliefs associated with childhood sexual abuse. *Journal of Social Work and Human Sexuality, 4*(1), 49–69.

Johnson, A. B., Gentile, J. P., & Correll, T. L. (2010). Accurately diagnosing and treating borderline personality disorder: A psychotherapeutic case. *Psychiatry*, 7 (4), 21–30.

Koerner, K., & Linehan, M. M. (2000). Research on dialectical behavior therapy for patients with borderline personality disorder. *Psychiatric Clinics of North America, 23*(1), 151–167.

Krueger, R. F., Derringer, J., Markon, K. E., Watson, D., & Skodol, A. E. (2012). Initial construction of maladaptive personality trait model and inventory for *DSM-5*. *Psychological Medicine, 42*(9), 1879–1890. doi: 10.1017/S0033291711002674

Krueger, R. F., Eaton, N. R., Clark, L. A., Watson, D., Markon, K. E., Derringer, J., . . . Livesley, W. J. (2011). Deriving an empirical structure for personality pathology for *DSM-5*. *Journal of Personality Disorders, 25*(2), 170–191. doi: 10.1521/pedi.2011.25.2.170

Krueger, R. F., & Markon, K. E. (2014). The role of *DSM-5* personality trait model in moving toward a quantitative and empirically based approach to classifying personality and psychopathology. *Annual Review of Clinical Psychology, 10*. doi: 10.1146/annurev-clinpsy-032813-153732.

Lehmann, C. (2003). Antipsychotics appear effective for borderline personality disorder. *Psychiatric News, 38*(2), 18.

Lenzenweger, M. F. (2008). Epidemiology of personality disorders. *Psychiatric Clinics of North America, 31*(3), 395–403.

Lenzenweger, M. F., Lane, M. C., Loranger, A. W., & Kessler, R. C. (2007). *DSM-IV* personality disorders in the National Comorbidity Survey Replication. *Biological Psychiatry, 62*(6), 553–564.

Linehan, M. (1993). *Skills training manual for treating borderline personality disorder*. New York: Guilford Press.

Linehan, M. N., Goodstein, J. L., Nielsen, S. L., & Chiles, J. A. (1983). Reasons for staying alive when you are thinking of killing yourself: The Reasons for Living Inventory. *Journal of Counseling and Clinical Psychology, 51*(2), 276–286.

Livesley, W. J. (2012). Disorder in the proposed *DSM-5* classification of personality disorders. *Clinical Psychology and Psychotherapy, 19*(5), 364–368. doi: 10.1002/cpp.1808

Maxmen, J. S., Ward, N. G., & Kilgus, M. (2009). *Essential psychopathology and its treatment* (3rd ed.). New York, NY: Norton.

McMain, S., & Ellery, M. (2008). Screening and assessment of personality disorders in addiction treatment settings. *International Journal of Mental Health Addiction, 6*(1), 20–31.

National Institute of Mental Health. (2009). *Borderline personality disorder*. Retrieved from http://www.nimh.nih.gov/health/topics/borderline-personality-disorder/index.shtml

Okasha, A., & Okasha, T. (2000). Notes on mental disorders in pharaonic Egypt. *History of Psychiatry, 11*(44), 413–424. doi: 10.1177/0957154X0001104406

Paris, J. (2002). Chronic suicidality among patients with borderline personality disorder. *Psychiatric Services, 53*(6), 738–742. doi: 10.1176/appi.ps.53.6.738

Perry, A., Tarrier, N., Morriss, R., McCarthy, E., & Limb, K. (1999). Randomised controlled trial of efficacy of teach patients with bipolar disorder to identify early symptoms of relapse and obtain treatment. *British Medical Journal, 318*(7177), 149–154. doi: doi.org/10.1136/bmj.318.7177.149

Perry, P. (1997, July–August). Personality disorders: Coping with the borderline. *Saturday Evening Post, 269*(4), 44–54.

Rettew, D. C. (2006). Avoidant personality disorder: Boundaries of a diagnosis. *Psychiatric Times, 23*(8).

Scheirs, J. G. M., & Bok, S. (2007). Psychological distress in caretakers or relatives of patients with borderline personality disorder. *International Journal of Social Psychiatry, 53*(3), 195–203. doi: 10.1177/0020764006074554

Sherry, A., Lyddon, W. J., & Henson, R. K. (2007). Adult attachment and developmental personality styles: An empirical study. *Journal of Counseling and Development, 85*(3), 337–348.

Sieleni, B. (2007). Borderline personality disorder in corrections. *Corrections Today, 69*(5), 24–25.

Sinclair, S. J., & Gansler, D. A. (2006). Integrating the somatic marker and social cognition theories to explain different manifestations of antisocial personality disorder. *The New School Psychology Bulletin, 4*(2), 25–47.

Stefansson, R., & Hesse, M. (2008). Personality disorders in substance abusers: A comparison of patients treated in a prison unit and patients treated in inpatient treatment. *International Journal of Mental Health Addiction, 6*(3), 402–406. doi: 10.1007/s11469-007-9134-0

Tillfors, M., Furmark, T., Ekselius, L., & Fredrikson, M. (2001). Social phobia and avoidant personality disorder as related to parental history of social anxiety: A general population study. *Behavior Research & Therapy, 39*(3), 289–298.

Walling, H. W. (2002). Antisocial personality disorder: A new heel for Achilles? *Western Journal of Medicine, 176*(3), 212–214.

Widom, C. S., Czaja, S. J., & Paris, J. (2009). A prospective investigation of borderline personality disorder in abused and neglected children followed up into adulthood. *Journal of Personality Disorder, 23*(5), 433–446.

Yen, S., Johnson, J., Costello, E., & Simpson, E. B. (2009). A 5-day dialectical behavior therapy partial hospital program for women with borderline personality disorder: Predictors of outcome from a 3-month follow-up study. *Journal of Psychiatric Practice, 15*(3), 173–182. doi: 10.1097/01.pra.0000351877.45260.70

Zanarini, M. C., Weingeroff, J. L., & Frankenburg, F. R. (2009). Defense mechanisms associated with borderline personality disorder. *Journal of Personality Disorders, 23*(2), 113–121. doi: 10.1521/pedi.2009.23.2.113

Zung, W. W. (1965). A self-rating depression scale. *Archives of General Psychiatry, 12*, 63–70.

APPENDIX

Quick References: Selected Disorders—Criteria and Treatment Plans

Overview and Treatment Plans for Selected Neurodevelopmental Disorders

Intellectual Disability
Autism Spectrum Disorders
Attention-Deficit/Hyperactivity Disorder

Overview and Treatment Plans for Selected Anxiety Disorders

Separation Anxiety Disorder
Generalized Anxiety Disorder

Overview and Treatment Plans for Selected Sleep-Wake Disorders

Insomnia Disorder
Hypersomnolence Disorder

Overview and Treatment Plans for the Eating Disorders

Anorexia Nervosa
Bulimia Nervosa

OVERVIEW AND TREATMENT PLANS FOR SELECTED NEURODEVELOPMENTAL DISORDERS

QUICK REFERENCE A.1

INTELLECTUAL DISABILITY (ID)*

Title Change: This condition was formerly titled mental retardation. Intellectual developmental disorder is the term used in *ICD-11*, and *DSM-5* uses the term intellectual disability.

Brief Description: This disorder has an onset during the developmental period and includes intellectual and adaptive functioning deficits that cross three primary domains: conceptual, social, and practical domains. Criteria for this disorder must be confirmed by both clinical assessment and standardized intelligence testing. This disorder becomes apparent during the developmental years and is characterized by an inability to maintain focus/concentration, an inability to complete tasks, and poor organization skills.

Abbreviated Criteria: Under abbreviated guidelines, all three of the criteria must be met: (1) deficits in intellectual functioning, (2) deficits in adaptive functioning, and (3) with onset during the developmental period.

Severity Specifiers: Severity uses the adaptive functioning, not IQ scores, and ranges from mild, moderate, severe, and profound.

Mild: Needs minimal assistance, may need some supervision and guidance, often lives in community or in minimally supervised settings.

Moderate: Needs moderate supervision, can attend to own personal care, can perform unskilled or semiskilled work, often lives in a supervised setting in the community.

Severe: Generally needs institutionalized care and has little or no communicative speech, possible group home with extensive support and follow-up to complete activities of daily living.

Profound: Generally needs total care required to meet activities of daily living.

Facilitating the Diagnostic Assessment

1. Deficits in intellectual functioning:
   Problems with reasoning (to supplement standardized testing, the practitioner can use scenarios of current everyday situations the individual will confront, consistent with developmental age, and document problematic responses)
   Problem-solving difficulties (to supplement standardized testing, ask basic questions that are age and/or developmentally appropriate, and document problematic responses)

* Criteria for the disorder are summarized from *DSM-5*, published by the American Psychiatric Association (APA), 2013.

Planning (to supplement standardized testing, ask questions related to expected daily tasks that are age and/or developmentally appropriate and how the individual approaches them, and document problematic responses)
Abstract thinking (to supplement standardized testing, ask age-appropriate questions related to conceptual or generalizable thinking and relevant to current everyday situations the individual will confront, and document problematic responses)
Judgment (to supplement standardized testing, ask age-appropriate questions related to basic decision making and relevant to current everyday situations that could affect the individual's health or safety, and document problematic responses)
Academic learning (to supplement standardized testing, gather information from parents and teachers related to academic interest and proficiency)
Learning from experience (gather information from parents and teachers related to ability to learn after making mistakes and other routine experiences to note how behavior improves based on experience)

2. Deficits in adaptive functioning (crosses multiple environments: home, school, work, community):
Personal independence (can individual complete age-appropriate tasks?)
Social responsibility (how does individual relate to others at home or supervised living facility, school, and other relevant situations?)

3. Onset during the developmental period.
Initial onset (e.g., birth, accident, injury, etc., with no specific age limit but during the developmental period)

Helpful Hints

- If this condition is present, the practitioner should always list it with supporting information from an intelligence test to verify the intelligence quotient (IQ) score. Must have IQ of 70 or below on an individual intelligence test.
- Individuals must have significantly subaverage intelligence and deficits in adaptive functioning. This disorder is slightly more common in males.

Source: Summarized criteria from the *Diagnostic and Statistical Manual of Mental Disorders,* Fifth Edition. Copyright 2013 by the American Psychiatric Association.

TREATMENT PLAN

Intellectual Disability

Signs and Symptoms to Note in the Record

- Subaverage intelligence; specifically, an IQ based on a standardized test with a score of 70 or below.

(continued)

TREATMENT PLAN (*Continued*)

- Limitations in communication, self-care, social and interpersonal skills, self-direction, and academic skills.
- List difficulties in coping with everyday demands.
- List difficulties in deficits in intellectual functioning, deficits in adaptive functioning, and with onset during the developmental period.
- Inability to follow through on assignments/tasks from beginning to end.
- Inattention to detail/often makes careless mistakes.
- Loses interest in activities/frequent shifting of focus from one project to another without completion.
- Messy working space/area.
- Dislike of activities that require sustained attention.

Goals

1. Behavior will correspond to appropriate level of functioning within social contexts, such as school, home, and community settings.
2. Maximize intellectual abilities to focus on strengths.
3. Reduce the number of socially inappropriate behaviors.
4. Increase attention/concentration span.
5. Adhere to firm limits as established by parents and teachers.
6. Increase self-esteem.

Supportive Care Goals

1. Parents and others (home, school, or work) will develop simple routines to help address frustration in completing tasks and positively reinforce compliance with the rules.
2. If needed, client will take medication as prescribed by the prescriber.

Objectives	Interventions
1. Maintain attention to activities for increasing intervals of time.	Assist parents and child in developing a routine; schedule child's chores and assignments each day and the time frame in which each is to be completed. Make recreational activities contingent upon completion of daily assignment while systematically increasing the length of time required to complete such tasks.
2. Improve self-confidence and self-worth.	Client will list, recognize, and focus on strengths and work on building interpersonal relationships.
3. Facilitate placements for completion of ADLs. Facilitate maximizing academic achievements in an appropriate school setting or possible employment setting.	Determine appropriate residential setting, depending on the client's abilities and the level of care required. Consult with teachers, parents, and mental health professionals to determine appropriate classroom setting, depending on the client's intellectual capabilities and skill level.
4. Introduce and utilize self-monitoring techniques to help	Introduce self-cues in the environment to serve as a reminder to the client to initiate or stay on task.

Objectives	Interventions
client initiate and stay on tasks.	Introduce the client to a nondisruptive, self-repeating tape of tones that regularly reminds the child to ask self, "Am I working on my assigned task?"
5. Develop an educational plan to maximize learning skills, identifying strengths and weaknesses.	Recommend, support, and/or implement a reward/token system for compliant behavior and positive academic performance.
6. Develop and implement a list of daily chores that the child is developmentally able to achieve, and positively reinforce achievements.	Parents will increase use of positive reinforcement at home.
7. Design a reward system to reinforce the child's socially appropriate behaviors.	Parents and teachers will recognize and verbally express when the child is behaving in a socially inappropriate way.
8. Medication consultation: determine whether medication would be helpful, and facilitate routine so it is taken as prescribed. Develop a mechanism to obtain consult and supportive information related to medications and how it can assist/affect completion of tasks.	Provide supportive problem-solving education related to need for medication and how it can assist/affect completion of tasks. Child will adhere to a daily routine of taking medications as established by parents. Parents will ensure that medication is taken in appropriate dosage and at specified time.
9. Develop, establish, and implement rules and consequences for the child when completing ADLs.	Assist the parents in determining clear rules for the child and developing a system of natural consequences for inappropriate behaviors.
10. Establish and reinforce task and developmentally appropriate behaviors.	Utilize verbal praise to reward compliance with rules involving support system. Utilize a reward system to reinforce on-task behaviors and completion of tasks at home and in the classroom.

QUICK REFERENCE A.2

AUTISM SPECTRUM DISORDERS (ASD)*

Title Change and Reclassification: This condition in *DSM-IV-TR* (2000) was a combination of conditions listed under the pervasive developmental disorders. Individual disorders combined into ASD include diagnoses previously titled autistic disorder (a severe form, onset in infancy or childhood, self-stimulating, self-injuring behaviors often present, i.e., rocking, spinning, head banging); Rett's disorder (females with

(*continued*)

* Criteria for the disorder are summarized from *DSM-5*, published by the APA, 2013.

QUICK REFERENCE A.2 (*Continued*)

deceleration of head growth, 5 to 24 months and problems develop with loss of previously acquired hand skills; loss of social engagement; appearance of stereotyped movements; impaired language functioning, associated with severe or profound mental retardation; related to a specific genetic mutation); childhood disintegrative disorder (normal development for 2 years and then a drastic decline, followed by a loss of previously acquired skills and development of autistic-like symptoms); Asperger's disorder (autistic-like symptoms without language impairment but severely impaired social interaction); and pervasive disorder NOS.

Brief Description: The essential characteristics of this disorder are repeated and persistent difficulties in both social communication and interaction. The symptoms are first evidenced in early childhood. Problematic communication and interaction behaviors are characterized by restrictive and repetitive patterns of behavior. All behaviors are severe enough to disturb daily functioning and other activities of daily living. Referred to as a spectrum disorder because the presentation and severity are highly affected by the condition, developmental level, and chronological age. In addition, the behaviors experienced in this disorder are not better explained by intellectual disability, as these disorders frequently co-occur.

Abbreviated Criteria: Under abbreviated guidelines, the two primary areas are social communication and interaction deficits across multiple domains, and restrictive and repetitive behaviors, interests, or activities.

Severity Specifiers: Due to the variability of the disorder, severity specifiers are required for both criterion A (deficits in social communication and interaction) and criterion B (restrictive and repetitive patterns of behavior). These two areas need to be rated separately, and the severity level for each area is rated as level 1 (requires support and has significant interference in one or more areas), level 2 (requires substantial support and interferes with functioning in a variety of contexts), or level 3 (requires substantial support; marked and extreme problems across all spheres). Additional specifiers include *with or without intellectual impairment, language impairment,* and whether it is *associated with another medical or genetic condition or environmental factor; associated with another neurodevelopmental mental of behavior disorder or catatonia.*

Facilitating the Diagnostic Assessment

1. Deficits in social communication and social interaction across multiple domains:
   Deficits with social emotional reciprocity (i.e., failure to respond to interactions consistent with developmental age)
   Deficits in nonverbal communications (i.e., inappropriate verbal and nonverbal responses to facilitate communication of own needs and with others)
   Deficits in developing and maintaining relationships (i.e., may also have a lack of interest in peer relationships)
2. Restrictive and repetitive patterns of behavior **manifested in at least two** of the following:
   Stereotyped or repetitive motor movements, speech, or use of objects

Problems responding to change and insistence on sameness; inflexible to change routines
Inflexibility and highly fixated, intense ritualistic behaviors
Sensory input and self-regulation is impaired with hyperactive or hypoactive sensitivity to aspects of the environment (e.g., temperature, textures, smelling or touching objects)

Helpful Hints

- If this condition is present, the practitioner should always determine whether *intellectual disability* also coexists and whether the behaviors are not better explained by another disability.
- Careful attention to identifying problems and concerns with social communication and interaction, as well as repetitive behaviors; should always be assessed for severity independent of each other.
- Characterization of ASD generally includes impaired reciprocal social interactions and stereotyped behaviors, with qualitative impairments, which deviate from expected communication and verbal or nonverbal responses.
- The skills exhibited are extremely limited and deficient, relative to the actual developmental level.
- The nature of these disorders can be lifelong, thus early and supportive assessment and intervention may result in improvement.

Source: Summarized criteria from the *Diagnostic and Statistical Manual of Mental Disorders*, Fifth Edition. Copyright 2013 by the American Psychiatric Association.

TREATMENT PLAN

AUTISM SPECTRUM DISORDERS (ASD)

General definition: The main features of autistic disorder are abnormal or impaired development in social interaction and communication, as well as a strict regimen of repetitive behaviors.

Signs and Symptoms to Note in the Record

Lack of interest in other people.

Failure to develop appropriate interpersonal relationships.

Delays in communication skills and language development.

Repetition of rituals or self-stimulating behaviors, such as rocking.

Self-injurious behaviors, such as head banging or biting.

Overreaction to changes in routine or environment.

Impairment in both intellectual and cognitive functioning.

(continued)

TREATMENT PLAN *(Continued)*

Goals

1. Increase and, when needed, develop basic language and communication skills.
2. Focus on strengths and highlight capabilities while problem-solving limitations.
3. Decrease and eventually eliminate all self-injurious behaviors.
4. Learn to relax and focus when experiencing extreme distress related to social communication or repetitive behaviors.
5. Learn to recognize environmental triggers that relate to unusual interests or repetitive behavior patterns.

Objectives	Interventions
1. Facilitate increased communicative speech and language.	Refer the client to a speech and language therapist to increase the child's development of speech and language skills. Work with client to facilitate communicative interactions patterns.
2. Increase interactions with others to help to improve communication skills.	Utilize positive reinforcement or modeling techniques to encourage interaction with others and increase communication skills. Assist others in support system and academic environment to also use positive reinforcement.
3. Establish and reinforce task and developmentally appropriate behaviors.	Use verbal praise to reward compliance with rules involving support system. Use a reward system to reinforce on-task behaviors and completion of tasks at home and in the classroom.
4. Decrease any self-injurious behaviors.	Problem-solve ways to address excessive anxiety related to communicative speech and repetitive behaviors Participate in a behavioral management plan with skills and techniques to identify triggers for self-injurious behaviors and how to prevent them.
5. Increase understanding of illness, highlighting realistic expectations to avoid excessive sensory stimulation.	Educate parents about ASD, explaining possible problems to anticipate as well as realistic expectations for performance. Refer to a support group for families to assist with learning how others address the child's individual needs. Encourage parents to identify when respite is needed and provide referrals as indicated.
6. Identify and reduce the incidence of unusual interests and sensory overload in everyday interactions.	Assist the client and his or her parents to identify environmental triggers, hyperreactivity or hyporeactivity to sensory input.
7. Learn and implement communication-related conflict-resolution skills.	Assist the client to identify potential social limitations and behavioral rehearsal strategies for addressing them in more socially responsive ways.

QUICK REFERENCE A.3

Attention-Deficit/Hyperactivity Disorder (ADHD)*

Brief Description: The essential characteristics of this disorder involve persistent difficulties in maintaining attention, as well as hyperactivity-impulsivity. The symptoms are first evidenced in early childhood and interfere with functioning or development. All behaviors are severe enough to disturb daily functioning and other activities of daily living and must be inconsistent with the individual's current developmental level. In addition, the behaviors experienced in this disorder are not better explained by another mental disorder, such as a mood or anxiety disorder or other related mental disorders.

Abbreviated Criteria: Under abbreviated guidelines, two primary areas are inattention and hyperactivity and impulsivity.

Severity Subtypes and Specifiers: Due to the variability of the disorder, subtypes and severity specifiers are provided. There are three subtypes for the disorder: combined presentation (the individual has inattention and hyperactivity-impulsivity), predominantly inattentive presentation (inattention is met for the last 6 months, but not hyperactivity-impulsivity), and predominantly hyperactive/impulsive presentation (hyperactivity-impulsivity but not inattention).

Additional specifiers include past and current signs and symptoms continue to be severe enough to make the diagnosis and are considered: mild (minor impairments to social and occupational functioning), moderate (symptoms between mild and severe are present), or severe (more symptoms than needed to make the diagnosis, severe symptoms are present and pronounced impairment when trying to complete tasks and other activities of daily living).

Facilitating the Diagnostic Assessment

1. Inattention with six or more of the following symptoms, lasting 6 months across social/academic/occupational multiple domains:
   Does not pay close attention to detail and often makes careless mistakes (quickly and incompletely finishes assignments and tasks).
   Cannot concentrate to complete basic tasks whether academic or at play.
   Does not pay attention to spoken directions or take verbal cues.
   Fails to follow through on directions and loses focus quickly (difficulty completing homework or work-related tasks).
   Difficulty in organizing tasks and daily activities.
   Limited concentration and avoids tasks that require sustained attention.
   Is disorganized and loses things needed to complete tasks.
   Easily distracted.
   Often forgetful.

(continued)

* Criteria for the disorder are summarized from *DSM-5*, published by the APA, 2013.

QUICK REFERENCE A.3 (*Continued*)

2. Hyperactivity and impulsivity with six or more of the following symptoms, lasting 6 months across social/academic/occupational multiple domains:
Fidgety behaviors (tapping feet, kicking chair, restless behaviors).
Leaves seat when expected to stay.
Feels restless with the need to get the energy out.
Cannot play or relax quietly.
Often has inner restlessness and is considered on the go.
Blurts out answers.
Has trouble waiting his or her turn.
Often interrupts and intrudes as cannot wait to speak and violates socially acceptable norms.

Helpful Hints

- When documenting the three subtypes for the disorder (combined presentation, predominantly inattentive presentation, and predominantly hyperactive/impulsive presentation), they are recorded as specify whether, rather than specify if.
- Pay careful attention to identifying problems and concerns based on inattentiveness and hyperactive and impulsive behaviors. All behaviors should be assessed for interference in social and academic situations, as well as within the family system.
- The skills exhibited are extremely impulsive and limited relative to the actual developmental level.
- The nature of these disorders is lifelong, and early and supportive assessment and intervention can lead to improved functioning.

Source: Summarized criteria from the *Diagnostic and Statistical Manual of Mental Disorders,* Fifth Edition. Copyright 2013 by the American Psychiatric Association.

TREATMENT PLAN

ATTENTION-DEFICIT/HYPERACTIVITY DISORDER (ADHD)

Brief Definition: A disorder that becomes apparent in childhood and is characterized by an inability to maintain focus and concentration, an inability to complete tasks, and poor organization skills. Primary areas of concern are inattention and hyperactivity and impulsivity.

Signs and Symptoms to Note in the Record

Inability to follow through on assignments and tasks from beginning to end.

Inattention to detail; often makes careless mistakes.

Loses interest in activities; frequently shifts focus from one project to another without completion.

Messy working space/area.

Dislike of activities that require sustained attention.

Inability to remain seated for an extended period of time.

Excessive fidgeting.

Excessive talking/noise.

Blurting out of answers, inability to think before speaking, inability to raise hand and wait to be called on.

Frequent interruption of conversations, activities, and so on.

Frequent accidents.

Goals

1. Focus on strengths and highlight capabilities while problem-solving limitations.
2. Learn to recognize environmental triggers that relate to inattention and impulsive behaviors.
3. When prescribed, client will take medication as recommended.
4. Focus on increasing attention/concentration span.
5. Set and adhere to task-oriented limits as established by parents and teachers.
6. Increase self-confidence and self-esteem.

Objectives	Interventions
1. Maintain attention to activities for increasing intervals of time.	Assist child in developing a routine; schedule child's chores and assignments to be completed each day, and the time frame in which each is to be completed. Make recreational activities contingent upon completion of daily assignment while systematically increasing the length of time required to complete such tasks.
2. Identify strengths and utilize them to increase self-confidence and self-esteem.	Will utilize verbal praise to reward compliance. Client will be able to identify and increase the frequency of positive self-statements. Client will identify things that he or she does well. Client will list, recognize, and focus on strengths and utilize them in interpersonal relationships. Help client make the connection between strengths and improving self-confidence and self-esteem.
3. Develop and utilize self-monitoring techniques to help client stay on task.	Introduce the client to a nondisruptive, self-repeating tape of tones that regularly reminds the child to ask self, "Am I working on my assigned task?"
4. Identify the consequences related to problematic behaviors and a plan for eliminating them	Client will discuss recent disruptive behaviors and explore alternatives on how the situation could be handled better next time. Assist the parents in determining clear rules for the child and developing a system of natural consequences for inappropriate behaviors. Work with the client on behavioral rehearsal outlining behaviors and subsequent consequences.

(continued)

TREATMENT PLAN (*Continued*)

Objectives	Interventions
5. Identify and reinforce appropriate behaviors increasing social interaction with peers, parents, and teachers.	Utilize verbal praise to reward compliance with rules. Utilize a reward system to reinforce on-task behaviors and completion of tasks at home and in the classroom. Assist parents and teachers in determining clear rules and boundaries for the client and responsibilities of the client. Parents and teachers will develop a system responsible for immediately alerting the child to impulsive or off-task behaviors (attention training system) at home or in school. Client will increase awareness of disruptive/impulsive behavior at home and in the classroom.
6. Education on medication usage.	Child will adhere to a daily routine of taking medications as established by the prescriber with oversight by parents. Client will be able to identify side effects related to the medications and express any concerns to prescriber and parents.

OVERVIEW AND TREATMENT PLANS FOR SELECTED ANXIETY DISORDERS

QUICK REFERENCE A.4

SEPARATION ANXIETY DISORDER*

Chapter Change: This condition was formerly listed under the disorders usually first diagnosed in infancy, childhood, or adolescence. When this chapter was eliminated from *DSM-5*, this disorder was moved to the anxiety disorders. All the disorders in that category, similar to this one, share excessive fear and anxiety related to behavioral disturbances.

Brief Description: This disorder becomes apparent during the developmental years and is characterized by what is considered developmentally inappropriate and excessive fear related to an inability to separate from those to whom the individual is attached. In children, this is most likely the caregiver. The excessive fear and anxiety has to be continuous and documented for a period of at least 4 weeks in children and adolescents and extended criteria of at least 6 months for adults. Like most diagnoses, the disturbance must cause documented clinically significant distress and impairment of functioning across multiple domains. This disorder is expected to create significant impairment in functioning in social, academic, occupational, or other areas of daily functioning. In addition, the diagnosis should never be better explained by another medical or mental health disorder.

* Criteria for the disorder are summarized from *DSM-5*, published by the APA, 2013.

Abbreviated Criteria: Regardless of the age, the primary characteristic is excessive fear and anxiety when separating from home or attachment figures. There are eight potential characteristics of the disorder, and to be diagnosed with the disorder, the individual must suffer from at least three of them.

Facilitating the Diagnostic Assessment

Excessive fear or anxiety that is related to separation from those attached that is clearly developmentally inappropriate with three of the following symptoms:

1. Recurrent and excessive distress related to separation from home or attachment figures (e.g., in children, beyond what would be expected for starting school or day care).
2. Excessive and constant worry related to losing attachment figures (e.g., death through injury, separation through other circumstances).
3. Excessive and constant worry related to individual experiencing an unfortunate event that results in being separated from attachment figures with an inability to return (e.g., kidnapping).
4. Persistent worry about leaving attachment figures, and based on this fear, will not complete expected life activities (e.g., leave home to go to school or work).
5. Persistent worry about being left alone at home, with subsequent refusal to be left alone and away from attachment figure(s) (i.e., will not stay home alone without attachment figure).
6. Persistent worry, anxiety, and subsequent refusal to sleep away from home without the attachment figure (e.g., refuses invitations from friends for sleepovers).
7. Repeated bad dreams and recurring nightmares involving separation and the inability to return home (i.e., often remembers dreams and worries the dreams will become real).
8. Repeated concerns and complaints related to physical ailments or unfounded physical reactions when anticipating leaving the home or significant other (e.g., vomits at thought of leaving).

Helpful Hints

- If this condition is present, be sure time frames are taken into account along with developmental age. For adults, the time frame is 6 months, but there is some flexibility. For children and adolescents, the time frame is 4 weeks.
- This disorder can easily be confused with agoraphobia (when the individual refuses to leave the home even with the significant other) or generalized anxiety disorder (worries about ill health and excessive anxiety).
- If the child with the disorder has had difficulty with attachments, look at the environmental and situational circumstances. Has the child been in repeated foster homes or subjected to a turbulent environment? Since life circumstances can clearly affect responses, supportive information should always be taken into account before placing this diagnosis.

(*continued*)

QUICK REFERENCE A.4 (Continued)

- Be careful placing this diagnosis with young children starting day care or school, as these transitions can be difficult for all individuals. Pay careful attention to process whether the symptoms are excessive enough, and the duration of the symptoms should always be taken into account.
- In assessment, there is not clear prevalence information related to gender. This disorder is equally common in males and females in clinical samples, but in the community, females appear to have a higher prevalence.
- Be sure to assess for cultural relevancy. Different cultural groups can have very different expectations related to child rearing and separation from the primary caregiver.
- The significant attachment figure may feel smothered or frustrated by the individual's behaviors. Be sure to involve this person in treatment; a referral for this person's own care may be in order.

Source: Summarized criteria from the *Diagnostic and Statistical Manual of Mental Disorders*, Fifth Edition. Copyright 2013 by the American Psychiatric Association.

TREATMENT PLAN

SEPARATION ANXIETY DISORDER

Definition: The main feature of separation anxiety disorder is an excessive anxiety and worry over being separated from the home or attachment figures.

Signs and Symptoms to Note in the Record

High level of distress when separated from parents or other caregivers.

Excessive worry about losing significant attachment figure or something happening to them while they are separated.

Fear of being alone without attachment figure nearby.

Frequent nightmares about separation from significant attachment figure.

Lack of participation in social, academic, or occupational activities due to excessive fear of being separated from either home or the significant attachment figure.

Goals

1. Decrease the anxiety and fear when a separation is anticipated or occurs.
2. Resolve the underlying issues that may be contributing to the fear.
3. The child should participate in activities with peers and spend time playing independently, away from parents.

4. Parents should establish clear boundaries and set firm limits on their child's acting-out behaviors that occur when separation is near.

Objectives	Interventions
1. Identify and describe fears and how those fears are irrational.	Taking into account the developmental level, explore why separation from home or significant attachment figure is feared.
2. Identify and describe events that trigger the excessive worry and fear and ways of addressing them.	Explore with client triggers for the excessive anxiety, and practice deep-breathing and behavioral rehearsal to better face and address the reluctance to complete tasks.
3. Identify the positive consequences related to completing tasks.	Use behavioral rehearsal to systematically approach situations that cause fear, with the focus on what would happen if completed.
4. Gradually increase the amount of time spent away from significant attachment figure.	Encourage the individual to express how fears are irrational. Encourage the individual to spend progressively longer periods of time completing independent activities without the significant attachment figure. Work with others in the support system to encourage independent activities in a slow and non-anxiety-producing way as possible.
5. Gradually increase the amount of time spent away from the home or safe environment.	Encourage the individual to express how fears of leaving home can be irrational. Encourage the individual to spend progressively longer periods of time completing independent activities outside the home, possibly reading outside of the house alone and the like. Use progressive experiences to assist client to relax while getting farther from the safe home environment. Work with others in the support system to encourage independent activities without them, away from the home in as slow and non-anxiety-producing way as possible.
6. Educate and problem-solve for the individual and significant attachment figure (s) the causes of excessive anxiety and worry and the factors that may contribute to its occurrence.	Encourage the child to examine and verbally express how fear may be related to past separations, trauma, or abuse. Encourage the parents to examine how they may be contributing to or reinforcing their child's anxiety and fears.
7. Assist significant attachment figure(s) to set limits on the individual's crying, clinging, pleading, and temper tantrums when separation occurs.	Teach the parent to set consistent limits when excessive worry results in temper tantrums, crying, and clinging. Educate the significant other about the need for space and privacy, and give permission to express feelings of frustration and/or acceptance of current behaviors.

QUICK REFERENCE A.5

GENERALIZED ANXIETY DISORDER*

Chapter Change: In previous versions of the *DSM*, this condition was part of a larger group of disorders also referred to as the anxiety disorders. In *DSM-5*, however, this original chapter was divided into three different disorders. This disorder and several others were retained under this chapter heading. Thus the title of the chapter is the same, but the disorders that are listed here have changed. One common characteristic that all disorders in this chapter share is excessive fear and anxiety related to behavioral disturbances.

Brief Description: This disorder becomes most apparent in the adult years (initial onset, in the 30s) that cause excessive worry and apprehension related to multiple and repeated life circumstances. The disorder is characterized by what is considered inappropriate and excessive fear and worry that may wax and wane across the life span. To meet the criteria for the diagnosis, the condition must be clearly documented as occurring most days, where the individual cannot escape the constant fears almost every day for a period of at least 6 months. Like most diagnoses, the disturbance must cause documented clinically significant distress and impairment of functioning across multiple domains. This disorder is expected to create significant impairment in social, academic, occupational, or other areas of daily functioning. In addition, the diagnosis should never be better explained by another medical or mental health disorder.

Abbreviated Criteria: Under abbreviated guidelines, there are six symptoms that are most characteristic of the disorder, and at least three must be present continually over the past 6-month period. In the rare case that it may be applied to children, only one recurring symptom is required).

Facilitating the Diagnostic Assessment

Excessive anxiety and worry that includes at least three of the following symptoms:

1. Inner restlessness, diffuse feelings of worry, and excessive distress related to several life circumstances (worry and distress can be all-consuming).
2. Easily fatigued with lack of energy to complete daily tasks (feels exhausted).
3. Difficulty concentrating (often reports being so stressed and worried the mind goes blank).
4. Persistent irritability and frustration with others and the life situation (i.e., the individual reports extreme irritation out of proportion to the event described or anticipated).
5. Bodily responses such as muscle tension (muscle tension is related to persistent worry behaviors).

* Criteria for the disorder are summarized from *DSM-5*, published by the APA, 2013.

6. Sleep disturbance (i.e., reports problems with sleep pattern disturbances; either falling asleep or staying asleep are the most common).

Source: Summarized criteria from the *Diagnostic and Statistical Manual of Mental Disorders,* Fifth Edition. Copyright 2013 by the American Psychiatric Association.

Helpful Hints

- This disorder becomes most apparent in the adult years, and of all the anxiety disorders, this one generally has the oldest age for initial onset (approximately age 30). Although this disorder can occur in children and adolescents, it is rare. To facilitate the diagnostic assessment, be sure to assess for other conditions, particularly anxiety-related conditions that manifest similar symptoms and are more likely to occur in children and adolescents (e.g., separation anxiety, social anxiety disorder).
- Multiple complaints and concerns can cross many domains. In assessment and treatment, one of the most difficult tasks may be helping the client to focus on the top three concerns and to address each one individually.
- In completing the diagnostic impression, the disorder can easily be confused with agoraphobia (when the individual refuses to leave the home) or worries about ill health and medically related conditions.
- Since anxiety-related symptoms are often threefold, involving cognitive, somatic, and behavioral responses, medical and other causes for the anxiety-like symptoms should be examined. Since many medications and/or medical conditions can be confused with the symptoms of generalized anxiety, a complete medical workup is always suggested prior to the diagnosis being placed or the start of treatment.
- When assessing the client, be sure to identify and address relationship, environmental, and other situational circumstances. These factors can clearly mimic, maintain, or increase the symptoms displayed. In addition, with this condition, relationship issues are almost always strained due to the relentless feelings of worry and apprehension involving so many different life circumstances. All of these supporting factors should be taken into account before placing this diagnosis.
- Be sure to assess for cultural relevancy, as different culture groups can have very different expectations related to approaching life circumstances.

Source: Summarized criteria from the *Diagnostic and Statistical Manual of Mental Disorders,* Fifth Edition. Copyright 2013 by the American Psychiatric Association.

TREATMENT PLAN

GENERALIZED ANXIETY DISORDER

Definition: Generalized anxiety disorder is characterized by excessive anxiety and worry about a number of events or activities that lasts for at least 6 months.

Signs and Symptoms to Note in the Record

Restlessness or feeling keyed up or on edge.

Easily fatigued.

Difficulty concentrating.

Irritability.

Muscle tension.

Sleep disturbance, such as restless sleeping or difficulty falling asleep.

Difficulty controlling the worry.

Goals

1. Reduce overall intensity and frequency of the anxiety.
2. Increase ability to function on a daily basis.
3. Resolve the core issue that is causing the anxiety.
4. Develop coping skills to better handle anxieties encountered in the future.

Objectives	Interventions
1. Complete a psychiatric evaluation, and when indicated, take medications as prescribed.	Arrange for a psychiatric evaluation for psychotropic medications, and monitor client for side effects of the medication.
2. Identify causes of anxious feelings.	Assign the client homework assignments to identify cognitive distortions that are causing anxiety.
3. Identify multiple stressors and focus on examining two or three to start the process.	Explore stressors and help client to start a cognitive restructuring plan to address only one or two of the worries identified. Highlight progress made related to addressing each problematic thought and worry and slowly moving to another, highlighting previous successful problem solving to foster encouragement and focus activities.
4. Identify how worries are irrational.	Psychotherapy to address client's cognitive distortions. Psychotherapy to assist client in developing an awareness of the irrational nature of fears.
5. Utilize thought-stopping techniques to prevent anxiety.	Teach client thought-stopping techniques to prevent anxiety-producing thoughts.
6. Identify triggers, and decrease level of anxiety by increasing positive self-talk.	Cognitive therapy to assist the client in developing more realistic thoughts that will increase self-confidence in coping with anxiety.
7. Identify alternative, more positive views of reality that oppose the anxiety-producing view.	Reframe the client's fears and anxieties by suggesting another way of looking at them and helping the client broaden his or her perspective.

Objectives	Interventions
8. Identify ways to relax, and develop a regular exercise program to decrease anxiety level.	Teach client the technique of guided imagery. Encourage regular exercise as a means of reducing anxiety.
9. Identify strained relationship issues related to excessive worry and apprehension and how this can be affecting the relationship.	Provide couple or family counseling as appropriate. Educate and problem-solve concerns and relationship issues that are increased by the disorder.

OVERVIEW AND TREATMENT PLANS FOR SELECTED SLEEP-WAKE DISORDERS

QUICK REFERENCE A.6

Insomnia Disorder*

Title Change: This condition was formerly primary insomnia in *DSM-IV* and *DSM-IV-TR*. The term *primary* was dropped from the title because of concern it would be related to primary versus secondary, when there was not meant to be any relationship between these terms and the diagnostic condition. In addition, there were several organizational changes made to the chapter, reclassifications and the addition of two conditions that replaced the NOS category from the previous edition of the *DSM* (rapid eye-movement sleep behavior disorder and restless legs syndrome).

Brief Description: This disorder is most commonly diagnosed in the adult years and focuses on problems of disturbed sleep patterns with dissatisfaction with sleep quality and quantity. In the assessment, although disturbed sleep problems predominate, it is possible that the individual will report some periods when restful sleep is maintained. The disorder is characterized by what is considered disturbing sleep patterns characteristic of early morning awakenings, maintaining sleep, or initiating it. To meet the criteria for the diagnosis the condition must be clearly documented as occurring at least 3 days a week and be present for at least 3 months. This difficulty persists even after the individual tries to control the sleep environment to be conducive to sleep and having an adequate opportunity for sleep in a temperature-controlled safe environment. Like most diagnoses, the disturbance must cause documented clinically significant distress and impairment of functioning across multiple domains. This disorder is expected to create significant impairment in social, academic, occupational, or other

(continued)

* Criteria for the disorder are summarized from *DSM-5*, published by the APA, 2013.

QUICK REFERENCE A.6 (*Continued*)

areas of daily functioning. In addition, the diagnosis should never be better explained by another medical or mental health disorder or related to substance use. This sleep disorder should not be confused with other sleep-wake disorders (e.g., narcolepsy or breathing-related sleep disorder, a circadian-rhythm sleep-wake disorder, or parasomnia).

Abbreviated Criteria: Under abbreviated guidelines, there are three types of symptoms related to sleep quality and quantity, and the individual will need to suffer from one or more of them for at least 3 nights a week over a 3-month period.

Facilitating the Diagnostic Assessment

Dissatisfaction with sleep quality or quantity with at least one of the three following symptoms:

1. Difficulty starting or initiating *sleep* (i.e., may try numerous ways to fall asleep with many unsuccessful, stressful attempts).
2. Frequent awakenings or trouble falling back to sleep once awake, and these events clearly frustrate the individual and disturb the sleep cycle (i.e., worry will not be able to go back to sleep or fall asleep; children may need caregiver to assist to return to sleep).
3. Early morning awakenings, repeated awakenings, or waking prior to expectation (i.e., planned sleep times are not completed, resulting in frustration and distress for the individual).

Severity Specifiers: Due to the variability of the disorder, specifiers are provided. There are three subtypes for the disorder: With non-sleep disorder mental comorbidity (includes the substance use disorders), with other comorbidity (occurs with another medical disorder), and with other sleep disorders (e.g., narcolepsy or breathing-related sleep disorder, a circadian-rhythm sleep wake disorder, or parasomnia). When coding this disorder, if a mental health or medical condition accompanies it, it should be listed immediately after the specifier.

In addition, the frequency of occurrence of the symptoms is noted, highlighting how often they lead to pronounced impairment in trying to complete tasks and other activities of daily living.

Symptoms lasting at least 1 month but less than 3 months are classified with the specifier *episodic.*

Symptoms lasting 3 months or longer are classified with the specifier *persistent.*

Symptoms with two or more episodes within the space of 1 year are classified with the specifier *recurrent.*

Source: Summarized criteria from the *Diagnostic and Statistical Manual of Mental Disorders*, Fifth Edition. Copyright 2013 by the American Psychiatric Association.

Helpful Hints

Be familiar with the term *nonrestorative sleep*. This occurs with poor sleep quality and can be identified by individuals' report that after sleeping, they are exhausted. Although this is a common symptom related to insomnia disorder, if it occurs alone without the other related symptoms, it is not considered insomnia disorder, and another disorder that captures this individual symptom should be considered. This symptom is very common in hypersomnolence as well; however, in hypersomnolence the concerns voiced usually surround symptoms related to excessive sleepiness.

- Polysomnography is a type of sleep study that involves multiple tests. An individual's air flow is monitored through the nose and mouth; blood pressure, electrocardiographic information, eye movements, and other bodily functions measure both sleep quality and type. Generally, it requires an overnight stay in a sleep laboratory. This can be a very helpful measure in assessing sleep disorders.
- Since sleep schedules vary, an intervention plan needs to fit the individual's own habits. Insomnia can occur as a symptom in many mental health disorders, making it an important intervention concern, whether it is the primary symptom or not.
- In the assessment phase, it is not uncommon for clients with this disorder to report on occasion having a good night with restful sleep. This positive occurrence may in itself become stressful as the individual may become frustrated with not being able to do it regularly.
- In assessing symptoms, be sure to look at sleep schedules, especially in children and adolescents, where diagnosing this condition is rare. Always examine bedtime behaviors and sleep-wake schedules with a particular emphasis on identifying problematic routines (cell phones and texting in bed, computers in bedroom) and developing healthy sleep routines.
- When assessing adolescents and younger adults, the biggest concerns are generally noted in trying to fall asleep; in older adults, just the opposite is true, and older adults often report trouble staying asleep.
- Identify life stressors and then their relationship to sleep patterns and reported quality. Many life events or being exposed to chronic stress can disturb sleep. This can be more pronounced when combined with a personality style that tends to be anxious or more worried than others.
- This disorder becomes most apparent in the adult years, and of all the sleep disorders, this one generally is the most commonly reported. To facilitate the diagnostic assessment, be sure to assess for other conditions, particularly anxiety-related conditions that would manifest similar symptoms, although they are more likely to occur in children and adolescents (separation anxiety, social anxiety disorder). All of these conditions can affect sleep patterns.
- There are often multiple complaints and concerns that cross many domains. Lack of sleep can be devastating to the individual and can affect every area of his or her life. Helping to educate how sleep affects daily functioning can be an essential part of the treatment to follow.

(*continued*)

QUICK REFERENCE A.6 (*Continued*)

- Always examine environmental conditions surrounding sleep. Is there noise in the environment, a comfortable and safe place to sleep, or could there be distractions or problems that occur at night (e.g., bedbug infestations)?
- Does the individual drink excessive caffeine, and could this be disturbing restful sleep? A careful evaluation of environmental circumstances is needed prior to placing the diagnosis. Assessing whether the symptoms an individual is experiencing are transient and short-term includes identifying causes such as jet lag, changes in shift work or activities of daily living (ADLs), excessive or unpleasant noise, or discomfort in room. These factors can clearly mimic, maintain, or increase the symptoms displayed. In addition, with this condition relationship issues are almost always strained due to the relentless feelings of worry and apprehension involving so many different life circumstances. All of these supporting factors should be taken into account before placing this diagnosis.
- Be sure to assess for cultural relevancy. Different cultural groups can have very different expectations of sleep-patterns and work-sleep schedules.

Source: Summarized criteria from the *Diagnostic and Statistical Manual of Mental Disorders,* Fifth Edition. Copyright 2013 by the American Psychiatric Association.

TREATMENT PLAN

INSOMNIA

Definition: The most common complaints are difficulty in initiating or maintaining sleep or of nonrestorative sleep. The sleep disturbance or daytime fatigue causes clinically significant distress or impairment in social, occupational, or other important areas of functioning. The sleep disturbance does not occur exclusively during the course of narcolepsy, breathing-related sleep disorder, circadian rhythm sleep disorder, or a parasomnia. The disturbance does not occur exclusively during the course of another mental disorder. The sleep disturbance is not due to direct physiological effects of a substance (e.g., a drug of abuse, a medication) or another medical condition.

Signs and Symptoms to Note in the Record

Difficulty initiating or maintaining sleep.

Reports experiencing nonrestorative sleep for a period of at least 3 months.

Note any psychological problems that may lead to insomnia, such as anxiety stressors.

Note any mental health conditions, such as schizophrenia, mania or hypomania (bipolar disorders), or depression, which may affect sleep patterns.

Note any medical conditions that may cause sleep disturbances, such as chronic pain syndromes, chronic fatigue syndrome, congestive heart failure, nighttime angina (chest pain) from heart disease, acid reflux disease, chronic obstructive pulmonary disease (COPD), nocturnal asthma (asthma with nighttime breathing symptoms), obstructive sleep apnea, degenerative diseases (such as Parkinson's disease and Alzheimer's disease), brain tumors, strokes, or trauma to the brain.

Note any medications or substances (legal and illegal) being taken, as they could interfere with sleep, and identify any strategy the client is using to deal with the disturbed sleep patterns (e.g., drinking herbs before bedtime, exercising before bed).

Goals

1. Identify sleep habits and ways to increase sleep scheduling and comfort.
2. Reduce preoccupation with stressors that disturb sleep-wake schedule.
3. Reduce thinking of unnecessary events or factors.

Long-Term Goals

1. Improve sleep-wake schedule.
2. Develop routine for initiating restful sleep.
3. Increase capacity to self-regulate thoughts and self-relaxation.
4. Increase ability to complete activities of daily living.

Objectives	Interventions
1. Physical exam to identify any medical or psychological illnesses that could contribute to sleep problems and disturbances.	Referral and discussion after a thorough medical history and assessment for medical conditions that might cause insomnia-like symptoms.
2. Polysomnography to identify sleep difficulties using multiple tests to measure bodily functions related to both sleep quality and type.	Referral and subsequent discussion of the results to see how information can complement treatment strategy suggested. Help to arrange appointment that will most likely involve an overnight stay in a sleep laboratory.
3. Complete a mental status exam, and assess for mental health–related problems and possible drug, substance, or alcohol abuse.	Assess for psychiatric disorders and drug and alcohol use. Seek input from a trained professional in psychiatry or substance abuse if needed.
4. Identify factors that trigger disturbed sleep patterns.	Complete a sleep diary for 2 weeks, identifying events and situations that seem to contribute to sleep-wake schedule difficulties. Offer optional devices that can be used to assist with sleep-wake patterns in addition to the diary. Explain actigraphy (a technique to assess sleep-wake patterns over time). An actigraph is a small, wrist-worn device (about the size of a wristwatch) that measures movement. It contains a microprocessor and onboard memory and can provide objective data on daytime activity.
5. Identify high-risk factors when becoming overtired.	Identify high-risk factors and situations with client and problem-solve what to do if these situations occur. Situations include: Difficulty with memory. Impaired motor coordination (being uncoordinated). Irritability and impaired social interaction. Motor vehicle accidents because of fatigue or sleep-deprived driving.

(continued)

TREATMENT PLAN (*Continued*)

Objectives	Interventions
6. Establish a sleep hygiene routine as part of the behavioral therapy routine. Steps include relaxation training, stimulus control, and sleep restrictions.	Introduce important sleep hygiene components, and help client develop a plan to improve sleep quality and quantity. Steps include: Sleep as much as needed until the client feels rested; do not oversleep. Increase exercise, and develop a routine to exercise regularly at least 20 minutes daily. This should be completed 4 to 5 hours before bedtime. Avoid forcing sleep. Develop and maintain a regular sleep and awakening schedule. Avoid caffeinated beverages in the afternoon, such as tea, coffee, and soft drinks. Avoid nightcaps (alcoholic drinks prior to going to bed). Do not smoke, especially in the evening. Do not go to bed hungry. Adjust the environment in the room (lights, temperature, noise, etc.). Do not go to bed with your worries; try to resolve them before going to bed.
7. Identify anxiety-causing and/or anxiety-producing cognitive mechanisms.	Client will be supported as he or she identifies and verbalizes feelings and emotions in response and when not in response to anxiety-producing cognitions that may affect sleep. Provide education on systematic desensitization, its mechanism, and applications. Educate client about self-relaxation techniques to alleviate fear, worry, terror, and/or stress. Assist client in practicing self-relaxation techniques in session to implement as needed.
8. Engage support systems.	Educate client and family regarding signs of insomnia and importance of keeping sleep hygiene routines.

QUICK REFERENCE A.7

HYPERSOMNOLENCE DISORDER*

Title Change: This condition was formerly primary hypersomnia in *DSM-IV* and *DSM-IV-TR*. The term *primary* was dropped because there was concern it would be related to primary versus secondary, and there is no relationship between these two terms and the diagnostic condition. In addition, the name was changed from *hypersomnia* to *hypersomnolence*. Both terms are interrelated and result in excessive sleepiness. The sleep-wake disorders chapter in *DSM-5* has also had several organizational changes, with reclassifications and the addition of two conditions (rapid eye-movement sleep behavior disorder and restless legs syndrome) that replaced the NOS category in the previous edition.

* Criteria for the disorder are summarized from *DSM-5*, published by the APA, 2013.

Brief Description: This disorder is most commonly diagnosed in late adolescence or early adulthood (age 17 to 24) and is most commonly characterized by self-reported excessive sleepiness. The average individual sleeps between 6 and 9 hours a night. In hypersomnolence, the sleep cycle often exceeds this 9-hour period, and the individual may have trouble waking up or staying awake. The individual with this disorder may be able to sleep at night for at least 7 hours, but when awake may require repeated daytime naps. Those suffering from this disorder generally report that even if they sleep normal amounts, the sleep was not restful and more is needed. In the assessment, although excessive sleepiness predominates, the individual may report some periods when restful sleep is maintained. To meet the criteria for the diagnosis, the individual reports these incidents of excessive sleepiness occurring at least 3 days a week for at least 3 months. This difficulty persists even after the individual tries to control the sleep environment to be conducive to sleep and has an adequate opportunity for sleep in a temperature-controlled, safe environment. Like most diagnoses, the disturbance must cause documented clinically significant distress and impairment of functioning across multiple domains. This disorder is expected to create significant impairment in social, academic, occupational, or other areas of daily functioning. In addition, the diagnosis should never be better explained by another medical or mental health disorder or by substance use. This sleep disorder should not be confused with other sleep-wake disorders (e.g., narcolepsy or breathing-related sleep disorder, a circadian-rhythm sleep-wake disorder, or parasomnia).

Abbreviated Criteria: Under abbreviated guidelines, three types of symptoms are related to excessive sleepiness, and the individual needs to suffer from one or more of them for at least 3 nights a week for at least 3 months.

Facilitating the Diagnostic Assessment

Dissatisfaction with sleep quality or quantity, with at least one of the three following symptoms:

1. Recurrent episodes of sleep or lapses in sleep within the same day (i.e., may need to take repeated naps, can develop dangerous automatic behavioral routines).
2. Can sleep more than 9 hours and still report nonrestorative and disturbed sleep. (i.e., always feels tired and reports sleep is not restful).
3. Difficulty waking up after an abrupt wakening (i.e., cannot seem to get moving to complete important tasks; very sluggish, resulting in frustration and distress for the individual).

Severity Specifiers: Due to the variability of the disorder, specifiers are provided. There are three subtypes for the disorder: with mental disorder (includes the substance use disorders), with medical condition (occurs with another medical disorder), and with another sleep disorder (e.g., narcolepsy or breathing-related sleep disorder, a circadian-rhythm sleep-wake disorder or parasomnia). In coding this disorder, if a mental health or medical condition accompanies it, it should be listed immediately after the specifier.

Clarification on the time frame is needed. It is termed *acute* if the criteria for the disorder are met but it lasts less than 1 month; it is termed *subacute* when the 1-month

(continued)

QUICK REFERENCE A.7 (*Continued*)

time frame has been met but the symptoms have been displayed less than 3 months; it is termed *persistent* if the duration is more than 3 months.

The severity of the condition is based on the degree of difficulty that results when the client is trying to maintain daytime or activity-time alertness. Individuals with this disorder find sleepiness irresistible, cannot maintain conversations when they want to, and have great difficulty overcoming these feelings and completing activities they usually find pleasurable or necessary. Reportedly, this happens multiple times during the day during what should be considered wakeful hours. When difficulty in maintaining activity (daytime) occurs once or twice a week, it is considered mild. When difficulty in maintaining alertness occurs 3 or 4 days a week, the specifier used is moderate, and when these symptoms occur 5 to 7 days a week, it is considered severe.

Source: Summarized criteria from the *Diagnostic and Statistical Manual of Mental Disorders,* Fifth Edition. Copyright 2013 by the American Psychiatric Association.

Helpful Hints:

- When assessing hypersomnolence, the most important first step is to make sure the client has had a complete physical exam. Medical conditions such as airway obstruction and obesity can clearly affect sleep patterns, and often addressing these medical conditions helps to resolve the sleep-related problems.
- Part of the medical workup needs to be assessment for the potential of substance use, legal or illegal. Medications can affect the symptoms experienced and should be evaluated along with the medical conditions as a first step in the assessment. In addition, does the individual drink excessive caffeine, and could this be disturbing restful sleep?
- Polysomnography is a type of sleep study that involves multiple tests. Air flow is monitored through the nose and mouth, and blood pressure, electrocardiographic information, eye movements, and other bodily functions measure both sleep quality and type. Generally it requires an overnight stay in a sleep laboratory. In this disorder, symptoms are almost always simply self-reported, and polysomnography could be helpful.
- Be familiar with the term *nonrestorative sleep.* It occurs with poor sleep quality, and individuals report they are exhausted after what would be considered an adequate amount of sleep. Although it is a common symptom related to hypersomnolence disorder, if it occurs alone without the other related symptoms, it is not considered hypersomnolence, and another disorder that captures this specific symptom should be considered.
- In the diagnostic assessment, be sure to differentiate between excessive sleepiness and fatigue. In excessive sleepiness, the individual may report being unable to stay awake during tasks such as driving, reading, and completing work tasks. In fatigue, the individual reports increased tiredness and an inability to complete tasks. Fatigue, in turn, can result in excessive sleepiness and a desire to rest rather than complete tasks.

- Some individuals with hypersomnolence disorder may engage in what is referred to as automatic behaviors. In these behaviors, the individual in a sleep state may, for instance, drive a car and be miles down the road and not sure how they got there. Other examples include dozing off at work, with friends, or during social gatherings. In the assessment, be sure to inquire about these types of dangerous behaviors.
- Since sleep schedules vary, an intervention plan needs to fit the individual's own needs and practices. Hypersomnolence can occur as a symptom in many mental health disorders, making it an important intervention concern, whether it is characteristic of this sleep disorder or related to crosscutting from another disorder.
- In the assessment phase, it is not uncommon for clients with this disorder to report occasionally having a good night of restful sleep. This positive occurrence may in itself become frustrating, as the individual often feels sleepy but because of anxiety will not be able to again reach restful sleep.
- In assessing symptoms, be sure to look at work or academic schedules and check whether the individual is able to complete tasks without being overwhelmed with feelings of sleepiness. Special attention should always be given to identify potential situations that might result in a danger to self or others.
- In adolescents and younger adults, the biggest concerns are generally not being able to escape feeling tired all the time; even after a nap, the feelings of tiredness do not leave.
- Identify life stressors and relationship factors that can make the person avoid responsibilities through being excessively sleepy.
- This disorder becomes most apparent in the late teens and early adult years. Although it can occur in children, this occurrence is rare. To facilitate the diagnostic assessment, be sure to assess for other conditions, particularly depression and anxiety-related conditions that manifest in similar symptoms and are more likely to occur in children and adolescents (e.g., separation anxiety, social anxiety disorder). All of these conditions can affect sleep patterns.
- Often multiple complaints and concerns cross many domains. Excessive sleepiness can be devastating to the individual and affect every area of his or her life. Help to educate clients and family members on how sleep affects daily functioning, as it can be an essential part of the treatment to follow.
- Always examine environmental conditions surrounding regular sleep activity that could result in excessive sleepiness. During regular sleep cycles, is there noise in the environment, a comfortable and safe place to sleep, or could there be distractions or problems that occur at night (e.g., bedbug infestations) that stop the person from sleeping at home? For adolescents, this is especially important to address; it may account for sleepiness in the academic setting. Also, is the individual bored, and sleeping is seen as a place of escape?
- Be sure to assess for cultural relevancy as different culture groups can have very different expectations of sleep patterns and work-sleep schedules.

Source: Summarized criteria from the *Diagnostic and Statistical Manual of Mental Disorders,* Fifth Edition. Copyright 2013 by the American Psychiatric Association.

TREATMENT PLAN

HYPERSOMNOLENCE DISORDER

Definition: Excessive sleepiness for at least 3 months shown by prolonged sleep episodes or by daytime sleep episodes occurring almost daily. For most, the duration of the major sleep episode lasts from 7 to 9 hours, with difficulty awakening in the morning. The excessive sleepiness causes significant distress or impairment in social, occupational, or other important areas of functioning. The excessive sleepiness is not better accounted for by insomnia, does not occur exclusively during the course of another sleep disorder, and cannot be accounted for by an inadequate amount of sleep. The disturbance is not caused by physiological effects of a substance or a general medical condition.

Signs and Symptoms to Note in the Record

Excessive sleepiness during wakeful times.

Symptoms related to excessive sleepiness: unable to complete tasks, read, or drive for extended periods without feeling the overall desire to sleep.

Symptoms related to fatigue where the individual is "just too tired" to complete tasks.

Reports experiencing nonrestorative sleep for a period of at least 3 months

Automatic behaviors completed in a sleeplike state (e.g., driving and not realizing how he or she got there, conversations with friends where the client slides into a trancelike state).

Psychological problems that may lead to hypersomnolence, such as depression or avoidance of current life expectations.

Mental health conditions, such as depression or schizophrenia spectrum disorders, may affect sleep patterns.

Medications or substances (legal and illegal) can increase incidents of sleepiness and interfere with sleep quality and quantity.

A medical condition that may influence current behaviors requires a referral for a comprehensive physical evaluation. Special attention needs to be given to the possibility of breathing concerns, airway obstructions, and obesity.

Goals

1. Identify sleep habits and ways to increase sleep scheduling and comfort.
2. Identify any underlying causes of the excessive sleepiness.
3. Identify automatic triggers that can lead to dangerous episodes of sleep-related behaviors.
4. Identify potentially dangerous work or other daily activities where increased episodes of sleepiness might create a danger to self or others.
5. Reduce thinking of unnecessary events or factors where sleep may be used as a type of escape.

Long-Term Goals

1. Improve individual functioning, and reduce episodes of excessive sleepiness.
2. Develop routine for initiating and ending restful sleep.
3. Increase capacity to self-regulate thoughts and self-relaxation.
4. Increase ability to complete activities of daily living and avoid potentially dangerous situations.

Objectives	Interventions
1. Physical exam to identify any medical or psychological illnesses that could contribute to feelings of excessive sleepiness and fatigue. Evaluate the need for medication such as stimulants and other wake-promoting drugs.	Referral and discussion after a thorough medical history and assessment for medical conditions that might cause hypersomnolence-like symptoms. If necessary, a referral for a psychiatric evaluation for the use of wake-promoting types of medications that may reduce feelings of excessive sleepiness.
2. Polysomnography to identify sleep difficulties by using multiple tests to measure bodily functions related to both sleep quality and type.	Referral and subsequent discussion of the results to see how information can complement treatment strategy suggested. Help to arrange appointment, which will most likely involve an overnight stay in a sleep laboratory.
3. Complete a mental status exam and assess for mental health–related problems and possible drug, substance, or alcohol abuse.	Assess for psychiatric disorders and drug and alcohol use. Seek input from a trained professional in psychiatry or substance abuse if needed.
4. Identify factors that trigger automatic types of behaviors related to excessive sleepiness and fatigue.	Complete a sleep diary for 2 weeks, identifying events and situations that seem to contribute to sleep-wake schedule difficulties. Complete self-report scales that can assist in identifying problematic behaviors in addition to the diary. Refer for Multiple Sleep Latency Test (MSLT), a measurement related to excessive sleepiness that can assist in determining REM sleep patterns.
5. Identify high-risk factors when becoming overtired, excessively sleepy, and fatigued.	Identify high-risk factors and situations with client, and problem-solve what to do if these situations occur. Situations include: Operating machinery Operating motor vehicles Other potentially dangerous activities
6. Establish a sleep hygiene routine as part of the behavioral therapy routine. Steps include: Relaxation training Stimulus control Identify sleep-induced triggers	Introduce important sleep hygiene components, and help client develop a plan to improve sleep quality and quantity. Increase exercise and develop a routine to exercise regularly at least 20 minutes daily. This should be completed 4 to 5 hours before bedtime. Develop and maintain a regular sleep and awakening schedule. Work to identify trigger events and create a strategy for addressing excessive sleepiness and fatigue.
7. Identify anxiety-causing and/or anxiety-producing cognitive mechanisms.	Educate client about self-relaxation techniques to alleviate fear, worry, terror, and/or stress. Assist client in practicing self-relaxation techniques in session to implement as needed.
8. Engage support systems.	Educate client and family regarding signs of hypersomnolence and the importance of keeping sleep hygiene routines.

OVERVIEW AND TREATMENT PLANS FOR THE EATING DISORDERS

QUICK REFERENCE A.8

ANOREXIA NERVOSA

Chapter Change: There were multiple changes made to this chapter in *DSM-5*. Although anorexia nervosa was not removed from this chapter, several additional diagnoses were added, and certain criteria were changed. Many of the eating-related disorders that used to be listed in infancy and early childhood are now together in the new feeding and eating disorders chapter. This chapter highlights the fact that eating disorders can cross the life span, and regardless of the age of the patient, the severity of the eating disorder is what matters in providing the appropriate treatment. Rumination disorder was moved from the childhood disorders with the clarification that this disorder was not limited to infancy and childhood and could occur at any age. In addition, the diagnosis feeding and disorder of infancy and childhood was renamed avoidant/restrictive food intake disorder. This broad category was expanded to include a wide variety of symptoms related to substantially restricting food intake, and this restrictive pattern can lead to a variety of physiological and psychological problems.

Brief Description: What all of the feeding and eating disorders share is a persistent disturbance related to eating or eating-related behaviors. These problematic eating patterns can result in altered consumption or absorption of food-related substances that can significantly impair physical health as well as the psychosocial functioning of the individual. In anorexia nervosa, three primary symptoms must consistently be present to place the diagnosis. The first relates to eating behaviors often referred to as energy intake. In anorexia nervosa, the energy intake behaviors are severely limited and restricted, based on the second symptom, a pronounced fear of gaining weight. As a result of this fear, these individuals are almost always underweight when compared with others of the same age, yet their third symptom is the misperception of being overweight.

Abbreviated Criteria: Three primary characteristics related to food intake need to be present in the disorder: an overriding desire to limit energy intake and consumption, intense fear of weight gain, and problems in perceiving weight and body shape when completing a self-evaluation.

Facilitating the Diagnostic Assessment

1. An overriding desire to limit energy intake and consumption (i.e., the intake is far below what is required for normal health).
2. An intense fear of gaining weight (i.e., what is considered unusual about this criterion is that often the individual who loses weight becomes more preoccupied with losing even more weight).
3. Problematic self-perceptions of body weight and body shape when completing a self-evaluation (i.e., although weight is substantially low for health, reduced caloric intake continues).

Severity Subtypes and Specifiers: Due to the variability of the disorder, subtypes and severity specifiers are provided. There are two subtypes for the disorder that occurs within the past 3 months: restricting type (specify whether weight loss is due to dieting only and not using other means) and binge-eating purging type (specify whether recent episodes relating to weight loss are due to binge eating or purging behaviors).

Additional specifiers include current and past signs and symptoms of the disorder that were met in the past and focus on the current presentation. The first relates to specify if partial remission, where the one of the three criteria is not met (low body weight), whereas the other two (intense fear of gaining weight and disturbances in self-perception) are. In full remission, although the disorder clearly was diagnosed based on the symptoms and the 3-month time frame, all three of the criteria of the disorder have not been met for a period of time. It is not specified how long this period of time should be, so practitioner judgment is expected.

Anorexia nervosa can also be coded based on level of severity. In this disorder, individuals are often underweight, and a concrete measurement of weight is needed to document the level of severity. The weight measurement used is the body mass index (BMI), a calculated number that takes into account an individual's height and weight to construct an ideal body weight. Although not a perfect test, it is a good indicator of whether an individual is over or under what is considered a healthy weight. In this disorder, when specifying if the condition is mild, a BMI greater than or equal to $17kg/m^2$ is expected. For moderate, a BMI of 16 to $16.99kg/m^2$ is required; for severe, a BMI of 15 to $15.99kg/m^2$ and to specify if extreme a BMI of less than $15kg/m^2$ is calculated.

Helpful Hints

- Because weight may be directly related to problematic medical conditions, a complete medical workup and physical exam is always recommended. Although death related to the disorder of anorexia nervosa is rare, if death occurs, it is most likely related to medical conditions that are the result of this mental disorder and problems that occur with persistent reduced energy intake.
- Use of the BMI and awareness of this measurement in terms of assessing whether the condition is mild, moderate, or severe is essential. It can be of particular help with adults and older adolescents but may not be much help with children. In these cases, BMI measurements and clinical judgment should always be combined to look at problematic weight loss patterns and urgency of treatment.
- In this disorder, the potential for suicide is elevated, and a careful assessment of danger to self should come early in the assessment process.
- This disorder generally begins in adolescents or young adults and rarely has an onset in adulthood. It is more common in females, with a 10:1 ratio, but it does occur in males, and it is important not to dismiss the possibility of a male suffering from this disorder.
- The fear of weight gain is a persistent criterion for this disorder. In assessing the individual, the practitioner may find that the more weight the individual loses, the more obsessed she or he becomes with losing more. Looking for rituals and

(continued)

QUICK REFERENCE A.8 (*Continued*)

behaviors consistent with weight loss is central to identifying triggers that can lead to continued and dangerous attempts at limiting energy intake.

- Individuals with this disorder may be preoccupied with dieting, what they will and will not eat, and exercise. Patterns of obsessively measuring caloric intake or weight may be prominent. If trigger points can be identified, they may be helpful in behavioral rehearsal designed to exemplify and avoid such behaviors.
- Be sure to assess for cultural relevancy: Different cultural groups can have very different expectations related to weight and appearance. In cultures where being thin is idealized, tremendous pressure may be put on the individual to maintain an unhealthy, unrealistic weight.
- Family members or significant others may feel extremely stressed; they know there is a problem, but the denial component of the individual's problematic beliefs and behaviors is pronounced. Family members and significant others often comment that the symptoms expressed are unshakable to reasoning, even though the individual appears able to engage in problem solving in areas unrelated to eating. In addition, those within the support system may have made numerous attempts to get the client help, but the individual denies having a problem. Recognition of key members of the individual's support system is essential, and inclusion in treatment will create the greatest possibility for success.

Source: Summarized criteria from the *Diagnostic and Statistical Manual of Mental Disorders,* Fifth Edition. Copyright 2013 by the American Psychiatric Association.

TREATMENT PLAN

ANOREXIA NERVOSA

Definition: This disorder is related to food intake, where the individual has an overriding desire to limit energy intake and consumption, an intense fear of weight gain, and problems in perceiving weight and body shape when completing a self-evaluation.

Signs and Symptoms to Note in the Record

Intense fear of gaining weight.

Refusal to gain weight or follow nutritional guidelines.

Behaviors representative of serious restricting of food.

Medical conditions: edema (swelling), hyperkeratosis (abnormal thickening of outer layer of the skin), carotonemia (pseudojaundice; excess carotene in the blood results in yellowish skin tone), hypotension or hypertension.

Emaciation.

Amenorrhea (absence of the menstrual cycle directly related to dieting and other problematic behaviors).

Lanugo hair (fine, soft hair).

Goals

1. Diminish feelings of anger and guilt, particularly regarding food and eating.
2. Establish healthy eating patterns.
3. Change and identify problematic beliefs related to food and weight.
4. Establish a sense of self-worth that is not paired with weight and body image.

Long-Term Goals

1. Accept body weight and image regardless of shape or size.
2. Reach improved nutritional and therapeutic quality of life.

Objectives	Interventions
1. Complete physical exam.	Refer client to physician for a physical exam.
2. Identify concerns related to eating disorders, and increase education related to problematic conditions that may develop.	Provide education related to problematic behaviors and consequences related to intense dieting and restriction of energy intake.
3. Identify dysfunctional eating patterns that may have resulted in physical problems.	Initiate keeping a journal of food consumption and any methods used to control gaining weight.
4. Increase understanding of the development of the body image disturbance and eating disorder.	Monitor diet-restrictive behaviors; in binge-eating purging type, develop a nutritional eating plan, and positively reinforce healthy eating patterns.
5. Identify the relationship among low self-esteem, a drive for perfectionism, a fear of failure, and the eating disorder.	Assist client in exploring how a drive for perfectionism and a need for control led to maintaining problematic behaviors. Encourage identification of positive qualities, and positively reinforce all of client's accomplishments.
6. Identify alternative coping strategies for dealing with the underlying emotional issues.	Assist in outlining trigger behaviors that lead to denial and food-restrictive practices. Problem-solve these behaviors, outlining alternate actions. Assist in developing assertive behaviors that allow healthful expression of emotions. Refer client to an eating disorder support group.
7. Identify beliefs regarding body image perceptions.	Keep record of negative body talk, and create a positive or neutral statement to counter each negative statement.
8. Identify positive characteristics of identity that are not based on body weight or size but on personal character, values, or personality traits.	Assist client to identify a basis for self-worth that is not based on body shape, weight, or size by assessing his or her talents, positive traits, and importance to significant others in life, such as family and friends.
9. Identify significant others and other family members essential to the identity of the client and treatment success.	Evaluate the family support system and identify significant individuals to assist in treatment. Provide education related to the condition. Share and discuss educational information regarding disadvantages of disordered eating (physical problems such as skin tone and color, hair loss, halitosis, low energy, lack of concentration). Initiate couple or family counseling to discuss present behaviors, concerns, and ways to work collaboratively together.

QUICK REFERENCE A.9

BULIMIA NERVOSA

Chapter Change: The feeding and eating disorder chapter of *DSM-5* has multiple diagnoses including bulimia nervosa. This chapter stresses that eating disorders can cross the life span, regardless of the client's age. This broad category was expanded to include a wide variety of symptoms where individuals engage in episodes of binge eating and the resulting pattern of binging and purging can lead to a variety of physiological and psychological problems.

Brief Description: What all of the feeding and eating disorders have in common is a persistent disturbance related to eating or eating-related behaviors. These problematic eating patterns can result in altered consumption or absorption of food-related substances that can significantly impair physical health and the client's psychosocial functioning. In bulimia nervosa, three essential features are indicative of the diagnosis. The first and second relate to recurrent episodes of binge-eating; the individual consumes large quantities of food, only to engage in compensatory behaviors to prevent weight gain, such as purging what has recently been eaten. Third, the individual is preoccupied with body shape, weight, and size and cannot seem to move beyond thinking about it. This disorder may have symptoms that overlap anorexia nervosa, but the episodes do not occur exclusively.

Abbreviated Criteria: Generally, bulimia nervosa has its first onset in adolescence or young adulthood. Compensatory behaviors must occur at least once a week for a period of 3 months.

Facilitating the Diagnostic Assessment

Recurrent Episodes of Binge Eating: These episodes occur at least once a week for an average of 3 months with clear recurrent episodes of binge eating with two of the following criteria:

1. Eating quantities of food much larger than most people would eat in a 2-hour period (i.e., eat large quantities of food fairly quickly).
2. Cannot stop eating. Often the individual feels a loss of control and cannot stop eating even when feeling full (i.e., rapidly consumes large volumes of food and appears preoccupied with consuming it).

Recurrent Inappropriate Behaviors to Prevent Weight Gain: Problematic compensatory behaviors include using laxatives to stimulate an immediate bowel movement and prevent food absorption, self-induced vomiting, and using other substances to prevent weight gain. The individual may also engage in excessive exercising.

Severity Specifiers: Due to the variability of the disorder, severity specifiers are provided. Specifiers include current and past signs and symptoms of the disorder that were met in the past and focus on the current presentation. The first is specify if partial remission, where the criteria for the disorder has been met in the past, and currently some of the criteria are still met but not all for a period of time. In full remission, although the disorder clearly was diagnosed based on the symptoms and the 3-month time frame, currently no criteria are met for a period of time. Since how long this period of time should be is not specified, practitioner judgment is expected.

Bulimia nervosa can also be coded based on level of severity. Compensatory behaviors such as purging and laxatives are monitored and used to quantify the level of problematic symptoms. In mild, the practitioner should specify if the individual is reporting one to three episodes of compensatory behavior per week. In moderate, the practitioner should specify if the individual is reporting four to seven episodes of compensatory behavior per week. In severe, the practitioner should specify if the individual is reporting 8 to 13 episodes of compensatory behavior per week; in extreme, 14 or more of the compensatory episodes are reported.

Helpful Hints

- Purging can lead to problematic medical and dental conditions. Thus a complete medical workup and physical exam and a dental checkup are always recommended. Medically, sialadenosis (the salivary glands become enlarged) is common and should be assessed. Clients may also have electrolyte imbalances from the repeated binging and purging.
- Repeated episodes of vomiting can lead to erosion of tooth enamel. This makes a dental examination essential to look at the current health of the teeth and gums.
- A medication evaluation by a psychiatrist is always recommended. Some individuals respond well to an antidepressant such as the selective serotonin reuptake inhibitors (SSRIs), including Celexa (citalopram), Prozac (fluoxetine), and Zoloft (sertraline). These antidepressants may take several weeks to produce the full effect, so early assessment is important; when combined with cognitive-behavioral treatment, they may be beneficial.
- This disorder generally begins in adolescents or young adults and rarely has an onset in adulthood. Although like anorexia nervosa, the female-to-male ratio is 10:1, this disorder can occur in males. Be careful not to dismiss the possibility of a male suffering from this disorder; when diagnosed, the treatment is similar.
- The fear of weight gain and the preoccupation with gaining weight is prevalent. Clients with this disorder spend an inordinate amount of time with negative self-talk related to body shape and image. They tend to be critical of self-flaws and find it difficult to refocus on a positive body image. Since individuals with this disorder are typically not underweight (normal to above normal), this eating disorder may be harder to diagnose than anorexia nervosa, in which clients are typically significantly underweight.
- Look for rituals and behaviors consistent with weight loss and practices such as forced exercise and misused laxatives.
- Individuals with this disorder may be preoccupied with dieting and generally are normal to possibly overweight. Family members are often the first to notice problematic patterned behaviors, such as not wanting to eat in public or in front of others.

(continued)

QUICK REFERENCE A.9 (Continued)

- Be sure to assess for cultural relevancy: Different cultural groups can have very different expectations related to weight and appearance. In cultures where being thin is idealized, there may be tremendous pressure on the individual to maintain an unhealthy, unrealistic weight.
- Family members or significant others may feel extremely stressed because they know there is a problem but are not sure how to help the loved one suffering from the disorder. Often the individual appears able to engage in problem solving in areas unrelated to eating. In addition, those within the support system may have made numerous attempts to get the client help, but the individual denies having a problem. Recognition of key members of the individual's support system is essential, and their inclusion in treatment will create the greatest possibility for success.

Source: Summarized criteria from the *Diagnostic and Statistical Manual of Mental Disorders*, Fifth Edition. Copyright 2013 by the American Psychiatric Association.

TREATMENT PLAN

BULIMIA NERVOSA (PURGING TYPE)

Definition: The main features of bulimia nervosa are binge eating and purging behaviors that are used as a means of preventing weight gain.

Signs and Symptoms to Note in the Record

Consumption of large quantities of food at one time, especially high-fat foods or sweets.

Self-induced vomiting, abuse of laxatives, or excessive exercise to prevent weight gain.

Preoccupation with body image and body size.

Constantly worrying and complaining of being fat.

Fear of becoming overweight.

Exercising too much.

Not wanting to eat in public restaurants or in places where others can see.

A distorted and negative body image.

Electrolyte imbalance and dental problems resulting from the eating disorder.

Going to the bathroom right after eating big meals.

Goals

1. Stop the pattern of binge eating and purging.
2. Restore a healthier eating pattern with appropriate nutrition to maintain a healthy weight.

3. Develop an understanding of cognitive and emotional struggles that have resulted in the eating disorder, and develop alternative coping strategies.
4. Change the perception of self so that it does not focus on body weight or size as the primary means of self-acceptance.

Long-Term Goals

1. Stop the cycle of binge eating and purging.
2. Build self-esteem and acknowledge a health body image.

Objectives	Interventions
1. Complete physical and dental exam and possible medication to help address symptoms and recurrent negative thoughts.	Refer client to physician for a complete physical exam and to dentist for a dental exam. Refer to a psychiatrist for a medication evaluation.
2. Identify food consumption patterns and any methods used to control gaining weight.	Discuss with client the dysfunctional eating patterns that may have resulted in physical problems.
3. Identify bingeing and purging behavior triggers and patterns of abuse.	Monitor client's bingeing and purging behaviors, develop a nutritional eating plan, and positively reinforce healthy eating patterns. Analyze the pros and cons of maintaining the disordered eating patterns—identifying functional higher-order goals of behavioral patterns and beliefs.
4. Identify the relationship of low self-esteem, a drive for perfectionism, a fear of failure, and the eating disorder.	Assist client in exploring how a drive for perfection and a need for control led to the eating disorder. Encourage client to identify positive qualities, and positively reinforce all of client's accomplishments.
5. Identify alternative coping strategies for dealing with the underlying emotional issues.	Assist client to develop assertive behaviors that will allow healthful expression of emotions. Refer client to an eating disorder support group.
6. State a basis for identity that is not body weight or size but personal character, values, or personality traits.	Assist client to identify a basis for self-worth that is not body size by assessing his or her talents, positive traits, and importance to significant others in life, such as family and friends.
7. Identify significant others and other family members essential to the identity of the client and treatment success.	Evaluate the family support system, and identify significant individuals to assist in treatment. Provide education related to the condition. Share and discuss educational information regarding the disadvantages of disordered eating (physical and dental problems, halitosis, low energy, lack of concentration, etc.). Initiate couple or family counseling to discuss present behaviors, concerns, and ways to work collaboratively together.

Author Index

Subject Index

About the Author

Sophia F. Dziegielewski, PhD, LCSW, is a professor in the School of Social Work, University of Central Florida (UCF), in Orlando. She also serves as editor of the *Journal of Social Service Research.* Dr. Dziegielewski is a licensed clinical social worker in the State of Florida and has been licensed for clinical practice in Tennessee, Georgia, and Ohio. She also serves as Chairperson for the University of Central Florida Human Subjects Review Board, where she presides over all human subjects research at this large (60,000 students) metropolitan university. Prior to this appointment, Dr. Dziegielewski served as Dean in the School of Social Work at the University of Cincinnati and had faculty appointments in the School of Social Work at the University of Central Florida, the University of Alabama, the Department of Family and Preventive Medicine and Psychiatry at Meharry Medical College, the University of Tennessee, and the U.S. Army Military College serving at Fort Benning, Georgia.

Dr. Dziegielewski has her MSW and PhD in Social Work from Florida State University, Tallahassee. Professional honors include the College and University Award for Excellence in Graduate Teaching at the University of Central Florida (2002) and the University Faculty Leadership Award (2002). In the national magazine *Social Worker Today* (2003), a feature story about Dr. Dziegielewski referred to her as a "legend" in her field. She is the recipient of numerous other awards and supports her research and practice activity with more than 135 publications, including eight textbooks, 95 articles, numerous book chapters, and hundreds of workshops and community presentations.

Her professional social work interests primarily focus on two major areas: health and mental health issues and time-limited evidence-based practice strategy. As a licensed clinical social worker and as Chair of the Institutional Ethics Review Board, she is firm on the importance of joining practice and ethical research and applying the concepts of measurement to establish treatment effectiveness in time-limited intervention settings.

MPM 070721
Printed in Singapore